Culture and Modernity

CULTURE AND MODERNITY

EAST-WEST PHILOSOPHIC PERSPECTIVES

Edited by

ELIOT DEUTSCH

University of Hawaii Press

Honolulu

Library of Congress Cataloging-in-Publication Data

Culture and modernity : East-West philosophic perspectives /
  edited by Eliot Deutsch.
      p.   cm.
  Essays presented at the Sixth East-West Philosophers'
Conference, August 1989 in Honolulu, Hawaii.
  Includes bibliographical references and index.
  ISBN 0-8248-1370-7 (alk. paper)
  1. Philosophy and civilization—Congresses.   2. Civilization,
Modern—Congresses.   3. East and West—Congresses.
4. Philosophy, Modern—Congresses.   5. Philosophy,
Oriental—Congresses.
I. Deutsch, Eliot.   II. East-West Philosophers' Conference
(6th : 1989 : Honolulu, Hawaii)
B59.C84   1991   91-19107
100—dc20   CIP

To Dr. Hung-Wo Ching
Enlightened Businessman

Contents

LANGUAGE AND NON-WESTERN CULTURAL TRADITIONS

CULTURE AND THE ETHICAL

CULTURE AND THE AESTHETIC

Preface

In his fine essay in this volume, Ferenc Feher describes the sextet in Mozart's *Don Giovanni* where each of the participants, while singing of "liberty," has his or her own very decided understanding of what the word means.

> For Don Giovanni, "liberty" is tantamount to the unhindered course of his predatory libertinism without the interference of police, religion, and the peevish complaints of petty moralizing. For Donna Anna, "liberty" will only be achieved in a world where the "intimate sphere" will no longer be threatened by moral monsters the likes of Don Giovanni. For Donna Elvira, "liberty" is a psychological category. She is not concerned with the world, only with her own spiritual equilibrium and her "freedom" from the haunting memory of the seducer. For Leporello, freedom means upward social mobility from the status of servant to a position that grants small pleasures and a pension. For Don Ottavio, the spiritual brother of Saint-Preux, the proto-Jacobin, "liberty" is entirely political in nature. It is tantamount to the stern rule of retributive justice and republican virtue. For Masetto, "liberty" is also political, but in a more concrete sense: it means freedom from the power of noblemen like Don Giovanni. Zerlina is not entirely sure whether it is freedom that she longs for most. But at least in one sense she, too, wants to be "free"—free from the whims of those silly men who are not capable of understanding that her intention is never to do them wrong; she merely wants to have a good time.

Feher, nevertheless, is quick to note that the six different "voices" are *participants* in a common enterprise, and that by extension there is a common *melos* which allows us "the very possibility of interpreting each other."

The essays in this volume from among many of the leading thinkers from numerous countries throughout the world were first presented at the Sixth East-West Philosophers' Conference, which was held in August 1989 in Honolulu, Hawaii, and which I had the honor to direct.[1] While never forming a melody quite as lovely as any of Mozart's, the authors did address several common problems under the general theme "Culture and Modernity: The Authority of the Past" in a spirit which sought mutual cross-cultural understanding through careful interpretation and frank critical engagement. Many voices were heard and listened to artfully.

Although there is always something of a tension among philosophers engaged in comparative work between those who are disposed to look for, find, and announce similarities and those who seek, discover, and celebrate differences in modes of thought, styles of argumentation, basic ideas, and presuppositions among diverse cultures and different individuals within those cultures, the conference on the whole was concerned more with the plurality issuing from differences than with the singularity following from sameness—while all the time its participants being very much aware of a common human/natural/spiritual world that has emerged so suddenly in world history and whose very fate rests so largely on the success of cooperative undertakings by those who represent very different worlds within that common matrix.

It seems quite obvious that often, and with good will, we look for a sameness or likeness in our encounter with other cultures and with persons from those other cultures—but a sameness that, in actuality, tends to assimilate the other to oneself; for it is given to each of us, especially those of us from cultures that happen to be dominant at a particular time, to believe that *we* are to define the measure and style of intelligibility of what can and what should not be said, and so on. I say we do this with "good will," which is to say that while we might be unaware of our cultural imperialism we do think that the other, while falling short of us, is intrinsically capable of being just like us, a thinking which may become condescending and patronizing.

Happily, even among those of us who were looking to secure universalist positions (Matilal, Apel . . .), this tendency was very much muted, and it was widely recognized that to celebrate difference in comparative philosophy means finally that one acknowledges when and where *distinctive* contributions to philosophical understanding obtain. Not all differences between philosophical traditions are worthy of the attention or care of philosophers, but only those that open up for them new possibilities of raising questions and that enrich their ability to think creatively. This might in its own way sound like a one-sided appropriation, but it need not be if at the same time we acknowledge the need for everyone to engage in this way in that appropriation. We then have, as we did have, a genuine mutual interchange.

Under its general theme, the Conference was structured so as to concentrate attention on several broad areas of philosophical interest, namely, on questions dealing with "incommensurability" and "relativism" and their bearing on ethical, aesthetic, religious, epistemological, scientific, and social-political issues.

One thing that seems obvious in the modernity/postmodernity controversy and becomes exceedingly apparent in many of the arguments put forward in the essays brought together here is the complex set of relations that obtain between the social-political, ethical, aesthetic, religious, and scientific dimensions of culture today. No longer is it possible to spell "culture" with a German capital "K" in such a way as to isolate various *geist* features and give exclusive attention and centrality to them. The "power" factors in human relations, and the distinctive discourses associated with them, are inseparably interwoven with the ethical needs of today (as so passionately addressed, for example, by Karl-Otto Apel); the aesthetic cannot be divorced from the historical, even if done only in a negative way, as suggested by Arthur C. Danto in his remark that "To be modern is to perceive the past as the locus of only negative messages, of things not to do, of ways not to be," or from changing psychological and social conditions as argued by Richard Wollheim, or from technological demands, as noted by Megumi Sakabe. And although it might very well once have been the case that the religious could rightfully claim to be the overriding cultural concern and foundational value, we now see it, with no less importance attached to it, as an inextricable part of what grounds cultural identity and cultural pluralism, especially in a cross-cultural context. Cultural identity, as R. R. Verma notes, for example, is bound up with ideas of progress and connects closely with modernity and authenticity. The concept of "progress" in turn, which so many of us were taught to deride as a last vestige of Enlightenment naivete, returns as a cultural issue in much contemporary thinking about science. Is there such a thing as scientific progress, and how does it, if it exists, bear on issues of rationality and truth? And can these essentially epistemological issues be isolated from what are—within the perspective now of "twentieth-century philosophy"—long-standing concerns about the nature of language and the formation of "conceptual schemes"?

Many of the heated debates over these various complex, interrelated issues and over the whole question of modernism and postmodernism and "the authority of the past" have taken place in the West as though Asian and other non-Western traditions were neither parties to, nor were to be affected by, the debate or its outcomes. In an essay "Modernity and Tradition," the late J. L. Mehta asks: "Is this 'modern' period [which he dates back to the end of the middle ages] a new epoch in Western history merely, or does it constitute something of a turning point in world history itself? The external facts are certainly episodes in Western history, but does not their meaning now encompass the entire world, enclosing it in a framework of ideas which it cannot escape, forming the present-day world civilization, carrying within it a whole variety of cultures, high and low, many of whom were once autonomous civilizations within their own right?"[2] The answer, now, seems to be "yes and no": "yes" insofar as many of the leading ideas of liberal democracy, of science and technology, of secularism, and the rest which we associate with modernity have challenged and informed the thinking of traditional societies throughout the world; "no" insofar as the wide "variety of cultures" (especially in East Asia and Africa) have refused to be "enclosed" by this "framework of ideas"—a framework that is itself being seriously questioned in the West today—and have rather struggled with varying degrees of success (as many of the essays here attest to) to forge creatively a new modernism appropriate to their own traditions. And, as Mehta notes, the interchange has not been entirely one-sided. "Leading Western writers," he states, "have become self-conscious of their own perspective. This involves an awareness of the possible validity of other perspectives and of the need to incorporate what one can of all that was so far excluded that lay outside the field of their 'single vision'."[3] As many of the essays here clearly and forcefully show (Hall, Herrera, Gyekye, Al-Azmeh), not only are non-Western societies such as Japan central players on the world economic scene, they have much to contribute on the basis of their own experience to the philosophical conversation concerning modernity and the authority of the past and may yet, on the basis of their own rich resources, alter fundamentally the very meaning of modernity in the West.

Writing of Habermas, Richard J. Bernstein has said that "Reason, freedom, and justice were not only theoretical issues to be explored, but practical tasks to be achieved—practical tasks that demanded passionate commitment."[4] It will, I think, be evident that the essays presented here exhibit precisely that rare combination of intellectual rigor (theory) and commitment to addressing concrete social and political issues (praxis) that is so badly needed by all thinking people today.

ELIOT DEUTSCH
University of Hawaii

Notes

1. The conference was sponsored by the Department of Philosophy at the University of Hawaii and the Society for Asian and Comparative Philosophy in cooperation with the East-West Center. It was funded, under the leadership of Dr. Hung Wo Ching, a prominent local businessman, entirely through donations by members of the Hawaii business community. Over 125 scholars participated in the conference with approximately 90 papers being presented over a two-week period. The distinguished scholar of Chinese thought Wing-tsit Chan was the honorary chairman of the conference. The director of the conference was assisted in its planning by a steering committee constituted by Roger T. Ames, Wing-tsit Chan, David Kalupahana, Kenneth Kipnis, Gerald Larson, Larry Laudan, Henry Rosemont, Jr., and Tu Wei-ming; and by an Interna-

tional Advisory Committee consisting of Richard J. Bernstein, Zhang Dainam, Alasdair MacIntyre, Daya Krishna, Mou Tsung-san, Yasuo Yuasa, and Tu Wei-ming (chair).

2. J. L. Mehta, *Philosophy and Religion: Essays in Interpretation* (New Delhi: Indian Council of Philosophical Research, 1990), p. 229.

3. Ibid.

4. *Habermas and Modernity,* ed. with an introduction by Richard J. Bernstein (Cambridge: The MIT Press, 1985), p. 2.

Acknowledgments

I would like to express my thanks to John Smith for his thoughtful assistance in the preparation of this work and to John Benson for his careful and precise copyediting. I would also like to express my appreciation to Sharon Yamamoto for her help in all phases of the editing and production of this rather complex book. I am especially grateful to my colleague Professor Roger T. Ames for the efficiency and graciousness with which he carried out so many tasks during, and in preparation for, the conference from which this volume derives.

The Crisis of Modernity

RICHARD RORTY

PHILOSOPHERS, NOVELISTS, AND INTERCULTURAL COMPARISONS: HEIDEGGER, KUNDERA, AND DICKENS

Suppose that the nations which make up what we call "the West" vanish tomorrow, wiped out by thermonuclear bombs. Suppose that only Eastern Asia and sub-Saharan Africa remain inhabitable, and that in these regions the reaction to the catastrophe is a ruthless campaign of de-Westernization—a fairly successful attempt to obliterate the memory of the last three hundred years. But imagine also that, in the midst of this de-Westernizing campaign, a few people, mostly in the universities, squirrel away as many souvenirs of the West—books, magazines, small artifacts, reproductions of works of art, movie films, videotapes, and so on—as they can conceal.

Now imagine that, around the year 2500, memory of the catastrophe fades, the sealed-off cellars are uncovered, and artists and scholars begin to tell stories about the West. There will be many different stories, with many different morals. One such story might center on increasing technological mastery, another on the development of artistic forms, another on changes in sociopolitical institutions, and another on the lifting of sexual taboos. There would be dozens of other guiding threads which storytellers might seize upon. The relative interest and usefulness of each will depend upon the particular needs of the various African and Asian societies within which they are disseminated.

If, however, there are *philosophers* among the people who write such stories, we can imagine controversies arising about what was "paradigmatically" Western, about the *essence* of the West. We can imagine attempts to tie all these stories together, and to reduce them to one—the one true account of the West, pointing out the one true moral of its career. We think of *philosophers* as prone to make such attempts because we tend to identify an area of a culture as "philosophy" when we note an attempt to substitute theory for narrative, a tendency toward essentialism. Essentialism has been fruitful in many areas—most notably in helping us to see elegant mathematical relationships behind complex motions, and perspicuous microstructures behind confusing macrostructures. But we have gradually become suspicious of essentialism as applied to human affairs, in areas such as history, sociology, and anthropology. The attempt to find laws of history or essences of cultures—to substitute theory for narrative as an aid to understanding ourselves, others, and the options which we present to one another—has been notoriously unfruitful. Writings as diverse as Karl Popper's on Hegel and Marx, Charles Taylor's on positivistic social science, and Alasdair MacIntyre's or Michael Oakeshott's on the importance of traditions have helped us realize this unfruitfulness.

Despite growing recognition that the essentialistic habits of thought which pay off in the natural sciences do not assist moral and political reflection, we Western philosophers still show a distressing tendency to essentialism when we offer intercultural comparisons. This comes out most clearly in our recent willingness to talk about "the West" not as an ongoing, suspenseful adventure in which we are participating but rather as a structure which we can step back from, inspect at a distance. This willingness is partly the cause, and partly the effect, of the profound influence of Nietzsche and Heidegger on contemporary Western intellectual life. It reflects the sociopolitical pessimism which has afflicted European and American intellectuals ever since we gave up on socialism without becoming any fonder of capitalism—ever since Marx ceased to present an alternative to Nietzsche and Heidegger. This pessimism, which often calls itself "postmodernism," is a rueful sense that the hopes for greater freedom and equality which mark the recent history of the West were somehow deeply self-deceptive. Postmodernist attempts to encapsulate and sum up the West have made it increasingly tempting to contrast the West as a whole with the rest of the world as a whole. Such attempts make it easy to start using "the East" or "non-Western modes of thought" as the names of a mysterious redemptive force, as something which may still offer hope.

In this essay, I shall be protesting against this recent tendency to encapsulate the West, to treat it as a finished-off object which we are now in a position to subject to structural analysis. In particular, I want to protest against the tendency to take Heidegger's account of the West for granted. There is, it seems to me, a growing willingness to read Heidegger as the West's final message to the world. This message consists largely of the claim that the West has, to use one of Heidegger's favorite phrases, "exhausted its possibilities." Heidegger was one of the great synoptic imaginations of our century, but his extraordinary gifts make his message sound more plausible than I think it is. We need to remember that the scope of Heidegger's imagination, great as it was, was largely restricted to philosophy and lyric poetry, to the writings of those to whom he awarded the title of "Thinker" or of "Poet." Heidegger thought that the essence of a historical epoch could be discovered by reading the works of the characteristic philosopher of that epoch and identifying his "Understanding of Being." He thought that the history of the West could best be understood by finding a dialectical progression connecting the works of successive great philosophical thinkers. Philosophers by trade are especially susceptible to the persuasive power of Heidegger's account of the West's history and prospects. But I think that this susceptibility is a professional deformation which we should struggle to overcome.

As a way of counteracting Heidegger and, more generally, the kind of post-Heideggerian thinking which refuses to see the West as a continuing adventure, I want to put forward Dickens as a sort of anti-Heidegger. I can sum up my sense of the respective importance of Dickens and Heidegger by saying that, if my imaginary Asians and Africans were, for some reason, unable to preserve the works of both men, I should much prefer that they preserve Dickens'. For Dickens could help them grasp a complex of attitudes that was important to the West, and perhaps unique to the West, in a way that neither Heidegger nor any other philosopher could. The example of Dickens could help them think of the novel, and particularly the novel of moral protest, rather than of the philosophical treatise, as the genre in which the West excelled. Focusing on this genre would help them to see not technology, but rather the hope of freedom and equality as the West's most important legacy. From the point of view I shall be adopting, the interaction of West and East is better exemplified by the playing of Beethoven's Ninth Symphony in Tienanmen Square than by the steel mills of Korea or the influence of Japanese prints on Van Gogh.[1]

To lay out this point of view, I shall do three things in the remainder of this essay. First, I shall offer an account of Heidegger as one more example of what Nietzsche called "the ascetic priest." Second, I shall summarize and gloss Milan Kundera's account of the novel as the vehicle of a revolt against the ontotheological treatise, of an anticlerical reaction against the cultural dominance of the ascetic priests. Third, I shall use Dickens to illustrate Kundera's suggestion that the novel is the characteristic genre of democracy, the genre most closely associated with the struggle for freedom and equality.

Heidegger's later work was an attempt to provide the one right answer to the question asked by my imaginary African and Asian philosophers of the future. Heidegger would advise these philosophers to start thinking about the West by thinking about what killed it—technology—and to work backward from there. With a bit of luck, they could then recreate the story which Heidegger himself told, the story he called "the history of Being." For Heidegger, the West begins with the pre-Socratics, with what he calls the separation between the "what" and the "that." This separation between what a thing is in itself and the relations which it has to other things engenders distinctions between essence and accident, reality and appearance, objective and subjective, rational and irrational, scientific and unscientific, and the like—all the dualisms which mark off epochs in the history of an increasing lust for power, an increased inability to let beings be. This is the history which Heidegger summarizes in Nietzsche's phrase *die Wüste wächst,* the wasteland spreads.[2]

As Heidegger tells this story, it culminates in what he calls the "age of the world-picture," the age in which everything is Enframed, seen as providing an occasion either for manipulation or for aesthetic delectation. It is an age of giantism, of aesthetico-technological frenzy. It is the age in which people build 100-megaton bombs, slash down rain forests, try to create art more thoroughly postmodern than last year's, and bring hundreds of philosophers together to compare their respective world pictures. Heidegger sees all these activities as aspects of a single phenomenon: the age of the world picture is the age in which human beings become entirely forgetful of Being, entirely oblivious to the possibility that anything can stand outside a means-end relationship.

Seeing matters in this way is an instance of what Habermas describes as Heidegger's characteristic "abstraction by essentialization." In 1935 Heidegger saw Stalin's Russia and Roosevelt's America as "metaphysically speaking, the same." In 1945 he saw the Holocaust and the expulsion of ethnic Germans from Eastern Europe as two instances of the same phenomenon. As Habermas puts it, "under the leveling gaze of the philosopher of Being even the extermination of the Jews seems merely an event equivalent to many others."[3] Heidegger specializes in rising above the need to calculate relative quantities of human happiness, in taking a larger view. For him successful and unsuccessful adventures—Ghandi's success and Dubček's failure, for example—are just surface perturbations, distractions from essence by accidents, hindrances to an understanding of what is *really* going on.

Heidegger's refusal to take much interest in the Holocaust typifies the urge to look beneath or behind the narrative of the West for the *essence* of the West, the urge which separates the philosophers from the novelists. Someone dominated by this urge will tell a story only as part of the process of clearing away appearance in order to reveal reality. Narrative is, for Heidegger, always a second-rate genre—a tempting but dangerous one. At the beginning of *Sein und Zeit,* Heidegger warned against the temptation to confuse ontology with the attempt to tell a story that relates beings to other beings, *mython tina diegeisthai.*[4] At the end of his career he takes back his earlier suggestion that what he called "the task of thinking" might be accomplished by *Seinsgeschichte,* by telling a story about how metaphysics and the West exhausted their possibilities. Now he realizes that he must cease to tell stories about metaphysics, must leave metaphysics to itself, if he is ever to undertake this task.[5]

Despite this suspicion of epic and preference for lyric, the ability to spin a dramatic tale was Heidegger's greatest gift. What is most memorable and original in his writings, it seems to me, is the new dialectical pattern he finds in the sequence of canonical Western philosophical texts. His clue to this pattern was, I think, Nietzsche's construal of the ascetic priests' attempts at wisdom, contemplation, and imperturbability as furtive and resentful expressions of those priests' will to power.

Heidegger, however, tried to out-Nietzsche Nietzsche by reading Nietzsche himself as the last of the metaphysicians. He hoped thereby to free himself from the resentment which, despite himself, Nietzsche displayed so conspicuously. Heidegger thought that if he could free himself from this resentment, and from the urge to dominate, he could free himself from the West and so, as he said, quoting Hölderlin, "sing a new song." He thought that he could become free of the will to power as a result of having seen through its last disguise. He thought that by leaving metaphysics to itself, turning from *Seinsgeschichte* to *Denken*, from *Sein* to *Ereignis,* he could accomplish the transition from epic to lyric, turn from the West to something Wholly Other than the West.

But on my reading, Heidegger was simply one more ascetic priest and his attempt to encapsulate the West, to sum it up and distance himself from it, was one more power play. Heidegger was intensely aware of the danger that he was making such a play. But to be intensely aware of the danger is not necessarily to escape it. On my reading, Heidegger is still doing the same sort of thing that Plato tried to do when he created a supersensible world from which to look down on Athens, or Augustine when he imagined a City of God from which to look down on the Dark Ages. He is opting out of the struggles of his fellow humans by making his mind its own place, his own story the only story that counts, making himself the redeemer of his time precisely by his abstention from action. All that Heidegger manages to do is to historicize the Platonic divided line. He tips it over on its side. The Heideggerian counterpart of Plato's world of appearance seen from above is the West seen from beyond metaphysics. Whereas Plato looks down, Heidegger looks back. But both are hoping to distance themselves from, cleanse themselves of, what they are looking at.

This hope leads both men to the thought that there must be some purificatory askesis which can render them fit for intercourse with something Wholly Other—for impregnation by the Form of the Good, for example, or for Openness to Being. This thought is obviously an important part of the Western tradition, and it has obvious analogues (and perhaps sources) in the East. That is why Heidegger is the twentieth-century Western thinker most frequently "put into dialogue" with Eastern philosophy.[6] Such Heideggerian themes as the need to put aside the relations between beings and beings, to escape from busy-ness, to become receptive to the splendor of the simple, are easy to find in the East.

But there are other elements in Western thought, the elements which

Heidegger despised, which are much harder to put into dialogue with anything in the East. In particular, as I shall be saying in more detail shortly, there is the novel—a Rabelaisian response to the ascetic priests. So, insofar as we philosophers become content either with a dialogue between Plato and the East or with one between Heidegger and the East, we may be taking the easy way out of the problems of intercultural comparison. Insofar as we concentrate on philosophy, we may find ourselves concentrating on a certain specific human type which can be counted upon to appear in *any* culture—the ascetic priest, the person who wants to set himself apart from his fellow humans by making contact with what he calls his "true self" or "Being" or "Brahman" or "Nothingness."

All of us philosophers have at least a bit of the ascetic priest in us. We all hanker after essence and share a taste for theory as opposed to narrative. If we did not, we should probably have gone into some other line of work. So we have to be careful not to let this taste seduce us into the presumption that, when it comes to other cultures, only our counterparts, those with tastes similar to our own, are reliable sources of information. We should stay alert to the possibility that comparative philosophy not only is not a royal road to intercultural comparison, but may even be a distraction from such comparison. For it may turn out that we are really comparing nothing more than the adaptations of a single transcultural character type to different environments.

Those who embody this character type are always trying to wash the language of their respective tribes off their tongues. The ascetic priest finds this language *vicious,* in Sartre's sense. His ambition is to get above, or past, or out of, what can be said in language. His goal is always the ineffable. Insofar as he is forced to use language, he wants a language which either gives a purer sense to the words of the tribe or, better yet, a language entirely disengaged from the business of the tribe, irrelevant to the mere pursuit of pleasure and avoidance of pain. Only such a person can share Nietzsche's and Heidegger's contempt for the people whom Nietzsche called "the last men." Only he can see the point of Heidegger's disdainful remark that the greatest disaster—the spread of the wasteland, *die Verwüstung der Erde,* understood as the forgetfulness of Being—may "easily go hand in hand with a guaranteed living standard for all men, and with a uniform state of happiness for all men."[7] Ascetic priests have no patience with people who think that mere happiness or mere decrease of suffering might compensate for *Seinvergessenheit,* for an inability to be in touch with something Wholly Other.

My description of the ascetic priest is deliberately pejorative and gendered. I am sketching a portrait of a phallocentric obsessive, someone whose attitude toward women typically resembles Socrates' attitude when he was asked whether there are Forms of hair and mud. Such a person shares Nietzsche's endlessly repeated desire for, above all else, cleanliness. He also shares Heidegger's endlessly repeated desire for simplicity. He has the same attitude toward sexual as to economic commerce: he finds it *messy*. So he is inclined both to keep women in their traditional subordinate place, out of sight and out of mind, and to favor a caste system which ranks the manly warriors, who bathe frequently, above the smelly traders in the bazaar. But the warrior is, of course, outranked by the priest—who bathes even more frequently and is still manlier. The priest is manlier because what is important is not the fleshly phallus but the immaterial one—the one which penetrates through the veil of appearances and makes contact with true reality, reaches the light at the end of the tunnel in a way that the warrior never can.

It is easy, with the help of people like Rabelais, Nietzsche, Freud, and Derrida, to make such seekers after ineffability and immateriality sound obnoxious. But to do them justice, we should remind ourselves that ascetic priests are very *useful* people. It is unlikely that there would have been much high culture in either West or East if there had not been a lot of ascetic priests in each place. For the result of trying to find a language different from the tribe's is to enrich the language of later generations of the tribe. The more ascetic priests a society can afford to support, the more surplus value is available to provide these priests with the leisure to fantasize, the richer and more diverse the language and projects of that society are likely to become. The spin-offs from private projects of purification turn out to have enormous social utility. Ascetic priests are often not much fun to be around, and usually are useless if what you are interested in is happiness, but they have been the traditional vehicles of linguistic novelty, the means by which a culture is able to have a future interestingly different from its past. They have enabled cultures to change themselves, to break out of tradition into a previously unimagined future.

My purpose in this essay, however, is not to arrive at a final, just evaluation either of Heidegger in particular or of ascetic priests in general. Instead, it is to develop an antithesis between the ascetic taste for theory, simplicity, structure, abstraction, and essence and the novelist's taste for narrative, detail, diversity, and accident. From now on, I shall be preaching a sermon on the following text from Kundera's *The Art of the Novel*:

> The novel's wisdom is different from that of philosophy. The novel is born not of the theoretical spirit but of the spirit of humor. One of Europe's major failures is that it never understood the most European of the arts— the novel; neither its spirit, nor its great knowledge and discoveries, or the autonomy of its history. The art inspired by God's laughter does not by nature serve ideological certitudes, it contradicts them. Like Penelope, it undoes each night the tapestry that the theologians, philosophers and learned men have woven the day before.

> . . . I do not feel qualified to debate those who blame Voltaire for the gulag. But I do feel qualified to say: The eighteenth century is not only the century of Rousseau, of Voltaire, of Holbach; it is also (perhaps above all!) the age of Fielding, Sterne, Goethe, Laclos.[8]

The first moral I draw from this passage is that we should stay on the lookout, when we survey other cultures, for the rise of new genres—genres which arise in reaction to, and as an alternative to, the attempt to *theorize* about human affairs. We are likely to get more interesting, and more practically useful, East-West comparisons if we supplement dialogues between our respective theoretical traditions with dialogues between our respective traditions of antitheory. In particular, it would help us Western philosophers get our bearings in the East if we could identify some Eastern cultural traditions which made fun of Eastern philosophy. The kind of fun I have in mind is not the in-house kind which we philosophers make of one another (for example, the kind of fun which Plato makes of Protagoras, Hume of natural theology, Kierkegaard of Hegel, or Derrida of Heidegger). It is rather that made by people who either could not follow a philosophical argument if they tried, or by people who have no wish to try. We need to be on the lookout not just for Japanese Heideggers, Indian Platos, and Chinese Humes, but for Chinese Sternes and Indonesian Rabelaises. I am too ignorant to know whether there *are* any people of the latter sort, but I hope and trust that there are. Somewhere in the East there *must* have been people who enjoyed unweaving the tapestries which the saints and sages had woven.

The need to unweave these tapestries can be thought of as the revenge of the vulgar upon the priests' indifference to the greatest happiness of the greatest number. This indifference is illustrated by the way in which Horkheimer and Adorno look for a dialectic of Enlightenment which will permit them to weave *Candide* into the same patter as Auschwitz, the way in which they allow contemplation of that pattern to convince them that Enlightenment hopes were vain. It is also illustrated by the way in which Heidegger blurs the distinction between automobile factories and death camps. We philosophers not only want to see dialectical patterns invisible to the vulgar, we want these patterns to be clues to the outcomes of world-historical dramas. For all our ascetism, we want to see ourselves, and people like ourselves, as engaged in something more than merely private projects. We want to relate our private obsessions, our private fantasies of purity, novelty, and autonomy, to something larger than ourselves, something with causal power, something hidden and underlying which secretly determines the course of human affairs.[9]

From Kundera's point of view, the philosopher's essentialistic approach to human affairs, his attempt to substitute contemplation, dialectic, and destiny for adventure, narrative, and change, is a disingenuous way of saying: what matters for me takes precedence over what matters for you, entitles me to ignore what matters to you, because I am in touch with something—reality—with which you are not. The novelist's rejoinder to this is: it is comical to believe that one human being is more in touch with something nonhuman than another human being. It is comical to use one's quest for the ineffable Other as an excuse for ignoring other people's quite different quests. It is comical to think that *anyone* could transcend the quest for happiness, to think that any theory could be more than a means to happiness, that there is something called Truth which transcends pleasure and pain. The novelist sees us as Voltaire saw Leibniz, as Swift saw the scientists of Laputa, and as Orwell saw Marxist theoreticians—as comic figures. What is comic about us is that we make ourselves unable to see things which everybody else can see—things like decreased suffering and increased happiness—by convincing ourselves that these things are "mere appearance."

The novelist's substitute for the appearance-reality distinction is a display of diversity of points of view, a plurality of descriptions of the same events. What the novelist finds especially comic is the attempt to privilege one of these descriptions, to take it as an excuse for ignoring all the others. What he or she finds most heroic is not the ability sternly to reject all descriptions save one, but rather the ability to move back and forth between them. I take this to be the point Kundera is making when he says:

> It is precisely in losing the certainty of truth and the unanimous agreement of others that man becomes an individual. The novel is the imaginary paradise of individuals. It is the territory where no one possesses the truth, neither Anna nor Karenin, but where everyone has the right to be understood, both Anna and Karenin.[10]

Kundera is here making the term "the novel" roughly synonymous with "the democratic utopia"—with an imaginary future society in which nobody dreams of thinking that God, or the Truth, or the Nature of Things, is on her or his side. In such a utopia nobody would dream of thinking that there is something more real than pleasure or pain, or that there is a duty laid upon us which transcends the search for happiness. A democratic utopia would be a community in which tolerance and curiosity, rather than truth-seeking, are the chief intellectual virtues. It would be one in which there is nothing remotely approximating a state religion or a state philosophy. In such a community, all that is left of philosophy is the maxim of Mill's *On Liberty,* or of a Rabelaisian carnival: everybody can do what they want if they don't hurt anybody else while doing it. As Kundera says, "The world of one single Truth and the relative ambiguous world of the novel are molded of entirely different substances."

One can, if one likes, see Kundera and Heidegger as trying to overcome a common enemy: the tradition of Western metaphysics, the tradition which hints at the One True Description that exhibits the underlying pattern behind apparent diversity. But there is a big difference between what the two men propose as an alternative to this tradition. For Heidegger the opposite of metaphysics is Openness to Being, something most easily achieved in a pretechnological peasant community with unchanging customs. Heidegger's utopia is pastoral, a sparsely populated valley in the mountains, a valley in which life is given shape by its relationship to the primordial Fourfold—earth, sky, man, and gods. Kundera's utopia is carnivalesque, Dickensian, a crowd of eccentrics rejoicing in each other's idiosyncracies, curious for novelty rather nostalgic for primordiality. The bigger, more varied, and more boisterous the crowd the better. For Heidegger, the way to overcome the urge to domination is to take a step back and to see the West and its history of power plays from afar, as the sage sees the Wheel of Life from afar. For Kundera the way to overcome the urge to domination is to realize that everybody has and always will have this urge, but to insist that nobody is more or less justified in having it than anybody else. Nobody stands for the truth, or for Being, or for Thinking. Nobody stands for *anything* Other or Higher. We all just stand for ourselves, equal inhabitants of a paradise of individuals in which everybody has the right to be understood but nobody has the right to rule.

Kundera summarizes his attitude toward the ascetic priest when he says:

> Man desires a world where good and evil can be clearly distinguished, for he has an innate and irrepressible desire to judge before he understands. Religions and ideologies are founded on this desire. . . . They require that somebody be right: either Anna Karenina is the victim of a narrow-minded tyrant, or Karenin is the victim of an immoral woman; either K. is an innocent man crushed by an unjust Court, or the Court represents divine justice and K. is guilty.

> This "either-or" encapsulates an inability to tolerate the essential relativity of things human, an inability to look squarely at the absence of the Supreme Judge.[11]

Kundera, in a brief allusion to Heidegger, politely interprets his term "forgetfulness of Being" as forgetfulness of this essential relativity.[12] But Heidegger never, even in his early "pragmatist" phase,[13] believed in essential relativity in Kundera's sense of the term. Heidegger's genre is the lyric, not the novel; his hero is Hölderlin, not Rabelais or Cervantes. For Heidegger the other human beings exist for the sake of the Thinker and the Poet. Where there is a Thinker or a Poet, there human life is justified, for there something Wholly Other touches and is touched. Where there is not, the wasteland spreads.

Whereas for Heidegger there are certain moments in certain lives which both redeem history and permit history to be encapsulated, for Kundera the thing to do with history is to keep it going, to throw oneself into it. But this throwing oneself into history is not the sort which is recommended by the ideological revolutionary. It is not a matter of replacing Tradition with Reason or Error with Truth. Kundera thinks that if we want to know what went wrong with the expectations of the Enlightenment we should read Flaubert rather than Horkheimer and Adorno. He says:

> Flaubert discovered stupidity. I daresay that is the greatest discovery of a century so proud of its scientific thought. Of course, even before Flaubert, people knew stupidity existed, but they understood it somewhat differently: it was considered a simple absence of knowledge, a defect correctable by education. Flaubert's vision of stupidity is this: Stupidity does not give way to science, technology, modernity, progress; on the contrary, it progresses right along with progress![14]

I take Kundera to be saying that the Enlightenment was wrong in hoping for an age without stupidity. The thing to hope for is, instead, an age in which the prevalent varieties of stupidity will cause less unnecessary pain than is caused in our age by our varieties of stupidity. To every age its own glory and its own stupidity. The job of the novelist is to keep us up to date on both. Because there is no Supreme Judge and no One Right Description, because there is no escape to a Wholly Other, this is the most important possible job. But it is a job which can only be undertaken with a whole heart by someone who is untroubled by dreams of an ahistorical framework within which human history is enacted, a universal human nature by reference to which history can be explained, or a far-off divine event toward which history moves. To appreciate the essential relativity of human affairs, in Kundera's sense, is to give up the last traces of the ascetic priest's attempt to escape from time and change, the last traces of the attempt to see us as actors in a drama already written before we came on the scene. Heidegger thought that he could escape from metaphysics, from the idea of a Single Truth, by historicizing Being and Truth. He thought that he could escape Platonic escapism by telling a story about the *Ereignis* which was the West, rather than about *Sein*. But from Kundera's point of view Heidegger's attempt was just one more attempt to escape from time and chance, though this time an escape into historicity rather than into eternity. For Kundera, eternity and historicity are equally comic, equally essentialist, notions.

The difference between Kundera's and Heidegger's reaction to the Western metaphysical tradition comes out best in their attitude toward closure. It is as important for Kundera to see the Western adventure as open-ended—to envisage forever new sorts of novels, recording strange new joys and ingenious new stupidities—as it is for Heidegger to insist that the West has exhausted its possibilities. This comes out in Kundera's insistence that the novel does not have a *nature,* but *only* a history, that the novel is a "sequence of discoveries."[15] There is no Platonic Form for the novel as a genre to live up to, no essential structure which some novels exhibit better than others, any more than there exists such a Form or such a structure for human beings. The novel can no more exhaust its possibilities than human beings can exhaust their hope for happiness. As Kundera says, "The only context for grasping the novel's worth is the history of the European novel. The novelist need answer to no one but Cervantes."[16]

The same point emerges when Kundera insists that the history of the novel and of Europe cannot be judged by the actual political future of Europe—or by the actual fate, whatever it may be, of the West. In particular, the West blowing itself up with its own bombs should not be read as a judgment on the novel, or on Europe—nor should the coming of an endless totalitarian night. To do so would be like judging a human life by reference to some ludicrous accident which ends it violently, or like judging Western technology by reference to Auschwitz. As Kundera says:

> Once upon a time I too thought that the future was the only competent judge of our works and actions. Later on I understood that chasing after the future is the worst conformism of all, a craven flattery of the mighty. For the future is always mightier than the present. It will pass judgment upon us, of course. But without any competence.

Kundera continues:

> But if the future is not a value for me, then to what am I attached? To God? Country? The people? The individual?

> My answer is as ridiculous as it is sincere. I am attached to nothing but the depreciated legacy of Cervantes.[17]

Kundera's phrase "paradise of individuals" has an obvious application to Dickens, because the most celebrated and memorable feature of his novels is the unsubsumable, uncategorizable idiosyncracy of the characters. Dickens' characters resist being subsumed under moral typologies, being described as exhibiting these virtues and those vices. Instead, the names of Dickens' characters *take the place* of moral principles and of lists of virtues and vices. They do so by permitting us to describe each other as "a Skimpole," "a Mr. Pickwick," "a Gradgrind," "a Mrs. Jellaby," "a Florence Dombey." In a moral world based on what Kundera calls "the wisdom of the novel" moral comparisons and judgments would be made with the help of proper names rather than general terms or general principles. A society which took its moral vocabulary from novels rather than from ontotheological or ontico-moral treatises would not ask itself questions about human nature, the point of human existence, or the meaning of human life. Rather, it would ask itself what we can do so as to get along with each other, how we can arrange things so as to be comfortable with one another, how institutions can be changed so that everyone's right to be understood has a better chance of being gratified.

To those who share Nietzsche's sense that the "last men" give off a bad smell, it will be ludicrous to suggest that *comfort* is the goal of human social organization and moral reflection. But this suggestion would not have seemed ludicrous to Dickens. That is why Dickens has been anathematized by Marxists and other ascetic priests as a "bourgeois reformer." The term "bourgeois" is the Marxist equivalent of Nietzsche's term "last man"—it stands for everything which the ascetic priest wants to wash off. For Marxism, like Platonism and Heideggerianism, wants more for human beings than comfort. It wants transformation, transformation according to a single universal plan; Marxists are continually envisaging what they call "new socialist man." Dickens did not want anybody to be transformed, except in one respect: he wanted everyone to notice and understand the people he or she passed on the street. He wanted people not to make each other uncomfortable by applying moral labels, but to recognize that all their fellow humans —Dombey and Mrs. Dombey, Anna and Karenin, K. and the Lord Chancellor—had a right to be understood.

Despite having no higher goal than comfortableness of human association, Dickens did an enormous amount for equality and freedom. The last line of Swift's self-written epitaph—"Imitate him if you dare: he served human liberty"[18]—would do for Dickens' tablet as well. But Dickens performed his services to human liberty not with the help of the "savage indignation" which Swift rightly ascribed to himself but with something more bourgeois—sentimental tears and what Orwell called "generous anger." Dickens strikes us as a more bourgeois writer than the man who described the Yahoos because he is more comfortable with, and hopeful for, human beings. One indication of this comfortableness is the fact on which Orwell remarked in the following passage:

> In *Oliver Twist, Hard Times, Bleak House, Little Dorrit,* Dickens attacked English institutions with a ferocity that has never since been approached. Yet he managed to do it without making himself hated, and, more than this, the very people he attacked have swallowed him so completely that he has become a national institution himself.[19]

The important point is that Dickens did not make himself hated. I take it that this was partly because he did not attack anything as abstract as "humanity as such," or the age or the society in which he lived, but rather concrete cases of particular people ignoring the suffering of other particular people. He was thus able to speak as "one of us"—as the voice of one who happened to notice something to which the rest of us could be counted upon to react with similar indignation as soon as we notice it.[20]

Dickens was, as Orwell says, "a good-tempered antinomian," a phrase which would apply equally to Rabelais, Montaigne, or Cervantes, but hardly to Luther or Voltaire or Marx. So I take "generous anger" to mean something like "anger which is without malignity because it assumes that the evil has merely to be noticed to be remedied." This was the kind of anger later found in Harriet Beecher Stowe and Martin Luther King, but not the kind of anger found in the ascetic priests. For the latter believe that social change is not a matter of mutual adjustment but of re-creation—that to make things better we must create a new kind of human being, one who is aware of reality rather than appearance. Their anger is *ungenerous* in the sense that it is aimed not at a lack of understanding of particular people by other particular people but rather at an ontological deficit common either to people in general or, at least, to all those of the present age. The generosity of Dickens', Stowe's, and King's anger comes out in their assumption that people merely need to turn their eyes toward those who are getting hurt and notice the *details* of the pain being suffered, rather than need to have their entire cognitive apparatus restructured.

As an empirical claim, this assumption is often falsified. As a moral attitude, it marks the difference between people who tell stories and people who construct theories about that which lies beyond our present imagination, because beyond our present language. I think that when Orwell identified a capacity for generous anger as the mark of "a free intelligence," he was adumbrating the same sort of opposition between the theorist and the novelist which I am trying to develop in this essay. Earlier I said that theorists like Heidegger saw narrative as always a second-best, a propaedeutic, to a grasp of something deeper than the visible detail, the true meaning behind the familiar and commonplace one. Novelists like Orwell and Dickens are inclined to see theory as always a second-best, never more than a reminder for a particular purpose, the purpose of telling a story better. I suggest that the history of social change in the modern West shows that the latter conception of the relation between narrative and theory is the more fruitful.

To say that it is more fruitful is just to say that, when you weigh the good and the bad that the social novelists have done against the good and the bad that the social theorists have done, you find yourself wishing that there had been more novels and fewer theories. You wish that the leaders of successful revolutions had read fewer books which gave them general ideas and more books which gave them an ability to identify imaginatively with those whom they were to rule. When you read books like Kolakowski's history of Marxism, you understand why the Party theoretician, the man responsible for the "correct ideological line," has always been, apart from the maximum leader himself, the most feared and hated member of the Central Committee. This may remind you that Guzman, the leader of the quasi-Maoist Sendero Luminoso movement in Peru, wrote his dissertation on Kant. It may also remind you that Heidegger's response to the imprisonment of his Social Democratic colleagues in 1933 came down to "Don't bother me with petty details."

The important thing about novelists as compared with theorists is that they are good at details. This is another reason why Dickens is a useful paradigm of the novel. To quote Orwell again, "The outstanding, unmistakable mark of Dickens' writing is the *unnecessary detail*"; "He is all fragments, all details—rotten architecture, but wonderful gargoyles—and never better than when he is building up some character who will later on be forced to act inconsistently."[21] If we make Dickens paradigmatic of the West, as I hope my fantasized Africans and Asians would, then we shall see what was most instructive about the recent history of the West in its increased ability to tolerate diversity. Viewed another way, this is an increased ability to treat apparent inconsistency not as something to be rejected as unreal or as evil, but as a mark of the inadequacy of our current vocabularies of explanation and adjudication.[22] This change in our treatment of apparent inconsistency is correlated with an increasing ability to be comfortable with a variety of different sorts of people, and therefore with an increasing ability to leave people alone to follow their own lights. This willingness is reflected in the rise of pluralistic bourgeois democracies, societies in which politics becomes a matter of sentimental calls for alleviation of suffering rather than of moral calls to greatness.

It may seem strange to attribute this sort of willingness to the recent West—a culture often said, with excellent reason, to be racist, sexist, and imperialist. But it is of course also a culture which is very *worried* about being racist, sexist, and imperialist, as well as about being Eurocentric, parochial, and intellectually intolerant. It is a culture which has become very conscious of its capacity for murderous intolerance and thereby perhaps more wary of intolerance, more sensitive to the desirability of diversity, than any other of which we have record. I have been suggesting that we Westerners owe this consciousness and this sensitivity more to our novelists than to our philosophers or to our poets.

When tolerance and comfortable togetherness become the watchwords of a society, one should no longer hope for world-historical greatness. If such greatness—radical difference from the past, a dazzlingly unimaginable future—is what one wants, ascetic priests like Plato, Heidegger, and Suslov will fill the bill. But if it is not, novelists like Cervantes, Dickens, and Kundera may suffice.[23] Because philosophy as a genre is closely associated with the quest for such greatness—with the attempt to focus all one's thoughts into a single narrow beam and send them out beyond the bounds of all that has been previously thought—it is among the *philosophers* of the West that contemporary Western self-hatred is most prevalent. It must be tempting for Africans and Asians—the principal victims of Western imperialism and racism—to see this self-hatred as about what the West deserves. But I would suggest that we take this self-hatred as just one more symptom of the old familiar quest for purity which runs through the annals of the ascetic priesthood in both East and West. If we set these annals to one side, we may have a better chance of finding something distinctive in the West which the East can use, and conversely.

Notes

1. The students were reported to have played a recording of this symphony as the troops were being held up by masses of people jamming the highways leading into the square. The same point about the impact of the West could be made by reference to the student speakers' repeated invocations of Thoreau and of Martin Luther King.

2. See Martin Heidegger, *What Is Called Thinking,* trans. by J. Glenn Gray (New York: Harper and Row, 1968), pp. 29 ff. (*Was Heisst Denken?* [Tübingen: Niemeyer, 1954], pp. 11 ff.).

3. J. Habermas, "Work and Weltanschauung: The Heidegger Controversy from a German Perspective," *Critical Inquiry* 15 (Winter 1989): p. 453.

4. Heidegger, *Sein und Zeit,* 10th ed. (Tübingen: Niemeyer, 1963), p. 6.

5. See Heidegger, *On Time and Being,* trans. by Joan Stambaugh (New York: Harper and Row, 1972), pp. 24, 41 (*Zur Sache des Denkens* [Tübingen: Niemeyer, 1969], pp. 25, 44).

6. See, for example, Graham Parkes, ed., *Heidegger and Asian Thought* (Honolulu: University of Hawaii Press, 1987). As what I say below makes clear, I have doubts about Parkes' claim (p. 2) that "Heidegger's claim to be the first Western thinker to have overcome the tradition should be taken more seriously if his thought can be brought to resonate deeply with ideas that arose in totally foreign cultural milieux, couched in more or less alien languages, over two millennia ago." This resonance can also be taken as a sign of regression rather than of transcendence—as a way of returning to the womb rather than a way of overcoming.

7. See Heidegger, *What Is Called Thinking?* p. 30 (*Was Heisst Denken?* p. 11). Heidegger goes on to say that Nietzsche's words *die Wüste wächst* "come from another realm than the appraisals of our age" *(ays einem anderen Ort als die gaengigen Beurteilungen unserer Zeit).* For another passage which brushes aside happiness as beneath the Thinker's consideration, see *The Question Concerning Technology,* trans. by W. Lovitt (New York: Harper and Row, 1977), p. 65 (*Holzwege* [Frankfurt: Klustermann, 1972], p. 204): "Metaphysics is history's open space wherein it becomes a destining that the suprasensory world, the Ideas, God, the moral law, the authority of reason, progress, the happiness of the greatest number, culture, civilization, suffer the loss of their constructive force and become void."

8. Kundera, *The Art of the Novel,* trans. by Linda Asher (New York: Grove Press, 1986), p. 160.

9. I discuss this urge, with reference to Heidegger, on pp. 107 f. and 119 f. of my *Contingency, Irony and Solidarity* (Cambridge: Cambridge University Press, 1989).

10. Kundera, *The Art of the Novel,* p. 159.

11. Ibid., p. 7.

12. Ibid., p. 5. Here, at the beginning of his book, Kundera thinks of Husserl's *Lebenswelt* and Heidegger's *In-der-West-Sein* as standing over against "the one-sided nature of the European sciences, which reduced the world to a mere object of technical and mathematical investigation," and casually assimilates both to his own notion of "the essential relativity of human affairs." But this assimilation is overly polite, and misleading. Husserl and Heidegger were insistent on getting down to the basic, underlying structure of the *Lebenswelt,* or of *In-der-Welt-Sein.* For Kundera, we make up this structure as we go along.

13. See Mark Okrent, *Heidegger's Pragmatism* (Ithaca: Cornell University Press, 1988), for an account of Heidegger's career that distinguishes the pragmatism, the emphasis on *Vorwurf* and *Bezuglichkeit,* in *Sein und Zeit* from the post-*Kehre* quietism.

14. Ibid., p. 162.

15. Ibid., p. 14.

16. Ibid., p. 144.

17. Ibid., p. 20.

18. Yeats' translation of Swift's ". . . *imitare si poteris, strenuum pro virili libertatis vindicem."*

19. George Orwell, *Collected Essays, Journalism and Letters,* vol. 1 (Harmondsworth: Penguin, 1968), pp. 414–415. In his illuminating *The Politics of Literary Reputation: The Making and Claiming of 'St. George' Orwell* (Oxford: Oxford University Press, 1989), John Rodden has noted both that Orwell in this essay "directly identified himself with Dickens" (p. 181) and that the identification worked, in the sense that "What Orwell wrote of Dickens [in the last sentence of the passage I have quoted] soon applied to himself" (p. 22). One facet of the identification was the patriotism common to the two men—a sense of identification with England and its history which trumped any theory about the place of England in universal history. From the theorist's point of view, patriotism is invariably suspicious, as is any loyalty to a mere sector of space-time. But for people like Orwell, Dickens, and Kundera, the only substitute for patriotism is attachment to some other spatiotemporal sector, to the history of something which is not a country—e.g., the history of the European novel, "the depreciated legacy of Cervantes."

20. Orwell, in *Collected Essays,* vol. 1, p. 460, says that "Even the millionaire suffers from a vague sense of guilt, like a dog eating a stolen leg of mutton. Nearly everyone, regardless of what his conduct may be, responds emotionally to the idea of human brotherhood. Dickens voiced a code which was and on the whole still is believed in, even by people who violate it. It is difficult otherwise to explain why he could be both read by working people (a thing that has hap-

pened to no other novelist of his stature) and buried in Westminister Abbey." If one had asked Dickens whether he had thought that ideal and that code inherent in human nature, or rather an historically contingent development, he would presumably have replied that he neither knew nor cared. That is the kind of question which "the wisdom of the novel" rejects as without interest or point.

21. These two quotes are from Orwell, *Collected Essays,* vol. 1, pp. 450 and 454, respectively.

22. I have argued elsewhere ("Freud and Moral Deliberation," in *The Pragmatist's Freud,* ed. Smith and Kerrigan (Johns Hopkins University Press, 1986)) that the increased popularity of Freudian explanations of untoward actions is an example of this changed attitude toward apparent inconsistency.

23. Byron is a good example of someone who saw the rising stock of tolerance and comfortableness as endangering the possibility of greatness. As my colleague Jerome McGann has pointed out to me, he took out this exasperation on, among other people, Cervantes: "Cervantes smiled Spain's chivalry away;/ A single laugh demolished the right arm/Of his own country;—seldom since that day/Has Spain had heroes" (*Don Juan,* XIII, 11). I have not said much about the poetry-novel contrast (as opposed to the philosophy-novel contrast) in this essay, but I would suggest that there is as much difference between Byron and Dickens as between either and Heidegger. That is why literature-vs.-philosophy is too course-grained a contrast to be useful. Mill and Dickens, or Farrell and Dewey, are closer to each other than Dickens is to Proust, or Byron to Hölderlin.

LUCIUS OUTLAW

LIFEWORLDS, MODERNITY, AND PHILOSOPHICAL PRAXIS: RACE, ETHNICITY, AND CRITICAL SOCIAL THEORY

The "Modernity" Debate

Currently, many intense efforts to characterize and assess contemporary historical developments as a total configuration center on whether we are in a "modern" or "postmodern" period. At the center of the philosophical wing of the debate are some of the most recent endeavors of Jürgen Habermas.[1] For him "modernity" is the name for a partial, but nonetheless quite significant, historical realization of key proposals from the progressive, humanist agenda of the European Enlightenment —the "project of modernity"—developed "within the horizon of Reason." Some of these developments and commitments are to be defended, even while critically refined and extended along with the "rehabilitation" of reason, against what he views as the naive—at worst self-contradictory—"Nietzscheanism" of critics of the project of modernity: Adorno, Foucault, Heidegger, and Derrida, among others.

On the other side of the critics are those who argue, among other things, that a dialectic of Enlightenment is at the heart of the modernity project and includes a false universalism that blocks an appropriation and appreciation of substantive differences (for example, race and ethnicity, or gender), and thus has contributed to totalitarian deceptions that mask various forms of domination. This has led the project to shipwreck on the shoals of (a) the reality of a pluralism of agendas emerging from the lifeworlds of diverse groups of persons who have exerted themselves politically and broken through reason-rationalized domination with a force sufficient to threaten social restructurings, and (b) social-structural developments (affecting the realms of culture, society, and socialization and individual psychic development) that transform the historical conditions of society in ways contrary to the agenda of modernity. "Reason," the critics conclude, is unable to secure universality or guarantee continuous historical progress in the form of material well-being, social peace and stability, and individual autonomy. At the very least, the project of modernity, as a fulfillment of the agenda of the Enlightenment, is incomplete; for some the project *cannot* be fulfilled. Historically, then, we are *beyond* modernity.

In this essay I join this wide-ranging debate by bringing into the discussion concerns from what Habermas has labeled a defensive, "particularist" cultural subgroup: that is, challenges to aspects of the project of modernity, especially its universalist philosophical anthropology, from the tradition of Black nationalism, one legacy contributing to a resurgence of what has recently been called the "politics of difference." My concern is with the social, cultural, and personal significance of life-worlds and practices that are conditioned, to a significant degree, by self-understandings partially shaped by matters having to do with race and/or ethnicity, and their importance for Habermas' proposal to rehabilitate reason as "communicative reason" as part of his project to develop a revised social theory.

The question motivating this discussion is whether a revised agenda for philosophical praxis along lines proposed by Habermas can contribute to the effort to chart a passage between anarchic pluralism and totalitarian universalism to a diverse but unified social world, locally and/or internationally, one that achieves and secures appropriate degrees of tolerance for diverse lifeworlds that is grounded in a consensus that provides practical universality. The discussion will include a review of the core of thought shaping the Enlightenment agenda, its philosophical anthropology in particular, as the script for the project of modernity, a review conducted against the historical backdrop of the politics of race and ethnicity in the American context, an ongoing and unfinished attempted revolutionary instantiation of Western modernity. I propose something of a middle passage, one that participates in the critique of some aspects of the Enlightenment project of modernity while redeeming and refining others, in arguing that the philosophical anthropology of the Enlightenment remains inadequate to the practical tasks of overcoming racism and invidious ethnocentrism while conceiving and realizing a just society. Hence, the Enlightenment-inspired project should be revised, and this revision ought to involve a reworking, as well, of the notion of "universality" that will serve as a key norm of likewise revised notions of "reason" and "reasonableness." Much of the promise of Habermas' effort is to be found here, that is, in its suggestiveness for just such a critical reworking of the theoretical underpinnings of social "modernization."

The Project of Modernity

A set of philosophical articulations forms the intellectual core of the agenda of the project of modernity and, for Habermas, was first problematized and connected to rationality by Hegel.[2] The central notion is "subjectivity," which, Habermas suggests, Hegel elucidated by means of the concepts of "freedom" and "reflection," with subjectivity carrying four basic connotations: individualism, the right to criticize, autonomy of action, and idealistic philosophy as the ultimate self-understanding of modernity, particularly in the philosophies of Descartes and Kant. It was Kant who "installed reason in the supreme seat of judgment before which anything that made a claim to validity had to be justified."[3] Within this "horizon of Western reason" the "rational content" of the project of modernity was constituted by self-consciousness, authentic self-realization, and self-determination in solidarity.[4] The rationality, in his words, was "subject-centered." Further, on the normative side a decisive position assumed by the thinkers of modernity was that the criteria by which the modern age would set its orientation could not be taken from the models of another epoch; rather, modernity would "create its normativity out of itself" through the resources of reason.[5] Thus, the "normative content" of the project of modernity was centered on fallibilism, universalism, and subjectivism.[6] For Habermas, these rational and normative "contents" were constitutive of the self-understanding of the intellectual executors of the project of modernity.

The contents were also internally connected with the processes of modern historical development. The Reformation, Enlightenment, and French Revolution were key historical events that validated the agenda of subject-centered reason and signaled the triumph of the "modern" age over the past. With the playing out of this agenda, historical development became the "objectification of rational structures" that, as described by Weber, Mead, and Durkheim, contributed to the rationalization, hence the secularization, of culture and society, processes characterized by: (1) "the reflective treatment of traditions" by virtue of which they "lost their quasinatural status"; (2) "the universalization of norms of action and the generalization of values, which set communicative action free from narrowly restricted contexts and enlarge the field of options"; and (3) "patterns of socialization that are oriented to the formation of abstract ego-identities and force the individuation of the growing child."[7]

With the onset of the project of modernity, all subsequent development—of self, society, and nature via exchanges with humans—would be under the aegis of reason. Thus was the modernity project informed by a distinctive philosophy of history, as well, one that characterized historical development, when guided by reason, as, to paraphrase Hegel, "progress in the realization of reason and freedom." The essence of modernity is carried in the historical realization of Enlightenment.

This was a decidedly *political* project, in the widest and most substantive senses. Through a confluence of circumstances, during the eighteenth century in particular, liberalism became the dominant social-political philosophy and vehicle for this project such that in continental Europe (though not in England) its history and the spread of the Enlightenment "must be regarded as aspects of one and the same current of thought and practice."[8] The grounds for this confluence are not hard to locate, for the definitive elements in the conception of "Man" and society within the liberal tradition are those of the project of modernity:

1. *Individualism:* ". . . It asserts the moral primacy of the person against the claims of any social collectivity."
2. *Universalism:* ". . . affirming the moral unity of the human species and according a secondary importance to specific historic associations and cultural forms."
3. *Egalitarianism:* ". . . confers on all men the same moral status and denies the relevance to legal or political order of differences in moral worth among human beings."
4. *Meliorism:* ". . . in its affirmation of the corrigibility and improvability of all social institutions and political arrangements."[9]

Thus, in the words of John Gray: "Liberalism . . . is the political theory of modernity."[10]

Race, Ethnicity, and the Politics of Difference

This broadly stroked characterization of the modernity project must be tempered by allowances for important differences in the formation of the project's agenda, and in its deployment, in response to the specific problems and historical conditions prevailing in different national contexts (continental Europe and France, England, Scotland, and America). What is true of each context, however, though with varying degrees of success and different consequences, is that the project of modernity brought about revolutionary social, cultural, political, and economic transformations during the seventeenth and eighteenth centuries.[11]

This is certainly true in the case of America, which became a grand experiment to realize the formation of a nation-state according to principles drawn from Scottish and French currents (among others) of the European Enlightenment, and from British and other European traditions. According to John Gray, the dominant influence on American liberalists was the Scottish social philosophers—Adam Smith in particular—who, more than French or American thinkers, aspired to develop "a science of society in which liberal ideals are given a foundation in a theory of human nature and social order. . . . "[12] In his reading of the *Federalist Papers,* Gray finds that the carriers of Enlightenment liberalism in America differed from the French *philosophes* and agreed with the Scottish Enlightenment thinkers in stressing human imperfectibility. In

this regard American liberalism shared a commitment of central importance to classical liberals: "that individual liberty and popular democracy are contingently but not necessarily related."[13]

This important distinction between the philosophical anthropology of
individualism and the political tenets of universal law and popular
democracy would prove decisive in the unfolding of America. The rea-
son-derived universalist and egalitarian aspirations of the project of
modernity notwithstanding, the liberals seeking to found America, as
were many Enlightenment thinkers, were particularly aware of the realities of human diversities and of their possible social and political consequences. Not all persons, as members of particular groups, were *initially*
at their best. Some (or their progeny) might be improved; others, by
virtue of their "nature," could not be. The egalitarian and universalist
elements of liberalism had to be tempered by the reality of human diversities, thus by the need to put into play, in some circumstances, the
meliorist element of the liberal conviction. These were the grounds on
which a circumscribed, dehumanizing, dominated subworld was constructed and institutionalized and into which Africans were herded and
confined as slaves and denied the rights to "life, liberty, and the pursuit
of happiness" otherwise available to males of European descent of the
appropriate class.

The enslavement of Africans was a crucible for the liberal modernity
project in America that was won through revolutionary battle and
enshrined in the Constitution, the Bill of Rights, and the Declaration of
Independence. The political philosophy that gave primacy to the *individual,* supposedly without regard to "race, creed, or national origin"
since "all men are created *equal,*" and to the rule of law with *universal*
binding force, had also to rationalize social distinctions, ultimately
group-based in terms of race (ethnicity, or gender), curb its own egalitarianism, and seriously distort the nation's subsequent historical development. Thus, while America became paradigmatic as a project of
modern Enlightenment with its capitalist, so-called free enterprise economic order, its representative democracy structured by a host of rights,
and its protected realm of civic privacy—all three resting on a (partially)
universalized and privileged Enlightenment notion of Man—it was also
equally paradigmatic of the self-contradictory tensions inscribed in the
core of Enlightenment thought and practice: on one side were the
universalist implications of the commitment to the "unity of mankind"
in the philosophical anthropology undergirding the political philosophy
of modernity anchored in ideas of reason; on the other side was the
attempt to manage human diversity and imperfectibility by elaborating
a hierarchy defined, in significant part, in terms of the purity, corruption, or level of development of reason (or even the presence or absence
of the ability to reason) in particular groups of persons. As the nation
was unfolding, the compromise on behalf of solidarity among the

colonies—increasingly regionalized by conflicting emerging political economies of neofeudal agricultural capitalism based on slave labor in the South, and of mercantile capitalism in the North and East—required a retreat from the enlightened norms of modernity. The deal was done with reason's sanction; but, in the process, reason was made the whore of political expediency. (Or, as we might now say, after Foucault: the nexus of power and knowledge, in which the latter served the former, was demonstrated with brutal frankness.)

But, the terms in which the deal was cut had been worked out much earlier. During the Greek Enlightenment Aristotle had articulated a scheme in which the recognition of human diversity in terms of hierarchical ordering was in accord with reason: groups of persons differed as a function of their *natures,* which determined their *end* or *telos,* the most that they were capable of being when fully developed. In his words: ". . . the nature of a thing is its end. For what each thing is when fully developed, we call its nature, whether we are speaking of a man, a horse, or a family. Besides, the final cause and end of a thing is the best. . . . "[14] The roles filled by persons of different groups demonstrated the practical truth of this "explanation" in Athens. Thus, it was "rational" to order social relations such that hierarchy brought the range of natures into functional relationships that were appropriate to those on each level: husband to wife, father to children, master to slave, Greek to barbarian:

> But is there any one thus intended by nature to be a slave, and for whom such a condition is expedient and right, or rather is not all slavery a violation of nature? There is no difficulty in answering this question, on grounds both of reason and of fact. For that some should rule and others be ruled is a thing not only necessary, but expedient; from the hour of their birth, some are marked out for subjection, others for rule.[15]

> . . . for in all things which form a composite whole and which are made up of parts, whether continuous or discrete, a distinction between the ruling and the subject element comes to light. Such a duality exists in living creatures, but not in them only; it originates in the constitution of the universe. . . .[16]

When Europeans encountered Africans, these valorizations were readily deployed in the rationalization of racial/ethnic differences into relations of superordination and subordination. Hegel, *the* philosopher of modernity, was quite explicit about the matter:

> Africa must be divided into three parts: one is that which lies south of the desert of Sahara—Africa proper—the Upland almost entirely unknown to us . . . ; the second is that to the north of the desert—European Africa (if we may so call it) . . . ; the third is the river region of the Nile. . . .

> Africa proper, as far as History goes back, has remained—for all purposes of connection with the rest of the World—shut up; it is the Gold-land com-

pressed within itself—the land of childhood, which lying beyond the day of self-conscious history, is enveloped in the dark mantle of Night. . . . The second portion of Africa is the river district of the Nile—Egypt; which was adapted to become a mighty centre of independent civilization, and therefore is as isolated and singular in Africa as Africa itself appears in relation to the other parts of the world. . . . This part was to be—must be attached to Europe. . . .

The peculiarly African character is difficult to comprehend, for the very reason that in reference to it, we must quite give up the principle which naturally accompanies all our ideas—the category of Universality. In Negro life the characteristic point is the fact that consciousness has not yet attained to the realization of any substantial objective existence—as for example, God, or Law—in which the interest of man's volition is involved and in which he realizes his own being. This distinction between himself as an individual and the universality of his essential being, the African in the uniform, undeveloped oneness of his existence has not yet attained; so that the Knowledge of an absolute Being, an Other and a Higher than his individual self, is entirely wanting. The Negro, as already observed, exhibits the natural man in his completely wild and untamed state. We must lay aside all thought of reverence and morality—all that we call feeling—if we would rightly comprehend him; there is nothing harmonious with humanity to be found in this type of character. . . .

At this point we leave Africa, not to mention it again. For it is no historical part of the World; it has no movement or development to exhibit. Historical movements in it—that is in its northern part—belong to the Asiatic or European World. Carthage displayed there an important transitionary phase of civilization; but, as a Phoenician colony, it belongs to Asia. Egypt will be considered in reference to the passage of the human mind from its Eastern to its Western phase, but it does not belong to the African Spirit. What we properly understand by Africa, is the Unhistorical, Undeveloped Spirit, still involved in the conditions of mere nature, and which had to be presented here only as on the threshold of the World's History. Having eliminated this introductory element, we find ourselves for the first time on the real theatre of History.[17]

This orientation rode the ships with the Europeans migrating to this land and was literally made-to-order for the situation of compromise faced by the thinkers in America who had to square slavery with the heritage of the American Revolution. Liberalism was reason-prepared, by both classical and modern Enlightenments, to handle diversity through a reason-privileged hierarchy that restricted egalitarianism to equality among equals. Africans had their differences fixed ontologically through reasoning strategies initially articulated by Aristotle, historically and culturally by Hegel, and spiritually and biologically by the Bible, to mention just a few participants in this grand conspiracy.

"Race" became a primary vehicle for this fixation and was later secured by the imprimatur of *science,* the rising authority-figure of modern reason in its exact, empirical forms. It was through the science of "race" that the executors of the project of modernity sought to take morphological, cultural, social, and historical distinctions among groups of peoples and erect them into a reason-certified hierarchy that had its proper place in the social and political arrangements of liberalism. This science of "race" is worth reviewing, in particular for what it reveals of the failure of the efforts to conscript scientific reason in the ploy to justify the institutionalization of exclusion and domination in the midst of the realization of the liberal project of modernity. This failure would serve to confirm the original tenets of liberal modernity's philosophical anthropology, namely, that beneath the differences all people were *essentially* the same. The recovery of this commitment would fuel the flames of struggle against oppression.

The career of "race" does not begin in modern science but predates it and emerges from a general need to account for the unfamiliar or, simply, to classify objects of experience, thus to organize the lifeworld. How —or why—it was that "race" came to play important classifying, organizing roles is not clear.[18] The nineteenth century development of the use of "race" to distinguish groups biologically was antedated by others in preceding centuries that apparently generated a more compelling need for classificatory ordering in the social world and, subsequently, the use of "race" as such a device. First, there were the tensions within Europe arising from encounters among different groups of peoples, particularly "barbarians"—whether defined culturally or, more narrowly, religiously. (And it should be noted that within European thought, and elsewhere, the color black was associated with evil and death, with "sin" in the Christian context. The valorizing power inherent in this was ready-to-hand with Europe's encounter with Africa.) A more basic impetus, intensified by these tensions, came from the need to account for human origins in general, and for human diversity in particular. Finally, there were the quite decisive European voyages to America and Africa, and the development of capitalism and the slave trade.[19]

The authority of "race" as an organizing, classificatory concept was strengthened during the unfolding of the project of modernity, in the eighteenth century in particular, when "evidence from geology, zoology, anatomy, and other fields of scientific inquiry was assembled to support a claim that racial classification would help explain many human differences. . . . "[20] "Race" contributed to a form of "typological" thinking—a mode of conceptualization that was at the center of the agenda of emerging scientific praxis at the time—that facilitated the classification of human groups. In the modern period the science of "race" began in comparative morphology with its stress on pure "types" as classificatory vehicles.

A major contributor to this unfolding agenda of classificatory thought was the botanist Linnaeus.[21] Other persons were particularly significant contributors to the development of such thought as it related to theories of racial types. According to Banton and Harwood, Johan Friedrich Blumenbach provided the first systematic racial classification in his *Generis humani varietate nativa liber* (*On the Natural Variety of Mankind,* 1775). This was followed by the work of James Cowles Prichard (*Generis humani varietate,* 1808).[22] Georges Cuvier, a French anatomist, put forth a physical cause theory of races in 1800 in arguing that physical nature determined culture. He classified humans into three major groups along an implied descending scale: whites, yellows, and blacks. As Banton and Harwood interpreted his work, central to his thinking was the notion of "type" more than that of "race": "Underlying the variety of the natural world was a limited number of pure types and if their nature could be grasped it was possible to interpret the diverse forms which could temporarily appear as a result of hybrid mating."[23] Other important contributions include S. G. Morton's publication of a volume on the skulls of American Indians (1839) and one on Egyptian skulls (1845). His work was extended and made popular by J. C. Nott and G. R. Gliddon in their *Types of Mankind* (1854). Charles Hamilton Smith (*The Natural History of the Human Species,* 1848) developed Cuvier's line of argument in Britain. By Smith's reckoning, according to Banton and Harwood, "The Negro's lowly place in the human order was a consequence of the small volume of his brain."[24] Smith's former student, Robert Knox (*The Races of Men,* 1850), argued likewise. Finally, there was Count Joseph Arthur de Gobineau's four-volume *Essay on the Inequality of Human Races* (1854) in which he argued that, in the words of Banton and Harwood, "the major world civilizations . . . were the creations of different races and that race-mixing was leading to the inevitable deterioration of humanity."[25]

Two significant achievements resulted from these efforts. First, drawing on the rising authority of modern science as the realization and guardian of systematic, certain knowledge, there was the legitimation of "race" as a gathering concept for morphological features that were thought to distinguish varieties of *Homo sapiens* supposedly related to one another through the logic of a *natural* hierarchy of groups. Second, there was the legitimation of the view that the behavior of a group and its members was determined by their place in this hierarchy.[26] Consequently, science-authorized and legitimated notions about "race," when combined with social projects involving the distinguishing and, ultimately, the control of "racially" different persons and groups—as in the case of the enslavement of Africans—took root and grew to become part of modern common sense. "Race" was an "obvious" factor of social life.

But the science of "race" was unstable: insights gained through attempts to secure racial distinctions scientifically in support of political projects of subordination and oppression subverted the projects themselves. The situation was both assisted and complicated by the work of Darwin and Mendel. Social Darwinism emerged as an effort by some (notably Herbert Spencer and Ludwig Gumplowicz) to apply Darwin's principles regarding heredity and natural selection to human groups and endeavors and thereby provide firmer grounding for the science of "race" (something Darwin was reluctant to do). Such moves were particularly useful in justifying the dominance of certain groups over others (British over Irish; Europeans over Africans . . .). On the other hand, however, Darwin's *Origins* shifted the terrain of scientific discourse from morphology and the stability of "pure types" to a subsequent genetics-based approach to individual characteristics and the effects on them of processes of change, and thus shifted the focus of science to the analysis of variety. In the additional work of Mendel, this development proved revolutionary:

> A racial type was defined by a number of features which are supposed to go together. . . . The racial theorists of the nineteenth century assumed there was a natural law which said that such traits were invariably associated and were transmitted to the next generation as part of a package deal. Gregor Mendel's research showed that this was not necessarily the case. . . . [It] also showed that trait variation *within* a population was just as significant as trait variations *between* populations. . . . [T]raits do not form part of a package but can be shuffled like a pack of playing cards.[27]

And, since environmental impacts that condition natural selection are important factors in the "shuffling" of traits, in addition to the roles played by heredity and the interplay between dominant and recessive traits, the notion of "pure" racial types with fixed essential characteristics was displaced: biologically (that is, genetically) one can only speak of "clines."[28]

The biology of "races" thus became more a matter of studying diversities within—as well as among—groups, and, of particular interest, of studying how groups "evolve" across both time and space. To these efforts were joined others from the *social* science of "race": that is, understanding groups as sharing some distinctive biological features—though not sufficient to constitute them as pure types—but with respect to which sociocultural factors are of particular importance (but in ways significantly different from the thinking of the nineteenth-century theorists of racial types).

For many scientists the old (nineteenth-century) notion of "race" had become useless as a classificatory concept, hence certainly did not support in any truly scientific way the political agendas of racists. Revolutions within science (natural and social) conditioned transformed approaches to "race." The conceptual terrain for this later, primarily twentieth-century approach to "race" continues to be, in large part, the notion of "evolution" and was significantly conditioned by the precursive work of Mendel and Darwin. In the space opened by this concept it became possible at least to work at synthesizing insights drawn from both the natural sciences (genetics, biochemistry) and the social sciences (anthropology, sociology, psychology, ethology) for a fuller understanding of "geographical races":[29] studies of *organic* evolution focus on changes in the gene pool of a group or groups; studies of *superorganic* evolution are concerned with changes in the "behavior repertoire" of a group or groups—that is, with their sociocultural development.[30] And it is a legitimate question—though one difficult to answer—to what extent, if at all, superorganic evolution is a function of organic evolution, or, to add even more complexity, to what extent, if at all, the two forms of evolution are mutually influential. The question of the relations between both forms of development continues to be a major challenge.

But what is a "race" in the framework of organic evolution and the global social context of the late twentieth century? Certainly not a group of persons who share genetic homogeneity. That is only likely in the few places where one might find groups that have remained completely isolated from other groups, with no intergroup sexual reproductions. Among other things, the logics of the capitalist world system have drawn virtually all peoples into the "global village" and facilitated much "interbreeding." But capitalism notwithstanding, "raciation"— that is, the development of the distinctive gene pools of various groups which determine the relative frequencies of characteristics shared by their members, but certainly not by them alone—has also been a function, in part, of chance. Consequently:

> Since populations' genetic compositions vary over time, race classifications can never be permanent; today's classification may be obsolete in 100 generations. More importantly, modern race classifications attempt to avoid being arbitrary by putting populations *of presumed common evolutionary descent* into the same racial group. Common descent, however, is inferred from similarity in gene frequencies, and here the problem lies. For . . . a population's gene frequencies are determined not only by its ancestry but also by the processes of natural selection and genetic drift. This means that two populations could, in principle, be historically unrelated but genetically quite similar if they had been independently subject to similar evolutionary forces. To place them in the same racial group would, as a step in the study of evolution, be quite misleading. In the absence of historical evidence of descent, therefore, it is difficult to avoid the conclusion that classifying races is merely a convenient but biologically arbitrary way of breaking down the variety of gene frequency data into a manageable number of categories.[31]

When we classify a group as a "race," then, at best we refer to generally shared characteristics derived from a "pool" of genes. Social, cultural, and geographical factors, in addition to those of natural selection, all impact on this pool, and thus on raciation: sometimes to sustain the pool's relative configuration (for example, by isolating the group—culturally or physically—from outbreeding), and sometimes to modify it (as when "mulattoes" were produced in the Americas in significant part through slave masters of European descent appropriating African women for their—the "masters" '—sexual pleasure). It is possible to study, with some success, the evolution of a particular group over time (a case of *specific* evolution)—that is, the grouping of all of the world's peoples in ordered categories "with the largest and most heterogeneous societies in the top category and the smallest and most homogeneous in the bottom."[32] In either case—of general or specific evolution—the concern is with superorganic evolution: changes in behavior repertoires. And such changes are not tied to the genetic specificities of "races."

But not all persons (or groups) think so. Though evolutionary—as opposed to typological—thinking, in some form, is at present the dominant intellectual framework for systematic reconstructions and explanations of human natural and social history, it, too, has been enlisted in the service of those who would have "science" pass absolution on their political agendas: that is, to legitimate the empowerment of certain groups, certain "races," over others. Even shorn of the more crude outfittings of social Darwinism's "survival of the fittest" (those who have power or seek power over others being the "fittest," of course . . .), the field of the science of "race" is still occupied by those offering orderings of human groups along an *ascending* scale with a particular group's placement on the scale being a function of the level of their supposed development (or lack thereof) toward human perfectibility: from "primitive" to "civilized," from "undeveloped" or "underdeveloped" to "developed" or "advanced."

Such arguments find fertile soil for nourishment and growth now that "evolution" (organic and superorganic, often without distinction), frequently conceived of as linear development along a single path which *all* "races" have to traverse, is now a basic feature of our "common sense" —Creationists excepted—and as we still face political problems emerging from conflicts among "racial" groups. "Race" continues to function as a critical yardstick for the rank-ordering of particular groups both "scientifically" and sociopolitically, the latter with support from the former. At bottom, then, "race"—sometimes explicitly, quite often implicitly—continues to be a major fulcrum of struggles over the distribution and exercise of power.

Certainly one of the more prominent contemporary struggles has centered on the validity of measurements of the "intelligence" of persons from different "racial" groups that purport to demonstrate the comparative "intelligence" of the groups. This struggle is propelled by the social weight given to "intelligence" as an important basis for achievement and rewards in a meritocratic social order. At its center is the question of the dominant roles played by either the genes or the environment in determining "intelligence" (and, by extension, in determining raciation). But, at basis we have in this struggle only a return of "reason" in disguise as the critical measure of humanity.

What, then, after this extended review of the science of "race," are we left with by way of understanding? With the decisive conclusion, certainly, that "race" is *not* wholly and completely determined by biology, but is only partially so. Even then, biology does not *determine* "race," but in complex interplay with environmental, cultural, and social factors provides certain boundary conditions and possibilities that affect raciation and the development of "geographical" races (again, the development of the distinctive gene pools of various groups which determine the relative frequencies of characteristics shared by their members). In addition, the definition of "race" is partly political, partly cultural. Nor does the modern conceptual terrain of "evolution" provide scientifically secure access to race-determining biological, cultural, and social development complexes distributed among various groups that fix a group's rank-ordered place on an ascending "great chain of being." Racial categories are fundamentally *social* in nature and rest on shifting sands of biological heterogeneity.[33] The biological aspects of "race" are conscripted into projects of cultural, political, and social construction. "Race" is a *social* formation.[34]

A review of the career of the concept of "ethnicity," which became paradigmatic for conceptualizing groupings of different humans during the 1920s and 1930s after having successfully challenged the then prevailing biologistic approach to races which had evolved after slavery to "explain" the "racial inferiority" of people of African descent—and, thereby, the "superiority" of the "white race"—reveals a legacy similar to that for race, in part because the terms have often been used as synonyms. With good reason, apparently, for the etymology of "ethnicity" reveals that the root term involved a physiological association that was retained in English: the word "ethnic" derives, via Latin, from the Greek *ethnikos*, the adjectival form of *ethnos*, a nation or race.[35] Later there were shifts from a biological (physiological) context of meaning to one that included cultural characteristics and political structures, though the shifts have been neither consistent nor unidirectional.[36]

First, prior to the 1930s, the focus on ethnicity was an insurgent approach that challenged the biologistic view of race, an attack that was led by "progressive" scholars, activists, and policymakers for whom what has come to be called the "Chicago school" of sociology was a decisive institutional site. In this intellectual and social context "race" was regarded as a social category and but one of a number of determinants of ethnicity or ethnic-group identity. Second, during the decades spanning the 1930s through the mid-1960s the ethnic paradigm served as the liberal/progressive "common sense" of race, a period in which assimilationism and cultural pluralism emerged as themes of discourses devoted to the articulation of strategies to guide the development of America into an "integrated" social whole in which racial/ethnic differences were "melted" away by the rationalist heat of egalitarian principles. This agenda, and the theorizing of "ethnicity" which was its intellectual articulation, were formed to meet the problems resulting from the migration and "culture contact" of European immigrants, hence the emphasis on—and the intellectual acceptance of the inevitability and desirability of—"integration."[37]

But the victory of the "ethnicity" paradigm in service to integration (that is, assimilation) was to prove hollow, in significant part because the paradigm and agenda were rooted in a framework structured so tightly around European experiences and concerns that there was a serious failure to appreciate the extent to which inequalities conditioned by biologically informed geographical raciations differed from inequalities that could be understood appropriately through the concepts of an "ethnicity" localized to groups of various lines of European descent. Thus, in the post-1965 period, when the Black Power movement ushered in an agenda decisively distinct from the assimilationism of the Civil Rights movement—and, in doing so, excited persons comprising other groups likewise to seek social justice in distributive terms referenced to their racial or ethnic identity, not just to their being Americans—"ethnicity" as paradigm for integration was sharply challenged. The responses of some proponents of its continued dominance defined the paradigm's third agenda of deployment: as a defense of "conservative" egalitarianism against the "radical" assault of proponents of "group rights"—Blacks, women, and "ethnics" who refused to surrender their cultural traditions and identities, their lifeworlds, to the homogenizing processes of America's "melting pot." And, once again, the defenders invoke the charge that the "ethnics" are being "unreasonable."

We are thus in the midst of "the rise of the unmeltables": that is, of social movements organized around a "new ethnicity"—"new" relative to the long dominance of the paradigm of assimilation—based on the use of cultural as well as biological characteristics by persons from various groups to identify *themselves* as being part of particular ethnic or racial groups, and to formulate their claims for social justice using these identifiers. One student of this "new ethnicity," Michael Novak, shares my reading of the times: this heightened awareness and articulation of "ethnicity" (he terms it "cultural awareness"), when politicized, makes this a major factor in global affairs, "perhaps even one of the major sources of political energy in our era."[38] Novak identifies a number of important components of the new ethnicity that are worth noting:

1. It is "post-tribal," that is to say, it arises in an era when virtually every cultural group has been obliged to become aware of many others.
2. It arises in an era of advanced technology that, paradoxically, liberates energies for more intense self-consciousness while, simultaneously, binding many cultures together in standardized technical infrastructures.
3. It arises during a period of intense centripetal and homogenizing forces; and in some cases it involves a rebellion against forces of technical power, and thus manifests a certain rebellion against the supposed moral superiority of modernity.[39]

But why this resurgence of political movements the central mobilizing terms of which involve valorizations of factors of difference, of particularity, such as race or ethnicity? Because, I think, the concrete existential concerns and actions of specific groupings of peoples to realize their particular(istic) interests, when pulled into the bounds of the theoretical and practical legacies of the project of modernity, have generally been poorly accommodated, if not eclipsed or eliminated, by the twin pressures of reductionist moves to individualism, and flights into abstract universalism, derivative of subject-centered reason. The historical, cultural, social lifeworld is the foundation and context of our lived experience, of our very being. And in the case of African people in America in particular, the projects of enslavement and subordination, facilitated by the hierarchizing, differentiating categories elaborated by some Enlightenment thinkers, helped to insure the preservation in revised form of a distinctive New World African lifeworld evidenced in our art, music, religion, literature, social life, and the very nature of our vernacular language. In addition, we also discovered—the reason-certified egalitarian, universalist promise of liberal modernity notwithstanding—that reason itself is never "pure," never without specific historical and cultural clothing appropriate to the particular projects of particular persons of particular groups situated in particular ways in a particular social order. Thus are we in the midst of a historical conjuncture that is highly charged by efforts to achieve democracy in a multi-"ethnic," multi-"racial" society where "group thinking" is a decisive feature of social and political life. Group-based particularity has become the basis of struggle. Neither liberalism nor the critical theoretical tradition of Marxism is a sufficient mediator.

In light of all this, how might the challenges of race and ethnicity be met successfully, both theoretically and practically? Are there insights that, when combined with critical social thought, will assist us in the practical realization of a social order structured, in part, by valorizations of race and ethnicity as substantive aspects of a democratic pluralism in which "difference" is prized over forced homogenization, or over the hegemony of one group and its values and practices over all others while disguising this dominance in the dress of liberal democracy, or of a party totalitarianism that invokes its legitimacy by repeating its mantras —"the proletariat," "the workers," "the people"—though always backing its stay in power and the enforcement of its agenda with willing use of brutal force?

In posing the questions in these terms it is obvious that the terrain on which theoretical and practical projects might be formed to accommodate "the politics of differences" cannot be that of the political theory of modernity (liberalism) alone. Nor can it be that of the revised, radicalized, but equally modern political project of Marxian-inspired social transformation. I find the philosophical anthropology of the liberal Enlightenment historically progressive but, at the same time, impoverished. The same is true of Marxism, since its core philosophical anthropology draws from the same well. For while race and ethnicity are without "scientific" bases in biological terms, this does *not* mean that the terms are completely void of positive, distinguishing social value—racism and invidious ethnocentrism notwithstanding. For me, race and ethnicity (and gender) are constitutive of the personal and social being of persons, and thus are not secondary, unessential matters: they make up the historically mediated structural features of human lifeworlds and inform lived experience. Further, they have both absolute (that is, in themselves) and relative (that is, in relation to other racial, ethnic, or gender groups) value *to the extent that, and for as long as,* persons *take them to be constitutive of who they are.* It is here that the philosophical anthropology of the Enlightenment comes up short. A theory of society that sets itself the task of understanding, scripting, and directing revolutionary social transformation that disregards these basic "social facts" is, in my judgment, seriously deficient.

In searching for new terrain and terms on and through which to fashion new theoretical and practical agendas I am committed to two basic beliefs. First, that a full appreciation of what it means to be human requires that we take proper note of human groupings the definitive characteristics of which (combining historically mediated physical, psychological, and cultural factors) are constitutive, in varying degrees, of the persons in the group. Second, that the principles on which we would base both the organization of sociopolitical life, and those intellectual enterprises whose objects are living human beings, take explicit account of these constitutive differences. Doing so can and ought to lead to the acknowledged and promoted substantial enrichment of our collective life given the wealth of messages, ideals, and practices contributed by various groups comprising our multidimensional social worlds. Not doing so results not only in our collective impoverishment, but, particularly when there is active opposition to those who are "different," the failure contributes directly to distortions of the cultural spaces we all occupy and to the deformation and self-deformation of members of those groups. Among the groups for whom these matters continue to be pressing issues are those constituted, at least in part, by factors termed "racial" and/or "ethnic."

There are many aspects to the challenge posed by the advocacy of forms of political, social, cultural, and intellectual life in which the "play of differences" is a normative, nurtured feature. One of the most important is the challenge to our basic conceptions of ourselves as individual persons and as ordered associates in sociopolitical structures and practices bequeathed by both liberal and radical (Marxian) traditions of modernity: namely, the requirement to look beyond what is often regarded as "accidental" differences, including "race" and "ethnicity," to the "substantial core" or *essence* which, ontologically, is the definitive constitutive factor of the human species, and thus is shared by all humans. For a long time now that "essence" has been identified as *reason*. Knowing and exercising this "essence" has been thought central to securing "universality" in epistemological matters as a foundation for unity and order in sociopolitical praxis.

For opponents of the project to give freer rein to the play of differences, the emphasis on *particularity* subverts these quests and, in practical terms, threatens the always tenuous achievements of cognitive and political normativity thought to be secured by the universality of reason: the achievement and perpetuation of knowledge (in science and philosophy, for example) become exposed to the acidic effects of "relativism"; and the freedom, peace, and prosperity of political stability won—or to be won—through liberal or revolutionary politics are jeopardized by possibilities of drift, chaos, or, at worst, anarchy.[40]

Such possibilities are real. Whether they are *probable* depends on a number of factors. But it is neither logically, socially, or historically *necessary* that such consequences follow from a greater play of differences. Achieving that increased play while preserving and enhancing social and intellectual life is precisely what I see as the challenge to be met in an appropriate valorization of race and ethnicity.

Philosophical Praxis: Critical Social Theory as "Cosmopolitan Liberalism"?

To this end I join others in calling for a serious revision of the traditions flowing out of the modern Enlightenment, traditions that have too often been a cloak for the hegemony of the complex metaphysics, ontology, and philosophical anthropology of a "white mythology" which "reassembles and reflects the culture of the West: the white man takes his own mythology, Indo-European mythology, his own *logos,* that is, the *mythos* of his idiom, for the universal form of that he must still wish to call Reason."[41] This notion of reason, articulated most forcefully by philosophers of the classical and modern Enlightenments, must be revised if it is to offer us guidance. In the words of Michael Novak:

> No one would deny that there is a perfectly straightforward sense in which all human beings are members of the same human family; every human being is bound by imperatives of reasoning, justification, and communication across cultural and other boundaries; and each human being is entitled to claims of fundamental human dignity. Still, it is also widely grasped today that reason itself operates in pluralistic modes. It would be regarded as "cultural imperialism" to suggest that only one form of reasoning is valid in all matters. It would be regarded as naive to believe that the content of human experiencing, imagining, understanding, judging, and deciding were everywhere the same. . . . It seems important for a liberal civilization today to thread its way philosophically between the Scylla of relativity and the Charybdis of too narrow a conception of universal reason.[42]

This challenge confronts philosophy directly. One of the central endeavors of Western philosophy continues to be that of attempting to provide the definitive characterization of what it is to be human (of what it is to be "Man"). And, in general, the terms in which the characterizations have been and are articulated are void of any explicit references to race and ethnicity. Certainly the Enlightenment was a partial triumph of precisely this mode of characterizing humans. And it was a triumph that made possible substantive progressive achievements in human history, won against some forces that, had they triumphed instead, would have given us a world not much to the liking of many of us, myself included.

But the victory was not without costs. At the very least, in focusing on what is shared in pursuit of unity and universality, the unique, the dissimilar, the individual, the particular is disregarded. And in this focusing a tension is created at the core of Enlightenment philosophy's view of Man: between its specification of the shared and universal in the characterization of the human species that makes us all "the same," and its emphasis on the free, rational *individual*. This tension, we noted, was handled, to some extent, by elaborating hierarchical categories for sorting different persons and groups. Further, the aspirations of universalist philosophy notwithstanding, where *generally* race, ethnicity, gender, and so forth were irrelevant to the formulations of key notions, the full truth of the matter disclosed the invidious ethnocentrism and racism, sexism, and class biases at the very heart of the enterprise: whether invoked in the Greek-barbarian distinction, the enslavement of non-Greeks and the constraining of women when fifth- and fourth-century Greece was at its zenith, or in the continued oppression of women and the enslavement and oppression of African peoples during and after the modern Enlightenment.

Of course, one might argue that where we find racism, ethnocentrism, class bias, or sexism in philosophy it is due to the failure of particular thinkers to live up to the terms of humanism called for by the universalist notions of humans as rational beings—for some, created in the image of God—who are rightly worthy of respect, and that a correction of such situations requires only that the guilty parties come to be governed by the logic of these notions. Consequently, no revision of the central notions about "Man" is required.

I disagree. While substantive in many ways in contributing to our sense of ourselves, and thus to the organization of our individual and collective life, the privileged notions are also insufficient in ways that can only be corrected by revising them to include space for an appreciation of group-based particularities. It is necessary to extend the privileged notions to groups of persons previously excluded from coverage (for example, women, Africans and people of African descent, and other peoples of color). We must rethink "Man" if some of the challenges to practical life are to be overcome.

But philosophy has seldom taken up such a project, having been much too preoccupied with the search for the invariant structures of experience, and the invariant operations of human understanding.[43] As important as this quest has been—and it has resulted in significant achievements in thought that have contributed, as well, to our practical life in very positive ways—it is not sufficient. Moreover, when it is allowed to dominate our efforts to give philosophical grounding to our collective and individual life, we sow the seeds that are harvested as the strife of renewed ethnicity and raciation as millions are unable to locate themselves in satisfying ways, or to find social justice, in the terms and practices of social ordering predicated on the stifling universalisms of the old liberalism and moribund attempted instantiations of dictatorial Marxism.

As in previous Enlightenments, philosophers can make substantial contributions to the project suggested by Novak. But we can do so only after adopting a more critical appreciation of difference, in part conceived in terms of "race" and "ethnicity," that preserves the progressive achievements of the old Enlightenments while contributing to our moving beyond them toward a new pluralist consensus. In promoting this development I do not seek refuge in Romanticism. Instead, what I desire is a new form of "liberalism," what Novak terms a *cosmopolitan* rather than a *universalist* liberalism, which should rest on two pillars: "a firm commitment to the laborious but rewarding enterprise of full, mutual, intellectual understanding; and a respect for differences of nuance and subtlety, particularly in the area of those diversifying 'lived values' that have lain until now, in all cultures, so largely unarticulated."[44] The elaboration of this new liberalism in its possible social-political realizations would be an important contribution from philosophy, something those of us involved in the discipline have not yet worked out as fully as we might.

This elaboration must include insights gained from explorations of the "other side" of race and ethnicity: namely, the lived experiences of persons within racial/ethnic groups for whom their race or ethnicity is a fundamental and *positive* element of their identity, and thus of their life-world, in ways that are far from detrimental to the social whole. A new liberalism that truly contributes to enlightenment and emancipation must appreciate such endeavors and appropriate the integrity of those who see themselves through the prisms of race and ethnicity, and who change their definitions of themselves. Certainly, the socially divisive forms and consequences of "race thinking" or "ethnic thinking" ought to be eliminated, to whatever extent possible. But we should not err, yet again, in thinking that "race thinking" or "ethnic thinking" must be completely eliminated on the way to an emancipated and just society, something that is both unlikely and unnecessary.

Such thinking has informed the tradition of critical social theory and left it divided on the issues of race and ethnicity, sometimes against itself: the Frankfurt School thought "race" to be without scientific basis as an explanatory notion; "official" Marxism in its classical form treated race and ethnicity as factors of conflict secondary to the primary contradiction of class struggle and which would be of no significance under socialism; the later "official" Marxism of 1928–1957 allowed that race—in the case of African Americans in particular—was the basis of a black *nation,* that is, a group whose members shared a common history and culture. A revised critical theory of society that helps to shape a cosmopolitan liberalism which contributes to the learning and social evolution that secure democratic emancipation in the context of racial and ethnic diversity would be of no small consequence socially and politically.

But would such a project require that we become "postmodern" and retreat from the progressive achievements of ancient and modern Western Enlightenments won through both liberal and Marxian traditions and practices? Perhaps, depending on how one proceeds. It also opens us to challenging possibilities for social learning that may provide us with bases for enhanced living, for realizing futures which we otherwise might not live due to our failure to learn and evolve. Here we rejoin Habermas, better prepared to appreciate the significance of what he offers as he takes up the philosophical challenge to elaborate a critical social theory that preserves the progressive achievements of the liberal and critical-Marxist projects of modernity while rehabilitating as "communicative reason" the reason of modernity of which I have been critical, and which he criticizes as "subject-centered" reason.

And how is this "communicative reason" different from "subject-centered reason"? Habermas offers the following distinctions:

"Rationality" refers in the first instance to the disposition of speaking and acting subjects to acquire and use fallible knowledge. . . . Subject-centered reason finds its criteria in standards of truth and success that govern the relationships of knowing and purposively acting subjects to the world of possible objects or states of affairs. By contrast, as soon as we conceive of knowledge as communicatively mediated, rationality is assessed in terms of the capacity of responsible participants in interaction to orient themselves in relation to validity claims geared to intersubjective recognition. Communicative reason finds its criteria in the argumentative procedures for directly or indirectly redeeming claims to propositional truth, normative rightness, subjective truthfulness, and aesthetic harmony. . . . This communicative rationality recalls older ideas of logos, inasmuch as it brings along with it the connotations of a noncoercively unifying, consensus-building force of a discourse in which the participants overcome their at first subjectively biased views in favor of a rationally motivated agreement. Communicative reason is expressed in a decentered understanding of the world.[45]

Habermas *wants* a form of understanding in which ". . . the paradigm of knowledge of objects has to be replaced by the paradigm of mutual understanding between subjects capable of speech and action," a form of reason that, at the same time, remains aware of the contexts of its own emergence and position, aware that even its most basic universalist concepts "have a temporal core"; but he must also take care to insure that communicative reason does not resurrect "the purism of pure reason."[46]

There are other worries for Habermas. There is the question of "whether the concepts of communicative action and of the transcending force of universalistic validity claims do not reestablish an idealism that is incompatible with the naturalistic insights of historical materialism . . . ," the idealism of "a pure, nonsituated reason" that reintroduces the chasm between the transcendental and the empirical.[47] The protection against idealism, for Habermas, is gained in the recognition of the fact that "the symbolic reproduction of the lifeworld and its material reproduction are internally interdependent . . . " and of the fact that the lifeworld provides the resources which nourish networks of communicative action and is "the *medium* by which concrete forms of life are reproduced."[48] In Habermas' rejoinder to these worries are to be found the challenges to be met in articulating a rehabilitated notion of reason that preserves universality while also preserving the particularity of historically situated lifeworlds:

There is no pure reason that might don linguistic clothing only in the second place. Reason is by its very nature incarnated in contexts of communicative action and in structures of the lifeworld. . . . The transcendent moment of *universal* validity bursts every provinciality asunder; the obligatory moment of accepted validity claims renders them carriers of a

context-bound everyday practice. Inasmuch as communicative agents recip-
rocally raise validity claims with their speech acts, they are relying on the
potential of assailable grounds. Hence, a moment of *unconditionality* is built
into *factual* processes of mutual understanding—the validity laid claim to is
distinguished from the social currency of a de facto established practice
and yet serves it as the foundation of an existing consensus. The validity
claimed for propositions and norms transcends spaces and times, *"blots
out" space and time;* but the claim is always raised *here and now,* in specific
contexts, and is either accepted or rejected with factual consequences for
action.[49]

We must wonder whether this is sufficient to support a theory of communicative reason and action as the means toward a socially realized
resting place between the universal and the particular, a theory that will
finally allow us to escape the "opposing impulses" that Habermas sees
as having dominated the history of philosophy since Plato and Democri-
tus.[50] Certainly, Habermas' efforts to elaborate such a theory are promising and, taken as a whole, represent one of the most consistent and
comprehensive attempts in recent social theorizing.

For me, much of that promise is provided by his appreciation of the
lifeworld—as the locus of cultural tradition, socially integrated groups,
and identity-formation and socialization, each dimension of which he
sees as having its own processes of reproduction and standards for evaluating them—and his incorporation of the insights gained through that
appreciation into his social theory. For it is through the notion of a life-
world that we can come to appreciate in our theorizing the constitution
of social groups—their cultural traditions, the identities of their members, and the forms of solidarity by which they achieve their social integration—appropriately characterized, in some cases, in terms of their
race or ethnicity. And we can do so without abandoning completely
modernity's quest for reason-sanctioned universality. For Habermas, at
least, rationality is still to be found grounding communication, the life-
blood of the lifeworld:

> . . . [T]he rational potential of speech is interwoven with the *resources* of
> any particular given lifeworld. . . . As a resource from which interaction
> participants support utterances capable of reaching consensus, the life-
> world constitutes an equivalent for what the philosophy of the subject has
> ascribed to consciousness in general as synthetic accomplishments. Now,
> of course, the generative accomplishments are related not to the form but
> to the content of possible mutual understanding. To this extent, *concrete*
> forms of life replace transcendental consciousness in its function of creat-
> ing unity. In culturally embodied self-understandings, intuitively present
> group solidarities, and the competencies of socialized individuals that are
> brought into play as know-how, the reason expressed in communicative
> action is mediated with the traditions, social practices, and body-centered
> complexes of experience that coalesce into *particular* totalities.[51]

We must note, however, that even as we understand the form of "transcendence" involved in the redeemed validity claims of historically situated speech during which consensus is reached to be different from the ahistorical "transcendental" of subject-centered reason, "transcendence" still trades off "transcendental" in securing universality for reason. Moreover, the universality achieved through reason-redeemed validity claims is still *formal:* the notion points us to *conditions of validity* for redeeming validity claims, not *which* claims are—or are not —valid. I do not think it quite as easy, nor in crucial cases even appropriate, as Habermas might make it appear, to have the only "force" operating in unconstrained dialogue be "the force of reason," where "force" is the universalistic binding power of redeemed claims which hold without regard to what he takes to be "particularistic" claims emerging from contexts of interests that are significantly linked to race or ethnicity.

But Habermas is fully aware of the limitations of what he offers as a critical theory that is free from the dialectic of impulses mentioned earlier that has dominated philosophy:

> . . . I have attempted to free historical materialism from its philosophical ballast. . . . A theory developed in this way can no longer start by examining concrete ideals immanent in traditional forms of life. It must orient itself to the range of learning processes that is opened up at a given time by a historically attained level of learning. It must refrain from critically evaluating and normatively ordering totalities, forms of life and cultures, and life-contexts and epochs *as a whole.* . . . Coming at the end of a complicated study of the main features of a theory of communicative action, this suggestion cannot count even as a "promissory note." It is less a promise than a conjecture.[52]

Again, the promise is in the theoretical—and if informed by it, the practical—spaces opened by the theory offered, up to now, as a conjecture. And, coming from one who deliberately seeks to further the progressive achievements of modernity in its liberal and Marxian moments, that is no insignificant offering. For African peoples have always been a force of difference for both traditions. Neither the full nature and extent of our oppression, nor our historical-cultural being as African and African-descended peoples, has been comprehended adequately by the concepts and logics involved in Marxian and liberal analyses and programs for the projects of modernity in societies in Europe and Euro-America.

In part this is a function of the subtle, but pervasive, racism mediated in the liberal and Marxian voices that narrated periods of the histories of particular European peoples as though, on the one hand, they were the histories of *all* peoples, and, on the other, as though Hegel had in fact provided the definitive word on Africans: a people without history because a people not yet sufficiently developed as to be makers of history. In part it was a function of the failure to deal with the heterogeneity of the populations of European centers of the rise of capitalism,[53] in part a failure to deal with racism as an indigenous element of European history and culture.[54] These failures were both institutionalized and compounded in the construction of the false universality that infected key concepts and strategies of the analyses and practices of liberalism and Marxism.

Could the articulation of a critical social theory leading to the formation of organizations and strategic implementations that promote social transformation take place in a context conditioned by the exploration of difference, by an explicit valorization of differences? There is the danger that we could well flounder on our differences and become a confusion of particularistic "interest groups" without transcending unifying principles that bind us into a real, living community. Instead of consensus, we could resurrect the Tower of Babel.[55]

This is indeed a real danger. But it cannot be removed theoretically. It is a danger that is concomitant to existential realities that should not be bleached out, as it were, by ahistorical, universalist categories intended to secure us against possible fragmentation. The new society must be won in the struggle to realize it. The excursion through "difference" involves, potentially, more than a concern on the part of women, of peoples of Amerindian, African, Hispanic, and Asian descents, of gays, and so forth to tell our own stories and, in doing so, to reaffirm ourselves. The important point is *why* the histories and cultures—the modalities of being, the lifeworlds—are meaningful and important, *why* they have an integrity worth preserving and struggling for while they are subjected to progressive refinement.

The issue, then, in its theoretical, practical, and *existential* realness, is whether there is sufficient commonality in our sufferings and our hopes —the modes and sources of our oppressions and in the requirements for a social order that would be void of them—as well as in our joys and accomplishments to allow our coming together and forging a concrete universal, a unity in diversity? If so, then we must move from theory to praxis in terms of moving from universality via conceptual strategies to universality in the form of democratically based shared unity as an existential project. The stress is on "project," that is, on constant practical efforts that are likewise constantly reconciled by the renewed recognition that no amount of "knowing" or "critical thought" secures the laws, meaningfulness, and trajectory of human history. Rather, it is a constant "doing" that is constituted in the very micro-cells of daily existence, and is structured by the powerfully binding and constituting forces of race, ethnicity, nationality, gender, and sexuality as mediated and mediating elements of cultural historicity. It is my sense—my hope —that posing and discussing this issue is in part the point of this conference, and that the motivation for organizing it comes in part from a recognition of the task we keepers of sometimes conflicting racial, ethnic, gender, sexual, cultural, and national legacies have been bequeathed by our shared and different histories.

Notes

1. For this discussion, the following works in particular: "Modernity—An Incomplete Project," in *Interpretive Social Science: A Second Look,* ed. by Paul Rabinow and William M. Sullivan (Berkeley and Los Angeles: University of California Press, 1987), pp. 141–156; *The Philosophical Discourse of Modernity,* trans. by Frederick Lawrence (Cambridge, Massachusetts: The MIT Press, 1987); *The Theory of Communicative Action,* vol. 2: *Lifeworld and System: A Critique of Functionalist Reason,* trans. by Thomas McCarthy (Boston: Beacon Press, 1987).

2. "Hegel was the first philosopher to develop a clear concept of modernity. We have to go back to him if we want to understand the internal relationship between modernity and rationality, which, until Max Weber, remained self-evident and which today is being called into question" (Habermas, *Discourse of Modernity,* p. 4).

3. Habermas, *Discourse of Modernity,* pp. 16–17, 18.

4. Ibid., p. 318.

5. Ibid., p. 7. Again, for Habermas Hegel is key: he ". . . was the first to raise to the level of a philosophical problem the process of detaching modernity from the suggestion of norms lying outside of itself in the past" (*Discourse of Modernity,* p. 16).

6. Ibid., p. 365.

7. Ibid., p. 2.

8. John Gray, *Liberalism* (Minneapolis: University of Minnesota Press, 1986), p. 16.

9. Ibid., p. x.

10. Ibid., p. 82.

11. The following discussion is taken from my *Philosophy, Ethnicity, and Race,* the Alfred P. Stiernotte Lectures in Philosophy, Quinnipiac College: Hamden, Connecticut, 1989, and my "Toward a Critical Theory of Race," in *Anatomy of Racism,* ed. by David Goldberg (Minneapolis: University of Minnesota Press, 1990).

12. Gray, *Liberalism,* p. 24. "It is in the writings of the social philosophers and political economists of the Scottish Enlightenment that we find the first comprehensive statement in systematic form of the principles and foundations of liberalism. Among the French, as among the Americans, liberal thought was bound up at every point with a response to a particular crisis of political order. It is not that the thought of the Scottish philosophers was not conditioned by the historical context in which they found themselves, but rather that they aimed, as perhaps the great French and American liberals did not consistently do, to ground their liberal principles in a comprehensive account of human social

development and a theory of social and economic structure whose terms had the status of natural laws and not merely of historical generalizations" (*Liberalism*, p. 24).

13. Ibid., p. 21.

14. Aristotle, *Politics,* bk. 1, chap. 5, 1252B.30–33.

15. Ibid., bk. 1, chap. 5, 1254A.18–24.

16. Ibid., bk. 1, chap. 5, 1254A.29–33.

17. G. W. F. Hegel, *The Philosophy of History* (New York: Dover Publications, 1956), "Introduction," pp. 91–99. This work is produced from lectures delivered by Hegel in the Winter of 1830–1831, though there had been two previous deliveries, in 1822–1823 and 1824–1825. See Charles Hegel's "Preface" to *The Philosophy of History,* pp. xi–xiii. It should be noted that these ideas were expressed, before the European cannibalization of Africa, by a person who was to become one of Germany's and Europe's most famous philosophers; these were ideas that were to help nurture the complex of beliefs that rationalized European racism vis-à-vis Africans.

18. "The career of the race concept begins in obscurity, for experts dispute whether the word derives from an Arabic, a Latin, or a German source. The first recorded use in English of the word "race" was in a poem by William Dunbar of 1508. . . . During the next three centuries the word was used with growing frequency in a literary sense as denoting simply a class of persons or even things. . . . In the nineteenth, and increasingly in the twentieth century, this loose usage began to give way and the word came to signify groups that were distinguished biologically" (Michael Banton and Jonathan Harwood, *The Race Concept* (New York: Praeger, 1975), p. 13).

19. Ibid., p. 14.

20. Ibid., p. 13.

21. "The eighteenth-century Swedish botanist Linnaeus achieved fame by producing a classification of all known plants which extracted order from natural diversity. Scientists of his generation believed that by finding the categories to which animals, plants and objects belonged they were uncovering new sections of God's plan for the universe. Nineteenth-century race theorists inherited much of this way of looking at things" (Banton and Harwood, *The Race Concept,* p. 46).

22. Ibid., pp. 24–25. Both works were closely studied in Europe and the U.S.

23. Ibid., p. 27.

24. Ibid., p. 28.

25. Ibid., pp. 29–30. These authors observe that while Gobineau's volumes were not very influential at the time of their publication, they were later to become so when used by Hitler in support of his claims regarding the supposed superiority of the "Aryan race."

26. "*Homo sapiens* was presented as a species divided into a number of races of different capacity and temperament. Human affairs could be understood

only if individuals were seen as representatives of races for it was there that the driving forces of human history resided" (Banton and Harwood, *The Race Concept,* p. 30).

27. Ibid., pp. 47–49.

28. "An article by an anthropologist published in 1962 declared in the sharpest terms that the old racial classifications were worse than useless and that a new approach had established its superiority. This article, entitled 'On the Non-existence of Human Races', by Frank B. Livingstone, did not advance any new findings or concepts, but it brought out more dramatically than previous writers the sort of change that had occurred in scientific thinking. . . . The kernel of Livingstone's argument is contained in his phrase 'there are no races, there are only clines'. A cline is a gradient of change in a measurable genetic character. Skin color provides an easily noticed example" (Banton and Harwood, *The Race Concept,* p. 62).

29. "When we refer to races we have in mind their geographically defined categories which are sometimes called 'geographical races', to indicate that while they have some distinctive biological characteristics they are not pure types" (Banton and Harwood, *The Race Concept,* p. 62).

30. Ibid., p. 63. "The main mistake of the early racial theorists was their failure to appreciate the difference between organic and superorganic evolution. They wished to explain all changes in biological terms" (Banton and Harwood, *The Race Concept,* p. 66).

31. Ibid., pp. 72–73, emphasis in the original.

32. Ibid., p. 77.

33. Ibid., p. 147.

34. Michael Omi and Howard Winant, *Racial Formation in the United States* (New York: Routledge and Kegan Paul, 1986).

35. William Petersen, "Concepts of Ethnicity," in *Harvard Encyclopedia of American Ethnic Groups* (Cambridge, Massachusetts: Harvard University Press, 1980), pp. 234–242; p. 234.

36. Ibid., p. 234.

37. For a fuller discussion of the career of paradigmatic "ethnicity" see Omi and Winant, *Racial Formation in the United States,* pp. 14–16.

38. Michael Novak, "Pluralism: A Humanistic Perspective," in *Harvard Encyclopedia of American Ethnic Groups* (Cambridge, Massachusetts: Harvard University Press, 1980), pp. 772–781; p. 774.

39. Ibid., p. 774.

40. This is one of Habermas' worries, and, in one of its expressions directed at an African American political tradition, is of particular concern to me: "After the American civil rights movement—which has since issued in a particularistic self-affirmation of black subcultures—only the feminist movement stands in the tradition of bourgeois-socialist liberation movements. The struggle against patriarchal oppression and for the redemption of a promise that has long been anchored in the acknowledged universalistic foundations of morality

and law gives feminism the impetus of an offensive movement, whereas the other movements have a more defensive character" (Habermas, *The Theory of Communicative Action,* vol. 2, p. 393).

41. Jacques Derrida, "White Mythology: Metaphor in the Text of Philosophy," in *Margins of Philosophy,* trans. by Alan Bass (Chicago: University of Chicago Press, 1982), pp. 207–271; p. 213.

42. Novak, "Pluralism: A Humanistic Perspective," p. 775.

43. Ibid., p. 775.

44. Ibid., p. 776.

45. Habermas, *Discourse of Modernity,* pp. 314–315.

46. Ibid., p. 300.

47. Ibid., pp. 321–322.

48. Ibid., pp. 322, 316.

49. Ibid., pp. 322–323.

50. "One relentlessly elaborates the transcendent power of abstractive reason and the emancipatory unconditionality of the intelligible, whereas the other strives to unmask the imaginary purity of reason in a materialist fashion. . ." (*Discourse of Modernity,* p. 324).

51. Ibid., p. 326.

52. Habermas, "The Tasks of a Critical Theory," *The Theory of Communicative Action,* vol. 2, p. 383.

53. "The bourgeoisie which led the development of capitalism were drawn from particular ethnic and cultural groups; the European proletariats and the mercenaries of the leading States from others; its peasants from still other cultures; and its slaves from entirely different worlds. The tendency of European civilization through capitalism was thus not to homogenize but to differentiate —to exaggerate regional, subcultural, dialectical differences into 'racial' ones." Cedric J. Robinson, *Black Marxism: The Making of the Black Radical Tradition* (London: Zed Press, 1983), pp. 26–27.

54. As Robinson noted (*Black Marxism,* p. 83):

. . . [T]here were at least four distinct moments which must be apprehended in European racialism; two whose origins are to be found within the dialectic of European development, and two which are not:

1. the racial ordering of European society from its formative period which extends into the medieval and feudal ages as 'blood' and racial beliefs and legends.

2. the Islamic, i.e. Arab, Persian, Turkish and African, domination of Mediterranean civilization and the consequent retarding of European social and cultural life: the Dark Ages.

3. the incorporation of African, Asian and peoples of the New World into the world system emerging from late feudalism and merchant capitalism.

4. the dialectic of colonialism, plantocratic slavery and resistance from

the 16th Century forwards, and the formations of industrial labour and labour reserves.

55. "There is a kind of progressive Tower of Babel, where we are engaged in building an edifice for social transformation, but none of us are speaking the same language. None understands where the rest are going" (Manning Marable, "Common Program: Transitional Strategies for Black and Progressive Politics in America," in *Blackwater: Historical Studies in Race, Class Consciousness and Revolution* [Dayton, Ohio: Black Praxis Press, 1981], p. 177).

DAVID L. HALL

MODERN CHINA AND
THE POSTMODERN WEST

China and Modernization

The belief that China has a serious long-term commitment to the project of entering the Modern Age is comforting to many, challenging to
some, and a source of anxious bemusement for others. However, the
majority of these opinions seem to have been formed by individuals who
have casually and unreflectively identified "modernity" with the institutions of liberal democracy, capitalist free enterprise, and the spread of
rational technologies.

Doubtless these are aspects of modernity which form the heart of contemporary Chinese interests (and anxieties) with respect to the West.
The deepening cultural crisis of "modernity" in the West, however,
bespeaks a far richer, more complex, and more consequential "modern
condition." It would be extremely foolish, therefore, for any modernizing nation, the Chinese included, to ignore the broader cultural accou-
trements associated with and embedded in the more practical elements
of the modern impulse. For some of these allied aspects carry with them
such disruptive potential as to suggest that the Western cure may be
more deleterious than the Chinese ailment.

In the past China has made precisely this assessment of its rather
half-hearted attempts at modernization and has sought on these occasions to reject all forms of Western influence. But for a variety of reasons associated with our present global situation, it does appear that
China now has little choice but to modernize, no matter what the risks
might be. The success of this enterprise, however, will depend upon the
recognition on the part of both the Chinese and the Anglo-Europeans
that the very notion of "modernity" has been called into question.
Under the banner of "postmodernism," cultural critics have raised
questions about the viability of the present forms of those very institutions of capitalism, democracy, and technology which seem to promise

50

to the Chinese the opportunity again to become one of the great nations of the world.

In this essay, I wish to argue that the intellectual culture of the Modern West is in such disarray as to be practically unusable as resource for the development of models of cultural accommodation which might ease the transmission of the practical elements of modernity China seeks to import. To demonstrate this fact I will, first, attempt to characterize the complexity of meanings associated with the concept of "modernity" and then show how the internal contradictions of the modern phenomenon have led to cultural crisis.

The second, equally important part of my argument will involve the presentation of the so-called "postmodern" critique of modernity and the illustration of how remarkably similar is the program and method of certain elements of classical Chinese thought to the postmodern sensibility.

A principal implication of my argument, one that I shall not in this context have occasion to spell out in any detail, is this:[1] it is unnecessary for the Chinese to reject their classical past in order to enter the modern age, since the modern age is itself entering into a period that is ideologically similar to the classical Chinese past. Therefore, instead of seeking modes of cultural accommodation in the institutions and rhetoric of the modern West, China could with much greater profit look to its own classical ("postmodern"!) past and, ultimately, to the *post*modern West to help resolve the very real tensions, conflicts, and contradictions attendant upon its entrance into a contemporary world defined by rational technologies and the capitalist impulse.

Strands of Modernity

What sense ought we to give the term, "The Modern Age"? What, specifically, is the cultural import of "modernity"? The vast number and variety of published responses to this question attest to the difficulty of giving a coherent response. Matei Calinescu describes "five faces" of modernity,[2] while David Frisby is content to assay "fragments" of its interpretation.[3] Both of these authors recognize that the search for a univocal definition of "modernity" would be in vain. Others who address this issue are often less modest[4]—though their treatments have in general shown that they have more reason to be.

Until the arguments were refined over the last several years, many philosophers were at least certain when the Modern Age *began*. It was with Descartes (1596–1650), he who made the significant double move that defines the Modern Epoch: the internal move toward the grounding of self-reflection, and the outward move from the self to the material world armed with the coordinates of analytic geometry.

What is modern about the Cartesian stratagem is not merely the provision of an unsullied vantage point from which reason could inventory the extended world. The modern impulse is found as well in Descartes' use of the "corpuscularian" theory rediscovered by his contemporary, Peter Gassendi.[5] Atomic theory, which characterizes the cosmos in materialist, mechanistic terms, is a principal motor of modernity, for it is the basis upon which the otherness of the world is both posited and overcome. Objective knowledge is possible as knowledge of objects. Whether it be in classical physics and chemistry, or in the biology of Charles Darwin (and his sociobiological kinsmen), or in the psychology of Freud (and that of his cousin, B. F. Skinner), or in the sociopolitical thinking of Marx and Engels—the knower becomes an object among other objects.

Of course, a more analytic, empirical, or pragmatic philosopher might locate the origins of modernity in the figure of Francis Bacon (1561–1626), who offered a slightly more direct access to the material world through the methods and tools of technical praxis. Bacon's move, too, was a double one which involved the practical, technical form of the Cartesian stratagem. The self-assertive organizer, manipulator, and transformer of the material world was himself to be a machine-like entity serving as the object of the same manipulation as that of any industrially grounded device.[6]

Without denying the importance of the two founders just mentioned, however, one could certainly shift a century forward from Descartes and cite Locke, Hume, or Adam Smith as the locus of yet another double moment of the modernist impulse, one which provides the conceptual tools for the analysis of the relation of the rise of the modern self to the redefinition of and increased emphasis upon the phenomenon of *property*.

In David Hume's (1711–1776) familiar consideration of the ground and consequence of human passions,[7] property plays the central role since the acquisition and maintenance of property insures the presence of pride, self-love, and the love by others of the propertied self. The absence of property and the means to acquire it guarantee that one shall be an object of the hatred of others and of one's self as well. The doubling that is effective in this gambit is one highlighted in advanced capitalist societies: property grounds both world and self. One comes into one's own by *owning*.

The so-called "romantic reaction" to the Age of Reason provided an alternative means of self-articulation. The alliance of *assertion* and *affect* was to insure that the emotional life would not be suppressed by rationality. Or, as a rather more accurate interpretation would have it: the removal of the locus of rationality and volition from the Mind and Will of God to the individual thinker and actor carried with it the implicit translation of affect as well. The Romantic contribution to the sense of modernity includes, therefore, the uncovering of both the creative and demonic potencies of the human being. Or, as both William Blake and Freud would suggest, the intimate connection between creativity and the irrational forces in the human being is intrinsic to his character.

At approximately the same period in which Hume was articulating his theory of the collusion of property and the passions in the creation of the modern self, the union of mathematical and physical science with technology was finally achieved through the increasing complexity and power of machine technology, which made sufficient demands upon the intellect and offered sufficient rewards so as to stimulate the scientific brain emerging *pari passu* with these changes.

It was a single, short step to the conspiracy of property interest and technological self-assertion in the rise of industrial capitalism that provided a framework in which the modern self's capacities for speculative rationality, active engagement with the natural world, and construction of economically productive enterprises were achieved.

Baudelaire's classic definition of modernity—"the ephemeral, the transitory, the contingent, the half of art the other half of which is the eternal and immutable"[8]—concentrates upon the aesthetic experiencing that is associated with the modern age. At the same time, Baudelaire's description of the artist as a pioneer of modernity hints at the essential connection between the economic and the aesthetic versions of the modern self: both are rooted in the passions. The former is concerned with production, the latter with creative expression. The distinctly aesthetic component of modern subjectivity emerged and exists still as a much prized but nonetheless ancillary element functioning in a visionary and critical capacity with respect to the general cultural milieu.

Modernity has its focus in the discovery, articulation, and ramification of the subjective self. The self which serves as the medium through which comes all experience of the external world, as well as all experience of the objects of consciousness, is a *modern* invention. The self which intends is likewise the intentional object of itself; the self which manipulates the environs can likewise manipulate itself and others, and the self as a more or less intimate bundle of impressions and memories comes into its own by *owning*—its "ownness" a function of its *proprius,* what properly belongs to it. This economic self is both source and object of the passions of pride and envy, love and hate engendered by this ownership. Finally, the self, which from its imagination and feeling creates the aesthetic objects variously prized, ignored, and condemned by *feigned* praise, promotes the reflection of imagination and affect back into itself.

Thus modernity in all its incoherent glory! The power of reason associated with the subjective autonomy of the human spirit forms an awkward alliance with the aggressive human desire to organize and control the natural environment, while the aesthetic impulse offers its embarrassed artifacts and advices aimed at moderating the excesses of reason threatened always by political assertion and economic desire. Self-reflection, self-assertion, self-gratification, and self-articulation are the contrasting, and conflicting, means of fabricating the modern self.

The Disintegration of Modernity

That there is a crisis in the modern age is well attested.[9] One of the surest signs of this crisis lies in the fact that we have developed a rabid (cultural) self-consciousness that has forced us above first-intentional considerations to the level of metatheoretical endeavors. In the absence of any consensus as to a theoretical grounding of culture, we feel the need to become aware of all the alternative semantic analyses that may be given any particular subject.

This phenomenon raises self-awareness to the second power. The understandings of modernity I have been listing *seriatim* (in conformity with this very obligation to rehearse all of the alternatives) become, in the hands of the metatheoreticians, objects of complex and nuanced classificatory schemes, which are meant to chart all once and future meanings of any theoretical concept.

The disease of "metamentality" prevents us from ascertaining the *truth* of this enterprise. We are left with the motivation to assess cultural *importance*. Schemes grounded in Aristotelian categories such as those of Richard McKeon and his epigoni,[10] or those rooted in Plato's Divided Line of the sort produced by Robert Brumbaugh,[11] or those associated with the "root metaphor" concept of Stephen Pepper[12] all chart the *important* world views without asking which, if any, is true.

Not all taxonomists are of this variety, however. Many attempt to read out of consideration the most facile sorts of perspectivism by attempting to emphasize not the theoretical alternatives per se but the fact that one has at last gotten a *true* theory of the sorts of theory possible. What makes this "modern" is the attempt to have the final say.

Such exercises in doublethink to the contrary notwithstanding, the fact remains that, with the growth of self-consciousness in the form of metamentality, it is no longer possible to believe in the viability of achieving a single theoretical explanation of the modern sensibility. Incoherences, contradictions abound. The modern age is a chaos of interpretations. This is the beginning of modernity's crisis.

We may assess the consequences of this fragmented cultural self-consciousness by recourse to one of the most influential treatments of modernity—that associated with Hegel's reading of Kant.[13] Philosophy, art, religion, science, and morality are the cultural interests with respect to which our modern sensibility has been expressed. Hegel's reading of modernity highlights the separation of these value spheres and the reshaping of our cultural sensibility in terms of the shift of priorities in the direction of a mutual critique which demands system.

For Hegel, Kant was *the* philosopher of modernity precisely because he articulated the autonomy of the ways of knowing involved in the aesthetic, moral, and scientific impulses. Kant's three critiques assessed the construction of and response to the scientific, ethical, and artistic spheres of cultural life. *Religion Within the Limits of Reason Alone* provided a more limited status for religion. In good Enlightenment fashion, Kant advertised the distinctive sense of the holy while denying it autonomy.[14]

According to Hegel, Kant was altogether too sanguine about the continued harmony of the value spheres for whose autonomy he argued. Hegel sought, therefore, to provide some guarantee for the unity and harmony of these spheres of cultural interest. On this reading, instead of seeing Hegel as the system monger who tried to say it all, once and for all, we might better interpret him as the true champion of modernity who recognized that system was necessary to preserve subjective freedom.

One way (but only *one* way) of rehearsing the collapse of the modern self into autonomous and mutually incoherent rational, volitional, and affective components of the sort I have outlined above is to speak of "secularization." Max Weber's sense of the movement from traditional to rational societies tells the story:[15]

The values of morality and art, science and religion are *implicit* in the culture as long as tradition reigns. They become *explicit* with the need to incorporate diversity of beliefs and customs, as in fact occurred in the sixteenth century and beyond. Secularization is another name for urbanization—the collection into a concentrated sphere of diversities which tradition could no longer balance.

In this manner the content of social and cultural life is raised to the level of consciousness and the ensuing recognition of conflict and relativity issues into a process of abstraction, formalization, and generalization which eschews differences by suppressing content. Formal rationality is the result.

Thus emerges the formal consciousness of the self as articulated into reason, appetite, and will—or thought, action, passion—or scientific, moral, and aesthetic interests. In becoming conscious of itself the modern self recognizes not only the internal contradictions associated with competing cultural spheres, but the contradictions of the self as the chaotic interspersal of rational, affective, and volitional impulses.

So we are brought again to the alternative expressions of modernity rehearsed above, but this time with the added insight that the cultural problem of modernity may be expressed in terms of the diremption of the value spheres as well as the internal diremptions of the self insofar as the self is its culture writ small.

The fading modernist sense of coherence might seem to receive some comfort from the recognition that the strains of the discourse and counterdiscourse of modernity match the fundamental interests which ground or focus the modes of construction and critique in intellectual culture—reason, volition, and passion. This sense of coherence is really a false one, however, for any attempt to see these various strands of modernity as tightly woven threads of a single fabric would be futile.

Rational analyses of the subjectivity of modern selfhood associated with the work of Jürgen Habermas[16] and volitional analyses of the sort Hans Blumenberg[17] provides, and aesthetic analyses of the kind found in Baudelaire and ramified in Walter Benjamin[18] or Jean-François Lyotard,[19] and economic analyses deriving from Hume, Adam Smith, Marx, et al.[20] are incompatible expressions of the sense of modernity. Not only is there an incommensurability among theoretical expressions of these positionings; there are, as well, serious practical disagreements and conflicts among the proponents of these positionings.

The main crisis in modernity is associated with the uncovering of the arbitrariness of cultural artifacts, including those artifactual constructs we term "theories." Michel Foucault's familiar analysis of the conspiracy of knowledge and power[21] demonstrates the manner in which discourse is always determined by the power relations in a society. This sort of analysis, begun with Friedrich Nietzsche at the end of the nineteenth century, has taken the heart out of all but the most obsessive of the modern reconstructionists.

But, of course, one person's crisis is another's long-awaited revolution. The modernist's frantic attempts to reconstruct the value spheres and the consequent sense of crisis with respect to the interpretations of culture and personality describe one contemporary ideological movement. A second, flying the paisley colors of postmodernism, accepts the condition of psychic fragmentation and its cultural implications as improvements over the rationally ordered psyche. The divided self is celebrated in its dirempted, deconstructed state. Postmodernism critiques the very idea of consensus, rejecting any theoretical grounding for culture.

It is crucial to recognize that each of the concrete activities and institutions most associated with modernization—namely, liberal individualism and the democratic institutions that uphold it, free-enterprise capitalism and the property interests that sustain it, and rational technology, motivated by the aim of the most efficient organization of means —originated in and, insofar as they remain intact are sustained by, the modalities of modern consciousness which are currently in crisis. These concrete modes of modernizing praxis are intimately connected with the fragmented, crisis-ridden culture of modernity.

Based upon the above argument, I would assert that it will become increasingly necessary as time passes to interpret modernization in its practical forms in terms of critical models drawn from a postmodern situation. Paradoxically, for reasons I shall now begin to articulate, this is a most promising turn of events for the Chinese.

Postmodernism and the Philosophy of Difference

The metaphysical tradition of the West is implicitly or explicitly grounded in a "philosophy of presence"—that is, the desire to make present the presence of Being in beings. Jacques Derrida terms this disposition to make *being* present "logocentrism."[22] The logocentric bias of Western philosophy motivates thinkers to attempt to present the truth, being, essence, or logical structure of that about which they think and discourse. The senses of modernity sketched above all had at their heart the attempt to characterize the capital "T" Truth of things. The failure of that undertaking is the failure of the philosophy of presence—and the failure of modernity.

The postmodern enterprise aims at the development of a philosophy of *difference.* Our purported inability to think difference and otherness in their most general senses threatens the entire metaphysical project of Western thought.

The most general question of difference concerns the difference between the "whatness" and the "thatness" of a thing. "A rose is a *rose. . . .*" Yes. In addition, "a rose *is. . . .*" Asking *what* a being is is a cosmological question; considering *that* it is is an ontological appreciation. A rose as an item related with the other items in its ecosystem in complex spatiotemporal and biochemical manners is a *cosmological* entity. *That* the rose is—its isness—indicates its *ontological* character.

Of course, the contrast of cosmological and ontological cannot be imagined without the cosmogonic tradition out of which it arises. For the ontological bias of Western philosophy derives from its attitude toward the chaos of beginnings.

The creation and maintenance of order from out of and over against the threat of chaos is the fundamental fact which establishes our sense of beginnings. Speculative philosophy, both as general ontology and as universal science, attempts to explain the fundamental fact of *order.* The ontologist asks the ontological question: "Why are there beings rather than no being?" Or "Why is there something rather than nothing at all?" Proponents of *scientia universalis* ask the cosmological question: "What kinds of things are there?" The cosmogonic tradition in the Hellenic West has determined that metaphysical speculation must involve the search for beings or principles which, as transcendent sources of order, account for the order(s) experienced or observed.

As traditionally interpreted, both the cosmological and ontological questions presuppose an ordered ground. It is this, of course, which defines the logocentric motive of Western philosophy—the desire to illumine and articulate the order and structure in things.

All this may seem extremely abstract and quite irrelevant to any discussion of the modernization of China. But I think not. There is a most serious issue at stake here. If our most general understandings of our world involve us always in presuming a universal ground such as the essence or structure of beings, we can easily lose sight of the particularities of both our experience of things and of the things themselves. Capital "T" Truth and capital "B" Beauty and capital "G" Goodness become the subject matters of our discourse instead of the truth, beauty, and goodness concretely realized by the insistent particularities of our world. We then claim to know generalities, universalities, absolutes, and essences, but we lose sight of the brute facticities of our world.

Any serious claim to objective truth involves us in insisting that reality shine through our assertions. The very being of things is present in one's theory or ideology. Our age is altogether too suspicious of such claims. The pluralism of doctrines and theories within a single culture such as ours, as well as the pluralism of cultures, makes any claim to the truth of things an implicitly political act. Dogmatism, totalitarianism, and narrow intolerance are all directly connected with unjustified claims to final truth.

The philosophy of presence is certainly not purposefully pernicious. Enlightenment rationality emerged from the idea that generic principles of logic and rationality may generate a common discourse for all cultures. Such rationalism was born from the need to connect diverse, pluralistic ideas, beliefs, and practices. Our reason was the gift of the ancient city-states, spread from Italy to the Peloponnesus, spun through the shuttles of Hebraic monotheism and Latin conceptions of *humanitas* and refined in the various furnaces of German, French, and English forms of colonialism.

The desire to see essential unity among cultures is a function of our missionizing activity expressed initially through Roman and Christian expansion, and now through our rational technologies motored by an incipient economic imperialism or, more politely put, an expanding market mentality. Proponents of Western values believe them to be exportable because they represent the grounds and consequences of a rational set of principles.

Our cultural values are housed in *doctrines*—propositions that may be entertained as beliefs. Philosophic and scientific principles are rational in form and are therefore open to public entertainment apart from specific cultural practices. Technology as a rational system carries with it the algorithms of its replication, requiring a minimum of human intervention.

In their attempts at modernization the Chinese are confronted with an uncomfortable dilemma. China must modernize, but the effects of a modernization understood in terms of liberal democracy, free enterprise, and rational technologies cannot but threaten its cultural integrity. China's ritual-based culture depends upon a commonality of traditions that liberal democracy renders quite fragile. The laws, rules, and values that define the Chinese sensibility are immanent within and relevant to the relatively specific character of the Chinese people. The paternalism of the Chinese form of government, its stress upon the solidarity of community over issues of abstract rights, its cultivation of and response to the psychological need for dependency are all delicate enough characteristics to be effaced by the impersonality of technology, the self-interest of free enterprise, and the individualizing ideals of democracy. Whatever benefits they might offer, each of these elements of modern culture leads to a bloating of the private sphere and threatens community.

Clearly, the problematic of distinctly modern Anglo-European philosophy is distinct from that of classical Chinese philosophy as regards the question of "difference." For a variety of reasons associated with the choices made at the origins of their cultural development, the Chinese find it easier to think difference, change, and becoming than do most of us. One the other hand, it has been easier in the modern West to think in terms of identity, being, and permanence.

I certainly have not failed to notice the dazzling incongruity that seems to lurk within my central claim. Could it really be the case that the country most identified with cultural continuity, inflexible tradition, and the most provincial intolerance toward other civilizations is expert in the philosophy of difference? My answer is—yes, certainly. Though I shall not discuss the background and significance of this question in any detail, I do hope to provide sufficient hints as to the plausibility of my affirmative response in the remarks which follow.

In defense of my somewhat exotic thesis I want to call attention to the evidence for thinking that Confucianism and philosophical Taoism share something like the problematic of postmodernism insofar as it is shaped by the desire to find a means of thinking difference. In its strongest and most paradoxical form my argument amounts to the claim that classical China is in a very real sense *postmodern.*

Two benefits may come from such an investigation as this. First, since it is rather obvious that the postmodern critique is neither an atavistic nor Luddite enterprise, one can hope that there may develop from out of the postmodern impulse alternative strategies for engaging and accommodating the practical consequences of the modern world. This means that China should be free to reflect upon the very difficult problems of modernization in terms of its own postmodern past.

A second benefit of the postmodern connection is that Anglo-European thinkers can discover in classical China supplemental resources for the development of a vision of cosmological difference and the language which articulates that vision. Certain of those resources may be found, as I now shall attempt to show, in the original Taoist and Confucian sensibilities.

Taoism and Cosmological Difference

I have argued elsewhere[23] that a philosophically coherent understanding of classical Taoism depends upon a recognition that neither of the two fundamental metaphysical contrasts of the Western tradition—that is, between "being" and "not being" and between "being" and "becoming"—is helpful in understanding the Taoist sensibility. In Taoism, the sole fact is that of process or becoming. Being and nonbeing are abstractions from that process.

The first words of the *Tao Te Ching* may be rendered in this way:

> The way *(tao)* that can be spoken of is not the constant way. The name that can be named is not the constant name. The nameless was the beginning of Heaven and earth.[24]

Throughout the *Tao Te Ching, tao* is characterized as both nameless and nameable. *Tao* per se is the total process of becoming, becoming-itself. Nameless and nameable *tao* function analogously to "nonbeing" and "being," respectively. Thus being and nonbeing are abstractions from the generic process of becoming-itself. *Tao* is the *that which*—a name for *process*. That which *is* and that which *is not*[25] are the polar elements of becoming-itself.

The fundamental truth of the Taoist vision is contained in this but mildly ironic send-up of Parmenides' infamous maxim: Only becoming is; not-becoming is not. That is, there is only coming into being which illustrates some mixture of being and nonbeing. Neither being nor nonbeing abstracted from its polar relationship with its opposite can be finally real.

Each particular element in the totality has its own intrinsic excellence. The Chinese term is *te. Te* may be understood as the "particular focus" or "intrinsic excellence" of a thing. The *te* of an element serves as the means in accordance with which it construes the totality of things from its perspective and thus "names" and creates a world.

The concepts of *tao* and *te* may be interpreted together in a polar fashion. *Tao-te* is best understood in terms of the relationships of field *(tao)* and focus *(te)*. The model of a hologram is helpful, for as in a holographic display each element contains the whole in adumbrated forms, so in the Taoist sensibility each item of the totality focuses the totality in its entirety. The particular focus of an item establishes its world, its environment. In addition, the totality as sum of all possible orders is adumbrated by each item.

Taoism is radically perspectival. "If a man lie down in a damp place," says Chuang Tzu, "he contracts lumbago. But what of an eel?"[26] The eel will be at least as uncomfortable as the man—but for the opposite reason. The Taoist totality is horizontal. There are no hierarchies; no great chain of being or ladder of perfections exists in the Taoist cosmology. For the Taoist, the anthropocentrism implicit in almost every form of Anglo-European ethical system is only one of a myriad of possible centrisms.

A familiar tale from the *Chuang Tzu* is enlightening in this regard:[27]

> The emperor of the South Sea was called Shu, the emperor of the North Sea was called Hu, and the emperor of the central region was called Hun-tun (Chaos). Shu and Hu from time to time came together for a meeting in the territory of Hun-tun, and Hun-tun treated them very generously. Shu and Hu discussed how they could repay his kindness. "All men," they said, "have seven openings so they can see, hear, eat, and breathe. But Hun-tun alone doesn't have any. Let's try boring him some!" Every day they bored another hole, and on the seventh day Hun-tun died.

Taoism is not a vision grounded upon order, but upon chaos. It is a vision in which harmony has a special kind of meaning associated with the breechless, faceless, orifice-free Lord Hun-tun. Assuming that *tao* is becoming-itself, and therefore the sum of all orders, provides a helpful response to Benjamin Schwartz' provocative query concerning the meaning of *"tao"* in *The World of Thought in Ancient China.* "How may a word which refers to *order*," he asks, "come to have a mystical meaning?"[28] The mystical meaning of *tao* lies in the mystery of chaos as the sum of all orders.

Tao is not organic in the sense that a single pattern or *telos* could be said to characterize its processes. It is not *a* whole but many wholes. Its order is not rational or logical but aesthetic—that is there can be no transcendent pattern determining the existence or efficacy of the order. The order is a consequence of the particulars comprising the totality of existing things.

This interpretation of *tao* makes of it a totality not in the sense of a single-ordered cosmos, but rather in the sense of the sum of all possible cosmological orders. Any given order is an existing world that is construed from the perspective of a particular element of the totality. But as a single world it is an abstraction from the totality of possible orders. The *being* of this order is not ontological, but cosmological. Such an abstracted, selected order cannot serve as fundament or ground. In the Taoist sensibility *all differences are cosmological differences.*

Taoism is based upon the affirmation rather than the negation of chaos. In the Anglo-European tradition, chaos is emptiness, separation, or confusion, and is to be overcome. In Taoism it is to be left alone to thrive in its spontaneity, for "the myriad things manage and order themselves."[29] Any attempt to make present a ground—the being of beings—is rejected. Chuang Tzu insists that "each thing comes into being from its own inner reflection and none can tell how it comes to be so."[30]

Taoism provides a model for thinking difference as strictly *cosmological* difference. Cosmological difference can be thought to the extent that we give up the distinction between cosmological and ontological realms. For it is the putatively ontological dimension that ultimately conceals the differences among cosmological entities by implicit appeal to the unity of being shared by all beings.

Reason and rationality presuppose the ontological philosophy of presence. But it is a simple-enough feat to demonstrate that rational ordering is an anthropocentric notion. For the various psychological and physiological uniformities defining the human species determine in advance the sorts of ordering that will be anticipated as defining the natural world. The sorts of beings we presume ourselves to be define the sorts of orders we may recognize and deem important. Alternative orders are recognized only from our anthropocentric perspective, since to know an order we must discern its pattern regularities, appreciate its realized uniformities, and establish plausible grounds for casual sequences among the elements serving to instantiate those uniformities.

The aesthetic ordering of the Taoist presupposes an alternative method of knowing. Such knowledge has as its subject matter insistently unique particulars which cannot be discussed in terms of pattern concepts defining regularities or uniformities. They can only be considered in terms of the cosmological differences grounded in the particularity of each item.

Confucius and the Language of Deference

One of the difficulties in communicating a vision of cosmological difference is that we lack a language which can adequately accommodate such aesthetic understandings. There is, of course, just such a language in philosophical Taoism and I could quite appropriately attempt to articulate it in the following paragraphs. Instead, I want to shift to the Confucian context to adumbrate the view of language and communication underlying the *Analects*. I shall do this in order to demonstrate that, however great the differences between Taoism and Confucianism *within* Chinese culture, judged from the perspective of Western thought they belong to essentially the same family. This is so because both Taoism and Confucianism presuppose the priority of cosmological difference over ontological presence—or, put another way, the priority of an aesthetic over a rational mode of understanding and discourse.

In the West two sorts of language have dominated the tradition. The first, the language of ontological presence, is that against which the postmodern thinkers are in full-scale revolt. Besides the language of presence, however, our tradition also allows the employment of language in a mystical or mythopoetic way. In this usage, language advertises the absence of the referent. This is the language of the mystical *via negativa* or the language of the poet who holds metaphor to be constitutive of discourse rather than merely parasitical upon a literal ground. We may call such expression the language of "absence."

A language of presence is grounded upon the possibility of univocal or unambiguous propositional expressions. This possibility requires criteria for determining the literalness of a proposition. For this to be so, literal language must have precedence over figurative or metaphorical language. This means that in addition to richly vague sorts of language associated with images and metaphors, there must be concepts as candidates for univocal meaning.

Since Aristotle's still-dominating discussion of metaphor, literal language has most often been privileged over figurative. And though to say this seems truistic and almost trivial, it is certainly *not* the case that such a preference was somehow built into the origins of language.

In the West, metaphors are usually deemed parasitical upon literal significances. Thus rhetoric, insofar as it employs the trope, metaphor, is rigidly tied to logic as ground. This serves to discipline intellectual and aesthetic activity, precluding untrammeled flights of the imagination.

If we are to have a language that evokes difference, however, we must find a new sort of metaphor. In place of metaphors which extend the literal sense of a term, we shall have to employ "allusive metaphors."[31] Allusive metaphors are distinct from the expressive variety since they are not tied to a literal or objective signification. They are free-floating hints and suggestions. They *allude;* they do not *express.* Their referents are other allusive metaphors, other things that hint or suggest. All language, at its fundamental level, may be nothing more than an undulating sea of suggestiveness.

Saussurean linguistics[32] and some semiologists influenced by Peirce and Saussure, as well as the poststructuralists who would expunge from language such "myths" as "authorial intent," "textual coherence," or "univocity," all employ something like allusive interpretations. Language as a system of differences, as a structure or context within which meaning is indefinitely deferred, is nothing more than an allusive system.

The Saussurean interpretation certainly may be said to apply to Chinese language and literature. The importance of context to meaning in Chinese language argues for the play of differences establishing meaning. Of course, in China almost all that may be said with respect to allusive metaphor may be said using the word "image."

In Anglo-European culture, the word "image" is used with distinctive connotations in literary criticism, psychology, and philosophy. The best understanding in this context is that an image is a sensory (that is, visual, auditory, tactile, olfactory) presentation of a perceptual, imaginative, or recollected experience. The form of the perception, memory, or imagination may be distinct from the mode of its presentation. For example, the olfactory or visual experience of a rose may be imaged in the words of a poet.

In such a case, the image is constituted by the word-picture as experienced by the celebrant of the poem and may or may not re-present the private experience of the poet. The most productive manner of insuring some resonance between the expressor of the image and the subsequent experiences of it is to reference them within a community of interpretation. Only communally experienced images are efficacious in promoting interpersonal and social relationships.

This suggests a real difference between Anglo-European and Chinese culture. In China, tradition, as a communal resource for meaning, more certainly disciplines the indefinite allusiveness of the language. In fact, it is tradition as the resource of meaning and value that serves to render plausible what seemed originally so paradoxical—namely, that Chinese culture has an appreciation of difference, which, historically, Western culture has never displayed.

Allusiveness requires vague[33] boundaries of self and world. The most desirable circumstance is one in which images, as richly vague complexes capable of a variety of evocations, are communally fixed and ritually protected as images. This is the aim of the classical Chinese, though it is obvious that Confucian orthodoxy was often guilty of providing a too narrowly fixed meaning for the relevant images. In any case, there is nothing behind the language in the form of a structure or logos to which appeal may be made to establish the presence of objective truth. Meanings derive from the allusive play of differences among the words and images of the language.

The images associated with the hexagrams of the *I Ching* are good examples of such communally fixed and ritualistically protected images. The images of the "creative" and the "receptive" associated with the first two hexagrams are housed in the communal memory and practices associated with the institutions, ritual practices, music, and literature which contextualize the book of oracles as a classic of Chinese culture. The concrete experiences of the individual consulting the *I Ching* resonate with the repository of significances in the larger communal context.

One of the signal consequences of a logocentric language is that there must be real independence of a proposition from the state of affairs it characterizes. This entails dualistic relations of propositions and states of affairs. Without such independence, in the senses of dualism and transcendence, nothing like logical truth may be formulated.

The presence of transcendent beings and principles in the formation of Western culture is uncontroversial. The dualism entailed by this transcendence, though often discomfiting to the theologically doctrinaire, is also a well-accepted characteristic of the rational interests of Anglo-European societies. Neither dualism nor transcendence is present in the original Confucian or Taoist sensibilities.

For a proposition to have a univocal sense, terms must be strictly delimitable. A polar sensibility precludes such delimitation in any but the grossest terms. Thus, the classical Chinese understanding of *yin* and *yang* as complementary concepts cannot coherently lead to dualistic translations or interpretations. *Yin* is becoming-*yang; yang* is becoming-*yin.* The locution "as different as night and day" would then have to mean "as different as night-becoming-day from day-becoming-night."

In a polar sensibility, terms are clustered with opposing or complementary alter-terms. Classical Chinese may be uncongenial to the development of univocal propositions for this reason. Without such propositions, semantic notions of truth are ultimately untenable. And without a capital "T" Truth lurking behind our acts of communication, notions such as "logocentrism" and "presence" cannot serve as standards for philosophical discourse.

The Confucian doctrine of the rectification of names well illustrates the way language is used concretely, evocatively, and allusively. This doctrine, central to Confucianism, is often outrageously misunderstood as a concern for univocity, for getting the definitions of terms straight and proper. Such an interpretation parodies the intent of Confucius' doctrine.

> Tzu-lu asked Confucius, "If the Lord of Wei were waiting for you to bring order to his state, to what would you give first priority?" Confucius replied, "without question, it would be to order names properly."[34]

The motive for the ordering of names is functional and pragmatic, rather than logical or strictly semantic. That is to say, the activity of matching name with role—calling a father a father when he is in fact a father—establishes coherence between roles already spelled out by ritual practices *(li)* and the actions of individuals—husbands, fathers, ministers, sons—whose ostensive identity as functionaries within the society may be in question.

It is quite interesting to see how closely related are the treatments of language in the sayings of Confucius and in the thought of a certain French thinker writing twenty-four hundred years later. I refer, of course, to Jacques Derrida. Derrida's well-rehearsed notion of *difference* tells the story.[35] The neologism *difference,* is meant to suggest that the differences investigated with respect to language have both an active and a passive dimension.

Meaning is always deferred. It cannot be present in language as *structure,* when that is the focus—for that omits the meanings associated with the use of the language. But focusing upon language as *event,* language as constituted by speech acts, does not solve the problem because, once more, the supplemental character of language—this time its structure—has been shifted to an inaccessible background.

To resonate most productively with Confucius, however, Derrida would have to accept an emendation to his notion of *difference* which would enrich the meaning of the deferring function. If one introduces the homonymic "defer," meaning "to yield," then the resultant notion of difference, as connoting both active and passive senses of differing and of deferring, well suits Confucius' rich use of language.

Confucius' language of difference is grounded in the sense of deference—a listening, a yielding to the appropriate models of the received traditions and to the behaviors of those who resonate with those models. In the *Great Preface* to the *Book of Songs,* traditionally attributed to Confucius, we read:[36]

> Poetry is the consequence of dispositions and is articulated in language as song. One's feelings stir within his breast and take the form of words. When words are inadequate, they are voiced as sighs. When sighs are inadequate, they are chanted. When chants are inadequate, unconsciously, the hands and feet begin to dance them. One's feelings are expressed in sounds, and when sounds are refined, they are called musical notes.

Confucius understands language after the analogy with music. Names are like notes. Harmony is a function of the particularity of names and notes and of their mutual resonances. Neither in Chinese music nor in Chinese language is there the stress upon syntax that one finds in the rationalistic languages of the West.

Confucian language is the bearer of tradition, and tradition, made available through ritualistic evocation, is the primary context of linguistic behavior. The sage appeals to present praxis and to the repository of significances realized in the traditional past in such a manner as to set up deferential relationships between himself, his communicants, and the authoritative texts invoked.

It is important to recognize that Confucius never tied the significances of language to the norms of present praxis. He insisted upon deferential access to the appropriate traditional models. If such models are not coopted by an authoritarian government or a rigid bureaucratic elite, as has been the case in the tawdrier periods of Chinese history, there is a rich and varied resource for the criticism of present praxis in spite of the fact that the language as a system lacks any transcendent reference.

The language of presence re-presents an otherwise absent object. The language of absence uses indirect discourse to advertise the existence of a nonpresentable subject. In either case there is a referent, real or putative, beyond the act of referencing. But the language of deference is based upon the recognition of mutual resonances among instances of communicative activity. There is no referencing beyond the act of communication as it resonates with the entertained meanings of the models from the tradition.

Conclusion

I have argued that the concept of "modernity" evokes an incoherent cluster of significances occasioned by and reflected in the actual disarray of modern Anglo-European culture. Thus there appears to be no viable context of modern cultural values to export to non-Western countries along with the concrete elements of modernizing praxis. On reflection, this may turn out to be of benefit to China since the values underlying the postmodern critique of modernity resonate more profoundly with the dominant cultural interests of the Chinese than ever did the interests and values of the Modern West.

As in all philosophical reflections, however, there is irony: at the very moment we in the West are drawn closer to the classical Chinese modes of thinking in search of a counterdiscourse in terms of which to critique modernity, the contemporary Chinese are confronted with the question of whether or not to accept the Trojan horse of Western technology, the meanest flower of that rational self-assertion against which postmodernism is in full-scale revolt.

There is a positive, hopeful element nestled among these difficulties. If we succeed in reshaping our culture after the fashion of the counterdiscourse of postmodernism, we shall develop styles of accommodating and refashioning technological, individualist, capitalist society into a form more compatible with the traditional Chinese culture. And in so doing we may be able to encourage the Chinese to look to their own presently neglected cultural roots to discover the most appropriate connections between their traditional past and their modernizing present and to discover, as well, the basis of a shareable present between China and the West.

In the absence of such a vigorous endeavor, there is reason to believe that we and the Chinese will be condemned by the mischievous demons of history to the sad, silly fate of falling under the spell of one another's rejected pasts.

Notes

1. Roger T. Ames and I are currently at work on a book, to be entitled *Anticipations of Culture—China and the West,* in which we shall elaborate upon this thesis.

2. See his *Five Faces of Modernity* (Durham: Duke University Press, 1987).

3. See his *Fragments of Modernity* (Cambridge, Massachusetts: MIT Press, 1986).

4. There are a number of attempts at a comprehensive investigation of the phenomenon of Modernity. All share a more or less self-consciously reductive approach. Among the better of these interpretations are: Hans Blumenberg's *The Legitimacy of the Modern Age* (Cambridge, Massachusetts: MIT Press, 1976); David Kolb's *The Critique of Pure Modernity—Hegel, Heidegger and After* (Chicago: University of Chicago Press, 1986); Jürgen Habermas' *The Philosophical Discourse of Modernity,* trans. by Frederick Lawrence (Cambridge, Massachusetts: MIT Press, 1987); Marshall Berman's *All That is Solid Melts into Air,* rev. ed. (New York: Penguin Books, 1988); and Lawrence Cahoone's *The Crisis of Modernity* (Albany: SUNY Press, 1988).

5. Gassendi's name is a convenient one to associate with the rediscovery of classical atomism, which captured the thought of numerous thinkers of the period. Besides Descartes, one might list Boyle, Hobbes, Locke, Newton, Harvey, and many lesser lights.

6. A principal virtue of Hans Blumenberg's *The Legitimacy of the Modern Age* (note 4 above) lies in its recognition of both the Cartesian and Baconian strands of modernity.

7. *A Treatise of Human Nature,* ed. by L. A. Selby-Bigge (Oxford, 1896). See especially bk. 2, i–ii, *passim.*

8. "The Painter of Modern Life," in *Selected Writings on Art and Artists* (New York: Penguin Books, 1972), p. 403.

9. See works cited in notes 1 and 2 above.

10. Most of McKeon's taxonomic work was presented in his "Idea and Methods" lectures during his tenure at the University of Chicago. A disciple, Walter Watson, has presented his version of the McKeon scheme in his recent *Architectonics of Meaning* (Albany: SUNY Press, 1987).

11. Robert Brumbaugh's typology is conveniently expressed in his *Compass of Philosophy,* written with Newton Stallknecht (New York: Longmans, Green & Co., 1954). Brumbaugh's typology has influenced the constructive work of Robert Neville and George Allan, among others. See the former's *Reconstruction of Thinking* (Albany: SUNY Press, 1981) and the latter's *Importances of the Past* (Albany: SUNY Press, 1986).

12. Stephen Pepper's *World Hypotheses* (Berkeley: University of California Press, 1966) contains the initial expression of his metatheoretical ruminations.

13. Hegel's interpretation of modernity is scattered throughout his writings, particularly *The Philosophy of Right* and *The Encyclopedia.* For summaries and critical interpretations of Hegel's understanding of "modernity" see Kolb, *The Critique of Pure Modernity,* pp. 20–117 *passim,* and Habermas, *The Philosophical Discourse of Modernity* pp. 23–44.

14. Nonetheless, Kant's separation of religion from the other value spheres did promote its becoming a *Fach,* a specialized discipline. And Rudolph Otto's defense of the autonomy of "the Holy" would hardly have been possible without Kant's initial speculations. See Otto's *The Idea of the Holy: An Inquiry into the Nonrational Factor in the Idea of the Divine and Its Relation to the Rational,* trans. by J. W. Harvey (New York, 1958).

15. See Weber's *Protestant Ethic and the Spirit of Capitalism* (New York: Scribners, 1958), *passim*, for discussions of the peculiarly "Occidental" character of the rationalization and secularization of tradition.

16. Habermas, *The Philosophical Discourse of Modernity.*

17. Blumenberg, *The Legitimacy of the Modern Age.*

18. Much of Benjamin's work is untranslated. In English, see *Illuminations*, trans. by H. Zohn (New York: Schocken, 1969), and *The Origins of German Tragedy*, trans. by J. Osborne (London: New Left Books, 1977).

19. See *The Postmodern Condition* (Minneapolis: University of Minnesota Press, 1979, 1983, 1984).

20. See Hume, *A Treatise of Human Nature;* Marx's *Economic and Philosophical Manuscripts of 1844*, trans. by M. Milligan (London, 1959); and Adam Smith's *The Wealth of Nations*, ed. by Edwin Cannan (New York, 1904).

21. The best example of this sort of analysis is to be found in Foucault's *Discipline and Punish: The Birth of the Prison*, trans. by Alan Sheridan (New York: Vintage/Random House, 1979).

22. Derrida's most sustained attempt at charting the "logocentric" bias of Western metaphysics is to be found in *Dissemination*, trans. by Barbara Johnson (Chicago: University of Chicago Press, 1981).

23. See my "Process and Anarchy—A Taoist Vision of Creativity," *Philosophy East & West* 28, no. 3 (July 1978): 271–285. See also the chapter "The Way Beyond Ways," in my *The Uncertain Phoenix* (New York: Fordham University Press, 1982).

24. See D. C. Lau, trans., *The Tao Te Ching* (New York: Penguin Books, 1963), p. 57.

25. In his "Being in Western Philosophy Compared with *Shan/Fei* and *Yu/Wu* in Chinese Philosophy," in *Studies in Chinese Philosophy and Philosophical Literature* (Singapore: Institute of East Asian Philosophies, 1986), pp. 322–359, A. C. Graham has indicated that the sense of *wu* ("have not," "there is not") contrasts with locutions entailed by the ontological sense of "Nothing" in that "Nothing" entails the sense of "no entity" while *wu* indicates merely the absence of concrete things.

This point, which concerns the concrete mode of the contrast between "being" and "not-being" is, I believe, at least obliquely relevant to my argument that Taoism is strictly concerned with cosmological differences and not at all with the contrast between the cosmological and ontological characters of things.

26. See Burton Watson, trans., *The Complete Works of Chuang Tzu* (New York: Columbia University Press, 1968), p. 56.

27. Ibid., p. 97.

28. *The World of Thought in Ancient China* (Cambridge, Massachusetts: Harvard University Press, 1985, p. 194).

29. See *Wang Pi's Commentary on the Lao tzu*, trans. by Arrienne Rump in collaboration with Wing-tsit Chan, Society of Asian and Comparative Philosophy monograph, no. 6 (Honolulu: University of Hawaii Press, 1979), p. 17.

30. See *Chuang Tzu,* chap. eight. The translation, admittedly a controversial rendering of an obscure segment of the text, is cited from Chang Chung-Yuan, *Creativity and Taoism* (New York: Harper & Row, 1963), p. 66.

31. See my *Eros and Irony* (Albany: SUNY Press, 1983), pp. 46–47, 180–182 and Roger T. Ames' and my *Thinking Through Confucius* (Albany: SUNY Press, 1987), pp. 192–198 for the characterization of "allusive metaphor" and "allusive analogy," respectively.

32. See Ferdinand Saussure's *A Course in General Linguistics* (London: Peter Owen, 1960).

33. The word "vague" is used in the systematic sense given it by Charles Peirce. The term means "open to rich and varied articulation." For a discussion of "vagueness" as a theoretical concept see Robert Neville's *Reconstruction of Thinking* (Albany: SUNY Press, 1981), pp. 39–42.

34. *Analects* 13/3; Roger T. Ames' translation.

35. See Derrida's *Writing and Différence,* trans. by Alan Bass (Chicago: University of Chicago Press, 1978), *passim.*

36. *Chih-ching,* Harvard-Yenching Institute Sinological Index Series, Supp. 9 (Peking: Harvard-Yenching Institute, 1934); Roger T. Ames' translation.

SVETOZAR STOJANOVIĆ

FROM MARXISM TO POST-MARXISM

Two Phases of Critical Marxism

As a reaction to the official "Marxism-Leninism" (Stalinism to a great degree), critical Marxism, especially in Eastern Europe and Yugoslavia, passed through two stages in the fifties, sixties, and seventies. The first was *Authentic Marxism* and the second *Revisionist Marxism*.

In order to destroy the "Marxist-Leninist" ideology, critical Marxists made a "back to authentic Marx" move. Their basic idea was that "Marxism-Leninism" is an essential distortion and not a creative development of the original thought of Karl Marx. True, in returning to the "real Marx" some naively expected to find a homogeneous thinker. Others knew, however, that their return to Marx had to be selective and critical from the very beginning, since his writings are full of important tensions and contradictions.

It was this insight that logically led to Revisionist Marxism;[1] significant and even crucial ideas of classical Marxism were increasingly subjected to transformation. From this fragmentation of Marxism there was, however, only one step to its radical revision; even the type of theorizing became the subject of revision.

But how much can one change the basic mode of theory construction and still remain a Marxist, no matter to what degree a revisionist one? In other words, radical Marxist revisionism was bound sooner or later to be transformed into post-Marxism, whether consciously or only *de facto*. It goes without saying that there may be considerable Marxist influences within post-Marxism (this is the case with my own latest book).[2] It is a theoretical and political orientation that draws upon multiple traditions and not just upon revisionist Marxism.

Marxist and Post-Marxist Dialectic

Marx's dialectic is, in essence, Hegelian, and to this Feuerbach's transformative method was indeed applied, though not quite consistently

71

and radically. In other words, the progressivistic framework of Hegelian dialectic remained unquestioned by Marx. Unlike Marx's dialectic, however, post-Marxist dialectic has to leave open the possibility of either progress or regress.

Aufhebung is one of the central categories both of Hegel's and of Marx's dialectic. As is well known, it means "negation, preservation, and elevation to a higher level of development." However, a completely open, directionless, post-Marxist dialectic has to allow for *Aufhebung* as well as *anti-Aufhebung*. The latter antonym, one that I proposed several years ago, means "negation, preservation, and falling to a lower level."

These are examples of *anti-Aufhebung:* first, the negation of the contradiction between the social character of production and the private character of appropriation through "primitive communism" (Marx's term); second, the negation of the separation of state and "civil society" by the statization of total social life (communist statism); and third, the "development" of Marxism from Marx through Lenin to Stalin.

Unlike the Marxist dialectic, the post-Marxist one should also be entirely open for nonsynthesizing forms of activity and social process. Indeed, the synthesizing categories of *Aufhebung* and *anti-Aufhebung* can play no central role in such a dialectic. Historical actors often opt not for the *Aufhebung* of opposites but for the preservation of them in a new configuration: combination, mutual complementariness, correction, balance, compromise, and control. More often than not the unintended outcome of their activity turns out to be such.

The illusion has to be dispelled that from opposing social entities the positive aspects can be separated at will by means of free deconstruction and then built into a new totality. We must not count on the possibility of completely eliminating the inner limitations of opposite entities; instead we should focus on combining such entities with a view to reducing the negative effects of these limitations to the inevitable minimums.

Upon reflection, one must conclude that surely there is no question that all realistic models of democratic socialism must be in conflict. The wisdom in building a new society rests largely in finding the right balance between opposite principles. Here are two examples: first, the criticism of the idea that socialism can "dialectically transcend" *(Aufhebung)* the separation of "civil society" and state; and second, the rejection of the assumption that socialist democracy can mean the "dialectical transcendence" of representative democracy by direct democracy.

Post-Marxist Theory and the Critique of Communist Statism

Since the Marxist study of the historical process is distinguished by the paradigm of "socioeconomic formation," it is important to determine the relevance of Marxism in relation to two basic formations, capitalist and statist, that dominate our world. The constant revision and perfection of this paradigm by Marxist revisionists is of no help; they have to accept that it has limited scope. This means that for each social formation in history its specific dominant factor and its precise nature needs to be established. Since capitalism doubtless constitutes a social totality with economic dominance, its corresponding paradigm is socioeconomic formation.

On the other hand, communist statism belongs to the family of sociopolitical formations. Pre-Stalinist, Stalinist, and post-Stalinist statism represents a social totality with political dominance, both in diachronic and in synchronic terms. Here political dominance takes the form of structural monopoly control by one class (statist) over the state and through it over the means of production. However, this paradigm of socio-political formation is no doubt an inverted Marxist or rather post-Marxist paradigm.

Moreover, not only this descriptive but also the critical (communist) dimension of the classical Marxist paradigm is now politically irrelevant in communist statism. As is well known, original Marxism stands for the "dialectical transcendence" *(Aufhebung)* of the separation of "civil society" and the state (or expressed metaphorically: the "withering away" of the state and law) as well as the complete elimination of the private property of the means of production and market-commodity relations in the new, communist society.

Admittedly, criticism of the existing (ruling) communism in the name of Marx's communism took on a subversive character in the fifties, sixties, and even seventies in some statist countries (for example, Hungary, Poland, Czechoslovakia and Yugoslavia) because (1) it successfully questioned the system's Marxist legitimacy, and (2) it challenged the ideological monopoly by the ruling class over public discourse. The bitter reaction by officials and the persecution of the critics showed that pointing to the gap between statist "Marxism-Leninism" and Marx's communism did indeed cause some irritation.

In addition to these two progressive functions, however, such criticism from the very beginning did play a potentially conservative role. But how could the idea of the withering away of the state serve to preserve a social order, the essence of which is a monopoly of control by a group over the state and, through it, over all key areas and means of social life? A realistic, and hence socially relevant, program would under these conditions focus on the reduction (liberalization) and in the long run the elimination of this monopoly (democratization). The program of the withering away of the state is an excellent example of how a utopia can indirectly contribute to preserving domination over people by drawing their attention away from real problems and ways to resolve them: by creating a legal and pluralistic state, separating it from "civil society," which has to be reconstituted, and so forth.

Symptomatically, the force of the Marxist critique of communist rule has increasingly waned as real prospects have opened up for its liberalization: for example, the decentralization of government, the reliance on the market, a certain rehabilitation of private property and initiative, and the establishing of the sphere of "civil society." However, even with the greatest possible conceptual elasticity, we cannot integrate such measures and changes into Marxism, and still less can we characterize them as Marxist. Indeed they are post-Marxist.

Unless this is understood, critics of the existing communism who rely on Marx's communism are threatened with a new, now deadly danger: that of becoming quite conservative and even reactionary. Marxism is unable to explain the emergence and nature of statism as a socio-political formation; all it needs now is to attack and hold back necessary changes. Unfortunately, it does not require great effort to use Marx's critique of bourgeois political economy against such liberal measures and changes. It is not hard to guess what Marx would say about them since he called even the principle of distribution according to work "bourgeois."

I believe that a difference should be introduced in classical Marxism between the principles of radical humanism and the idea of communist social organization. These familiar principles include: praxis, de-alienation, de-reification, meeting authentic human needs, accepting the freedom of each and every individual as the condition for the freedom of all, and others. Marx linked their realization with classless and stateless social organization, where private property and a commodity-monetary economy were to be abolished, and the distribution of the social product was, in the first phase, to be carried out in accordance with the work invested, and later, in accordance with needs. Life has proven Marx's idea of a communist society to be in part irrelevant to the prospect of feasible and viable socialism, and in part incompatible with it.

This, of course, is not to say that Marx's humanistic principles need have the same fate. Provided we separate them from communist utopia and understand them as ultimate regulative and critical, not constitutive and operative, principles, they can, with numerous necessary mediations, be useful in assessing existing societies (whether capitalist or statist) and projects of democratic socialism.

Post-Marxist Ideas About the Liberalization of Communist Statism and About Democratic Socialism

We are already witness to the fact that communist statism is feasible, but whether it will remain viable depends on the possibilities for radical self-reformation. The statist class is now at a historical turning point; in order to preserve selective-strategic control over the state and the means of production, it will ultimately have to sacrifice total, supercentralized and detailed control. Only the first is necessary to preserve the basic identity of the communist statist system. Between these two limits lies the structural possibility of the liberalization of statism. Whether it will be actualized no doubt depends on contingent historical factors, including the emergence of strong reformist leaders like Gorbachev. In some statist countries—for example, Yugoslavia, Poland, and Hungary—the process of liberalization has advanced substantially indeed.

We could also call reformed statism "statism with a civil and bourgeois face." Admittedly, a comprehensive civil society calls for a completely legal and pluralistic state. However, by definition, statism in self-reformation could not go that far. That would be revolution, not reform.

In saying that only liberalization, not democratization, is possible within the framework of statism, I of course do not rule out the possibility of the democratization of individual groups, organizations, or institutions, but only the possibility of establishing a truly democratic state, since this would mean eliminating the monopoly over the state, in which case it would no longer be a statist society.

Without the existence of a strong civil society, which would inevitably also have important bourgeois components, socialism also looks very unlikely and unattainable, and one of the reasons is that it must be organically integrated into the world market economy.

The only feasible and viable socialism for today's and tomorrow's world is socialism with a civil and bourgeois face. This is not a "transition period" between capitalism and communism, or a "lower phase" of communism, but a new social formation with a fairly mixed type of ownership, economy, civil society, and entire social organization.

Capitalism and statism are two dominant world systems, whereas democratic socialism is a major social force within them. Nobody doubts that capitalism is not only feasible but viable as well. On the other hand, more and more there are those who doubt that a system of democratic socialism could be feasible and viable.

There is an important lesson to be learned from the fact that the most productive and humane countries in the world are capitalist ones, but with a social-democratic face. It is imperative for both liberal statists and democratic socialists to study in detail the arrangements and achievements of this Western mix of capitalism, democracy, and socialism. This combination is highly instructive for both statism and socialism with a civil and bourgeois face.

In addition to political pluralism, pluralism of democracies, and pluralism in forms of ownership, democratic socialism must be based on an even more fundamental pluralism of principles of social organization. Thus an economy has to based on the profit motive, whereas the state to a great degree must be based on the opposite principle of solidarism (social state). Enterprise also in socialism must be a profit-making institution and not a basic unit of social policy of the state. This is a good illustration of the idea expressed in the section on dialectic that socialism should not try to "dialectically transcend" opposite principles in order to make an organic unity, but rather try to preserve and combine such principles of social organization.

Post-Marxism and Post-Christianity in the Shadow of the Apocalypse

Dialogues between Marxists and Christians all over the world are taking place at an already post-Marxist and post-Christian time, whether we are conscious of it or not, whether we like it or not. It goes without saying that this "post" does not mean "without" (Marxism and Christianity), let alone "anti." Rather, I have in mind both crisis and development within these great traditions. In other words, both post-Marxism and post-Christianity should be defined by basic discontinuities as well as by fundamental continuities with their roots and previous (Marxist or Christian) stages. A post-Marxist like myself naturally could still be very much under the influence of (revisionist) Marxism.

Our century is characterized by two basic contradictory experiences: on the one hand there is democracy versus totalitarianism (Nazism and Stalinism), and on the other hand unprecedented creativity versus the potential for the self-destruction of the human race through nuclear war or ecological catastrophe. The former is typical of the first half of the century, the latter of the second half. The experience of totalitarian evil and of the possibility of collective suicide has put an unbearable burden on our generation.

I would like now to say a few words about the experience of Stalinist evil, particularly against the background of Marx's anthropology. Marx made his generalizations about human nature on the basis of work situations and work relations. It is this model that led him to his ideas about the human potential for creativity, sociability, freedom, and so forth. (Another essential influence on him was Feuerbach's anthropology.)

However, the human potential for great evil, not to speak of totalitarian evil, cannot be recognized if work is taken as a basic anthropological model. A more promising analysis would have to be made against the background of power relations. However, compared with totalitarian evil, even the Hegelian paradigm of master and servant seems to be quite innocent. After all, Auschwitz and the Gulag brought about the ultimate extreme in master-thing relations (the absolute reification of human beings) and not merely master-servant relations.

Unprepared for such great evil in "its" midst, Marxism had to enter a crisis from which it is extremely difficult to recover. Unlike Marxism, however, Christianity has not been taken by any great surprise. It is, however, faced with an unresolvable problem of theodicy.

There have been numerous repercussions of the experience of Stalinist totalitarianism on Marxism and on perspectives of socialism: for example, in the field of political theory and practice. After this experience a naive approach to power cannot be excused. In this respect liberalism has obvious advantages over Marxism. Since its inception, liberalism has been pressing for the division and control of power, for the opposing of one will to power with another so that neither could be extended too far and become independent of society. To the slogan "power tends to corrupt, and absolute power tends to corrupt absolutely," utopian Marxists had nothing better to answer than, as it were, "proletarian power tends to fight corruption, and absolute proletarian power tends to fight corruption absolutely."

Marx's altogether too optimistic conception of human "species being" has to be revised to such an extent that we can speak only about a post-Marxist (post-utopian) philosophical anthropology. It was Marx who defined the potential for good (creativity, sociability, freedom, and so forth) as belonging to "human essence" and the potential for evil (destructivity, egotism, loss of unfreedom, and so forth) as inherent only in "human existence." Unlike Marx, a post-Marxist sees both these opposite potentials as inherent in "human essence." In other words, we are dealing here with an internal contradiction of "human essence" rather than with an external contradiction between human "essence" and "existence."

In a long discussion on whether a Marxist normative ethics is possible and needed, much time has been wasted. Those who have argued that such ethics is impossible rely on Marx's idea that communism will bring about the final elimination of the contradiction between human being *(Sein)* and human ought *(Sollen)*. Others, myself included, have put forth the opposite thesis that Marx's discourse itself is full of normative-ethical statements, such as when he criticizes capitalism and writes about the "transition period" between capitalism and communism and about the lower phase of communism. It is high time to replace this dispute with the insight (post-utopian and post-Marxist) that the contradiction between human being and ought, being rooted in the human "essence" itself, can never be totally removed. Hence a normative ethics will always be necessary.

Anthropologically, ontologically, historically, morally, and theologically speaking, we have been in an absolutely new situation since 1945. If we start counting from that same year, we are now in the forty-sixth year of the new calendar. This condition clearly points up the crisis not only in Marxism and Christianity, but also in all ways of thought, feeling, and action to date.

Even in its revisionist versions, Marxism seems to have forgotten about man's consciousness of his own morality and his ability to suppress it as a basic characteristic of "generic being." This potential also exists at the collective level. Even though we live with the real possibility, and even probability, of collective self-destruction, we go on thinking, feeling, and acting as though this absolute *novum* did not exist. Marx's premise about the self-producing being of man is ironically confirmed; we have added collective self-destruction to our own potentials.

Mention should also be made, in this context, of some obsolescence in the problematic of human intentional evil. The accent should be shifted to the unconcern, indifference, nonchalance, and carelessness of humankind. Who suffers from a nightmare of the apocalypse? Awareness of its possibility is suppressed so much that it cannot manifest itself even in daydreaming. Given these traits, do we have any real chance of avoiding an apocalyptic fate? Confronting us is a new, most dangerous form of collective self-delusion.

Most important of all, the human race's self-destruction can happen quite by chance. It would be an absolute irony of history if human beings, although defined as intentional beings, bring about a definite end to their own intentionality. The "easiest" thing, therefore, is to be fatalistic and say that in the final analysis there is nothing serious that can be done against chance anyway.

Mankind can accidentally cause absolute evil. Does it mean that the Christian Satan has chosen contingency as his medium? On the other hand, Marxists take a structural approach to alienation. But this does not help here; the question is how to deal with the possibility of contingent and yet absolute alienation. Scientists calculate probabilities, but what use or consolation is there in calculating the probability of an apocalypse?

As I have already said, we are living in an entirely new ontological situation. Marx spoke of two kingdoms (realms): the kingdom of necessity (material production) and the kingdom of freedom, which develops on the basis of the former (material abundance). Of course he did not expect the sociohistorical being to remain divided in world terms; in one part of the world there is real hope in the kingdom of freedom. But most of the world still lives in the kingdom of poverty, wherein is rooted the kingdom of unfreedom.

However, it is not my intention to dwell on this contradiction in the sociohistorical being or on the fact that this may well be one of the causes of mankind's self-reckoning. The point I am trying to make is that a third kingdom should be added in sociohistorical ontology: the kingdom of fatal man-made contingency. This is the framework of living, acting, and feeling wherein mankind can only hope and try to survive and attain the kingdom of freedom. However, what kind of freedom is it which is constantly under the threat of such contingency? After all, freedom cannot be defined as recognition of contingency. And yet, we ought to add to the principle of contingency the principle of active hope embodied in a supercategorical imperative of a new planetary ethics defining as supreme duty and supreme value the survival of human-kind.

It is the danger of simple and absolute negation, and not the question of the possibility or impossibility of dialectical negation, that should be of prime concern to us. How naive today appears the example of the simple negation, so dear to Engels, of a grain being trampled by man. We are now living in the shadow of the possible annihilation of the whole human race. Many Marxists still write about the negative dialectic of human intentions and goals resulting in their opposites. But what about the possibility of an irrevocable and at the same time accidental triumph of negative dialectic over humankind?

The apocalyptic rebellion of things against their human creator may be in the offing. This would be the anthropological version of the Last Judgment. A cynic would say that the final disappearance of alienation can coincide with its final and absolute triumph. Dogmatic "dialectical materialists" are left to delude themselves with a dialectics of nature without human beings!

Marxists hope that mankind will manage to overcome the "natural-ness" of the historical process, its blind occurrence "behind man's back." This would be a fundamental turnabout from "prehistory" to the start of real history. We would finally find the key to the enigma of history, in terms both of understanding and of mastering history. We, however, are going in the opposite direction, toward absolute prehistory; having been at least a kind of subject, we have now become a toy in the hands of contingency for which we have only ourselves to blame.

How can we talk about human dignity and hold our heads high in the face of such fatal contingency? The problematic of utopia also needs to be posited differently. It is ironic but true that the most radical utopia now is the survival of humankind. But is there any more minimal utopia than that? A negative utopia would have to talk about an earth from which people had eliminated themselves. This, however, leaves even science fiction speechless, let alone Marxism and Christianity.

What is the purpose of politics today? Traditionally speaking, politics concerns power over people, society, and nature. Now, however, politics is confronted with man's powerlessness in the face of the fatal chance of man's doing. The legitimacy of governments, authorities, states, and politics appears quite different in this light. A policy that is not preoccupied with the question of mankind's survival cannot be legitimate.

We are also witness to the fact that democracy has lost much of its substance. If democracy is the possibility of the citizen to influence the conditions under which he lives, then what is the purpose of it if he can influence all other decisions except the decision of all decisions. Michel Foucault criticized the inherited view of power and pointed out that in the modern world power is quite diffuse and spread out like capillaries.

But I am thinking of the far more radical diffusion of power and power-lessness. Where is that power concentrated that could accidentally destroy humankind or prevent that from happening?

We also have to change our approach to justice. Many Marxists have been quite critical of those communist regimes that have sacrificed present generations in the name of future generations. But present generations pass decisions and nondecisions which can prevent the emergence of future generations. Would that not be absolute injustice?

The philosophical dispute between existentialism and essentialism is also largely *passé*. Existentialism came onto the scene by criticizing many earlier philosophers for their essentialistic approach and claiming that it is not true that human essence precedes human existence, but the other way around. However, in our day and age, man's existence and essence are open to the whims of a contingency that is our product.

I am proposing a transpolitical philosophy of contingentialism. There is the real possibility and even probability of the circle of human contingency closing once and for all, from man's biological contingency in the universe to the contingency of humankind's survival thanks to its own creativity.

Christianity certainly cannot accept the contingency of man's appearance in the universe. If mankind destroys itself, however, it will commit an absolute, irreparable, irredeemable sin. In my view, Christianity as Christianity is unable to permit such a possibility. Humankind needs a post-Christianity that concerns itself less with original sin and more with definitive sin. We need a new supercommandment.

I do not deny, of course, that other forms of religion are possible which would not stand in contradiction to the threat of the apocalypse. They say, for example, that there was once an Indian tribe that believed that God had not finished creating the world and that he would return to it when people had disappeared.

In my opinion, however, no Christian (but only post-Christian) theology, no matter how revisionist it may be, can see the Judgment Day as human judgment in disguise. The self-apocalypse brings into question other Christian teachings as well—for example, divine love, mercy, salvation, and so forth—none of which can be unconditional. What theodicy could justify the Christian Almighty? He himself would "die" if the human race destroyed itself! Anyway, have we not already committed an unforgivable blasphemy by coming to the brink of the abyss and teetering over it?

It is high time for religions to give absolute priority to concern for the continuation of humankind. A theology of the survival of humankind would be even more radical than the theology of liberation. Everyone should join the cry of the famous Christian socialist Walter Dirks: "A good end is improbable but imperative."

Christians, especially if they are statesmen, who are nonchalant about the real danger of the human race's self-destruction are no better than their atheistic counterparts on the other side of the ideological divide. We do not need any Strategic Defense Initiative but a Strategic Historical Initiative for the salvation of humankind.

On the other hand, atheists should give deep thought to whether the notion of a completely profane world gives us any chance at all to avoid the apocalypse. Is an atheism conceivable for which the continuation of the human species would be a sacred cause?

Notes

1. Svetozar Stojanović, *Between Ideals and Reality* (New York: Oxford University Press, 1969, 1973); and *In Search of Democracy in Socialism* (Buffalo: Prometheus Books, 1978, 1981); both of these books were written under this circumstance.

2. Svetozar Stojanović, *Perestroika: From Marxism and Bolshevism to Gorbachev* (Buffalo: Prometheus Books, 1987, 1988).

Incommensurability

RICHARD J. BERNSTEIN

INCOMMENSURABILITY AND
OTHERNESS REVISITED

I

"Incommensurability," "otherness," "alterity," "singularity," *"différance,"* "plurality." These signifiers reverberate throughout much of twentieth-century philosophy. For all their differences, they are signs of a pervasive amorphous mood—what Heidegger calls a *Stimmung.* It is a mood of deconstruction, destabilization, rupture, and fracture—of resistance to all forms of *abstract* totality, universalism, and rationalism. In the most diverse philosophic currents—ranging from Anglo-American postempiricist philosophy of science to Continental poststructuralism, we can detect family resemblances in this complex reaction against some of the dominant tendencies in the history of Western philosophy. Sometimes the object of attack is what Richard Rorty calls the Cartesian-Lockean-Kantian tradition of modern epistemology. Sometimes the rebellion is against the Enlightenment legacy. Sometimes, as in Nietzsche, Heidegger, and Derrida, it is the entire tradition of Western metaphysics that is made to tremble. But whatever is the specific target of destabilization and deconstruction, and regardless of the philosophic "vocabulary" in which these objections are articulated, there is also a profound convergence in the mood that they express.

I want to unravel some of the threads that are interwoven by these signifiers—especially those that cluster around the notions of incommensurability and otherness. What is at issue here? Why have these themes become so central in our time? What can we learn from the intensive debates concerning them? And what is to be rejected as misleading and/or false?

In order to orient my questioning, let me step back to gain some perspective. One of the oldest and most persistent questions in Western philosophy—and as far as I understand it, in Eastern thought, too—has been the "problem" of the one and the many and/or identity and difference. One might even argue that Western philosophy began with this

85

"problem." I speak of *the* "problem" in scare quotes, because—as so often happens in philosophy—we are really dealing with *many* problems under this rubric. Nevertheless, we can say that philosophers have always been concerned with understanding what underlies and pervades the multiplicity, diversity, and sheer contingency that we encounter in our everyday lives. Is there some fundamental, essential unity that encompasses this multiplicity? Is there a one, *eidos,* universal, form, genus that is essential to the multiplicity of particulars? What is the character of this essential unity? It can be—and indeed has been—argued that the dominant tendency in Western philosophy and metaphysics has been to privilege and valorize unity, harmony, and totality and thereby to denigrate, suppress, or marginalize multiplicity, contingency, particularity, and singularity. The problem of the one and the many and/or identity and difference can take on many different ontic forms—it arises not only in metaphysics, but also in epistemology, ethics, politics, and religion. Even the recent debates between so-called communitarians and anticommunitarians can be viewed from this perspective. Anticommunitarians are deeply suspicious of any claim that compromises the independence and ontological irreducibility of individuals, while communitarians argue that a theory of the individual or self that does not acknowledge the reality of common shared bonds that unite individuals leads to a shallow and inadequate understanding of social and political life.

If we read the history of philosophy as an attempt to reconcile identity with difference, then we can understand why Hegel might be seen as the culmination of this tradition. More systematically and thoroughly than any previous philosopher, Hegel sought to think through a "final solution" to this problem. Hegel himself claimed that the entire tradition of Western philosophy achieves its *telos* with the unity of identity with difference. Ironically, almost every philosopher since Hegel has rejected his "solution."

But Hegel already brilliantly noted and indeed anticipated what has been deeply troubling for many post-Hegelian thinkers. We can see this clearly in the section "Absolute Freedom and Terror" in the *Phenomenology of Spirit.* Hegel adumbrates the dialectic of what happens when an abstract universalism, an abstract "universal will" ascends the throne "without any power being able to resist it."[1] The demand for (of) abstract universal freedom inevitably leads to terror. "In this absolute freedom, therefore, all social groups or classes which are the spiritual spheres into which the whole is articulated are abolished. . . ."[2] It is doubly ironic that even though Hegel contrasts the terror of abstract universal freedom with the struggle for, and actualization of, concrete freedom as the *telos* of history, post-Hegelian philosophers have not only been skeptical of Hegel's relentless drive toward a grand *Aufhebung,* they have also accused him of furthering a new, more subtle and pernicious form of terror in his demand for *totality*. Indeed this charge has become a cliché for those who think of themselves as "postmodern." Jean-François Lyotard concludes his essay, "What is Postmodernism?" with a rhetorical flourish directed toward Hegel and his legacy.

> The nineteenth and twentieth centuries have given us as much terror as we can take. We have paid a high enough price for the nostalgia of the whole and the one, for the reconciliation of the concept and the sensible, of the transparent and the communicable experience. Under the general demand for slackening and for appeasement, we can hear the mutterings of the desire for a return of terror, for the realization of the fantasy to seize reality. The answer is: Let us wage war on totality; let us be witnesses to the unpresentable; let us activate the differences and save the honor of the name.[3]

But I am getting ahead of my story. Let me turn to the question of incommensurability.

II

"Incommensurability" was thrust into the center of Anglo-American philosophic debates because of Thomas Kuhn's provocative book, *The Structure of Scientific Revolutions*. Kuhn tells us that "In applying the term 'incommensurability' to theories, I had intended only to insist that there was no common language within which both could be fully expressed and which could there be used in a *point-by-point* comparison between them" (emphasis added).[4]

Now it is important to remember the context in which Kuhn introduced incommensurability—just as it is essential to distinguish carefully commensurability, compatibility, and comparability.[5] Kuhn never intended to deny that paradigm theories can be compared—indeed *rationally* compared and evaluated. In insisting on incommensurability, his main point was to indicate the ways in which paradigm theories *can* and *cannot* be compared. Furthermore, incompatibility is not to be confused with, or assimilated into incommensurability. For incompatibility is a logical concept that presupposes—as Kuhn himself notes—a common language in which we can specify incompatible logical relations. What, then, is the meaning and significance of the incommensurability of paradigm theories?

Kuhn's main (although very brief), explicit discussion of incommensurability occurs in the context of his analysis of the resolution of scientific revolutions. Kuhn seeks to explain why proponents of competing paradigms "may [each] hope to convert the other to his way of seeing his science and its problems [but] neither may hope to prove his case."[6] He specifies three reasons why "the proponents of competing paradigms must fail to make *complete* contact with each other's viewpoints" (emphasis added).[7] These are the reasons for claiming there is "incommensurability of the pre- and post-revolutionary normal scientific traditions. . . . In the first place, the proponents of competing paradigms will often disagree about the list of problems that any candidate for a paradigm must resolve. The standards of their definitions of science are not the same. . . . However, more is involved than the incommensurability of standards."[8] Secondly, then, "within the new paradigm, old terms, concepts, and experiments fall into new relationships one with the other."[9] But there is a third—and for Kuhn, this is the "most fundamental aspect of the incommensurability of competing paradigms."[10] In a provocative and ambiguous passage he writes:

> In a sense that I am unable to explicate further, the proponents of competing paradigms practice their trades in different worlds. One contains constrained bodies that fall slowly, the other pendulums that repeat their motions again and again. In one, solutions are compounds, in the other mixtures. One is embedded in a flat, the other in a curved, matrix of space. Practicing in different worlds, the two groups of scientists see different things when they look from the same point in the same direction. Again that is not to say that they can see anything they please. Both are looking at the world, and what they look at has not changed. But in some areas they see different things, and they see them in different relations to the other. That is why a law that cannot even be demonstrated to one group of scientists may occasionally seem intuitively obvious to another. Equally, it is why, before they can hope to communicate fully, one group or the other must experience the conversion that we have been calling a paradigm shift. Just because it is a transition between incommensurables, the transition between competing paradigms cannot be made a step at a time, forced by logic and neutral experience. Like the gestalt switch, it must occur all at once (though not necessarily in an instant) or not at all.[11]

It is passages like this one that provoked strong reactions among philosophers. Such expressions as "different worlds," "conversion," and "gestalt switches" led (or rather, misled) many sympathetic and unsympathetic readers to think that his conception of a paradigm is like a total self-enclosed windowless monad—and that a paradigm shift necessitates an "irrational conversion." Even Karl Popper interpreted Kuhn as being guilty of "the myth of the framework"—the myth that "we are prisoners caught in the framework of our theories; our expectations; our past experience; our language."[12] Presumably we are so imprisoned in these frameworks or paradigms that we cannot even communicate with those imprisoned in "radically" incommensurable paradigms. In another context I have argued that this is an inaccurate and distortive reading of Kuhn—although, unfortunately, a very common one.[13] Despite Kuhn's repeated protests that he never intended to suggest that paradigm switches involve an irrational mystical conversion, the rhetoric of extreme relativism has continued to haunt the appeal to incommensurability.

Although there are many ambiguities in Kuhn's discussion of incommensurability, one point is clear. Kuhn is primarily concerned with the incommensurability of *scientific* paradigms. But the very idea of incommensurability became so fertile and suggestive that it was soon generalized and extended to problems and contexts far beyond Kuhn's original concern to analyze scientific inquiry.

We can witness this in Richard Rorty's use of incommensurability in *Philosophy and the Mirror of Nature.* Rorty stretches the idea of commensuration and incommensurability to call into question the main tradition of modern epistemology—the "Cartesian-Lockean-Kantian tradition."[14] He characterizes "commensurable" as follows:

> By "commensurable" I mean able to be brought under a set of rules which will tell us how rational agreement can be reached on what would settle the issue on every point where statements seem to conflict. These rules tell how to construct an ideal situation, in which all residual disagreements will be seen to the "noncognitive" or merely verbal, or else merely temporary—capable of being resolved by doing something further. What matters is that there should be agreement about what would have to be done if a resolution *were* to be achieved. In the meantime, the interlocuters can agree to differ—being satisfied of each other's rationality the while.[15]

According to Rorty, "epistemology proceeds on the assumption that all contributions to a given discourse are commensurable."[16] The dominating assumption of epistemology is that to be rational, to be fully human, to do what we ought, we need to be able to find agreement with other human beings."[17] Hermeneutics, according to Rorty is a struggle against the assumption of commensuration; hermeneutics indicates the desire to keep open the cultural space that opened up after the demise of epistemology. Rorty is calling for the ever new "invention" of incommensurable vocabularies—ever new forms of dissensus, not epistemological consensus. By generalizing and pressing the incommensurability thesis to this extreme, Rorty has not only raised the specter of an extreme relativism but has provoked strong and hostile reactions. We can see this backlash in the reassertion of the varieties of metaphysical and scientific realism that has dominated so much of recent analytic philosophy.[18]

Instead of attempting to sort out the tangled issues involved in the crossfire of realist and antirealist arguments, I want to discuss briefly the significance of Donald Davidson's contribution to the debate about incommensurability in what has become a "classic" paper, "On the Very Idea of a Conceptual Scheme." Davidson questions the intelligibility of the idea of a conceptual scheme, a framework, a paradigm that is presupposed—but rarely critically examined—in the debates about incommensurability. The main force of his argument is to show that the very idea of a conceptual scheme (in which we use sentences with truth values) that is presumably "radically" incommensurable with alternative conceptual schemes is—when we think it through—incoherent.

Summing up his conclusion, Davidson writes:

> It would be wrong to summarize by saying we have shown how communication is possible between people who have different schemes, a way that works without need of what there cannot be, namely a neutral ground, or a common coordinate system. For we have found no intelligible basis on which it can be said that schemes are different. It would be equally wrong to announce the glorious news that all mankind—all speakers of language, at least—share a common scheme and ontology. For it we cannot intelligibly say that schemes are different, neither can we intelligibly say that they are one.[19]

Davidson is not denying that there may be a sense in which different languages or vocabularies are incommensurable. Rather he is rejecting the "dogma of scheme and reality" whereby we assume that different conceptual schemes are partial representations of a common uninterpreted reality. He is challenging the idea that we can intelligibly conceive of different conceptual schemes so that it makes sense to say that the truth values of sentences in "one" conceptual scheme may not share any of the truth values of sentences in different alternative conceptual schemes.[20]

Before drawing out the lessons of what can be learned from the use and abuse of appeals to incommensurability, I want to consider briefly one further appropriation of this controversial concept. Alasdair MacIntyre applies the concept of incommensurability to what he calls "tradition-constituted and tradition-constitutive" inquiries. In this respect, MacIntyre wants to show how rival traditions themselves may be incommensurable—especially traditions where the concepts of justice and practical rationality are central. The position developed by MacIntyre in *Whose Justice? Which Rationality?* is complex and nuanced —and, I would argue, not completely persuasive.[21] Let me outline some of his main theses. MacIntyre presents a "rational reconstruction" of three primary traditions—the Aristotelian, the Augustinian, and the Scottish "common sense" tradition—in order to show how each of these traditions can be viewed as *rationally* resolving conflicts (or failing to resolve conflicts) generated *within* each of these traditions. Although each of these traditions is formed by historically contingent beliefs, nevertheless *within* each of these traditions universal claims are made about what is justice and what is practical rationality—claims which are, in important ways, incompatible and incommensurable with those made in rival traditions. Each of these traditions develops its own standards of rationality. But despite this incommensurability we are not forced into an epistemological situation of relativism or perspectivism.[22] The rational superiority of a tradition can be vindicated without (falsely) presupposing that there are universally neutral, ahistorical standards of rationality. There is not "rationality as such." However, it is possible to show that a specific tradition—say the Aristotelian tradition—can be rationally vindicated and shown to be rationally progressive by its own "standards of rationality." Furthermore, we can show— and MacIntyre thinks he has shown this—that rival incompatible and incommensurable traditions fail, not only according to Aristotelian standards of rationality, but according to their own standards of rationality. This is precisely what MacIntyre claims to have demonstrated about the "tradition" of liberalism that has its roots in the Enlightenment. We cannot ever hope to provide a *final* rational vindication for any "tradition-constituted and tradition-constitutive inquiry" because there cannot be an epistemological guarantee that a living tradition will be able to continue to solve the problems and conflicts it inevitably generates. Traditions undergo what MacIntyre calls "epistemological crises." We cannot know in advance whether or not a specific tradition will be able to resolve these "epistemological crises." But this claim does not mean we should be agnostic about the traditions in which we participate. Rather it means recognizing our historical finitude and fallibilism. Fallibilism itself presupposes that there is a truth which can be known. We can support our allegiance to a tradition by showing how it is rationally progressing according to its own historically developing "standards of rationality" and how it can successfully meet the challenges of rival traditions. There is no way to jump "out" or "over" history.

Now despite MacIntyre's apparently tolerant claims in acknowledging the "legitimacy" of radically incommensurable traditions of justice and practical rationality, there is an *implicit* cultural imperialism in his view. For it is a necessary consequence to his claims that a given tradition *may* contingently turn out to be rationally superior to all its rivals. And indeed MacIntyre does believe he has shown that:

> an Aristotelian tradition with resources for its own enlargement, correction, and defense, resources which suggest that *prima facie* at least a case has been made for concluding . . . that those who have thought their way through the topics of justice and practical rationality, from the standpoint constructed by and in the direction pointed out first by Aristotle and then by Aquinas, have every reason so far to hold that *the rationality of their tradition has been confirmed* in its encounters with other traditions. . . . (Emphasis added)[23]

I have indicated that I do not find MacIntyre's complex argument fully persuasive. Specifically I do not think he has justified the claim that the Aristotelian-Thomistic tradition of justice and practical rationality *is* rationally *superior* to its rivals—even the few rival traditions he has analyzed. But this is not the place to develop fully the reasons why I think he fails to justify *this* claim.[24] However, I do think MacIntyre deepens our understanding of incommensurability by applying this concept to a "thick description" of traditions. Furthermore, I agree with MacIntyre that acknowledging such incommensurability does not mean giving up the universality of truth claims made within a given tradition. The incommensurability of traditions does not entail relativism or perspectivism.

But the time has come to sum up what I think are the proper conclusions to be drawn from the debates about incommensurability. Although I cannot develop a full-scale justification for these claims here, I do believe they can be adequately justified. I want to sum up these conclusions in a series of theses.

1. The controversies concerning incommensurability have challenged and raised serious doubts about the belief that there is—or must be—a determinate, universal, neutral, ahistorical framework in which all languages or "vocabularies" can be *adequately* translated and which can enable us to evaluate rationally the validity claims made within these disparate languages. In this respect one of the most fundamental foundational claims of Western philosophy and epistemology has been called into question.

2. The incommensurability of languages and traditions does not entail a self-defeating or self-referentially inconsistent form of relativism or perspectivism.

3. The concept of incommensurability is not to be confused with, or reduced to logical incompatibility or incomparability. Incommensurable languages can be compared and rationally evaluated in *multiple* ways. Practically, such comparison and evaluation requires the cultivation of hermeneutical sensitivity and imagination.

4. Incommensurable languages and traditions are not to be thought of as self-contained windowless monads that share nothing in common. In Wittgenstein's phrase, this is a (false) picture that holds us captive. There are always points of overlap and crisscrossing, even if there is not perfect commensuration. We must not succumb to "the myth of the framework." Our linguistic horizons are always open. This is what enables comparison, and even sometimes a "fusion of horizons."

5. We can never escape the real practical possibility that we may fail to understand "alien" traditions and the ways in which they are incommensurable with the traditions to which we belong.

6. But the response to the threat of this practical failure—which can sometimes be tragic—should be an ethical one, namely, to assume the responsibility to listen carefully, to use our linguistic, emotional, and cognitive imagination to grasp what is being expressed and said in

"alien" traditions. We must do this in such a way that we resist the dual temptations of *either* facilely assimilating what others are saying to our own categories and language without doing justice to what is genuinely different and may be incommensurable *or* simply dismissing what the "other" is saying as incoherent nonsense. We must also resist the double danger of imperialistic colonization and inauthentic exoticism—what is sometimes called "going native."[25]

7. Within a given language or tradition which may be incommensurable with its rivals, participants are always already making universal validity claims that "transcend" their local contexts.

8. Above all, we must always strive to avoid a false essentialism when we are trying to understand the traditions to which we belong or those alien traditions that are incommensurable with "our" traditions. For frequently discussions of East-West lapse into such a false essentialism where we are seduced into thinking that there are essential determinate characteristics that distinguish the Western and Eastern "mind." This false essentialism violently distorts the sheer complexity of overlapping traditions that cut across these artificial simplistic global notions.

9. Learning to live with (among) rival pluralistic incommensurable traditions—which is one of the most pressing problems of contemporary life—is always precarious and fragile. There are no algorithms for grasping what is shared in common and what is genuinely different. Indeed, commonality and difference is itself historically conditioned and shifting. The search for commonalities and differences among incommensurable traditions is always a task and an obligation—an *Aufgabe*. It is a primary responsibility for reflective participants in any vital substantive tradition. In this sense the plurality of rival incommensurable traditions imposes a *universal* responsibility upon reflective participants in any tradition—a responsibility that should not be confused with an indifferent superficial tolerance where no effort is made to understand and engage the incommensurable otherness of the Other.

I agree with a theme which has been just as central for Gadamer as it has been for Derrida—that it is only through an engaged encounter with the Other, with the otherness of the Other that one comes to a more informed textured understanding of the traditions to which "we" belong. It is in our genuine encounters with what is other and alien that we can further our own self-understanding.

III

Let me abruptly switch contexts and take up the themes of otherness and alterity. But I hope to show—as my last remarks suggest—that this is not really an abrupt change at all. Although the thematization of "otherness" has not been in the foreground of twentieth-century Anglo-

American philosophy, it has been at the very center of twentieth-century Continental philosophy—especially German and French philosophy. Michael Theunissen begins his impressive book *The Other* with the following claim—a claim with which I fully agree:

> Few issues have expressed as powerful a hold over the thought of this century as that of "The Other." It is difficult to think of a second theme, even one that might be of more substantial significance, that has provoked as widespread an interest as this one; it is difficult to think of a second theme that so sharply marks off the present—admittedly a present growing out of the nineteenth century and reaching back to it—from its historical roots in the tradition. To be sure the problem of the other has at times been accorded a prominent place in ethics and anthropology, in legal and political philosophy. But the problem of the other has certainly never penetrated as deeply as today into the foundations of philosophical thought—the question of the other cannot be separated from the most primordial questions raised by modern thought.[26]

But what precisely is the "problem" of the Other. Here, too, we must be careful to avoid a false essentialism. When we "look and see," we discover that it "names" a cluster of problems related by family resemblances rather than a single, well-defined problem. Theunissen tells us: "Generally speaking, 'the Other' comprehends all those concepts by means of which contemporary philosophy has sought to set out the structure of being-with, or its original transcendental form. Thus, among other things, it comprehends the difference between 'Thou' on the one side and the 'alien I'—the 'alter ego' or being-with-the-other—on the other side."[27] But even this broad formulation does not encompass all the issues raised by the question of "the Other." Indeed it does not explicitly mention those analyses where "the Other" is taken to be a generic term for what is excluded, repressed, suppressed, or concealed. Thus, for example, one can speak of "the Other" of Reason—regardless of how this "Other" is characterized. Theunissen primarily intends to call attention to the "problem of the other," where the other is understood as a *personal* other, whether a first-person "alien I" or a second-person "thou" (although what is meant by "personal" is itself problematic and contested). In French, for example, this systematic ambiguity in the neutral English term "Other" is reflected in the distinction between *"autre"* and *"autrui."*[28]

To pursue the vicissitudes of reflections on "the Other" would require nothing less than a comprehensive narrative of twentieth-century Continental philosophy. The theme of "the Other"—and specifically what constitutes the otherness of "the Other"—has been at the very heart of the work of every major twentieth-century continental philosopher. But in order to leap into the center of controversies concerning "the Other," I want to begin by considering one of the most extreme and radical formulations of the problem of "the Other"—the one developed by the French Jewish thinker, Emmanuel Levinas.

Levinas, perhaps more than any other French thinker, is responsible for the original French encounter with, and appropriation of Husserl and Heidegger. It was from Levinas' early writings on Husserl that even Sartre first learned of the importance of phenomenology. But, for my purposes, I want to focus on the way in which "the Other"—specifically *autrui*—becomes increasingly predominant in Levinas' thinking. This notion becomes a lever for a questioning and challenging of the entire project of philosophy, including the phenomenology of Husserl and the fundamental ontology of Heidegger. According to Levinas, both Husserl and Heidegger still think in the shadow of Greek philosophy—which has set the terms for the entire tradition of Western philosophy. Simplifying to the extreme, we can say that Levinas reads the entire project of the history of Western philosophy, whose destiny has been shaped by the classical Greek problematic, as functioning within what he calls "the Same and the Other." Furthermore, the primary thrust of this Western tradition has always been to reduce, absorb, or appropriate what is taken to be "the Other" to "the Same." This is manifested not only in ontology but also in epistemology and in the main traditions of Western politics and ethics. This drive to reduce or assimilate "the Other" to "the Same" is already reflected in the Parmenedian identification of thought and being—where difference and otherness disappears. This imperialistic gesture—this gesture to conquer, master, and colonize "the Other"—reveals the violence that is implicit in the reduction of "the Other" to "the Same." For Levinas, this violence reaches its apogee in Hegel. Commenting on Hegel, Levinas tells us:

> The I is not a being that always remains the same, but is the being whose existing consists in identifying itself, in recovering its identity throughout all that happens to it. It is the primal identity, the primordial work of the identification. . . . Hegelian phenomenology, where self-consciousness is the distinguishing of what is not distinct, expresses the universality of the same identifying itself in the alterity of objects thought and despite the opposition of self to self.[29]

To illustrate what he means, Levinas cites a famous passage from the *Phenomenology of Spirit* where Hegel declares:

> I distinguish myself from myself; and therein I am immediately aware that this factor distinguished from me is not distinguished. I, the selfsame being thrust myself away from myself; but this which is distinguished, which is set up as unlike me, is immediately on its being distinguished no distinction for me.[30]

Levinas reads this as affirming that "the difference is not a difference; the I, as other, is not an 'other'."[31] In short, even though "alterity" drives the Hegelian dialectic, this "alterity" is ultimately *Aufgehoben*, swallowed up in the Absolute Subject. Consequently, "alterity" has no singular *metaphysical* status outside what is *ontologically* the same—it is only a "moment" within "the Same."[32] Of course, Levinas is not the first to raise this type of objection against Hegel. We find variations on it in thinkers as diverse as Kierkegaard, Nietzsche, Adorno, Sartre, Heidegger, Foucault, and Derrida. What is distinctive about Levinas, what makes him so "radical," is his claim that even Husserlian phenomenology and Heidegger's fundamental ontology—despite protests to the contrary—do not escape this reduction of "the Other" to "the Same."

Levinas boldly seeks to escape this philosophical imperialism of "the Same" and "the Other" by opening the space for the absolute exteriority of the metaphysical Other *(autrui)*, which he sharply distinguishes from the ontological other *(autre)*. The metaphysical other is an "other with an alterity that is not formal, is not the simple reverse of identity, and is not formed out of resistance to the same, but is prior to every initiative, to all imperialism of the same. It is other with an alterity constitutive of the very content of the other."[33] To acknowledge the otherness of the Other *(autrui)*, to keep it from falling back into the other of the same requires Levinas to speak of it as the "absolute other." It is the Stranger *(L'Etranger)* who genuinely dis-turbs or ruptures the being at home with oneself *(le chez soi)*.[34] It is this radically asymmetrical relation between the I and the other (a "relation" that defies reduction to reciprocal equality) that characterizes what Levinas calls *the ethical relation*. As he boldly pursues this pathway of thinking, he categorically asserts the metaphysical priority and primacy of the ethical (which is not to be confused with the Kantian primacy of practical reason)—a primacy that reigns over all ontology. We can see just how radical Levinas' thinking is when he distances himself from Heidegger.

> Even though it opposes the technological passion issued forth from the forgetting of Being hidden by existants, Heideggerian ontology, which subordinates the relationship with the Other to the relation with Being in general, remains under obedience to the anonymous, and leads inevitably to another power to imperialist domination to tyranny.[35]

Initially, Levinas' idiom may strike us as idiosyncratic (which it is) and abstract (which it is not). We can begin to relate these reflections on "the Other" *(autrui)* to our discussion on incommensurability. For by argumentation and phenomenological description, Levinas seeks to elicit the incommensurability of "the Other" with the I. This incommensurability and asymmetry of "the Other" *(autrui)* is manifested in what he calls the "face-to-face," the primary ethical relation that can never be reduced to the "totality" of "the Same" and "the Other." Against the tendency so deeply ingrained in Western discourse that highlights and valorizes reciprocity, likeness, and symmetry in "personal" relationships—for example, in Western discourses on friendship *(philia)*—Levinas emphasizes the lack of reciprocity, unlikeness, asymmetry—and indeed incommensurability—in the ethical relation of the "face-to-face." This even has consequences for understanding the asymmetry of responsibility, where I, in responding to "the Other" *(autrui)*, am always responsible for (to) "the Other" *(autrui)*, regardless of "the Other's" response to me.

We can appreciate the thought-provoking quality of Levinas' thinking when we realize that he is at once reiterating and radicalizing a theme that has been sounded over and over again in the aftermath of Hegel and which has become so dominant in what is loosely and vaguely called "postmodern" thought. This is the theme that *resists* the unrelenting tendency of the will to knowledge and truth, where Reason —when unmasked—is understood as always seeking to appropriate, comprehend, control, master, contain, dominate, suppress, or repress what presents itself as "the Other" it confronts. It is the theme of the violence of Reason's imperialistic welcoming embrace.

The metaphors of "imperialism," "colonization," "domination," "mastery," and "control" are not to be taken as "dead" metaphors. For the "logic" at work here *is* the "logic" at work in cultural, political, social, and economic imperialism and colonization—even the "logic" of ethical imperialism, where the language of reciprocal recognition and reconciliation masks the violent reduction of the alterity of "the Other" *(autrui)* to "more of the same." What is at issue here is the acknowledgment of the radical, incommensurable *singularity* of the Other *(autrui)*, to recover a sense of radical plurality that defies any facile total reconciliation. (I hope it is becoming clear how relevant this is to understanding the treacherous dynamics of the forms of cultural imperialism that have been played out in East-West relations.)

In "using" Levinas as exemplar of a radical thinker who seeks to take us beyond the limits of the "logic" of "the Same" and "the Other"— which *he* takes to be the logic of Western philosophy shaped by the Greek problematic—I do *not* want to suggest that I agree with him. Derrida's own brilliant deconstruction of Levinas' texts exposes the double-bind logic that ensnares Levinas. For Derrida's close reading brings out the aporetic quality and instability of Levinas' "position." Derrida's reading has consequences that reach far beyond the interpretation of Levinas. For Levinas comes precipitously close to reinstituting a new set of rigid dichotomies, for example, ontology/metaphysics, philosophy/ethics, Greek/Jew.

Derrida questions the intelligibility of Levinas' notion of *the* Absolute Other and absolute exteriority. He even shows how "Levinas is very close to Hegel, much closer than he admits, and at the very moment when he is apparently opposed to Hegel in the most radical fashion. This is a situation he must share with all anti-Hegelian thinkers."[36]

Derrida agrees with Levinas that "the other is the other only if his alterity is absolutely irreducible, that is, infinitely irreducible. . . ."[37]

But, contrary to Levinas, who claims that "to make the other an alter ego . . . is to neutralize its absolute alterity," Derrida argues that "if the other was not recognized as ego, its entire alterity would collapse."[38] Against, Levinas' reading of Husserl, Derrida (rightly) claims that according to Husserl "the other as alter ego signifies the other as other, irreducible to *my* ego, precisely because it is an ego, because it has the form of the ego. . . . This is why, if you will, he is face, can speak to me, understand me, and eventually command me."[39]

Derrida presses this point even further when declares: "the other, then would not be what he is (my fellowman as foreigner) if he were not alter ego. . . . [T]he other is absolutely other only if he is an ego, that is, in a certain way, if he is the same as I."[40] This last claim sounds *as if* Derrida is siding with Hegel against Levinas. But to draw this inference would miss the subtlety (and instability) of Derrida's point. His "logic" here is a "both/and" rather than an "either/or"—but it is not the "logic" of *Aufheben* in which all differences and oppositions are ultimately reconciled. In short, there is both sameness and radical alterity, symmetry and asymmetry, and identity and difference in my relation with "the Other," and above all in the ethical relation.

Just as Derrida plays off Hegel and Husserl against Levinas (indeed with Levinas' *own* reading of Hegel and Husserl), Derrida also turns Heidegger against Levinas. When he does this, the ethical (or rather the metaethical) implications of Derrida's deconstruction and destabilization become vivid. For Derrida writes:

> Not only is the thought of Being not ethical violence [as Levinas claims], but it seems no ethics—in Levinas' sense—can be opened without it. . . . [The thought of Being] conditions the *respect* for the other *as what it is*. Without this acknowledgement, which is not a knowledge, or let us say, without this "letting-be" of an existent (other) as something existing outside me in the essence of what it is (first in its alterity), no ethics would be possible . . . to let the other be in its existence and essence as other means that what gains access to thought, or (and) what thought gains access to, is that which is essence and that which is existence; and that which is the Being which they presuppose. Without this, no letting-be would be possible, and first of all, the letting be of respect and of the ethical commandment addressing itself to freedom. Violence would reign to such a degree that it would no longer even be able to appear and be named.[41]

Derrida, who begins his essay on Levinas with a citation from Matthew Arnold—

> Hebraism and Hellenism,—between these two points of influence moves our world. At one time it feels more powerfully the attraction of one of them, at another time of the other; and it ought to be though it never is, evenly and happily balanced between them.[42]

—concludes his essay with a much more ambiguous—and what he would call "undecidable"—question:

And what is the legitimacy, what is the meaning of the *copula* in this proposition from perhaps the most Hegelian of modern novelists: "JewGreek is
greekjew. Extremes meet"?

Derrida's citation above from Matthew Arnold can be read as allegori-
cal—and it is just as applicable to EastWest. For playing with Derrida's
citation of Joyce's *Ulysses,* we can ask: "And what is the legitimacy,
what is the meaning of the *copula* in the proposition: 'EastWest is west-
east. Extremes meet?' "

Now despite the allusions to my earlier discussion of incommensurability in exploring the alterity of the other, one may wonder what does
this strange continental talk about "the Other" have to do with the original problematic of incommensurability? If there are "family resemblances" aren't they only extremely superficial? I do not think so. So—
in a manner that roughly parallels the theses that I advanced in the
discussion of incommensurability—let me conclude with a number of
theses concerning the alterity and singularity of the otherness of the
Other that interweave with the discussion of incommensurability.

1. The controversies concerning the otherness or alterity of "the
Other" do highlight a deep tendency in Western philosophy to reduce
(violently) "the Other" to "the Same." And they deeply question and
challenge this tendency—showing us the consequences of this reduction. They show us what is silenced or obliterated when we fail to
acknowledge the alterity (the incommensurability) of the Other.

2. This irreducible alterity does not mean that there is nothing in
common between the I and its genuine "Other." If there were nothing
in common, we would once again find ourselves in the *aporias* of self-
defeating relativism and/or perspectivism.

3. Acknowledging the radical alterity of "the Other" does not mean
that there is *no* way of understanding the other, or comparing the I with
its other. Even an asymmetrical relation is still a *relation.* Alternatively
we can say that to think of "the Other" as an "absolute Other" where
this is taken to mean that there is *no* way whatsoever for relating the I to
"the Other" is unintelligible and incoherent. We must cultivate the
type of imagination where we are at once sensitive to the sameness of
"the Other" with ourselves *and* the radical alterity that defies and resists
reduction of "the Other" to "the Same."

4. Acknowledging radical alterity does not mean that we should think
of the "terms" of this relation of the "I" or "we" to its "other" as windowless monads completely impenetrable to each other.

5. We can never escape the real practical possibility that we will fail
to do justice to the alterity of "the Other."

6. But the response to the threat to this practical failure should be an
ethical one—to assume the responsibility to acknowledge and not to violate the alterity of "the Other." Without such acknowledgment and recognition no ethics is possible. We must resist the dual temptation *either*

facilely to assimilate the alterity of "the Other" to what is "the Same" (this is what Levinas so acutely emphasizes) *or* simply to dismiss (or repress) the alterity of the Other as being of no significance—"merely" contingent. We must also resist the double danger of imperialistic colonization and inauthentic exoticism when encountering "the Other."

7. Contrary to Levinas there *is* a reciprocity between the I and "the Other" *(autrui)* that is compatible with their radical alterity. For *both* stand under the reciprocal obligation to seek to transcend their narcissistic egoism in understanding the alterity of the Other.

8. Above all, we must always strive to avoid a false essentialism that sees *only* more of the Same in the Other—that fails authentically to confront "the terror of Otherness."[43]

9. Learning to live with the instability of alterity—learning to accept and to encounter a radical plurality which fully acknowledges *singularity* —is always fragile and precarious. It makes no sense even to speak of a "final solution" to this problem—*the* problem of human living. No one can ever fully anticipate the ruptures and new sites of the upsurge of alterity. This is a lesson that we must learn again and again. And it has been painfully experienced in our time whenever those individuals or groups who have been colonized, repressed, or silenced rise up and assert the legitimacy and demand for full recognition of their own nonreducible alterity. The search for commonalities and precise points of difference is always a task and an obligation—an *Aufgabe*. Without a *mutual* recognition of this *Aufgabe,* without a self-conscious sensitivity to the need always to do justice to the Other's *singularity,* without a heightened awareness of the inescapable risks that can never be completely overcome, we are in danger of obliterating the radical plurality of the human condition.[44] It is an *Aufgabe* not only when we seek to understand our own traditions (whether "West" or "East") but also when we authentically try to encounter and understand Eastwest and Westeast.

Notes

1. G. W. F. Hegel, *The Phenomenology of Spirit,* trans. by A. V. Miller (New York: Oxford University Press, 1977), p. 357.

2. Ibid., p. 357.

3. Jean-François Lyotard, *The Post-Modern Condition: A Report on Knowledge,* trans. by G. Bennington and B. Massomi (Minneapolis: University of Minnesota Press, 1984), pp. 81–82.

4. Thomas Kuhn, "Theory-Change as Structure-Change: Comments on the Sneed Formalism," *Erkenntnis* 10 (1976): 190–191. In this passage Kuhn speaks of the incommensurability of *theories.* Kuhn has not always carefully distinguished between theories and paradigms. Not all theories are to be construed as paradigms. But in this context it is clear that Kuhn is referring to paradigm-

theories. See my discussion of Kuhn's "ambiguous concept of a paradigm" in *The Restructuring of Social and Political Theory* (Philadelphia: University of Pennsylvania Press, 1978), pp. 84–93.

5. See my discussion of incommensurability in *Beyond Objectivism and Relativism* (Philadelphia: University of Pennsylvania Press, 1983), pt. 2, "Science, Rationality, and Incommensurability."

6. Thomas Kuhn, *The Structure of Scientific Revolutions,* 2d ed. enl. (Chicago: University of Chicago Press, 1970), p. 148.

7. Ibid., p. 148.

8. Ibid., p. 148–149.

9. Ibid., p. 149.

10. Ibid.

11. Ibid., p. 150.

12. Karl Popper, "Normal Science and Its Dangers," in *Criticism and the Growth of Knowledge,* ed. by I. Lakatos and A. Musgrave (Cambridge, England: Cambridge University Press, 1970), p. 56.

13. See Bernstein, *Beyond Objectivism and Relativism,* pp. 79–93.

14. Richard Rorty, *Philosophy and the Mirror of Nature* (Princeton: Princeton University Press, 1979). See especially chap. 7, "From Epistemology to Hermeneutics," pp. 315–356.

15. Ibid., p. 316.

16. Ibid.

17. Ibid.

18. See Rorty's discussion of the "backlash" of realism in his "Introduction" to *Consequences of Pragmatism* (Minneapolis: University of Minnesota Press, 1982).

19. Donald Davidson, "On the Very Idea of a Conceptual Scheme," *Proceedings and Addresses of the American Philosophical Association* 47 (1973–1974): 20.

20. Giving up the dualism of "scheme and world" does not entail relinquishing the notion of objective truth:

> In giving up dependence on the concept of an uninterpreted reality, something outside all schemes and science, we do not relinquish the notion of objective truth—quite the contrary. Given the dogma of a dualism of scheme and reality, we get conceptual relativity, and truth relative to a scheme. Without the dogma, this kind of relativity goes by the board. Of course, truth of sentences remains relative to language, but that is as objective as can be. In giving up the dualism of scheme and world, we do not give up the world, but reestablish unmediated touch with the familiar objects whose antics make our sentences and opinions true or false. ("On the Very Idea of a Conceptual Scheme," p. 20)

21. Alasdair MacIntyre, *Whose Justice? Which Rationality?* (Notre Dame: University of Notre Dame Press, 1988). See especially the last three chapters: "The Rationality of Traditions"; "Tradition and Translation"; and "Contested Justices, Contested Rationalities."

22. MacIntyre distinguishes between the "relativist" challenge and the "perspectivist" challenge. "The relativist challenge rests upon a denial that rational debate and rational choice among rival traditions is possible; the perspectivist challenge puts in question the possibility of making truth-claims from within any one tradition" (p. 352). MacIntyre develops and seeks to answer these challenges in his chapter, "The Rationality of Traditions," pp. 349–369.

23. MacIntyre, *Whose Justice? Which Rationality?* pp. 402–403.

24. My main reasons for arguing that MacIntyre fails to justify *this* central claim concern some of the aporetic consequences of his analysis of "truth," and how truth claims about justice and practical rationality are legitimated. Furthermore I do not think that MacIntyre squarely faces the issue of how much disagreement there can be about what *are* the standards of rationality even *within* a "tradition-constituted and tradition-constitutive inquiry." For he fails adequately to indicate how disputes about "standards of rationality" (whether *within* a tradition or among rival traditions) are to be *rationally* resolved. But to justify my objections requires a more detailed analysis and critique of MacIntyre's understanding of "truth" and "rationality" (including both practical and theoretical rationality).

25. See Clifford Geertz' sensitive and subtle discussion of this double danger in "From the Native's Point of View: On the Nature of Anthropological Understanding," in *Interpretive Social Science,* ed. by Paul Rabinow and William Sullivan (Berkeley: University of California Press, 1979). See also my discussion of Geertz in *Beyond Objectivism and Relativism,* pp. 93–108.

26. Michael Theunissen, *The Other,* trans. by Christopher Macann (Cambridge, Massachusetts: MIT Press, 1984), p. 1.

27. Ibid.

28. In distinguishing the neutral generic sense of "the Other" from the personal senses of "the Other"—as it is investigated, for example, in what is sometimes called "the problem of intersubjectivity" or "sociality"—I do *not* want to suggest that these are unrelated. On the contrary, what characterizes most treatments of "the Other" is the interweaving of the multiple senses of "the Other."

29. Emmanuel Levinas, *Totality and Infinity,* trans. by Alphonso Lingis (Pittsburgh: Duquesne University Press, 1969), p. 36.

30. Ibid.

31. Ibid.

32. Levinas sharply distinguishes *metaphysics* from *ontology:* "The metaphysical desire tends toward *something else entirely,* toward the absolutely other" (p. 33). "Thus the metaphysician and the other cannot be *totalized*" (p. 35). But ontology involves "a reduction of the other to the same by interposition of a middle and neutral term that ensures the comprehension of being" (p. 43). According to Levinas, "Western philosophy has most often been an ontology . . ." (p. 43). See *Totality and Infinity,* "Metaphysics and Transcendence," pp. 33–52.

33. Levinas, *Totality and Infinity,* p. 38.

34. Ibid., p. 39.

35. Ibid., pp. 46–47.

36. Jacques Derrida, "Violence and Metaphysics: An Essay on the Thought of Emmanuel Levinas," in *Writing and Difference,* trans. by Alan Bass (Chicago: University of Chicago Press, 1978), p. 99.

37. Ibid., p. 104.

38. Ibid., p. 125.

39. Ibid.

40. Ibid., p. 127.

41. Ibid., p. 138.

42. Ibid., p. 79.

43. This is David Tracy's phrase. See David Tracy, *Plurality and Ambiguity: Hermeneutics, Religion and Hope* (New York: Harper & Row, 1987).

44. This allusion to Hannah Arendt is deliberate. Although I have discussed the "problem" of "the Other" primarily with reference to Levinas and Derrida, I might have concentrated on Arendt's own analysis of plurality as a fundamental characteristic of the human condition. Indeed Arendt—with a specific emphasis on action, speech, public space, and politics—develops one of the most perceptive analyses of plurality that does justice to both singularity (alterity) *and* togetherness (commonality). See Hannah Arendt, *The Human Condition* (Chicago: University of Chicago Press, 1958). See also my discussion of Arendt's understanding of plurality in "Judging—the Actor and the Spectator" and "Rethinking the Social and Political," included in Richard J. Bernstein, *Philosophical Profiles* (Philadelphia: University of Pennsylvania Press, 1986).

ALASDAIR MACINTYRE

INCOMMENSURABILITY, TRUTH, AND THE CONVERSATION BETWEEN CONFUCIANS AND ARISTOTELIANS ABOUT THE VIRTUES

Nothing would be accounted a theory of the virtues in either Eastern or Western philosophy unless it provided an account of the excellences and perfections of human activity and achievement as such. The theory itself may be of Chinese or Greek or other particular cultural provenance; and what it presents as the excellences of human beings as such may well seem to outsiders to be excellences of what are specifically Chinese or Greek forms of activity. But the claims of such a theory must concern human rather than Chinese or Greek excellence. It is unsurprising that philosophers who have recognized this truth should also have supposed that adequate grounds for holding any particular theory of the virtues must themselves in a similar way concern human nature as such, characterized in some way independent of the highly particular cultural and conceptual frameworks, through which Chinese or Greek or other thinkers express their culturally idiosyncratic understandings of reality. Such philosophers have indeed commonly hoped that an appeal to such culturally neutral grounds would provide moral philosophers with the resources for adjudicating rationally between the rival and competing claims about the virtues and other moral matters, advanced from the standpoint of a variety of different cultures.

I was once one of them. In *A Short History of Ethics* (1966) I attempted to give an account of just such a universally human, culturally neutral grounds, in order to distinguish between that which in Aristotle's theory of the virtues is permanently valuable and that which I then took merely to reflect the ideological and cultural biases of Aristotle and his milieu. The grounds which I then invoked concerned certain very general features of human life, some arising from physical and biological needs, wants, and vulnerabilities, others from social and institutional considerations. This could have been done, and since has been done by others much better than I did it.[1] But in an article on "Human Nature and the Virtues in Confucius and Aristotle,"[2] George H. Mahood argued compellingly that what was at fault was not so much the inadequacy of my attempt as the attempt itself. Let me not simply repeat, but also expand his argument, giving him the credit for exposing my errors, but not holding him liable for the way in which I now try to correct them.

What Mahood showed was that in trying to identify the relevant features of human life as such, as though this was a straightforward empirical task, carried out from some neutral vantage-point, I had begged the prior conceptual question of how such features are to be identified and characterized. When that question is posed, it becomes clear that major rival theories of the virtues, deriving from very different cultural contexts, such as those advanced by Aristotelians and Confucians, characteristically each have internal to them their own conceptually idiosyncratic account of those features and of their relationship to the theory and practice of the virtues.

It is not that an account, neutral with respect to any two such competing bodies of theory, because genuinely independent of either, cannot be supplied concerning such universal or near universal features of human life as certain desires and needs of individuals and the social and institutional constraints imposed upon the expression of those desires and needs. But any such account which is in this way independent will be so at so bare a level of characterization that it will be equally compatible with far too many rival bodies of theory. And any account which is rich enough in its identifications and characterizations to be genuinely relevant to the evaluation of a set of theoretical claims concerning the virtues will in fact turn out already to presuppose in those identifications and characterizations some one such theoretical stance regarding the virtues, rather than its rivals. That is to say, every major theory of the virtues has internal to it, to some significant degree, its own philosophical psychology and its own philosophical politics and sociology. These dictate for the adherents of each such theory how the relevant empirical findings concerning human life are to be construed, classified, and characterized. There is just no neutral and independent method of characterizing those materials in a way sufficient to provide the type of adjudication between competing theories of the virtues which I had once hoped to provide and to which some others still aspire.

Mahood's criticism did not itself issue in this conclusion, perhaps because his concern was not so much, if at all, with Aristotelian and Confucian accounts of the virtues as competing rivals, as with the extent of the resemblances between them. Drawing upon the work of Wing-tsit Chan,[3] he emphasized those central virtues which the adherents of both standpoints agree in praising and the extent to which some of these, at least, are understood in similar ways. It is of course true that there are such significant areas of agreement. Both doctrines, for example, describe and endorse a method of moral education according to which we first have to learn from others in particular situations what courage or justice or whatever requires from someone circumstanced as we are and then learn how to extrapolate, how to extend our practical grasp of these virtues to other very different types of situation. Both recognize that this central moral capacity, this practical knowledge of how to judge and to act rightly by going on and going further from what we learned initially, is not itself a kind of rule-following. Yet these important areas of agreement coexist with equally striking areas of disagreement. Indeed in their overall doctrines and perspectives Confucianism, whether that of Confucius or that of the Neo-Confucians, and Aristotelianism, whether that of Aristotle or that of Aquinas, present crucially different and incompatible accounts of the best way for human beings to live, so that even those theses about which there is substantial agreement function in significantly different ways.

Confucius, it seems generally to be agreed, had a relatively small place for explicit theorizing within the moral life itself. And the end internal to that life, conceived in Confucian terms, is simply to live an excellent way. By contrast, for Aristotelianism, although practical intelligence is something very different from theoretical, and a large measure of practical intelligence can be had by those lacking in theory, nonetheless theory, by supplying a knowledge of that *telos* which is *the* human good, a knowledge from which the first premise of all practical deliberation "Since the good and the best is such and such" derives, not only corrects the deficiencies of practice, but also directs us toward that kind of understanding which is the *telos* of every rational being. This relationship of theory to practice, and of both to the human *telos,* gives expression to the relationship of part to part and of parts to whole in a well-ordered *psychē.* And it is in terms of the right ordering of the *psychē* that the virtues and their relationship to each other are to be understood. This is why defectiveness in any one virtue in an individual person, being a sign of disorder in that *psychē,* is a sign of defectiveness with respect also to the other virtues.

Confucianism denies this type of strong thesis about the unity of the virtues. "A courageous man does not necessarily possess *jen,* "[4] although one cannot have *jen* without courage. But courage can, on Confucius' view, be put to the service of wickedness, without thereby ceasing to be courage,[5] and this disagreement with Aristotelianism arises from a way of understanding the relationship of the virtues which has no place for and no need for either a conception of a substantial *psychē* or for the kind of *telos* which is *eudaimonia.* And this exclusion by Confucius of Aristotelian concepts extends, as we might expect, to Aristotle's conception of the type of community in which the social relationships are such as to give socially embodied expressions to the virtues and which provide the arena within which movement toward the *telos* takes place. That is to say, in the Aristotelian scheme of things the concepts of the particular virtues find application and exemplification only if and insofar as the concepts of *psychē, telos,* and *polis* also find application and exemplification in some way or other.

In some way or other, it has to be said. For at least on a Thomistic understanding of Aristotle this whole family of concepts may find application and exemplification even in cultures in which local idiom and doctrine to some degree obscure or prevent recognition of these concepts, as would be the case in a Confucian culture. Equally there are central Confucian conceptions for which Aristotelianism does have and can have no corresponding place. So neither Aristotle nor Aquinas is able to connect the rightness of action, *yi,* with its issuing from *li,* the ordering of action in accordance with ritual formality, such that whether that formality governs participation in rites required for respect to ancestors or such everyday activities as conversation and meal-taking, *li* renders the relevant actions appropriate both to oneself and to their social context.[6] And different understandings of human life at the level of fundamental concepts issue in different catalogues of the virtues, different understandings of particular virtues, and different styles and modes of deliberation and action, symbolized by the very different modes of discourse, with respect to theoretical argumentation, and of the uses of empirical material and of aphorism and anecdote in the *Analects* and other Confucian classical texts, on the one hand, and in the *Nicomachean Ethics* and the *Politics* and Aquinas' commentaries upon them, on the other.

David L. Hall and Roger T. Ames have argued recently that there is the sharpest of contrasts between the presuppositions of traditional Western metaphysical thinking, informed by conceptions of rational order, and those of classical Chinese thinking, informed instead by conceptions of order which they describe as aesthetic. But I do not think that I misrepresent their intention in formulating matters in this way, if I suggest that what their arguments really show is that within the Confucian mode of thinking there is no place for the classical Western contrast between the rational and the aesthetic as modes of ordering. Confucian modes of expression are themselves ordered in accordance with the modes of ordering which they expound. Hence there is even a problem about how to state the nature of the contrast, more generally between classical Western and classical Chinese modes of thought, and more particularly between what I have been describing up to this point as Confucian and Aristotelian moral stances. And Henry Rosemont has drawn our attention to the importance of the fact that the classical Chinese language has no terms for, and that correspondingly Confucian texts contain no discussion of, the most familiar Western moral concepts, including that of morality itself.[7] It follows that up to this point, without acknowledging it, I have been characterizing the differences between Aristotelianism and Confucianism from what is more generally a Western and more specifically an Aristotelian point of view, both in the terms which I have used and in the type of order of exposition which I have employed, and, as it will turn out, inescapably so.

For as we move from level to level within these two systems of thought and practice, posing questions of interpretation, explanation, and justification, it becomes clear that each has its own internal structure in terms of which these are understood. Consider first Confucianism. In his exposition of Hsün Tzu's Confucian moral epistemology, A. S. Cua understands the knowledge of *tao* as the *telos* of ethical argumentation and of *t'ung-lei* as the understanding of that whole of which the various aspects of the virtuous life are parts.[8] To justify a particular judgment or course of action is to see it in the light afforded by this insight into the whole, sometimes by engaging in creative analogical projection from other cases.

What must impress any reader who follows through the details of Cua's interpretation of Hsün Tzu's reflective and rationally organized Confucianism is twofold. First it is clear that it is indeed precisely by using terms so as to characterize parts or aspects of that whole which is the moral life in terms of the whole, and in moving between knowledge of the whole and knowledge of the parts that ethical argumentation takes place. But such argumentation, and the use of terms in accordance with it, has just those qualities of aesthetic insight and judgment which one would expect, if the whole to be discerned by the morally aware and wise person had those properties of aesthetic order identified by Hall and Ames. And that is to say that to enter at any point on those activities of interpretation, explanation, and justification elucidated by Hsün Tzu will be already to have presupposed the fundamental conclusions and insights toward which these activities move. To speak in any radically different and alternative idiom will be to have excluded oneself from the Confucian discourse in a way that precludes entering into debate with its exponents.

This large circularity is to be found in Aristotelianism as well as in Confucianism and, I suspect, in any large-scale system of thought of sufficient scope and power. For Aristotle and for Aquinas there are two ways of justifying first principles, and both of them involve analogous types of circularity. We may argue dialectically against opponents on the basis of prior common beliefs (what T. H. Irwin calls 'weak' dialectic);[9] but it is of course by virtue of the extent to which these beliefs already give expression to Aristotelian principles that the Aristotelian is able to use this kind of dialectical appeal successfully. And we may also argue, using what Irwin calls 'strong' dialectic, to a conclusion that without certain first principles the kind of objectivity and knowledge which the sciences provide cannot be had; but that objectivity and knowledge is already itself understood in a specifically Aristotelian way as both presupposing and employing formal and teleological principles alien to many rival modes of thought, including the dominant modes of thought of Western modernity. So that once again our conclusions are to a significant degree already presupposed by the premises from which the argument begins.

There is of course nothing logically vicious about these large circularities internal to large-scale systems of thought. But in identifying them in the Confucian and Aristotelian moral systems we are discovering that each system has its own standard and measures of interpretation, explanation, and justification internal to itself. And the many points of resemblance to be observed between the two, both in matters of substance and of procedure, do nothing to modify a reiteration of the conclusion that there are indeed no shared standards and measures, external to both systems and neutral between them, to which appeal might be made to adjudicate between their rival claims. The two systems of thought and practice are incommensurable in the sense made familiar to us by Thomas Kuhn—the concept, if not the word, was anticipated both by Bachelard and by Polanyi, and has in the last thirty years in various conceptual guises played a key part in the writings not only of Kuhn and Feyerabend, but also of Foucault and Deleuze. But just because there have been importantly different versions of the concept of incommensurability, carrying with them very different implications, it is necessary to say in what sense its use here illuminates the relationship of Confucianism and Aristotelianism.

First of all, incommensurability is a relationship between two or more systems of thought and practice, each embodying its own peculiar conceptual scheme, over a certain period of time. The reference to periods of time brings out the fact that conceptual schemes have a historical existence, that the identity of conceptual schemes through time is compatible with large changes in both their internal structures and their external relationships, and that two different and rival conceptual schemes may be incommensurable at one stage of their development and yet become commensurable at another. How this can be the case can only become clear if we first state some of the conditions which must be satisfied if two or more schemes are to be held genuinely incommensurable over a certain stretch of time.

During such a stretch of time it will be the case that those who inhabit each of the two or more rival schemes of thought and practice embody them in their beliefs, actions, judgments, and arguments in such a way that it is both the case that the members of the two or more rival parties can agree, each from their own point of view, that they are referring to, characterizing, and conducting their inquiries about what is indeed one and the same subject matter, and yet also in their characterizations of and questions about that subject matter employ, to some large and significant degree, concepts whose applicability entails the nonapplicability, the vacuousness, of the conceptual scheme or schemes employed by their rivals. It is not that what is according to the one scheme true is according to its rivals false; it is rather that the standard or standards which determine how the true-false distinction is to be applied are not the same. And there is, during this stretch of time at least, no higher standard yet available to judge between these rival standards.

It follows that two or more rival and incommensurable conceptual schemes, as embodied in theory and practice, must share a certain structure. There has to be first some shared level of descriptive characterization and of associated reference at which each provides sufficient grounds for asserting that it is of one and the same subject matter that they speak. So Aristotelian and Galilean physicists had to be able to agree to some significant extent both in their conceptions of moving bodies in general and in their references to some particular moving bodies in order to have a common subject matter about which to disagree. Similarly there must be, as we have already seen that there is, considerable agreement about the virtues in general and about some particular virtues between Confucian and Aristotelian moralists if they likewise are to identify that about which each is committed to accusing the other of misunderstanding.

It is at a second level of characterization that predicates are applied in accordance with standards internal to and peculiar to each of the rival standpoints and such that each set of standards excludes the possibility of application for key predicates of its rivals. And this use of predicates will give expression to distinctive modes of observation, of seeing as and of imagining, as well as of reasoning. So, to use Kuhn's famous example, while the theoretically committed Galilean will see and report one and the same stone swinging from one and the same line—as will indeed the person innocent of physical theory and inquiry—the former will observe and report an instance of constrained natural motion, the latter a pendulum. And so likewise, while both the Confucian and the Aristotelian moralist will see and report one and the same person giving freely and liberally to someone else in need, the Confucian may observe an absence of *li,* of that ritual formality which is an essential characteristic of *jen,* a type of absence necessarily invisible to the Aristotelian, who has no words in either Aristotle's Greek or William of Moerbeke's Latin to translate *li,* an expression captured neither by such Greek words as *hosia, orgia,* or *teletai* used of religious rituals, nor by such words as *ethos,* signifying the customary and habitual, nor by their medieval Latin equivalents. By contrast, the Aristotelian will observe, as we noted earlier, an example of a disposition evidencing a particular ordering or disorder of the *psychē,* a conformity or lack of it to what is required of a citizen of a *polis,* both understood in terms of an ultimate *telos* conceived in a highly specific way, all of which must be invisible to the Confucian who has no words for *psychē* or *polis* either in the ancient Chinese of Confucius or in the later Chinese of Sung Neo-Confucianism.

What this juxtaposition of the type of example from the history of Western physics by which Bachelard and Kuhn introduced recent discussions of incommensurability with examples from Confucian and Aristotelian moral theory brings out is that incommensurability may, but need not, be associated with and arise from untranslatability. Galileo and the last heirs of Aristotelian physics, the impetus theorists, did after all speak the same natural languages. Indeed when Galileo moved from being the last great impetus theorist to being the first Galilean, his radical shift in perspective and in theoretical standpoint required a large enrichment of the natural languages which he employed in terminology and idiom, but this kind of change often occurs within one and the same natural language. Yet even if translatability does not entail commensurablity, it may be, it surely must be, one initial step toward making possible a type of conversation between originally incommensurable standpoints which could over time transform their relationship. And yet even making this initial move depends upon recognizing a prior and more fundamental task.

When the incommensurability of two rival conceptual schemes, embodied in thought and practice, arises from the untranslatability of one natural language-in-use into another, the kind of untranslatability which is characteristically a sign of profound differences in culture, it does not follow that all mutual understanding is precluded. But such understanding is possible only for those adherents of each standpoint who are able to learn the language of the rival standpoint, so that they acquire, so far as is possible, that other language as a second first language. Inhabiting both standpoints, only such persons will be able to recognize what is translatable and what is untranslatable in the transitions from one such language to the other. And it is they therefore who will be able to understand what would have to be involved by way of an extension and enrichment of their own first language-in-use if it were to be able to accommodate a representation of the other.

Cicero long ago confronted this type of problem in contriving accounts of Greek philosophy in a Latin hitherto generally inhospitable to philosophical uses of language; and moral theorists, such as ourselves, who communicate in natural languages extended and enlarged in their possibilities of philosophical and moral usage by generations of Cicero's successors, including those Jesuits who first provided accounts of Confucianism in European languages, accounts first integrated into European philosophical usage by Leibniz, cannot but be aware of how what cannot be said at one stage of some particular natural language-in-use may come at a later period to be sayable in an enriched and extended successor version of that same natural language.

Suppose, then, that the adherents of at least one of two such incommensurable schemes of thought and action are in fact provided in their own language-in-use with what is, so far as the genuinely bilingual translators can discern, an adequate representation of the rival point of view. They can now in some sense understand what it is that they reject, but that they must reject it remains the case, for what is now presented to them *within* the framework of their own standpoint as an alternative to their own theorizing on some particular subject matter will inescapably be judged false by the standards informing that framework. So if a set of Confucian theses about the virtues had been presented within the framework of some scholastic version of Aristotelianism, and had been correctly translated and rightly understood, it would inevitably in the light of Aristotelian principles have been rejected. So an advance may have been made, but it has after all only been one from mutual incomprehension to inevitable rejection. How does this constitute an advance in the conversation?

It does so, if and only if the conversation then moves one stage still further. That stage is one at which one at least of the contending parties extends its conceptual grasp by acquiring the concept of incommensurability itself and in the light thus afforded comes to recognize two things: that its own rejection of the rival alternative up to this point was indeed inevitable and that, were the adherents of that rival alternative in like manner to understand their opposing point of view, the same inescapable act of rejection would have to ensue. But once this had been understood by Aristotelians—I cannot on this point speak for what a Confucian response could be—they would have to conclude that no rational encounter, no dialectical appeal to mutually acknowledged principles of any kind, whether principles embodied in shared established opinions or principles necessary for the achievement of scientific explanation and understanding, had taken place or could so far have taken place. Why would this matter?

Without rational encounter with some other rival theory, whether incommensurable or not, we have not tested its claims to truth. Even if we are right in taking it to be erroneous, it is only in the results provided by rational encounter that we provide grounds for diagnosing and identifying its error. So that without rational encounter the rival theory becomes a subject matter concerning which we have not achieved that truth which is *adaequatio intellectus ad rem*. And notice that it is a conception of truth which is at stake here which is neither reducible to nor explicable in terms of warranted assertibility.

Questions concerning the warranted assertibility of the rival incommensurable views can at this stage of comparative inquiry already be given completely unproblematic answers. By Aristotelian standards of rational warrant, the rival view, Confucian or other, simply fails, and of course vice versa. Just because it has become clear that there are rival incommensurable traditions of rational thought and action, each no doubt sharing certain principles with its rivals, but only to a point insufficient by the standards of each to provide substantive warranted conclusions, it has also become clear that progress in rational inquiry, although it may lead toward and characteristically does lead toward, agreement within any one such tradition, need not lead toward any kind of agreement, any convergence of views, between the adherents of rival and incommensurable traditions. Warranted assertibility is always from the point of view of and in accordance with the standards of some one out of the rival incommensurable points of view. But what makes the concept of truth distinctive is precisely that it holds or does not hold independently of point of view. To claim truth for some expression of the relationship of a mind to its objects or for that relationship itself is to claim that this is how things are, no matter how they seem from points of view.

Of course anyone who makes a claim to truth for a judgment or theory or conception or the relationship of mind to object expressed in these does so from some one particular point of view, from within one particular tradition of inquiry rather than from that of its incommensurable rivals. But what is then claimed is *not* that this is how things appear in the light of the standards of that point of view (something which the adherents of a rival and incompatible point of view need have no reason to deny), but how they are, a claim in terms of fundamental ontology. It follows that any claim to truth involves a claim that no consideration advanced from *any* point of view can overthrow or subvert that claim.

Such a claim, however, can only be supported on the basis of rational encounters between rival and incommensurable points of view, in which one such point of view has been vindicated in such a way as to provide support for its claims to truth vis-à-vis rival standpoints. So that for any Aristotelian, Thomistic or otherwise, the problem of how rational encounters between rival and incommensurable points of view can be possible is a crucial one. And there could be no subject matter of such a confrontation for which it is both philosophically and morally more important to provide an account of this possibility than the theory and practice of the virtues, as understood by Confucians on the one hand and Aristotelians on the other, since the radical conflicts involved, combining as they do a certain measure of agreement on important matters together with intractable and incommensurable differences, make it something of a paradigm case for the conversation between different cultures. How then to proceed further?

At this point we have to take note of a contemporary thesis which, if true, would show that we ought not to proceed further, because we have already taken a false turn. There is a view of translation, advanced by Donald Davidson and others, according to which—I state the view without the nuances and qualifications which an adequate statement of it would require—the problem of understanding an alien point of view, expressed in some natural language other than one's own, is no more and no less than that of translating it into one's own language. If we do so successfully, we shall discover that in the very act of translating we have understood what is said from that alien point of view, in that other language, as governed by the same standards of assertibility, of argument, and of evaluation which govern our own theory and practice.

Because to understand *them* is to translate *their* language into *ours*—rather than, as I have suggested, for us to learn *their* language as well as our own—and because to share a language is to share a conceptual scheme, even although in terms of the only conception of conceptual scheme which has mattered since Hegel, Galileo, and his opponents plainly shared the same languages, but differed as physicists in their conceptual scheme, radical incommensurability is on this view impossible and, therefore, when it actually occurs, invisible. But it is a view made plausible by, and which offers a rationale for, a way of translating texts from alien and different cultures, and of responding to them, which is central to the cosmopolitan cultures of those modern internationalized languages-in-use, such as contemporary Trans-Atlantic and Trans-Pacific English, one of whose central features is that utterance in them presupposes only the most minimal of shared beliefs. These are languages, so far as is possible, for anyone at all to use, for those who are equally at home everywhere and therefore nowhere. Every national language-in-use can in time become like this, substituting, for example, in order to achieve this condition, for those highly specific expressions of respect by which different types of person of inferior and superior status address one another, in a way which presupposes a shared belief in a particular hierarchical ordering of society and perhaps of nature, a belief incompatible with many other standpoints and incommensurable with some, neutral and anonymous courtesies, meaning and presupposing as little as possible, by which anyone can address anyone. They are the standard languages, alas, of international conferences.

What happens, if we accept the thesis that translatability into such a language by removing incommensurability from the debate enables such rival doctrines as those of Aristotelianism and Confucianism concerning the virtues to enter a genuinely rational encounter? Suppose that we do indeed translate both the Greek of Aristotle or the Latin of William of Moerbeke and the ancient Chinese of Sung Confucianism, languages which, as we have already seen, cannot to a significant degree and at key points be translated into each other, into one of those modern internationalized languages which present themselves as languages for anyone, and therefore languages into which every text can be translated: will this solve our problem?

What then occurs is familiar to us all. The particular texts which are the bearers of each of the competing bodies of theory come to be for the most part read in such translation in large abstraction from the cultural and historical contexts in and through which they originally derived their intelligibility as part of the sequence constituting that kind of tradition of inquiry which is the bearer of a developing theory. Each such theory, or rather each such theory at some particular stage in its development, is presented as making claims, which the reasons advanced from within the theory itself necessarily appear insufficient to sustain. For each such theory, when thus presented, is viewed *ab extra* from the standpoint of that dominant mode of modernity for which there are a variety of competing modes of rational justification and no sufficient reasons available for deciding between them.

The next step, however, is not to admit the concept of incommensurability. It is instead to substitute for the traditional notion of the rational justification of one among competing rival bodies of theory some notion of pragmatic context-bound justification, according to which justification is relative to the contingent purposes and agreements of those who engage in activities of justification in the course of their conversation with each other. In such contexts claims to truth *can* amount to no more than claims to warranted assertibility. And theories which, as originally presented in the contexts of rational inquiry in which they were first elaborated, were understood and rightly understood as mutually incompatible, may now, when detached from these contexts, and presented in detachment also from the classical conception of truth, come to be regarded as matter for personal choice, perhaps eclectic choice, in accordance with whatever criteria happen to seem pleasing to a particular person.

It was Protestant Christianity that was first—as early as the nineteenth century—afflicted by this kind of pragmatic aestheticism, but since then the same kind of aestheticization has invaded such disparate areas of life as morality, politics, and even attitudes toward and interpretations of the natural sciences, if not the practices of those sciences. Notice that this kind of aestheticism is very different from the sense of aesthetic order which Hall and Ames understand as underlying Confucius' social and political theory and cosmological vision. For that harmony of vision into which, on the Confucian view, each individual has to integrate his own insights as constitutive parts of a harmony underlying the practice of the virtues, a practice whose claims are universal, even if the universal envisaged is very different from, for example, an Aristotelian conception of rational universality, is quite alien to this modern individualism of aestheticized personal choice, in which each person constructs his or her own *collage*.

In such a cultural milieu, that of the dominant modes of Western modernity, fundamental theoretical standpoints become objects of choice and, if not of criterionless choice, of choice in accordance with criteria adopted because they serve to give expression to the nonrational and prerational attitudes of the person who so chooses. The theories between which such choices are made seem at first sight almost indefinitely various: a range of theories drawn from the Western past and present, of which Aristotelians of different kinds are only one species, supplemented by a similar range of theories drawn from the Eastern past and present, of which in like manner Confucianisms of different kinds are only one species. Yet this picture of a smorgasbord of theoretical standpoints laid out before a clientele of metaphysical and moral consumers, each expressing his or her own personal tastes in his or her choice of items, is an illusion. What are in fact available for choice are often enough not the theoretical standpoints which are purportedly on display, but instead a series of counterfeits. How so?

It is a central characteristic of both Aristotelian and Confucian moral theory and practice that, however someone may come to embody one or the other such theory and practice in his or her own life, so that he or she becomes in some full sense an Aristotelian or a Confucian, it cannot be by some act of aetheticized choice, nor indeed by an act of choice at all. Indeed, according to both doctrines, albeit in very different ways, choosing is itself something that we have to learn how to do from within the practice of the theory, something that can be learned only by those who have already committed themselves, or perhaps more often found themselves already committed, to Confucianism or, as it may be, Aristotelianism. One cannot become an Aristotelian or a Confucian by an act of choice, but only by and through a systematic initiating education. But, it may be asked, does not one choose, may not one at least be said to choose—in some sense—to embark on such an education which will in time lead to the formation of either a Confucian or an Aristotelian character? Indeed one may. But since at the outset of such an education one does not and cannot as yet understand in any adequate way what it is to be a Confucian or an Aristotelian, either theoretically or practically, since that type of understanding is what such an education has as yet to supply and what only such an education can supply; any act of choice prior to or at the outset of such an education cannot be a choice of genuine Confucianism or of genuine Aristotelianism. All that can be offered on the smorgasbord of theories for acts of consumer choice are counterfeit versions, reinterpreted to fit the pragmatic and aesthetic modes of modernity, and so not at all the substantive theories with whose incommensurability I have been concerned in this essay.

It follows that the problem of constructing a rational debate and encounter between an Aristotelian theory of the virtues and a Confucian, arising from the incommensurability of these two standpoints, cannot be solved by translation into the idioms of and presentation in terms of the forms of discourse of cosmopolitan modernity. Does there then remain any way of bringing these two particular standpoints into a potentially creative dialogue, in which genuinely rational encounter can take place, or must we rather conclude, as some have done, that where two standpoints are in fact incommensurable rational encounter is precluded? The first step toward avoiding this latter pessimistic conclusion is to recognize that both Aristotelianism and Confucianism have long and complex histories of internal development in which each has been confronted by successive sets of problems and difficulties, problems and difficulties identified by the standards internal to each of these developing modes of moral thought and practice. Moreover, each has, by these same standards internal to each, been more or less successful at dealing with, solving, or dissolving such problems and difficulties. Indeed each has in so doing partially transformed and sometimes added to the standards which provide it with the resources for identifying and for responding to such problems and difficulties.

Insofar as each of these two incompatible and incommensurable bodies of theory and practice has passed beyond the initial stage of partial incomprehension and partial misrepresentation of the other, by so enriching its linguistic and conceptual resources that it is able to provide an accurate representation of the other, it follows that accurate representation will be of the other as a historically developing body of theory and practice, succeeding or failing at each stage, in the light of its own standards, in respect of the difficulties or problems internal to it. That is, what the Aristotelian will have had to provide for his or her own use will be a history of Confucianism, written and understood from a Confucian point of view, and what the Confucian will similarly need will be a history of Aristotelianism, written and understood from an Aristotelian point of view. To what might the construction of such histories lead?

Any particular tradition of inquiry, any body of well-developed theory and practice, may come in the light of its own standards of rationality, theoretical and practical, to be recognized by its own adherents as rationally inferior to some other rival and incompatible tradition, embodying in its theory and practice some alternative and incommensurable standpoint, if two conditions are both satisfied. The first is that its own history, as narrated in the light of its own standards, the standards internal to it, should lead in the end to radical and, so far as it is possible to judge, irremediable failure, perhaps by reason of its sterility and resourcelessness in the face of some set of problems which its own goals require it to solve, perhaps because, in trying to frame adequate solutions to its problems and an adequately comprehensive account of the subject matter with which it deals, it lapses into irreparable incoherence. Notice that for this first condition to be satisfied it does not follow that such failure should actually be acknowledged by the adherents of such a tradition of inquiry; it is enough for it to be the case that, if these adherents did in fact view matters as the standards of rationality internal to their standpoint require them to be viewed, they would recognize that failure. And those external to that standpoint, who have incorporated within their own structures of understanding an accurate representation of that standpoint and its history, may on occasion be able to

recognize such a condition of failure, even when it has gone unacknowledged by the adherents of the tradition of inquiry which has failed.

A second condition which has to be satisfied, if the adherents of such
a body of developed theory and practice, which has issued in failure, are
to be rationally justified in acknowledging that some alternative, incompatible, rival tradition is rationally superior to that to which, until this
point in time, they have given their allegiance, is that the adherents of
this alternative rival tradition be able to provide the resources to explain
why their own tradition failed by its own standard of achievement and,
more precisely, why it succeeded and why it failed at just the points and
in just the ways in which by those same standards it did succeed and
fail. Moreover, the resources for such explanation must not be available
in anything like the same way within the body of theory and practice
whose failure is being explained. When both these conditions are satisfied, then it is rational for the adherents of the tradition of inquiry which
has failed to transfer their allegiance to that which has provided the
explanation of its failure.

Since these two conditions can both be satisfied when each of the two
standpoints involved is evaluated as succeeding or failing only by the
standards of rational evaluation internal to each, and since there is
therefore no need, in order for them to be satisfied, for there to be any
set of common or shared standards sufficient for the task of rational
evaluation, let alone neutral and independent standards, it follows that
these two conditions can be satisfied when the two competing and
incompatible bodies of theory and practice are incommensurable. And
it has indeed been the case that when one body of theory and practice,
incommensurable with another rival such body, has established its
rational superiority over that other, these two conditions have in fact
been satisfied. So it was, in perhaps the most notable case in Western
thought, when the new Galilean physics and later its Newtonian heir,
established their superiority over the impetus theory of late medieval
Aristotelian physics, in such a way that it became possible not only to
contrast the fertility, comprehensiveness, and coherence of the later
scheme (by its own standards) with the incoherence and sterility of the
earlier (by its own standards, standards incommensurable with those of
the theory by which it was defeated), but also to explain exactly why
and how impetus theory had to fail at just the points and in just the ways
it did in fact fail. Incommensurability, it turns out, does not after all
preclude rational debate and encounter.

One might of course make this point in another way. When the histories of two rival, incompatible, and hitherto rationally incommensurable systems of thought and practice reach a point at which it is possible
to pose the question, in a detailed and substantive way, of whether or
not the outcome of these two histories is such that the two conditions
which I have specified have already been satisfied, or seem likely in the

future to be satisfiable, then these two systems of thought and practice have become commensurable. Their earlier incommensurability turns out to belong to those stages in their respective histories at which that question could not yet be posed in a sufficiently detailed way.

It thus becomes clear why if the adherents of two hitherto rationally incommensurable bodies of thought and practice, such as the moral theories of Confucianism and Aristotelianism, come to understand the importance of making rational debate and encounter between them possible, then a necessary first step is for each of them to provide for themselves a history of the other, written from that other's point of view and employing the standards of rational success or failure internal to that other's point of view. Aristotelians need to understand the history of Confucianism as a form of moral inquiry and practice, as it has been, is, or would be written from a Confucian point of view, in order to be able to learn to identify those episodes in which Confucianism becomes in some way problematic for a sufficiently tough-minded and insightful Confucian. Confucians similarly need to understand the history of Aristotelianism as a theory and practice of the virtues in order to be able to learn to identify those episodes in which Aristotelianism is at least in danger of foundering, as judged by the Aristotelian standards of a sufficiently tough-minded and insightful Aristotelian.

What would it be to write such histories, to acquire these parallel kinds of historical understanding? This question is far too large to be answered here. At best I can only gesture toward an answer. Consider, for example, the part that would necessarily be played in such a history by the successive prefaces and postscripts to the *Pei-hsi tzu-i* (translated as *Neo-Confucian Terms Explained*),[10] the encyclopaedic dictionary of Neo-Confucianism which summarizes and elucidates the thought of Ch'en Ch'un's teacher, Chu Hsi (1130–1200). I remarked much earlier in this essay that Confucius did not give a large place to explicit theorizing within the moral life. But the life of the Confucian teacher, whose role and function is to transmit the Confucian way of life, involves continuously renewed reflection upon the canonical texts and upon those who have best commented upon them and understood them. And the successive prefaces and postscripts to the *Pei-hsi tzu-i,* written before 1226, in 1247, 1490, 1492, 1508, 1670, 1695, and 1714, afford us points of entry to successive stages in Neo-Confucianism's self-scrutiny. Are there to be found there or elsewhere in the history of similar texts signs of Confucianism exhibiting strains and becoming at least to some degree problematic in its own terms?

One area in which such strains seem to become recurrently evident is that in which Confucianism aspires to reconcile a largely particularist morality in which the exercise of the virtues is defined in terms of highly specific types of social, especially familial, relationships with some account of what we owe to human beings as such. So, in the first preface to the 1714 edition of the *Pei-hsi tzu-i,* the writer renews the criticism of Han Yü's mistake, made nine hundred years earlier, of confusing the virtue of *jen* with universal love, in a way that suggests that there had been more recent renewals of that mistake. And already in the sixteenth century, Ho Hsin-yin (1517–1579), because of his attempt to formulate a standard by which the specific social relationships in terms of which Confucius had defined virtues and duties could themselves be criticized morally, a standard therefore to be defined independently of those relationships, had been accused of having in consequence discarded four out of the five relationships crucial to the Confucian doctrine of virtues and duties, retaining only that between friend and friend.[11]

That is to say, Confucianism appears to face a recurrent type of dilemma: *either* it retains its highly specific and concrete character, thus tying itself to particular Chinese forms of social relationships of a traditional kind and, while not necessarily exempting the concrete embodiments of these forms altogether from moral criticism, rendering its moral standpoint inseparable from loyalty to these now often radically changing forms, *or* it makes itself relevant to types of social order in which these forms of social relationships do not or no longer exist, but in so doing it empties itself of specific moral content and so diminishes its doctrine of the virtues by specifying them only in barren generalities.[12] Whether or not this dilemma can in fact be somehow overcome is perhaps what is centrally at stake in that contemporary revival of Confucianism for which Tu Wei-ming has been the most distinguished voice in English.[13]

What in a similar way would constitute an example of something deeply problematic about the Aristotelian theory of the virtues for an Aristotelian, which has emerged in the successive stages of the history of Aristotelianism? Interestingly a dilemma parallel to that internal to Confucianism appears within Aristotelianism. For Aristotle, as we have already noticed, defined the specificities of the virtues in terms of the social relationship of the *polis.* Does it then follow that in societies in which there is no longer a *polis* the Aristotelian theory of the virtues cannot but become empty and irrelevant? It was Aquinas who, following the example of his Islamic predecessors, undertook the task of recasting the Aristotelian doctrine of the virtues so that it might retain specific requirements for social relationships and yet be a doctrine of the virtues for human beings as such and not just for Greeks inhabiting a *polis.* Did Aquinas succeed or fail? There is as much at stake for contemporary Thomistic Aristotelians in answering this question as there is for contemporary Neo-Confucians in responding to their own parallel dilemma.

What these examples, inadequately stated as they are, may seem to bring out is not only something of the way in which we have to write our histories if we are to bring rival and incommensurable theories of the virtues to a point at which genuine rational debate and encounter can occur, but also more generally something of how conversation between rival bodies of theory and practice, rooted in very different cultures, has to proceed, if its interchanges are not to be sterile. Two features of all such conversations are crucial.

The first is this: the only way to approach a point at which our own standpoint could be vindicated against some rival is to understand our own standpoint in a way that renders it from our own point of view as problematic as possible and therefore as maximally vulnerable as possible to defeat by that rival. We can only learn what intellectual and moral resources our own standpoint, our own tradition of theoretical and practical inquiry possesses, as well as what intellectual and moral resources its rivals may possess, when we have understood our own point of view in a way that takes with full seriousness the possibility that we may in the end, as rational beings, have to abandon that point of view. This admission of fallibilism need not entail any present lack of certitude, but it is a condition of worthwhile conversation with equally certain antagonists.

A second condition is that we do not allow ourselves to forget that in comparing two fundamental standpoints at odds with each other, in the way in which and in the degree to which the Confucian theory and practice of the virtues are at odds with the Aristotelian, we have *no* neutral, independent standpoint from which to do so. We may compare Confucianism and Aristotelianism from a Confucian standpoint, or from an Aristotelian; or we may compare both or either with some third, different, equally incompatible and incommensurable standpoint, such as that of Buddhism or of Kantianism, but we cannot find any legitimate standing ground outside the context of the points of view. And when we have undertaken comparative study in a manner which recognizes this, we shall soon find that our task is not so much that of comparing Confucianism and Aristotelianism as that of comparing Confucian comparisons of Confucianism and Aristotelianism with Aristotelian comparisons of Confucianism and Aristotelianism. The key to comparative studies is the comparison of comparisons.

Against all this one complaint may finally be made. It is that not only did I begin by comparing the Confucian theory of the virtues with the Aristotelian in terms which are themselves already Aristotelian and which presuppose the truth of an Aristotelian standpoint, but that more generally the argument of this essay is framed in terms of and presupposes just that conception of rational order which Hall and Ames judge to be characteristic of Western metaphysics and to exclude just that conception of aesthetic order which they take to be fundamental to Confucianism. Yet if the argument of this essay is correct, how could I, as an Aristotelian, have done otherwise? What I have presented is indeed an Aristotelian account (albeit one which perhaps many Aristotelians would reject) of what is at issue between a Confucian theory of the virtues and an Aristotelian. To elicit from some Confucian a no doubt very different account of what is at issue is one of the principal aims of this essay. We have to begin by disagreeing even on how to characterize that about which we disagree, if we are to make any movement, even a stumbling and halting one, in the direction of rational agreement.

Notes

1. Notably by Martha Nussbaum in "Non-Relative Virtues: An Aristotelian Approach," *MidWest Studies in Philosophy* 13, ed. by P. A. French, T. E. Uehling, and H. K. Wettstein (Notre Dame: University of Notre Dame Press, 1988).

2. *Journal of Chinese Philosophy* 1, nos. 3–4 (1974).

3. Wing-tsit Chan, "The Evolution of the Confucian Concept Jen," *Philosophy East and West* 4, no. 4 (1953).

4. *Analects* XIV, 4.

5. *Analects* VIII, 10; XVII, 23.

6. David L. Hall and Roger T. Ames, *Thinking Through Confucius* (Albany: SUNY Press, 1987), p. 99.

7. Henry Rosemont, "Against Relativism," in *Interpreting Across Boundaries,* ed. by Gerald J. Larson and Eliot Deutsch (Princeton: Princeton University Press, 1988).

8. A. S. Cua, *Ethical Argumentation* (Honolulu: University of Hawaii Press, 1985).

9. T. H. Irwin, *Aristotle's First Principles* (Oxford: Oxford University Press, 1988).

10. Ch'en Ch'un (1159–1223), *Pei-hsi tzu-i (Neo-Confucian Terms Explained)* trans. and ed. by Wing-tsit Chan (New York: Columbia University Press, 1986).

11. Ronald G. Dimberg, *The Sage and Society: The Life and Thought of Ho Hsin-yin,* Monograph of the Society for Asian and Comparative Philosophy (Honolulu: University of Hawaii Press, 1974), p. 142.

12. See David B. Wong, "Universalism versus Love with Distinction: an Ancient Debate Revived," forthcoming in *Journal of Chinese Philosophy.*

13. See his *Humanity and Self-Cultivation* (Berkeley: University of California Press, 1979).

KARL H. POTTER

THE COMMENSURABILITY OF INDIAN EPISTEMOLOGICAL THEORIES

What follows is an attempt to confront and come to terms with what I call the "incommensurability thesis" about Indian epistemic theories. The thesis I have in mind is this: that though the epistemological theories of the various schools of classical Indian philosophy appear to be addressed to problems common to all parties they are not really so, because each of these different schools addresses a separate topic using a conceptual scheme incommensurate with the schemes used by the others. If the incommensurability thesis is correct, and the various systems of Indian philosophy base themselves on incommensurate conceptual systems, we ought to draw a relativistic conclusion about Indian theories of knowledge. The conclusion would be that the various Indian systems, while appearing to present alternative answers to a set of common epistemological problems, one or more right and others wrong, are in fact not disagreeing about anything at all, since the terms they are using have different meanings in each system.

The thought that epistemic theories are actually incommensurate is, or ought to be, a disturbing one indeed. Among many related implications is this one: that the question "Which epistemic theory is the correct theory?" is at least incapable of answer, and is probably incoherent. Epistemology is about as basic as anything can be—even logic. If there is no correct epistemological theory, if anything goes in epistemology, it seems unavoidable that the same incoherence holds everywhere, that anything goes anywhere—that there is no objective standard of truth.

I believe that a growing number of serious thinkers are coming to accept the incommensurability thesis about knowledge and truth. For example, I read Nelson Goodman's beautifully crafted theory of "versions" as a sophisticated way of learning to live with incommensurability. "Truth cannot be defined or tested by agreement with 'the world',," he writes;[1] all that can be maintained are mutually incompatible versions that satisfy various standards of "rightness."[2] Yet, much as I respect and admire Goodman's reasoning, I remain hopeful that he is

123

mistaken, and the following remarks are offered in the hope, and in the tentative assumption, that there is only one fully correct version and that the various philosophical attempts—such as are found in Indian philosophy—to characterize *the* correct version are not doomed to fail from the outset.

Rejecting incommensurability commits us to finding a way to measure alternative conceptual schemes. In a previously published paper[3] I attempted to suggest such a way. Broadly put, I suggested that two theories of knowledge share a conceptual scheme if there are intentional equivalences that obtain among the concepts employed in the two theories. But I now believe this to be a mistaken way to proceed. The fault lies in the assumption that a conceptual scheme is a set of concepts in the sense of "concept," in which a concept answers to the intentional *sense* of a term, that is, a "criterion in mind" for applying or withholding the term to or from an object. Intentions, I have come to realize, are precisely things whose nature is confined to that scheme in which they function. A conceptual scheme is a closed network of interrelated concepts, each of which is understood through its relations to the others in the net. While there may be "primitive" concepts that have no equivalents expressible through concepts in the system, this does not allow the user of the scheme to escape these concepts' incommensurability, since the primitive concepts are not measured *at all,* either within the scheme *or* outside it. And if we enlarge the net (the scheme) to include an appropriate explanation for the concepts considered primitive before, the same problem recurs at a higher level and we generate an infinite regress that brings our efforts to naught. So my earlier suggestion fails.

What I want to suggest instead is that in the case of India the terminology in which many, indeed practically all, things are discussed relates to a conceptual scheme shared by the users of these terms through *pragmatic,* rather than semantic or syntactic, dimensions of meaning. More specifically, I suggest that the original meanings of many classical terms should be sought in those terms' functioning to guide action, in particular to guide actions toward realizing the ultimate purposes of men.

I

We in the Western world find it almost impossible to imagine that there could be any mode of meaning more primary than the semantic one. The function of language to describe is automatically taken to be the fundamental reason for having words, language, at all. True, Wittgenstein and those under his influence have attempted to bring this notion into question, but the thrust of our own heritage is difficult to throw over. Nevertheless, I suggest that such a preoccupation with semantics is a parochial habit on our part.

Evidence that traditional Indian assumptions about language and thought make pragmatics fundamental is easy to locate. Historically it seems evident that the Vedas were the earliest formal linguistic products of India. The science of exegesis of the thoughts conveyed in the Vedas is known in India as *Mīmāṃsā*. Mīmāṃsā traditions, which go back to Vedic times, are significant in what they suggest about how people thought then. As is generally recognized, but little studied and appreciated, Mīmāṃsā exegetics made pragmatics basic to language. Scripture was understood as primarily injunctive in nature. The function of Vedic words in guiding actions was considered to be their essential meaning. Commenting on this view of language and its implications from a Buddhist perspective, Mervyn Sprung writes:

> . . . [A]t no level and at no point does language in fact name anything. It does not *refer*, as we say. Its function is rather to bind together a world which is by nature disjointed and meaningless, and to be the means of moving about with practical effectiveness in it. Language, in short, has no cognitive capacity; its role is instrumental; it suggests what to expect from things and what to do with them; it conducts. Words are guides, they preserve proven ways of coping with things. They are, to risk a neologism, ductal or ducational. A name suggests a way. . . .[4]

This view of language, which Sprung ascribes to Madhyamaka Buddhism, seems to represent the consistent working out of the implications of a scheme in which pragmatic meaning is assumed to be primary.

The Indian tradition of Vedic times postulated an ordered, threefold set of human aims *(puruṣārtha)*, namely, *artha* (politico-economic), *kāma* (erotic-aesthetic), and *dharma* (ethical). These are ordered so that the ethical is the superior aim, whose fulfillment includes and transcends the other two. Complete achievement of *dharma* leads to heaven. The means to this end involves the proper performance of positive actions. Acts are of three sorts: bodily, mental, and vocal. Activities of these types exhausted the field of actions, and the function of Indian "science" was to tell us how to act in these three ways in order to achieve prosperity, satisfaction, and eventually heaven.

It is especially important to notice that under "action" the Mīmāṃsakas understood mental and vocal as well as overt bodily activity. One may say that the fundamental sciences were the science of *dharma,* which tells us how to choose our overt actions; grammar, which tells us how to speak properly; and logic, which tells us how to think clearly and cogently. Other sciences (for example, astronomy, medicine, agriculture, and architecture) develop understanding of the specific subject matters about which people with particular roles and concerns spoke and thought; these three are of special interest because they abstract from such specific subject matter and tell men in general how to use their bodies, minds, and voices to maximal effect.

Thus, linguistic acts should be performed if they are conducive to human aims, and they are likely to be so if they utilize words which were originally established as useful in this respect, originally established either in the nature of things (as Mīmāṃsā doctrine has it) or by God or by the ancient sages, wise men of yore. Grammar tells us what right speech consists of; other sciences tell us what it is good for. The feature which makes a word an appropriate one for discussing grammar is not its capacity for ranging over a precisely determined domain of objects. Rather, it is the word's function in guiding us to proper speech, a function whose evidence is just the fact that it is found used in the oldest discussions. There may be differences of opinion over what such a word actually denotes or connotes, since men now do not always understand clearly the precise intentions of the ancient sages or God or the impersonal source of language. But despite the differences of semantic meaning which different interpreters may attach to a traditional word, if they are in agreement about the pragmatic function of the word in guiding action, they are speaking to the same end; the interpreters are all practicing the same science.

Logic was to be viewed in parallel fashion. Mental acts should be performed if they are conducive to human aims, and they are likely to be so if they measure things out (pra + mā) in a fashion that fits the requirements of human purposes as established by tradition, provided the understanding of tradition is not defective. The terminology for speaking correctly about mental acts is, once again, established by traditional authority, and, once again, it is not the semantic content of these words which fixes their function but rather their practical role in guiding men to the performance of mental acts, proper habits of thought, which are conducive to human aims. Again, there may be differences of opinion over what such a word actually denotes or connotes, differences which arise because we do not now remember clearly what the semantic content (if any) of those words was according to the original intent (if any) of the first speakers. But again, despite wide divergences of interpretation, if the interpreters are in agreement about the practical role of the word in guiding mental activities, they are speaking to the same end, practicing the same science. And to this extent the incommensurability thesis cannot be unqualifiedly made out.

All this makes excellent sense as long as we are assuming that positive activity (pravṛtti) is the purport of the sciences. And it appears that in the earliest, Vedic period this was indeed so. The attitude was extroverted, and serious men were concerned with achieving a better state ("heaven") through positive acts leading to such a state. But these assumptions were brought into question when a new human aim came to be recognized, that end of man which is liberation (mokṣa, nirvāṇa) from existence altogether. This new aim of man, according to suggestions in the Upaniṣads, according to various sectarian teachings such as those found in Jainism, Buddhism, and so forth and according to an increasingly impressive number of teachers down through the centuries, is to be achieved not by positive activity but by what is precisely its opposite, withdrawal from action (nivṛtti). The new goal of liberation gradually comes to be accepted as superior to the other three. By the ancient logic, which dictates an order among human purposes, the relation among the new group of four aims of man should likewise have been one of progressive support and transcendence. On the face of it, however, the relation between positive activity and withdrawal from action is one of opposition, not support and transcendence. A tension was thus created between the active tradition of ancient Vedic times and the withdrawal tradition of "philosophy" as suggested in some Upaniṣadic passages and spelled out in a number of important views of life, the Indian philosophical systems of classical times.

The history of the tension between activity and withdrawal is worthy of extended attention, but is not the subject of this essay. What is important for my argument is to emphasize that the new goal of liberation seems to constitute an example of a "scientific revolution" in Thomas Kuhn's sense,[5] involving what he calls a "paradigm shift." As Kuhn himself points out, a shift of paradigm is not inconsistent with the cumulative development of facets of the new paradigm within the previous one. In the case we are now considering, action is the center of the older, Vedic paradigm, and the development of theories about the relation between action and the mechanism by which it produces its results led eventually to the paradigm shift in question. Once the shift was recognized, attempts began to be made to reconcile the two paradigms through some sort of synthesis. Eventually these attempts culminated in still another paradigm shift, this time to devotionalism, which I believe must be understood as opposing both Vedic activity and the classical withdrawal paradigms.

If this understanding is correct, it would not be surprising if we found that the terminology of the sciences changes radically from paradigm to paradigm. What is surprising, then, is that in India the terminology did not change all that much. Rather than abandoning the terms in which the activity scheme was enunciated and preserved, those who accepted the new withdrawal paradigm made great attempts to preserve the older terminology, while revising the old conceptual content to the extent that it now expressed an alien paradigm. To some extent, as I mentioned, there were attempts made to marry the two paradigms utilizing the terminology of early times; philosophers differed in the degree to which they were willing to recognize the incompatibility of the paradigms. Śaṃkarācārya is the philosopher most insistent on the incompatibility; the Bhagavadgītā is the best-known example of an attempt at compromise.

Indian philosophical systems, then, share a common paradigm, the paradigm of withdrawal from activity. My contention is that it is this shared paradigm that makes the disparate assumptions of those systems *commensurable*. If I am right, one should be able to trace the meanings of the fundamental concepts of Indian philosophy back to origins in the paradigm of positive activity, and should be able to reconstruct a change of emphasis in the use of these terms reflecting the paradigm shift from activity to withdrawal. It should be possible to justify this reconstruction by appealing to the later use of those concepts that were first used at a time prior to the first paradigm shift.

II

I now wish to examine the epistemological terminology of Indian philosophical systems to determine whether my contention appears viable, that is, to see whether it is plausible that epistemic terms have a history of development from an originally pragmatic meaning, in the activity paradigm in which they were born, to a liberation-dominated paradigm of withdrawal, in the period in which the philosophical schools flourished.

The student of Indian theories of knowledge, and for that matter the general student of India, is regularly astonished by the number of different terms which get translated as "truth." Consider: we have the term *vidyā,* suggesting an understanding which undermines and replaces "ignorance" *(avidyā)* by its opposite, knowledge. But we also have the term *satya,* a term which Gandhi was fond of and used in such a famous conception as *satyāgraha,* by which he meant a kind of activity. The term derives from *sat,* meaning "being," and is opposed to *asat,* "nonbeing." *Satya* suggests reality, what is actually the case. In addition we have *prāmāṇya,* deriving from *pra + mā,* which, as we saw, literally means the measuring out of things in some appropriate fashion. Its opposite is *apramā,* types of which include not just erroneous judgments and illusions, but also doubts and even *reductio ad absurdum; apramā* seems to suggest whatever is *not* a measuring out in an appropriate manner. There are still other terms which get translated regularly as "truth"; these will suffice for now.

All three of these terms—*vidyā, satya,* and *prāmāṇya*—go back to the earliest usage, to the time when the liberation ideal had not yet created the first paradigm shift. If epistemology is a subject which is properly developed using terms such as these three, one must admit that there were at least incipient epistemological references in those times.

Now it is a common expository habit to class epistemology as a branch of philosophy, and thus to count Indian epistemology as a branch of Indian philosophy. But what is meant by "Indian philosophy?" This is not an easy question to answer. The term "philosophy," "love of wisdom," can probably be given a Sanskrit rendition, but that is not at all what either Indian or Western scholars, classical or modern, have meant by "philosophy" in the phrase "Indian philosophy." What they have regularly meant by it is that which constitutes the subject matter of the literature of the several *darśanas,* the so-called six systems of Hindu thought plus the several systems of Buddhist thought as well as Jainism. "Materialistic" *(cārvāka)* thought is also philosophy. What all these systems have in common is that they relate to the aim of liberation: they all, whatever else they do, explain what do and do not constitute bondage and liberation. Most of them do a good deal more, and that more regularly overlaps subjects that in the West are regularly labeled philosophical. Such central philosophical subjects as logic, ontology, and epistemology (though not ethics) are found discussed in the *darśana* literature, and so it is not surprising that such literature is called philosophy by Western and European-oriented Indian writers.

These systems, however, arose in the liberation-dominated period of Indian thought, and their accounts of logic, ontology, and epistemology are clearly guided by the requirements of a world view which countenances the theory of karma, transmigration, and eventual liberation. The result is that if by "epistemology" we choose to mean the theories of knowledge developed in the *darśanas,* the three terms for "truth" that I have identified, whose usage goes back prior to the philosophical period, were not originally philosophically epistemic in content. Then what *did* they mean in their original, preliberation context?

Pramā, which literally has to do with measuring out, had as its practical function the indication of the way one should think about things so as to be most likely to achieve the highest human values. *Prāmāṇya,* then, originally could be applied to anything which played that role. Such a thing was called a *pramāṇa.*

Vidyā appears in the earliest literature and tradition, among other things, as a term for the kind of understanding which is to be gleaned from correct scientific awareness. One hears mention of various *vidyās,* meaning essentially the subject matters of various disciplines, whose theory guided the correct practice of major types of human activities. Bodily acts were likely to be conducive to human purposes if they were oriented by *vidyā.* If they were not they would lead to frustration. Thus the major causal condition of frustration is *vidyā.*

Satya occurs very early in a context of action, and appears to mean action that is effective, that works. Thus, in the ancient version of the lie-detector test, the "truth" *(satya)* is ascertained by discovering whether an act is or is not effective.

It would seem, then, that in the earliest preliberation paradigm the correctness of a thing, such as its truth, was a function of its practical efficacy. That notion reappears in various guises in the classical period. For example, the mark of truth in general according to many Buddhists is *arthakriyākāritva,* the capacity of a judgment to bring about the acquisition of worthwhile things and the avoidance of danger. It is also interesting to note that even in classical liberation paradigms, explanations of the meanings of these terms can suggest the preliberation understanding of truth. For example, in classical Nyāya *prāmāṇya* is frequently explained as necessarily involving *yāthārthya*. The term *yāthārthya* is gorgeously ambiguous. It appears to be understood in Nyāya, a realistic system, as connoting correspondence to an independent external reality. But the term could as well mean "fitting the purpose intended," in which case this definition of *prāmāṇya* as what possesses *yāthārthya* exactly matches the understanding that I am proposing held sway in preliberation usage.

It would appear that these three terms for truth had mainly to do with actions in their earliest usage. Specifically, they were used to indicate that an action is efficacious, conducive to human purposes. By extension, anything which occasioned or causally conditioned such conduciveness was likewise spoken of using these words and their derivatives. Notice that I am alluding to the practical use of such terms, not to their semantic content. Just what things the terms were supposed to describe is something else again. Indeed, that topic—what sort of a thing could be a *pramāṇa*, be *satya,* or have to do with *vidyā*—is one about which early writers even in the second or liberation stage sometimes appear remarkably vague. Nyāya writers—both Hindus and Buddhists—in the first few centuries of the first millennium sometimes seem to be conducting strange exercises attempting to discover just what things are *pramāṇas*. For example, it is queried whether a *pramāṇa* is always a cognition—or might it be any kind of thing as long as it regularly helps to produce true awareness, that is, as long as it leads to successful activity?

If this account is correct, the terms for truth did not have, in their earliest usage, any necessary relation to what we now think to be characteristic epistemological issues. The question of idealism versus realism, for example, was not automatically raised by using terms like *satya, vidyā,* or *pramā*. It was an open question whether efficacious action involved correctly judging how an external world actually is ordered. If one held the view that it necessarily must do so, this was a theory about what was true, not an analysis of the meaning of "true." In short, it was an open possibility that the truth did not correspond to reality, if by "reality" one means some fixed order of nature antecedently established. That is not to say that the point of view of this first stage was idealist, or even that it was skeptical. It is to say that the words in question had their meanings fixed by their function to guide actions toward ends deemed of human value. The question of the entities to which the terms might or might not be applied comprised a distinct, unfixed aspect of their meaning, a matter to be explored.

Let us say that the meaning of a term of language users L is "fundamentally pragmatic" if and only if it is the case that its semantic range for L is determined by its use in action-contexts. A term's semantic range is determined by its use in action-contexts if and only if its proper application to *x* depends on deciding whether *x* is involved in (an) action of the relevant sort. And the ways in which an *x* can be involved in an action include, for example, being its agent *(kartṛ),* its object *(karman),* its purpose *(kartavya),* its fruit or result *(kārya, phala),* or being an action itself *(kriyā, kṛti),* or some direct abstraction from these such as being the property of being an agent, and so forth.

A large number of words used in what we in the West call "epistemology" had fundamentally pragmatic meaning for the Indians of Vedic times. For the most part, these words retained this fundamentally pragmatic meaning for speakers in classical times as well.

The terms that display pragmatic meaning are not confined to abstract terms. Consider, for example, *ghaṭa,* "pot." We would be inclined to think that this word is not fundamentally pragmatic, but we would be mistaken, since originally the word appears to have been used to indicate anything that can be used to hold water, and using something to hold water is an action. Indeed, most common words for material objects were likewise fundamentally pragmatic in meaning.

Matters change when a different question about a pot is asked—not "what is it good for?" but "what is its nature?" Though this might be answered by defining a pot in terms of its function in action, it need not, and one finds different opinions offered about the nature of objects belonging to natural kinds or classes. For example, if one believes in universal properties one may say that a pot is anything which possesses potness. Or if one is concerned with how to tell a pot from other things one may point to characteristic marks, for example, its shape, as its differentium.

Were there any terms which were not fundamentally pragmatic? Perhaps. Consider *cit* and its derivatives. *Cit* means consciousness, not in the sense of a mental act, but rather by analogy with light—just as light shines from the sun without the sun doing anything, so consciousness shines (some say) from the self without any effort. Action does not have any relevance here, it would seem.

Most words in epistemology, however, are just ambiguous in this regard. *Jñāna* is sometimes translated as "knowledge," mistakenly since a *jñāna,* unlike knowledge, need not be true or even be the kind of thing that could be true or false. Better as translation of *jñāna* is "awareness," as in "he became aware of the pot." Now being aware of a specific thing is a kind of mental act, although it seems that we are not fully in command of what we are made aware of—it seems to happen to us whether we wish it to or not, unless we render ourselves unconscious or dead. So "awareness" can go either way, as an action or as a passive state. (This, by the way, explains how *jñānayoga,* as in, for example, the *Bhagavadgītā,* can make some sense: since awareness is or may be an action, disciplining it is possible.)

Another term which causes confusion is *viṣaya.* Regularly rendered as "object," the word appears initially to mean any content of awareness. Thus it has fundamentally pragmatic meaning. For a system which believes that the only being things have is as contents of awareness, such contents are the only "objects" recognized. For other systems, which recognize a distinction between reality and appearance, a term is needed to pick out the real objects from those that are apparent (mere contents) only. One characteristic term for picking out a real thing is *vastu*.

What in general is the procedure for deciding whether a word is used in a fashion reflecting its fundamentally pragmatic meaning? It seems to me that here the analogy between mental acts and vocal acts is helpful. Just as many epistemic words have a fundamentally pragmatic meaning in virtue of their relation to mental acts, so many words describing aspects of language have a fundamentally pragmatic meaning by virtue of their relation to speech acts. For example, the term *vākya*, usually translated as "sentence," fundamentally applies to things by virtue of their playing a certain role in acts of speech. Again, the great significance of mere labeling seems also to derive from the practical importance of speech as an activity with (broadly speaking) ritual import. This may help explain the (from our semantic point of view) rather puerile citing of the name of a thing as of central importance in analyzing the thing's makeup or origination.

The suggestion, then, is that just as one is likely to discover the fundamentally pragmatic meanings of words apparently descriptive of language by considering the (kinds of) speech acts it was used in, so one may be able to identify the fundamentally pragmatic meanings of epistemic words by considering the kinds of mental acts they were used in connection with. And since thinking about these things necessarily involves speaking about them (if only to ourselves), the relation between vocal and mental acts and their respective terminologies is especially close. Thus there may be expected to be analogies between the speech act of, say, asserting and the mental act of believing.

III

In part I it was suggested that there is a paradigm shared by the various classical systems of Indian philosophy that makes their different ontologies commensurable, and that what is shared is a general commitment to a value—the ultimate purpose of liberation. This value, it was argued, was superimposed on a previously established terminology of positive activity; the new "negative" value of liberation gave new and different meaning, in a systematic way, to the older terms of action theory. A new value—liberation—was made supervenient on the order triad of values—*artha, kāma, dharma*—which are determinants of the Vedic period's thought, as refined most evidently in Mīmāṃsā. In part

II, I illustrated how this worked itself out in the terminology of one particular area, the field of epistemology.

But it is still unclear why I should suppose that this answer to incommensurability succeeds where the previous answer failed. Why should it be that replacement of one paradigm by another should make any difference to the question of incommensurability? Isn't the logic of the matter the same whatever the paradigm involved? I don't think so. And the reason why the new answer succeeds where the other failed is that the new answer specifically invokes a hierarchically ordered set of *values,* where the previous attempt did not.

A way of summarizing my argument concerning Indian epistemology is this: those awarenesses that are called "true" in Indian philosophy are just those which tend to satisfy our purposes, and the ones that are "false" are those that do not satisfy. The philosopher can hardly leave the matter there, however. He will wish to know why one sort of awareness satisfies our purposes and another does not. And one cannot answer *this* question by merely saying "that's the way the world is." For now we are precisely questioning whether the world is any one way at all. If the world is any way we want it, as was pointed out at the start, if there is no single correct version of how things are, then skepticism wins the day and any one person's belief is as good as any other's.

But there *is* an answer, or correct response, to the skeptic on this point. For the question why one awareness satisfies and another does not can be answered by appeal, not to how things *are,* but to how they should be thought to be. There is an alternative source of justification that lies in the nature of the drives which motivate action, in the normative ordering of these drives. What we find through experience is two things: (1) that some ways of being satisfied are more satisfying than others, and (2) that no positive pattern is entirely satisfying, since there always remain other drives as yet unsatisfied and so productive of frustration. The first point suggests that drives can be ordered in terms of the quality of their satisfaction. The second suggests that the ultimate human aim both is and ought to be the complete quiescence of all drives without residue.

The first point is frequently enough made in Western thought, although its significance is nowadays hidden behind a kind of skepticism about values known as noncognitivism or nonnaturalism. The noncognitivist skeptic, when faced with a claim that certain drives or purposes are of greater value than others, that their satisfactions are qualitatively orderable, challenges the proponent of that claim to vindicate it, pointing out that the claimer cannot appeal to experience since values are not acts and *de gustibus non est disputandum.* This skepticism is misplaced. The normative ordering of drives, and the values implicit in their satisfaction, are in principle justifiable as facts. The justification comes in terms of criteria of rational satisfactoriness, stemming from commitment to certain methodological values—to the preferability of explanations of greater adequacy (they explain *more*), of consistency (inconsistent explanations, since they make contradictory explanations true, explain nothing), of accuracy (in a sense which does not require correspondence but does require that the explanans be *germane* to the explanandum), and of greater economy or power (fewer terms explaining more experiences).[6]

The experiences whose explanation requires an ordering of values include those which cause our admiration for those who sacrifice so that others may succeed, our contempt for those who cheat, our preference for long-term positive satisfactions of a moderate sort in comparison with short-term highs and lows, our conviction that harming others unnecessarily is wrong, and so on. These experiences are inconsistent with the value-skeptic's position that any satisfaction is as good or as bad as any other. Such a skepticism is analogous to a parallel sort with respect to sense experience, by a skeptic who would say that appearance is reality, that if one sees red then one ought to conclude that the thing is really red, though we all know perfectly well that people who acted on that basis would be completely uncritical in their account of how things behave and so would be at the mercy of their environment. The sense-skeptic's position is inadequate, inaccurate, inconsistent, and without power; likewise the value-skeptic's.

It is true that people have found it woefully difficult to arrive at a basis for ordering values that satisfies these methodological requirements. But one should not conclude from that difficulty that there is no such ordering rationally called for by our drives. If the higher norms tend to arise from the social context in which human beings interact with one another, which is what many moral philosophers have concluded, then that context provides a broad base for value-ordering. If a satisfaction of passions turns out in general to be fleeting and productive of more frustration, while the quiescence of drives arising from concerns for the long-term well-being of oneself and others produces longer-term satisfaction and less immediate frustrations, then (other things being equal) that suggests an ordering in which the latter drives are to be ranked more worthy of quiescence than the former.

Such an ordering of values is promulgated over the centuries as a cornerstone of traditional Indian thought in the familiar doctrine of human aims—*artha, kāma,* and *dharma,* capped eventually by a fourth, *mokṣa.* This hierarchy of values is grounded in the experiences of human beings and is justified by those groundings together with the methodological requirements mentioned before—of adequacy, accuracy, consistency, and simplicity.

Suppose that there is a hierarchy of values—how does that help us in justifying an ontology? It does so because there is a selection process generated by an acknowledgement of the hierarchy of values, a process by which certain candidates for ontological priority are preferred to other candidates. If interpersonal *(dharma)* values are ranked higher than material *(artha)* ones, say, then concepts implicit in the formulation of those higher-ranked values also come to play a fundamental role in ontology—to constitute the categories or primitives of one's metaphysical system. In Vedic India the result of the recognition of *dharma* as supreme value had its natural outcome in the ontology of Mīmāṃsā, in which human action is the fundamental ontological principle. Elsewhere, a physicalistic world view is one which ranks the manipulation of physical and physiological factors as the source of highest value. Of course, these characterizations are highly oversimplified. We are talking always about a complex set of interrelated norms involving all the features of our experience, and the resulting metaphysics will eventually, if it is to be rationally acceptable, have to find a place within it for those features which are not projections of highly valued norms but nevertheless have to be accommodated. Thus reluctantly the physicalist wrestles with consciousness, morality, and other features of experience not easily encompassed in physical categories. Likewise, the Mīmāṃsaka wrestled with those aspects of experience which do not easily fit under the rubric of action or activity.

So it is understandable that different ontologies correspond to different hierarchies of values and find their source of justification there. An ontology is a "version" (once again to use Goodman's term) which adopts certain concepts as primitive, concepts whose choice has been dictated by the recognition of a certain ranking of types of satisfaction and of the drives which involve them. To convince a philosopher that his ontology is mistaken requires convincing him that his value-ordering is misguided. This is not a matter of taste. Quite the reverse; it involves the deepest and broadest possible assessment of how the values found in our experience hang together. Its justification, though, is ultimately in terms of the experienced satisfactions of inquirers. Accuracy, adequacy, consistency, and economy are themselves justified because it has been found that a purposive activity which proceeds on the basis of notions satisfying these methodological norms is more likely to be successful, more likely to produce satisfaction, than purposive activity that ignores these norms.

What is real, then, is what has a place in a scheme generated by a hierarchy of values. A world or version is relative to that hierarchy. It follows that if some hierarchy can be justified as being the most satisfactory basis for purposive activity, that hierarchy is the one that generates the really real, the highest reality. The Sanskrit term here is, suggestively, *paramārtha*, the highest purposive value or goal object, from which is derived the adjective *pāramārthika*, used to describe that set of ontological principles which constitutes *paramārthasat*, the highest reality. And what is "true," ultimately, is precisely these principles and the version which they alone generate. It is that which is *satya* and whose appreciation is termed *vidyā,* understanding or knowledge. We have now found a natural home for the expressions of both Indian and Western epistemology, though we have not yet established what their proper designata are, since it has not yet been determined how to identify this highest reality or truth.

The key to that discovery, as conceived in Indian philosophy, is to reflect on the point that the ultimate criterion which grounds any ontology is satisfaction. Satisfaction derives from quiescence of drives.[7] The paradox about satisfaction is that it never comes unmixed with frustration. We are always driven by a multiplicity of drives, and so, no matter how obsessively we pursue quiescence of one of them, the rest remain unsatisfied. Indeed, more than that, our situation is such that in the very process of achieving quiescence of one drive we generate more drives which will require future quiescence. Positive activity is undertaken relative to one drive out of many. The thought then arises: is it possible to quiesce *all* our drives? That would be *ultimate* satisfaction, satisfaction unmixed with frustration. Surely, that must be—if it is indeed feasible—the highest value in the hierarchy. And indeed, it is so conceived in classical Indian thought. That highest value is liberation *(mokṣa, nirvāṇa),* the fourth and most supreme of the aims of men.

Since all values are fundamentally achievement values stemming from quiescence of drives, it is clear that without changing that understanding of values, liberation, complete quiescence of drives, *must* be the highest value, since upon its achievement no drives will remain to be quiesced which might generate other values higher than liberation. And thus we can now answer the question as to which is the final ontology, the highest reality: it is that version or world whose fundamental concepts arise from the ultimate value of liberation. Just how that is to be fleshed out is precisely what is argued out, using commensurate terminology, among the various *darśanas,* the several classical systems of Indian philosophy.

Notes

1. Nelson Goodman, *Ways of Worldmaking* (Indianapolis: Hacket Publishing Co., 1978), p. 17.

2. Ibid., pp. 109–110.

3. Karl H. Potter in *Self, Knowledge and Freedom: Essays for Kalidas Bhattacharyya,* ed. by J. N. Mohanty and S. P. Banerjee (Calcutta, 1978), pp. 17–30.

4. Mervyn Sprung in *"Language" in Indian Philosophy and Religion,* ed. by H. G. Coward, SR Supplements 5 (Canadian Corp. for Studies in Religion, 1978), p. 47.

5. Thomas Kuhn, *The Structure of Scientific Revolutions* (Chicago: University of Chicago Press, 1962, 1970).

6. For a remarkable discussion of these methodological norms and an insight into how they work see Nelson Goodman, *The Structure of Appearance* (Cambridge, Massachusetts: Harvard University Press, 1950; Bobbs-Merrill, 1966; D. Reidel, 1977), especially part one.

7. The terminology of "drive" and "quiescence" derives from Stephen C. Pepper, *A Digest of Purposive Values* (Berkeley and Los Angeles: University of California Press; London: Cambridge University Press, 1947).

Relativism

BIMAL K. MATILAL

PLURALISM, RELATIVISM, AND
INTERACTION BETWEEN CULTURES

Pluralism versus Singularism

Singularism is to be understood as defying the thought that there may be a variety of conceptions of good cherished by different groups of human beings. Pluralism, on the other hand, allows for the multiplicity of the concept of the common good as well as freedom of choice on the part of the individual to choose his or her own community life. Relativism goes a little further than this and holds that one such conception of good is as good as any other, there being no overarching standard. Pluralism keeps the possibility open for ranking these different concepts of good. The burden on the pluralist as well as on the relativist is to devise a judicious blending of social and political institutions that will accommodate such diversity. The pluralist, therefore, is usually regarded as a liberal and has the desire to make accommodation for such diversities. However, even a conservative can be a pluralist. In fact one may claim that a conservative who preaches noninterference with the rights of others to pursue their own good is better equipped to be a pluralist. He would demand that the state should be as far as possible neutral over questions of personal morality and common conceptions of the good, and the aims of life. Besides, the state should provide a framework of law and other institutions—a framework within which individuals and communities would pursue their own goals. Pluralism stipulates that we do not need substantive moral agreement, except only for the basic agreement about the indispensability of mutual toleration. Conservatism does not mean authoritarianism. The conscience of a conservative can allow authoritarianism only at the risk of hypocrisy.

One may say that a conservative person does not only prefer one conception of good to another, but also believes that his own conception is the best one. However, such blindfolded conservatism suffers from a basic inconsistency. A pluralist conservative must first accept the diversity of the notion of "good." In principle, it may be conceded that one particular notion of good is better than another's, but we really do not

141

know which one. Besides, short of indulging in a dogma, we cannot say that one particular way of life ("form of life," if you like) is best for the whole of humanity. Besides, even if we believe in a pluralist ideal, it does not mean that we have to believe that every ideal of human flourishing is as good as any other. Pluralism is not relativism, not quite. What is important politically is to emphasize the following fact: interference with the rights of others to pursue their own good should not be allowed or justified under any circumstances, except when such pursuit causes *harm* to others. However, what causes "*harm* to others" is another difficult matter in regard to which there is no unanimity. I shall return to this point later.

Our awareness of the diversity of human groups, the variety of races, classes, castes, and communities, and consequently the presence of the plurality of human goals, desires, aptitudes, abilities, and aims, is very ancient. But still it has not fostered what we understand today by the ideals of pluralism. Singularism has always been a seductive ideal. Even the enlightened sociopolitical thinkers of the nineteenth and twentieth centuries (being influenced by their predecessors) talked in terms of a singularistic goal to be sought after, in terms of a single and unified conception of good that is valid and desirable for all types of human beings. This is the concept of "a harmonious universe." The general pattern of the arguments they used in order to reach their antipluralistic conclusions can be given as follows. Freedom, or rational self-direction, is inherent in every man and woman. The obvious problem, however, is said to be that this all-important faculty lies dormant in most people, and hence the problem of diversity of goals arises. Not everybody can judge what is best for him or her. The clearest example would be the case of children. Rationality lies dormant in them but can be awakened through training, discipline, force, coercion, or even occasional violence (slapping, and so forth). Using such premises and supporting examples (Nyāya's *sādharmya-dṛṣṭānta*), these enlightened thinkers of Europe reached, by a not too circuitous road, a paradoxical conclusion which gave unequivocal support to the most abject forms of authoritarianism. It was paradoxical, for they were regarded as both enlightened and liberal.

This type of authoritarianism has been the breeding ground of singularism and antipluralistic ideals. It is still important for us to note the steps of this argument. For despite the fact that the fallacies and mistakes of these honored thinkers (we must remember that they are still our "heroes" in the field of sociopolitical thought and that this particular case does not detract any glory from these thinkers) have been pointed out by many today who comment upon them, the argument as well as the conclusion in question still holds its charm, and many even today assume its validity and become unconsciously its victims. Hence it must be rewarding to rehearse the steps of this old argument.

Sir Isaiah Berlin, in a slightly different context, has identified the mistakes of these thinkers (whom he also admires most). I shall quote from his famous essay, for it would be no exaggeration to say that nobody has been able to surpass Sir Isaiah in presenting this argument in its simplicity, elegance, and profundity. Sir Isaiah was defending his "two concepts of liberty":

> Comte put bluntly what had been implicit in the nationalist theory of politics from its ancient Greek beginnings. There can, in principle, be only one correct way of life; the wise lead it spontaneously, that is why they are called wise. The unwise must be dragged towards it by all the social means in power of the wise; for why should demonstrable error be suffered to survive and breed?[1]

A few pages later, Sir Isaiah sums up:

> Let me state them once more: first, that all men have one true purpose, and one only, that of rational self-direction; second, that the ends of all rational beings must of necessity fit into a single universal, harmonious pattern, which some men may be able to discern more clearly than others; third, that all conflict, and consequently all tragedy, is due solely to the clash of reason with the irrational or the insufficiently rational—the immature and undeveloped elements of life—whether individual or communal, and that such clashes are, in principle, avoidable, and, for wholly rational beings, impossible; finally, that when all men have been made fully rational, they will obey the rational laws of their own natures, which are one and the same in them all, and so at once wholly law-abiding and wholly free.[2]

Need we add anything more? However, if anybody has the slightest worry about the relevance of this rather long quotation to my main concern, it must be set at rest already. The premises here unequivocally challenge the ideals of pluralism. These ideals can be defended, I believe, even without our making concession to the pernicious form of relativism.

In fact, I shall try to do more than that. For I believe that though excitement over relativism today may force us to reject the dogmas of singularism, some relativists still find the argument above attractive, and in this way they are inclined to collect ammunition to silence their opponents. The popular form of relativism goes several steps further than accepting the pluralistic ideals. However, I believe it is possible to accept the pluralistic ideals without giving in to this popular form of relativism—that is, without proclaiming loudly, as is often done, that since every truth is relative, there is no such thing as good or bad, right or wrong, true or false, for it is all relative.

To return to our quotation from Berlin. The first two premises are obviously identical with the two complementary sides of the singularistic doctrine that defies pluralistic ideals. They can even be reformulated to support another conclusion: the plurality that we experience all over the world throughout history is only apparent or falsely created; our rational wisdom, which some of us may be fortunate enough to have fully developed, can easily see through this veil of appearance and experience directly the deeper unity of mankind. A so-called deeper insight into the conflict-free, harmonious universe, a new Garden of Eden, as not only the ultimate truth but also the ultimate goal of all of us, is such an attractive and charming idea that many people in different ages have *fallen* for it (if one excuses the biblical metaphor). Even today we have a considerable number of its optimistic followers. Hence the warning is worth repeating.

The third step in the argument above (the quotation from Berlin) is almost patently false. For the historical evidence is that the actual clashes and conflicts and their resulting bloodshed and massacres are not always due to the disharmony between reason and unreason, but actually due to the clash of one irrational choice over another by different human communities. However, it is easy to see why the singularist's contention, that a rational resolution of these conflicts would bring down the kingdom of heaven upon earth, would be a too simplistic solution for an utterly complex situation. Apart from the romantic overtures towards a *unified* Garden of Eden, the idea has no substantive base. It is difficult to see how we can promise a "Rose Garden."

Pluralism and Relativism

One may argue that if pluralistic ideals are conceded, if one denies that there is a common goal and a unified good for all human beings and that the kingdom of heaven on earth is possible if every human being becomes enlightened enough to exercise rational wisdom and rational self-direction, then are we not giving in to a sort of pernicious form of relativism? Of course, in the field of ethics and morality today, relativism has many things going for it. Since the beginning of social anthropology along with the rise of liberal colonialism, we have learned to "respect," if not to justify, the ethical and moral standards of others. Even if we do not understand fully why the native calls a particular act "good," we have no right to condemn it or force the native to explain it in the light of reason. It becomes another question of morality to use such language of "qualitative contrast" (a term taken from Charles Taylor)[3] to describe the native practices, which the outsiders do find obnoxious. This is, on the face of it, a kind of tolerance that should be practiced, for it also amounts to a value and hence involves a sort of moral obligation. However, *tolerance* ought to be practiced with *sincerity* (both being moral virtues). It is on the other hand next to impossible for a singularist (or one who believes *firmly* in the superiority of one's own way of life over all others') to be tolerant and sincere (that is, unhypocritical) at the same time as far as *respect* for another's way of life is concerned.

Modern developments in epistemology and philosophy of language have supplied much ammunition to the moral relativists and moral skeptics. W. V. Quine (1960) formulated his celebrated thesis of indeterminacy of translation which has had far-reaching effects. Some implications of this thesis have been used, rightly or wrongly, by the cultural anthropologists in support of their thesis of cultural relativism. It is often emphasized that transcultural evaluation of norms is not possible. If the languages of "qualitative contrast" are not interculturally valid, the notion of ethical or moral absolutes must be rejected as dogmas of singularism. Comparative ethnography induces moral skepticism. Ethical norms are regarded as being immanent or imbedded in the cultural norms, and when these cultural norms vary or are incommensurate with one another, ethical relativism becomes an inevitable conclusion. Such relativism, however, has often been criticized for being basically inconsistent and confused, if it is seriously held by anyone as part of his ethical thinking. Bernard Williams has called it "vulgar" relativism.

There are several ways by which a defensible nonvulgar form of (moral) relativism can be formulated. Relativism, in fact, has been formulated and defended by several philosophers today. A few specimens will do. We start with the following observation. Each culture has its own axiomatic construction of reality which is an integral part of what we call its world view. The ethical system of each culture is imbedded in such an axiomatic construction of reality.

We can now formulate the thesis of ethical relativism by using such notions as "real confrontation" and "real option" and introducing a watertight distinction between "real" and "notional" options. Each ethical system is unique to its own culture and there cannot be any real confrontation between one such culture and another, and hence one cannot be a *real* option for the other. The concept of "notional confrontation" is very important here; it saves the thesis from the charge of inconsistency. The concept of the "notional," it is argued, allows us to think of moral concerns of the "alien" culture so that we can use such language of condemnation and admiration across cultural boundaries, but it does not lead us to think of there being any substantive relation between our moral concerns with theirs. As long as such a *substantive* relation is not thought to exist, the question of appraisal of theirs with ours does not arise. For, as Bernard Williams has argued, it is the presence of some substantive relation between moral concerns of different cultures "which alone can give any *point* or *substance* to the appraisal."[4]

The above is my reconstruction of the thesis on the basis of the formulation of Bernard Williams in his earlier writings. I do not wish to attribute the above entirely to Williams, for he has recently talked about some important "riders" to his formulation and patently used it as a heuristic device to clarify our understanding of relativism. Hence let us call the above the view of some philosophers whom I regard as my *pūrva-pakṣa* ("opponent") and not hold Williams responsible for the entire argument. However, I believe his "notional confrontation" somewhat arbitrarily excludes the substantive relation between the moral concerns of different cultures. It is not made clear why and how such thinking of relating the moral concerns must be excluded. In fact, if the member of one culture-group is fully exercising his well-developed rational wisdom (which alone can sustain his practical reasoning), he is bound to raise the question of substantive relationship between our moral concerns and theirs, and this will give *point* to the transcultural evaluation. In fact the borderline between the "real" and the "notional" confrontation tends to vanish under pressure, unless of course we are talking about two completely individuated cultures, a society of the bygone ages and a contemporary society.

In short, this type of relativism receives support, for the possibility of "real confrontation" is excluded between cultures. However, such a possibility can be excluded only if the cultures are very remote from each other (either in time or in space). The relativism or incommensurability of the values of a society of bygone ages (Bronze Age, for instance) with those of a modern society is philosophically uninteresting. Hence, as long as the proper individuation or separation of two contemporary cultures (conceiving them as two "windowless monads," to use Bernstein's phrase)[5] does not seem possible, we can argue against such relativism. I call this "the Impossibility of the Individuation of Cultures" (IIC) argument.

Another way is to introduce a sharp distinction between two types of language of appraisal or contrastive choices: one is "right-and-wrong" and the other is "good-and-evil." The former belongs to the agent's own ethics or moral frame of reference while the latter does not. A moral agent is conceived here as belonging to a group or community which has its own special set of ethical principles. The agent reaches his "inner moral judgment" on the basis of such principles as he and his peers have consciously or unconsciously agreed to keep. If the agent acts on the basis of such inner moral judgment, it should be considered *right,* no matter whether such an act is in fact good or evil from our point of view. This means that when a member of Murder Incorporated performs his duty, that is, kills somebody following the ethics of the society he belongs to, that is, Murder Incorporated, we cannot judge him to be doing something wrong although we can call him an *evil* human being.

This formulation is derived from the thesis of moral relativism, formulated by Gilbert Harman.[6] I must say again that my formulation may not exactly represent the views of Harman. The protagonists of the view above would also depend upon the possibility of the proper individuation from group moralities, and they assume a sharp distinction between what is wrong and what can be called evil. We may insist that each group has its own particular code of ethics which its members must follow, no matter what. Here probably one may suggest that the ethics could be distinguished from morality in the sense that the former is group-related while the latter is not. Ethics on this view is something like the honor code of a particular group. However, such a distinction does not resolve the basic problem of morality. Elsewhere I have shown that there is a striking resemblance between such a view of "group-related morality" and some version of the classical *varṇadharmas* ("class-duties") of the Hindus. Thus Arjuna was asked, in the *Bhagavadgītā*, to follow his "inner moral judgment" and thereby decide to fight the Kauravas because it was what a Kṣatriya ("warrior") should do.[7]

This type of moral relativism has its own problems, although it is based upon an impeccable logic. First, it has some repugnant consequences where one has to support the action of people like Hitler as *right* from the point of view of the agent's own moral frame of reference. We can only call such actions *evil*, that is, not good, from our point of view. But this separation of the concept of evil from that of wrongdoing is highly questionable. I call this the "Repugnant Consequence" (RC) argument. Besides, why should every code of conduct which is unique to a particular group be honored as its *moral* code of conduct, or moral frame of reference? It seems to defy our linguistic intuition of the word "morality" if the code of conduct of Murder Incorporated is to be called a moral code among others. Must every code of conduct of any fanciful club be regarded as an ethical code? Must the diabolical action dictated by some diabolically minded human beings belonging to a club be glorified as constitutive of the morality of its members? People are different all over the world, but the pertinent question is: How much? or To what extent? It is true that they belong to different societies which are historically and geographically conditioned and hence have developed different faiths, myths, rituals, kinship systems, standards of interpersonal behavior. The culture's "ethical" system may be built upon all of these which motivate them to act. But this is not everything. It does not exhaust the domain of morality or what the motivation for some fundamental moral action is all about. Besides, the pervasive presence of moral dilemmas in this world shows, among other things, that the moral agent cannot be exclusively the member of one particular group. Crisscrossing the group loyalties gives rise to almost unresolvable moral dilemmas for which the service of rational wisdom is required. In sum, this formulation of relativism suffers from both defects. That is, both arguments, the IIC and the RC, can be leveled against it.

Relativism and Realism

Moral relativism has recently been receiving support from the rise of some form of relativism in other fields, such as theoretical science. Quine, who is not himself a relativist, had said (in 1960) that, of the native's sentence there may be two or more translations which are sometimes in conflict and there is no fact of the matter to help us to choose any particular one among them.[8] In 1970 Thomas Kuhn, who is also not strictly a relativist, propounded his thesis, according to which we have very little to go upon in choosing among incommensurable theories.[9] In fact, Kuhn has argued that we cannot depend upon the avoidance of error as a criterion without running into the problem of circularity or the question-begging situation. For we cannot specify the truth condition of one of the rival theories, say T1, unless we specify it relative to the other theory, T2, in a way that would entail the falsity of T1 and the truth of T2. This type of assessment begs the question unabashedly. We may depend, Kuhn says, upon such epistemic issues as simplicity, fruitfulness, accuracy, and so forth, but here again there may be genuine differences regarding what constitutes, for example, simplicity. Without settling such disputes, we can hardly make a rational choice among incommensurable theories. Simplicity, and so forth are epistemic or cognitive values. Besides, scientific inquiries are, according to Kuhn, value-laden in many ways. Now, since the disputes regarding such cognitive values are not settleable, the only way to settle disputes regarding value commitments is through persuasion or coercion.

Such well-argued views have given strong impetus to the rise of modern relativism. Since conflicts are not to be resolved through further inquiry, disputes concerning values of different kinds—cognitive, moral, political, or aesthetic—would be and actually are settled overtly or covertly by persuasion. What we have called one's rational wisdom has not been able to yield (even when used properly) satisfactory results: for example, agreement as regards the choice. Kuhn has of course been criticized for his view. Isaac Levi, for example, rejects the conclusion that avoidance of error cannot be a critical desideratum in any inquiry,[10] and perhaps further inquiry and marshaling of more information may even be desirable in some cases. However, moral conflict should be seen in the broader perspective of conflict in values in other areas. Levi insists that there are similarities between decision-making under unresolved conflict in scientific inquiry and practical deliberation.

All these, however, do not endorse the rather facile and unacceptable form of relativism. It only requires that the singularist's picture of the unified universe, his notion of Truth and of the Good, needs revision or modification. I believe the pluralist ideals can be better formulated so as not to imply necessarily the facile form of relativism. Pluralism and some form of realism are compatible.

Even on the nonobjectivist view of ethics, one's ethical reflections do not stop at the boundary of one's own culture but extend beyond to the others. No stance of pseudoliberalism, using the notion of hypercommensurability as a ploy, can deflect our ethical censure or praise of the *other's* actions. Some sort of universal obligation is implicit in our modern conception of the ethical so that we are apt to censure someone, even in our own culture, if he fails to meet some basic ethical obligation under the pretext of some group loyalty or loyalty to his own self or his family.

I also believe that the notion of incommensurability is what often obfuscates the issue here. For this notion is sometimes claimed to imply material unintelligibility, and therefore mutual uncriticizability. But, if incommensurability or undercommensurability of standards (or lack of a common denominator in terms of which we can transcend the problems of intertranslatability) does not stand in the way of mutual appreciation and respect, it cannot by the same token stand in the way of mutual criticism, intelligibility, and understanding.

Realism, that is, a sort of hardheaded metaphysical Realism, has recently been very much in the firing line and criticized today as an old legacy of what we used to call "science." Putnam has called it the *externalist* perspective, and found it almost indefensible. Some philosophers, like Richard Rorty, have found the old controversy between realism and relativism or idealism to be useless and counterproductive and suggested that the sooner we give up this style of philosophizing the better.[11] However, a sort of popular or vulgar pragmatism or relativism has become widespread today which has been extended from the field of metaphysics to ethics and morality. It has been hailed as the "liberating" message and has generated insouciance. From the strictures of a number of academic philosophers against the viability of metaphysical realism (and these philosophers no doubt have had good and well-reasoned arguments for their views) it has spread all over at the popular level, where any belief in the absolutist's conception of truth and good is instantly ridiculed: "Do you believe in witches and unicorns?" Cultural diversity is often conflated with the relativity of good and bad about almost everything and it puts on the garb of pseudoliberalism where it is further conflated with freedom, openness, and equality. What was regarded as a serious academic discussion or controversy between relativism and realism in metaphysical and moral fields conducted with informed sophistication and technicalities has now been vulgarized and regarded by a majority of uninformed students and common people as a useless enterprise, for they all claim to *know* that everything is relative. The situation became so much worse that it irritated not without justification many well-known writers and professors like Allan Bloom, who

wrote the best-seller, *The Closing of the American Mind*,[12] rebuking and
ridiculing at every step, sometimes unfairly, the new wave of relativism,
where, he rightly observed, the extreme left and the extreme right might
converge. Bloom, however, displayed, somewhat unwittingly, an embarrassing ignorance of any other culture and thereby might have for-
feited his claim to be critical of any seriously formulated relativism. A
critical stance toward the popular and uninformed version of relativism,
perhaps on just grounds, can be greeted with cheers. However, Bloom
went to the other extreme and argued in favor of the old, blindfolded
singularism. And this, to be sure, must be regretted.

Cultural Confrontation

Cultural and ethnic diversity does not lead to the type of relativism that
Bloom and others have criticized. Even plurality of goals may be made
compatible with realism. I believe there is a minimal universal moral
standard which is applicable to all human beings irrespective of race,
sex, color, religion, culture, national or social origins, birth, or other
status. Given the prevalent mistrust today in any forms of abstract totality, universalism or rationalism, it might indeed be like going against
the current to argue for a minimal universal ethic. Some, having even
acknowledged that human beings as biological creatures may share
some common features, may contend that such universalism is boring
and unexciting. Shylock's claim in *The Merchant of Venice*, for example,
was true but uninteresting, on this view. However, the two qualifications "universal" and "minimal" should be emphasized. The sense of
"universal" has already been indicated. I shall further amplify it in the
course of this essay. I believe our notion of the ethical law demands
some sort of universality, as I have already mentioned. The qualification "minimal" is what makes it nonantagonistic to cultural and moral
diversity as well as to the partial incommensurability of such diverse
values. In fact, the view that I wish to defend seems more defensible not
in spite of, but because of, the fact that it is arguable in full awareness of
the pervasive presence of moral and cultural diversity. Besides, this theory of minimal morality, which is claimed here to be universally applicable, should be distinguished from the view of the protagonists of the
"Natural Law" doctrine, and certainly from the singularism that people like Allan Bloom prefer. It is important to emphasize the distinction
because, in spite of the obvious similarity between them as regards their
universality (and probably inalienability), the Natural Law doctrine
lacks the flexibility as well as amenability to contextual interpretation in
the background of cultural and social diversity that the former, minimal
universal morality doctrine enjoys. Plurality of morals, cultural norms,
and social obligations are facts that are not in dispute here. Nor is the
fact that there are irreducible residues in each cultural norm which are

claimed in part to be incommensurate with those from another norm. What is in dispute is whether the following argument holds. If there does not exist any universal, context-neutral rational standard to judge the relative merit or demerit of such different culture-dependent values and practices, or if, *à la* Bernard Williams, there is no *real* confrontation among them such that one cannot be a *real* option to another, then we are forced into a position of relativism, which, if true, runs counter to the claim of universality of the minimal moral standard that I am inclined to support. I believe the argument does not hold. Even if we concede the incommensurability, that is, the argument in favor of relativism of a majority of cultural and ethical values (such that a rational choice among them seems not sometimes impossible but in fact unnecessary), it is not contrary to the claim made here about a minimal number of universal, that is, culture-neutral or context-neutral, moral values which are and should be constitutive of the ethos of any human society. The qualifier "human" in "human society" is important, although we need not appeal to any universal essence of man. I do not believe that this minimal ethics has to be based upon such universal essence. It can be based upon some empirically given concerns of humans.

Elsewhere I have argued that cultural confrontations do take place and have often taken place in the history of mankind, and some of them are also *real* even in the sense that Williams wishes to attach to the adjective in his phrase "real confrontation."[13] Cultures and societies, or at least, the present-day cultures, are not like water-tight compartments, which may seldom confront one another in reality and interact. They do interact with each other, sometimes generating violence, sometimes peacefully and almost unconsciously accepting value trade-offs and value rejections. That is why the IIC argument holds. For the Williamsian kind of *notional* confrontation we have to imagine two self-contained and totally isolated cultures with guaranteed immunity from external influence, and hence with guaranteed immunity from evaluation and criticism from outside. Such cultures are mostly theoretical constructs, which sustain this defensible type of relativism. Williams himself recognized this and in his later publication talks about "the Relativism of distance" which exists between past and present societies or between past and future societies.[14]

But what does this empirical evidence prove? It does not, of course, prove that a coherent construction of the relativistic position on the basis of *notional* confrontation is impossible. In fact, such construction helps us to understand a culture and most of its values from an internalist's point of view, and that is an acceptable device in comparative ethnology or ethnography. But in practice, in today's world, cultures and subcultures do flow into each other, interacting both visibly and invisibly, eventually effecting value-rejection and value-modification at every stage. This only shows the vitality of cultures, which are like living organisms in which internal and external changes are incontrovertible facts. As indicated earlier, a culture as well as its constitutive values, moral and nonmoral, basic and nonbasic, faces both the internal critique (originating from human rationality) and the external challenge from the confrontation with other cultures, both causing change, development, and mutation as well as acceptance of different values within that culture. A culture that does not react and change with time is as good as a dead one or it is dying, or at best it maintains a fossilized form of existence, fit to be turned into a museum piece. A culture is also compared with a language (a reflex of the anthropological discipline); a living culture is like a living language which keeps changing (though slowly) over a period of time, assimilating new idioms and phrases, new structures and forms (which we often call the creative aspect of a language). A dead language does not change nor does a dead culture.

Here we may make another point about Quine's celebrated thesis about the indeterminacy of translation. It is a coherent theory-construction comparable to some extent to the relativism of distant cultures, and it has the same character of being a heuristic device for a better understanding of the nature of meanings as translational constants, and so forth. Radical translation, however, assumes that the native's language is unchanging, and the Gavagai culture does not interact through assimilation and modification on being confronted with the linguist's culture over a period of time. But empirical evidence goes against it, and eventual intertranslatability with negligible traces of indeterminacy are not only possible but actually take place after a period of time. This is not a criticism of Quine, for we concede the point about the indeterminacy of the mental at a certain level.

Comparative ethnographers have often pointed out that there are certain core values unique to each culture which show resilience, resist change, or even possess immutability in the midst of confrontation and interaction with other cultures. The culture's ethical system being immanent, such core values are not available for *real* confrontation or transcultural evaluation. Hence a sort of relativism is still inescapable for the pluralists. My critique of this view is twofold. First, it assumes an "essentialist" view of culture; particular cultural essences constituted by its particular core values are immutable much like the essence of a particular species of animal. (This is not exactly the "false essentialism" that Bernstein has warned us about in his essay. However, it is something similar.) Once we give up the essentialist dogma admitting mutation and changes, the analogy does not work. We are, after all, creatures of history and we must concede our finitude and fallibilism. Second, it assumes too much on the basis of too little as evidence. Granted that one experiences "culture shocks," sometimes very odd and quaint and sometimes very bizarre feelings, when one is getting acquainted with an "alien" culture, and consequently also with its values and mores, but this does not supply enough evidence for the conclusion which embraces uniqueness and immutability of the core values. In fact, certain historically conditioned and geographically or environmentally generated values and practices, sharpened and shaped by local myths, rituals, and kinship systems, and so forth are the hardest to give up for a member of a particular culture and hence they offer the greatest resistance to change. They are also the hardest for outsiders to comprehend or to translate into their own culture, for commensurable values and concepts are not often available. It is for this reason we tend to look upon them as *essential* constituents of the uniqueness of a particular culture. But they also yield to slow change almost imperceptibly as the causal factors keep changing and disappearing. Of course, cultural conservatism would like to preserve some of them, and fundamentalism would like to revive a few practices and beliefs, but the preserved historical relics, and the revived practices, when they are being taken out of their contexts, can never be the same. The life of a Bronze Age chief or a medieval samurai can be, *par contra* Williams, real options for us only if they are "revived" or "reconstructed" today, although they would not be the *same* lifestyles of the bygone ages. We cannot go back in history.[15]

On the Idea of the Basic Moral Fabric

Some sort of relativism (in the sense of an absence of any transcultural standard of evaluation or of incommensurability or undercommensurability of cultural and ethical norms) does exist between cultures and correspondingly between their moral codes or values at a certain level. This is not denied here. However, there are limits to how much individual moral systems can differ from each other. In order to be recognized as moral systems there must be a common reference point, or system of coordinates, as Davidson demands for alternative conceptual schemes.[16] We can again borrow concepts from the field of linguistics and say that just as there are many context-sensitive rules in the description of any language, there are context-sensitive ethical codes in communities, but this does not preclude the presence of some context-neutral rules. I submit the following thoughts for consideration: supposition of the context-neutral rules assumes that there is a basic moral fabric in all societies, all communities and cultures, which holds their members, human beings, together. This should not be conflated with the old universalism, nor with any objectionable form of essentialism (namely, that all humans have the same essence). Since we talk about minimal agreements in norms, this view concedes relativism up to a limit but rejects it when it militates against the basic fabric of the human world.

There are many faces of morality, but at least two main sides of morality deserve our attention here. One side can be called the rational side, the general or common morality dictated by the common concerns of humans and being the necessary constituent of any human society. The other is the less than rational, the historically and environmentally conditioned, hence the contingent side of morality, which varies from culture to culture. If we are not too squeamish about the use of certain words, we may call the first the universal or general morality, which constitutes the basic fabric or minimal moral standard that I have talked about, and the second, the particular morality, most of which arises from the loyalty of a group to a preferred way of life, such preference being also historically conditioned. A sort of relativism may exist with regard to the latter, but the former, by definition, should be nonrelativistic. It is the latter kind that creates the hardest problems for our understanding and for commensurability of the "alien" 's values. Much talk about a facile form of relativism that I have alluded to in the previous section and that has sometimes captured the minds of the soft-headed liberalists today, is due to a lack of understanding of these problems. It has persuaded most people to take seriously the (illicit) generalization that all moral standards are relative. Very often the locally conditioned mores of a society pass for its morality. We may call the latter the *ethical* code of a particular society to distinguish it from the basic minimal moral standard, which is or should be, I claim, common to all societies today. Here I am drawing from the insights of the traditional ethicists of India, who, entangled as they were in the complicated labyrinth of the group- and caste-related ethical duties, made a fundamental distinction between the *sādhāraṇa dharma* (general moral duties) and *viśeṣa dharma* (particular moral codes).

The particular side of morality may be unique to each culture or individual community, for it is connected (causally or otherwise) with the particular community's distinctive way of life, its institutions, membership conditions, and values. Each culture has certain unique rules, virtues, and obligations. Family relationship, marriage rules, interpersonal behaviors, some rules of sexual conduct, and so forth are examples of such particular morality. Religion adds another dimension to the diversity of morals. Each religion has its own particularity as well as its sectarian varieties. Each religion consists of a belief in the superhuman origin of a doctrine embracing norms and ultimate goals as well as of a group of people who hold the belief and have an obligation to comply with such norms (for example, a particular way by which to live and behave with others). In this way diversity in world religions is a major contributory factor to diversity as well as to the relativity of a particular morality.

The general and culture-invariant side of morality can, on the other hand, be illustrated in very general terms and sometimes be left open to contextual interpretation. This, however, need not, and should not, detract anything from its universality or generality. Formulation of a principle depends upon the contingencies of a particular linguistic convention generating a limited number of expressions, and hence the universality of such formulation may often be open to challenge.

In fact one can use the point made by Bernard Williams about a "thicker" ethical concept of some "hypertraditional" society by referring to the main example of a certain school slang.[17] The ethical concepts of this hypertraditional society may be such that the external observer (anthropologist) may be barred from saying what the locals say, but not barred from recognizing that what they say can be true. Even the well-known "disquotation principle" about truth does not in this case require that what the members of the hypertraditional society say, involving such "thicker" ethical concepts, cannot be true.

It may be worthwhile to start with the common elements in the ethicoreligious teachings of the three or four Indian religions. (One may inquire whether they are associated with certain "thicker" ethical concepts or not.) There are at least four moral virtues which they all recommend and they are also common to other world religions. First, there is what we call respect for life, which I would like to call nonviolence (not strictly in the Gandhian sense), thereby slightly broadening its scope. It is presumably derived from the virtue of kindness or compassion for others. One of the fundamental constituents of common morality entails this principle, and it is also necessary for the adequate maintenance of any worthwhile social life. We do not, however, need a supernatural agency for the imposition of this value (or any other value); human rationality can be the legitimate arbiter of value. It is significant to note that in Indian traditional religions, such as Buddhism, no supernatural power is invoked as the legitimate arbiter of value.

Respect for life or nonviolence requires that human life should not unnecessarily be endangered, and that wanton killing (of humans as well as animals) must be prohibited. No person should act in such a way as to harm the life of his fellow beings. Some qualifications may be necessary, for there may be moral justification for taking an animal's life or even a human life. Besides this justification may vary from person to person, or from society to society. Self-preservation or self-defense (against *real* but not *perceived* threats) may be one allowable justification which has universal application. Besides, abortion and euthanasia are examples of wanton killing according to some, not according to others. Hence, some sort of contextual interpretation may be necessary here. But I am personally skeptical of such justification according to the varying contexts. For in most cases such justification is hardly moral; it is prudential or otherwise. Hence, if from a moral point of view we have to maintain the universality of the said principle, we have to exclude most of such contextual interpretation. Mahatma Gandhi's famous example was that of a snake: whether to allow it to bite a saint or have it killed. And even there he was not sure whether an exception can be made. (On this point, see P. S. Jaini.)[18] Besides, if certain killings (for personal gain, or sadistic pleasure, or because the victim is "racially inferior") are permitted by certain particular moral codes—if, in other words, there is conflict between universal and particular morality— then according to the view I am defending, the universal morality should override the particular. Otherwise it will go against the basic fabric of the human society as a whole. To allow somebody to kill a human being for a reason, justifiably or not, is also to use the person as a means, not an end. This goes against the celebrated Kantian doctrine: "Treat humanity, whether in your own person or in that of another, always as an end withal and never merely as a means." Kant's own explanation is, of course, that a human being must be treated as an autonomous agent.[19] But even so, the connection between the respect for life and an interpretation of this Kantian universal principle can possibly be shown, although I shall not go into it here.

Among other moral virtues, claimed to be universal, is truth-telling or the prohibition against lying. Again, social life would be impossible without this prohibition. Kant claimed this prohibition to be absolute. Here, the Indian religions, especially Hinduism in its *dharma-śāstras* (treatises on moral duties), make an exception. As against Kant they hold that the obligation to tell the truth to a would-be murderer in search of his intended victim can be violated. There is an interesting *Mahābhārata* episode which illustrated and illuminated various facets of this argument nicely.[20] The other two moral virtues recommended by the Indian religions may or may not constitute the fabric of universal morality today. But therein lies some insight which seems worth exploring. One is the prohibition against stealing, conditional upon the presence of the institution of property. We can take property here not necessarily as personal or private, for there are public and community properties. The simple Buddhist way of formulating the virtue is "not grabbing or taking what is not yours." As long as the institution of property remains a common factor of all human societies, the universality of this prohibition would not be unfounded. Besides, "free-loaders" and "free-riders" are even today terms of moral reproach in most societies. Excessive greed for money, power, or personal gain is condemned, even in today's society.

The universality of the fourth prohibition would perhaps be most debatable. The prohibition of adultery is conditional upon the institution of marriage. But it cannot be universal. However, I prefer again the Buddhist way of putting it: "not to play false, in the sexual intimation, with the partner." This may not depend upon the institution of marriage. Violation of sexual ethics, when such ethics might be allowed contextual interpretation, depending upon the societies or groups, seems to be morally reprehensible. Rape may be a particular case of this prohibition.

One question now lurks behind, which I must answer at this stage. By occasionally allowing contextual interpretation, albeit to a limited extent, am I not conceding some sort of relativism, which I have previously denounced? My answer is simple: if this sort of relativism is conceded, it is still very different from the very "exciting" sort of relativism that I have denounced already. Alternatively, we may rule that the last virtue may not constitute the fabric of the universal morality. Contextual interpretation is needed because the universality of some of these principles suffers (and shrinks) when we deal, as we must, with a particular formulation of them in reference to particular languages or social practice.

There may be other moral virtues or principles or obligations which could form the fabric of the basic universal morality in the same vein. For example, we could add justice, social responsibility, and obligation to choose good (or a lesser evil) rather than evil. Even some notion of justice was not absent from the set of virtues extolled in traditional India. For instance, in the *Sāṃkhya-kārikā,* verse 2, the Vedic religious rituals were denounced, for they supposedly produced results (wealth for some and poverty and unhappiness for others) that were unfair, unjust, and iniquitous *(aviśuddhi-kṣayātiśaya).* Besides, a common argument against theism (in Buddhism and Jainism) was that if God created the world, how could he create inequalities (see also *Vedānta-sūtra,* 2.1. 32–34).

I base this moral fabric upon what I take to be the common concerns of all *known* human societies. They may be called *relative to all known reasons,* all things considered (reminiscent of R. Carnap's notion of total evidence in inductive reasoning). If any human society is discovered by the anthropologists on the face of this globe where one or several of such concerns are *proven* to be absent, I believe this notion of universal moral fabric should be modified. I concede this possibility.

Proceeding from a different vein, one may develop the notion of a general morality taking the happiness of all creatures and the alleviation of their pain or suffering as basic and then recommend action guides which must be obeyed by all. Alternatively, one can formulate a defensible concept of *human need* and then talk about such a need-based general ethic which would be culture-invariant and agent-neutral. Human beings as biological creatures need food, clothing, and shelter; there is need for nutritional requirements, for participation in social life, and so forth. Pluralism or even occasional allowance for context-dependence does not stand in the way of defending the view that there is a basic or minimal moral fabric which is universal and context-transcendent. This does not deny the diversity of human goals, nor does it concede the old singularism or moral jingoism or even the convergence of all human goals through rationality as conceived by the nineteenth-century liberals. Phillipa Foot has remarked:

> Granted that it is wrong to assume identity of aims between people of different cultures; nevertheless there is a great deal that all men have in common. All need affection, the cooperation of others, a place in a community and help in trouble."[21]

I concede that the formulation of the principles above may be shown to be inadequate to meet the claim of universality. I have said that their universality seems to shrink when we deal, as we must, with a particular formulation of them in a particular language with a given culture. The fault here, it seems to me, lies more with the contingencies of a given linguistic apparatus, and/or of the cultural condition (in the context of which the particular formulation has been given) than with the principles themselves. Arguably, one may say that the particular formulation captures the principle in the sense of illustrating it, although the formulation itself suffers from lack of generality. This is, I believe, the problem with any notion of universality.

I have touched upon the politics of relativism in my introductory comments. However, there is more to this politics of relativism. It has been noted by some postmodernists in Europe that the traditional non-relativistic (singularistic) self-understanding of the West has thrust itself towards the reduction, absorption, and appropriation of "the Other" to itself. The Western conquest of the world, its imperialism and its domination (both in the material world and in the thought-world), and the resulting violence (in both thought and action)—all these can be seen as the attempt to avoid and contain the disturbance and ruptures that the strangers, the absolute other, may create. Against this background, the concession to the incommensurability of the other and the acceptance of a relativistic stance has been, and certainly would be, welcome. However, even relativism can be a tool in the hand of the oppressor. For example, a "liberal" colonialist may follow a policy of benign and not-so-benign neglect and thereby resist successfully the liberal forces in the native's own tradition and let superstitions, conservatism, and fundamentalism take over. The important point is that singularism does not always foster imperialism, nor does relativism necessarily encourage liberalism. It may encourage pseudoliberalism and love for exotic rituals. The latter can easily be a subterfuge for the implicit claim of superiority for one's own cultural practice. Prolonged political domination of the *other* cannot be stopped (even by the politics of relativism), short of a cultural conquest and the cultural bankruptcy of the *other*. However, during confrontation and interaction, both sides, the dominant and the subordinate, are bound to change almost imperceptibly, and there will be, as I have already said, value change, value rejection, and value mutation. For (resounding a comment once made by Hegel, we may say) the slave can change or influence the master much as the master can change the slave.

In conclusion, I wish to point out that in order to sustain any acceptable form of social life, a basic fabric of universal morality is absolutely necessary. And if our talk of human rights in today's world has to receive any significant defense (if, that is, the Declaration of Human Rights of 1948 is to have any point), such rights should be based upon the notion of the basic universal moral fabric that I have tried to explore here.[22] Imitating our poet-philosopher Tagore, I might add that "where knowledge is free" and "where the clear stream of reason has not lost its way into the dreary desert sand of dead habit," there and then probably we can make this basic and universal moral fabric a little bit more visible to others than in today's world mad with war, bigotry, fundamentalism, and power-brokerage.

Notes

1. Sir Isaiah Berlin, *Four Essays on Liberty* (London: Oxford University Press, 1969), p. 151.

2. Berlin, *Four Essays,* p. 154.

3. Charles Taylor, "The Diversity of Goods," in *Utilitarianism and Beyond,* ed. by Amartya Sen and Bernard Williams (Cambridge: University of Cambridge Press, 1982).

4. Bernard Williams, *Moral Luck* (Cambridge: Cambridge University Press, 1981); emphases added.

5. Richard J. Bernstein, "Incommensurability and Otherness Revisited," in this volume.

6. Gilbert Harman, "Moral Relativism Defended," in *Relativism: Cognitive and Moral,* ed. by Jack W. Meiland and Michael Krausz (Notre Dame: University of Notre Dame Press, 1982).

7. Bimal Matilal, *Confrontation of Cultures: S. G. Deuskar Lectures on Indian History and Culture* (Calcutta: C.S.S.S., 1988), p. 15; also "Ethical Relativism and Confrontation of Cultures," in *Relativism,* ed. by M. Krausz (Notre Dame: University of Notre Dame Press, 1989).

8. W. V. Quine, *Word and Object* (Cambridge, Massachusetts: Massachusetts Institute of Technology Press, 1960).

9. Thomas Kuhn, *The Structure of Scientific Revolutions* (Chicago: University of Chicago Press, 1970), 2d ed.

10. Isaac Levi, *Hard Choices* (Cambridge: Cambridge University Press, 1986), pp. 40–41.

11. Richard Rorty, *The Consequences of Pragmatism* (Minneapolis: University of Minnesota Press, 1982).

12. Allan Bloom, *The Closing of the American Mind* (New York: Simon and Schuster, 1987).

13. Matilal, *Confrontation of Cultures,* p. 15.

14. Bernard Williams, *Ethics and the Limits of Philosophy* (London: Fontana and Collins, 1985).

15. Matilal, "Ethical Relativism."

16. Donald Davidson, "On the Very Idea of a Conceptual Scheme, in *Inquiries into Truth and Interpretation* (Oxford: Oxford University Press, 1984).

17. Williams, *Ethics and Limits,* pp. 143–145.

18. P. S. Jaini, *The Jaina Path of Purification* (Berkeley: University of California Press, 1979), p. 315, in a review of Jaini by Bimal K. Matilal, *Bulletin of the School of Oriental and African Studies* (London, 1980).

19. Immanuel Kant, *Fundamental Principles of the Metaphysic of Morals,* 10th ed., trans. by T. K. Abbot (London), sec. 2, p. 56.

20. Bimal Matilal, "Moral Dilemmas: Insights from Indian Epics," in *Moral Dilemmas and the Mahābhārata,* ed. by Bimal K. Matilal (Delhi: I.I.A.S., Shimla, 1989).

21. Philippa Foot, "Moral Relativism," in Jack W. Meiland and Michael Krausz, eds., *Relativism: Cognitive and Moral* (Notre Dame: University of Notre Dame Press, 1982), p. 164.

22. A. J. M. Milne, *Human Rights and Human Diversity* (Albany: State University of New York Press, 1986).

JIANG TIANJI

THE PROBLEM OF RELATIVISM

The problem of relativism is a complex one. There are many relativistic doctrines, and relativism is variously contrasted with realism, objectivism, foundationalism, rationalism, and, of course, with the alternative absolutism or universalism, by different authors. For a clarification of the problematic, I propose first of all to distinguish semantic concepts from epistemic concepts in the discussion of this problem. The concept "truth" on the standard two-value logic is a semantic concept denoting the relationship between a belief or a sentence and an extra-linguistic fact, however you construe this latter term. As a semantic concept, "truth" is thus absolute. One has to redefine the concept as an epistemic one, by introducing the cognitive subject or speaker for whom the sentence is accepted or acceptable, to obtain the doctrine of relative truth. And a critique of relativism which would condemn this doctrine as being self-refuting has again returned to the concept's semantic sense instead of following the relativist's redefinition of it. This is not, of course, the intent of relativism.

"Rationality," on the other hand, is an epistemic concept, denoting the relationship of an action or belief and the reasons for its choice in distinction to the causes for determining it. Having reasons seems to be a distinctive characteristic of human action and belief. It has been obvious to everyone that different people may have different reasons for the same belief or action, which they choose from among alternatives. That rationality is relative to the subject or speaker seems to be unquestionable. I believe that what I term the doctrine of local rationality would express the real intent of cognitive relativism. This is because speakers belonging to different communities, relying on different basic beliefs or background assumptions and armed with different intellectual resources, will naturally have different, but never the same, reasons for their beliefs and actions dealing with the same or similar problems in similar situations in life.

Relativism, therefore, is simply defined as the doctrine that there are no universal standards: no universal standards of rationality for cognitive relativism, or no universal standards of morality for moral relativism, or no universal standards of aesthetic appraisal for aesthetic relativism. The primary focus of this essay is on cognitive relativism, and our discussion will concentrate on the doctrine of local rationality, given that universal standards of rationality are denied by relativists. The doctrine of relative truth is neglected altogether, because it is a controversial and very complicated doctrine. Anyway in the two most important forms of relativism, the semantic concept "truth" need not be used at all, while the epistemic concepts—"reason," "knowledge," "acceptance," and "consensus"—occupy a central place.

Transcultural Relativism and Transtheoretical Relativism

There are two opposing paradigms within cultural anthropology: unilinear evolutionism and cultural relativism. The evolutionists identify rationality with science and conclude that primitive people lack rationality because they lack science. Later, primitive societies are granted some sort of rationality that is deficient because of its pseudo-scientific and prescientific cognition. Tylor and Frazer saw scientific method and its product as the progressive force that would sooner or later vanquish superstition and other forms of unreason altogether. This science-based arrogance of the nineteenth-century evolutionists considers Western science the highest achievement of rationality, and the society that uses science and technology tops all the rest. They see anthropology's goal as charting the growth of reason through the long convoluted human career. Frazer did so by describing the evolutionary pattern in the tangled skein of human thought in which the primordial black threads of magic give way slowly to the red stain of religion, itself ultimately to be purified into the clean white cloth of science. Thus to discern the forms and the developmental pattern of thought and to chart the growth of rationality should be the prime focus of anthropology.

Cultural relativism, on the contrary, objects to this simple-minded unilinear evolutionism, which sins against alien cultures by imposing one's own standards and values on them. It advocates actually the thesis of incommensurability between different cultures, even though this term is not explicitly used. It insists that each alien culture and each society has to be understood in terms of its own values, beliefs, and ideals rather than by adopting a transculturally neutral standpoint which takes them all to be measured by a single standard. Franz Boas and his followers refused to see any hierarchy among peoples, and an evolutionary scheme linking different phases of cultures in the manner of Tylor and Frazer. Cultural anthropology, as put by Herskovits, shall lead us to see "the validity of each set of norms for the people whose lives are guided by them and the values they represent."[1] Most important is how to interpret and understand alien peoples and alien cultures. This problem has been brought into focus by hermeneutics and neo-Wittgensteinians. They insist that our ability to make sense of social phenomena is ultimately dependent on their relation to forms of activity that we have learned to participate in. The practices of one's own society form the innermost core of one's study of alien cultures. These constitute the paradigms to which we ultimately revert, whether for the sake of bringing forward similarities or differences. This implies that in interpreting and trying to understand an alien culture we cannot but employ our own background beliefs, values, and standards—in a word, our own conceptual framework; but this would not be imposing on other peoples if we did not use our own standards to evaluate alien cultures and measure their status in the development of rationality. Rationality within a given society can only be measured by the standards of the society itself. As a result, most or all beliefs and actions of different peoples are found to be more or less equally rational by their own standards. This is local rationality. But the rationality of the local standards themselves is a further question yet to be tackled. Relativism usually allows comparison but disallows evaluation. It argues that all evaluations are in terms of some standard or other, and standards derive from cultures; no evaluation can escape the web of culture, and hence all evaluation is culture-bound.

Now the crux of the divergence and opposition between the evolutionary paradigm and the relativist paradigm is the question of whether or not we can discriminate a better or worse society or a more or less successful culture. Before expatiating on this question, let us first touch on the parallel paradigm shift in the history and philosophy of science since the early sixties.

The rationality debates in the history of science are more remarkable still than those in cultural anthropology, because natural science, usually considered the most objective part of human knowledge, is least expected to be vulnerable to relativism. In the period of the ascendancy of logical empiricism, philosophers were eager to work out different techniques for theory choice or different sets of rules for reaching rational agreement in scientific issues. Their efforts were without avail. It seems to be generally agreed that no algorithm can be constructed for choice among competing scientific theories. Kuhn, in his *Structure of Scientific Revolutions* (1962), introduced scientific communities to replace logical calculi for taking charge of the job. The philosopher of science who used to be "the guardian of scientific rationality" has now to concede his place of honor to the sociologist and/or psychologist. Inspired by Kuhn's insight, the sociology of science has started and elaborated a "Strong Program" with its radical relativism. Developing Kuhn's ideas about theory-choice and extending them beyond the boundaries of exact science, Barry Barnes and David Bloor of the Strong Program have propounded a sociological theory of local acceptability to substitute for the principle of universal rationality of the modern scientific method. They have argued that local acceptance goes with local modes of cultural transmission, of socialization and social control, of power and authority; the scientific task is to trace these links, investigating the "specific local causes" of beliefs being held.[2] So the explanation of theory acceptance, and not reasons of theory/choice, is sought. On their doctrine that "rules of arguments and criteria of truth are internal to a social system," that "truth" and "rationality" are to be redefined as "internal to given societies," and that it is "the relevant local consensus" (Mary Hesse)[3] which determines what to accept, there could not be any valid distinction between what is true, reasonable and explanatory and what counts as knowledge, on the one hand, and what is locally accepted as such on the other. "For the relativist," Barnes and Bloor have said, "there is no sense attached to the idea that some standards or beliefs are *really* rational as distinct from merely locally accepted as such."[4] In the history of science, Kuhn has only detected a "rationality gap" during scientific revolutions, with rationality still prevailing in normal science. But what the Strong Program sociologists are espousing is a version of radical relativism. The rationality debates between opposing camps are still going on.

The parallel paradigm shifts sketched above have brought forth transcultural and transtheoretical relativisms. They support each other, just as their opponents, unilinear evolutionism and inductivism, have strengthened each other's positions. All these versions of universalism see science and the scientific method as the apex of human rationality, a measuring rod for ranking peoples and cultures in terms of the stage of their intellectual development, or a "big ditch" for dividing the modern scientific world-view from all the traditional world-views. But the thesis of incommensurability has brought modern science and its method under suspicion, hence undermined any evolutionary scheme of the Tylor-Frazer type. Moreover, conceptual incommensurability seems to be explanatory for the more obvious fact of cultural divergence and cultural incommensurability, and it has consolidated much more the gains of cultural relativism, just as cultural relativism and its anthropological method have inspired and given birth to the cognitive relativism in natural science in the first place.

Arguments Pro and Con

The most plausible arguments for relativism are as follows. (1) It is an obvious fact that diverse religions, moral systems, customs, social institutions, and belief systems have been discovered. The extent of cultural divergence is often so astounding that it can only be explained by different criteria of validity and different standards of rationality. Now if, as amply demonstrated by anthropological evidence, universalism and unilinear evolutionism are to be discarded, for we could never have a cross-cultural super-standard to adjudicate between diverse standards, the only alternative seems to be relativism. (2) The recent sociological turn in philosophy and the human sciences generally has effected a radical change in the fundamental notions of philosophy, meaning, truth, and rationality. The internal, individualized epistemology of both empiricism and rationalism seemed to give way to an external, socialized epistemology, of which the central idea is community practice. That different practices bring forth different norms to govern individual behavior and beliefs attests to a diversity of rationality standards. These norms may be initially only descriptive of the diverse ways and manners of social activities,[5] but they would begin to have prescriptive force if most members of the community follow them and judge the actions of each other by them. Different practices thus generate different standards of rationality. Once you admit local rationality, relativism seems to follow. (3) Traditional philosophers may advance the objection that even if diverse religions, moralities, and belief systems—in a word, diverse cultures—are an undeniable fact, radical incommensurability, and hence relativism, does not follow. For diversity is explicable by different environments and different forms of social organization wherein peoples make their livelihood and carry on their social activities. That they must make a living and carry on much the same kind of social actions—laboring, getting married, procreating, dominating and being dominated, oppressing and being oppressed, exploiting and being exploited, slaying and making war—is also an undeniable fact. Even if their diverse behavior could not be measured by the use of a universal standard and arranged along an evolutionary scale, we may still adjudicate on their comparative degrees of function-fulfilling, of efficiency, of success in self-realization—in a word, on their comparative degrees of "being civilized." But this objection presupposes a transcultural super-standard, which gains its plausibility only from men everywhere being the same kind of animal having the same sort of biological functions, and possessing roughly the same pattern of psychological traits. It can be countered by relativists that the inference from a common biological and psychological base to a civilizational and cultural universal is incorrect. The gap between them has not been bridged, and the inferential "leap" is therefore unjustified. (4) Finally, the strength of relativism also rests on the fact that we have so far been unable to give a unique characterization of the methodology of science and, *a fortiori,* that we cannot expect to draw on the theory of scientific method for a unique model of rationality. Divergent and incompatible theories of science are bound to be matched by divergent and incompatible models of rationality. That no universal paradigm-independent and culture-independent standards of scientific rationality, and also of morality and aesthetic appraisal are ever to be hoped for, as relativists insistently claim, is most plausible.

Now for the objections to relativism: (1) Critics usually object to the so-called myth of the framework which takes speakers of various communities for prisoners trapped in closed linguistic frameworks. The critic identifies relativism with what the "myth" claims, and thinks that to explode the myth is to refute relativism. Perhaps no relativist ever denies the possibility of interpreting and understanding an alien framework or an alien culture. The proper endeavor of anthropology and the history of science, for relativism, is just that. The relativists have tried their utmost by employing special techniques to interpret and understand alien belief systems and alien behavior. The notion that different cultures and paradigms have their own particular rules or methodologies does not imply the partition of either human beings or scientists into a number of windowless capsules, that is, communities between which all communication is impossible. Relativism does not preclude cross-cultural or cross-theoretical intelligibility. (2) Perhaps the myth of the frameworks implies also what is sometimes termed the "tyranny of the framework," that each community or culture is a law unto itself, because it prescribes its own rules for justification of beliefs and behavior, and all outside criticisms and any evaluation in terms of external standards are automatically eliminated. This objection is only half true, for relativists do not recognize any supercultural standard for adjudication on the rules that are culture-bound. But this does not mean that we must always evaluate any exotic and bizarre manner and custom by the alien standards. Whenever I make an evaluation of anything, I make it in terms of the standards of my own culture—otherwise it cannot be my evaluation—only that I may not impose the standards I accept and operate by on alien cultures as universal standards for ranking them. Certainly we should try to *understand* what other people say and do in terms of their own standards, but understanding is not equivalent to acquiescence. It is possible for us to understand cannibalism as practiced formerly by some tribes, in terms of the categories and values of the alien culture; that does not commit us to condoning it. For instance, Jarvie has made the accusation that "relativism cannot function as a basis for anthropology because it leads to an all-tolerant nihilism."[6] Such facile condemnation of the relativistic program is unfounded. (3) Now we come to the well-known "bridgehead argument." As Steve Lukes puts it, "Barnes and Bloor claim that the accumulating evidence from anthropology and the history of science overwhelmingly supports thoroughgoing relativism; but from this argument it follows that, unless relativism is denied, that evidence would never show up."[7] But does it? The argument rests on the claim that identification of beliefs, seeing the actor's world from within, requires a bridgehead of true and rational beliefs. Successful translation and radical interpretation of alien beliefs must presuppose "what a rational man cannot fail to believe in simple perceptual situations, organized by rules of coherent judgment, which a rational man cannot fail to subscribe to."[8] This claim develops from Davidson's logical argument about how to discriminate a meaningful disagreement from meaningless one. For Davidson this "depends entirely on a foundation—some foundation—in agreement."[9] What constitutes this foundation or bridgehead is either ordinary perceptual judgments (Hollis) or "primary theory" (Horton), which are regarded as common to all cultures. The knot is: are all these beliefs necessarily shared by all cultures? Does it not beg the question of understanding an alien culture? Relativists could object that, in the first place, we have to know how the world is "cut up" by different cultures, because the ontology underlying a culture depends entirely on the classification scheme it uses. We cannot simply assume that these schemes are all the same. In the second place, the only possible means of identifying an alien belief is through the observation of a person's overt behavior, for we do not understand his or her speech. But to understand the meaning of even a piece of overt behavior, we have to take into account the role it plays in the context of other activities of the alien. This presupposes that we already have an independent understanding of the alien's life. Therefore, there are no conceptual grounds for supposing that the so-called bridgehead actions (not to speak of perceptual *judgments* and primary *theory*) enjoy a privileged status in the interpretation and understanding of an alien life-form. *A fortiori,* we have no reason to suppose that they are necessarily common to and shared by all cultures. That the evidence about all these divergent belief systems and behavior in alien cultures and divergent theories in different paradigms "show up" at all, and, moreover, are to be understood, is mainly due to the use of hermeneutic techniques by anthropologists and the historians of science. (4) More important still is the "big ditch argument." It develops from the science-based criterion of nineteenth-century evolutionism. Modern science and technology are regarded as a gulf separating Western culture from all primitive and traditional cultures. As Lukes pointed out, "from this argument it follows that judgments of cognitive superiority of later over earlier phases of science and of scientific over prescientific modes of thought are not and cannot be relative to a particular scheme."[10] This means that there is a superparadigmatic standard of rationality after all. This argument, most emphatically voiced by Ernst Gellner, has also been very circumspectly employed by Charles Taylor. Taylor makes several important points in his discussion of rationality. First, he agrees with the relativist's point of view that we must speak of a plurality of standards of rationality because there are incommensurable cultures and activities. Second, a plurality of standards does not rule out judgments of superiority. On the contrary, it is precisely incommensurability that opens the door to such judgments. This is where he disagrees with relativism. Third, judgments of comparative superiority are not made by any super-cultural standard already accepted by both sides. *Such* standards are not available. Here he seems to agree with the relativist again. Fourth, different standards can be rated as superior or inferior; hence the rationalities can also be ranked as higher and fuller or lower and poorer. Here he seems to disagree with relativism again. But some standard, explicit or implicit, must be used in any ranking. This would be a superstandard for ranking different forms of rationality. The superstandard may not be accepted by both sides, nay, it is rarely so accepted. It is rather used by a third party, in this case by an anthropologist or a historian of science, who first formulates the criterion for the evaluation of different belief systems and cultures. The crucial point now is: is this super-standard "internal" to the evaluator's culture? Lukes has emphatically denied such culture-dependence to the judgments of superiority, and affirmed that they are derived from the "Cartesian absolute conception of knowledge"[11] that furnished the super-standard for comparative appraisal. Taylor ranks rationalities by the super-standard—achievement of a more or less perspicuous order, or, in other words, achievement of a greater or smaller understanding of the world. But he does not say whether or not this standard is "internal" to our theoretical culture in contrast to other atheoretical cultures. This has to be decided. Whether comparative appraisal is possible or not hinges on this question.

Local Rationality and Global Rationality

I propose to distinguish moderate from radical relativism by its recognition of global rationality standards besides local ones. Radical relativism would regard any rationality as local, internal to a particular culture or community, whereas universalism upholds a unique standard of rationality in place of a plurality of standards, hence any violation of the unique standard would be condemned as irrational. Moderate relativism, with its admitting the global standard of rationality, is confronted with the question, whence does it come? If it is the most recent form of rationality, then it cannot but be an imposition of our own local rationality on other communities and cultures. Science-based nineteenth-century evolutionism is just such an example. If, on the other hand, it comes *a priori,* being presuppositions or ultimate conditions of linguistic communication and human thinking that render rational justification of beliefs or behavior possible in the first place, then it is abstract and absolute, offering no clues at all to the explanation of the growth of rationality and the occurrence of a plurality of rationalities in cultures of the world. This is why universalism has now been generally discarded. But radical relativism fares no better. With a plurality of windowless communities or closed cultures, which do not interact with one another, any culture would be precluded from going through a regenerating process due to outside influence, and would cling to traditional practices or even rigid formalities in dealing with all situations. The culture will by and by become exhausted and the people domesticated to this culture will sooner or later disappear from the face of the earth. Such an account of imagined situations will not be borne out by anthropological and historical evidence. Some cultures are bound to react on each other, and there would be a great number of people participating in them, thus belonging to different communities and submitting to different normalities or norms during their lifetimes. The spectacle of many separate and isolated isles of culture spread diachronically or synchronically all over the world is extremely unbelievable. This is the *reductio ad absurdum* of radical relativism which, just like universalism, could not explain the fact that rationality extends as well as grows. It is just unreasonable to deny, I think, an overall or global rationality as it is to deny a plurality of local rationalities. But whence the standards of global rationality? How are they to be distinguished from those of local rationality?

Here we have to rely on the difference between what is just normal and what is both normal and normative. What is initially only normal for any community or culture might in time become normative for other cultures as well. But it is perhaps never the case that everything that is normal for a particular culture, even for the most recent and advanced one, becomes normative for all other cultures. This is because what is normal or norms (in the sense of customary behavior) for a particular culture are of diverse natures. Some norms are conventional, and are valid only for the said culture. Others may be natural, and hence are potentially, and even actually, normative for other cultures, some of them or all of them. The difference between what is just normal and what is both normal and normative rests on the distinction between what is conventional and what is natural. For instance, certain forms of technology or a minimum degree of technological control are needed for every society, including primitive ones. They are therefore natural, whereas complete submissiveness to nature is only normal and conventional for some Oriental societies or some religious communities in them, and is therefore unnatural. Again, a certain degree of convenience and comfort is normal and natural, but the artificial wants and extravagances of modern consumer society or of some groups in it are conventional and normal only for those who can afford to indulge in them. They are conventional wants instead of natural needs and hence unnatural. Here we have to draw on Wittgenstein's general view on the normal and the normative for clarifying our distinction between local and global rationalities.

Both conventionalists and relativists appeal to what is normal and traditional to justify a practice, or a certain way of seeing and doing things. They claim that no justification in what we say and do can be found by attending to what goes on in individuals, as foundationalists of both empiricist and rationalist schools used to maintain. On the contrary, such justification could only be found in what is normal. But conventionalists would consider normalcy the sole basis of justification; for them the ways of talking and doing things that are normal in a community must be accepted. Wittgenstein did not advocate such uncritical conventionalism. That he was continuously concerned with the shifting of forms of life, the availability of alternative ways of doing things, and the conventionality of criteria suggests that rational justification for a practice cannot depend on mere normalcy alone. Perhaps there could be no justification for our practices at all. Here Wittgenstein looked more like a relativist than a conventionalist. All such labeling of Wittgenstein is, however, controversial. But his account of what is normal and what is normative will make his position clearer in this regard.

Wittgenstein's account is primarily about the elementary practices: ways of counting, assessing volumes, classifying biological species, and using names generally. But we could extend Wittgenstein's arguments and conclusions to include other cases, those complex practices investigated by anthropologists and historians of science.

Wittgenstein emphasized that normal ways of seeing and describing things are subject to some evolution. Appeals to what is normal in a given moment cannot by themselves rationally justify our manners of seeing and doing things. Our ways of thinking and speaking of things would be normal and justifiable only for us. But Wittgenstein would not say this is a rational justification. Justification only for a social group or a community is what we term local rationality.

According to the Strong Program of Barnes and Bloor, knowledge is taken to be what is accepted as such in our culture. Now that "knowledge," "truth," and "rationality" have been redefined as "internal to given societies," they proceed to deny that there is any valid distinction between what is true and reasonable, and what counts as knowledge, on the one hand, and what is locally accepted as such, on the other. "For the relativist," they say, "there is no sense attached to the idea that some standards or beliefs are really rational as distinct from merely locally accepted as such."[12] Thus, what epistemologists study is the rules accepted as rational in their own society. Although Barnes and Bloor make a distinction between cognitively binding rules and mere social conventions, this distinction is not the same as what Wittgenstein distinguished as the normative from the merely normal. Their locally accepted "rational" rules are not what is normative for Wittgenstein. Wittgenstein would not say that what is normal in a community or a culture must always be accepted. Only when what is normal is also in part constitutive of our forms of life must it be so. The distinction between what is normative from what is merely normal is just what distinguishes the cases in which there are no alternatives for us to a normal practice from the cases in which there are. When a practice is constitutive of our form of life, there are no genuine alternatives, which means that the practice could not be other than it is. Hence it cannot be abandoned or altered. It belongs to what Wittgenstein could term "the common behavior of mankind" (*Philosophical Investigations,* 206). Wittgenstein accepted a translation of "Lebensform" as "ways of life of human beings" (*Nachlass* no. 226). He claimed: "And thinking and inferring (like counting) is of course bounded for us, not by an arbitrary definition, but by natural limits corresponding to the body of what can be called the role of thinking or inferring in our life. Nevertheless, the laws of inference can be said to compel us, that is to say, as other laws in human society" (*Remarks on the Foundations of Mathematics,* Part I, 116.). All these quotations indicate that "our form of life" should not be interpreted as "life of a group" or "communal life," or "the common behavior of mankind" but rather as "ways of human life." Evidently what is constitutive of our form of life is not merely what is normal in a given community, but what is normative for our life as human beings.

Wittgenstein, of course, unlike universalists, also takes notice of the cases in which there are alternatives to the normal practice prevailing in a community. Given that these normal practices are not constitutive of our form of life, there naturally are diverse ways of thinking and doing things under different circumstances. Hence a plurality of local rationalities, as relativists invariably claim we have obtained even in natural science, not to speak of religions, ideologies, and moral systems, is nothing but local acceptance or consensus. It is the classification scheme or conceptual framework of a culture that furnishes criteria of identity for things, that is, conditions under which things may be called thus and so; without such criteria there would be no possibility of making sense of the world. But criteria will not make logically sufficient conditions of the state of affairs for which they are criteria, and the satisfaction of them does not justify our saying "X is F" or "here is an F." Yet Wittgenstein nevertheless supposed that "To use a word without a justification does not mean to use it without right" (*Philosophical Investigations,* 289). Criteria are needed especially when a normal practice of calling things is abrogated. According to Stanley Cavell, "Wittgenstein's criteria are appealed to when 'we don't know our way about', when we are lost with respect to our words and the world they anticipate. Then we start to find ourselves by finding out and declaring the criteria upon which we are in agreement."[13] But under what circumstances would our description of things be rationally justifiable? Is it justified when we recognize ourselves by finding out that we are in agreement with others in community? Cavell emphasized that "the search for community" is also the "search for reason" or the claim to reason. Of course it is. But the *claim* to reason is not identical with rationality itself. It is only when our beliefs are expressed by sentences that "we would all say" in certain circumstances; then they are rationally justifiable. And this "all" should not be confined to any given community, but be inclusive of most or all human beings. Therefore what is much wider than communal agreement is needed for rational justification of our beliefs, and such agreement is dependent on circumstances being what they are.

Wittgenstein's strategy of imagining practices radically different from our normal ones is intended for testing the possibility of our self-recognition in such practices. That we are unable to recognize ourselves in such cases makes it evident that our idea of what is human includes finding certain of our normal practices—of counting, conceptualization, and following rules—natural. What is normal for us when subjected to such a test of unintelligible examples appears as natural to human beings in general. The examples of practices are ones "in which the idea of normalcy upon which the strength of criteria depends, is seen to be an idea of naturalness."[14] We ourselves are partially determined by the practices we find natural. Hence it is necessary for our self-recognition that certain normal practices be shared. Moreover, it is necessary for our being human that certain of our current practices be normal and natural for human beings in general. Such is the way in which Wittgenstein has caught a glimpse of human universals. Wittgenstein's well-known rejection of a private language as empty for us makes it clear that some practices can be shown to be constitutive of our form of life and hence necessary for us as human beings.

Wittgenstein's strategy of imagining ourselves doing things otherwise renders possible the discovery of some normal practices being natural. These elementary practices would constitute practice-governing principles for belief systems, moral systems, and cultures. With some of the normal ways, in various communities, of thinking and doing things found to be natural for human beings in general, such beliefs and practices are rendered globally justifiable. These practice-governing principles will serve as guidelines for the comparative appraisal of different cultures.

There are two fundamental problems for moderate relativism: how to interpret and understand alien cultures and how to compare and assess their varying degrees of worthiness. Wittgenstein, far from being a radical relativist, has undermined radical relativism with his discovery of some practice-governing principles. These principles not only furnish "the system of reference" (*Philosophical Investigations,* 206) for the interpretation and understanding of alien languages and alien cultures, but also give a clue to the comparative appraisal of diverse belief-systems and cultures. Wittgenstein's insight thus renders a great help to anthropologists and historians of science in their attempt to solve the above-mentioned problems.

It is a hopeful sign that Wittgenstein beckons us to a nonethnocentric and fuller understanding of aliens and their cultures. We may use the practice-governing principles to find out which alien belief system or culture or which parts and elements thereof are normal and conventional, and hence locally justifiable for the aliens only, and which one or which parts and elements thereof are normal and natural, and hence globally justifiable for us as well as for aliens.

Relativism cannot, of course, be refuted; it can only be kept within bounds.

Notes

1. Melville J. Herskovits, *Man and His Works* (New York: Knopf Publishers, 1947), p. 76.

2. Barry Barnes and David Bloor, "Relativism, Rationalism and the Sociology of Knowledge," in *Rationality and Relativism,* ed. by Martin Hollis and Steven Lukes (Cambridge: MIT Press, 1982), p. 22f.

3. Mary Hesse, *Revolutions and Reconstructions* (Bloomington: Indiana University Press, 1980), p. 45.

4. Ibid., p. 27.

5. Avrum Stroll, "Norms," in *Dialectica* (Neuchatel: Editions du Griffon, 1987), p. 10ff.

6. Ian C. Jarvie, "Rationality and Relativism," in *The British Journal of Sociology* vol. 34, no. 1 (London: Routledge & Kegan Paul [March, 1983]).

7. Steven Lukes, "Relativism In Its Place," in *Rationality and Relativism,* p. 298.

8. Martin Hollis, "The Social Destruction of Reality," in *Rationality and Relativism,* p. 74.

9. Donald Davidson, *Inquiries into Truth and Interpretation* (New York: Clarendon Press, 1984), pp. 196–197.

10. Steven Lukes, "Relativism in Its Place," p. 298.

11. Ibid.

12. Barney Barnes and David Bloor, "Relativism, Rationalism and the Sociology of Knowledge," p. 27.

13. Stanley Cavell, *The Claim of Reason* (New York: Clarendon Press, 1979), p. 34.

14. Ibid., p. 122.

FERENC FEHER

BETWEEN RELATIVISM AND FUNDAMENTALISM: HERMENEUTICS AS EUROPE'S MAINSTREAM POLITICAL AND MORAL TRADITION

The *nunc stans* of today's Europeans is the feeling that the "European project" or tradition has increasingly become problematic. At the same time, it is gradually dawning upon us that hermeneutics, which for a long time transpired as an innocent Romantic innovation within the sanctuary of Academia, has been an inherent and permanent constituent of the European project, a factor which has irreversibly shaped Europe's *political* and *moral* physiognomy.

Europe, as we now know from Agnes Heller's pioneering essay,[1] has been a late, basically eighteenth-century substitute for the Christian umbrella culture under whose shadow the European project was slowly maturing. The Christian prehistory of "Europe" showed, from the Council of Nicea to Luther's challenge to the universal Church, very little propensity for that cultural and political hermeneutics which we associate with the European project. The political scope granted to a pluralistic interpretation of the only accepted text of European culture in which terms sociopolitical conflicts could articulate themselves was not wider but narrower than in other cultures outside of Europe. In Nicea, it was Constantine's all-powerful verdict that distinguished the orthodox from the heretical. And, in turn, all regional heresies almost immediately raised themselves to the rank of limited, though equally exclusive and intolerant, orthodoxies. More than a thousand years later, the Wittenberg break with the exclusive Catholic text was initially largely bent on repeating the old story of Nicea. Paradoxically, for almost a millennium the European *differentia specifica* had been, in contrast to Islam (Europe's major competitor), whose prophet recognized the distinguished role of all "peoples of the Book,"[2] universalistic intolerance. Europe was not prepared to bear with more than one text, one divine authority within its orbit.

After the extremely savage wars of religion, the unmitigated brutality of which often foreshadowed the charming face of our century of genocides, the turning point, a turn unexpectedly propitious for the emergence of the hermeneutical political tradition, came with a *wave of toler-ance,* a specifically European innovation. On a formal level, it is of course possible to read Lessing's celebrated parable of "the three rings" in his *Nathan The Wise* as the European edition of Mohammed's concil-iatory stance. The three interconnected rings of the Christian, Moslem, and Jewish cultures are indeed literally identical to Mohammed's ges-ture of singling out "peoples of the Book." And yet there is a fundamen-tal difference pregnant with serious political consequences between the respective structures of these trinities. Mohammed's principal stance developed into a nonproselytizing indifference towards the religious, albeit certainly not towards the political, existence of various conquered groups living under the Moslem umbrella. This indifference barely con-cealed a strict political-cultural inequality, but for the infidel this was for centuries incomparably more endurable than was the Christian zeal for converting the infidel and crushing the heretic. By contrast, Lessing's project of a conciliatory, universal, and rational world religion, which stands here as the metaphor for a great variety of European trends of tolerance, was fundamentally different in nature. The project acknowl-edged the theoretical, practical, and moral equality of all three rings, all the cultures involved in this early ecumenical arrangement. Further-more, the relationship between them was not one of indifference, but one of active curiosity for one another and genuine eagerness for recip-rocal learning.[3]

With the "Copernican turn" of the seventeenth and eighteenth cen-turies active tolerance, the heroes of which were Montaigne, Spinoza, Lessing, Condorcet, Herder, and Humboldt, the bases of a new herme-neutical political culture were established. The practical consequences of this innovation proved immense, and despite cataclysmic setbacks, they continue to influence our way of thinking today. The pragmatic end result of the wars of religion, viewed with bitter resignation on both poles, was a stalemate in which neither of the contending factions suc-ceeded in demolishing the other and restoring the dominance of the one and only correct text. This stalemate now appeared as an asset, as a dis-tinctive feature of Europe. Thus, Europe alone seemed capable of giv-ing shelter and a legitimized existence to various creeds without aban-doning the idea of truth, without relapsing into that absolute and cynical relativism which was an unmistakable sign of the decadence of aging Rome. And the new continent, a consistent completion of the European project in this and many other respects, was familiar with bias, but never with the concept of heresy.

This new constellation implied above all a new understanding of free-dom which appraised the degree of its own liberty by the yardstick of the other, by the liberty of those thinking differently. Furthermore, it became, beyond the indifferent tolerance of liberalism, the foundation of a new *hermeneutical* culture, political and moral. First, it questioned the institution qua institution as the source of interpretive authority. This tradition fed on Luther's monumental challenge to the Church as the sole repository of an authoritative exegesis and as the guarantor of the ultimate sanctity and relevance of "The Text," although the latter continued to be for Luther the only divine and correct one. The Protestant initiative of making *le travail du texte,* the individual and critical reading of the normative code, an indispensable precondition of deciphering, even constituting the text's meaning, was the initiating gesture of hermeneutics and one which, once secularized, also became a major citizen virtue.[4] Second, it followed from the new constellation that, in an unintended step beyond Luther, the existence of a variety of heterogeneous texts was recognized as beneficial, and thus variety and plurality were increasingly promoted. The hermeneutical reader-actor could no longer *a limine* deny that valuable findings may be hidden even in such texts whose ultimate untruth was for him or her a foregone conclusion. Even the institutional outlook of the new Europe, the idea of the representative system, was shaped not only by raising individual liberties to the level of ontological data and by recognizing various earlier, suppressed, interests as legitimate, but also by building the newly found hermeneutical dimension into the European political and oral tradition.

However, the postrevolutionary world had a Janus-face. On the one hand, it was a universe of irreducible heterogeneity, the disparate elements of which (classes, class interests, and separate national entities) had become legitimized in the heat of great revolutions. On the other hand, this world claimed universality by being capable of reading each and every text and mediating between them. But it could validate universality only by imposing sheer power upon other regions of the world, and it could only conceal the absence of the power by sheer hypocrisy.

Marx's towering figure and his grand narrative provided the paradigmatic answer to this impasse of political hermeneutics. Marx was the ultimate hermeneutician of the European project. With an unfailing eye, he re-read all of its texts and found the "deep texts," the "real meaning," beneath them. This was a unique performance. A new all-embracing universal had been substituted for the old one. Marx emphatically stated that it was not the Christian umbrella culture, but its offspring, which had for centuries been slumbering in its womb, that was the overarching category in this text reconstruction. In good Hegelian fashion, the truth of the old was now to be found in the new which transpired as the more general, the more universal; the truth of the Christian universal was to be found in the European (or Western) universal. The latter alone could, as Marx and later Weber understood it, become the progenitor of the irresistible vehicle of universalization: industrial capitalism. However, all traditional European universals were unmasked hermeneutically by Marx as so many particulars with false claims and unbacked credentials. The theory of "ideology" was a direct yield of the centuries-long European skill of spotting the "deep text" beneath the text. Furthermore, Marx supplied a causative explanation of the European hermeneutical self-delusion in his theory of classes and class limitations. Finally, with a dialectical *bravura aria,* the unmasking of pretended and pretentious universals resulted in the positing of the ultimate universal: the philosophical construction of the universal class of the proletariat, which was to emancipate the supreme universal, the human species.

The hermeneutical aspect of the Marxian reconstruction was apparently perfectly balanced by its (Hegelian) promise to complete, and to terminate, philosophy at the very moment when it reached the one and only absolute truth. Once all ideologies were unmasked, all texts critically re-read, philosophy would complete its theoretical task. What would remain would be the practical task alone: the transformation of the world under the guidance of the self-purified theory. This was a perfect dialectical construct with one fatal conclusion later brutally drawn by the only philosophical genius of Marxism after Karl Marx: Georg Lukács. Lukács, who apparently had the intellectual ambition to become the new Augustine of a new *ecclesia universalis et militans,* argued that textual exegesis had come to an end with Karl Marx, alias Absolute Truth. The future task of the theorist, who is simultaneously a functionary, consists, therefore, of upholding *the new orthodoxy.*[5] The terminus of the Marxian hermeneutical odyssey was thus a relapse, culturally as well as politically-institutionally, into the pre-hermeneutical concept and practice of orthodoxy.

However, long before the truly fatal cycle of transforming the Marxian dialectic into a self-repetitive and self-reproducing orthodoxy was set in motion and the this-worldly kingdom of the Grand Inquisitor established, the newly established hermeneutical politics of Europe had already been bitterly grappling with certain inherent and ineliminable problems of its own. The major one was the *tension between the voice and the text.* Pre-hermeneutical cultures, with their central category of "revelation," a European coinage which, under different names, existed in each of them, had not been familiar with this tension. Moses saw God "face to face"; Mohammed never did—he only heard his voice—but this was a difference of no major consequence. The Ultimate Authority was vocal, not textual; the written is only a trace of this vocal authority. The laws emanated from the Voice and they found their ultimate justification in its unquestionable authority. However, once a long line of criticism of the Holy Script turned a skeptical ear toward the transcendental voice and came to the conclusion that it was not, or at least it was no longer, audible, and that, therefore, the divine authority, guarantor of the eternal and unquestionable authority of the time-honored texts had evaporated, an unexpected dilemma emerged.[6] New texts with authority were now needed, and indeed Europe went about manufacturing a cornucopia of such new texts: constitutions, moral and penal codes, blueprints for utopias of the best possible world. Nor did these remain in the solitary semidarkness of private studies. In the clashes of great revolutions, they entered the public space and offered themselves as the new slabs of stone. But the vexing question was persistently there: Whose is the authoritative voice behind the text? What is the source of its authority?

The hermeneutical politics of Europe initially had a great degree of self-confidence in the easy solution to this dilemma. And its different branches offered various options. The American solution was only inconsistently stripped of the transcendental aura of foundation. It was not for nothing that the first compacts and agreements were named "covenants." Yet this solution was only apparently a relapse into a pre-hermeneutical stage of political culture. At this point, the great break-through of the "protestant ethic," its insistence on *le travail du texte*, proved crucial. The voice behind the text transpired in reality as the dignified tenor of "citizens in congress" with each other. These citizens honestly believed that the serious and independent reading and wording of texts of foundation, a virtue they had learned while studying their Bible, was applicable to politics as well. Their mutual covenant strongly resembled their consultation with their God, and it was therefore sufficiently transcendent and immanent at the same time. The foundation of the text in this dual voice was admittedly fictitious, but it was a *longue-durée* fiction.[7]

In the English version, the early spirit of empiricist skepticism had prevailed centuries before reaching its theoretical peak in Hume's philosophy. The hermeneutical politics of the English development, based on the veneration of traditions (in the plural) and the conception of common law, allowed for a certain degree of textualization without which the so crucial practice of legislation, administering justice, and law enforcement, would simply have collapsed.[8] The British empiricist-skeptical spirit also could unhesitatingly account for the voices giving vent to the constantly changing opinions of those who, in quick succession, entered into and cancelled bargains and temporary agreements with one another in the public space and in the market place. As such, the voices behind the texts were real and not fictitious. No mysterious carrier of "deeper texts" beneath the surface texts needed to be looked for in lieu of them. However, owing to their often inarticulate and constantly changing character, these voices, individually or in aggregate, were certainly lacking in any kind of supreme, not to mention transcendental, authority. For that reason, British political hermeneutics has up until this day consistently denied the need for one all-embracing text and the assumption of a single ultimate voice behind it.

The French resolution of the tension between text and voice, one born in the Great Revolution, has often, and rightly, been criticized as the myth of reason. A new mythological entity, termed *la nation,* alias *le peuple,* made its appearance beneath the text. This entity was, in every stage of its quick metamorphoses, an all-encompassing one speaking with the authority of a voice whose existence was philosophically asserted and politically coercively enforced. In the French political theater, hermeneutical license very quickly reached the level of an almost total arbitrariness. The radical hermeneuticians, from Sièyes through Robespierre to the First Consul, invariably pretended to hear the allegedly majestic, sonorous, and easily decipherable message of their mythological entity behind the cacophony of inscrutably violent quarrels. The pragmatic result of this often deliberate and always manipulative mis-hearing of the Voice behind the text was, as Raymond Aron has correctly remarked, the chronic breaking down of all French texts of foundation one after the other, for two centuries.

The general political consequences of this permanently unresolved, or only partially resolved, tension between voice and text for the European project were manifold, each of them equally grave. First, this culture increasingly became characterized by a hypertrophic cult of self-legitimizing texts while the search for the underlying and authorizing voices was gradually and increasingly repressed. If today Derrida probes into the problematical character of *écriture* with such an emphasis and with unmistakably mystical overtones, this apparently surprising philosophical inquiry, its topicality and relevance, can be traced back, at least in part, to precisely this unresolved tension.

Second, and exactly to the degree that European political hermeneutics proved less and less capable of coping with the problem of foundation, an artificially bolstered, therefore exaggerated and aggressive self-confidence vested in the European text transpired all over the world in the process of global cultural colonization. The key term of this operation was "to teach human groups without a text, the reading, understanding and copying the Text," the text of Europe. The very term "primitive" was in many ways constructed on the basis of a contrast between human groups with, and others allegedly without a text.[9] In the process of imposing the European text on the world, of degrading all other systems of self-expression to the rank of nontext, and of gradually losing interest in reading, deciphering, and understanding them in the zeal for substitution, the conquering European culture began to undermine its own hermeneutical foundations. As Hannah Arendt has correctly emphasized, the results of colonization always boomerang, the chickens indeed come home to roost.[10] And the hermeneutical politics of Europe, this great emancipatory achievement, was no exception to that rule.

The nineteenth century saw the process of concocting some of the most fatal home-made European potions as panacea to the tension between the voice and the text. The first was the emergence of hero-worship from Carlyle via Wagner and Napoleon III through Nietzsche. This cult was invariably accompanied by a deliberately manufactured political mythology. The synthetic authority of the new hero was supposed to replace the vanished authority of the Voice behind the Text. However, this was an unequivocally antihermeneutic subject, in addition to being a capricious-tyrannical one. The Hero of Carlyle, whose metamorphoses may become identical with World History, Siegfried, Zarathustra or the "New Emperor," increasingly tended not just to lend an overtly arbitrary authority to shattered texts in their lightningly short appearance in the political theater, but to eliminate texts outright and replace them by these respective voices. Wotan in Wagner's political mythology still had a shaky legitimacy of a kind. Siegfried had none apart from that of his sword. Zarathustra was a prophet (and a legislator) in a highly ambiguous constellation where the audience had to accept upon his word that God had died and—perhaps—was resurrected in the voice of the prophet.

Out of the anti-hermeneutic drive in the public space, charismatic politics was born. Weber, who introduced the principle into the domain of legitimation, and thus justified it as part and parcel of political practice, knew best that it was a religious principle irreconcilable with rationality and, we would add, with hermeneutics.[11] The warrior-prophet, the model of charismatic action, bore his own justification in himself, and his enunciations and messages tolerated no individual reading. And yet, having recourse to this irrational and antihermeneutic authority, in each and every case when the text and its prestige broke down for want of a backup voice became common practice in European politics.

The parallel development, the *aestheticization of politics,* pointed in the opposite direction. The hero, the warrior-prophet, the resurrected God after the death of gods, or the new emperor, were all also supreme artists whose raw material was the world (or "history" or "society") itself. It was from this living raw material that they conjured up their spectacular artworks. The charismatic politician felt justified to shape the world, this artifact lying passively around him, almost as if it were waiting to be molded, with *poetica licentia.* The very categories of politics became aesthetic in nature. The politician had "inspiration." Great designs, common to no one else, appeared to him in his solitary musing. He, a public figure by definition, lived in the creative solitude of the genius amidst the cheers of a vulgar audience, not worthy of him. (Leni Riefenstahl magnificently captured this artistic feature of the Führer in *Der Parteitag.*) Politics had self-consciously become theater already in the scenes of the French Revolution, which simply copied the theatricality of Poussin's paintings and the Versailles setting of the *tragédie classique* and which inspired in turn the similarly theatrical great art of Jacques-Louis David. Trotsky's theatrical politics (and the theatrical historiography of Deutscher, Trotsky's hagiograph and the only significant follower of Carlyle's style of history writing) were not simply histrionics. Rather, they were manifestations of this dominant trend of aestheticizing politics and shaping the world according to the inspiration of the artist-politician.

The comeback of the self-eliminated emancipatory tradition of moral and political hermeneutics occurred when people in Europe sifted through at least part of the debris, a by-product of the *Götterdämmerung* brought upon them by charismatic cataclysm-mongers, and when the empires, these great training grounds of the supremacy of the European text, disappeared. Cataclysms teach modesty, sometimes even excessively. This is how political and moral hermeneutics, the intellectual product of the European project, turned against the very project after the fall.

The quickly drawn conclusion of the present era of increasing relativism is that Europe is but one text among many. In a merciful reading, the European text transpired as being not better or worse than the other texts, but simply different. To the degree that the European self-laceration for the crimes of colonization had been emerging and the new anthropology had completed its emancipatory mission by unearthing and deciphering unknown and mysterious alien texts, the hermeneutic infatuation of Europeans for the Other went to the opposite extreme, the zeal of anti-ethnocentrism. For a typical new advocate of hermeneutical (anti-European) anti-ethnocentrism, preoccupation with the European text means a hidden cultural colonialism, and the attempt to uphold at least some of the battered European universals implies a version of gunboat diplomacy.

In a follow-up to the external relativization of the European text, this text is now being undermined internally as well. The replacement of universals by great consecutive historical waves was the very process of "making Europe." First the universal of the Roman Empire—a model which never entirely vanished from the old continent and which in fact recurred twice, in the abortive dreams of Charlemagne and Napoleon —was replaced by the universal City of God, the Christian paradigm. Later the paradigm of Europe was supplied in lieu of the Christian universal. The new wave now emerging turns against the very idea of universals and wishes to replace them by "mini-discourses" which are self-sustaining and self-legitimizing (from within). The success of the project of mini-discourses would be a paradigmatic case of Pyrrhic victory. For it would establish a fragmented world order in which the communication between mini-discourses systematically breaks down, and could only be temporarily and provisionally restored via the "translation" of one particular text to another.

The opposite trend, the aggressive counteroffensive of *political fundamentalism with a religious coloring* against political and moral hermeneutics is now similarly emerging. Not an altogether new story, it is merely the latest of the consecutive waves of the European effort to create political (or civic) religions. The pioneering attempt, made almost in the hour of collapse of the Jacobin dictatorship, was Robespierre's frantic effort to erect a new authority beyond the reach of heterogeneous and contending interpretations: the cult of the Supreme Being.[12] State-sponsored and enforced adoration of Marxism-Leninism, with the Georgian seminarist raised to the rank of a deified Roman Caesar, was a half-hearted and inconsistent, yet crucial, continuation of this tradition. But it was certainly a chapter in the old story of "hermeneutical incertitude," of the tension between the text and the voice. As long as the Bolsheviks had genuine self-confidence, they remained perfectly indifferent to any legitimizing authority other than violence. Only when their authority remained in the long run without firm foundations did they embark on the fabrication of a supreme and authoritative, quasi-religious voice. But their attempt at a synthetically produced civic religion had to remain a half-hearted experiment. There was too much Enlightenment in the Marxist tradition to declare overtly that the new authority was transcendental. But in practice, the Bolshevik rule was that of the Grand Inquisitor wrapped in secrecy, relying on hierarchy and the prestige of the sword. Nationalism, at the other extreme of the political diapazon, a perfectly straightforward this-worldly business in its early period, developed into a quasi-religion in an era when nations got systematically entangled in a cycle of deadly and biased conflicts in the course of which alien texts were rather *ab ovo* rejected as false and threatening messages, instead of being peacefully and patiently unraveled.[13] In its further development, nationalism reached the level of the mystique of the Grail, in which the in-group, the exclusive repository of the mystique of separation and distinction, felt legitimized to whatever it wished with the out-group.

The present religiously colored political fundamentalism is an incomparably more timid phenomenon. It has strong inhibitions about appearing in an overtly religious form in the business of politics in its fearing the accusation of sectarian rule. Equally, it has an in-built reluctance to display its actual ethnocentrism. Therefore, its religious façade is weak and one without serious appeal. Yet its antihermeneutical posture is unmistakable. The hermeneutical versus antihermeneutical political debate appears clearly in the Bork-Dworkin controversy. Bork is one of those rare conservative ideologues who is aware that the elimination of hermeneutics, that is, the license of interpreting certain fundamental texts (for example, the Constitution, which in his view should remain uninterpreted and as such, almost sacred) is indispensable for bringing the post-modernist wave of deconstruction to a halt. It is also mandatory to terminate the scenario of moral nihilism, if need be, coercively. As a fundamentalist conservative, Bork is concerned neither with the social price the world would pay for such a ban on hermeneutics nor with the curtailment of our liberties resulting therefrom. Being concerned about both, Dworkin, a man of liberal principles, regards the ongoing interpretation of the Constitution (in other words, the continuation of the European tradition of hermeneutical politics) not just as a fundamental citizen right but also as a precondition of an even relative social harmony.[14]

We are now indeed at a crossroad. If the absolute relativism of certain postmodernist trends will prevail, we will no longer have concepts to explain why the Holocaust was any more than an unpleasant event for one mini-discourse demolished by another, considerably larger mini-discourse, which, without a doubt, justified its act "from within." We will no longer be capable of theoretically justifying our practical and emotional judgment that the Holocaust, the Gulag, and colonial genocide were the negative limit of human performance, and, as such, infinitely evil. Driving the great European discovery of emancipation, hermeneutics, beyond certain limits destroying the European project with our own hands, would not merely be an act of theoretical and political masochism. It would also be an act with such grave political consequences that sometimes non-Europeans, who nevertheless articulate their needs in a very European vocabulary, are worried about it. On the other hand, all conservative attempts at stopping, if need be forcibly, the process of practical hermeneutics for fear of self-deconstruction would endanger our accumulated emancipation. But where are the limits? In many ways, Dworkin was right: we must have principles which serve us in a dual function, both as guides and as limits to our expansion and prohibition. We must have at least two principles with which to interpret and at the same time to curb, the excesses of interpretation. These principles should be the supreme values of freedom and life.

Nothing demonstrates the state of "lingering on the crossroads" more vividly than the present *debate on humanism.* The concept was the crowning achievement of the Enlightenment. Substituting "mankind" or "humanity" for the "Christian community" brought unexpected results in almost every field of social orientation. It served as basis for the assertion of *the unity of the race* and for the declaration of the "rights of Man." Although for obvious reasons this was a defective and one-sided formula ("Man" being the codename for only half of our race), there is no inherent substance in the concept which would prevent it from including the other half of mankind. "Humanism" as an overarching term, provided a theoretical foundation for the rationality and liberties of all human beings, as well as for their communication on totally new, "republican" grounds. Humboldt was the first of this great generation of humanists to observe that *Humanität* could provide a firm guidance for hermeneutics in a dual sense. It is *Humanität* toward which we are striving in our interpretive work, and we gain in humanity while we make progress in interpretation.[15]

Today humanism is the main target of deconstructive philosophical criticism. And this campaign has serious consequences for the status of hermeneutics as politics. Major objections have been made to the concept. In the famous debate between Sartre and Heidegger, which in the main was a confrontation between "Existentialism as Humanism" and "Brief über den 'Humanismus'," the problem of human imperialism was raised.[16] Heidegger reacted sharply to the paradoxical character of post-Copernican development. While natural sciences were emptying "the human center of the universe," philosophical humanism, in its own bid for the deification of Man, moved into the void and made "Man" the philosophical axis of world interpretation. Heidegger rightly detected the major dilemma of this conception: it provides an arrogant technological culture with a license for inflicting devastating damages on the interior and the exterior of the human world.

Another obvious critique is the understanding of "humanism as an oppressive universal." In terms of this criticism, humanism is in fact a European scenario. "Man" is seen as identical with the European man who embarked on the project of remaking the world in the image of the only progressive arrangement he was familiar with as well as prepared to recognize: nineteenth-century Europe. This European scenario of humanism forcibly blended all differences. Within its own world, its own nation state and colonies, it tolerated neither particularity nor singularity. "Difference" (for example, the female difference, the difference of races or that of sexual deviation) was persecuted or outright exterminated by an ethnocentric and oppressively universalistic humanism. This is clearly a *libertarian* objection different from the line of *Brief über den Humanismus*. It not only has its strong points but it also formulates the general dilemma of devising a universal category which is meaningful and all-embracing without being oppressive or intolerant.[17]

A third objection refers to the illicit extension of the Cartesian cogito —a specifically modern and European *Weltanschauung*—to the rest of our race who allegedly live under different stars. Vestiges of this kind of thinking can indeed be found in every description of humanity as "a community of rational beings" as, for example, in the Kantian version. But I strongly doubt if this propensity necessarily leads to colonialism. Kant's own passionately negative attitude to the colonization of the "primitives" in the name of civilizing them, a stricture in perfect harmony with the whole of his philosophy, is a refutation of the necessity of such a linkage. Kant believed that the "civilizers" acted out a shameful parody of the Enlightenment, their apparent frame of reference. The Enlightenment can only have one meaning: emancipation *through our own deeds* from *self*-incurred tutelage. Emancipation through the deeds of others is tantamount either to more intensive tutelage or to outright slavery.[18]

There is a fourth and final objection to the Enlightenment scenario of humanism. Humanism qua the overarching category of our world-interpretation is either formulated in a *strong substantive sense* or as a *mystical "mana,"* as the Mozartian "melody" which surrounds our aesthetic

vision of the world. The latter, to use Heidegger's term, is a moral-aes-
thetic anthropology. If it is understood in a strongly substantive sense,
our interpretation can be accused of racism, for the "substance" with
which "humanity" is identified will, in all probability, be identical with
the "substance" of one particular race, group or nation, excluding all
others from the community. If it is mere *"mana"* or "melody," it may
color our vision, but it will certainly not serve as an antidote against
anti-humanistic temptations and threats.[19]

The diverse rebellions against the concept of "humanism" have
therefore both strong and weak points, varying from scenario to scenario. But what would happen if, under the impact of multiple criticism, we were to resign the concept altogether? Ernst Troeltsch made
the interesting observation that all conceptions of "world history" in
which freedom prevails and which are not based on theodicy, *present the
human universe as an exception in the kingdom of nature.* The feeling of being
an exception is one of *horror vacui,* the state of mind which is peculiar to
the space explorer. Troeltsch remarked that Kant had already felt this
horror and speculated on the possibility that nature could "suck us
back" in order to eliminate this island of deviation.[20] In a more historicist rendering, this ontological anxiety surfaces as the hallmark of
modernity triggered by "living against nature." (For modernity, with
its insistence on freedom, rationality and self-perfection, is indeed a
countercurrent in the sea of our natural existence in history.) But "living against nature" takes not only audacity; it also requires *the solidarity
of the human bond.* Resigning the concept of "humanism" would be tantamount to relinquishing this solidarity, to the cancellation of the project
of modernity.

Are there ways to overcome the crisis? The writing on the wall is legi-
ble enough. The "European text," more of a museum prospectus these
days than a gospel, is taken to task from within and without. It is made
responsible for colonizing the past. It is labeled "ethnocentric" by guilt-
ridden Europeans and "irrelevant" by those excluded from the European text. Its universalism is treated as oppressive on the one hand and
impotent on the other. Micro-discourse is declared by the ingenious theories of post-modernity to be the ultimate acceptable extension of
(micro-) universals. Even philosophy's volunteering to translate the
parlance of micro-discourses into one another's dialect has been pronounced illicit or at least futile. The "theory of two worlds," this innovation of totalitarianism (now perhaps on the wane), has further
aggravated the condition of the hermeneutical community. It is not
unreasonable to describe the present situation as a constant oscillation
between relativism and fundamentalism.

And yet, there seems to be no viable alternative to the restoration of
the "text" of interpretation and the universal hermeneutic community
through the revitalization of (European) humanism. "Restoration"

does not necessarily mean "redefinition." Above all, it implies a *new covenant,* one in which the moral earnestness of a commitment is more important than the philosophical accuracy of a new definition. Why "covenant" rather than "redefinition"? First, because in our practical-moral decisions—and it is the domain of practical reason where the term "humanism" really matters—we are living under time duress. We need to act toward common understanding, instead of common destruction, and we simply cannot wait until a new definition with a consensual validity has established itself. Furthermore, the achievement of such a consensually valid definition is not even desirable, for it would almost certainly become yet another oppressive universal, with more cases of exclusion than inclusion.[21]

If "the new covenant" is meant to be a rational, rather than an emotional, community, it must possess certain features of cohesion. It must be explicitly stipulated by its participant members that the practical definitions of "humanism" and "universal hermeneutic community" will widely vary, but it must be equally assumed that every participant member will have some definition of "humanity." It must be recommended in the community that every participant be aware of the criticisms of the previous definitions of humanity, lest people fall into the same old traps. But it will not be mandatory to have discarded any one of the earlier "erroneous" concepts. More importantly, in every practical conflict situation, the individual should behave toward the other as if the other fit his or her own definition of membership in the human race and the hermeneutic community—even if this attitude cannot be supported with theoretical arguments. In other words, humanism and the universal hermeneutic community can only be restored *under the primacy of practical reason.*

In Kant's political philosophy, *res publica noumenon,* perpetual peace and humankind are three ways of describing one and the same state of affairs. And although his political philosophy explicitly excluded the utopia of world government, the ideal of a unified world legislation qua the ultimate standard of appraising our actions, was always in the background of his project of perpetual peace. It is my firm belief that today a universal community of interpretation can only be restored if the prerogatives of even a fictitious, or merely implicitly suggested, universal republic or world legislation are excluded from that community's sphere of authority. For an authority of this kind would become transcendental to the process of interpretive work and would appear as a subtly coercive power. The idea of the covenant should not aspire to the homogenization of a highly heterogeneous world; in such a case, it would simply repeat the old mistakes of oppressive universals. It must avoid the trap of becoming the universalist apparel of the cultural imperialism of a particular region.

Yet merely procedural principles are not sufficient to reestablish worldwide hermeneutical politics, the legacy of Europe. In which direction shall we search in order to remedy this predicament? I cannot recommend a better guide than what has been termed by Agnes Heller the "moral maxims of democratic politics."[22]

* * *

In one of the culminating great moments of *Don Giovanni,* in the immortal sextet at the end of the first part, Don Giovanni, Donna Anna, Donna Elvira, Don Ottavio, Leporello, Masetto, and Zerlina sing *unisono "Viva la liberta"*—and each of them means something radically different by the same words. For Don Giovanni, "liberty" is tantamount to the unhindered course of his predatory libertinism without the interference of police, religion, and the peevish complaints of petty moralizing. For Donna Anna, "liberty" will only be achieved in a world where the "intimate sphere" will no longer be threatened by moral monsters the likes of Don Giovanni. For Donna Elvira, "liberty" is a psychological category. She is not concerned with the world, only with her own spiritual equilibrium and her "freedom" from the haunting memory of the seducer. For Leporello, freedom means upward social mobility from the status of servant to a position that grants small pleasures and a pension. For Don Ottavio, the spiritual brother of Saint-Preux, the proto-Jacobin, "liberty" is entirely political in nature. It is tantamount to the stern rule of retributive justice and republican virtue. For Masetto, "liberty" is also political, but in a more concrete sense: it means freedom from the power of noblemen like Don Giovanni. Zerlina is not entirely sure whether it is freedom that she longs for most. But at least in one sense she, too, wants to be "free"— free from the whims of those silly men who are not capable of understanding that her intention is never to do them wrong; she merely wants to have a good time.

The sextet is an incommensurable expression of the new age born with the French Revolution and its new concept of the political. "Freedom" will be the common vocabulary in which the "will of all" is going to express itself. But behind this apparent total consensus, there will be a cornucopia of almost irreconcilable interpretations. It is also the most plastic portrayal of what I have called here the moral and political hermeneutics of modernity. Right at its peak, when the unrestrained, sensuous singing of all six protagonists celebrates the intoxicating moment of the birth of the new principle, the principle immediately displays its Janus-face. We are all one in aspiring to "liberty"; this creates the common *melos* among us, the very possibility of interpreting each other. But we are also different within this common *melos* to the point of mutual indiscernibility. We regularly misread each other, subsume others under our own motivations, over- and under-estimate each other. And when interpretation breaks down, in our rage, we solve by violence, or by resorting to transcendental powers (to the Comtur) what we cannot solve by our this-worldly means. But the blessed predicament of modernity is that we cannot abandon either the common *melos* or the individual difference unless we want to destroy the new modern world, our own creation, with our own hands.

Notes

1. Agnes Heller, "Europe: An Epilogue?" in Agnes Heller and Ferenc Feher, *The Postmodern Political Condition* (Cambridge and New York: Polity Press and Columbia University Press, 1989).

2. For the Prophet's attitude to the "Peoples of the Book" see Maxime Rodinson, *Mahomet* (Club français du livre, 1961).

3. For the characterization of Lessing's new concept of "tolerance" see Wilhelm Dilthey, *Das Erlebnis und die Dichtung: Lessing, Goethe, Novalis, Hölderlin* (Göttingen: Vanderhoeck & Ruprecht, 1965); and Agnes Heller, "Enlightenment Against Fundamentalism: The Example of Lessing," *New German Critique* 23 (Spring-Summer 1981): 13–26.

4. The inseparable ties between Protestantism and hermeneutics are emphasized in Wilhelm Dilthey, *Leben Schleiermachers,* first half of vol. 13; *Gesammelte Schriften* (Stuttgart-Göttingen: Taubner-Vandenhoeck & Ruprecht, 1961). See especially the chapters dealing with the prehistory of hermeneutics prior to Schleiermacher.

5. The works Lukács had been struggling in vain to complete, almost until his conversion to communism at the end of the war, *Heidelberger Philosophie der Künst* (1912-1914) and *Heidelberger Asthetik* (1916-1918) (Darmstadt and Neuwied, Hermann Luchterhand Verlag, 1974), concluded on a tragically relativistic note. In certain aspects, Lukács' classic of Marxist orthodoxy, *History and Class Consciousness,* can be regarded as Lukács' reply to his own, increasingly relativistic, hermeneutics.

6. The deeper implications of the critique of the Bible for the emergence of a "hermeneutical politics" have been elaborated in Leo Strauss' excellent book *Spinoza's Critique of Religion* (New York: Schocken Books, 1965). In particular see chap. 10, "Spinoza's Conception of the Bible and Bible Science."

7. The early American covenants' "discourse with God" and their continual practice of *political* text interpretation in their townships and assemblies has been brilliantly described by Hannah Arendt in her *On Revolution* (New York: Viking Press, 1965), pp. 166–176.

8. It is Hannah Arendt again who understood Burke's critique of the French Revolution as an interpretation from the position of the English text. For Burke, as Arendt perceived the merit of the issue, every conception of rights which was not based on the empirical evidence of tradition, but which was regarded as a "natural" and inalienable attribute of "man," was a contradiction in terms. Burke was still the thinker of the age for which the Latin *homo* was

equivalent to the *lawless* person. And he interpreted the French innovation as sophism and lawlessness, consistently from his own position (Arendt, *On Revolution*, p. 38).

9. For the definition of the understanding of the "primitive" by the "civilized" and the modern see Stanley Diamond, *In Search of the Primitive* (New Brunswick, New Jersey: Transaction Books, 1974). The problematic aspect of this highly original book is spelled out by the sympathetic writer of the foreword, Eric R. Wolf, in the following words: ". . . Diamond sets for us and for himself a triple task; to comprehend the primitive world as primitives do, to see our world from the vantage point of the primitive, and to link this understanding to the unexpressed aspects of our nature" (p. xiii). One could ask: what about the traditional task of anthropology, namely, to see the primitives from the vantage point of our own world?

10. Arendt explains in detail the meaning of the "boomerang effect" of colonization on "home culture." See Hannah Arendt, *The Origins of Totalitarianism* (New York: Harcourt, Brace, Jovanovich, 1958), 2d ed., revised and enlarged, in particular in the chapter "The Inheritance of Lawlessness."

11. The description and definition of political charisma can be found in Max Weber, *Wirtschaft und Gesellschaft* (Tübingen: J. C. B. Mohr–Paul Siebeck, 1972). In particular see the chapters "Die drei reinen Typen legitimer Herrschaft" and "Charismatische Herrschaft."

12. I have analyzed the Cult of the Supreme Being as an attempt at creating an "authoritative voice" behind the "text" in "The Cult of the Supreme Being and the Limits of the Secularization of the Political," in *The French Revolution and the Birth of Modernity*, ed. by Ferenc Feher (Berkeley-Los Angeles: University of California Press, forthcoming).

13. For a classic example of an antihermeneutical concept of the political see Carl Schmitt's *The Concept of the Political*, trans. by George Schwab, with comments by Leo Strauss (New Brunswick, New Jersey: Rutgers University Press, 1976).

14. Ronald Dworkin, "From Bork to Kennedy," *The New York Review of Books* 34, no. 20 (December 17, 1987): 36–42.

15. For Humboldt's thesis of the role of *Humanität* see "The Nature and Conformation of Language," in *The Hermeneutics Reader*, ed. by Kurt Mueller-Vollmer (New York: Continuum, 1985).

16. Martin Heidegger, "Brief über den 'Humanismus' " (1946), *Wegmarken* (Frankfurt: Vittorio Klostermann, 1978).

17. The (critical) characterization of humanism as "European" is, surprisingly, the deed of Sartre *after* the phase of "existentialism as humanism." In *L'idiot de la famille*, Achille Flaubert, the father, appears as the epitome of the oppressive (European and rationalist) humanism generating cripples through his tyranny. In *Saint Genet*, the same principle manufactures criminals and expels the sexually deviant from the community of the "normal ones." In his famous preface to Frantz Fanon's *Wretched of the Earth*, the idolization of the opposite of European humanism is explicit.

18. Immanuel Kant, *Zum Ewigen Frieden* (Frankfurt: Werke, Suhrkamp Verlag), vol. 11, pp. 214–215. Kolakowski's, in my view false, understanding of Kant's position is that Kant wants to "impose" his theory on mankind. See Leszek Kolakowski, *Religion* (London: Fontana, 1985), p. 190.

19. Agnes Heller characterized humanism as "mana" in her "The Moral Situation of Modernity," in *The Post-Modern Political Condition*. I have pointed out, in analyzing Weber's conception of music, the organic interrelationship between the understanding of "rationalized" music as "European" and "the mana of humanism." In this we are following in the footsteps of *Doktor Faustus* by Thomas Mann. Adrian Leverkühn's rebellion against humanism, his pact with the Devil can only lead to another version of the same: anti-*humanism,* to the revoking of the *Ninth Symphony.*

20. Ernst Troeltsch, *Der Historismus und seine Probleme,* vol. 11, *Gesammelte Schriften* (Tübingen: J. C. B. Mohr–Paul Siebeck, 1922), p. 274.

21. The concept "covenant" raises the correlative concept of the "we," the collective subject of hermeneutics as ethics. Maurizio Ferraris, in his "Etica e ermeneutica," *Aut Aut,* n.s., no. 228 (Milan: Nov.-Dec. 1988): 87–95, discusses the "radical" proposal of Gianni Vattimo, in the latter's "Metafisica, violenza, secolarizzazione," *Filosofia* '87 (Roma-Bari, La Terza, 1987), and the possible "we" or collective subject of a hermeneutical ethics. In Vattimo's view, as Ferraris presents it, there is an element of violence in the Nietzsche-Heidegger-type rejection of the classical-humanist tradition and Heidegger's stricture on metaphysics (which also seems to be negative and therefore sterile according to Vattimo). The assumed violence is comprised in the "must not" of the position: "you must not think in terms of the classical transition"; "you must not think metaphysically." This kind of violent arbitrariness does not create a subject for an ethics of hermeneutics; it only assumes its existence. Vattimo rejects equally the Habermas-Apel-Gadamer solution, viz., their (explicit or implicit) return to the classic community of humanism. This recourse is strongly foundationalist and therefore dogmatic. Its "we," or collective subject, is the illusory subject of nineteenth-century philosophy and politics. Vattimo's own recommendation is as follows: "Non un *logos* e una comunita storica devono fare da orizzonte di riferimento, ma l'idea di un indefinito allargamento del *logos* di fronte a una comunita sempre in via di farsi" (Ferraris, p. 91). This "community-in-the-making" does not mean a simple break with religion (or the substitution of technology for it), but rather *an ongoing process of secularization.* Although I have several objections to both Vattimo's critique and his recommendation, my idea of the "covenant" is extremely similar to his "community-in-the-making" as a process of secularization and as the "we" of a hermeneutical ethics. See also Gianni Vattimo, "Etica delia communicazione o etica dell'interpretazione?," *Aut Aut* no. 225 (May–Jun. 1988): 1–11.

22. Agnes Heller, "Moral Maxims of Democratic Politics," *The Power of Shame: A Rationalist Perspective* (London: Routledge & Kegan Paul, 1982).

Language and Non-Western Cultural Traditions

A. C. GRAHAM

CONCEPTUAL SCHEMES AND LINGUISTIC
RELATIVISM IN RELATION TO CHINESE

Philosophers discussing conceptual schemes seem generally to treat them as assumptions in propositional form behind the thought of different cultures, cosmologies, or phases in the history of science. On the one hand, conceptual schemes appear as conflicting systems of assumed truths which are only imperfectly testable by observation, and bring us uncomfortably near to epistemological chaos; on the other, suspicion arises that the notion of a conceptual scheme may not be coherent at all. As Donald Davidson argues in his paper "On the Very Idea of a Conceptual Scheme," we seem to end up with nothing definite but "the simple thought that something is an acceptable conceptual scheme or theory if it is true."[1] For inquirers into the thought and language of other cultures, the issue is inescapable. That very idea is one of their indispensable tools, to which Davidson's objections do not directly apply, since their own tendency is to think of it in terms not of propositions[2] but of classification by naming, and perhaps in terms of syntactic structures. I wish to argue that examination of their usage can open up a different perspective on the philosophical problems. At the roots of the systems of propositions called "conceptual schemes" by philosophers there are patterns of naming, pre-logical in the same sense as patterns of perception are pre-logical, and I shall myself use the term exclusively of these. As an example of the usage I quote a few paragraphs written by myself before having read Davidson.

> That all thinking is grounded in analogization shows up especially clearly when we try to come to grips with the thought of another civilization. The concepts which it assumes as self-evident, until persistent failure to solve a problem calls attention to them, appear to an outsider as strange metaphorical structures to be examined and re-examined as he learns to find his way around the conceptual scheme. To take an example from my own professional field, sinology, the first Christian missionaries in China were confronted with the Neo-Confucian cosmology, for which the universe is com-

posed of something called *ch'i* and ordered by something called *li*. *Ch'i* is a universal fluid out of which bodies condense and into which they dissolve. At its densest, as in a stone, it is inert, but the more tenuous it is the more freely it moves, for example as the air we breathe; even the void is *ch'i* at the ultimate degree of rarification. Inside the denser *ch'i* of the living body flow more rarified currents which circulate and activate it, moving freely as breath, less freely as blood. The concrete meaning of the word in ordinary language is in fact 'breath', and the alternations of breathing out and in are the paradigms for the *ch'i* in its active phase moving, expanding, rarifying as the 'Yang', and in its passive phase reverting to stillness, contracting, solidifying as the 'Yin'. This duality accounts for the generation and alternation of opposites throughout nature, light and dark, moving and still, male and female. Since *ch'i* occupies the place in Chinese cosmology corresponding to matter in ours, Westerners took a long time to grasp how very different it is from what we understand by matter. Early in the present century S. Le Gall was still translating *ch'i* by *matière*. A passage by the Neo-Confucian Chang Tsai (1020–1077), translatable as

'The assembly and dispersal of the *ch'i* in the *T'ai-hsü* ("Supreme Void") is like ice congealing and melting in water'

is rendered by Le Gall

'La condensation et les dispersions *des atômes* (my italics) dans la T'ai-hiu peuvent se comparer à la fonte de la glace dans l'eau.'

Although Chang Tsai's comparison with water shows clearly that the *ch'i* is a continuum and not an aggregate of atoms, the analogy with matter is so deep in Le Gall's preconceptions that he assumes the component atoms to be implicit in the word *ch'i* of the Chinese text. A reader asking the important question 'Is there atomism in Chinese philosophy?' would find the wrong answer embedded in an actual quotation from a Chinese philosopher.

As of *li,* it is pattern, structure, order; the concrete uses of the word are for veins in jade and the grain of wood. The *li* as a whole is the cosmic pattern which lays down the lines along which nature and man move, which harmonizes opposites with complementary functions, Yang and Yin, ruler and subject, father and son, and alternates day and night, birth and death, the rise and fall of dynasties, in regular cycles diverging downwards to the minutest detail of texture and converging upwards to the unity in which everything is interrelated. The *li* is not obeyed or defied like a law, one goes either with or against the grain of it, as in chopping wood. Le Gall translated it by *forme,* thus by the choice of two words remolding the whole Neo-Confucian cosmology after the analogy of Aristotelian form and matter. J. Percy Bruce chose for his equivalent 'law', and so incorporated into the Neo-Confucian terminology itself the wrong answer to the question "Are there laws of nature in China?", a misunderstanding which Joseph Needham in elucidating the concepts of Chinese science had to analyze at length. But to think of Le Gall and Bruce as making mistakes which we now avoid would miss the whole point. There are no exact equivalents for *li* and *ch'i* among our concepts, and there is no way of approaching them except by breaking out from or awakening to one analogy after another.

Approaching this cosmology, it is natural for an outsider to suppose that the Chinese can think only concretely, after the analogies of breathing or the veins in jade (a supposition encouraged by misunderstandings of Chinese script as a kind of picture-writing), while he thinks abstractly; that the Chinese are wrong and he is right (for is not the universe in fact composed of matter obeying the laws of nature?); that the Chinese are trapped within an unchanging conceptual scheme while he is free to go wherever reason bids. However, to take the first point first, the Chinese concepts appear concrete to us only because the enquiring outsider, unlike the insider who habitually thinks with them, needs to fix his attention on their metaphorical roots. He is much less conscious of the metaphors behind his own "matter" and "law," which however he must rediscover if he wants to explore the differences to the bottom. He himself thinks of matter after the analogy, if not actually of the timber which is the concrete meaning of Greek *hule* and Latin *materia,* at any rate of the "materials" utilized in making an artefact; and the usage of "matter" has behind it a larger model, of a universe created by God for a purpose, from which the transparently metaphorical "laws of nature" also derive. Indeed, we no longer employ the word with full assurance, or are confident of what we mean by philosophical "materialism," now that we are forbidden to think of atoms as little balls out of which a universe could be constructed; twentieth century physics has less substantial entities which would slip through one's fingers. As for the metaphor of "law," its persisting power is evident whenever someone, pondering the determinist thesis that even his own actions are "bound by," are "subject to," "obey" the laws of nature, finds himself thinking as though he ought to be conscious of his own resisting will, as he is when submitting to human laws.[3]

To approach the pre-logical patterning of names we require in the first place the tools not of philosophy but of semiology. The most useful for our purposes are Roman Jakobson's "paradigm/syntagm" and "metaphor/metonym."[4] A sentence is formed, on the one hand by selecting words, on the other by combining them. Words are related "paradigmatically" in the sets from which they are selected, "syntagmatically" in the phrases or sentences which combine them.

A	B	Paradigm
1. He	They	
2. posted	collected	
3. a	the	
4. letter.	mail.	

Syntagm

Verbal thinking draws from a stock of paradigms already grouping syntagmatically in chains of oppositions which at their simplest are binary. The following chain (in which we number only for convenience) guides the formation of such English compound words as 'daylight' and such formulas as 'the light of knowledge' or 'the darkness of evil' before they enter into sentences.

	A	B	Paradigm
1.	Day	Night	
2.	Light	Darkness	
3.	Knowledge	Ignorance	
4.	Good	Evil	

Syntagm

In Jakobson's terminology, paradigmatic relations are of "similarity/contrast," syntagmatic of "contiguity/remoteness." There are consequently two kinds of proportional opposition guiding our thinking:

$A1 : B1 :: A2 : B2$ (Day compares with night as light with darkness):

$A1 : A2 :: B1 : B2$ (Day connects with light as night with darkness).

When relations tend to similarity rather than contrast, contiguity rather than remoteness, one pair may substitute for the other, by the figures of speech called "metaphor" and "metonymy."

	A	B	Paradigm	A	B
1.	King	Lion		King	Chairman
2.	Man	Beast		Throne	Chair

Syntagm

King compares with Lion as men with beasts, so by metaphor the lion is king of the beasts and the king is a lion among men. King connects with throne as chairman with chair, so by metonymy the monarchy is called the throne and the chairmanship the chair.

In these chains of opposition we find the beginnings of a conceptual scheme, in which the thinking we shall call "correlative" in contrast with "analytic" will tend to fill a vacancy by its place in the pattern. We conceive it as spontaneous and pre-logical, the completion of a *Gestalt* as in perception, indispensable at the foundations of thought but requiring analytic thinking to test it. It is at this level that one would begin a comparison of Western with Chinese conceptual schemes. The relevance of chains of opposition, easily overlooked when we try to uncover our own preconceptions, is immediately obvious when examining Chinese thought, since the structures are exposed nakedly by the tendency to parallelism in the classical language, and are overtly formulated in the Yin-Yang cosmological scheme.

A	B
Yang	Yin[5]
Light	Darkness
Motion	Stillness
Heaven	Earth
Male	Female
Ruler	Subject

It is this scheme which has called attention to the most often noticed difference between Western and Chinese thinking, that the Western tends to center on conflicting opposites (truth/falsehood, good/evil), the Chinese on complementary polarities. We may illustrate the latter tendency from the *Chuang-tzu:*

> If then we say 'Why not take the right as our authority and do without the wrong, take the ordered as our authority and do away with the disordered, this is failing to understand the pattern of heaven and earth, and the myriad things as they essentially are. It is as though you were to take heaven as your authority and do without earth, take the Yin as your authority and do without the Yang; that it is impracticable is plain enough.[6]

Some of the English chain of opposition with which we started (day/night, light/darkness) fits neatly into the Yang/Yin scheme; but in the latter A and B are interdependent, with A only relatively superior, and the chain does not lead to "good/evil." Here our conceptual schemes differ, not in assuming the truth of contradictory propositions, but in including or excluding different pairs of words. That the Western chains of oppositions, like the Chinese, are right at the foundations of thought, has only been suspected quite recently. For Derrida[7] our "logocentric" tradition has a chain in which it strives to abolish B and leave only A, "signified/signifier, speech/writing, reality/appearance, nature/culture, life/death, good/evil. . . ." Contemplating it, one begins to see an affinity, for example, between Western positions as far apart as the Christian faith in the immortality of the soul and the scientist's (before quantum mechanics) in universal causation; given the pairs "life/death" and "necessity/chance," the West struggles to eliminate B in favor of A. More recently, David L. Hall and Roger T. Ames[8] have directly contrasted Western and Chinese oppositions, with the West habitually treating A as "transcendent" in the sense that A is conceivable without B but not B without A; for a Westerner there could be God without world, reality without appearance, good without evil.

On the paradigmatic dimension, vocabularies class as similar or different each in its own way; to the extent that languages are like English and Chinese in lacking a common ancestor, words will approach synonymy only when, in our Jakobsonian terminology, they name things closely similar to each other and distinctly remote from everything else, such as organisms and human artifacts. If, for example, an English speaker says "The cat sat on the mat," and a Chinese *Mao wo tsai hsi-tzu-shang,* only the cat is satisfying these conditions. For the English, its posture is similar to a man sitting in a chair, for the Chinese to a man lying *(wo),* whether face forward or on his back. As for the mat, we cannot expect an unrelated language to share precisely our classification of floor coverings as mats, rugs, carpets; *hsi-tzu* is used of straw mats. In addition the verb is tensed in English but not in Chinese. The sentences are not therefore fully intertranslatable, do not express the same proposition; *Mao wo tsai hsi-tzu-shang* is true even if the cat has never before now sat on the mat, false if it sat on a cloth mat. That Chinese and English divide up and organize the world differently shows up still more clearly in the classical language, with its neat parallelism and explicit classifications. For "Grass is green" one might find *Ts'ao ch'ing*—at any rate where a two-word parallel excluded the need for grammatical particles. Here the meaning of *ts'ao* depends on a division of vegetation into *ts'ao mu* "grass and trees," implying a wider scope than our 'grass'. *Ch'ing* is one of the Five Colors, the blue-green which contrasts equally with red, yellow, white, and black. If grass were blue, "Grass is green" would be false, but *Ts'ao ch'ing* would be true. It will be said perhaps that anything factual may be translated into any language by expanding with qualifications. But this claim, besides being unprovable by any number of examples, seems to assume that there are indeed atomic divisions in nature and culture which will impose themselves on the speakers of all languages.

Synonymy will of course be even harder to find in the terminology of philosophy and morals. We might say that apparently synonymous words will be like exactly equal lines; with a further focusing of the microscope a difference will appear. When a discipline is borrowed from another culture precise equivalents may be stipulated (the names of elements in physics will in any language have the same Latin formations or assigned native words), but this consideration does not apply to ancient China. Since logical operations are independent of language structure—a point to which we shall return later[9]—we might expect true synonymy among logical and mathematical terms; we can hardly deny that the numbers are the same, or that the Mohist's *Huo yeh che pu chin yeh*[10] is if correctly then exactly translated " 'Some' is not all." But in philosophical terminology, even when there are commonly agreed equivalents—*Tao*/"Way," *hsing*/"nature," *T'ien*/"Heaven"—there can be no question of perfect synonymy; they are satisfactory because if used consistently they enable the reader of a translation in which they recur to develop a sense of how they are diverging from the same words in an English context, an insight which is no more than assisted by the explanations in the introduction or notes of the book. Students of the ethical, political, scientific, or philosophical thinking of China are often amazed to discover that some crucial Western concept ("truth," "being," "liberty") is missing in this civilization; but granted that the classical language has no exact synonyms for the words, neither has it for "ethics," "politics," "science," "philosophy," or "civilization." The point is always to compare and contrast Chinese concepts with our own, not to go looking for our own in other cultures.

It may seem that these proposals commit us to an extreme form of linguistic relativism. Of *Ts'ao ch'ing* and "Grass is green," neither entails the other, since there is *ts'ao* which is not grass and *ch'ing* which is not green; nothing said in Chinese can imply or contradict anything in English, and likewise with all conceptual schemes. Since schemes overlap and run into each other, and each person has his own continually changing blend, the result should be epistemological chaos. Plainly we have to respect the evidence of experience that in international and other intercourse we do succeed in exchanging facts, and do know how to take into account that the other person is not saying quite the same thing. Whatever explanation we give for making this concession to common sense will apply also to statements within philosophical and scientific schemes. On the present line of argument the explanation will be that we come to understand the words by correlation within the scheme, a pre-logical process which analysis assists but cannot replace. We are in command of English only when we have stopped analyzing and applying a rule for singular and plural, and the gap in the chain "dog/ dogs, tree/trees, house/? "spontaneously fills with 'houses'." Learning Chinese, we start by translating with equivalents from the dictionary: *an*/quiet, still, peace, tranquility; *wei*/dangerous, perilous, lofty. But we are at home with these words only when we have become acquainted with them in different contextual patterns, in particular when we notice that, as we would never have guessed from these entries in Mathews' dictionary, *an* and *wei* are opposites. We may think of them as basically "secure/insecure," but our analyses of the words never catch up with our understanding of them in context. But if I learn the words primarily by correlating them, with analysis secondary even if employed at all, I understand the Chinese as I understand the English, and can confirm the truth of either *Ts'ao ch'ing* or "Grass is green" by looking at grass and other herbs without bothering about translatability. If in a particular context a Chinese reports what he saw by *Mao wo tsai hsi-tzu-shang,* I am orientated toward what he saw as toward things I have seen myself, possibly but not necessarily by visually imagining as in my own case I visually remember. I can then say "The cat sat on the mat" as I might say "You still have that cat, then," responding to the event which he observed without concern for whether I am saying what he said. I do have to coordinate the Chinese and English sentences, but will do so most accurately by correlation sensitive to more difference and similarity than I can analyze; there is no need to relate them logically because if I want to infer from one of them it will be in the same language. On this account the only connection between truth and translatability, *pace* Davidson,[11] will be that *if* a true statement does have a translation equivalent (as with scientific statements using stipulated equivalents), the latter will be true as well.

To think of the conceptual scheme as a pre-logical pattern of names—understanding by 'names' the products of the classifying act of naming, not the singular terms of logic—does not have the revolutionary consequences of treating it as a system of logically related propositions. The position remains the same as with dating by a calendar. That for a Muslim this is not the year 1990 does not open up the terrifying thought that in another conceptual scheme I am living hundreds of years ago; having compared the Muslin and Christian calendars I find that we agree. If there is a single goat in plain sight, and X says *yu yang,* "There is a *yang*" (conventionally translated 'sheep'), and Y "There is no sheep," I may be startled if I fail to appreciate that *yang* includes goats as *shan yang,* 'mountain *yang*'; but for anyone who has fully correlated the Chinese and English words the observation confirms both sentences. Davidson offers a similar case of agreement disguised by different usages of 'yawl' and 'ketch';[12] our account however differs from his in not having to assume (even if it is indeed the case) that the extensions of *yang* and 'sheep and goats' precisely coincide, that they are intertranslatable like the dates of the two calendars. When reading explanations in two languages of a vocabulary difference between them, one is positively grateful that they do not say exactly the same thing, much as when collecting information about an incident one wants photographs taken from different angles at different moments. Davidson remarks that "Whorf, wanting to demonstrate that Hopi incorporates a metaphysics so alien to ours that Hopi and English cannot, as he puts it, be 'calibrated', uses English to convey the contents of sample Hopi sentences,"[13] but there is no paradox here; Whorf would hardly have denied that bilingual readers would be clearer about the divergence with an equally sophisticated Hopi account to compare with his.

Our account of the incommensurability of statements in English and Chinese may seem at first sight to have the same consequences as Feyerabend's of the incommensurability of some scientific theories, according to which a crucial experiment cannot refute an old theory and confirm a new one, because terms change in meaning with the change of context; the reason for going over to the new theory is that the experiment described in relation to the old is incompatible with the old, but in relation to the new is compatible with the new.[14] Agreeing with Kuhn that, of Popper's methods of rationalizing science, "the one that can be applied, refutation, is greatly reduced in strength," Feyerabend draws a more radical conclusion than Kuhn's, that "what remains are aesthetic judgments, judgments of taste, and our own subjective wishes."[15] Our present approach, without necessarily excluding his epistemological anarchism, does not in itself imply more than we already know, that to confirm or refute requires not only logic and observation but checking whether words have the same sense and whether the calendar is Christian or Muslim. What distinguishes our approach from Feyerabend's is that as long as the scheme is conceived as propositional, all truth dissolves into "verisimilitude," but when it is conceived as a pattern of names, we have two clearly defined poles, with truth irrelevant to the pre-logical pattern and required for the observation statements; we ignore for the moment what lies in between.[16]

To treat schemes as systems of propositions makes it hard to interpret those paradigm switches by which, according to Kuhn,[17] science moves from an old one to a new. Davidson's abolition of the conceptual scheme is already implicit in his own description of the supposed switches: "We get a new out of an old scheme when the speakers of a language come to accept as true an important range of sentences they previously took to be false (and of course vice versa)," but with the meanings of the sentences changed.[18] But granted that Kuhn's paradigms are not Jakobson's, and that they are disciplinary matrices with the theories inside them, his choice of the term "paradigm" calls attention to the point he takes as crucial, that a scientific theory is not fully intelligible outside the practice in which the experimenter assumes his problem to be *similar* to those of classic cases taken as exemplary. A crisis comes when scientists lose faith in the similarity, leading in due course to the sudden insight which shifts the classification of the similar and the different. On Kuhn's account as on ours the switch is pre-logical, like the flash of metaphor in a poem. The conceptual scheme as pattern of the matrix as a whole is of course neither true nor false, but the truth of predictions which follow from the old and new theories can be checked as one checks the Chinese and English sentences against the cat on the mat, the green grass, and the goat in the field.

As the paradigm for the paradigm shift we may take the argument of Ryle's *Concept of Mind,* and restate it in terms of the proportional ratios of our semiological description.[19] Ryle sets out to discredit the dichotomy of a body which is extended in space and a mind which is not. He points out that to assume that mind is different in kind from, yet interacts with, the body, which is a machine, implies crediting it with a similarity, that its activities like the body's have causes and effects. The mind as "ghost in the machine" has to be conceived as a "spectral machine." This leads to familiar difficulties; how can willing, which is nonspatial, cause the limbs to move in space, or the mind's perception of a color be the effect of a process in the optic nerve? Ryle sees the problem as arising from an improper correlation in the metaphorizing at the back of thought, "Mind : head, hands, feet : : ruler : subjects" (the "para-political myth"), adjusted after the advent of mechanistic science to ". . . . . : : governor engine : other engines" (the "para-mechanical myth"). He invites us instead to try out other correlations : "Mind : head, hands feet : : University : colleges, libraries, playing fields," or ". . . . . . : : the British constitution : Parliament, judiciary, Church of England." It is implied that the correlations deposited by habit or initiated by fresh insights are prior to the possibility of logical demonstration; when a new one occurs to the philosopher he chooses which to prefer by whether the arguments which start from him lead into or avoid logical difficulties.

Ryle's change of approach is not a matter of questioning the *proposition* "Mind is to head, hands, feet, as ruler is to subjects." We may illustrate this point, and also the fluidity which makes the paradigm switch possible, by adding two more pairs to the chain with which we started. The added pairs include one to race and gender prejudices formulable as propositions; the conflict of the propositions with observation stimulates a break with the paradigm ejecting them from the scheme.

	A	B
1.	Day	Night
2.	Light	Darkness
3.	Knowledge	Ignorance
4.	Good	Evil
5.	White man	Black man
6.	Blonde	Brunette

The scheme imposes a pressure to think of white man as contrasting with black as day and good with night and evil, of black man as connecting with ignorance and evil as white with knowledge and good. Someone who yields to it may formulate a couple of the syntagmatic connections (B5 with B3 and 4) in the sentences 'Black men are ignorant' and 'Black men are evil'. But even the least rational of racialists guided by the correlation is unlikely to base his case on, or even to accept, the propositionalized "White man is to Black man as. . . . ."; he will offer examples to prove "Black men are ignorant" and "Black men are evil." Or again, in responding to certain kinds of art and entertainment, we allow ourselves to expect that the blonde woman will be the heroine and the brunette the villainess; but not only have we never formulated "Blondes are to brunettes as. . . .," we do not in ordinary life expect blonde women to be sweet and innocent, and brunettes sultry and dangerous. The propositions from which our rational thinking starts do not belong to the conceptual scheme as we are using the term; they are formulations of syntagmatic connections within it. Once formulated, they can be tested by observation from within the scheme, which confirms that there is generally light by day and darkness by night, but not that the white or blonde are generally good and the black or brunette evil, and forces ejection of the last two pairs from the scheme.

Let us suppose that in X's scheme propositions formulating syntagmatic connections have grown into a magical system which entitles him to predict that by reciting certain spells the ritually pure become invulnerable to bullets, in Y's into a scientific system entitling him to predict that they will be as vulnerable as anyone else. X seeing his comrades fall assumes that they have ritually defiled themselves, until finally the slaughter compels him to admit that in this case his system has no predictive value. Then X and Y agree in assenting to both X's "Your magic is stronger than mine" and Y's "My science is more effective than your magic," sentences which are not intertranslatable. If we make X speak Chinese and Y English, the word with which they assent will differ in semantic scope, but each if bilingual will respond to X's sentence with *jan* ("so") *hsin* ("trustworthy") (for convenience we make them speak the classical language of Chinese philosophy) and to Y's with "true." X is now driven to the conclusion that to defend China it will be necessary to master Western magic; and in doing so he finds himself, at least while utilizing the discipline which he is now coming to conceive as science, forced into a paradigm shift from his own to Y's conceptual scheme. At this point X and Y agree that Y's system of propositions is more adequate for prediction, perhaps also that X's is or was more adequate for integrating a community in harmony with nature. Does it follow that for both of them X's is false and Y's true? That will depend on whether they judge truth solely by utility for prediction. We use the word "true" unanimously only of factual statements such as "The cat sat on the mat" and "No one is invulnerable to bullets." Its variable metaphorical extensions (different from those of comparable Chinese words), to moral, spiritual, metaphysical, logical, or scientific truths, or to the truth to life or nature of works of art, are a matter of preferred terminology; nowadays one can even accept a religion without insisting on its truth. The issue which concerns us here has nothing to do with whether one decides to apply 'true' to theories only relatively adequate for prediction, which we accept in expectation of abandoning them when they are superseded by the work of some future Noble Prize winner. To escape the conclusion that all truth is relative to incommensurable conceptual schemes it is enough to show that the schemes themselves are patterns of names neither true nor false, and that factual statements depend on them for their meaning but not for their truth; we need not bother about what lies between these extremes.

We have imagined X and Y as learning each other's languages. The mere fact that they can do so forbids us to suppose that what is true at one end of the Old World may be false at the other, or that, schemes being incommensurable, an English speaker and a Chinese can never

judge the truth of anything the other says. However, it makes no difference whether the schemes belong to different natural languages or to the
same. If we make X an English practitioner of modern witchcraft saying "My magic is stronger than yours" to the man of science Y, the
appeal to judgment by results is the same as if we make him Chinese.
There is always the danger of thinking of language communities with
their conceptual schemes as distinct entities like persons, so that getting
out of the scheme of one's own seems to raise the same difficulties as
escaping solipsism in the case of the individual. But for the philosophical issue it does not matter whether, within language in general, differences are of total vocabulary or of technical terminology or of elevated,
colloquial, or slangy levels of speech, any more than it matters for children at the stage when they effortlessly pick up a language and as
quickly forget it. (A friend of mine trying to halt the rapid erosion of the
Chinese which his children had been speaking before returning to England was asked "Why do you keep on talking in that funny way?") For
the issue which we are discussing there is no such thing as a monolin-
gual speaker, and the language in which any one person thinks
embraces every variety in varying degrees comprehensible to and utiliz-
able by him. If his French is perfect he can no more translate it perfectly
into English than his scientific into liturgical language or his poetry into
officialese.

As we noticed in the first paragraph of this essay, conceptual schemes
may be taken to include not only the syntagmatic connections of pairs in
a chain but the syntactic structures which organize them in sentences,
although not on our account the sentences themselves. We may see
Indo-European and Chinese syntax as converging towards a shared distinction between the nominal and the verbal unit, much as their vocabularies approach synonymy in naming organisms, artifacts, and other
"natural kinds." On closer inspection of nouns, differences appear;
Hansen argued that classical nouns in general are closer to our mass
than to our count nouns.[20] Harbsmeier has more recently divided them
into three classes:

1. Mass nouns, counted with a preceding sortal as in modern Chinese (yi pei shui, "one cup of water").
2. Count nouns, counted individually without sortal or with the
   sortal following the noun (san ma or ma san p'i, "three horses").
3. Generic nouns, with kinds variously divisible and countable without sortals (ssu min, "the four classes of people").[21]

Hansen argues that Western thought is predisposed by number termination to conceive of the world as an aggregate of distinct objects,
and Chinese by the mass noun to conceive of it as a whole variously
divisible into parts. Le Gall's inability to understand the ch'i except as a
collection of atoms[22] would be a good illustration. The hypothesis sur-
vives Harbsmeier's classification; most or all philosophical terms would

presumably be not count but generic nouns. This is plainly the case with *ch'i;* the *yi ch'i/*"one *ch'i*" divides into the *erh ch'i/*"two (sorts of) *ch'i*," the Yin and Yang, and so on through the *wu ch'i/*"five (sorts of) *ch'i*" down to the *wan wu/*"myriad (sorts of) things." That Chinese thought would be conditioned to divide down rather than add up is in any case suggested by other features of the language. In classical Chinese one affirms existence not by "X exists" but by *Yu X/*"(It) has X" (the 'it' of the translation being the stop-gap 'it' of the English 'It' is raining'), tends to ask of a particular object not *Ho yeh/*"What is it?" but *Ho mu yeh/*"What tree is it?" or *Ho niao yeh/*"What bird is it?" and asks for the agent of an action not with *ho/*"what?" but with *shu/* "which?"[23] We may even catch Davidson, that blasphemer against the conceptual scheme, in taking a wrong turning because predisposed by grammatical number to think of the world as an aggregate of constant and discrete units. He is denying the coherence of claiming that a scheme organizes "reality (the universe, the world, nature)."

> We cannot attach a clear meaning to the notion of organizing a single object (the world, nature, etc) unless that object is understood to contain or consist in other objects. Someone who sets out to organize a closet arranges the things in it. If you are told not to organize the shoes and shirts but the closet itself, you would be bewildered. How would you organize the Pacific Ocean? Straighten out its shores perhaps, or relocate its islands, or destroy the fish.
>
> A language may contain simple predicates whose extensions are matched by no simple predicates, or even by any predicates at all, in some other language. What enables us to make this point in particular cases is an ontology common to the two languages, with concepts that individuate the same objects. We can be clear about breakdowns in translation when they are local enough, for a background of generally successful translation provides what is needed to make the failures intelligible.[24]

Here the example of the Pacific Ocean is well chosen. Language divides up and organizes its indeterminate parts (its 'seas', its 'shores', its 'bays'—unless the shores have been straightened out) and its individual objects ('islands', 'fish'). The differentiation of objects from parts is relative to the degree of Jakobsonian similarity and contiguity; Indo-European languages draw a sharp and at some places arbitrary line between them, preferring for our convenience to treat the Pacific spray with its transient drops, and the sand with its enduring grains, as masses rather than as collections of individuals. Why then does Davidson treat this example as without significant difference from the much less apposite illustration of the closet, of a space occupied by the artifacts (shoes, shirts), which like organisms are especially clearly individuated? Surely because he is thinking in a language which sharply contrasts the singular with the plural, 'the closet itself' with 'the shoes and shirts', 'the Pacific Ocean' with 'its islands' and even 'its shores' (which are parts rather than objects), 'the world, nature, etc.' with 'objects'. There would be no such compulsion to assume the primacy of individuals if English, on the analogy of classical Chinese, lacked number termination, and we said "this closet" and "its shoe and shirt" as we say "its dust" or "its smell." The effect of number termination is such that we cannot even make the simple statement that language classifies things as similar or different without implying in advance that the "thing-s" are different.

Davidson recognizes that different languages may individuate differently over a certain range of words, but sees this as only a local difficulty for translation. That we could not explore such differences without sharing "concepts that individuate the same objects" seems to him self-evident, requiring no further explanation or illustration. But let us suppose, reverting to one of our previous examples, that a Chinese student of English has been assuming that *yang* and 'sheep' are synonymous but begins to doubt it. He points out a sheep and a goat, asks of both "Is that a sheep?" and in the second case I answer "No, a goat." He has no need to guard against the danger that I might take him to be pointing at the horn; I cannot answer "No, a horn," because 'horn', unlike 'goat' is not on the same paradigmatic level as 'sheep'. It would be less appropriate to his problem to ask the "What is that?—which allows me to answer "A horn," forcing him to introduce a shared concept by narrowing his question to something like "What is that animal?"

As this criticism of Davidson illustrates, logic is independent of syntactic structure, which in any language is logically untidy, and can guide argument in a direction which, irrespective of language, may be wrong. An obvious example is the ambiguity of 'or'; the absence of a linguistic marker of the distinction between exclusive and inclusive 'or' has not stopped Westerners from establishing it and Chinese from learning it from them. The mysteries of the *Lao Tzu* and the *Yi Ching,* and the systematic but seemingly quite alien thinking of Yin-Yang cosmology, has often tempted Westerners to speculate that Chinese thought has a logic peculiar to itself. But Harbsmeier's examination of classical Chinese particles from the logician's angle[25] leaves no doubt that logical operations were always the same in China as they are here. Even Yin-Yang thinking, which is pre-logical, is the same elaboration of correlative thinking as that of Western protoscience right up to the Renaissance. Chinese syntax does affect both the subject/predicate distinction and, as I have argued elsewhere,[26] the categories; but we no longer think like Aristotle that these belong to logic. It is convenient to speak of the Chinese *verb* as having a subject, but this refers to the agent of the action rather than the topic of the sentence, and in sentences divisible into topic and comment the verb may have a subject inside the comment. However, Aristotle's assumption that the grammatical subject provides what the sentence is about and the predicate what is said about it does not work well even for Indo-European language ("Who was the writer? *Shakespeare* was the writer"). It is not required for the validity of the syllogism; if asked for an example of a particular which is demonstrably mortal, I could answer "All *men* are mortal; *Socrates* is a man; therefore, *Socrates* is mortal." When the occasional syllogism with both premises explicit happens to turn up in early Chinese literature, there is no doubt that it is functioning precisely as it would for us, as in this one from Wang Ch'ung (A.D. 27–c.100):

> Man is a thing : though honored as king or noble, by nature he is no different from other things. No thing does not die, how can man be immortal?²⁷

Here it may be noticed that with the tightening of logical organization sentences do approach intertranslatability. It would seem pointless to extend our doubts about "The cat sat on the mat" to "No thing does not die" as a translation of Wang Ch'ung's *Wù wu pu ssu,* which, word-for-word, is roughly "Thing not-have not die." In Chinese as in standard English the double negative amounts to an affirmative (and would be so understood in such a sentence even in languages which are logically less tidy in this respect, such as Greek, in which negatives can pile up without a switch to the affirmative). Doubt as to whether the Chinese sentence can be analyzed as subject and predicate does not affect the point that *wù* and *ssu* have the same logical relation as 'thing' and 'die'. *Wù* has a narrower extension than 'thing' (for "things to do" there is another Chinese word, *shih*), but the logical relation to *ssu,* 'die', narrows the extension of each to 'living thing'. Granted that in traditional Chinese medicine there is not even an exact synonymy of *ssu* and 'die', this raises only the same sort of problem as the difficulty of defining clinical death in our own medicine; the general difference between a functioning and a decomposing body is among the least impugnable distinctions between natural kinds.

As for the categories, it has been shown by Benveniste²⁸ and others that Aristotle's relate closely both to the Greek interrogative pronouns, adjectives, and adverbs and to Greek grammatical distinctions. Thus the last four (posture, state, action, passion) are illustrated by verbs in the middle, perfect, active, and passive respectively; since modern languages lack the middle voice and an equivalent to the Greek perfect, the categories of posture and state are barely intelligible to us. I have tried the experiment of similarly relating classical Chinese interrogatives and sentence units to the vernacular category-words, and found that the resulting classification often diverges from Aristotle's. Thus questions such as *Ho jo/* "What is it like?" when asked of a thing, are answered by describing its *chuang,* "appearance, characteristics," comparable with Aristotelian quality. But interrogatives such as *Wu-hu/* "whence, where, whither?" will, depending on the direction implicit in the succeeding verb, ask for the source, position, or destination, in agreement with the common generalization that Chinese thinking is in terms of process rather than of static entities. The corresponding category would have to be much wider than Aristotelian place; it seems to be *tao*, 'path','way', with *so*, 'place', as a position on it. It is notable that what we would call moral qualities seem never to be included in a person's *chuang;* they belong to his *tao*, the way he acts, and to his personal *te* (variously translated as 'virtue','power','potency'), the source from which the action starts.[29] Here we catch a glimpse of answers to such questions as why the Tao is central to Chinese thought, why it is regularly paired with *te*, why it is conceived as the source of all things as well as their path. But although convinced that syntactic structure guides categorization in both Greek and Chinese, I fully agree with Reding's observation[30] that, for example, Aristotle recognizes logical relations even when they are not marked by the genitive case, which in the Greek distinguishes his initial examples of the category of relation. This would only be further evidence that syntactic structures are logically irregular and have to be tidied up. Since the interrogative words of different languages are not synonymous, and connect with their syntactic structures, it seems inevitable that Aristotle or anyone else asking questions with them will be categorizing along lines initially set by the language in which he thinks.

Introducing syntactic structure into the conceptual scheme does not, therefore, bring us any nearer to epistemological relativism. Truths of fact are independent of the scheme, and so are logical 'truths', if that is what you want to call them. Moral 'truths' we leave out of the present discussion. By 'independent', it may be necessary to repeat, I do not mean that factually true statements are translatable into any natural language, but that to confirm or refute a factual statement by reason and observation you have only to understand its place in the appropriate conceptual scheme; you do not have to share the scheme. Nor do I want to suggest that if schemes could be perfectly corrected by logic and observation they would all become the same. In reading Chinese thinkers, as in reading the poets of unfamiliar literatures, one welcomes—to use the inevitable visual metaphor—looking out on the world from a new perspective, and has the impression of seeing the world more clearly as more perspectives are opened. This is not simply because much Chinese philosophizing *is* poetry; one has the same impression in reading the great philosophers of the West, who do not, like the great scientists, become obsolete. In treating schemes as equal, with one or another more adequate for solving one or another kind of problem, it becomes possible to use one to criticize something in another, as Fingarette uses Confucius to undermine our inner/outer dichotomy, Rosemont the problematic of moral choice, Hall and Ames the concept of transcendence.[31] Thus one oddity of the Western tradition, as I have argued elsewhere,[32] is an ontology in which the concept of Being covers the whole range of the Indo-European verb 'to be', the various uses of which are distinguished by different words and constructions in many or most languages, including Chinese. It was in Arabic, which like Chinese has no common word for existence and the copulative functions, that the concepts of existence and essence divided out.[33] Here we have a good instance of a logical distinction which is more visible in one language than in another but is not created or abolished by either. Aristotle, alone among the Greeks, did perceive the distinction between existence and the copulative; and the Latin scholastics did see the point of the Arabic concepts and borrow them, although only to incorporate them into their own concept of Being.

In this example, the syntactic structures guiding Chinese thought happen to be logically tidier than the Indo-European guiding ours. Like symbolic logic, classical Chinese deals differently with existence and copulas, and although it does not distinguish class membership from class inclusion, it has had from the early centuries A.D. a separate copula *chi* distinguishing identity. The existential *yu* X/"(It) has X/there is X" is analyzable as verb-object, not subject-verb, so like the existential quantifier of logic, *yu* cannot be mistaken for the predicate. Again as in logical symbolism, there is no copula linking the subject to what corresponds to our predicative adjective, in Chinese a stative verb as in *Ts'ao ch'ing*/"Grass is-green." Finally, there is no word for a concept of Being covering all these, any more than there is a symbol for it in logic. That symbolic logic is a Western discovery confirms that our thought has not been permanently imprisoned by Indo-European language structure. Nevertheless, Being has never quite lost its place in our conceptual scheme. Even in refuting the assumption that existence is a predicate, Kant, passing from "God is omnipotent" to "God is, or there is a God" *(Gott ist, oder es ist ein Gott)*, thinks of the 'is' as still the same word positing the subject as previously it posited the predicate in its relation to the subject.[34] Modern languages, unlike Greek and Latin, distinguish existence from the copulative relations almost as clearly as Arabic and Chinese, using "the is", *il y a* and Kant's *es ist* for existence and reducing 'is' to a copula. However, we still have the abstract noun 'being' embracing all the functions of Greek *einai* and Latin *esse,* now detached from both our natural and our artificial languages, but all that is needed for the ghost of the old concept still to walk.

We may see the question of the conceptual scheme as emerging because in recent thought the relation between correlative and analytic thinking has unobtrusively become a problem. Western philosophy (like one ancient Chinese school, the Later Mohists)[35] strives to detach analytic thinking from correlative and make it the sole authority for knowledge as distinct from opinion. This enterprise has no place for correlative thinking as spontaneous patterning in which a gap is filled by a flash of insight; it has to propositionalize it as the loose inference by analogy outside the bounds of strict logic, allowable for everyday commonsense thinking, where indeed it is indispensable, and in the creative thinking which precedes exact formulation (as Popper affirms, what matters in science is how you test the hypothesis, not how you arrived at it). As for the more exuberant excesses of correlative thinking in the Chinese proto-sciences and in the Western up to the sixteenth century, for the seeker of exact knowledge they are not only fallacy-ridden but scarcely intelligible, and thinkers who (like most of the Chinese) seldom analyze except to correct correlations[36] do not count as philosophers at all. However, modern philosophy has to take increasing notice of the models, analogues, metaphors, and paradigms, which still refuse to be expelled from its realm. It is driven from several directions (by Wittgenstein, Ryle, Kuhn, Derrida) to admit that if we dig below the surface of our supposedly exact knowledge we still find the correlative at its foundations. This recognition is the same as the sinologist's when, in searching for the metaphorical roots of a Chinese concept, he discovers that to compare and contrast it with Western concepts he has to explore their roots as well.

But a philosopher habituated to assume the complete independence of analytic thinking cannot fully adapt to this changed situation. A conceptual scheme is intelligible to him only as a system of propositions presupposed as true. In our longest quotation from Davidson[37] it may be noticed that, where we would speak of distinguishing things by naming them 'sheep' and 'goat' or assimilating them by their Chinese name *yang,* Davidson speaks of "simple predicates whose extensions are matched by no simple predicates" (the extension of 'is sheep' or 'is goat' not matching that of *yang yeh,* 'is *yang*'). For him the act of naming being outside logic cannot be taken into account. But to accept the idea of the conceptual scheme on these terms has the result that as observational tests become progressively weaker our propositions about the world threaten to become disconnected from the world. In the extreme case of Derrida, the similarities and differences between things are wholly excluded from consideration, difference is confined to the "identity/difference" of Saussurian linguistics, and language, instead of returning analytic thinking to its correlative roots, breaks out of its bounds to fly away into the void. Then it comes as a relief when Davidson shows that a conceptual scheme conceived as propositional does not even make sense, and we are back where we started.

The solution, I suggest, is to accept and come to terms with the thought that analysis starts from the results of spontaneous correlation. Modern philosophy no longer treats thought as distinct from and "clothed" by language; modern linguistics confirms our intuition that for the full exercise and understanding of language analysis is insufficient. The thinking which is fully adequate, for linguistic as for other skills, is spontaneous correlation. To the extent that we lose the faith that, by definitions and stipulated translation equivalents, we can detach words from their dependence on variable patterns of syntagm and paradigm, to achieve true intertranslatability, it becomes urgent to recover the engagement of analytic with correlative thinking. It may be humiliating at first for the pure rationalist to admit that reason has never after all escaped dependence on structures maintained by habit or shifted by unanticipated insight. But he is being asked only to relinquish his hope of a knowledge which is more than critically tested opinion; and by now we are all getting used to that. Is not reason more secure when credited only with testing and building on the results of spontaneous patterning, which, although erratic, is corrigible, than when, insisting on its independence, it turns against itself, persistently refuting all its traditional supports? Do we not already assume that it does merely test and build on results at the level below, perceptual patterning?[38]

Notes

1. Davidson, in *Post-analytic Philosophy,* ed. by John Rajchman and Cornel West (New York: Columbia University Press, 1985), p. 139.

2. For practical reasons I shall speak of 'propositions' where Davidson and others say 'sentences', reserving the latter for sentences in natural languages, English, Chinese.

3. *Reason and Spontaneity* (London: Curzon Press, and Totowa, New Jersey: Barnes & Noble, 1985), p. 57 f.

4. Roman Jakobson, "Two Aspects of Languages," in *Selected Writings,* vol. 2, (The Hague and Paris: Mouton, 1971), pp. 239–259.

5. As Henry Rosemont has pointed out to me, there are few exceptions (such as English 'black and white') to the rule that the preferred member of a pair is said first, and the Chinese *Yin/Yang* is perhaps the most remarkable.

6. *Chuang-tzu,* chap. 17, trans. by A. C. Graham, in *Chuang-tzu, the Inner Chapters* (London: George Allen & Unwin, 1981), p. 147.

7. Jacques Derrida, *On Grammatology,* trans. G. C. Spivak (Baltimore: Johns Hopkins University Press, 1976).

8. David L. Hall and Roger T. Ames, *Thinking Through Confucius* (Albany, New York: SUNY Press, 1987).

9. Cf. pp. 206–209 above.

10. *Mo-tzu,* chap. 45, trans. by A. C. Graham, in *Later Mohist Logic, Ethics and Science* (London and Hong Kong: Hong Kong University Press, 1978), p. 471.

11. Cf. Davidson's argument that there can be no notion of truth independent of the notion of translation (Davidson, in *Post-analytic Philosophy,* p. 140).

12. Ibid., p. 141.

13. Ibid., p. 130.

14. P. K. Feyerabend, *Problems of Empiricism* (Cambridge: Cambridge University Press), p. 158 f.

15. Ibid., p. 160.

16. Cf. p. 203 above.

17. Thomas S. Kuhn, *The Structure of Scientific Revolutions* (Chicago: University of Chicago Press, 1970).

18. Davidson, in *Post-analytic Philosophy,* p. 133.

19. Gilbert Ryle, *The Concept of Mind* (London, Hutchinson's University Library, 1949).

20. Chad Hansen, *Language and Logic in Ancient China* (Ann Arbor: University of Michigan Press, 1983).

21. Christoph Harbsmeier, "Language and Logic in Ancient China," in Joseph Needham, *Science and Civilization in China* (Cambridge: Cambridge University Press), vol. 7, no. 1 (forthcoming).

22. Cf. p. 194 above.

23. Cf. "Relating Categories to Question Forms in Pre-Han Chinese Thought," in my *Studies in Chinese Philosophy and Philosophical Literature* (Albany, New York: SUNY Press, 1990), pp. 373–378, 380–385.

24. Davidson, in *Post-analytic Philosophy*, p. 137.

25. Christoph Harbsmeier, *Aspects of Classical Chinese Syntax* (London: Curzon Press, 1981).

26. "Relating categories."

27. *Lun heng,* chap. 24 *(Tao hsü p'ien),* trans. by Alfred Forke, *Lun Heng, Essays of Wang Ch'ung* (New York: Paragon Book Gallery, 1962), vol. 1, 335 f.

28. Emile Benveniste, *Problèmes de linguistique générale* (Paris: Gallimard, 1966).

29. A. C. Graham, "Relating categories," pp. 385–374, 400–404.

30. Jean-Paul Reding, "Greek and Chinese Categories," *Philosophy East & West* 36, no. 4 (October 1986): 349–374, criticizing Benveniste and myself on this question.

31. Herbert Fingarette, *Confucius, the Secular as Sacred* (New York: Harper & Row, 1972); Henry Rosemont, Jr., "Why Take Rights Seriously? A Confucian Critique," *Human Rights and the World Religions,* ed. by L. Rouner (South Bend: University of Notre Dame Press, 1988). Hall and Ames *ut supra.*

32. "Being in Western Philosophy Compared with *shih/fei* and *yu/wu* in Chinese Philosophy," in *Studies in Chinese Philosophy,* pp. 322–359.

33. I discuss the linguistic side of the Greek-Arabic-Latin transmission of Western ontology in "Being in Linguistics and Philosophy," in *The Verb 'To Be' and Its Synonyms,* ed. by John Verhaar, Foundations of Language Supplementary Series, vol. 5 (Dordrecht, Holland, D. Reidel, 1972), pp. 225–233. The same series has a version of "Being in Western Philosophy" designed for the non-sinological reader, " 'Being' in Classical Chinese," in vol. 1 (1967).

34. Cf. "Being in Western Philosophy," in *Studies in Chinese Philosophy,* p. 354 f.

35. Cf. A. C. Graham, *Later Mohist Logic.*

36. As in the dialogues of Mencius and Kao-tzu, analyzed by D. C. Lau, *Mencius* (Harmondsworth: Penguin Classics, 1970), pp. 235–263.

37. Davidson, in *Post-analytic Philosophy,* p. 137.

38. For this essay I am indebted to the criticisms of Henry Rosemont.

THOMAS P. KASULIS

THE ORIGINS OF THE QUESTION:
FOUR TRADITIONAL JAPANESE
PHILOSOPHIES OF LANGUAGE

What is the nature of religious language? Of the various types of language use, speech acts, or language games, which best apply to the way we use language in religious contexts? These are some of the primary questions in the philosophy of religion as practiced in the West today. There is no consensus on how these questions should be answered, but the questions still tend to frame the arena within which the discussions and disagreements occur.

The early positivists like A. J. Ayer, for example, applied these questions to religious discourse in a way that influenced much of the Anglo-American philosophy of religion to follow. Using an impoverished understanding of the kinds of discourse, Ayer assumed that religious language had to be one of two kinds. Either it asserted empirically verifiable propositions or it merely expressed emotions without making any claim to truth. In short, religious language either represented bad science (which is to say, superstition) or it was no more than a series of propositionally meaningless "oohs!" and "ahs!"

Subsequent philosophers tried to save religious discourse from this oversimplified critique. There were a variety of approaches. Some looked harder at the idea of verifiability, noting that certain religious claims were indeed empirically verifiable although only after death or at the Last Days, for example. This is admittedly an odd set of conditions for verifiability, but in theory no different from meaningful scientific claims whose truth cannot yet be determined because of the lack of sophisticated enough equipment or the proper set of conditions. Other defenders of religious discourse examined more closely the notion of assertion. Our analytic epistemological categories were enriched by comparing the assertions characteristic of belief, knowledge, and faith. Still others rethought the problem of reference. Perhaps religious assertions were not about external states of affairs, but rather about internal, personal dispositions to act or behave in certain ways. According to this view, verifiability lies in correlating religious statements with religious behavior. Related to this line of thinking, some philosophers of religion used J. L. Austin's theories to pursue the performative dimensions of religious language: religious sentences often do something as well as say something.

Our point is to note that even with all this variety, and it is merely a small sampling of the diverse analyses of religious language, basically the same questions are being asked. Of the kinds of discourse, which do we use in making religious statements? Of the kinds of knowledge, which do we find in religious contexts? As we shall now see, the twentieth-century European continental approaches have not been significantly different in this regard.

Probably the most significant movement in continental thought to influence the philosophy of religion in this century has been the philosophy and theology of symbols. The semiotic philosophers denied special status to scientific forms of knowing. For Neo-Kantians like Ernst Cassirer and theologians like Paul Tillich, science was only a single, non-privileged instance of human knowing based on the manipulation of symbolic structures. Following the thrust of Cassirer's work, Susanne Langer called for a reevaluation of such human phenomena as art and ritual, finding epistemic implications in what the positivists had excluded from philosophical consideration.[1]

We note, however, that even in the case of the philosophies of symbols the enterprise has been, as it was for the analytic philosophers, to locate religious language, or religious claims to knowledge, within the larger categories of language or knowledge itself. We continue to ask: what is the nature of religious language? what kinds of language use are found within religious discourse? where does religious discourse fit under the broader theories of language and knowledge?

We do not take the time to reexamine the questions themselves, however. Where do the questions come from? What do they assume? For example, our contemporary Western line of inquiry seems to assume that some forms of language are religious and some are not. In other words, we assume that language itself is not religious, but only some kinds of language are religious. On the surface that assumption is innocent enough. It seems an obvious truth. But is it really so?

The historian of Western philosophy might point out that for Thomas Aquinas, for example, this "truth" was not so obvious. In fact, he explicitly denied it. For him all words ultimately came from the "inner word" or "word of the heart," the point of contact between the individual and the divine.[2] This suggests that *all* language is sacred, not that religious language is only one category of linguistic expression alongside others.

If we look comparatively at the history of religions, we find the assumption that language in itself is sacred to be more the norm than the exception. The *Ṛg Veda* upholds speech *(vāc)* as the supreme principle or deity of sustenance (see, for example, X.125.4). The *Tao Te Ching* says it is the *named* which is the mother of the variegated universe of things. In Genesis, God says "let there be . . ." when creating things, even though there is no one to hear the words other than the divine ear itself. The Gospel of John says that the Word is in the creation of all things. Of course, we might discount all this as the reflection of an archaic and now antiquated world view. But that is precisely the point. The modern Western assumption that language is not intrinsically spiritual is just that—a modern Western assumption.

It would seem that in at least our historical and cultural context, we should be able to ignore the issue of the origin of language and simply take the presence of language as our starting point. Or can we? Wilbur Marshall Urban makes the following observation:

> It is often maintained that origins do not affect validity, but notoriously they do and nowhere more clearly than in this sphere of language. It is, as we have seen, almost universally assumed that what speech was originally made for determines in some significant way what it is capable of doing now. . . . In any case, . . . historical origins may not affect values, but metaphysical concepts of ultimate origin certainly do.[3]

So our question now becomes: what difference does it make to a philosophy of religious language whether we assume that the origin of language is itself spiritual? This brings us to our comparative enterprise. Let us now briefly examine four traditional Japanese philosophies of religious language, showing how they related the question of spiritual origins to the secondary question of distinguishing religious from nonreligious functions of ordinary language. We may then conclude with observations about what this comparative analysis can teach us about our current situation in the Western philosophy of religion.

Let us begin with the metaphysics of language developed by Kūkai (744–835), Japan's first major philosophical thinker and the founder of Japanese Shingon Buddhism. At the heart of Kūkai's philosophy was his theory about the nature of words. From the Shingon standpoint, each thing in the universe is a "symbolic expression" *(monji)* of the *dharmakāya buddha*. The universe as a whole is the "symbolic embodiment" *(samayashin)* of the *dharmakāya* as the specific Buddha Dainichi Nyorai (Sanskrit: *Mahāvairocana*). Contrary to the exoteric schools, which understand the *dharmakāya* to be the *abstract* identity between the Buddha and reality, Shingon maintains that the identity is *concrete* and *personal*. It is helpful to think about this relation on three levels: the cosmic, the microcosmic, and the macrocosmic; that is, the supersensible, the subsensible, and the sensible planes of reality.

On the cosmic level, the universe is just Dainichi Nyorai's act or function *(yū)*. Dainichi is in an enlightened state, mentally envisioning reality (the *maṇḍala*), verbally intoning the sacred sounds *(mantra)*, and physically enacting the sacred gestures *(mudrā)*. The universe is, therefore, the natural expression of Dainichi's self-enjoyment *(jijuyū sammai)*. The *dharmakāya* is just being itself and in its so doing, the universe is as it is. What we know as the cosmos is actually Dainichi's mental, verbal, and bodily activity, the three intimacies *(sanmitsu)*. On this cosmic level, the goal of the Shingon Buddhist is to recognize the universe as the stylized expression, the intimation, of these three intimacies.

On the microcosmic level, Dainichi's enlightened activity is manifest as subperceptible resonances *(kyō)*. These resonances harmonize into various structural configurations: physically as the five (or according to Kūkai's later thought, six)[4] elements, mentally as the five wisdoms (and the buddhas associated with each), and phonetically as the base units of all language. In terms of the latter, at the subperceptible, inaudible level every word is necessarily a "truth word" *(shingon)* in that it is a surface (macrocosmic) manifestation of a microcosmic expression within Dainichi's enlightened activity.

On the macrocosmic level, the realm of perceptible reality, we are ordinarily oblivious to the cosmic and microcosmic dimensions. Shingon practice aims at revealing Dainichi's activity by making one more intimately aware of one's own activity. Through the ritualized practice of the *maṇḍalas, mudrās,* and *mantras,* one realizes that one's own participation is itself Dainichi's act. Since it is the domain most directly related to language, let us consider the practical aspects of mantric practice.

Shingon ritual recognizes five (or six) seed *mantras* that, when properly intoned, attune the practitioner to the elemental resonances out of which all language is constituted. Through mantric practice, one knows directly the truth words *(shingon)* inaudible to ordinary hearing. This is intended to enrich the practitioner's awareness in two ways. First, one recognizes these microcosmic resonances to be the imperceptible building blocks of the universe. In this respect, the ordinary macrocosmic world becomes the surface appearance of a deeper spiritual reality. Second, that deeper microcosmic level is not the world of quantum mechanics, an atomistic system probabilistically structured. Rather, there is a pattern to the microcosmic resonances, a pattern which is ultimately the self-expressive force of the cosmic buddha, Dainichi Nyorai.

In terms of our concern about the religious nature of language, therefore, we can say the following. Kūkai's esoteric Buddhist metaphysics maintained that all things in the universe are the Buddha's spiritual expressions. Everything we experience is only a manifestation of a microcosmic resonance or vibration, which in turn is nothing but the self-expression of the personal being that cosmically constitutes the universe. Language, therefore, is in one respect no different from any other phenomenon—it is a symbolic expression of the absolute spiritual principle. In another respect, however, language (as well as other formal structures such as art, bodily postures, conceptual frameworks) has a special function. Language may not only express spirituality; it may also *refer* to it. It is through these formal structures that we initially come to know about the cosmic and microcosmic realities behind the macrocosmic world experienced through the ordinary use of the senses. For Kūkai, the phenomena of the world, just as they are, are telling us something, but only through teachings formulated in language, diagrams, art, and postures do we become attuned to what they are telling us. We become capable of harmonizing with the style of the universe's self-expression only through our exposure to the teachings of Shingon Buddhism.

In this regard we can say that Kūkai found a dual relationship between language and spirituality. On one level, all language (indeed everything whatsoever) is inherently religious. Without the spiritual presence of the Buddha Dainichi, there would be no language. On another level, however, we can distinguish truly spiritual forms of language use (what Kūkai would think of as esoteric teachings) from secularized forms of linguistic expression (the exoteric teachings). Only the former point to language's sacred foundation as they simultaneously express that foundation. Sacred words (epitomized by the *mantra*) express the sacred as sacred, whereas ordinary words merely express the sacred as something else. Sacred language directs us to the root of language and, therefore, to the root of reality.

Of course, Kūkai's view technically represents only Shingon Buddhism and Shingon has not been a dominant tradition in Japan for over a thousand years. Yet, the esoteric Buddhist world view also influenced the Tendai Buddhist tradition and, by extension, the popular schools arising in the Kamakura period such as Pure Land, Zen, and Nichiren —themselves all originally offshoots of Tendai. We can here briefly examine aspects of Shinran's and Dōgen's views of religious language to see how Kūkai's theory about the religious nature of language prevailed, although in a transformed (sometimes radically transformed) mode.

Let us begin with Shinran (1173–1262), the founder of Shin Buddhism or, more technically Jōdo Shinshū, the "True Pure Land School." The relevant issue for him was how we should try to read a religious text so that we may enter into its true meaning. In his *Kyōgyōshinshō* Shinran, following T'an-luan, writes:

> The openings of the sutras declare: "thus" [*sutras* typically begin with the phrase "thus have I heard"]. This clarifies the fact that faith is what makes possible our entrance.[5]

The important point in this rather trenchant passage is Shinran's association of "faith" or "entrusting" *(shinjin)* with "thus" *(nyoze)*. In his articulation of the faith experience in Shin Buddhism, Shinran emphasized that faith can never be self-consciously willed or calculated *(haka-*

rai). Rather, it must be a surrender to the natural (*jinen*) presence of the "other-power" (*tariki*), that is, the compassion of Amida Buddha which prepares the way for our enlightenment. Amida's compassion is immediately available to us in all things, but we must allow ourselves to be open to it.[6] If we depend on our own power, Shinran maintained, the ego would obstruct any progress toward enlightenment.

This presents an interesting problem for Shinran's hermeneutic theory. Since he follows the traditional stance that he himself does not know the nature of Amida or his soteriological role but rather that it "has been made known" to him through the *sutras* and the teachings of the Pure Land patriarchs, it is crucial that Shinran have an infallible way of reading and understanding such texts. He cannot trust his own ability to "figure things out" (*hakarai*) since that would be an instance of trying to save himself through his "own power" (*jiriki*). Hence, he must be a literalist who protects himself at all times from eisegesis, from reading his own ideas into the text.

Normally, when we think of literalist interpreters, we envision scholars who pour over the philological, historical, and contextual components of the text or, alternatively, fundamentalists who believe that the text is patently obvious and one should simply read it naively. Shinran would have good reasons for rejecting either of these models of literalism, however. The scholarly approach itself smacks of *hakarai*, the ability to figure things out by trusting one's own knowledge and technical skills. The fundamentalist approach, on the other hand, overlooks the pernicious presence of ego and its ability to delude us in our attempts to "just see what the text says."

Shinran's readings of the texts clearly fit neither model of literalism. In the opening of his *Ichinen tanen mon'i*, for example, he quotes a passage from Shan-tao, a passage that surely means by any ordinary reading of the Chinese: "May everyone always desire that *at the time of death* [the Pure Land] will appear before them" and interprets it to say instead: "Everyone should always, *up to the time of death,* desire that [the Pure Land] will appear before them."

The key to Shinran's position is in how he understands "other-power" to inform his reading of a text. Shinran's position is that one must submit to the text, but not to its letters; one must yield to the spiritual power behind it, the power of Amida's Vow. For Shinran, the Shin Buddhist reader should approach the text without preconceptions, without special technical skills, and without the confidence that one can understand. We should see the text as something open to our entering into it.

This explains why Shinran's reading emphasizes the terms "thus" (*nyoze*), "faith" (*shin*), and "enter" (*nyū*) in T'an-luan's statement. In Shinran's understanding of the power of Amida's Vow, *shinjin* or faith is the dynamic through which thusness and the thus-come (*nyorai*, that is, the Buddha Amida) work naturally through the person so that the person may enter the Pure Land. By approaching the text with *shinjin,* the reader trusts not the text but the compassionate vow of Amida Buddha to help us.

How can we trust ourselves to be honest? How can we trust ourselves not to deceive ourselves? According to Shinran, we can't. Faith, which includes the denial that I can figure out things on my own, must inform the reading of the text from the start as well as follow from it. A religious reading requires of the reader that one not trust oneself: such a misplaced trust is simply own-power, *jiriki.* The only effective form of trust is the trust in Amida's Vow, and that trust is nothing other than the natural function of the Vow's power itself. From the *tariki* standpoint, *I* do not read the text; the text expresses itself to me and through me.

What does this mean in broader philosophical terms? Shinran's point is that there is no such thing as a religious text *per se,* but only religious *readings* of sacred texts. More precisely, if a text is read nonreligiously, it is not a religious text. If it is read religiously, it may or may not be a religious text, depending on whether it possesses the capacity to affect the reader's spiritual self-reflection. Interestingly, if the reader leaves the reading with the sense of "now I know the answer," the text read is not religious. The point of the religious text is to make us more acutely aware of our inadequacy, our failings, our limitations. Similarly, a reading that leaves the reader in utter despair also fails to qualify as religious because it has not instilled the reader with the sense of "other-power" essential to the faith necessary in spiritual development. Indeed, according to Shinran, without such faith, the text cannot be read religiously.

Now let us consider Dōgen (1200–1253), the founder of the Japanese Sōtō Zen tradition. We have seen that in both Kūkai and Shinran there was a metaphysical assumption that all language is expressive of the sacred power of the Buddha, but that religious language is distinctive in its ability to refer to that fact and to lead the audience to recognize that truth. We find a similar situation in Dōgen. For Dōgen, like Kūkai, all of reality is the self-expression of the Buddha. In Dōgen's terminology, this is the ubiquitous nature of the Buddha's "expression" *(dōtoku).* Dōgen even states that mountains and rivers, just as they are, are *sūtras.*[7]

Dōgen's approach to religious language differs from that of many other Zen masters. First, some interpreted the traditional dictum that Zen be "outside letters" to mean that the Zen transmission from master to disciple must be nonverbal. Dōgen explicitly denied this interpretation. One focus of the nonverbalist interpretation was the traditional Zen story of the transmission of insight from the historical buddha, Śākyamuni, to his disciple Mahākāśyapa. The story states that the Buddha, seated before a group gathered for a lecture on the Dharma, silently twirled a flower and winked. Only Mahākāśyapa reacted—by smiling. Pleased with his response, the Buddha said he would transmit the treasury of the correct Dharma-eye *(shōbōgenzō)* directly to Mahākāśyapa.

In his *Shōbōgenzō* fascicle "Mitsugo," Dōgen gives his own interpretation of the story. He notes that many would take the Buddha's behavior to mean that esoteric, nonverbal transmission is superior to the verbal. That is, one might think the twirling and winking were *mitsugo* or esoteric language. Dōgen rejects that reading. First he points out that only after the nonverbal exchange did Śākyamuni speak about transmitting the Dharma. It seems, then, that the transmission itself did not take place with the silent exchange. As Dōgen states:

> If Śākyamuni dislikes the verbal and prefers to twirl the flower, he should save the twirling for after (speaking). (13:58)[8]

If the Zen transmission can be verbal, Dōgen must explain how a particular verbalization may have a spiritual function. Here it is significant to see how he reinterprets the classical sense of the term *"mitsugo,"* a word that would ordinarily be translated "esoteric language" in the Shingon or Tendai schools and have the connotations of an extraordinary, secret, ritualistic communication directly linking the minds of master and student. In contrast, Dōgen considers *mitsu* to be part of our everyday experience. He writes:

> The *mitsu* words, meanings, and actions [in other words, the three 'intimacies' discussed by esotericists like Kūkai] of the Buddha's truth *(buppō)* are not the way [the anti-verbalists argue]. On the occasion when you meet someone, you hear and express *mitsu* words. When you know yourself, you know *mitsu* action. (13:58–59)

In other words, Dōgen maintains that *mitsugo* is not a mystical and recondite form of transmission at all. If it is true that, as Dōgen says, "on the occasion when you meet someone, you hear and express *mitsugo,*" *mitsugo* must be instead the very basis of interpersonal communication. It is what makes conversation a meeting ground for human intimacy. Dōgen, in fact, says as much:

> This word *mitsu* indicates the fact of *intimacy (shinmitsu).* . . . Intimate action is not knowledge of self and other [such that] I alone can know my private self and do not understand each other private person. Because [as we say] "intimacy is what is near you," everything exists through intimacy; each half exists through intimacy. Personally investigate such facts with clarity and diligence in your practice. (13:59)

For Dōgen, it seems, language becomes religious when the speaker and audience are each involved in their respective practices, and the expression *(dōtoku)* of that combined practice is verbalized as intimate language. To make this point, Dōgen again modifies the traditional understanding of a classical Zen term, *kattō,* a word which usually indicates a deluded person's "entanglement" in words. Since he rejects the idea that verbalization is necessarily deluded and an obstruction to the transmission of enlightenment, Dōgen added a positive meaning to the term *kattō*, attaching the nuance of "intertwining" to the verbal exchange of master and disciple. In his *Shōbōgenzō* fascicle *"Kattō,"* Dōgen explores this point, explaining how one must "use *kattō* (intertwining) to cut through *kattō* (entanglement)." That is, the master uses words to entangle both the student and the master, and together they use the words to cut through that entanglement.

> Therefore, the very utterances are lines that leap out of themselves; student and master personally practice together. The very listenings are lines that leap out of themselves; student and master practice together. The common personal investigation of master and disciple is the patriarchal intertwining *(kattō)*. The patriarchal intertwining is the life of (Bodhidharma's) skin-flesh-bones-marrow. (Shākyamuni's) very twirling of the flower and winking are the intertwining.[9] (12:428)

Dōgen's general interpretation of religious language can be summarized as follows. Like Kūkai and Shinran, Dōgen believed every phenomenon is an expression of the buddha. In this respect, every event—verbal or nonverbal—has a spiritual source. Therefore, Dōgen restricts the idea of distinctively religious language *(mitsugo)*—language that refers to as well as expresses spirituality—to the context of language arising within the intertwining of a master's and student's mutual practice, that is, language within the context of *kattō*. For Dōgen, it should be noted, Zen practice is not the means to Zen enlightenment, but rather is identified with it. Dōgen uses the term *shushō*, "practicing enlightenment" or "cultivating the authentication" of the enlightenment already within us. The event of truly religious language arises only when the people in dialogue are in the process of expressing *(dōtoku suru)* their authentic selves and, as Dōgen says at one point, when "each person brings one's own half of the intimacy." Religious language only occurs when both people are referring to, as well as expressing, their radical enlightenment *(hongaku)*. According to Dōgen's theory of *dōtoku*, every statement, indeed every phenomenon, is expressive of a radical spirituality filling the cosmos, but only the religious language of *mitsugo* points out the expressive process and brings both speaker and audience into the awareness of that omnipresent process.

Obviously, Dōgen's primary model of religious language is oral, but his own unorthodox readings of traditional terms and classical passages suggests that he believed even written texts can exemplify *kattō*. Indeed, in another essay, I argued that such a point of view influenced his unusual writing style in his major work *Shōbōgenzō*.[10]

As our final historical example, let us turn to the case of Motoori Norinaga (1730–1801), a major philosopher in the Shintō tradition and crucial to the revival of Shintō as a national religion in the nineteenth and twentieth centuries. Motoori was a philologist who turned his attention to deciphering one of the earliest texts recorded in Japanese, the *Kojiki*. The *Kojiki* was first recorded in the eighth century and it supposedly preserved the most ancient Japanese stories of the creation, stories that had been preserved only in the oral tradition up to then. The orthography used in recording those stories, however, had not been used for a millennium and much of it was unintelligible to Motoori's contemporaries.

Motoori's purpose in spending most of his adult life decoding the text went beyond philology, however. Motoori was a fundamentalist who believed the *Kojiki* to be the actual words of the gods *(kami)* spoken at creation. Hence, the ancient Japanese language (the *Yamato no kotoba*) was not simply the earliest language, but the *Ursprache* of all languages. This devotional attitude led Motoori to believe in a rather intriguing theory of religious language.

In his study of the ancient Japanese language, Motoori identified with the perspective of the Native Studies *(kokugaku)* scholars who emphasized that the same term, *koto,* originally meant both "word" and "thing." This semantic range assumed a parallelism or even interdependent relation between the linguistic and the ontological. This resonance between word and referent was sometimes called *kotodama,* the "spirit of words/things." The Native Studies scholars made that notion central to their reconstruction of the original Japanese world view.

Of course, the nativists generally conceded that words today may refer in only a crude, indefinite way to nonlinguistic realities, but for them this was proof that the primal power of verbal expression has been lost. Motoori hoped to recapture it, however. His line of thought was as follows. Insofar as the *Kojiki* is the story of origins and is the earliest extant text written in Japanese, it must describe what had originally been orally transmitted about how word-things *(koto)* came into being. In the unfolding of the words-things found in the *Kojiki,* therefore, we find the reenactment, not merely the description, of creation itself. That is, if the *Kojiki*'s words are internally related with realities, when you capture the full resonance and semantic range of the word, you also capture the reality as well. To uncover the meaning of the ancient words is to participate ritually in the creation itself.

This theory of the Yamato language was in accord with Motoori's theory of poetry. For him, a poetic text is not simply the expression of fact; it also is a direct expression of *kokoro*. *Kokoro* is a term ordinarily embracing both heart and mind, the seat of personal intentionality both emotional and intellectual. Motoori did not, however, limit this term to the feelings of the experiencer alone, as being only subjective as opposed to objective. There is also *kokoro* in things *(mono no kokoro)* and events *(koto no kokoro)*. If a person has sensitivity *(kokoro ga aru hito*—a person with heart), he or she will be aware of the *kokoro* of things as well. An affective knowledge occurs when the event's *kokoro* and the person's *kokoro* are expressions of the total affective context. According to Motoori, this affective resonance between the *kokoro* of the person and thing is called in classical literature *mono no aware,* literally (following Motoori's analysis of the word), "the ah-ness of things." The *aware* is the natural expression (like "ah") of being so in touch with a thing or event that we are in turn touched by it.

In this way, Motoori connected the spiritual and aesthetic into a single theory of the power of word-things. When the *kokoro* of the reader or the poet is in accord with the *kokoro* of things and events, the creative act of spirituality is enacted or reenacted: the words and realities find their completeness of expression in each other. It was, incidentally, this view of language *(kotoba)* as the budding of leaves *(ha* or *ba)* springing from the thing-words *(koto)* that Heidegger discussed in his "A Dialogue on Language between a Japanese and an Inquirer," in his *On the Way to Language.*[11]

In summation, although devoutly Shintō in his perspective, Motoori was in accord with his Buddhist predecessors in believing the origin of language to be a spiritual event, an event whose significance is lost in ordinary discourse. Only when the heart-mind-intention *(kokoro)* of the individual is attuned to the spiritual power of language *(kotodama),* does the discourse both express and refer to that spiritual source.

To conclude this essay, we can now focus on some general principles in this analysis that reflect on our initial discussion about the philosophy of religious language in our contemporary Western context. First, we have noted how all four of our traditional Japanese philosophers believed that language itself is sacred in its very source. Modern Western philosophies of language, of course, are not interested in the issue of origins, but as Urban argued, insofar as a philosopher makes an assumption about what language is for, there is at least a metaphysical if not historical assumption about why there is language at all, about whence language derives. Of twentieth-century Western philosophers, perhaps only Heidegger has made this metaphysical question about language central to his philosophical ruminations. It may be more than historical accident that modern Japanese philosophers have gravitated more toward Heidegger's work than that of any other twentieth-century Western thinker.

We also noted at the outset that the idea that language and things came into being together, emerging out of a common spiritual principle, seems to be remarkably widespread among the world's religions. Given this context, it is strange to limit our philosophical analysis of religious language to assertional functions: representatives of those traditional religions would argue we have already robbed the language of its spiritual basis. At least our four classical Japanese philosophers would agree with such a criticism. Perhaps religious language is meant to be about not what already is, but rather about the source of the what-is, that process which makes the what-is into the what-it-is. This circumlocution is reminiscent of Heidegger's odd phrase: the "thinging of things," a phrase which tries to capture the phenomenological fact that the things of experience come into being as experiential content in an organismic, rather than static, manner.

Second, our four classical Japanese philosophers have each, in his own way, argued that religious discourse is not a text, but the hearing or reading of a text. What makes a text or an utterance religious is not simply where it came from, the context in which it was expressed, or the nature of the object to which it refers. The audience and its state of heart or mind is a necessary condition for the religious character of the expression. This relation between the religious discourse and the audience is reciprocal. On one hand, the religious language has a performative function: it is meant to do something to or for the audience. Yet, on the other hand, it is the audience which imbues the discourse with its power. The religious language has power only insofar as the audience gives it its specialness. The members of one religious tradition are often left cold when they read the text of another tradition. As Kūkai, Dōgen, Shinran, and Motoori all insisted, the audience must participate with, or enter into, or become entangled in, or intend the text with the proper attitude.

Our final point concerns wisdom and its relation to philosophizing. One of the trends of modern Western philosophy has been the increasing movement away from the classic Greco-Roman and medieval emphasis on wisdom toward the almost exclusive focus on knowledge. The study of wisdom—both practical and intellectual—has given way to narrowly defined epistemological concerns. In doing so, philosophy has become the love of knowledge instead of the love of wisdom. The problem has been compounded ever since modern philosophy has turned its attention to religion, losing sight of the fact that religion also has more to do with wisdom than knowledge. If our postmodern philosophy of religion is going to deal more fruitfully with the nature of religious discourse, it would seem that philosophy must first reexamine itself and once again love that aspect of human life from which it derives its name—*sophia*. Only then might we again stand in a place where we can hear what religious discourse really has to say.

Notes

1. Our survey could continue, showing in particular how some of these ways of doing philosophy of religion have run aground. The analytic approach has exhausted its repertoire of simplistic forms of language use and has moved increasingly into the area of figures of speech, metaphors, and so forth. There is

still so much analysis to be done in these areas that the philosopher of religion cannot simply call on any agreed body of analysis as a tool to use in evaluating religious discourse in any sophisticated way. On the other side of the English Channel, the poststructuralist deconstructionists have detached symbolic forms from their claim to any Neo-Kantian transcendental necessity or their claim of being based in a "natural kinds" realism. Symbols, it seems, refer only to other symbols in some form of culturally, socially, and historically relative episteme.

2. For a detailed discussion of the Thomistic theory, see Bernard Lonergan, *Verbum: Word and Idea in Aquinas* (Notre Dame, Indiana: University of Notre Dame Press, 1967). See also my comparison on this point in my article "On Knowing the Mystery: Kūkai and Thomas Aquinas" in *Buddhist-Christian Studies* 8 (1988): 36–45.

3. Wilbur Marshall Urban, *Language and Reality* (New York: Macmillan, 1939; reprint, 1961).

4. Up to the writing of his *Sokushin jōbutsu*, Kūkai seems to have referred to the traditional list of only five elements *(godai)*, rather than the list of six *(roku-dai)*, which adds consciousness to the former list of earth, water, air, fire, and space.

5. Translated from *Shinshū shōgyō zensho (SSZ)* (Kyoto: Kōkyō Shoin, 1940–41), vol. 2, p. 65. There are two textual points to note here. First, T'an-luan probably meant to emphasize that the "thus having heard" aspect makes the texts reliable and worthy of our serious attention. (This, at least, is the point made in a recent unpublished paper by Roger Corless, "Shinran's Proofs of Buddhism.") Shinran, on the other hand, emphasizes the aspect of faith as entrance, as the experience grounded in the "thus" *(nyoze)* of Amida's vow. The second textual point is that there is an apparently slight deviation in the *kunten* between the Bando and Honpa Honganji versions of the *Kyōgyōshinshō*. My translation here is closer to what I take to be the intent of the Bando version. In any case, the translation is meant to be consistent with Shinran's overall discussion.

6. See, for example, the following famous quotation in which Shinran identifies entrusting or faith *(shinjin)* with the *dharmakāya*, and therefore with reality, itself.

Because all sentient beings in their hearts entrust themselves to the vow of the dharmakāya-for-us *(hōben hosshin)* [that is, to Amida's Vow], this very faith *(shinjin)* is itself buddha-nature, this very buddha-nature is itself dharma-nature *(hosshō)*, this very dharma-nature is itself the *dharmakāya*. *(Yuishinshō mon'i (SSZ 2:630))*

7. See, for example, his *Shōbōgenzō*, fascicle *Sansuikyō*.

8. Quotations from the *Shōbōgenzō* are translated from Mizuno and Terada, eds., *Dōgen shū*, volumes 12 and 13 of the Iwanami shoten series *Nihon shisō taikei*.

9. The phrase "skin-flesh-bones-marrow" refers to the transmission of enlightenment from Bodhidharma, the founder of the Zen tradition in East

Asia to his disciple Hui-k'o. For Dōgen's unorthodox interpretation of this story see his discussion in *"Kattō"* or my discussion of that interpretation in "Dōgen on How to Read *Shōbōgenzō,"* in William LaFleur, ed., *Dōgen Studies* (Honolulu: University of Hawaii Press, 1987).

10. LaFleur, *Dōgen Studies.*

11. Martin Heidegger, *On the Way to Language,* trans. by Peter D. Hertz (New York: Harper & Row, 1971), pp. 1–54.

ROGER T. AMES

MEANING AS IMAGING: PROLEGOMENA
TO A CONFUCIAN EPISTEMOLOGY

The Project

My essay will involve the attempt to import the classical Chinese term *chih* into a Western philosophical vocabulary. I want to give an account of how the conventional translation of *chih* as "to know" or "knowledge," while foregrounding our philosophical importances, pays the unacceptable penalty of concealing precisely those meanings which are most essential to an appreciation of its differences. This penalty is unacceptable because it is surely the possibility of identifying and appropriating what is not already ours that motivates the project of translation in the first place.

The movement among cognate Indo-European languages lulls us into a sense of shared conceptual ground that is illusory when addressing the more exotic traditions. After all, each of the world's languages is "specialized" in saying particularly well those things necessary to address the unique features of its own natural and social conditions, and hence, the greater the degree of difference among cultures, the greater the degree of difference in translating among the languages that express them.

In reconstructing *chih,* I want to try to recover what has been lost in traditional translation. To do this, the first step must be the discovery and articulation of those presuppositions which make it fundamentally different from what we mean by "to know."

In the attempt to give definition to these "uncommon assumptions" in *Thinking Through Confucius,* David L. Hall and I argue that a notion of transcendence in various guises has been a recurrent and dominant feature since the inception of classical Western philosophy.[1] We further suggest that one obvious signal of this notion of transcendence is the inventory of dualisms which have been generated as the vocabulary of philosophic reflection. Dualistic concepts such as reality and appearance, knowledge and opinion, theory and praxis, God and world, form

and matter, mind and body, reason and experience, cognitive and affective, and so on are derived from a notion of transcendence, where one
element in the dualism has ontological priority over the other. For
example, where "appearance" strictly requires "reality" for its explanation and justification, "reality" does not in any strict sense depend
upon "appearance." This independence of knowledge from opinion
reflects an ontological disparity between two kinds of reality.

Thinking Through Confucius is an attempt to "think through" Confucius and the philosophical tradition that he inspired as an alternative to
our own dialectic in which this notion of transcendence has played such
a significant role. If we are going to understand *chih* in its own terms, it
will be necessary to reinstate implications of "knowing" that are precluded by the assumption of ontological transcendence.

Chih as Imaging a World

A careful reading of the *Analects* reveals that an extraordinary amount of
the vocabulary used to present Confucius' philosophical insights is concrete "way" imagery—a characteristic that our standard English translations have yet to reflect. When Confucius modestly describes his own
project, he literally says: "I follow along the way, I don't construct it."[2]

The contemporary philosopher Feng Ch'i appeals to the *Analects* passage "as for my Way *(tao),* there is a consistency that runs through it"[3]
to argue that Confucius must be treated as a systematic philosopher.[4]
But I think that this rationalization of Confucius privileges concept over
image in a text that can most profitably be read as sustained image.
This sustained image, like the detailed biographical portrait of Confucius in the central chapters, is a signature of the text. In insisting that
coherence makes Confucius a systematic philosopher, Feng Ch'i seems
to overlook an important distinction between the conceptual edifice of
systematic philosophy constructed from a ground of univocal meanings,
and an aesthetic coherence which eschews meaning understood as
objective reference in favor of meaning inherent in the process of
imaging.

It is important at this juncture to clarify the meaning of "image." In
our tradition, image in the vernacular combines the notions of perception and imagination, where the mimetic, representative, figurative,
and fictive connotations of image are derived from the ontological disparity between a transcendentally "real" world and the concrete world
of experience. The absence of such ontological disparity in the Confucian model will mean that image is the presentation rather than the representation of a configured world at concrete, literal, and historical
level. Disengaged from an ontological prejudice that renders image fictive in some process of comparison and substitution, or of transference
and analogy, the image assumes considerably more force as a mode of

evidence alternative to *logos* in understanding and articulating our world.[5] As the act of generating meaning by circumscribing, isolating, and compositing "things," it is the very differentia and character of reality.

Willard J. Peterson in fact argues that the term *hsiang,* generally translated as "image" or "model" in the *Book of Change,* ought to be rendered "figure" in the sense of "to give or to bring into shape."[6] This is what is meant in the *Book of Change* when it states:

> The Sages having the means whereby to perceive the mysteries of the world and to calculate their shapes and contents, they "imaged *(hsiang)*" what is appropriate for things. For this reason, we call them images *(hsiang).*[7]

There is a reported conversation in the *Book of Change* between Confucius and his disciples that is an encouragement to read the *Analects* itself as a sustained image:

> The Master said: "Writing cannot give a full account of words, and words cannot give a full account of meaning."
>
> "Then one cannot grasp the meaning of the superior persons and sages?"
>
> "The superior persons and sages established images to give a full account of their meaning."[8]

The meaning resident in the image as established is the act of establishing the image itself. Contrary to one's own naive expectations—and the advice of many subtle aesthetic theories—what one finally "sees" in a work of art is the creative act that produced it. The creative process, not the object, is the repository of meaning. What is imaged is the process.

Perhaps a useful analogy for this sense of imaging is the traditional art of calligraphy. The personal style of the calligraphy as contrasted with the text is nonreferential and nonrepresentational—yet it is revealing of the artist himself. His moods, his time, his joy and pain, his place are all resident in the Chinese character. One's calligraphy is biographical—but a biography that transmits the tradition rather than merely one's own idiosyncrasies.

George Lakoff most recently, and Stephen Pepper before him, are persuasive in arguing that the development and extension of metaphors is one of the most fundamental ways through which a culture interprets and understands its world.[9] As a third-century statement of this same insight, Wang Bi in his commentary to the *Book of Change* attempted to explain the relationship between image (which in this tradition does the work of metaphor), word, and meaning:

> The image gives off meaning; words elucidate the image. To give a full account of the meaning, nothing is as good as the image; to give a full

account of the image, nothing is as good as words. Because words are produced from images, we can seek out words as a window on the image. And because the image is produced from meaning, we can seek out the image as a window on meaning. Meaning is given full account with the image, and the image is articulated with words. Hence, words are whereby we elucidate the image. Having gotten the image, we can forget the words. The image is whereby we preserve meanings. Having gotten the meaning, we can forget the image. . . . For this reason, preserving the words is not getting to the image; preserving the image is not getting to the meaning.[10]

In classical Western epistemology, a distinction between object and idea is assumed. Idea is a representation of the essential structure of the object in the subject. Essentialistic "things" can be explained by causal chains, and allow for the isolation of reasons or causes. Language mediates this distinction between object and subject, and derives its meaning and its clarity as the articulation of what is essential in the world for the mind. Language is not reality, but is an instrument for capturing and explaining what is univocal and essential about it. "Knowing" occurs through the categories of language as a valid explanation of the correspondence between world and idea.

In this model, the limits of our language are indeed the limits of our world, because beyond explanation there is only indeterminacy. It is this disjunction between objective world and subjective representation which grounds the classical epistemic vocabulary of "to conceive, to comprehend, to perceive" which etymologically combines the notions of "to take effectively," "to take to oneself," "to take in and hold" with the sense of "formal, in set form." In this model, concepts are necessary conditions for knowing. A concept is a grasping of the form of something, what is essential to it.

In the Confucian world, as expressed here by Wang Pi, there is not the familiar disjunction between reality and the concrete world of phenomena. There is an unbroken line between image as what is real, image as the presentation (*not* re-presentation) of what is real, and image as the meaning of what is real. Image *is* reality. It is because this line is unbroken that the epistemic vocabulary of the *Analects* and classical Chinese more broadly is a language of tracing relationships—of "unraveling *(chieh),*" and "getting through without obstruction *(ta* or *t'ung).*" Perhaps one of the more vivid images is the frequently encountered appeal to the chariot metaphor where, with varying degrees of facility and varying pedigrees of horses, one courses through the cosmos from one end to the other, partaking of all its mysteries.[11]

The construction of human imagery is natural, pursued as a complement to the patterning of the heavens and the veins and relief of the earth's topography.[12] Importantly, the human enterprise of configuring the world takes the structures implicit in the heavens and the earth as models to inspire rather than as objects of imitation and replication.

Further, where a continuum is assumed between subject and object and the subject thus participates in the imagistic play which configures the world, images, far from being identical, are necessarily multivalent.[13]

Words as the articulation of the image do not identify and describe an independent reality, but inscribe it and participate in it. What is "known" exists as a function of being able to know—it does not exist prior to it. There is a natural "awakening to and manifesting *(chüeh)*" of a reality to which one has immediate access as something within *(wu or chüeh)* as opposed to the conceptual notion of "grasping something from without." And it is only by following the inscription—the image, the words, the path—that one comes to know the world.

In contrast with knowing as the grasping of what is essential—the making present of the being or *logos* of beings—knowing in a Confucian world involves a tracing out without obstruction of the correlated details and the extended pattern of relationships which obtain among them. Instead of a classical rationalistic epistemology dependent upon the categories of rational faculty, substance and accident, necessity and contingency, essence and attribute, and linear causal chains, Confucian knowing has as its goal a comprehensive and unobstructed awareness of interdependent conditions and their latent, vague possibilities, where the meaning and value of each element is a function of its own particular network of relationships.

Imaging permits direct access to concrete detail and nuance—the immediate noninferential intuition of a world—unmediated by abstract and intellectualized discourse. For example, one may appeal to the categories of correlative "kinds *(lei)*" to organize and explain items in the world. But the inclusion in any particular "kind" is a function of analogy and a dynamic mutual responsiveness rather than any set theoretical identity.[14] And the correlations that one can pursue among the welter of concrete details serves an analogous function to concept, where clarity is necessarily the high price paid for concreteness and immediacy.

The Chinese have traditionally attracted respect for their compilations of a quite astounding variety of data, which, by virtue of its concreteness, discloses the subtlety, detail, and particular relief of the historical terrain. On the other hand, they do not have the same pride of place when it comes to the broad strokes of theory, sweeping generalizations, and grand methodological programs which are willing to sacrifice a degree of nuance for the power to elucidate over vast tracks. The commentarial tradition that attends Confucius, for example, is a sustained effort to clarify richly vague images. The *hsün-ku* approach entails *"hsün,"* the tracking down of a particular meaning at a particular place and time, and *"ku,"* the identification and explanation of old objects: plants, minerals, animals, and so on. This approach stands in obvious contrast to a more conceptual and theoretically oriented methodology.

Chih as Modeling a World

In the *Analects,* the wise person—the person of *chih*—is frequently described as "not being confused *(pu-huo),"* in the sense of distinguishing clearly among alternatives and putting this discernment to work in selecting what is most appropriate.[15] When asked by one of his disciples to explain how to discriminate amid confusion, the student is presented with a concrete and specific scenario of what such confusion would look like: "In a fit of rage to forget the safety of one's own person, or worse, to forget the safety of one's family—is this not confusion?"[16] Even in explaining discrimination, Confucius does not appeal to concept, but rather appeals to concrete illustration or example. To what extent, then, does Confucian judgment require a conceptualized world?

It is at this point that we want to determine the role of correlative, imagistic thinking in the classical Chinese world as a basis for exploring what tends to be understood as the conceptual implications of *chih.* Above it has been observed that in classical Confucian thought, meaning emerges as a tension between the complementary and oppositional dispositions revealed in configuring or "imaging" the concrete world in a fruitful and efficacious way. "Imaging" a world is accomplished through tracing effective correlations among interdependent details. These correlations are effective to the extent that some interpretations tend to maximize difference, diversity, and opportunity, and, hence, are more productive of harmony than others.

Jacques Gernet observes that in the manipulation of the Chinese language, meaning is achieved in precisely this same way:

> Given that Chinese is an uninflected language, all that helps to guide one through a phrase, with the aid of a very limited number of particles, are the links between terms of similar meaning, the oppositions between terms of opposite meaning, the rhythms and parallelisms, the position of "words" or semantic units and the types of relationship between them; and yet the infinite possible combinations of two semantic units are the source of an inexhaustible fund of meaning. At every level, meaning stems from the way terms are combined. No doubt this is what accounts for the predominant role played by complementary pairs of opposites and correspondences in Chinese thought and above all for its fundamental relativism. Nothing has meaning except through opposition to its contrary. Everything depends upon position *(wei)* and timing *(shi).*[17]

I cite Gernet at such length here because what he has to say about the Chinese language can be applied broadly to the Chinese sense of order. He himself describes the Chinese culture as "a global universe where all things—dominant ideas, morality, religion, politics—were mutually related and echoed one another."[18]

In Gernet's analysis of the relationship between the Chinese language and correlative thinking, perhaps his sensitivity is most in evidence when, even though he believes this correlative world of the Chinese contrasts so starkly with our own that we find ourselves "in the presence of a different kind of humanity,"[19] he still stretches his own efforts at understanding to conclude:

> The lack of those mental categories which we take to be constitutive of all rational thought does not imply an essential inferiority, but rather different modalities of thought, the strength and flexibility of which may, on further consideration, be seen as advantages. In the manipulation of the Chinese language, the mental mechanisms and aptitudes that are at work are different from those which have been favoured in the West.[20]

By contrast with Gernet, Hellmut Wilhelm tends to characterize correlative thinking as protoconceptual:

> What we observe here is apparently an attempt to create and formulate concepts for specific purposes, if not to define them. We stand witness here to the first manifestation of a new stage in the self-realization of the human mind in which the faculty of judgment is first exercised and leads to abstractions distinct from images. . . . It would be a fallacy, however, to reduce these concepts entirely to their image antecedents and to deny to the authors of these early texts the faculty of abstraction that is reflected in these terms. It is a different mental faculty, newly awakened, than the one that contemplates and represents images. A realization of this faculty only renders to the hexagrams their tension, their clarity, and their authority.[21]

In Wilhelm's discussion of the polarity in the human mind between the "contemplated" image and the "reflective" concept, the reduction of the dynamic and performative effort of "imaging" to passive contemplation privileges conceptual thinking—the awakening of some hitherto unstimulated faculty. That is to say, the "compositioning" of particulars in the process of imaging is the functional equivalent of conceptual "judgments." It would seem that the operative difference between image and concept in Confucius could be more clearly construed culturally and historically where authoritative images gradually lose their specificity and detail in the process of appropriating them from one concrete situation and applying them analogously to another. *Hsiang* as "particular images" emerge to become "models." Through analogizing, then, models come to do the work that we expect of concepts. What is significant here is the fact that, given the historical and emergent nature of the Confucian "model," the assumption that these generalizations are in any sense univocal—justified either by some self-same identical characteristic or by some shared rational faculty—is simply not present. As one would anticipate in the classical Confucian context, the relationship between "image" and "model" is appropriately described in the language of polar opposition rather than dualism.[22]

One feature of classical Chinese philosophy that has been much noticed is the application of a common vocabulary to elaborate fundamentally disparate ideas. Each philosopher, regardless of his orientation, seems to appeal to a similar set of locutions to express what are radically differing positions. It is within the bounds of these models or "quasi-concepts" that the philosophers, through greater or lesser imagistic play, detail their unique insights.

A. C. Graham has observed that Hsün Tzu is the first philosopher in the classical Chinese tradition to make a distinction between the intellect or faculty of knowing, and the process of knowing something.[23] Hsün Tzu states that "the means whereby one knows (chih) inherent in a person is called the intellect (chih)."[24] This would suggest that, for Confucius at least, no distinction is drawn between a superordinate faculty of cognition and what is cognized. What one knows and how one knows are mutually determining. This is not to suggest that Confucius denies the biological basis of human experience, but to claim that for him the structure of human rationality is importantly contingent—an ongoing process specific to social, cultural, and, of course, natural conditions.

There is much in the ongoing conversation among contemporary philosophers—Thomas Kuhn, Paul Feyerabend, Richard Rorty, Alasdair MacIntyre, and Hans-Georg Gadamer—that amounts to an assault upon classical notions of rationality. This critique, meant as it is to free us from "the myth of the given," enables us to consider the possibility of a tradition in which rationality emerges largely as the product of a historical and cultural process. Alasdair MacIntyre is almost representative of the current climate in insisting that "the teaching of method is nothing other than the teaching of a certain kind of history."[25] For Confucianism, rationality is coherence in experience that is ultimately historically and culturally grounded.

Chih as Historical Experience

I want to recall that in the Confucian model, chih does not refer to the application or operation of some essentialistic intellect or faculty of mind. For this reason, the early tradition will not support a rationalist/empiricist kind of distinction. Chih is irreducibly experiential. And as experience, it is culturally and historically constructed. While we tend to associate "knowing" with the mind of the individual knower, an alternative model would see knowledge, especially where it is importantly imagistic, emerging from out of the social and cultural dynamics of experience in the world. Chih is chih tao—knowing the "way," a specific cultural tradition. My claim is not that chih is some universal human enterprise which, in different situations and under varied conditions, takes on its cultural particularity. Rather, I want to underscore the extent to which a career of experience shapes chih and makes it profoundly particular. Chih is formed dialectically amid cultural and social forces, both shaping and being shaped by them.

In A. S. Cua's analysis of argumentation in Hsün Tzu, the most "rationalistic" of the classical Confucians, Cua is concerned that the function of history, the repository of experience which makes the exercise of Confucian rationality invariably "concrete," be fully appreciated.[26] Valid reasoning in Confucius is the discovery and articulation of appropriate and efficacious historical instances of reasonableness.

As David L. Hall suggests, standards of historical and philosophical explanation are analogous.[27] The criteria applied in the compilation of historical records and the criteria for ascertaining the nature, extent, and veracity of knowledge are one and the same. The historian is philosopher. This being the case, what do the peculiarly didactic, hagiographic, and moralizing commitments of Chinese historiography mean for its philosophic standards?

In our tradition, dating back to the classical Greeks, there is an epistemic hierarchy which encourages the notion that the purest forms of ratiocination are of a "scientific" character in the sense that they are free of the affective and the moral.[28] A distinctive feature of both Chinese philosophy and historiography is the absence of any attempt to separate out and privilege the "cognitive" logical and ostensibly objective explanation (logos) from the more subjective "affective" (pathos) and "volitional" (ethos) means of persuasion. In our attempt to understand the standards governing Chinese historiography, the ritual and religious purposes served in the preparation of dynastic histories must be taken into account.[29] In thinking, talking, and writing about historical events, the discourse is clearly and explicitly moral, and revealing of a value system which the philosopher-historian seeks to promote.

One recurring feature of the Chinese tradition which is certainly evident in the *Analects* is the degree to which it seems to appeal to history rather than an established mythology as its primary resource for imagery. This, I suspect, is due to the intimate relationship between myth and history in the Chinese world. That is, myths have their origins in and are elaborations upon historical events, and hence, are inseparable from them. Although Chinese mythology looks euhemeristic in character—the emergence of myth out of historical personages and incidents—one hesitates to use "euhemerism" in explanation of Chinese *mythos* because it implies a rationalization of mythology—a reduction of *mythos* to the *logos* of history in order to recover its authority.

In the Chinese case, the situation is reversed. *Mythos* is the gradual "mythologization" of history as a means of investing the historical record with additional authority. The assumption that the historical record has greater veracity than the mythological explanation, or even that there is some standard for separating these two, is not important in the tradition.

A distinction between biography and hagiography is dependent upon a separation of the secular and the sacred that is not characteristic of early Chinese thought. Rather, the mythological and hagiographic explanation is a fortified and more adequate historical explanation.

Chih as Social

With respect to the locus of *chih,* we must begin from the commonly observed feature of classical Confucianism that the person is irreducibly social. The arguments for the composite, aggregate, and relationally defined person have been made rather persuasively, and yet the implications of this relational definition of person have not been very vigorously pursued. For example, this definition of person applied to an epistemological model would mean that those psychological assumptions dependent upon the existence of some discrete *psyche* as locus of "the solitary knower" would lose place to a sociology of knowledge. Epistemic terminology certainly defines the relationship between oneself and one's world, but what is at issue here is the extent to which the Confucian focus is on self or on world, and the extent to which the self is to be understood as private and autonomous. The problem that I want to pursue is this: where in our tradition, to whatever degree "knowing" may be construed as the condition of an individual mind and knowledge as a kind of private property, this characterization would serve poorly as an explanation for *chih.* In fact, as we shall discover, *chih* is not only communal, but its status and value are a function of the extent to which it fosters social cohesiveness. To interiorize *chih* is to degrade it.

There is one passage in the *Analects* which on the surface would seem to challenge a sociological basis for a Confucian epistemology, but which, on closer scrutiny, can in fact serve to elucidate the position. D. C. Lau translates *Analects* 16/9 as follows:

> Confucius said: "Those who are born with knowledge [*chih*] are the highest. Next come those who attain knowledge through study. Next again come those who turn to study after having been vexed by difficulties. The common people, in so far as they make no effort to study even after having been vexed by difficulties, are the lowest."

There are many scholars who would read this as a reason/experience distinction. To clarify what is in fact intended by this passage, Ch'en Ta-ch'i appeals to a second related passage (7/20):

> The Master said, "I was not born with knowledge but, being fond of antiquity, am quick to seek it."

If being "born with knowledge" referred to rational as opposed to empirical knowledge, Confucius would be going beyond the demands of modesty in denying that he, unlike other human beings, was lacking this capacity. Ch'en Ta-ch'i then goes on to argue that Confucius is not establishing a distinction between rational and empirical knowledge, but rather is attempting to distinguish and describe three different grades of innate intelligence.

While Ch'en Ta-ch'i's critique on the rational/empirical distinction is persuasive, I am reluctant to allow that Confucius is referring to an individuating innate intelligence that entails an otherwise unnoticed nature/nurture distinction.[30] First, the character *sheng* that D. C. Lau translates as "born" is one of those terms I referred to above as being defined by a cluster of several isolated meanings which must, to capture the full sense of the term, be reintegrated as a textured and interpenetrating field of meaning. Lau translates the same term *sheng* elsewhere as "life,"[31] and "to live."[32] *Sheng* means "to be born, to grow, and to live a life"—the maturation of a continuing growth. Hence, the passage cited above should read: "those who are born, grow and live a life with *chih*," rather than "those who are born with *chih*."

Given that a person is irreducibly social and relational, he can intuit *chih* from the *ethos* or character of the culture in which he lives. In fact, rather than thinking in terms of the characteristics of sovereign individuals who cumulatively constitute a cultured community, we must reverse the gestalt, and think of the cultural ambiance in its "personal" character. A person derives *chih* from his environing conditions. One dimension of these environing conditions is the pattern of interpersonal bonds invested with cultural importances which tie a person into a family and community. A person whose world was the golden age of the Chou dynasty would, by virtue of the environing conditions which constitute him, have immediate access to a higher quality of *chih* than someone living in the chaos of the Warring States period or on the barbarian frontier.

A second point to be made from this passage is that the category of persons who are wise without learning illustrates the recurrent play between *historia* and *mythos* that I want to suggest is comparable to the importance of the *historia* and *logos* relationship familiar in our tradition. Although Confucius defines himself in terms of *hao hsüeh*—his fondness for learning—he is quite ready to allow that there may exist a category of persons for whom wisdom is more readily available in the network of relationships that constitute their world.

One clear signal of the Confucian sociology of knowledge is the presumption that *chih* is productive of communal harmony and enjoyment. There are two passages in the *Analects* that make the link between *chih* and enjoyment explicit:

> Those who are *chih* enjoy water; . . . those who are *chih* find enjoyment.
> . . . Being fond of something is better than simply *"chih"*-ing it; finding enjoyment in it is better than simply being fond of it.[33]

The person of *chih* is a master communicator, and acts to reinforce those social relationships that establish consensus and conduce to happiness. His is a social intelligence and sensibility to which communication is integral.[34]

Chih and the Affective

Among the many dualisms that have structured our early philosophic dialectic, one of considerable prominence that has pervasive implications is our willing separation of the cognitive and the affective. This dualism has many labels: thinking and feeling, reason and passion, mentality and sentimentality, thought and emotion. As was observed above, it is typical of these dualistic categories that one—in this case, the cognitive element—is valued over the other—the affective. Catherine Lutz, in her synopsis of the traditional Western attitudes toward thinking and emotion, lays out a complex picture which, for want of space, can be summarize1 as contrasting sets of associations.

THOUGHT (COGNITIVE)	EMOTIONS (AFFECTIVE)
rational	irrational
intentional	unintentional
mental	physical
cultural	natural
universal	personal
predictable	unpredictable
controlling	uncontrollable
detachment	attachment
fact	value
logic	rhetoric
decisive	dispositional

This is not intended to paint an overly simple picture, but merely is a point of departure for understanding the contrast between Western and Confucian contextualizations of emotion.

The first indication that this dualism is not operative in the classical Confucian world is the identification of both the cognitive and affective with the *hsin*, requiring that we translate what is physically the heart as the "heart-and-mind." It is not that *hsin* sometimes means one thing, and sometimes the other, but rather that it always means both. Mental events do not simply evoke an emotion—they are not attended by an emotion. Rather, the cognitive and the affective are integrally and inextricably intertwined: one "feels" one's thoughts. Thoughts are colored rather than black and white.

This claim that the passions are not separate from thinking is borne out by A. C. Graham's insistence that *ch'ing*, conventionally rendered "passions" in our translations of classical texts, may *refer* to the passions as integral to our genuine selves, but in the pre-Han literature it never *means* "passions."[35] This means that there is no superordinate category that translates "emotions" or "passions" in counterdistinction to "cognition." Situations are always experienced and interpreted both cognitively and emotionally.

Above in the discussion of "imaging" a world, I observed that the underlying image in the *Analects* is *tao*—the "way." It is important in the context of recognizing the affective dimension of tracing the *tao* to understand that in addition to emerging as a determinate "model" for being human, *tao* also refers to the "mode" and "mood" of being human—the indicative (fact) and subjunctive (desire) as well as the imperative (command) moods. *Tao* refers to the emotional consciousness or temper that attends and shapes all human experience, including mental acts.

In the classical language, and in the language of the *Analects* more specifically, there is no indication that *chih* is dispassionate. On the contrary, there are repeated cases where Confucius himself expresses the gamut of emotions, from humor to anger to exasperation. What is different about this celebration of the passions is that those which are encouraged are invariably productive and prosocial—emotions reflecting broad community concerns stimulated by a sense of what is appropriate *(yi)*, as opposed to idiosyncratic, disruptive responses that are at best self-serving *(li)* if not antisocial. Even anger can be educated to become a generous passion where it really does represent a just cause. Community leadership—social, political, and moral—is always emotional leadership.[36]

It is because *chih*, resisting dualistic distinctions, is both cognitive and affective that the holistic process of achieving authoritative personhood *(jen)* in Confucius is repeatedly defined in tandem with *chih*. For Confucius, *chih* is a necessary condition for *jen*.[37] Feng Ch'i, insisting that *jen* entails both emotion and rationality, has collected the many passages in the *Analects* which treat *jen* and *chih* together in his section on "A Discourse on the Unity of Authoritative Person *(jen)* and *chih*."[38] Confucius' two most prominent disciples in the classical period—Mencius and Hsün Tzu—both describe Confucius as "both *jen* and *chih*."[39] Feng Ch'i concludes that, since *chih* and *jen* are mutually entailing, this is the same as saying that for Confucius, epistemology and ethics are inseparable as a moral epistemology.[40]

Chih as Performative

Elsewhere David L. Hall and I have argued that *chih* in Confucius is fundamentally performative—it is "realizing" in the sense of "making real."[41] At issue in Confucius is first and foremost the transformation of human life. Without restating the arguments and illustrations, our points were basically three.

First, there is no "knowledge"/"wisdom" distinction in classical Chinese. This would indicate an unwillingness to allow for the separation between theory and praxis and between fact and value that distinguishes knowledge from wisdom in our own tradition.

Second, *chih* refers to a propensity for forecasting accurately the outcome of a coherent set of circumstances of which the forecaster himself is a constituent and participatory factor. It also entails a casting of the form of the future in such fashion and with such persuasive authority as to invite sympathy and participation.

Third, and corollary to the second point, *chih* requires the ability to articulate a future in language as a communal act, and to bring it to pass. Using Rylean language, *chih* is an "achievement" rather than an "attempt" word—a "performance verb."[42] It is speech and deed that effects an intended consequence.

Chih as Moral Prompting

Above, performative *chih* has been identified with the authoritative person as insistently prosocial—as appropriate and significant *(yi)* action rather than action which is only self-serving *(li*)*. The communal leader displays *chih* at the appropriate time and place to the benefit of his community, and in turn becomes the object of and occasion for their deference. His conduct establishes a bearing for moral behavior from whence society takes its direction.

I use "moral prompting" rather than "prescription" here to avoid the sense of external imposition that prescription entails, and to avoid the identification of morality with any particular person. Confucian ethics are participatory. The ethical force of *chih* lies in the achievement of the *ethos* or aesthetic character of the community.

The emphasis on the quality of particular detail as opposed to external principle as the source of harmonious engagement reveals the nature of the Confucian sense of harmony—it is an aesthetic as opposed to a logical order. It is the seeming unwillingness on the part of the positivistic and rule-oriented interpreters of Confucianism to understand the distinction between logical and aesthetic harmony that occasions their misreading of Confucian ethics.

For Confucius, talk of an "ideal language" is no more relevant in the moral sense than in the scientific. There is no "moral stuff" to which language may refer. The act of expressing, which presupposes in a crucial fashion, the act of *imaging* determines the elements which are candidates for social harmony. There is no antecedent moral pattern or structure to reflect in language. Moral harmony is not an imitation of some ideal moral reality—it is realized in the act of imaging and modeling as discussed above.

By contrast, A. N. Whitehead's definition of beauty resonates immediately with the underlying aesthetic sensibility of Confucian ethics:

Beauty is the internal conformation of the various items of experience with each other, for the production of maximum effectiveness.[43]

Whitehead goes on to disassociate this sense of harmony from the logical:

Now Harmony is more than logical compatibility, and Discord is more than logical incompatibility. Logicians are not called in to advise artists. The key to the explanation is the understanding of the prehension of individuality. This is the feeling of each objective factor as an individual "It" with its own significance. . . . An analogous substitute may deceive, but when discovered never does as well. The analogy may claim affection. But the original *It* commands a poignancy of feeling.[44]

In the Confucian world, in the absence of the reality/appearance distinction that generates a correspondence theory of truth, truth is not going to have the same philosophic import. As Whitehead says, "Truth is a qualification which applies to Appearance alone. Reality is just itself, and it is nonsense to ask whether it be true or false."[45] Given the aesthetic commitment of the Confucian sense of order, "Beauty is left as the one aim which by its very nature is self-justifying."[46] Instead of the dualistic truth/falsity distinction which leads to a propositional expression of truth, Confucius recognizes a world of unique particulars, and is concerned to distinguish the qualitatively authentic from the counterfeit. There is Confucius' concern for the inadequacy and impertinence of the "analogous substitute" that Whitehead alludes to above.[47]

Moral actions are not imitation of some ideal—that would render them counterfeit. They serve to "educate" the moral sphere, not to imitate it.[48] That is, every creative imaging and modeling activity manifests internal articulations of the elements of social life which leads to the "mutual adaptation of the several factors in an occasion of experience."[49]

In this essay, I have attempted to recover those dimensions of the classical Chinese term, *chih*, that have been concealed by the conventional translation, "to know." From this exploration of *chih* and its range of meaning, it becomes clear at least that a formulaic translation of this term as simply "to know" puts at risk a great deal that is philosophically significant. Without detailing the welter of competing theories of knowledge which comprise the inventory of Western philosophy, it still is apparent that *chih* denotes a cluster of meanings that are not all coincident with any in our tradition.

Given the implications of *chih*—namely, performative, productive, social, affective, and, above all, fundamentally aesthetic as well as cognitive—it would seem that as a term it comes closer to a broad notion of cultivation rather than some more sharply defined cognitive exercise. This seeming broadness, of course, is much muted by the parochializing constraints that these implications impose on the range of knowledge. That is, for the same reasons that early Confucianism sponsors a graduated rather than a universal notion of love, it also sponsors a kind of knowledge that is narrowly focused. If the degree of "cultivation-as-knowledge" is burdened by participatory and productive demands, the penalty one pays for the depth and quality of detail is the range of jurisdiction and validity. *Chih* means a successful configuring of one's world through the process of modeling. In the *Analects,* when Fan Ch'ih asks Confucius what he means by *chih,* Confucius defines it as *chih jen*—"*chih* others."⁵⁰ While this expression is most frequently translated as "know others," in fact Confucius' own explanation to Fan Ch'ih, who complains that he does not understand, is that *chih* is "the process of applying the straight to true up the bent."⁵¹ The point is that to "*chih* others" entails the cultivation of the people by providing a concrete, evocative, and effective model.

Notes

1. See *Thinking Through Confucius* (Albany, New York: SUNY Press, 1987), in particular, "Some Uncommon Assumptions," pp. 11–25.

2. *Analects* 7/1. The primary meaning of *shu* is "to follow along the path." By extension, it means "to record," "to transmit."

3. See *Analects* 4/15 and particularly 15/3.

4. See Feng Ch'i, *Chung-kuo ku-tai che-hsüeh te lo-chi fa-chan* (The logical development of ancient Chinese philosophy) (Shanghai: Shanghai Peoples' Press, 1983), vol 1: 84.

5. In fact, just as *cosmos* means an elegant as well as an ordered, so *logos* means *oratio* as well as *ratio.* That is, the aesthetic and rhetorical side of cosmology tends to go unnoticed in our contemporary interpretation of the classical tradition.

6. See Willard J. Peterson, "Making Connections: 'Commentary on the Attached Verbalizations' of the *Book of Change,*" *Harvard Journal of Asiatic Studies* 42, no. 1 (June 1982): 67–116, especially pp. 80–81.

7. See *Yi Ching* 41/*hsi shang*/6. Cf. Peterson, "Making Connections," p. 114.

8. See the *Chou Yi* in the Harvard-Yenching Index Series, 44/*hsi shang*/12. Cf. *The I Ching or Book of Changes,* by Richard Wilhelm, translated into English by Cary F. Baynes, 3d ed. (Princeton: Princeton University Press, 1967), p. 322.

9. See George Lakoff and Mark Johnson, *Metaphors We Live By* (Chicago: University of Chicago Press, 1980), and more recently, George Lakoff, *Women, Fire, and Dangerous Things* (Chicago: University of Chicago Press, 1987). See also Stephen C. Pepper's classic treatment of metaphors underlying our meta-

physical traditions, in *World Hypotheses* (Berkeley: University of California Press, 1942).

10. See Wang Pi, "Ming Hsiang" (Elucidating the image), in his *Chou Yi lüeh-li* (A summary introduction to the *Book of Change*), in the *Pai-pu ts'ung-shu chi ch'eng* 10b–11b.

11. The *Huai Nan Tzu* is replete with this epistemic imagery in the most hyperbolic terms.

12. Hellmut Wilhelm, in his discussion of imagery in the *Yi Ching* collects passages from the text that connect the formulation of human imagery with the patterning of heaven and earth. See *Heaven, Earth, and Man in the Book of Changes* (Seattle: University of Washington Press, 1977), especially pp. 198–199.

13. For a discussion of the function of image in Chinese thought, see Pauline Yu's *The Reading of Imagery in the Chinese Poetic Tradition* (Princeton: Princeton University Press, 1987), especially chapter one: "Setting the Terms." See also Stephen Owen, *Traditional Chinese Poetry and Poetics* (Madison: University of Wisconsin Press, 1985), especially chapter one: "Omen of the World: Meaning in the Chinese Lyric."

14. See A. C. Cua, *Ethical Argumentation: A Study in Hsün Tzu's Moral Epistemology* (Honolulu: University of Hawaii Press, 1985).

15. See, for example, *Analects* 9/29 and 14/28.

16. *Analects* 12/21.

17. See Jacques Gernet, *China and the Christian Impact: A Conflict of Cultures,* (Cambridge: Cambridge University Press, 1985), p. 242.

18. Ibid., p. 247.

19. Ibid.

20. Ibid., p. 242.

21. H. Wilhelm, *Heaven, Earth, and Man,* pp. 200–201.

22. See *Thinking Through Confucius,* pp. 17–21, for an elaboration of this distinction.

23. See A. C. Graham, *Studies in Chinese Philosophy and Philosophical Literature* (Singapore: Institute of East Asian Philosophies, 1986), p. 15.

24. See *Hsün Tzu* in the Harvard-Yenching Concordances, 83/22/5.

25. I have borrowed this passage from Richard Bernstein's citation of a pre-revision article of MacIntyre's that was later published in an abbreviated form in the *Monist* 60 (1977): 453–472. See *Beyond Objectivism and Relativism* (Philadelphia: University of Pennsylvania Press, 1983), p. 57.

26. A. S. Cua, *Ethical Argumentation,* pp. 96–97.

27. See David L. Hall, "Cultural Requisites for a Theory of Truth in China" (manuscript), p. 19.

28. See Catherine Lutz, *Unnatural Emotions* (Chicago: University of Chicago Press, 1988).

29. See Michael Loewe's discussion of "The Structure and Practice of Government," in Michael Loewe and Denis Twitchett, eds., *The Cambridge History of China,* vol. 1 (Cambridge: Cambridge University Press, 1986), p. 468 and pp. 493–494.

30. See my article, "Does *renxing* in the *Mencius* really mean 'human nature'?" in *Texts and Contexts: Studies in Chinese Philosophy in Honor of A. C. Graham,* ed. by Henry Rosemont, Jr. (New York: Open Court, 1991).

31. See *Analects* 11/12, 12/5, 12/10, and 15/9.

32. Ibid., 6/19.

33. *Analects* 6/20 and 6/23.

34. See the discussion of "The Sage *(sheng jen)* as Master of Communication," in *Thinking Through Confucius,* pp. 296–304.

35. See A. C. Graham, pp. 59–65.

36. See Catherine Lutz, *Unnatural Emotions,* p. 160.

37. In *Analects* 5/19, Confucius says of Ling Yin Tzu-wen and Ch'en Wen Tzu, "They are not *chih*—how could they be *jen?*"

38. Feng Ch'i, *Chung-kuo ku-tai che-hsüeh,* vol. 1, pp. 82–89.

39. See *Mencius* 2A:2 and *Hsün Tzu* 79/21/26.

40. Feng Ch'i, *Chung-kuo ku-tai che-hsüeh,* pp. 89–90.

41. See my paper, "Confucius and the Ontology of Knowing," in Gerald J. Larson and Eliot Deutsch, eds., *Interpreting Across Boundaries: New Essays in Comparative Philosophy* (Princeton: Princeton University Press, 1988), pp. 265–279. See also *Thinking Through Confucius,* pp. 50–62.

42. See Gilbert Ryle, *The Concept of Mind* (London: Hutchinson & Co., 1949), pp. 130–131 and 149–153.

43. A. N. Whitehead, *Adventures of Ideas* (New York: Free Press, 1967), p. 265.

44. Ibid., pp. 261–262.

45. Ibid., p. 241.

46. Ibid., p. 266.

47. For the prominence of Confucius' concern over dissemblance, see D. C. Lau's Introduction to *The Analects.* See also *Thinking Through Confucius,* p. 279.

48. Ibid., pp. 270–271. "Art is the education of nature."

49. Ibid., p. 252.

50. *Analects* 12/22.

51. Ibid. In another related passage—2/19—Confucius uses this same expression, "apply the straight to true up the bent," in a political context as a method for attracting the deference and respect of the people.

ON THE DUAL NATURE OF TRADITIONAL CHINESE THOUGHT AND ITS MODERNIZATION

Chinese intellectuals living at a time when history and contemporary reality converge may often find themselves greatly perplexed by certain questions. How is it that China, having created so splendid a culture and having stood for so long at the forefront of world civilization, has come to lag so far behind the West in modern times? Why does she proceed with such difficulty, pacing back and forth along the road to modernization?

In the wake of the "culture mania" that has swept China since 1980, people have felt an urge to take a closer look at traditional Chinese thought. This essay is in no way intended as a comprehensive study of traditional thought, but rather is devoted to a brief discussion of its dual nature and the process of modernizing it; thereby it is hoped that some tentative answers will be provided for the questions just raised.

The Dual Nature of Logical Thought

In ancient China, there were two modes or models of logical thought. One was formal logic, represented by the *Mo Jing* (Mohist Canon), and the other was dialectical logic, represented by Xun Zi, the *Yi Zhuan* (Appendixes of the Book of Changes), the *Nei Jing* (Classic of Internal Medicine), and so on. Dr. Joseph Needham, the renowned authority on the history of science in China, has pointed out that "While the Greeks and Indians paid early and detailed attention to formal logic, the Chinese showed a constant tendency to develop dialectical logic."[1] This argument is quite reasonable. It is true that dialectical logic was fully developed in China after the Han dynasty, while formal logic fell short in its development, and that there was a general indifference to the latter. A *concept* is the cell of logical thinking, and the concepts employed by the Chinese usually bear the characteristics of dialectical thinking.

The first of these characteristics is flexibility. The pre-Qin philosopher Zhuang Zi held that "there is no movement through which things do not become modified, no time when they are not changed"; therefore, change could only be comprehended by a kind of changeable *zhi yan* (language which flows over, as from a goblet), namely, a kind of flexible language. And Xun Zi also noticed the mobility of concepts, just as he pointed out that names (concepts) were established by usage according to historical changes.

The second characteristic is polysemy. This means that a concept may actually cover different meanings. What is called *ren* (humanity) by Confucius has dozens of definitions: for example, "It is to love man," "Humanity is the denial of self and response to the right and proper," "Do not do to others what you do not like yourself," and so forth. Lao Zi discussed the concept of *Tao* in the same way.

The third characteristic is multiple function: a concept may often have different functions in Chinese traditional philosophical thought. For example, *qi,* can sometimes refer to natural forces (the "Six Energies"), or to mind (the "noble spirit"), or to material original principle ("subtle matter," "original matter"), or to substance or noumenon ("*qi* made up of *yin* and *yang*").

The fourth is integration. In ancient Chinese language, an abstract concept usually consists of one monosyllabic character; only by explaining it from various angles can it be delineated as a whole. For example, the concept of *zhi* discussed in the Mohist Canon must be viewed as a whole involving three integral parts: "Knowing *(zhi)* is a faculty" (the ability to know), "Knowledge *(zhi)* is a meeting" (the cognitive process), and "Mind-knowledge *(zhi)* is an understanding" (the effect of knowledge).

Now let us examine the method of reasoning in traditional Chinese thinking. It occurs as a kind of systematic inference (that is, a system that can be inferred from another system), which is different from Western propositional inference. The Chinese inference is also full of dialectical concepts.

The first concept is of dynamism. The two opposite symbols "——" and "— —" form a dynamic system of strong and weak. Combining these two symbols, the *Yi Jing* (Book of Changes)—which signaled the beginning of Chinese philosophy—inferred a more complex dynamic system of eight trigrams and sixty-four hexagrams, with the latter derived from a combination of any two of the original eight trigrams. Thus it was said that "through the interplay of the strong and the weak, change and transformation become manifest."

The second concept is of organicism. For example, the *Classic of Internal Medicine* says that a doctor can measure, discriminate, and explain the functions of a patient's internal organs simply by feeling the patient's pulse. Obviously it considered the "*yin-yang* and five elements," the five internal organs, and the patient's physiological and mental changes as an organic and interconnected whole.

The third is a concept of the unity of opposites. Xun Zi pointed out that reasoning ("dialection and explanation") involved contradictions and was a process by which to comprehend "the way of movement and quiescence." And Wang Fuzhi held that reasoning was a contradictory movement between good and bad luck, joy and anger, gain and loss.

It should be said that one of the merits of traditional Chinese thought was that it paid such great attention to dialectical logic; however, its neglect of formal logic has resulted in a good number of grave drawbacks.

First of all, its concepts and methods of inference were not strict. Since its concepts were polysemous and flexible, they were ambiguous and inexact at best; thus the concrete aspects of objects were hard to grasp from a narrow perspective. Since its systematic inference lacked definite rules and procedures and depended simply on analogous inference, there were always a good number of strained interpretations. For example, when the norms of the Way of man were derived from the Way of Heaven, or when the mysteries of the Way of Heaven were derived from the Way of man, the differences between systems with regard to their levels, features, and elements were usually overlooked.

Second, the degree of systematization and formalization of Chinese logic was decidedly inferior to that of the West, and this has had a direct influence on the backwardness of modern Chinese science. Ancient Chinese science failed entirely to produce a theoretical system of mechanics. Though in the Mohist Canon there are studies of some forms of the physics of statics—the lever, the pulley, and so forth—this sort of investigation eventually ceased, and there was no further progress. Modern science, however, began with precisely this subject of mechanics, mainly with investigations into mechanical motion—and this type of investigation depended particularly on the principles of formal logic. But in China the conditions for such research did not exist.

Ancient Chinese science also failed completely to construct a system for forming hypotheses. For example, Chinese astronomy had quite a few advantages in the areas of astronomical observation and date calculation—there was but one step between the celestial globe created by Zhang Heng, a scientist of the Han dynasty, and the geocentric system advanced by his contemporary Ptolemy. But subsequent Chinese astronomers could not make this one step forward, because what concerned them was merely exposition and technique, and they lacked a system for creating hypotheses that could attempt to explain the movements of the celestial bodies that made up the universe. This deficiency is also related to the lack of formal logic in China.

Ancient Chinese theories of mathematics likewise lacked logical systematization. Many mathematicians such as Liu Hui, Zu Chongzhi, and Shen Kuo put emphasis on revealing the dialectical aspects of mathematical logic, and they regarded calculation as superior to demonstration, and algebra as superior to geometry. Undoubtedly these predispositions hampered the development of systems for axiomatic deduction like Euclidean geometry, the formalization of symbols, the simplification of operational signs, and the achievement of greater accuracy in mathematical conceptualization, operational rules, and relations between number and shape. All of the foregoing are naturally related to formal logic.

Thus it can be seen that dialectical logic played a positive role in ancient Chinese thought—but at the same time it hindered the development of modern science.

The Dual Nature of the Theory of Knowledge

Viewed in the context of its epistemology, the traditional Chinese way of thinking clearly bears the imprint of dialectics. In this respect, there are two important characteristics, which are discussed in what follows.

1. The Integrative Connection

In correspondence with the fact that traditional Chinese philosophy views the Universe as organic, the first characteristic of traditional Chinese thought is its integrative connection, which is involved in two specific models.

One is the model of the "mysterious union between the *yin-yang* and the five elements." The *yin-yang* was seen as an integral whole representing the things that were opposite to each other and interrelated in space and time. The five elements (metal, wood, water, fire, and earth) were also seen as a whole. As this whole expanded outward, some relevant wholes such as the five colors, five tones, five flavors, five internal organs, and the like were derived from it; as it developed inward, the doctrine of mutual promotion and restraint among the five elements came into being and became a model of the vital and interconnected phenomena of nature. The *yin-yang* and the five elements had originally been two independent wholes until the late Warring States period and the early Han dynasty, when the two were integrated into one great whole in such writings as *Lu's Almanac,* the *Classic of Internal Medicine,* the *Huai Nan Zi,* and so on, with the advancement of the concept of *yuan qi.* In the words of Zhou Dunyi, "The essences of Two (*yin* and *yang*) and Five (elements) unite in mysterious union so that consolidation ensues." This kind of model represents the deep-rooted conception of the universe and nature that existed in Chinese thinking.

The other model is of the "interaction between Heaven and man." This model, whether in the form of the "unity of man with Heaven" or of the "distinctive functions of Heaven and man," regarded Heaven and man as an integral whole with unified laws and a rhythm of changes. In Wang Fuzhi's opinion, though "heavenly Heaven" (thing-in-itself) differed from "man's Heaven" (thing-for-us) in its form and qualities, it could still be transformed into "man's Heaven" and man could "make his own destiny" and would "conquer Heaven," since Heaven and man had combined into one. This was a correct attitude toward the relationship between Heaven and man, according to the traditional way of thinking.

2. The Inseparableness of Ti and Yong

The traditional Chinese way of thinking that is reflected in the knowledge of the substance and cause of motion in things can be expressed in terms of the inseparableness of *ti* (substance) and *yong* (function).

Wang Pi, a thinker of the Mysterious Learning, of the Wei period, was the first to advance this idea. According to Wang, the *function* of "nonbeing" could not separate itself from the *substance* of "nonbeing"; the function of "being" was also the manifestation of the function of "nonbeing." Similarly, Guo Xiang held that if there was some substance, then it had some function. Later, both the Buddhistic scholars of the Sui and Tang and the Neo-Confucianists of the Song and Ming periods also advocated the idea of the inseparableness of *ti* and *yong;* the former thought that substance and phenomenon were unified on the basis of heart (mind), and the latter (especially Zhu Xi) united *ti* with *yong* on the basis of "principle" *(li)*.

Some materialist philosophers tried to prove the inseparableness of *ti* and *yong* through the doctrine of *qi*. Zhang Zai, for example, pointed to the "Great Void in which no shapes exist; such is the *qi* in its original substance." This was his summation of the debate over "being and nonbeing." This kind of thinking displays the characteristic theoretical orientation of the Chinese with regard to the knowledge of the category of cause *(gu)*.

3. The Harmony of Opposites

This is a theoretical framework for a way of thinking about the law of development of things *(li)*.

The *Yi Zhuan* (Appendixes of the Book of Changes) says: "One *yin* and one *yang* constitute what is called *Tao,* " and "Through the interplay of the strong and the weak, change and transformation become manifest," assuming that though the world is full of various contradictions it has achieved a harmonious development.

Taoism advocates the idea of harmony of opposites as well. Lao Zi says: "The movement of Tao consists in reversion," holding that everything in the world is produced from opposites in contradiction—for example, *yin* (negative forces) and *yang* (positive forces)—and everything moves towards its opposite: "Being and nonbeing produce each other, difficult and easy complete each other, long and short contrast each other, high and low distinguish each other, sound and voice harmonize with each other." Taoism holds that the two opposites in a contradiction are mutually conditional and interdependent. Thus it can be seen that the relationship between the two opposites in a contradiction is a sort of dynamic harmony between two things in mutual antithesis, connection, and involvement.

This kind of thinking is widely prevalent in traditional Chinese culture and provides the Chinese theory of knowledge with a multidimensional structure of antitheses: righteousness and profit, humanity and righteousness, past and present, propriety and law, Heaven and man, names and actualities, being and nonbeing, principle and desire, and so forth.

Moreover, this way of perceiving things can be popularly formulated into two propositions. One is that everything in the world can be divided into two. The other is that two can harmoniously combine into one, just as Lao Zi says: "It is on the blending of the breaths of the *yin* and the *yang* that their harmony depends." The idea of a harmony of opposites is substantially aimed at a solution to the problem of the dialectical unity of "two" with "one," and it signifies the law of the unity of opposites within things and things at their best state.

However, traditional Chinese dialectical thinking has its faults. One of these faults is that the attempt to know an integral whole by blanket intuition has hampered the preciseness of thought. Chinese philosophy often made no distinction between subject and object since the image, properties, and features of the object and the experiences and feelings of the subject were merged into a single whole. This has imposed restrictions on the subject's ability to confirm the objective reality and its images, and has made it difficult to classify, sift, and abstract the perceptual material in terms of the intension and extension of a particular concept. On the other hand, ancient Chinese philosophers at times made a general survey of, and had a caricature-like understanding of, the objective world, comprehending the actual connection within things by means of fantasies or divinations. For example, in his prose poem "Heaven Asks," Qu Yuan raised more than 170 questions on the structure of the cosmos, but they were merely brilliant divinations and fell short of a concrete analysis and definite views of his own. Moreover, the Chinese liked to use ambiguous concepts and expressions of infinite capacity as their equations for solving all problems on nature, society, mind, and so on. An example is the saying that "One *yin* and one *yang* constitute what is called *Tao.*" In fact, the mysteries of nature and the essence of things cannot be expounded in this way.

The second fault is that mystical intuition has replaced conceptual thinking. Namely, it is through intuitive perception instead of conceptual analysis and linguistic expression that we are able to comprehend objects and truths. This is the common approach advocated by Confucianism, Taoism, Mysterious Learning, and Buddhism. For example, Zhu Xi, the eminent representative of Neo-Confucianism, maintained that the extension of knowledge lay in the investigation of things, but the prerequisite for grasping absolute truth was that "when one has exerted oneself for a long time, finally a morning will come when complete understanding will open before one." In Lao Zi's opinion, *Tao* was eternal and had no name, so one must abandon sageliness and discard wisdom if one wanted to grasp the *Tao*. And the Chan (Zen) school of Buddhism held that one could become a buddha by practicing meditation without the use of written texts, and so forth. All of this is sheer mysticism.

The third fault is that the dogmatism adopted by classical learning has checked the development of independent thinking. This dogmatism has three main characteristics: (1) *Adhere to the one:* one need not seek the truth; all one has to do is to follow the teachings of the sages (Confucius, Mencius, and so on) or to interpret and copy their teachings. (2) *Preserve uniformity with the one:* one should make idols of the sages, consider their teachings as absolute truth, and take the classics and the interpretations of them made by imperial order as the standard for judging everything. (3) *Reduce to the one:* on the one hand this means that "Many" should be reduced to "One," and that "One" should replace "Many" in order to keep a balance in one's thinking between subtle forces of attraction. This latter is actually an eclecticist doctrine of compromise. On the other hand, it refers to the case in which one is infatuated with the solution for the object as a whole while doing little quantitative analysis and making little use of one's intellect. This is the doctrine that everything has only one aspect. Obviously it is not sufficiently comprehensive.

In short, the dogmatism of classical learning represses individual expression in thought and smothers one's independence, critical spirit, and creativity.

The Impact of Modernization

In 1840 the roar of British cannons brought China fully into contact with the Western world; all manner of new ideas swarmed in, changing the direction of Chinese culture and the traditional ways of thinking, including philosophy, which had evolved in isolation over several thousand years. The bonds with classical learning were severed, hastening the modern transformation of Chinese thought.

At the outset of the modern period, Gong Zizhen, looking down from his philosophical heights, held in esteem the idea of "self." Of course, this was a new idea that ran counter to the traditional thought of classical learning. Wei Yuan said of Gong that "his principle usually regards reversion as a major event." Kang Youwei further put forward the proposition that the task of the new learning was to break with convention—that is, to be bold enough to go against the tide of classical learning. Liang Qichao, who claimed to be a modern Chen She or Wu Guang of the contemporary world of ideas, proposed to demolish the mind-set of classical learning through a principle of destruction: first, tear off the Confucian mask; second, break away from dependence on Confucius; and third, break with the "slavery of study" and the "enslavement of the mind." What Liang longed for, he said, was freedom: "Freedom is the acknowledged truth of the world and the essential tool for life," and "Truth issues where there is freedom of thought." During the May Fourth Movement of 1919, Chen Duxiu and others upheld the two banners of science and democracy. Chen wanted to use the weapon of science to "purge thoroughly" the way of thinking of classical learning, while at the same time he wanted to safeguard the "right of personal freedom," "independent personal self-expression," and "freedom of individual thought." These were certainly powerful lances actively directed at the mind-set of classical learning.

The introduction of Western formal logic was a major step toward the modernization of the traditional way of thinking. Yan Fu, with the perception of an enlightened thinker, independently pioneered the introduction of Western systematic logic. He pointed out that logical thinking was "the method for studying all principles and rules, a science with which to learn all other sciences." In particular, he spoke highly of the inductive method. Zhang Taiyan, another proponent of logical thought, laid stress, however, on the deductive method; he was the first to make a valuable study of the similarities and differences between Aristotelian logic, Indian classical logic, and the Chinese Mohist Canon. Liang Qichao made a study of history using the deductive method, offering the following points of emphasis: "View the matter comprehensively," "There are expositions as well as inference," "Pay attention to the cause as well as to the effect," and "Understand the randomness of historical events occurring down through thousands of years." Wang Guowei made a timely translation of one textbook on logic written by W. S. Jevons, and gave the following summary of the book: "For all things in the world, the part could not be known without reference to the whole and vice versa." This comes close to the idea of the unity of the particular and the general, of analysis and synthesis, and of induction and deduction.

Hu Shih not only exhumed the system of formal logic existing in the pre-Qin Mohist Canon but also offered the following observations: "Let the evidence be produced then," "Be bold in making hypotheses and be cautious in proceeding with verification," and "Behave as if in a scientific laboratory" in order to transform the traditional way of thinking. Chen Duxiu concluded that the scientific method was no more than inductive logic and proposed to employ a logical system as the basis for scientific thinking. During the 1930s and 1940s, Jin Yuelin provided a systematic introduction to Western deductive logic (especially the mathematical logic of Bertrand Russell) and included some innovations. In some of his writings Jin established a theory of formal logic. This counts as a major achievement in the modernization of Chinese thought.

Since the May Fourth Movement, the introduction of Marxism has added a note of sobriety to the effort to modernize Chinese thought. Based upon an ideological analysis of culture, Marxism was welcomed by progressive Chinese intellectuals at that time, perhaps because it was realized that the Western learning that had been introduced thus far was alone not powerful enough to overcome the shortcomings of the old, established feudalistic way of thinking. There was an urgent need for a new philosophy.

What was the role played by the newly imported Marxism in the modernization of Chinese thought? Generally speaking, Marxism used the concept of unity of the general and the particular in its historical method of analyzing China's national predicament; it pointed out where China was heading and elevated the materialist concept of history to the level of a dialectical concept of development. Based on this methodology, along with a dynamic theory of reflection, a theory of the movement of cognition, and a method for the analysis of contradictions, Mao Zedong constructed an interpretation of a fundamental principle: he elevated a primitive dialectics to the level of dialectical materialism.

Now there is no need to be reticent over the fact that in the process of the application of Marxism to China and the modernization of the traditional Chinese way of thinking there have also been many shortcomings.

First, the close connection between the modernization of traditional thought on the one hand and the development of science and logic on the other has been neglected. In modern China some advanced thinkers like Kang Youwei, Liang Qichao, and Sun Yat-sen, and Marxists such as Li Da, Ai Siqi, Mao Zedong, and others all devoted too much attention to the political function of philosophy; they failed to relate philosophy to the natural sciences. At the same time, they did not make a conscious effort to change the traditional way of thinking in its weakest area: the want of a formal logic. On the contrary, they continued to follow, and even consolidated, the old traditional ways. For example, both Ai Siqi and Li Da downplayed and even denied a place for formal logic, believing that formal logic had lost its utility and had become a historical relic; dialectical logic was seen as the only "scientific" method of thinking. As Ai Siqi said, "Since there is already an advanced dynamic logic (dialectical logic), there is no need for formal logic." Mao Zedong made a great contribution to the theory of dialectical logic, but he barely touched on the subject of formal logic. This could not but constitute a barrier to the modernization of thought.

Second, traditional thought, characterized as it is by integration and intuition, often displays a tendency toward empiricism and an eagerness for quick success and immediate rewards, and this is diametrically opposed to the process of scientific thinking.

Take, for example, the attitude toward foreign ideas: most modern Chinese thinkers introduced certain aspects of Western philosophy according to their relevance to real-life, political themes and their utilitarian applications; the Chinese understanding of Western philosophy as a whole tended to be generalized, intuitive, and superficial. Yan Fu, for example, concerned himself mainly with the introduction of such Western ideas as were expounded in T. H. Huxley's *Evolution and Ethics and Other Essays,* whereas Yan chose to downplay Adam Smith's doctrine of individualism, Montesquieu's advocacy of the separation of powers, J. S. Mill's principle of induction, and the philosophy of Kant. And Liang Qichao introduced the Chinese to the idea that "sovereign power lies in the people," as represented in Rousseau's social contract—but Liang made little effort to preach the philosophies of Hobbes, Kant, and Bentham. Why *Evolution and Ethics* and *Social Contract* had such tremendous appeal in China can be explained by the fact that the choices made by the Chinese public from Western philosophy were very practical in nature. They chose ideas that were relevant to their experience.

Moreover, the Chinese interest in Marxism came about chiefly out of a concern for "saving China," and what was learned came mainly from Soviet publications. But knowledge of the Western cultural background which gave birth to Marxism—of its development and of the completeness and the scientific nature of its theory—was deficient. A certain degree of dogmatism was able to enter which precluded the assimilation of Western philosophy, under the pretext that this was Chinese Marxism; thus Marxism was converted into something conservative and stagnant. Even today, in an era of reform, there are still cases where instead of following well-established theories and doctrines, there are some persons who indiscriminately follow one particular theory for a moment and then flit on to a second theory the next moment, all in search of a panacea.

As for the attitude toward tradition, this, too, has been dependent on prevailing conditions. When it becomes necessary to inspire the people, to revitalize their natural confidence, the traditional culture is more useful; when there is a need to break away from the bondage of feudal autocracy, then the slogans for violent attack against the traditional culture are put up in readiness; and then, when idealism turns into disillusionment, some of the would-be radical reformers who were once so anti-tradition and anti-authority now become dispirited and seek to reinstate the old tradition, to the point of advocating a new authoritarianism.

And as for the relationship between theory and practice, there are some who neither believe in advanced theories from abroad nor aspire to create a uniquely Chinese system; they engage in neither logical analysis nor experimental verification, but grope in the dark, as if feeling their way across a river. The result is that they have become blind and have committed blunders in their attempt to provide guidance: for example, allowing prices to rise, deprecating education, and inhibiting democracy.

In the foregoing, it can be seen that empiricism, or the desire for rapid success and immediate reward, reflects the limitations of traditional Chinese thinking.

The third shortcoming is the dogmatism of classical learning, which frequently manifests itself in ideological intolerance. This dogmatism suits both feudal autocracy on the one hand and peasant sentiments on the other. Chinese peasants are both a diligent, revolutionary class and a superstitious, conservative class; they are apt to show reverence for persons in authority—a condition under which dogmatism can develop and spread unchecked. In this regard, history has provided two severe lessons.

One was the May Fourth Movement of 1919. At that time the two great banners of science and democracy were flown—the symbols of a revolution in which the dogmatism of classical learning was criticized by Chinese intellectuals. Some people of that period, however, declared that they would completely break with and abandon the traditional culture and instead absorb and improve on the better aspects of that tradition, in this way actually establishing a new culture. This example shows that the way of thinking embodied in classical learning still had influence on the Movement itself.

The other lesson was the so-called Great Cultural Revolution of 1966–1976. Those who mobilized this movement tried to destroy with one ideology all other forms of thought, referring to them as the "four olds" (old ideas, old culture, old customs, and old habits), and in the entire country only one brain was allowed to think, judge, and command. In this way a revolutionary cult was established to get rid of the old, to make way for the new, and thus establish a new proletarian, socialist culture. But on the contrary, the actual result was that dogmatism and certain decadent aspects of the tradition were allowed to spread unchecked under the mantle of Marxism. This was a historical tragedy for all Chinese.

To grant exclusive authority to one ideology by means of violence or administrative decree can only turn "the contention of a hundred schools of thought" into a condition where "not even a crow or sparrow can be heard—silence reigns." Intolerance in ideology strangles individual freedom and the willingness to participate on the part of the masses—and the consequence is that culture withers.

Prospects and Expectations

Since the Opium War the Chinese have gone through the Taiping Revolution, the "Hundred Days" Reform of 1898, the 1911 Revolution, the May Fourth Movement, the founding of the People's Republic, and the Great Cultural Revolution, and now the nation is carrying out modern reconstruction and political and economic reforms. Historical changes and the unremitting efforts of generations of thinkers have provided many favorable turns in the modernization of the traditional Chinese way of thinking, and some reasonable elements of Western civilization have more or less been assimilated. Yet since the traditional way has been followed for generations, it will always be characterized by stability, solidity, and exclusivity, and the innermost core of its structure will be hard to change. Even some changes that did occur have had a checkered career and often have been manifested as a retreat on the road of advancement or a setback after achievement. Thus it is not easy, even today, to go through a transition and attain the modernization of traditional ways of thinking.

However, the modernization of ideas is far more important to a revolution than the modernization of a political system or an economy. So the traditional way of thinking, even the entire structure of ideas of a society, must be changed in accordance with modern standards.

Moreover, history and contemporary reality tell us that to achieve the modernization of traditional Chinese thought is not simply a philosophical problem to be solved by a few philosophers and other thinkers, but also a problem which needs to be studied and dealt with from a multiplicity of angles including politics, economics, ideology, and culture; solutions must rely on the strength of the whole society and must cover the development of science and the productive forces, the promotion of political democratization, the encouragement of a spirit of criticism and creativity, the establishment of a variety of schools of thought, and the enhancement of the quality of cultural expression throughout the nation.

The modernization of traditional Chinese thinking cannot be accomplished simply by casting aside traditional dialectical methods entirely or by strictly following the same course of evolution that occurred in the West and rigidly turning to that precise mode of thought characterized by reductive analysis. This is because contemporary thought, to include science, is developing in a synthetic and systematic direction, toward a unity of the definite and the indefinite and of the precise and the inexact, especially after some outstanding scientists (for example, Niels Bohr) have been greatly inspired by traditional Chinese dialectics; some of the more recent scientific discoveries such as quantum mechanics and relativity theory have had a long and informative dialogue with ancient Chinese philosophy. This means that the modernization of traditional Chinese thought is heading in the direction of a new hybrid, based on the confluence of Chinese and Western thought rather than on either tradition alone.

In today's world, mutual alliance has replaced one-sided plunder, and cooperation is taking the place of confrontation. And in today's China, most Chinese expect to see seclusion give way to openness, the cult of violence and dictatorship set aside for a new material civilization with spiritual values, and intolerance replaced by tolerance. A new age of confluence between Chinese philosophy and culture and Western philosophy and culture has already begun. To this end, it is advantageous to develop a more modern way of thinking.

Of course the realization of this modernization will require time and effort. As a first step, however, the confluence of Chinese and Western philosophy will certainly lead to good prospects for the renewal of an ancient Chinese civilization, through the continued development of its national wisdom and the transformation of its traditional way of thinking.

Note

1. Joseph Needham, *Science and Civilisation in China,* vol. 3, *Mathematics and the Sciences of the Heavens and the Earth* (Boston: Cambridge University Press, 1959), p. 151.

Culture and the Ethical

KARL-OTTO APEL

A PLANETARY MACROETHICS
FOR HUMANKIND: THE NEED,
THE APPARENT DIFFICULTY, AND
THE EVENTUAL POSSIBILITY

I

In what follows I would like to deal in succession with the three aspects
of the problem of a macroethics as indicated in the title of this essay.
First I would like to point to the urgent need for a macroethics; this, in
my opinion constitutes the most important new task of philosophical
ethics in our age. Second, I will outline and explicate the apparent difficulties which, on the level of professional (academic) philosophy during
the last three decades, have suggested that the problem of a rational
grounding of a macroethic of humankind cannot be solved, or that it is
not even a meaningful problem. Third, I will try to suggest a possible
solution to our problem from the point of view of a transcendental pragmatics of human communication, or, more precisely, of argumentative
discourse as a reflexive form of human communication.

To begin with, however, I should answer the question of what I mean
by a macroethics of humankind and why, or in what respect, it can be
considered as a new feature in the historical development of ethics that
should correspond or answer to a new stage in the cultural evolution of
humankind. I think there are few aspects of contemporary civilization
where the structural noncontemporaneity (or nonsynchronism) of the
different sectors of sociocultural development is more striking than in
the dimension of conventional morals, especially if it is compared or
confronted with the actual requirements of a common and joint responsibility for the global consequences of human activities. A conventional
morals in all peoples or cultures is still essentially restricted to human
relations in small groups or, at best, to the fulfilling of the duties of professional roles within a social system of norms: for example, within a
national state. I would designate these two levels of conventional morals
by the terms microethics and mesoethics, respectively. And I would
emphasize that even the usual tensions and conflicts between moral

demands are still experienced and articulated as those of an antagonism between the levels of micro- and mesoethics.

Thus, for example, the demands of the roles and norms that are defined by a social system (of law and order) impose themselves on and enter into, the intimate relations of sympathy, interest, and loyalty that constitute the social mastic of small groups, such as families and clans; and they have done so most successfully up to now in cases of mobilization of national or religious or quasi-religious feelings: for example, in connection with wars or revolutions. Less spectacular, but usually working in a sufficiently efficient form, are the norms of the social systems which are brought to bear by public acceptance and the sanctions of law. But it also happens again and again in many countries that the state of law and the moral norms of the social system lose their authority and efficiency. Then their functions may, so to speak, fall back to families and clans as a consequence of general corruption, as for instance in the case of Mafia rule.

Now, in the middle of these persisting features of conventional morals, that is, of tensions and conflicts from the demands of micro- and mesoethics, new features of moral demands have emerged and developed in industrial societies during this century: features that can no longer be understood in terms of the conventional moral categories, that is, neither by those of microethical loyalty within small groups nor by those of the mesoethical norms of the social systems of law and order.

What I mean here may be elucidated along the lines of two directions of cultural evolution which may be traced down to the beginnings of humankind, that is, to the breaking through the barriers of animal instincts that must have given rise to the progressive development of social institutions and moral norms.[1] The first direction of cultural evolution from point zero, so to speak, may be characterized, I suggest, as *Homo faber*'s breaking through the natural equilibrium between the world of causal effects of actions and the world of the perceptible signs that could trigger those actions within the feedback circle of animal behavior.[2] One may assume that *Homo faber*'s invention of tools and especially of weapons has definitively canceled this equilibrium by opening up a scope of possible effects of action that were not foreseen, so to speak, in the realm of the triggering of instinctive behavior.[3]

Thus, for example, the murder of Abel by Cain, or, in other words, the phenomenon of war, in contradistinction to the restricted fighting of animals, may perhaps be explained by the expansion or increase of the causal effectivity of human actions beyond the original scope of those triggering signs that previously appealed to inhibition instincts. And this development went further, up to the invention of nuclear warheads, whose possible effects cannot even be imagined in terms of man's original world of the perceptible signs that could appeal to our quasi-instinctive feelings.

Now, the need for the moral regulation of human actions which are no longer regulated by instincts could up to now have been fulfilled, or answered, somehow, by the development of social institutions, which makes up the other dimension of cultural evolution. That is to say, the development of those two stages of conventional morals of family clans and of states (under law), which I have called the micro- and mesoethical stages, has, up to now, coped somehow with the challenge of *Homo faber*'s constant increasing of the range of efficacy of human actions. Some anthropologists or anthropological philosophers have even suggested that institutions and conventional morals of the kind that I have outlined may be considered to be the definitive analogue to and equivalent of animal instincts on the level of human culture; and from this premise they have sometimes drawn the conclusion that all questioning of contingent institutions and conventions in the spirit of enlightenment or reason has to be rated as a dangerous and pathological tendency of cultural development.[4] Thus, on the level of the mesoethics of national states, even war could be considered as an institution for settling conflicts and distributing living space (*"Lebensraum"*) and resources.

But I think the possibility of looking at the global situation of humankind in this way has come to an end in this century for at least two reasons. The first reason is that the development of social institutions itself has passed that stage where the regulation of human interaction can find its most integrative form and its highest moral authority in the (national) state, as had been suggested by Hegel. In the meantime, not only religion and philosophy have questioned that suggestion, as they did in Hegel's time, but the social institutions themselves have differentiated themselves into subsystems that more or less determine or condition human behavior far beyond the legal power or the moral authority of the state. The most illustrative example of this development is provided by the social subsystem of the international economy.[5] This example shows that a new and up to now unanswered challenge to moral responsibility has come about: for certain kinds of human interaction are mediated by the world market—the signals which direct this interaction are prices, while the medium of actual communication is money. It is an interaction carried out from a great distance by anonymous persons, hence it leaves almost no opportunity for face-to-face meetings between real people with moral sensibilities. And while the effects of this everyday economic activity may be felt by other human beings in other parts of the world (for instance, the Third World), these effects are as unimaginable to us as (or even more unimaginable than) the possible consequences of our use of atomic weapons. This comparison of the effects of human actions leads us to consider the second reason why, in my opinion, conventional morals in the sense of micro- and mesoethics can no longer cope with the new challenges of human responsibility for the distant consequences of our actions. The second reason, which in many ways is related to the first—especially in connection with the development of social subsystems of our global economy—is that there is a new relationship between humankind and nature, or, rather, between us and our ecosphere. The novelty of this relationship, as is well known, consists in the fact that nature, as it constitutes our biosphere and the wealth of our economic resources, is no longer undamageable and inexhaustible, as people have thought it to be throughout history, up until now.

It seems that this state of affairs has come about through the technological skills to increase and expand the effects of human actions—and these same skills can be traced back to *Homo faber*'s accomplishment of breaking through the barrier of animal instinct. Since then, one might say, the technological achievements of *Homo faber* have always been ahead of the moral responsibilities of *Homo sapiens,* but in this century we have had to confront this fact. For now, for the first time, it has slowly become clear that, at least with regard to our ecosphere, we are compelled to organize, somehow, a collective sense of responsibility for the consequences of our activities in science and technology.

Thus it turns out that we in the developed world are now confronted, in our relation to the environment, with the same novel—and almost outrageous—moral demands as confront us in our long-distance economic interactions with people. For each of us is now expected to share at least some responsibility for the emissions of industrial plants into the air and water, or for the preservation of forests on a global scale, for the very climate and atmosphere of the entire planet, and at the same time each of us must feel responsible as a citizen—for example, as the reader of a newspaper or as a voter—for the politics, say, of the World Bank with regard to Third World debt. Thus it appears that in both dimensions of cultural evolution, namely, that of technological interventions in nature and that of social interaction, a global situation has been brought about in our time that calls for a new ethics of shared responsibility, in other words, for a type of ethics that, in contradistinction to the traditional or conventional forms of ethics, may be designated a (planetary) macroethics.

The problematic novelty of the demands of this new form of ethics may be illustrated by some characteristic comments from those who are rather skeptical, or even upset, about the possibility of such a "hyperethics," as it has been characterized.[6] For example, in a review of Hans Jonas' book *The Principle of Responsibility,*[7] a pioneering work in that it forcefully suggests the need for a new type of ethics, the reviewer reminded his readers, by a reference to Arnold Gehlen's philosophy of institutions, of the fact that nobody can be responsible for something outside her or his role or function within a social system.[8] Here, by way of negation, or nonunderstanding, at least one important feature of the new macroethics was indirectly distinguished: the demand for coresponsibility for the consequences of our collective activities. For it seems clear that individual persons, taken in isolation, cannot indeed take responsibility for these consequences. What, then, does it mean to be coresponsible?

Another feature of the desired ethics was indirectly illuminated by the booklet "The Seven Mortal Sins," by the famous ethologist and Nobel prizewinner Konrad Lorenz. From the perspective of his well-known thesis that a human morals is essentially based on quasi-instinctive dispositions or residual instincts which correspond to the quasi-moral behavior of animals, Lorenz ascertains, and deplores the fact, that in modern mass society, with its complex but anonymous human relations, the moral dispositions of human beings—for example, feelings of sympathy and readiness to help—are hopelessly overcharged. Hence, Lorenz can only place his hope on the possibility of a mutation in the continuing process of biological evolution in humankind, such that human beings would acquire a new quasi-instinctive disposition of morality.[9] What is indirectly illuminated in this conclusion by an ethologist is, in my opinion, the fact that the new ethics of coresponsibility that is called for cannot indeed be provided in our day by the quasi-instinctive dispositions of humankind but has to be provided rather by human reason as a compensation for the lack of quasi-instinctive dispositions.

For that matter, it has to be realized that Lorenz' assessment of the situation has been confirmed, in a sense, by another Nobel prizewinner, namely, the economist Friedrich August von Hayek. Hayek is also convinced that moral feelings and dispositions in the sense of traditional ethics, including that of Christianity, must be restricted to the archaic level of human relations within small groups. Above this level, demands for an ethics of human solidarity, not to speak of coresponsibility on a global scale, become ideological and thus harmful, because human freedom can only be guaranteed by the undisturbed functioning of a market system of economy, with its anonymous relations of remote interaction. Therefore, on Hayek's account, the current demand for "social justice" is also simply ideological and ultimately harmful, and the only feature of the traditional ethics of justice that can and must indeed be preserved, and even cultivated, in the present situation of humankind is the obligation of honesty in regard to concluding and keeping contracts. Thus Hayek's recourse is to the minimal morality of an institutional domestication of the strategical interaction of commerce by simultaneously excluding any further demands of a morality of solidarity and coresponsibility.[10]

I think that the indirect illumination of our problematic of a macroethics of humankind that we may indeed derive from Hayek's comments as well as from those of Konrad Lorenz and Arnold Gehlen lies in the insight that the new ethics, if it should be possible at all, calls for a rational foundation that transcends all traditions; for so much has been clearly shown, precisely by the quoted skeptical comments: a macroethics cannot be based either on the quasi-instinctive feelings and dispositions of loyalty within small groups or on the conventional morals that is represented by the present social institutions, including the spirit of the present state of law.

But what have the representatives of professional ethics, in the sense of (moral) philosophy, to say on our problem of a rational foundation for a universally valid macroethics of humankind? With this question I proceed to the second part of my essay.

II

A first stage of the answer we are seeking in this century may be characterized by Max Weber's conception of value-free science in contradistinction to the complementary dimension of the irrational, but authentic, decisions about one's private choice of ultimate value-axioms.[11] This suggestion of a division of labor, so to speak, between scientific rationality and irrational morality has impregnated, and for a long time dominated, Western ideology as the complementarity system of Positivism and Existentialism, where ethics like religion could only be conceived of as a matter of private emotions and decisions that could not lay claim to universal public validity.[12]

This complementarity system of Western ideology implied a strange or even paradoxical answer to the twentieth century's challenge to moral reason. For, in the complementarity system, the part of rationality was definitively defined by the value-neutral rationality of science (that is, of technologically relevant natural science)—whereas, on the other hand, it is precisely the technological consequences of science in the life-world of our day that has called for a new rational foundation of a planetary ethics of coresponsibility. Thus it appears that it is science that at the same time has called for a new rational ethics and, by its monopoly on the definition of rationality,[13] has blocked the way of a rational grounding of ethics by showing that it is impossible.

I am afraid that this blocking mechanism still works today with many tough-minded thinkers, although there is a knockdown argument available that overthrows the whole mechanism. The counterargument shows up at the moment when we realize that scientific research, including the operations of ascertaining its intersubjective validity, is not only a matter of the subject-object relation of cognition but also, and always at the same time, a matter of the subject-cosubject relation of communication and interaction between the members of a scientific community. It then becomes clear that it is even, or precisely, value-free natural science, that is, the value-neutral objectification of nature along the line of the subject-object relation, that must presuppose an ethics of an ideal communication community with regard to the subject-cosubject relation, which is complementary to the subject-object relation. And it becomes clear immediately that the ethic of an ideal communication community that is presupposed by science cannot be an irrational one of mere emotions and private, subjective decisions. For it is precisely the purpose of deciding about claims of intersubjective validity by rational arguments that presupposes in principle an ethic of the community that implies equal rights and equal responsibility on the level of arguing.[14]

Hence, this much may be concluded already at this stage of the argument: the fact that the rationality of science is value-neutral, in regard to its objects, cannot entail that a nonvalue-neutral rationality, and hence a rationality of ethics, is impossible. For the existence of value-neutral science as an enterprise of a human community has presupposed, as the condition of its possibility, the normative validity of a rational ethics, at least for the community of scientists.

Now, by this argument it has not yet been shown that a rational foundation of a universally valid ethics of coresponsibility for human beings is possible, for the scientific community is not identical with the community of humankind, and the interests of the first are not the same as the interests of the latter. The ethically relevant difference between both types of community has been correctly indicated, I think, by Charles Peirce, who postulated that the members of an ideal community of investigators must surrender all their self-interests in favor of the community's interest in searching for the truth.[15] This self-surrender cannot be generalized as a moral obligation of all members of the human community; for, from the point of view of the latter, it may even be asked whether or not science ought to be. And also this question has to be answered by a universally valid ethics of coresponsibility for humankind.

One might ask already at this point: what is it that could be reasonably imputed as an obligation of all members of an ideal community of humankind? Surely, it could not be a self-surrender of all self-interests in favor of the interest of searching for the truth? But could it not be a principle of self-surrender in the sense of acknowledging a principle of transubjectivity in settling all conflicts only by intersubjectively acceptable arguments?

I shall come back to this point. But first I have to continue my report about professional philosophy's stand with regard to our problem of a new macroethic of humankind. Although the answer of the first stage, the complementary system of Positivism and Existentialism, is still very influential, it could not prevent a "rehabilitation of practical philosophy," nay even a boom of ethics, in the last decade in Europe and in the United States. But it seems to be characteristic for this second stage of the philosophical answer to our problem that most positions do not try to refute the positivistic verdict against the possibility of a rational foundation of a universally valid ethics but rather accept it tacitly by recourse to some kind of a neo-Aristotelian (or neo-Hegelian) rehabilitation of the traditional ethos of a specific sociocultural form of life.

Thus one could follow the line of Aristotle's distinction between "epistēmē" or "theoria" on the one hand and "phronēsis" on the other hand and claim, somehow along with Aristotle's *Nicomachian Ethics,* that the faculty of practical reason cannot provide strict universal validity of principles but only, indeed, habits and attitudes of moral reflection and of prudent decision-making within the context of concrete situations and according to the self-evident norms of the substantial ethos of a specific tradition or sociocultural form of life. (This perspective of a pragmatic neo-Aristotelianism, which emancipated itself from its traditional background of a teleological metaphysics of the cosmos,[16] and hence of natural law qua universal law, was strongly confirmed and supplemented in recent decades by a post-Wittgensteinian relativism of the different or even incommensurable forms of life and by a post-Heideggerian hermeneuticism and super-historicism of the epochal clearings of truth or at least of the meaning of being within the occidental tradition of thought.)[17]

Thus it is within the scope of the historicist and relativist neo-Aristotelian turn, and accompanied by more or less strong invectives against post-Kantian deontological universalism, that a broad stream of ethics of the good life according to the reflection of local traditions has emerged in the Western world. Whereas in Anglo-Saxon quarters, with Williams, MacIntyre, or the American "Communitarians," the accent is placed primarily on the need for substantial values or material norms as against Kantian formalism,[18] in Germany the hermeneutic-historist trend of neo-Aristotelianism is rather neo-conservative and even skeptical, with a strong aggressive turn against the so-called erroristic utopism of recent neo-Marxist emancipatory philosophy (for example, of the Frankfurt School).[19]

The neo-Aristotelian turn here takes on an air of pretended sobriety (in German: *Abwiegelung*), as in the often repeated Gadamerian outline of what is needed for an ethics of the good life in a good polis: namely, in Greek, *phrōs dei* plus *phronēsis* (I would translate this as: "that which is usual or customary in a good civil society" plus "prudent application of the implicit norms of the local tradition").[20] A good illustration of this attitude was provided in a recent (Hegel) Congress by the following countersuggestion (which was directed against Kant's comparison of the "categorical imperative" with a "compass" for the moral life): in a good polis, that is, a city, we do not need a compass, because there are street signs.[21]

Now, I think that these neo-conservative trends toward the so-called "rehabilitation of practical reason" provide no solution whatever to the problem of a macroethics of coresponsibility of humankind which I have tried to expose in the preceding; they rather represent an evasive or even escapist attitude with regard to the very problem that is posed to us in our day. And the slogans of at least the German representatives of neo-Aristotelianism seem to my eyes almost as paradoxical and anachronistic as the positivist blockings of a rational ethics of responsibility for the technological effects of science. This is especially illustrated by the reception of the book by Hans Jonas, who is himself a neo-Aristotelian of sorts. But Jonas, in his recourse to Aristotle's teleological metaphysics of the cosmos, arrives at results that are diametrically opposed to those of the neo-conservative neo-Aristotelians: for Jonas, from the value-conservative perspective of caring for the survival of humankind and preserving human dignity, comes to demand a quite new cosmopolitan ethics of collective responsibility for the consequences of the collective activities of the industrial societies with regard to the future of humankind.

Now, I do not think that Jonas succeeded in providing a rational foundation for the desired ethics from his metaphysical premises.[22] But at least his vision of the problem may be easily integrated into a postulative program that could be set up against the neo-Aristotelian retreat to local traditions. In my own words it could read as follows.

We are not living today in quasi-autarchical societies or "poleis" as in the classical tradition of Greek civilization (which, by the way, was overthrown already by Alexander in the lifetime of Aristotle in favor of a political anticipation of a "cosmopolis"). We are living today, for the first time in history, in a planetary civilization that at least in some vital respects—culture, science, technology, and economy—has been unified to such an extent that we have become members of a real communicating community or, if you will, members of the crew of one boat, for example, with regard to the ecological crisis. Here I must strongly contradict the diagnosis of Jean-François Lyotard, who from the undeniable breakdown of the speculative philosophy of history drew the conclusion that in our day we have to give up the very idea of a common human history and moreover even the idea of a "we" as a possible subject of human solidarity.[23] I would suggest, to the contrary, that the vague ideas of the eighteenth-century philosophers concerning the unity of human history have today been realized in a sense. To be sure, they have not been realized in the sense of the Marxist conception of a unity of scientific theory and praxis with regard to the known and controlled "necessary course of history," but they have been realized as an ethically desirable and partly existing unity of cooperation with regard to the shaping, preserving, and reshaping or reforming of the common conditions of the present world civilization.

To sum up: what we need today is indeed a universally valid ethics for the whole of humankind; but this does not mean that we need an ethics that would prescribe a uniform style of the good life for all individuals or for all the different sociocultural forms of life. To the contrary: we can accept and even oblige ourselves to protect the pluralism of individual forms of life so long as it is guaranteed (warranted) that a universally valid ethics of equal rights and of equal coresponsibility for the solving of the common problems of humankind is respected in each single form of life. It appears to me that a fatal mistake of philosophical thought in our day consists in supposing a fundamental antagonism or even a contradiction between the called-for universalism of a post-Kantian ethics and the pluralism of a quasi-Aristotelian ethics of the good life, or of *"souci de soi,"* to speak along with M. Foucault. At least the whole history of human rights speaks against this supposition, as Foucault had to acknowledge in the last days of his life.[24]

But let me proceed now to the last part of my essay. Until now I have only pointed to the *called-for* macroethics of humankind by criticizing the insufficient conceptions of the professional ethics of our day. But what about the real possibility of a rational grounding of the called-for type of ethics? Are there no promising approaches in this respect?

III

In order to introduce the arguments of a discourse-ethics, as it is proposed by Jürgen Habermas and myself, let me start out once more by way of a critical discussion. I will try to win my point of departure by offering some critical comments on the most recent turn of a great philosopher who, standing in the Kantian tradition, has perhaps made the most important contribution to an up-to-date ethics of justice. I mean, of course, John Rawls. I will only mention here his two principles of justice,[25] especially the famous "principle of difference," which, I think, functions in our day as the permanent ethical counterargument against the most suggestive current temptation of Western democracy, namely, the temptation of the politics of the so-called "two-thirds society," that is, of a social politics that exploits the majority mechanism of parliamentary democracy just by caring only for the satisfaction of two-thirds of the population at the cost of the last third. It seems clear that Rawls' "difference principle" is directed precisely against such a politics, which, as we know, may be very successful for a time.

However, in his last turn, in his essay "Justice As Fairness: Political Not Metaphysical,"[26] Rawls seems to deny, or, respectively, to revoke the universality-claim of his earlier foundation of an ethics of justice as fairness in favor of a neo-Aristotelian or historistic recourse to the specifically American tradition of the "sense of justice." Richard Rorty has elucidated this turn in his confession of an extreme form of ethnocentric historicism, telling us that, as an American, he has to insist on the priority of the Constitution of and the political institutions his country over and against every claim of a philosophical critique or legitimation of this local tradition. If it came to a discussion with people like Ignatius of Loyola or Nietzsche, that is, people who in principle would deny the democratic tradition, he could not, he says, try to defend this tradition by philosophical arguments, that is, by recourse to universally valid principles or criteria, but would eventually have to consider the other side as "mad."[27] It seems clear that this also would have to be his attitude in a discussion with representatives of Eastern communism or with Islamic fundamentalists defending a conception of theocracy. Now, in answering Rorty, I would not deny the possibility of a total breakdown of discussion, that is, of argumentative discourse, but, in my opinion, such a breakdown should never be caused by my own dogmatic recourse to my own tradition, but, in the worst case, it could be forced by the very refutation of philosophical arguments by one of the partners of the discussion, be it Rorty or Nietzsche or Lenin or Khomeini or Deng Xiaoping.

But, in our present context, it seems to me more important to ask for the reasons for John Rawls' own recourse to the local tradition as a contingent historical basis for "the sense of justice as fairness." I think the reason for this turn hangs together, in a strange way, with the fact that Rawls had indeed good reasons for being dissatisfied with the rational foundation of his original approach by the conception of the "original position," that is, of the rational choice of the best order of justice by voters who follow the strategic rationality of decision-making under the restrictive conditions which Rawls had imposed on the original situation of choice, such as the "veil of ignorance" about each voter's place in the social order that had to be chosen.

The later Rawls had to realize first that it was very misleading to suggest that, with regard to the grounding type of rationality, his theory of justice was part of the theory of rational choice (that is, of strategical decision theory). On the one hand, the real foundation of his theory was rather provided by Rawls' own conception of "justice as fairness," which made him impose the restrictive conditions on the original position; on the other hand, Rawls was even compelled, already in his former work, to suppose a special "sense of justice" as fairness as the equipment of ideal rational voters;[28] for otherwise those voters might follow the purely strategic rationality of Hobbesian wolves, by entering the original contract with the criminal proviso of breaking it at the next best occasion, in order to enjoy the criminal-strategic surplus advantage from the other people's keeping the contract.[29]

Now, realizing these ambiguities in his "theory of justice," the later Rawls saw himself compelled to make a clear decision between the Hobbesian and the Kantian conception of practical reason or, respectively, rationality; and he did so in favor of the Kantian conception.[30] But in doing so, he had not yet solved the problem of the rational grounding of his own choice of the nonstrategic conception of reason qua sense of fairness which he also presupposed with the original voters. For he conceived of the Kantian solution as a kind of moral constructivism on the background of the intuitions of common sense (as in his theory of the "reflective equilibrium" between philosophical constructions and the people's common sense).[31]

At this point everything depends on the notion of a common sense that could be presupposed by a philosophical reflection on moral intuitions. If it is taken as the contingent background of the personal competence of concrete voters or, for that matter, of philosophers, then it can hardly be avoided that the claim to universal validity has to be given up. For then the whole thrust of this century's insights into the contingent "prestructure" or "background" of the "life-world" comes in: from Collingwood's insights into the historical structure of the "metaphysical presuppositions," and from Heidegger's and Gadamer's analysis of the "pre-understanding" of the life-world, up to Wittgenstein's conception of the paradigmatic presuppositions of language games as parts of different forms of life, and to John Searle's analysis of the "background" of our meaning-intentions.[32] All these insights seem to suggest that, as Rorty puts it, there can only be a "contingent basis for possible consensus" that we may presuppose as a commonsense basis even for ethics.[33] For a concrete person cannot avoid being dependent in his or her prenotions of the good on the historical background of his cultural tradition.

This looks quite plausible, but let us ask the following question: why is it impossible to deny the presupposition of universally valid norms, such as that of equal rights, in a discussion about these matters, even in a discussion between representatives of quite different sociocultural forms of life? Or, speaking more correctly: why do many of those philosophers who, on the level of their propositions, in fact deny the necessity of presupposing any universally valid norms actually contradict this by the performance of their propositions as long as they succeed in advancing (bringing forth) meaningful, that is, intelligible arguments? I have never seen, for instance, that Rorty, in any of his long pleadings against the possibility of presupposing universal norms, ever behaved as if he did not know that all partners in the actual discussion must of course follow universally valid norms of communication.

May one perhaps say that the procedural norms that must be followed in an argumentative discourse about any subject matter have nothing to do with the searched-for moral norms for the life-world, since they are simply instrumental in relation to the common, but nonetheless contingent purpose of the ongoing discussion?

I would answer to this last argument in the first place as follows: the fact that we have to discuss any subject matter that is controversial by way of an argumentative discourse is not contingent or incidental, since there is no reasonable alternative to that procedure, if we do not wish to fight or to negotiate but to find out by arguments of reason who is right in the matter at stake. But this (that one wishes to find out who is right) is presupposed in any philosophical discussion. Hence the procedure of argumentative discourse is nonsurpassable *(nicht hintergehbar)* in philosophy; it is, as I would claim, the transcendental-pragmatic a priori of any philosophy whatever, or, in other words, it belongs to the noncontingent "fact of reason" in Kant's sense. One may dispute it by propositions but not by performatively self-consistent acts of arguing.

Now, as I intimated already, this noncontingent fact of reason cannot be external or incidental with regard to the real moral controversies of the life-world, since it is the only human institution that can provide a possible, reasonable solution to these controversies. This fact is reconfirmed indeed by the fact that in all human controversies on the level of prediscursive communication the controversialist partners spontaneously bring forth universal validity claims as long as they do not break off or restrict the communication.[34] How, then, may these facts of communication be reconciled with the insights into the contingent historical background of all our notions about the good in the different sociocultural forms of life?

I think that a mistake is being made in the present discussion of the topic of historical contingency versus universality of norms, a mistake that is similar to the one that is being made in the contraposition of the particular ethics of the good life to a formal deontological ethics of justice or the right. In both cases it is overlooked that those people, that is, the philosophers, who discuss the historical contingency of the background conditions of all forms of life have already reflectively transgressed (surpassed) those contingent conditions. They have done so by entering into the new postenlightenment institution of argumentative discourse, which, from the beginning up until now, has provided the procedural conditions for the possibility of philosophy and all the sciences. Now, by relying on these preconditions of argumentation, which no philosopher can avoid,[35] they have also acknowledged certain normative preconditions for any communication using arguments that cannot be reckoned with the historically contingent background conditions of the different cultural traditions of morality.

Of course, the noncontingent, normative presuppositions of argumentative discourse must be *formal* and *procedural.* They cannot directly prescribe the material norms that are needed in concrete situations of human interaction, but they prescribe indeed as a regulative principle that the concrete norms, which are always fallible and subject to revisions, ought to be grounded in such a way—if possible, by real discourses—that they are acceptable to all affected people (even the next generations), and not, say, only to the partners of a bargaining agreement who care only for their shared interests at the cost of third parties. Even less than concrete norms the concrete valuations or values of the good life in the different sociocultural forms of life may or should be prescribed by the universally valid forms of argumentative discourse, but these latter may very well prescribe those obligations and restrictive conditions of self-realization that make possible the coexistence and the cooperation of the different forms of life. Now this difference and complementarity between the level of universal procedural principles and that of concrete norms, and finally forms of life, may also elucidate the relationship between the universal principle of justice as fairness and the particular American tradition of morals in the case of Rawls. One may easily concede that Rawls could not have developed his two principles of justice and their very detailed explication without a connection with and constant inspiration from the specific American tradition of morals and of political institutions. Thus far his book provides only fallible proposals for the practical discourse of humankind as does any other moral philosopher who suggests material norms, being of course inspired by that philosopher's own particular tradition.

But this concession does not entail any surrender of ethical universalism to historism-relativism. For the commonsense intuition of justice as fairness—which, according to the principle of "reflective equilibrium," provides the guiding principle for Rawls' approach—is not only determined by the contingent local tradition of American culture (or, more precisely expressed, by the contingent elements of this tradition), but it can and must also be based on those moral intuitions which are provided by the noncontingent presuppositions of the institution—or rather philosophical meta-institution—of argumentative discourse. For in this meta-institution every philosopher must participate, in order to argue, that is to say, in order to think with a claim to the intersubjective validity of his thought. Here we have indeed found that Archimedean point of a transcendental-pragmatic foundation of the universality of morality without which a planetary macroethics of humankind would indeed be impossible. This Archimedean point is easily overlooked by a philosopher because it is, so to speak, too close to his actual thought. But it actually makes up that "original position" of strict reflection, from which every philosopher as such has to start out and from which also Rawls in fact started out when he imposed his restrictive conditions on the "original position" of his voters.

However, at the conclusion of my essay, I want still to emphasize that a morality of justice as fairness is not enough from the point of view of the called-for macroethics, although very much would have been reached if we could have realized something like Rawls' program, for example, with regard to the relationship between the First and the Second and the Third World. It would amount to the establishment of an international order of law as it was postulated by Kant, and this would indeed fulfill a requirement of the called-for macroethics. But, as I have tried to suggest in the preceding, we need also an ethics of coresponsibility with regard to the effects of our collective activities, especially in view of the ecological crisis. Coresponsibility, it seems to me, is a principle of ethics that is different from, or goes beyond, the sense of justice (even if the range of reciprocal obligations between people is extended to the relationship between different generations, as it would indeed be demanded by a macroethics). And the specific problem of a macroethics in my opinion refers to the question whether a postconventional, that is, a rational and universally valid, foundation of coresponsibility, that is of everybody's personal obligation to solidarity with humankind, can be given. For the conventional forms of coresponsibility and solidarity which are restricted to small groups or, at best, to nations, will not suffice, as I have pointed out in the preceding.

Now, I think we can also in this respect find out the Archimedean point of a transcendental-pragmatic foundation by thoroughly reflecting on what we must have acknowledged in a serious argumentative discourse about these problems. For, in my opinion, every serious question that is asked in this context shows that by asking questions we implicitly take coresponsibility, in principle, for the progressive solution of all those problems of the life-world that can be posed and possibly solved by cooperation on the level of practical discourses. This apparently esoteric philosophical foundation is, in a sense, well confirmed in our day by its standing in a "reflective equilibrium" with those public declarations which go along with the hundreds of dialogues and conferences on vitally important questions (of humankind) which take place every day on all political, economic, and cultural levels. For these conferences and dialogues at least *pretend* in most cases to be something like practical discourses, striving for solutions that are acceptable for all affected human beings. I do not think that the testimonial value of these symptomatic facts is completely reduced by the insight that in most cases the public declarations are more or less incompatible with the bargaining character of the real communication procedures. For the public declarations—in general, the humanitarian language games of the media—show at least that a consciousness, and conscience, according to the standard of a macroethics of coresponsibility is possible today.

I have to finish with this very short and insufficient remark about what I think is the main problem of a discourse-ethics today: the problem of organizing somehow the collective coresponsibility of all members of the human community of communications. But this problematic of course goes far beyond the transcendental-pragmatic foundation of simply a universally valid principle of coresponsibility.[36]

Notes

1. Cf. A. Gehlen, *Der Mensch* (Bonn, Frankfurt: Äthenäum, 1978).

2. Cf. J. von Uexküll, *Theoretische Biologie* (Frankfurt/M.: Suhrkamp, 1973).

3. Cf. K. Lorenz, *Über tierisches und menschliches Verhalten*, 2 vols. (München: Piper, 1965).

4. Cf., e.g., A. Gehlen, *Urmensch und Spätkultur* (Wiesbaden: Athenäum, 1977); and *Moral and Hypermoral* (Frankfurt: Athenäum, 1973).

5. Cf. N. Luhmann, *Die Wirtschaft der Gesellschaft* (Frankfurt/M.: Suhrkamp, 1988); F. A. von Hayek, *New Studies in Philosophy, Politics and Economics* (London: Routledge & Kegan Paul, 1978); and "The Fatal Conceit," in *Collected Works of F. A. von Hayek* (London: Routledge & Kegan Paul, 1987), part one: Ethics, The Taming of the Savage.

6. Gehlen, *Urmensch und Spätkultur.*

7. Cf. Hans Jonas, *Das Prinzip Verantwortung: Versuch einer Ethik für die technologische Zivilisation* (Frankfurt/M.: Insel, 1979).

8. Cf. G. Maschke, *Frankfurter Allgemeine Zeitung* (7.10.1980).

9. Cf. K. Lorenz, *Die acht Totsünden der zivilisierten Menschheit* (München: Piper, 1973); and *Das sogenannte Böse: Zur Naturgeschichte der Aggression* (Wien: Borothea-Schoeler, 1963), p. 413.

10. See Luhmann, *Die Wirtschaft;* also G. Radnitzky, "An Economic Theory of the Rise of Civilization and Its Policy Implications: Hayek's Account Generalized," in *Jahrbuch für die Ordnung von Wirtschaft und Gesellschaft* 38 (1987): 47–85.

11. Cf. Max Weber, "Politik als Beruf," in *Gesammelte politische Schriften* (Tübingen: Mohr, 1958), pp. 493–548; and "Der Sinn der Wertfreiheit" and "Wissenschaft als Beruf," English translation in Max Weber, *The Methodology of Social Sciences* (Glencoe, Illinois: Free Press, 1949).

12. Regarding the "complementarity-system" of Western liberal ideology, cf. Karl-Otto Apel, "Das Apriori der Kommunikationsgemeinschaft und die Grundlagen der Ethik," in *Transformation der Philosophy,* vol. 2 (Frankfurt/M.: Suhrkamp, 1973); English translation in *Towards A Transformation of Philosophy* (London: Routledge & Kegan Paul, 1980).

13. Cf. Karl-Otto Apel, "The Common Presuppositions of Hermeneutics and Ethics: Types of Rationality beyond Science and Technology," in *Phenomenology and the Human Sciences* (Humanities Press Inc., 1979), pp. 35–53; and "Types of Rationality Today: The Continuum of Reason between Science and Ethics," in *Rationality Today,* ed. by T. Geraets (Ottowa: University Press, 1979), pp. 307–340.

14. See Apel, "Das Apriori" and "The Common Presuppositions."

15. Cf. C. S. Peirce, *Collected Papers,* ed. by C. Hartshorne and P. Weiss (Cambridge: Harvard University Press, 1931–1935), vol. 5, pp. 354 ff.; also Karl-Otto Apel, *Charles S. Peirce: From Pragmatism to Pragmaticism* (Amherst: University of Massachusetts Press, 1981), pp. 52 ff.

16. Cf. H. Schnädelbach, "Was ist Neoaristotelismus?" in *Moralität und Sittlichkeit,* ed. by W. Kuhlmann (Frankfurt/M.: Suhrkamp, 1986), pp. 38–63; and Karl-Otto Apel, *Diskurs und Verantwortung* (Frankfurt/M.: Suhrkamp, 1988), Sachregister.

17. Cf. Karl-Otto Apel, "Wittgenstein und Heidegger: Kritische Wiederholung und Ergänzung eines Vergleichs," in *Der Löwe spricht und wir verstehen ihn nicht* (Frankfurt/M.: Suhrkamp, forthcoming); and "Sinnkonstitution und

Geltungsprechtfertigung: Heidegger und das Problem der Transzendental-philosophie," in *Martin Heidegger: Innen und Außenansichten* (Frankfurt/ M.: Suhrkamp, 1989), pp. 131–175.

18. Cf. B. Williams, *Ethics and the Limits of Philosophy* (Cambridge: Harvard University Press, 1985); Alasdair MacIntyre, *After Virtue: A Study In Moral Theory* (London: Duckworth, 1981); and *Whose Justice? Which Rationality?* (London: Duckworth, 1988).

19. Cf., e.g., O. Marquard, "Das Über-Wir: Bemerkungen zur Diskursethik," in *Das Gespräch (Poetik und Hermeneutik),* ed. by K. Stierle and R. Warning (München: Fink, 1984), vol. 11.

20. Cf. Hans-Georg Gadamer, "Über die Möglichkeit einer philosophischen Ethik," in *Kleine Schriften* (Tübingen, 1967), vol. 1, pp. 179 ff.

21. Cf. Karl-Otto Apel, Günther Bien, and Rudiger Bubner, "Podiumsdiskussion unter Leitung von Walter C. Zimmerli," in *Hegel-Jahrbuch* (1987), pp. 13–48.

22. Cf. Karl-Otto Apel, "The Problem of a Macroethics of Responsibility to the Future in the Crisis of Technological Civilization: An Attempt to Come to Terms with Hans Jonas' 'Principle of Responsibility'," in *Man and World* 20 (1987): 3–40; German version in Apel, *Diskurs und Verantwortung.*

23. Cf. J. -F. Lyotard, "Histoire universelle et différences culturelles," in *Critique* 456 (1985): 559–568.

24. Cf. Luc Ferry and Alain Renaut, *La Pensée* 68 (Paris: Gallimard, 1985), vol. 68, p. 45.

25. Cf. John Rawls, *A Theory of Justice* (Cambridge: Harvard University Press, 1971), chap. 11.

26. Cf. John Rawls, "Justice as Fairness: Political not Metaphysical," in *Philosophy and Public Affairs* 14 (1985): 223–251.

27. Cf. Richard Rorty, "The Priority of Democracy to Philosophy," in *The Virginia Statute of Religious Freedom,* ed. by M. Peterson and R. Vaughan (Cambridge: Cambridge University Press, 1988); and my critical discussion of this article in *Diskurs und Verantwortung,* p. 397 ff.

28. Cf. Rawls, *A Theory of Justice,* chap. 25.

29. Cf. Karl-Otto Apel, "Normative Ethics and Strategical Rationality: The Philosophical Problem of a Political Ethics," in *Graduate Faculty Philosophy Journal,* vol. 9, no. 1 (New York: New School for Social Research, 1982): 81–108; reprinted in *The Public Realm: Essays on Discursive Types in Political Philosophy,* ed. by R. Schurmann (New York: SUNY Press, 1989), pp. 107–131.

30. Cf. Rawls, "Justice as Fairness," p. 237 n. 20.

31. Cf. John Rawls, "Kantian Constructivism in Moral Theory," in *Journal of Philosophy* (September 1980): 519.

32. Cf. Apel, "Wittgenstein und Heidegger" and "Sinnkonstitution."

33. Cf. Rorty, "The Priority of Democracy."

34. In this sense "negotiations," i.e. "bargainings," may amount to a restriction of communication, since they replace morally relevant validity claims and their discussion by offers and threats (that is, "discursive rational-

ity" by "strategical rationality"); another type of restricted communication is rhetorical persuasion in the sense of *Überredung* (i.e. covertly strategic rationality). A new beginning—but, I think, only a beginning—in the analysis of these intricate problems has been made by J. Habermas in *Theorie des kommunikativen Handelns* (Frankfurt/M.: Suhrkamp, 1981); English translation, *The Theory of Communicative Action,* Boston: Beacon Press, 1987). Cf. also *Kommunikatives Handeln,* ed. by A. Honneth and J. Joas (Frankfurt/M.: Suhrkamp, 1986); Karl-Otto Apel, "Läßt sich ethische Vernunft von strategischer Rationalitat unterscheiden?" in *Archivio di Filosofia* 51 (1983): 373–434; and "Sprachliche Bedeutung, Wahrheit und normative Gultigkeit: Die soziale Bindekraft der Rede im Lichte einer transzendentalen Sprachpragmatik," in *Archivio di Filosofia* 55 (1987): 51–88.5.

35. Cf. Karl-Otto Apel, "The Problem of Philosophical Foundation in Light of a Transcendental Pragmatics of Language," in *Philosophy: End or Transformation?* ed. by K. Baynes, J. Bohman, and T. McCarthy (Cambridge: MIT Press, 1987), pp. 250–290; and "Fallibilismus, Konsenstheorie der Wahrheit und Letztbegründung," in *Philosophie und Begründung* (Frankfurt/M.: Suhrkamp, 1987), pp. 116–211.

36. In particular, there is the moral problem of how to act if, or, respectively, when, the conditions of the applicability of discourse ethics are not given. I have dealt with this problem under the label "part B of ethics" in *Diskurs und Verantwortung.*

ANTONIO S. CUA

REASONABLE CHALLENGES AND PRECONDITIONS OF ADJUDICATION

This essay proposes a Confucian response to reasonable, external challenges to an ethical tradition. Section I presents the conception of Confucian tradition as a living tradition as reflected in the attitude of Hsün Tzu and Chu Hsi toward orthodoxy. Of special importance are the critical learning of the classics, the reasoned assessment of the views and conduct of contemporary adherents and external critics, and the authoritative role of exemplary individuals. Section II deals mainly with the problem of responding to challenges of normative ethics. It is maintained that a Confucian moral philosopher, by reflecting on the significance of *tao* (the Way) and by reshaping such basic notions as *jen* (humanity), *li* (rituals), and *yi* (rightness), for the purpose of discourse on intercultural value conflict, can develop a coherent set of transcultural principles as preconditions for or ground rules of adjudication.

I

Confucianism, in the words of Thomé Fang, is "a constructive philosophy of comprehensive harmony invested with creative energies of life."[1] Although this is a compendious statement of the outcome of Fang's metaphysical inquiry, it is an apt characterization of the vitality of the Confucian *tao* (Way) as an ethical vision of the good human life, an ideal amenable to varying interpretations of its concrete significance in different times and places. As I understand it, the *tao* is an ideal theme rather than an ideal norm or supreme principle of conduct.[2] It is fundamentally a unifying perspective for harmonizing the diverse elements of moral experience. To adopt the *tao* is to see human life, in its morally excellent form, as possessing a coherence in which apparently conflicting elements are viewed as eligible components of an achievable harmonious order. It is this vision of *tao* that renders intelligible the idea of a Confucian ethical tradition as a living tradition enriched by its historic past, and interpreted by adherents as having a present and prospective significance.[3]

Hsün Tzu and Chu Hsi are perhaps the most articulate spokespersons of the importance of learning the classics as an indispensable means to inculcate a respect for the historical aspect of tradition. Hsün Tzu points out that learning is an unceasing process of accumulation of goodness, knowledge, and practical understanding. "If a superior man *(chün-tzu)* studies widely and daily engages in self-examination, his intellect will become enlightened and his conduct be without fault."[4] In general, the program of learning "commences with the recitation of the classics and ends with the study of rituals *(li)*." Its purpose, however, is "first to learn to become a scholar and ultimately to become a sage."[5] The classics are presumed to embody the concrete significance of *tao*. For example, "The *Odes (Shih)* give expression to the will *(chih)* or determination (to realize *tao*); the *History (Shu)* to its significance in human affairs; the *Rituals (Li)* to its significance in conduct; the *Music (Yüeh)* to its significance in promoting harmony; and the *Spring and Autumn Annals (Ch'un-Chiu)* to its subtleties."[6] Notably, these classics are not self-explanatory, thus guidance from perceptive teachers is required. For example, "the *Rituals* and *Music* present us with models, but no explanations; the *Odes* and the *History* deal with ancient matters and are not always pertinent; the *Spring and Autumn Annals* are terse and cannot be quickly understood."[7]

Indeed, for Confucius, Mencius, and Hsün Tzu, the rituals *(li)* represent an ethical, cultural tradition. The observance of ritual *(li)* is stressed in self-discipline in order to attain the virtue of humanity *(jen)* *(Analects* 12:1). For Confucius, rituals *(li)* "were a body of rules governing action in every aspect of life and they were the repository of past insights into morality."[8] Learning to be a moral agent, in part, consists in appreciating "the accumulated wisdom of the past."[9] Compliance with these rituals *(li)* as a set of formal prescriptions of proper behavior without regard to humanity *(jen)* and particular circumstances would be deemed unreasonable. It is, perhaps, for this reason that Confucius stresses the sense of rightness *(yi)* rather than preconceived opinions in coping with novel and exigent situations *(Analects* 4:10). Mencius is emphatic that the relevance of a *li* requirement must be considered in the light of weighing *(ch'üan)* particular circumstances.[10] In a similar spirit, Hsün Tzu emphasizes the exercise of rightness *(yi)* in responding to changing circumstances of human life *(i-yi pien-ying)*.[11] In general, the enforcement of laws and other rules of conduct depends on superior or exemplary persons *(chün-tzu)* who have not only a knowledge of the subject matter, but also an understanding of their underlying purposes, in addition to having a sense of priority and an ability to respond appropriately to changing affairs.[12] Learning to become a sage *(sheng-jen)* must begin with the study of the classics with a view to discerning their actuating significance in living contexts.

The Confucian respect for the authority of the past in relation to the present requires not only a critical understanding of the practical significance of the classics, but, more importantly, a critical assessment of the ethical character and achievement of contemporary adherents of the tradition. Thus Hsün Tzu urges his readers to distinguish common people from three sorts of Confucians (ju); the vulgar or conventional (su-ju), the refined or cultured (ya-ju), and the great or sagely Confucians (ta-ju). Common people neither seek nor respect scholarship. Devoid of any sense of justice and rightness (cheng-yi), they regard wealth and profit as the ultimate end of human life. In attire and deportment, the conventional Confucians are no different from common people. They are, however, men of pretension; that is, they uncritically adopt erroneous doctrines, since they have no real comprehension of the classics and the rationales for exalting ritual (li) and rightness (yi). With only a sketchy understanding of the words of former kings, they would invoke "former kings" to deceive the stupid and seek a living. The refined Confucians, on the other hand, are men of integrity who honor the rituals (li) and rightness (yi) and the classics; yet they do not possess sufficient intelligence and experience to comprehend the coherence of their rationales. As men of integrity, they would candidly avow their knowledge and ignorance, free from self-deception and desire to deceive others. It is for this reason that they honor the worthy and fear the law without remissness or pride. The great or sagely Confucians are those who have the knowledge of the unity of ritual (li) and rightness (yi), that is, their rational coherence and prospective significance. Thus they can deal with the present by means of knowledge of the past. On matters pertaining to humanity (jen) and rightness (yi), they render discriminating judgments without error, as if "distinguishing white from black."[13]

The foregoing distinction between three types of Confucians may be seen to be motivated by Hsün Tzu's desire to respond to the internal challenges or challenges within the Confucian tradition—a reminder and warning, so to speak, to his fellow Confucians against uncritical intellectual and practical affiliation. His critique of Mencius on the relation between morality and human nature is a well-known illustration of an internal conflict between different interpretations of a key aspect of Confucian ethical tradition.[14] Like Mencius, Hsün Tzu is also quite aware of the need to engage in argumentation to answer external challenges to the Confucian tradition. For Mencius, there was no alternative but to engage in disputation,[15] since the tao of the sages, embodied in Yao and Shun, has been obscured by the prevailing teachings of Yang Chu and Mo Tzu.

In a similar spirit, Hsün Tzu attacks the views of a number of philosophers, for example, Mo Tzu, Hui Shih, Sung Tzu, and Shen Tao, as well as Lao Tzu and Chuang Tzu. Hsün Tzu considers pernicious most of their doctrines, which are often presented in elegant language and composition, because they present erroneous conceptions of the distinction between right and wrong and between order and disorder. However, it is noteworthy that Hsün Tzu's critique explicitly acknowledges that "some of what they advocate has a rational basis, and their statements have a perfect logic *(ch'eng-li)*."[16] In the light of his holistic conception of *tao,* many philosophical views are unacceptable, not because they are totally erroneous, but mainly because they grasp only partial aspects of *tao* and exaggerate these at the expense of other aspects. In Hsün Tzu's terms, their minds are beclouded or preoccupied *(pi)* with exclusive attention to the importance of one item in a distinction without weighing the importance of the other. For example, Mo Tzu exaggerates the importance of utility without appreciating the beauty of elegant form; Chuang Tzu exaggerates the importance of Heaven at the expense of understanding humans. It is perhaps his holistic conception of *tao* that enables Hsün Tzu, for example, to learn from Chuang Tzu on the nature of the mind and from the Mohists on the need to emphasize certain standards of argumentative competence.[17]

In sum, in Hsün Tzu we find a Confucian philosopher who exemplifies a concern with defending the Confucian *(ju)* tradition against both internal and external challenges, and who is at the same time quite capable of critical adoption of non-Confucian views that he deems reasonably acceptable. Let me briefly turn to Chu Hsi's conception of the Confucian tradition, *tao-t'ung,* commonly rendered "transmission of *tao*"—a conception central to the orthodox tradition of Neo-Confucianism. Because of its religious connotation, the notion of orthodoxy quite naturally suggests an uncritical adherence to conventional or currently accepted beliefs as possessing an unquestioned authoritative status. As de Bary has instructively shown, *tao-t'ung* is better construed as "repossession of *tao*" or "reconstitution of *tao.*" For distinguishing the conservative and liberal tendencies in Neo-Confucianism, it is important to differentiate two contrasting attitudes toward orthodoxy, the "prophetic" and the "scholastic." de Bary writes:

> "Prophetic" I use here to indicate an extraordinary access to and revelation of truth not vouchsafed to everyone, which by some process of inner inspiration or solitary perception affords an insight beyond what is received in scripture, and by an appeal to some higher order of truth gives new meaning, significance, and urgency to cultural values or scriptural texts. . . . By contrast I use "scholastic" to represent an appeal to received authority by continuous transmission, with stress on external or public acceptance of it as a basis of its validity.[18]

Chu Hsi's attitude is "prophetic" rather than "scholastic." His own study of the classics represents "serious efforts to revitalize the tradition [which] involved creative adaptation as well as faithful interpretations."[19] For example, in his detailed recommendations of classics for examination, apart from some commentaries, Chu Hsi stresses the self-critical study of original texts: "In studying the classics one must have regard for the considered views of former scholars and extrapolate from them, aware that they are not necessarily conclusive but must be weighed as to what they understood and what they missed; then finally all this must be reflected upon in one's own mind to verify it."[20] Chu Hsi would also recommend nonorthodox philosophers of early China such as Hsün Tzu, Han Fei Tzu, Lao Tzu, and Chuang Tzu.[21] As de Bary reminds us, Chu Hsi's notion of *tao-t'ung* should not be construed in a manner that suggests a passive reception and transmission of the Confucian Way, for it involves an activity of revitalization and rediscovery, as well as recovery of the meaning of tradition, or, in contemporary language, an activity of constructive or reconstructive interpretation of the tradition. "In fact, Chu Hsi emphasized the discontinuities in the tradition almost more than the continuities, and underscored the contributions of inspired individuals who rediscovered or 'clarified' the Way in new forms."[22]

The stress on the role of inspired and insightful persons regarding classical learning, in both Hsün Tzu and Chu Hsi, recalls Confucius' notion of *chün-tzu* or paradigmatic individuals, that is, persons who, through their life and conduct, embody humanity *(jen)*, ritual *(li)*, rightness *(yi)*, and other ethical excellences. The *chün-tzu* are the exemplars of the actuating significance of the Confucian tradition, serving as standards of inspiration for committed agents.[23] These paradigmatic individuals are generally ascribed an authority by their contemporary adherents. The authority, however, is based on the acknowledgement of their superior knowledge and achievement, and especially their exercise of rightness *(yi)* in interpretive judgments concerning the relevance of rules in exigent situations, or, in Hsün Tzu words, on *tao* and virtue *(te)*.[24] Quite in the spirit of Hsün Tzu or Chu Hsi, a Confucian thinker would concur with Gadamer's remark that "the authority of persons is based ultimately, not on the subjection and abdication of reason, but on recognition and knowledge—knowledge, namely, that the other is superior to oneself in judgment and insight and that for this reason his judgment takes precedence; that is, it has priority over one's own."[25] However, while possessed of an authoritative ethical status, as standard bearers and interpreters of culture, the *chün-tzu* are not arbiters of moral disputes, for their interpretations of the Confucian tradition represent individual efforts toward the repossession or reconstitution of *tao*, thus essentially contestable and subject to reasoned assessment of their contemporaries and posterity.[26]

II

In general, understanding any living ethical tradition or cultural way of life, from the internal point of view of a reflective, committed agent, involves an appreciation of the interaction of the consensual and dissensual aspects of tradition.[27] As MacIntyre forcefully points out, "A tradition is an argument extended through time in which certain fundamental agreements are defined and redefined in terms of two kinds of conflict: those with critics and enemies external to the tradition who reject all or at least key parts of those fundamental agreements, and those internal interpretative debates through which the meaning and rationale of the fundamental agreements come to be expressed and by whose progress a tradition is constituted."[28]

Given his or her commitment to *tao,* a Confucian thinker today would view those critical, external challenges from modern and contemporary Western moral philosophy not as rival alternatives but as reasonable challenges in the reconstitution of the Confucian ethical tradition. Whether he or she should participate in the rational resolution of theoretical issues is a question to be postponed, pending the development of an approach that can appropriate these challenges as a resource for a viable redefinition of the Confucian tradition, amenable to reasoned discourse concerning its adequacy. Reasonable challenges are thus those that provide an occasion for rethinking about the presumed values of the tradition, for an exploration of avenues of self-transformation consistent with *tao;* and at the same time they provide an occasion for inquiring into the projective possibility of the significance of its basic notions and concerns in dealing with the problem of intercultural conflict. Such an inquiry inevitably confronts the Confucian philosopher (who deems his or her tradition as a mature tradition) with the problem of articulating a conception of rational inquiry. For as MacIntyre justly says, "One of the marks of any mature tradition of rational inquiry is that it possesses the resources to furnish accounts of a range of conditions in which incoherence would become inescapable and explain how these conditions would come about."[29] Embarking upon such an inquiry entails no less than constructing a metaphysical system—in Fang's words, "a philosophy of comprehensive harmony."[30] For this writer, there are, however, the more modest, perhaps more fundamental, tasks for an "underlabourer" in moral philosophy.[31]

The metaethical challenge pertains to conceptual and epistemological reconstruction. At issue is not the development of a conceptual scheme as a rival alternative to those in Western traditions,[32] but the explication of the Confucian conceptual scheme, based on selective, internal classical sources, as consisting of *tao* and virtue *(te),* and the general specification of their concrete significance in terms of humanity *(jen),* ritual *(li),* and rightness *(yi)* as basic and interdependent notions of virtue.[33] With this conceptual scheme as a foundation, it is possible, as I have shown elsewhere, to formulate a plausible Confucian conception of ethical argumentation as a cooperative enterprise aimed at securing agreement on solutions to problems of common concern among participants. In this conception, disputes and disagreement are considered against the background of *tao* as a unifying perspective along with various standards of competence.[34]

The challenge of normative ethics, however, points to an extremely difficult task of accommodating the role of objective principles in Confucian ethics as a form of virtue ethics. In an earlier essay, I explored this problem through the distinction between voluntary mediation or arbitration and adjudication as methods of conflict resolution.[35] In this proposal, emphasis on the centrality of virtues is at home in arbitration. The basic task of an arbitrator is not only to give a sound interpretation of the meaning of a current practice, but also to shape the expectations of conflicting parties along the line of mutual concern, that is, to get them to appreciate one another as interacting members in a community. The aim is thus to direct attention to the importance of reconciliation of persons rather than to the subject matter of conflict. The key to conflict resolution in arbitration lies in the restoration of harmonious personal relationships, in making people aware of the importance of living together in spite of their differences. Virtues or desirable character traits, especially the cooperative ones, are germane to arbitration. When disputes cannot be thus resolved, an appeal to adjudication is essential in order to settle disputes. Here objective principles have an indispensable role to play in deciding the rights or wrongs of contending parties. Toward the end of this earlier essay, I indicated that it is quite consistent with the Confucian conception of ethical argumentation to formulate a coherent set of transcultural principles, not as universal, substantive normative principles comparable, say, to those of the Kantian or utilitarian, but as ground rules or preconditions of adjudication, that is, conditions that must be satisfied prior to seeking convergence of substantive values. In what follows, again provisionally, I make more explicit the background assumptions and the sort of transcultural principles that may be developed in consonance with the spirit of Confucian argumentation.[36]

The background assumptions comprise my philosophical, Neo-Confucian reading of the significance of *tao* regarding reasoned discourse on intercultural ethical conflict.[37] I take it that the *tao* is a proper subject for ethical discourse. In the words of Wang Yang-ming, "The Way *(tao)* is public and belongs to the whole world, and the doctrine is also public and belongs to the whole world. They are not the private properties of Master Chu [Hsi] or even Confucius."[38] My reading of *tao,* indeed indebted to Wang Yang-ming, is thus open to critical evaluation by fellow Confucian moral philosophers.

At the outset of the present essay, an allusion is made to *tao* as an overarching vision of the good human life, an ideal theme of excellence, a holistic, unifying perspective for harmonizing diverse and conflicting elements of moral experience. While it is fundamentally homocentric,

the vision has a comprehensive scope, encompassing all existent entities. A commitment to the realization of *tao,* or alternatively humanity
(jen), involves an acknowledgment and concern for the integrity or
intrinsic value of every existent thing. What is envisaged in *tao* may be
characterized as an ideal of the universe as a moral community.[39] Metaphorically put, *tao* is the vision of "the genuinely ethical symphony"[40]
or "congeniality of excellences."[41]

In light of *tao,* the desirable interplay between humans and between
humans and other things is one of concord *(ho).* In actuality, such a state
of affairs is a rare occurrence. There is an antinomic character to all
values.[42] Without a doctrine of hierarchy of values, a reflective, sincere
(ch'eng) Confucian would regard value conflict, especially among
humans, to be a matter of regret, yet also an invitation to employ persistently one's abilities and resources in order to bring about a state of
harmonious coexistence or equilibrium *(chung).*[43] Dealing with the
problem of conflict requires influence and response *(kan-ying),* an imaginative model or schema for mediating the ideal *tao* and the actual world.
The vertical aspect of influence and response *(kan-ying),* so to speak,
consists in practical causation with respect to nature. In this manner,
natural events are viewed as actual and potential factors that affect
human life, but subject to human control with due cognizance of its limitations. Differently put, events are challenges to action. The point of
commitment to *tao* is in part to alter natural circumstances and states of
affairs along the line of the vision of the good human life. The task
posed by the horizontal aspect of influence and response *(kan-ying)* pertains to conflict in human intercourse. It is as formidable as the vertical
task, perhaps even more complex in that humans are actuated by a wide
cultural diversity of conceptions of value. It calls for the exercise of the
art of accommodation *(chien-shu),*[44] involving coordination of diversity
of goods or ideals implicit in various ways of life.[45]

A recognition of the varieties of cultures as coherent ways of life is
compatible with what Hampshire calls "the no-shopping principle," for
"one cannot pick and choose bits of one picture to put besides bits of
another; the coherence of the pictures comes from their distinct histories."[46] For a Confucian, such an appreciation of cultural diversity is a
prelude to an endeavor to explore the areas of common interest as candidates for arbitration in cases of conflict or radical disagreement.
Moreover, since *tao* is the *telos* of ethical argumentation, the disputed
questions of value, rooted in different ethical traditions, admit of reasonable solution, on the presumption that the participants have a
shared interest in the common problem. When such a presumption is
defeated, arbitration will probably not secure the desired outcome of
agreement. Failure in arbitration thus calls for adjudication. I assume
that the theoretical Confucian task here lies in reshaping humanity
(jen), ritual *(li),* and rightness *(yi),* the general specifications of the con-

crete significance of *tao,* for the purpose of developing a set of trans-cultural principles of adjudication.[47] These principles, as I suggested in the earlier essay, could be formulated by reflecting upon Hsün Tzu's conception of those desirable qualities of participants or the *ethos* of Confucian argumentation: for example, humaneness *(jen-hsin)* and fair-mindedness or impartiality *(kung-hsin),* and ritual *(li).*[48] Impartiality may be considered an aspect of rightness *(yi),* since the exercise of right-ness *(yi),* as noted in section I, requires impartial weighing of circum-stances.

Given the assumptions above, with no claim to completeness, I pro-pose the following principles as a point of departure for further inquiry:[49]

P1 nonprescriptivity
P2 mutuality
P3 procedural justice
P4 rectification
P5 reconsideration

Before proceeding to discuss these principles, let me say something more about their status in adjudication. These transcultural principles are to be viewed as heuristic or leading principles of inquiry into the possibility of achieving consensus of substantive norms.[50] As ground rules for intercultural discourse, they are, so to speak, protocols of ethi-cal diplomacy, reflecting in part the basic sense of ritual *(li)* as a set of formal prescriptions for proper behavior with a focus upon both their delimiting and supportive functions, that is, conditions that acknowl-edge the necessity of constraints that set the limits of proper behavior and conditions that facilitate the satisfaction of tradition-oriented value claims within the prescribed limits.[51]

The principle of nonprescriptivity may also be called the principle of integrity. It is a principle of respect for the integrity of ethical traditions. More generally, from the *tao* perspective, it is the principle of respect for the diversity of goods, for various experiments of living in distinct cul-tural forms of life. In particular, the principle captures an aspect of humaneness *(jen-hsin).* Mencius is emphatic on this theme of integrity exemplified in different, worthy ways of pursuing humanity *(jen)* in the light of personal situations.[52] This principle is valuation-neutral regard-ing the substantive content of different ethical traditions. Acceptance of this principle, however, does not preclude the possibility of the adher-ents of different traditions learning from one another. While traditions that survived the crucial test of their long history deserve respect, it is a Confucian faith that healthy interaction of modern cultures of the East and the West will eventually lead to the "higher form of creative synthe-sis which will emerge as a new culture of the future with both the East and the West as its necessary ingredients."[53] As Winch reminds us, "the concept of *learning from* which is involved in the study of other cultures is closely linked with the concept of *wisdom*. We are confronted not just with different techniques, but with new possibilities of good and evil, in relation to which men may come to terms with life."[54]

Accepting this principle as a precondition for discourse on issues of substantive cultural norms is also compatible with Williams' view of "relativism at a distance," in that an encounter with an alien tradition, from each culture-oriented point of view, may be merely a matter of notional rather than real confrontation. But, as Williams says, "Today all confrontations between cultures must be real confrontations." Unlike Williams, a Confucian would cast doubt on his thesis that "reflection might destroy knowledge, because thick ethical concepts might be driven from use by reflection, while the more abstract general ethical thoughts that would probably take their place would not satisfy the conditions of propositional knowledge."[55] Consider Williams' examples of "thick" ethical concepts such as treachery, promise, brutality, courage, lying, and gratitude. These concepts seem "to express a union of fact and value" as contrasted with such "thin" concepts as good, right, and ought. A Confucian would view this distinction as a distinction between levels of abstraction. Given his or her faith in the creative synthesis of the cultures of the East and the West, the "thick" culturally operative concepts are in principle subject to conceptual transformation via analogical projection of the significance of humanity *(jen)*, ritual *(li)*, and rightness *(yi)*. Thus in spite of their usual locus of ethical significance, these concepts may be shaped into "thin" general notions, subject to specification of their concrete significance in different cultural habitats. Moreover, for the Confucian, the basic issue concerns the possibility of reasoned agreement to conflict resolution in the light of acknowledged preconditions of discourse and not the adoption of some version of moral realism. This does not mean that conflicting value claims cannot be assessed in terms of their truth dimension. Rather, such an assessment depends on a context of discourse consisting of a particular rather than a universal audience. As Austin once remarked, "In real life, as opposed to the simple situations envisaged in logical theory, one cannot always answer in a simple manner whether it [a statement] is true or false."[56]

Confucius disclaimed himself to be a man of humanity *(jen)*, for commitment to humanity *(jen)*, as it involves persistent effort in extending benevolence, is a heavy burden. However, the practice of humanity *(jen)* "depends on oneself alone and not on others."[57] On one occasion, in response to the question whether there is a single word that can serve as a guide to one's whole life, Confucius said, "It is perhaps the word *'shu'*. Do not impose on others what you yourself do not desire *(yü)*."[58] As a method for the practice of humanity *(jen)*, *shu* calls for "the ability to take as an analogy what is near at hand," that is, using "oneself as a measure" (*Analects* 6:29).[59] The notion of *shu,* reminiscent of the Golden Rule, includes two elements: desire (*yü*) and the use of analogy. The desire in question pertains to second-order, reflective, rather than to first order, occurrent desire, that is, desire as mediated by reason or reflection. And this reflection is conducted with due regard to humanity (*jen*), the concern for the well-being of another.[60] The element of analogy may be viewed as an imaginative projection of one's concern for humanity (*jen*) in taking into account other peoples' desires and interests.[61] As Fingarette put it, analogy or comparison is "an act of creative imagination." "The spirit of such teaching as *shu* and the Golden Rule is obviously to call upon us to take the other person's situation into account in some central way."[62]

Reflection on the significance of the notion of *shu* for intercultural discourse suggests what I call the principle of mutuality or consideration, a collateral principle of integrity, which enjoins the parties in dispute to exercise sympathetic imagination in appreciating the integrity of an alien, conflicting tradition and to endeavor, whenever the opportunity arises, to transform disagreement into an occasion for exploring the possibility of a convergence of values. One's desire for imposing one's own norms must thus be mediated by a reflection that attends to the other's similar desire. Analogical projection of the extensive significance of one's cultural norms is not discouraged, but it must be moderated by due consideration for the other's own conception of her or his locus of operation. Given the real possibility of "relativism at a distance," the principle of mutuality remains a procedural rather than a substantive requirement. Of course, in light of *tao,* the aim of attaining congenial coexistence within the limits of ritual (*li*) also calls for *supporting* or facilitating the realization of the ideals of other ways of life. Coupled with this concern, the principle of mutuality would enjoin sustaining the vitality of different ways of life, as seen by their adherents to be worthy of continuing preservation.

The argumentative role of ritual (*li*) as a set of formal prescriptions for proper behavior and rightness (*yi*) as fairmindedness or impartiality (*kung-hsin*) may be construed as a concern for consistency or the principle of procedural justice. Consistency is not just a matter of compliance with the requirements of deductive logic, for "these formal requirements tell us nothing about what in particular is to *count* as consistency, just as the rules of the propositional calculus limit, but do not themselves determine what are to be proper values of p, q, etc."[63] The principle of procedural justice, in Rawls' terms, is that of pure procedural, as distinct from perfect or imperfect procedural justice. Unlike the former, the latter has no substantive criterion of justice that is presupposed for insuring just outcome; and unlike the latter, the former has no guarantee that any given substantive criterion will yield the desired outcome. "Pure procedural justice obtains when there is no independent criterion for the right result: instead there is a correct or fair procedure such that the outcome is likewise correct or fair, whatever it is, provided that the procedure has been properly followed."[64]

The principle of procedural justice embodies a concern for the establishment of three different and related sorts of procedures as preconditions for adjudication: (1) procedures that maintain the argumentative process as an orderly way of presenting competing value claims, (2) even more important, procedures that ensure equal participation of the disputing parties in an open forum, and (3) procedures that pertain to the impartial enforcement of any agreed solution to the problem of common concern. The first sort of procedure reflects the concern of ritual (*li*) in its basic focus on form, manner, and order of conduct; the second and the third that of fairmindedness. For further exploration, a Confucian theorist may appropriate some insights into the process theory of judicial review without taking a position on its adequacy as an explanatory *cum* justificatory theory of American Constitutional law. The stress on the procedural side of due process, on the preservation of structure rather than "identification and preservation of specific substantive values," is a dominant theme in the Constitution of the United States and some of its Amendments.[65] The Due Process and Equal Protection Clauses of the Fourteenth Amendment, for example, as a matter of minimum interpretation, seem to address the guarantee of fair procedures, say, for airing the grievances of the citizenry against unjustified treatment by its government. This dominant theme suggests the primacy of procedural justice over agreement on substantive norms for settlement of disputes. More generally, when competing substantive value claims have implicit reference to a divergence of tradition-oriented ideals, it is plausible to maintain that the hope for peaceful resolution depends on an acknowledgment of some procedural rules as a precondition for negotiation and for consideration of the possibility of mutual accommodation.[66]

Coupled with *tao* or humanity (*jen*) as an overarching ideal of extensive concern for the integrity and well-being of every existent thing, the principle of procedural justice must be supplemented by the principle of rectification or restoration of the values lost in conflict resolution. Accommodating coherently the diversity of competing goods and ideals, with due regard to fairmindedness (*kung-hsin*), inevitably involves the loss or sacrifice of values. The problem of influence and response (*kan-ying*) or coordinating the satisfaction of the demands of varieties of ethical excellence is, so to speak, a design problem "akin to that of landscape gardening or interior decoration."[67] In this setting, we are concerned with the meshing of elements in a life arrangement. The possibility of obtaining the desired solution depends on recognizing the constraints imposed by limited natural resources as well as those of human nature and culture. Factors such as partiality or limited benevolence, foresight, and vulnerability, as well as those of cultural traditions need to be taken into account in an overall design of life.[68] Cognizance of these constraints points to the need for making comparative judgments of importance.[69] In light of *tao*, the loss or degradation of one value in such a judgment is a matter of regret, but more important, the experience has a prospective significance in that it calls also for an active concern for restoration of the value lost or its functional equivalent.[70] In addition to the principle of rectification we may also propose a principle of reconsideration, that is, that any substantive ethical agreement reached in argumentation is subject to reasonable reconsideration in the light of changing local cultural circumstances as well as their relevance to future issues of value conflict.[71]

Notes

1. Thomé H. Fang, *Chinese Philosophy: Its Spirit and Development* (Taipei: Linking, 1980). See also Fang, *The Chinese View of Life: The Philosophy of Comprehensive Harmony* (Taipei: Linking, 1980). For a discussion of Fang's view as a contribution to moral philosophy, see my "Ethical Significance of Professor Thomé H. Fang's Philosophy" (Presented at the International Symposium of Thomé H. Fang's Philosophy, Taipei, Taiwan, August 15–18, 1987), published under the title *Philosophy of Thomé H. Fang* (Taipei: Youth Cultural Enterprises, 1989).

2. For the general distinction of ideal theme and norm, see my *Dimensions of Moral Creativity: Paradigms, Principles, and Ideals* (University Park: Pennsylvania State University Press, 1978). For application to Confucian ethics, see my "Chinese Moral Vision, Responsive Agency, and Factual Beliefs," *Journal of Chinese Philosophy* 7 (1980); and *The Unity of Knowledge and Action: A Study in Wang Yang-ming's Moral Psychology* (Honolulu: University of Hawaii Press, 1982), chap. 3.

3. See my "Status of Principles in Confucian Ethics," in *Proceedings of the International Symposium on Confucianism and the Modern World* (1987). A revised version appeared in the *Journal of Chinese Philosophy* 16, no. 3 (1989).

4. Li Ti-sheng, *Hsün Tzu chi-shih* (Taipei: Hsüeh-sheng, 1979), *ch'uan-hsüeh p'ien*. See Burton Watson, trans., *Hsün Tzu: Basic Writings* (New York: Columbia University Press, 1963), p. 15; cf. John Knoblock, *Xunzi: A Translation and Study of the Complete Works*, vol. 1 (Stanford: Stanford University Press, 1988), p. 135; H. H. Dubs, trans., *The Works of Hsüntze* (Taipei: Ch'eng-wen, 1966), p. 31. Asterisks below indicate my emendation.

5. *Ch'üan-hsüeh p'ien;* Watson, *Hsün Tzu*, p. 19.*

6. *Ju-hsiao p'ien;* Dubs, *Works of Hsüntze*, p. 104.*

7. *Ch'üan-hsüeh p'ien;* Watson, *Hsün Tzu*, p. 20. For further discussion of the pedagogical and other functions of the use of historical characters and events, see my "Ethical Uses of the Past in Early Confucianism: The Case of Hsün Tzu," *Philosophy East & West* 35, no. 2 (April 1985).

8. D. C. Lau, trans., *Confucius: The Analects* (Middlesex: Penguin Books,

1979), Introduction, p. 20. For further discussion on the different functions of *li*, see my "The Concept of *Li* in Confucian Moral Theory," in Robert E. Allinson, ed., *Understanding the Chinese Mind: The Philosophical Roots* (New York: Oxford University Press, 1989).

9. D. C. Lau, *Confucius: The Analects*, p. 45.

10. See my *Dimensions of Moral Creativity*, chap. 6; and *Ethical Argumentation: A Study in Hsün Tzu's Moral Epistemology* (Honolulu: University of Hawaii Press, 1985).

11. *Hsün Tzu, pu-kou p'ien* and *chih-shih p'ien.*

12. Ibid., *chün-tao p'ien.*

13. This discussion of the three types of Confucian *(ju)* is a partial interpretive reading of a long passage in *ju-hsiao p'ien*. For further discussion of the great or sagely Confucian as distinct from the superior man, see my *Ethical Argumentation*, pp. 67–78. (Cf. Dubs, *Works of Hsüntze*, pp. 110–112.) For an anticipation in the *Analects* 6:13: "The Master said to Tzu-hsia, 'Be a gentleman *(chün-tzu) ju*, not a petty *ju'*."

14. See my "The Conceptual Aspect of Hsün Tzu's Philosophy of Human Nature"; "The Quasi-empirical Aspect of Hsün Tzu's Philosophy of Human Nature"; and "Morality and Human Nature," *Philosophy East & West* 28, 29, 32 (1977, 1978, 1982). It must be noted that in an essay entitled "Against Twelve Philosophers *(fei shih-erh tzu)*" Hsün Tzu's terse critique of Mencius and Tzu-szu as having only a sketchy or fragmentary understanding of the *tao* of Ancient Kings has done much more damage to his reputation than his other essays. As Knoblock points out, "In other books, we have seen his critique of 'worthless' and 'base' Ru (Confucian) philosophers, but in none was criticism so directly aimed at particular heroes of the conventional, officially sanctioned Confucianism of the imperial period." See Knoblock, *Xunzi*, p. 212. Knoblock provides an informative, philosophical introduction to this essay.

15. Mencius' critique is rather terse: "Yang advocates everyone for himself, which amounts to a denial of one's prince; Mo advocates love without discrimination, which amounts to a denial of one's father. To ignore one's father on the one hand, and one's prince on the other, is to be no different from the beast." See D. C. Lau, trans., *Mencius* (Middlesex: Penguin Books, 1970), 3B:9.

16. This is Knoblock's excellent interpretive translation along with his gloss: "That is, they were able to offer facts in evidence to support their doctrines, could give them a foundation, observed the forms of argumentation of the day, used discriminations, and were skilled in debate" (Knoblock, *Xunzi*, pp. 223–224, 302 n. 30). For my reconstruction of Hsün Tzu's standards of argumentative competence, see *Ethical Argumentation*, chap. 1.

17. See *chieh-pi p'ien* and *cheng-ming p'ien;* Watson, *Hsün Tzu*, pp. 120–156; Dubs, *Works of Hsüntze*, pp. 259–299. For further discussion on this notion of *pi* in connection with *tao*, see my *Ethical Argumentation*, esp. chap. 4; and "Hsün Tzu and the Unity of Virtues," *Journal of Chinese Philosophy* 14, no. 4 (1987).

18. Wm. Theodore de Bary, *Neo-Confucian Orthodoxy and the Learning of the Mind-and-Heart* (New York: Columbia University Press, 1981), p. 9; and *The Liberal Tradition in China* (Hong Kong and New York: Chinese University of

Hong Kong Press, 1983), pp. 15–16. See also Tu Wei-ming, "Reconstituting the Confucian Tradition," in his *Humanity and Self-Cultivation: Essays in Confucian Thought* (Berkeley: Asian Humanities Press, 1979), chap. 9. For a detailed discussion, see Chan, "Chu Hsi's Completion of Neo-Confucianism," in W. T. Chan, *Chu Hsi: Life and Thought* (Hong Kong: Chinese University of Hong Kong Press, 1987); and "The New *Tao-T'ung,*" in W. T. Chan, *Chu Hsi: New Studies* (Honolulu: University of Hawaii Press, 1989). For a plausible defense of Chu Hsi's doctrine, see Liu Shu-hsien, "The Problem of Orthodoxy in Chu Hsi's Philosophy," in W. T. Chan, ed., *Chu Hsi and Neo-Confucianism* (Honolulu: University of Hawaii Press, 1986), chap. 24.

19. Tu, *Humanity and Self-Cultivation,* p. 134.

20. Cited in de Bary, *Neo-Confucian Orthodoxy,* p. 58.

21. Ibid., p. 99. For an insightful discussion of the role of book learning in Chu Hsi's thought, see Yü Ying-shih, "Morality and Knowledge in Chu Hsi's Philosophical System," in Chan, *Chu Hsi and Neo-Confucianism,* chap. 15.

22. Ibid. For an instructive study of Wang Yang-ming's philosophy against the background of the problem of "orthodoxy," see Julia Ching, *To Acquire Wisdom: The Way of Wang Yang-ming* (New York: Columbia University Press, 1976). For a similar view on the Christian tradition, see Jaroslav Pelikan, *The Vindication of Tradition* (New Haven: Yale University Press, 1984); and on some principal Western traditions of practical rationality and justice, see Alasdair MacIntyre, *Whose Justice? Which Rationality?* (Notre Dame: University of Notre Dame Press, 1988). Hereafter cited as *WJWR.*

23. For further discussion of the role of paradigmatic individuals in morality and *chün-tzu,* see my *Dimension of Moral Creativity,* chaps. 3 and 5; in education, see my "Competence, Concern, and the Role of Paradigmatic Individuals *(chün-tzu)* in Moral Education," *Philosophy East & West* 42, no. 2. For the notion of paradigm as a means, rather than a method, of representation of a standard within a language game, see L. Wittgenstein, *Philosophical Investigations,* 3d ed. (New York: Macmillan, 1969), sections 50–51.

24. *Hsün Tzu, ch'iang-kuo p'ien.* Hsün Tzu is also emphatic that just as there are cases in which a filial son can reasonably go against his father's wishes in following *yi,* there are also cases in which a minister can oppose his ruler in following *tao.* (See *tzu-tao p'ien* and my *Ethical Argumentation,* p. 64.)

25. Hans-Georg Gadamer, *Truth and Method* (New York: Seabury Press, 1975), p. 248.

26. For a general discussion of the reconstitutive dimension of morality, see my *Dimensions of Moral Creativity,* chap. 6.

27. Ibid., pp. 92–106.

28. MacIntyre, *WJWR,* p. 12. See also Pelikan, *Vindication of Tradition,* pp. 72–73.

29. MacIntyre, *WJWR,* p. 393. See also, p. 327.

30. See note 1 above.

31. Recalling Locke's conception in his "Epistle to the Reader," *An Essay Concerning Human Understanding* (New York: Dover, 1959), p. 14.

32. Cf. MacIntyre, *WJWR,* chap. 18.

33. A compendious statement of the results of my conceptual inquiry is given in my "Confucian Ethics" in Lawrence C. Becker, ed., *Encyclopedia of Ethics* (Garland Publishing, forthcoming). This inquiry, as well as the conception of argumentation, is inspired by and in part indebted to Ch'en Ta-ch'i, *K'ung Tzu Hsüeh-shuo* (Taipei: Cheng-chung, 1976); and *Hsün Tzu Hsüeh-shuo* (Taipei: Chung-hua wen-hua she, 1954). For methodological consideration, see my "Reflections on Methodology in Chinese Philosophy," *International Philosophical Quarterly* 11, no. 2 (1971): 244–247; "Tasks of Confucian Ethics," *Journal of Chinese Philosophy* 6, no. 1 (1979); and "Reflections on Moral Theory and Understanding Moral Traditions," in Gerald James Larson and Eliot Deutsch, eds., *Interpreting Across Cultures: New Essays in Comparative Philosophy* (Princeton: Princeton University Press, 1988). Cf. Ronald Dworkin, *Law's Empire* (Cambridge: Harvard University Press, 1986), chap. 2.

34. See my *Ethical Argumentation.* For more extensive discussion of a nondeductivist conception of moral reasoning, see my "The Possibility of a Confucian Theory of Rhetoric" (Presented at the Conference on Rhetoric: East and West, East-West Center, Honolulu, June 12–18, 1988; the proceedings will be edited by Kathleen Hall Jamieson, the director of the conference).

35. See "The Status of Principles in Confucian Ethics."

36. I leave open the question of the plausibility of MacIntyre's conception of "rationality of traditions," thus freeing myself from his preoccupation with the relativist and perspectivist challenges. I am more concerned with exploring the significance of his suggestion that, though conflict between alternative traditions may take the form of rivalry, "it can also happen that two traditions, hitherto independent and even antagonistic, can come to recognize certain possibilities of fundamental agreement and reconstitute themselves as a single, more complex debate" (MacIntyre, *WJWR,* p. 12). However, my stress is on prior agreement on the preconditions of discourse in the light of the non-agonistic conception of Confucian ethical argumentation.

37. These assumptions are my response to what I take to be a common aspiration of Chinese thinkers today for creative synthesis of Chinese and Western cultures. See, for example, the recurrent theme in the journal *Che-hsüeh yü wen-hua (Universitas);* the "Proceedings of the First World Conference on Chinese Philosophy" (Taipei, August 19–25, 1984), published in the *Bulletin of the Chinese Philosophical Association,* vol. 3 (1985), 763 pages; and the 1987 proceedings of the International Symposium on Confucianism and the Modern World, which contained 1827 pages (see note 3 above). Samples of earlier studies may be found in Arne Naess and Alastair Hannay, eds., *Invitation to Chinese Philosophy* (Oslo: Universitetsforlaget, 1972). The synoptic statement below is derived from a series of studies inspired by Wang Yang-ming. Apart from the works cited in note 2 above, see also my "Practical Causation in Confucian Ethics" and "Confucian Vision and Experience of the World," *Philosophy East & West* 25 nos. 1 and 3 (January and July 1975); "Ideals and Values: A Study in Rescher's Moral Vision," in Robert Almeder, ed., *Praxis and Reason: Studies in the Philosophy of Nicholas Rescher* (Washington: University Press of America,

1982); and "Between Commitment and Realization: A Study in Wang Yang-ming's Vision of the Universe as a Moral Community," in Tu Wei-ming, ed., *Confucian Spirituality* (Crossroad/Continuum, forthcoming).

38. Wing-tsit Chan, *Instructions for Practical Living and Other Neo-Confucian Writings by Wang Yang-ming* (New York: Columbia University Press, 1963), p. 164. See also Julia Ching, trans., *The Philosophical Letters of Wang Yang-ming* (Columbia: University of South Carolina Press, 1972), p. 76.

39. As Wang writes: "The great man regards Heaven, Earth, and the myriad things as one body. He regards the world as one family and the country as one person. . . . Forming one body with Heaven, Earth, and the myriad things is not only true of the great man. Even the mind of the small man is no different. Only he himself makes it small. Therefore when he sees a child about to fall into a well, he cannot help a feeling of alarm and commiseration. This shows that his humanity *(jen)* forms one body with the child. . . . Again, when he observes the pitiful cries and frightened appearance of birds and animals about to be slaughtered, he cannot help feeling an 'inability to bear" their suffering. This shows that his humanity forms one body with birds and animals." Wang goes one to point out that a man of *jen* also forms one body with plants, stones, tiles, mountains, and rivers. See Chan, *Instructions,* p. 272.

40. See William James, *Essays on Faith and Morals* (New York: Longmans, Green & Co., 1949), p. 212.

41. This notion, according to Norton, is said to be implicit in Plato's *Lysis.* See David Norton, *Personal Destinies* (Princeton: Princeton University Press, 1982), pp. 306–307, 362–262. For my use with qualification in connection with Rescher's moral vision, see "Ideals and Values," pp. 181–184 and 202–203.

42. Nicolai Hartmann, *Ethics* (London: George Allen & Unwin, 1932), vol. 2, p. 76.

43. This reading of *chung* and *ho* in *The Doctrine of the Mean (Chung Yung)* is indebted to Wang Yang-ming. See "Confucian Vision and Experience of the World," pp. 325–326.

44. See *Hsün Tzu, fei-hsiang p'ien.*

45. As Rescher put it: "Each ideal can—and should—be pursued and cultivated in consonance with the realization of other values. The pluralism of ideals, the fact that each must be taken in context, means that in the pursuit of our ideals we must moderate them to one another." See Nicholas Rescher, *Unpopular Essays on Technological Progress* (Pittsburgh: University of Pittsburgh Press, 1980), p. 59. And, more recently, see Rescher, *Ethical Idealism* (Berkeley: University of California Press, 1987), pp. 76–78. Further discussion may be found in my "Ideals and Values," pp. 185–190.

46. Stuart Hampshire, *Morality and Conflict* (Cambridge: Harvard University Press, 1983), p. 148. See also Ruth Benedict, *Patterns of Culture* (Boston: Houghton Mifflin, 1934), and "Configurations of Culture in North America," in Margaret Mead, *Ruth Benedict* (New York: Columbia University Press, 1974).

47. For samples of these efforts with respect to the problem of conceptual

unity, see my "The Problem of Conceptual Unity in Hsün Tzu and Li Kou's Solution," *Philosophy East & West* 39, no. 2 (April 1989); "Hsün Tzu and the Unity of Virtues"; and "The Concept of Li in Confucian Moral Theory."

48. See "The Status of Principles in Confucian Ethics," section 2; and "The Possibility of a Confucian Theory of Rhetoric," section 1.

49. P1, P2, P3, and P4 are adumbrated in my "The Status of Principles in Confucian Ethics." But, again, my discussion of these principles is intended as no more than another sketch in a progress report toward the development of a systematic Confucian moral philosophy.

50. With Rawls, I suppose that "one of the aims of moral philosophy is to look for possible bases of agreement where none seem to exist. It must attempt to extend the range of consensus and to frame more discriminating moral conceptions for our consideration." However, given radical disagreement rooted in tradition-oriented perspectives, the prior task is to look for those principles, à la Scanlon, that cannot be reasonably rejected given "the aim of finding principles which could be the basis of informed, unforced general agreement." The proposed transcultural principles may be construed in the sense of Scanlon's principles, but they are not intended to be contractarian normative principles. See John Rawls, *A Theory of Justice* (Cambridge: Harvard University Press, 1971), p. 582; John Rawls, "Justice and Fairness: Political and Not Metaphysical," *Philosophy and Public Affairs* 14, no. 3 (1985); and T. M. Scanlon, "Contractarianism and Utilitarianism," in Amartya Sen and Bernard Williams, eds., *Utilitarianism and Beyond* (London: Cambridge University Press, 1982), p. 111.

51. For detailed explanation and justification of these two functions of *li,* see my "The Concept of *Li* in Confucian Moral Theory."

52. While this principle recalls Kant's Principle of Humanity, it is not a formula of the Categorical Imperative, and thus pretends to no status of being an apodictic and universal principle of conduct. For Mencius, see *Mencius,* esp. 5A:7; 6B:6; and 6A:10.

53. Thomé H. Fang, *Creativity in Man and Nature* (Taipei: Linking, 1980), p. 141.

54. Peter Winch, *Ethics and Action* (London: Routledge & Kegan Paul, 1972), p. 42. See also MacIntyre, *WJWR,* pp. 394–395.

55. Bernard Williams, *Ethics and the Limits of Philosophy* (Cambridge: Harvard University Press, 1985), pp. 129, 140, and 169.

56. J. L. Austin, *How to Do Things With Words* (Cambridge: Harvard University Press, 1962), p. 142. For the distinction between the universal and the particular audience, see Ch. Perelman and Anna Olbrechts-Tyteca, *The New Rhetoric: A Treatise on Argumentation* (Notre Dame: University of Notre Dame Press, 1969), p. 87; and my "Some Aspects of Ethical Argumentation. A Reply to Daniel Dahlstrom and John Marshall," *Journal of Chinese Philosophy* 14, no. 4 (1987): 509–512.

57. *The Analects,* 7:34; 8:7; 12:1; 15:21.

58. Ibid., 15:24. See also 5:11; 6:20; 12:2; and 4:15. *Chung* (doing one's best) and *shu* are said by Tseng Tzu to characterize the thread of Confucius' *tao*

(ibid., 4:15). I here focus only on *shu* with Lau's reminder that *"chung* is the doing of one's best and it is through *chung* that one puts into effect what one had found out by the method of *shu"* (ibid., p. 16). I take it that *chung* here may be construed as an expression of one's sincere commitment to *jen.* For further discussion, see my "Confucian Vision and the Human Community," *Journal of Chinese Philosophy* 11, no. 3 (1984). For fuller alternative readings of relevant passages, see Herbert Fingarette, "Following the 'One Thread' of the *Analects,"* *Journal of the American Academy of Religion* 47, no. 35 (1979); and David L. Hall and Roger T. Ames, *Thinking Through Confucius* (Albany: SUNY Press, 1987), pp. 283–304.

59. Lau, *Confucius: The Analects,* p. 15.

60. See Harry Frankfurt, "Freedom of the Will and the Concept of a Person," *Journal of Philosophy* 68, no. 1 (1971): 10. This distinction is implicit in Hsün Tzu: "A single desire which one receives from nature *(t'ien)* is regulated and directed by the mind in many different ways. Consequently, it may be difficult to identify and distinguish it in terms of its original appearance. . . . If the guidance of the mind is in accord with reason, although desires are many, what harm will this be to good government" (Watson, *Hsün Tzu,* 151*). See my "Dimensions of *Li* (Propriety): Reflections on An Aspect of Hsün Tzu's Ethics," *Philosophy East & West* 29, no. 4 (October 1979): 380–381. For a similar interpretation, see Liang Ch'i-hsiung, *Hsün Tzu chien-shih* (Taipei: Shang-wu, 1978), p. 323.

61. For a detailed discussion of analogical projection, see my *Ethical Argumentation,* esp. pp. 78–86.

62. Fingarette, "Following the 'One Thread' in the *Analects,"* p. 383.

63. Winch, *Ethics and Action,* p. 34.

64. Rawls, *A Theory of Justice,* pp. 85–86.

65. This appropriation of Ely's insight is consistent with an appreciation of Dworkin's moral theory of judicial review, in particular, that the Due Process and Equal Protection Clauses of the Fourteenth Amendment are best viewed as embodying "abstract intention" rather than particular conceptions of justice. It must also be noted that in light of *tao,* the right sort of procedures to be spelled out may well involve competing substantive value judgments to be resolved within argumentation. Again, like the question of truth, the question here is a matter of context of discourse consisting of particular rather than universal audience. See John Hart Ely, *Democracy and Distrust* (Cambridge: Harvard University Press, 1980), p. 92; and Ronald Dworkin, *A Matter of Principle* (Cambridge: Harvard University Press, 1986), p. 49. For Dworkin's emphasis on procedural due process, see *Law's Empire,* pp. 166–167, passim.

66. For the priority of moral rules over the pursuit of ideals, see my *Dimensions of Moral Creativity,* esp. pp. 135–139.

67. Rescher, *Unpopular Essays on Technological Progress,* p. 60.

68. Hsün Tzu, like Hume, Hart, Warnock, and Rawls, regards these factors in human nature and the scarcity of resources as causes of human conflict. I take it that these same factors are equally germane to conflict resolution, for

they act as constraints on the articulation of feasible objectives—a theme that pervades Rescher's various writings on values. For further discussion, see "The Quasi-Empirical Aspect of Hsün Tzu's Philosophy of Human Nature" and "Ideals and Values."

69. See *Mencius*, 7A:46. Also, 6A:10 and 6A:14.

70. See my *The Unity of Knowledge and Action*, pp. 37–42. For similar concern with rectification in Weiss' metaphysics, see "The Structure of Social Complexes," *Review of Metaphysics* 41, no. 2 (1987): 340–341.

71. For the Confucian notion of reasonableness, see my *The Unity of Knowledge and Action*, pp. 94–100. For affinity to Rescher's notion, see "Ideals and Values," pp. 193–198.

THE FRENCH REVOLUTION
AND THE HOLOCAUST:
CAN ETHICS BE AHISTORICAL?

In recent years, philosophers like Stuart Hampshire, Bernard Williams, and Alasdair MacIntyre (responding, perhaps, to arguments by anthropologists like Clifford Geertz and political scientists like Michael Walzer) have given increasing centrality to the question as to whether ethics should be universalistic or should rather be rooted in the forms of life of particular traditions and cultures. I want to consider that question in the following light: On the one hand, John Rawls—whom I consider to be the greatest living social ethicist—has said that he is not discussing the "foundations" of ethics, but rather addressing the main question confronting Western bourgeois democracies after the French Revolution, that is, the tension between Equality and Liberty.[1] This suggests that Rawls is pessimistic about the prospects for "universalistic" ethical theory (perhaps more so than when he wrote *A Theory of Justice*). On the other hand, George Steiner has suggested that after the Holocaust it may be impossible to believe that the values of the West have any vitality at all.[2] But to understand this thought, it is necessary to understand how Steiner is using the notion of "the Holocaust."

Steiner is not using the phrase in its accepted denotation, the execution (I write "execution" to bring out the horrible "legality" of the proceeding, as contrasted with a mere "slaughter") of six million Jewish women, men, small children, and even infants. Instead, and very tellingly, he is using the term to cover the killing, by war, genocide, and so on, of *seventy million people* in the thirty seven years beginning with 1914. He is, for example including the slaughter of Europe's youth in World War I, itself one of the most suicidal acts by any civilization in history, and also the purges of Stalin, the deportations of peoples, the planned starvations, and so on.

Elsewhere, Steiner connects the self-destructive proclivities of European civilization with a loss of the concept of "tragedy" and with an alarming loss of what he calls "flexibility."[3] Discussing this aspect of Steiner's thought would require me to become a futurologist or a sociol-

ogist, neither of which I am. But, thinking about this as a mere philosopher, and putting these remarks—Rawls' and Steiner's—together, I
find myself in the following "bind": if Rawls is right, ethical theory
seems to require the framework of a tradition to give its questions substance, and to provide a shared framework of assumptions within which
questions can be discussed. On the other hand, the horrors to which the
regnant Western tradition have led call into question, at least for some,
the possibility of doing what Rawls suggests, that is, just assuming the
basic values of the Enlightenment and calmly discussing how to adjudicate tensions between them.

When I accepted the invitation to speak at the Sixth East-West Philosophers' Conference, I wrote the director that "Needless to say, I do
not expect to resolve these dilemmas. I hope, between now and the
summer of 1989, to find something to say about them." Let me say that
I now feel very glad that I did not promise to resolve the dilemmas! But
before saying something about them, let me get out of the way a reason
that may occur to any liberal person for not taking seriously enough this
thought of Steiner's.

The obvious reason one might give for dismissing Steiner's views is
that there is nothing wrong with the great Enlightenment *values;* it is just
the West's *compliance* with those values that is faulty. In a sense, this is
perfectly true. I, for one, cherish and want others to cherish the Enlightenment values of liberty (expanded by Kant and others to include
autonomy and toleration), fraternity, and equality. And the events of
the Holocaust—in Steiner's extended sense—were a violation of those
values, even if some of the participants in the extended Holocaust
claimed that their actions would bring about the reign of those very
values on earth in due course.

But the distinction between our values and our "compliance" is too
simple, and in two different ways. In the first place, our values are not
all that *clear.* This is the problem to which Rawls' work is addressed. In
the real world, our values of liberty and of equality conflict, and the
conflicts are difficult to adjudicate. In principle, I suppose, one could
have perfect economic equality (equality of political power is a far more
difficult notion). At one time, the more left-wing *kibbutzim* in Israel
required all their members to have the same *furniture* in their apart-
ments, to make sure that no invidious inequalities would arise; but most
of us would feel that this degree of equality requires an inadmissible
interference with individual freedom. On the other hand, the wide-open
"freedom" of economic enterprise on which the United States and England today pride themselves has led to massive inequalities, including
the inequality between the homed and the homeless.

In the second place, the massive and long-continued failure of the
West's societies to comply with their own supposed values suggests that
large numbers of people find them insufficient in some way. If the

Enlightenment were a recent event, one might say "Well, naturally people are nostalgic for old verities, old faiths, old ways, however superstitious or unjust. Give them time." But the Holocaust—using the term now in it narrower sense—took place two centuries after the Enlightenment, and was perpetrated by a nation that prided itself on its contributions to Western philosophy, literature, music, science, and so on. If there is a felt dissatisfaction with Enlightenment values, we must not turn our eyes away from that fact.

Two Meanings of "Universal Ethic"

In a conversation, my old friend Sidney Morgenbesser once remarked that many philosophers confuse the notion of a "universal ethic" with the notion of a "universal way of life." Thinking about the present topics has caused me to wonder whether that confusion may not be intrinsic to the Enlightenment itself, or perhaps, even to Western philosophy itself. Aristotle's *Politics* poses the question as "What is the Best Constitution for a *polis*—for *any* group of civilized human beings?" And it is undeniable that many Enlightenment thinkers framed the question in the same way. As Isaiah Berlin recently put it, "Voltaire's conception of enlightenment as being identical in essentials wherever it is attained seems to lead to the inescapable conclusion that, in his view, Byron would have been happy at table with Confucius, and Sophocles would have felt completely at ease in *quatrocento* Florence, and Seneca in the *salon* of Madame du Deffand or at the court of Frederick the Great."[4]

This tendency, the tendency to think that the right ethical principles must be concretized in the form of an "ideal society" or an "ideal way of life"—I know that these are not the same, but a blueprint for one tends to become a blueprint for the other—has been reinforced by the successes of science, successes that went far beyond even what the most optimistic Enlightenment thinkers expected. In the wake of those successes, it was inevitable that some thinkers, if not by any means the majority, would begin to suggest that human welfare, too, was a problem which could benefit from a technical solution. A special case of this is the development of the nineteenth-century socialist movement in a particular direction, a direction heavily influenced by Karl Marx's notion that he had taken socialism from its "utopian" phase to its "scientific" phase.

In the light of these facts, is it to be wondered at if many people began to feel that much of what they valued in their traditions—and above all their religious beliefs and their sense of their own history—was in peril? To be sure, such feelings are especially likely to arise if one is superstitious or chauvinist or racist or all three at once, but is it fair to *equate* such a worry with superstition and chauvinism and racism? This, I think, is the question that will not go away. As communitarian thinkers like Michael Sandal and Charles Taylor have recently been pointing out, to dismiss such feelings as "reactionary" is to hand a potent issue —in the long run, perhaps the most potent of all issues—over to reactionaries.

The Wealth of Cultural Diversity

But even posing the issue of cultural diversity, and of the sense that cultural diversity is in tension with the Enlightenment, in terms of "religions" (perhaps the concept of "religions" is itself a uniquely Western concept)[5] and "history" (a notion that has come to have a special sense in the West in the last two or three centuries) is itself unduly parochial. Perhaps we in the West have far too narrow a sense of the wealth of human cultural diversity, and perhaps this makes it easier for some of us to contemplate the idea of a world with one language, one literature, one music, one art, one politics—in a word, one culture.

Let me make it clear that I am not saying that most, or even many, Enlightenment thinkers would endorse such an idea. But some have done so and some still do. Rudolf Carnap—a philosopher whose stature both as a thinker and as a human being were undeniable—felt strongly that for all x, planned x is better than unplanned x. I know this from conversation with him, and it is also evident in his Intellectual Autobiography.[6] Thus the idea of a socialist world in which everyone spoke Esperanto (except scientists, who, for their technical work, would employ notations from symbolic logic) was one which would have delighted him. And I recently had a conversation with a student who remarked quite casually that it would not really be so bad if there were only one language and one literature: "We would get used to it, and it might help to prevent war."

Part of what lies behind such attitudes is a simple failure to appreciate the real wealth of cultural diversity in the world, a failure to appreciate *what* we are in danger of losing as the result of cultural *Gleichschaltung*. My own awareness was recently heightened by reading Ben Ami Scharfstein's description[7] of a number of cultures whose way of life is *really* "different" from any I have personally experienced, and in an unexpected way—the artistic creativity and spontaneity that is normal in those cultures. Permit me to quote a short passage from Scharfstein's book:

> In Chattisgarh, a great, mostly arid plain of northeastern India, every subject goes into poetry, much of which, for that reason, is prosaic; but much is sensitive and eloquent. Many of the songs are known to everyone, and gifted individuals continue to augment their number. "Life in Chattisgarh is hard, dusty and unrewarded; it might well be hopeless were it not for the happiness that song brings to the meanest hovel."[8]

Scharfstein goes on to describe a number of other peoples in whose ways of life the arts of poetry and song play a role which is almost incomprehensible to my contemporaries, for whom "poetry and song" almost always are products produced by "artists" and enjoyed by consumers few of whom are "artists." I quote Scharfstein again: "In the Andaman Islands, everyone composes his own songs, even the small children. To end this disorderly paragraph, I repeat the sneer of an Eskimo woman at a rival, 'She can't dance, she can't even sing,' the latter part of the sneer meaning, 'She can't even compose songs.' "

The possibility of making oneself conscious of other modes of human fulfillment and the terrible difficulty of doing this are themes to which I shall return later in this essay.

Individualism and Egotism

In addition to the confusion between the idea of a universal ethic and the idea of a universal way of life, there is another confusion of ideas which is associated with the Enlightenment, and that is the confusion between individualism and egotism. That the confusion (or identification) exists has long been noticed, as witness the following remark by Horace Greeley in 1853: "This is preeminently an age of Individualism (it would hardly be polite to call it Egotism) wherein the Sovereignty of the Individual—that is the right of every man to do pretty nearly as he pleases—is already generally popular and is visibly gaining ground daily."[9]

Again, let me make it clear that I am *not* joining the host of critics of "bourgeois individualism." "Individualism" is not the name of one single thing, and some of the ideas that go under the name of individualism are to be cherished. For example, individualism can mean, simply, the idea that individuality is precious—even sacred. In the Jewish tradition, one often quotes the parable about Rabbi Zusiah, who, on his death bed, told his grieving disciples that he was terrified of the judgement of his Maker. "But you are a holy man," the disciples protested. "You have been as faithful as Abraham; you have been as holy as Moses; you have been as learned as Hillel." "The Lord is not going to ask me, 'Have you been Abraham?' 'Have you been Moses?' or 'Have you been Hillel?' " was the sage's reply. "The Lord is going to ask me 'Have you been Zusiah?' "

Again, individualism can mean the doctrine of individual rights; and this is a precious doctrine. Those who attack this doctrine as bourgeois ought to reflect more on what happens when individual rights are suppressed in the name of a supposed solution to all human problems (a useful case, in that it reveals how two tendencies of the Enlightenment can conflict: the emphasis on individual rights, and the emphasis on finding a solution to the problems of life by the use of Reason). But there is no doubt that the doctrine of individual rights easily becomes popularized as "the right of every man to do pretty nearly as he pleases."

There have been philosophers for whom the confusions and excesses of the Enlightenment have constituted the Enlightenment itself. I am thinking especially of Heidegger. For Heidegger, the desire for the Esperanto-speaking planned society and the world of capitalist greed and competitiveness are both manifestations of ends-means rationality, unbridled subjectivity, and the will to power; and the Enlightenment is simply the pretty face of an age whose real inner compulsion is to ends-means rationality, unbridled subjectivity, and the will to power. I am the last to say that there is nothing to Heidegger's critique; yet, even if Heidegger himself had never joined the Nazi movement, that critique would remain hopelessly one-sided. As a one-sided critique it has real power, however (as does Marx's *Capital,* from a different direction); what Heidegger focuses on are just the issues that I have located as the points of greatest dissatisfaction with Enlightenment values.

To locate dissatisfactions is very different from offering solutions, however, and I have promised *not* to solve these problems! Indeed, I do not think that one can solve them in the study. Durkheim remarked that the problem of alienation can only be solved in life, not in the study, and that the thing to do to hasten a solution is to eliminate concrete injustices and exclusions,[10] and one can only applaud his wisdom. But part of eliminating injustices is to eliminate the injustices we do to the interests and sentiments of others by too hastily labeling those interests and sentiments "reactionary." We have to become more aware of the enormous value of cultural diversity, we have to recognize the need for and the value of cultural roots, and we have to know and *say* that if everyone *should* have the *legal* right to "do pretty nearly as he pleases," it does not follow that one *deserves* that right as a matter of course. Some people are *morally* undeserving of rights that it would be wrong to take away from them. Some of one's rights should be *earned,* morally speaking.

The Return of Relativism

There is another side to the coin, however. If the idea of a universal ethic leads (however invalid the logic!) to the idea of a universal way of life, then there are many thinkers who would advocate *modus tollendo tollens:* since a universal way of life is a bad idea, so is a universal ethic. (Bernard Williams' *Ethics and the Limits of Philosophy* is a recent example of this way of thinking, and, philosophically speaking, one of the most powerful. Of course, Williams also believes on metaphysical grounds that a universal ethic with objective validity is an impossibility.)[11]

The relativist position faces a problem which is simultaneously obvious and deep. Relativism is not itself an ethics but a metaethics, one which, as Bernard Williams is aware, is corrosive of all ethical positions and views. That *reflection destroys ethical knowledge* is something Williams tells us again and again; this could be the motto of his whole book. To the extent that the relativist wants to be more than just a *meta*-ethicist, he is in a difficult position. As I said, Williams is aware of this problem, and one way in which he tries to meet it is the following. He accepts the now familiar dichotomy between "thick" and "thin" ethical concepts. "Thick" ethical concepts (the terminology comes, I believe, from anthropology) have a heavy descriptive content. The importance of such concepts, though not the terminology, was already familiar to Ortega y Gassett: "Language evinces—for deep reasons which we cannot go into in this essay—an economizing tendency to express phenomena of value by means of a halo of complementary signification that surrounds the primary, realistic signification of words. . . . Similarly [Ortega has just discussed the word 'noble' as an example of this] the words 'generous', 'elegant', 'skillful', 'strong', 'select'—as well as 'sordid', 'inelegant', 'gauche', 'weak', 'vulgar'—mean simultaneously realities and values. What is more, if we explored the dictionary in order to gather all the words with a completely evaluative sense, we would undoubtedly be astonished by the fabulous decantation of characters and tinges of value in ordinary language."[12] By "thin" ethical concepts, Williams means such abstract ethical concepts as "right," "wrong," "good," "bad," "virtue," "vice," "duty," and "sin."

Following the lead of John McDowell,[13] Williams rejects the view that "thick" ethical concepts can be explicitly factored into a "descriptive component" and an "evaluative component"; that is, he rejects the view that, for each thick ethical concept (see, for example, Ortega's little list that I just quoted) one can construct a value-free concept which has exactly the same extension. McDowell's argument—which Williams considers to be probably correct—is that a speaker cannot tell how these concepts will be applied to hard cases, or just to novel cases, by skilled speakers unless he is able to identify imaginatively with the values of the group whose concepts they are.[14]

But Williams goes still farther, and denies that there are any *entailments* connecting "thick" and "thin" ethical concepts. He considers a hypertraditional society which he imagines as lacking our thin ethical concepts altogether, and he argues that when someone in that society says, as it might be, that some action is "sordid" his statement does not *entail* that the action is *wrong*: after all, "wrong" is *our* notion, and it is a kind of logical parochialism (Williams claims) to hold that all valuations in all languages implicitly involve *our* thin ethical concepts. I think Williams' conclusion is right but the argument is terrible! There *are* circumstances in which it would not be self-contradictory to say "That was a sordid thing to do, but it had to be done" (where the "had to be done" clearly has the force of "was morally required"); that is why I agree that (for example) "sordid" does not *entail* "morally wrong." But the *fact that a concept does not belong to some language does not show that statements in our language containing that concept cannot be entailed by statements in the other language*; "I have one pear in each hand" entails "I have an even prime number of pears in my hands," whether or not the concepts "even" and "prime" belong to the language in which the first statement was made.

Williams needs this complicated philosophical machinery, because he wants to argue that, in a hypertraditional society, ethical truths (expressed in the thick ethical vocabulary of that society) can be *true* (in accordance with the rules of the local language game) without having any *universal* implications whatsoever. In effect, Williams' machinery is designed to allow precisely what some critics of the Enlightenment seem to want; a number of local ethical outlooks, each of which can be regarded as "true" by its adherents, but whose truth does not have any universalistic implications whatsoever.

An example may make it clearer how this works. Suppose we have lost an ethical concept ("chastity," I fear, is a good example). Then even if that concept is alive and well in society S, if society S's way of life is too "distant" from ours, if we could not adopt that way of life without being brainwashed or going mad, and if, in the same sense, our way of life is too "distant" from society S's, then, if all these conditions are met, according to Williams, the knowledge of people in S that some forms of behavior are "unchaste" is simply *irrelevant* to us. (In Williams' jargon, any confrontation between our outlook and the outlook of S is *notional* and not *real*.) Indeed, if we have really lost the concept, we will be "disbarred" from even expressing what people in S can express by saying that those forms of behavior are "unchaste." (Here Williams is pretty obviously using the machinery of "incommensurability" introduced into the philosophy of science by Kuhn.) Nor does the truth of the statement that those forms of behavior are unchaste (made by a member of society S) entail that those forms of behavior are "morally reprehensible" (something we *can* express), for such an entailment would be just the sort of "thick to thin" entailment that Williams is at pains to deny.

One wonders, however, to just *what* societies Williams' doctrine, assuming or imagining it to be correct, would ever apply? Examples are hard to come by in Williams' writing: the three that I remember are a "bronze age chieftain," a "medieval samurai," and the Aztecs!

It seems appropriate here, to comment on the inclusion of the "medieval samurai." As we know, the medieval samurai was extremely likely to be a student of Zen Buddhism and possibly also of Confucianism. As such, he may not have been inclined to use our Western "thin" ethical concepts, but he was certainly acquainted with an abstract vocabulary suitable for making universalistic claims. When a Zen Buddhist says that one way of life leads to *satori* and another way of life leads to pain, he is making a claim of universal significance: that is, so to speak, the *point* of Buddhism. And when Confucius tells us how we should treat our family members, our superiors, and our subordinates, it is, I reck-lessly say, fair to use the words "should" and "ought" in explaining his thought in English even if the uses of these words in English do not exactly line up with their uses in Chinese (the language in which Confu-cianism was studied in Japan). Certainly, by the time of the "medieval samurai," rich systems of *thin* ethical concepts had become widely known in Japan.

Indeed, the whole idea of a culture which has only "thick" ethical concepts and no "thin" ones is a philosopher's myth. Homer tells us a lot about "bronze age chieftains" and *they* certainly had "thin" ethical concepts, starting with χϱή meaning "it is right and proper"; one must, one ought to." Again, I am not claiming that χϱή is *synonymous* with any of these dictionary entries; but any philosophical doctrine which requires for its defense the claim that this common Greek word is totally *uninterpretable* in English is as bankrupt as the bugaboo of total "incom-mensurability" itself, while the claim that the use of what was restricted to class-bound obligations (so that an aristocrat could not even express —or think—the thought that *anyone,* including commoners, "ought to" defend his home or feed his children) is pure fabulation. As for Nahuatl (the Aztec language), even though I wrote my Senior Paper for Zelig Harris on the Nahuatl plural many years ago, I no longer know (if I ever did) what the Nahuatl ethical vocabulary was like, but I would be astounded if it, too, did not have its "thin" as well as its "thick" con-cepts.

The problem, in short, is that traditional societies—the traditional societies that actually have existed, not Williams' fictitious "hypertradi-tional society"—don't just have "thick" ethical concepts; they also have *philosophical* conceptions, conceptions about how *everyone* should live, and attach great importance to those conceptions. What we in the West refer to as the "religions" of traditional peoples, for example, are con-cerned with problems that are meant to *transcend* the culture-bound, as well as with problems that arise in particular "traditional" cultures. The impossibility of discussing ethical problems without assuming the value framework of a particular culture, if it is an impossibility, suggests the impossibility of any significant notion of a "universal" or "eternal" existential problem. Yet every sane person does believe deep down that there are universal human problems.

That Williams himself does not think that his doctrine of a "relativity of distance" helps us very much *today* is indicated by his remark (p. 163): that "Relativism over merely spatial distance is of no interest or application in the modern world. Today all confrontations between cultures must be real confrontations. . . ."

Isaiah Berlin on Relativism

If Williams' version of relativism is ultimately unsatisfying, it is in part because the *constraints* he places on an adequate ethical outlook seem so very weak. True, he often says that such an outlook must be such that we could "live reflectively and stably in it"; but he often expresses a certain pessimism as to whether *any* ethical outlook can really survive very much reflection. Apart from that, the only standard of human flourishing that he mentions is "the ecological standard of the bright eye and the bushy tail"—a revealing bit of reductionism, that!

A very different conception arises when one begins to see that there are alternative good ways of life, alternative fulfilling conceptions of the good, in (if you please) a "thicker" sense of "fulfilling." I should like to quote Berlin again:

> Communities may resemble each other in many respects, but the Greeks differ from Lutheran Germans, the Chinese differ from both; what they strive after, and what they fear or worship is scarcely ever similar.
>
> This view has been called cultural or moral relativism. . . . It is not relativism. Members of one culture can, by the force of imaginative insight, understand (what Vico called *entrare*) the values, the ideals, the forms of life of another culture of society, even those remote in time or space. They may find those values unacceptable, but if they open their minds sufficiently they can grasp how one might be a full human being, with whom one could communicate, and at the same time live in the light of values different from one's own, but which nevertheless one can see to be values, ends of life, by the realization of which men could be fulfilled.[15]

To say with Berlin that one can *entrare* the "values, the ideals, the forms of life" of another society is not to say that one must regard all "values, ideals, forms of life" as equally good. Berlin spoke of "another culture or society," but very often what is hard to "enter" is our own culture, or our own culture as it conflicts with itself inside each of us. These conflicts are hard to bear; but the refusal to understand imaginatively one or another part of one's own culture is often a refusal to understand oneself. Wittgenstein once said that "To imagine a language is to imagine a form of life." Citing this passage, Stanley Cavell has written,

> In philosophizing, I have to bring my own language and life into imagination. What I require is a convening of my culture's criteria, in order to confront them with my words and life as I pursue them and may imagine them; and at the same time to confront my words and life as I pursue them with the life my culture's words may imagine for me; to confront the culture with itself along the lines in which it meets in me.[16]

This form of philosophy, Cavell adds, may be called "education for grown ups."

Pragmatism and Relativism

Is there a danger of relativism in the wider and deeper knowledge of traditions (including the traditions of one's ancestors) with which one does not fully identify? To some, Berlin's denial that his position amounts to "cultural and moral relativism" might seem a little facile. After all, he condemns moral absolutism in sharp terms. "I conclude that the very notion of a final solution is not only impracticable but, if I am right, and some values cannot but clash, incoherent also. The possibility of a final solution—even if we forget the terrible sense that these words acquired in Hitler's day—turns out to be an illusion, and a very dangerous one. For, if one really believes that such a solution is possible, then surely no cost would be too high to obtain it; to make mankind just and happy and creative and harmonious forever—what would be too high a price to pay for that? To make such an omelette, there is surely no limit to the number of eggs that should be broken—that was the faith of Lenin, of Trotsky, of Mao, for all I know, of Pol Pot."[17] Or, if Berlin is not a relativist, is he not just saying that there are a number of optimal moral and political and religious philosophies around, and that one must just make one's own subjective choice among the optimal ones?

Berlin is certainly defending pluralism, but pluralism should not be confused with naive cultural relativism. Since he does not discuss this issue in detail, I would rather look at another thinker who had a lifelong preoccupation with these questions—William James. James, just as much as Isaiah Berlin, defended pluralism and condemned dogmatism and absolutism. At the same time, James famously (or notoriously, depending on your point of view) defended the right to believe.

> Our passional nature not only lawfully may, but must, decide an option between propositions, whenever it is a genuine option that cannot by its nature be decided on intellectual grounds, for to say under such circumstances, "Do not decide, but leave the question open," is itself a passional decision—just like deciding yes or not—and is attended with the same risk of losing the truth.[18]

How does James reconcile the right to believe with "passion" with his condemnation of dogmatism and authoritarianism?

For pragmatists the answer lies in the following reflection. The notion that history has thrown up a number of "optimal" ways of life—optimal but irreconcilable—is much too simple. Every way of life, every system of values, traditions, and rituals that humans have so far invented has defects as well as virtues. Not only are there imperfections that can be exposed from within the way of life, imperfections that a reflective person of good will can point out and try to change from within, but there are defects that we come to see from the outside, as the result of increased knowledge and/or a widened sense of justice (from what

James called "listening to the cries of the wounded").[19] For example, all historical ways of life suffer from male chauvinism, from prejudice against homosexuals, and from other kinds of insensitivity or cruelty. Simply to declare any way of life perfect is to violate a maxim which should govern the search for truth in *every* area of life: do not block the path of inquiry! That truth cannot be secured once and for all by revelation applies to ethical and religious truth just as much as to scientific truth. Our problem is not that we must choose between an already fixed and defined number of optimal ways of life; our problem is that we don't know of even one *optimal* way of life.

In this predicament, we have no choice but to try to reform and improve the ways of life we have, as well as to try new ones if we believe them to be better; but these trials must not be at the expense of the right of others to make their trials. There is nothing wrong with the choice of the person who chooses to stay within a traditional way and to try to make it as good and as just and as fulfilling as possible—as long as he or she does not try to force that way on everyone else. This is, of course, a democratic idea; for pragmatists, however, it follows not just from the idea of democracy, but, more fundamentally, from the recognition that a truth worthy of the name has to be world-guided and subject to public discussion.[20] This is what William James meant when he wrote that "The practical consequence of such a philosophy is the well-known democratic respect for the sacredness of individuality. . . . [It] is, at any rate, the outward tolerance of whatever is not itself intolerant. . . . Religiously and philosophically, our ancient national doctrine of live and let live may prove to have a far deeper meaning than our people now seem to imagine."[21]

When Berlin describes what "all these views" (Platonism, traditional theology, the Enlightenment, progressive thought in the nineteenth century) had in common he writes:

> [W]hat all these views had in common was a Platonic ideal: in the first place that, as in the sciences, all genuine questions must have one true answer and one only, all the rest being necessarily errors. In the second place, that there must be a dependable path toward the discovery of these truths. In the third place, that the true answers, when found, must necessarily be compatible with one another and form a single whole, for one truth cannot be incompatible with another—that we know *a priori*. This kind of omniscience was the solution of the cosmic jigsaw puzzle. In the case of morals, we could then conceive what the perfect life must be, founded as it would be on a correct understanding of the rules that governed the universe.

Pragmatism agrees with Berlin in rejecting the first and third items in this list: the idea of one true answer (which does not really apply to science either,[22] except in an oversimple picture of what science is like), and the resulting idea of a single set of rules which describe both the universe and what would be a "perfect life." Pragmatism does not believe that there can be an "ethical theory dogmatically made up in advance," James tells us;[23] and it requires that we tolerate pluralism. But pragmatism's attitude towards Berlin's second point—the idea of "a dependable path toward the discovery of these truths"—is nuanced. There is no *algorithm* or mechanical procedure, no set of fixed ahistorical "canons of scientific method" which will lead us to the truth in every area, or in any, but there is the imperfect but necessary "path" of struggling for and testing one's ideals in practice, while conceding to others the right to do the same.

The ethic to which this conception of truth leads is, it seems to me, the ethic that is needed to combine the great Enlightenment value of tolerance with the respect for the particularity of tradition, and with the recognition of the need for thick conceptions of the significance of life whose absence in Enlightenment thought left people feeling a huge void. To some this ethic will seem dull—a mere restatement of "liberalism." To this the reply must be that the desire for views which are "exciting," "original," "radical," views which "deconstruct" everything which we thought before, is not in general the same as the desire for truth. The clash of traditions and conceptions of the good will certainly continue. If that clash is not accompanied and tempered by the effort to understand values and conceptions of the good which are not our own and the willingness to compromise, our worst fears will certainly come true. Writing of the very failing I have been discussing, the failure (James calls it a "blindness") to understand the "values and meanings" of others, James writes that "No one has insight into all the ideals. No one should presume to judge them off-hand. The pretension to dogmatize about them in each other is the root of most human injustices and cruelties, and the trait in human character most likely to make the angels weep."[24]

Notes

1. Cf. Rawls' "Justice as Fairness: Political not Metaphysical," *Philosophy and Public Affairs* 14, no. 3 (Summer 1985).

2. I am referring to a lecture Steiner gave a few years ago at the Van Leer Foundation in Jerusalem.

3. In *The Death of Tragedy* (New York: Knopf, 1963).

4. "On the Pursuit of the Ideal," *New York Review of Books* 35, no. 4 (March 17, 1988): 14.

5. This was suggested by Wilfred Cantwell Smith, in his *The Meaning and End of Religion: A New Approach to the Religious Traditions of Mankind* (New York: Macmillan, 1963); see esp. chap. 2, "Religion and the West."

6. Cf. *The Philosophy of Rudolf Carnap,* ed. by P. A. Schilpp (LaSalle, Illinois: Open Court, 1963).

7. Cf. chap. 3 of Scharfstein's *Of Birds, Beasts, and Other Artists* (New York: New York University Press, 1989).

8. In the last sentence, Scharfstein is quoting from V. Elwin, *Folk Songs of Chattisgarh,* (Bombay, 1946), p. 1.

9. Greeley was thinking about divorce, but the remark has, of course, much wider pertinence (quoted in N. M. Blake, *The Road to Reno: A History of Divorce in the United States* (Macmillan, 1962; reprint, Greenwood, 1977)).

10. At the end of *Of the Division of Labor,* trans. by George Simpson (New York: Free Press, 1964, c. 1933).

11. For a detailed critique of Williams' arguments, see my "Objectivity and the Science/Ethics Distinction," in my *The Place of Facts in a World of Values* (Cambridge, Massachusetts: Harvard University Press, forthcoming).

12. "Introducciòn a la estimativa," *Obras Completas* 6 (1923), 317, 320–321.

13. Cf. McDowell's "Are Moral Requirements Hypothetical Imperatives?" *Proceedings of the Aristotelian Society,* suppl. vol. 42 (1978), and "Virtue and Reason," *Monist* 62 (1979).

14. For a somewhat different argument to the same effect, see my *Reason, Truth and History* (Cambridge: Cambridge University Press, 1981).

15. "On the Pursuit of the Ideal" (cited in n. 4), p. 14.

16. *The Claim of Reason* (Oxford, 1979), p. 125.

17. "On the Pursuit of the Ideal," p. 16.

18. "The Will to Believe," in *The Will to Believe and Other Essays in Popular Philosophy* (New York: Dover, 1956, c. 1897).

19. Cf. "The Moral Philosopher and the Moral Life," in *The Will to Believe and Other Essays.*

20. This pragmatist idea of a connection between democratic ethics and scientific method has recently been revived and elaborated by two famous Frankfurt philosophers: Jürgen Habermas and Karl-Otto Apel. For a discussion of their work and its relation to pragmatism see my *The Many Faces of Realism,* (La Salle, Illinois: Open Court, 1987), pp. 53–56.

21. *Talks to Teachers on Psychology and Some of Life's Ideals* (Cambridge, Massachusetts: Harvard University Press, 1983, c. 1899), pp. 4–5.

22. On this, see my *Realism and Reason, Philosophical Papers Volume III* (Cambridge: Cambridge University Press, 1983).

23. This is the first sentence of "The Moral Philosopher and the Moral Life."

24. "What Makes a Life Significant?" in *Talks to Teachers on Psychology,* p. 150.

JOEL J. KUPPERMAN

TRADITION AND MORAL PROGRESS

This essay will examine only a few aspects of a very large subject. In the first section I will explain what a moral tradition is, and what functions it fulfills. In the second I will explain what I mean by moral progress, and will argue a view that in some quarters is highly unfashionable, namely, that there is, or at least recently has been, moral progress. Clearly the most interesting philosophical questions concern the relations, if any, between moral tradition and moral progress. This is a subject that I have taken up elsewhere, focusing both on the ways and also on how criticism within a tradition makes progress possible.[1] In the third section I will look at a different set of issues, focusing on how exposure to alternative traditions can be conducive to moral progress. This can be taken not only as ethical analysis but also as a defense of pluralism and of the usefulness of comparative philosophy.

I

The simplest view of what a moral tradition is consists of equating it with a set of general moral recommendations or prohibitions. Thus the moral tradition of the Old Testament might be held to consist of the Ten Commandments plus perhaps a supplementary list of commands having to do with such matters as diet and ritual. One difficulty with this as a general account of moral tradition is that it works less well for an ethics, such as an Aristotelian or Confucian ethics, that is not as strongly rule-centered as is the Old Testament. It would be exceedingly peculiar to attempt to grasp the recommendations made by Confucius and Aristotle in terms of a set of "Thou shalt" 's and "Thou shalt not" 's. Some elements of the teaching, such as Aristotle on adultery and Confucius on filial impiety, might lend themselves to this treatment without too great a distortion; but other elements would not.

A deeper difficulty with equating a moral tradition with a set of general recommendations is that the practice of moral life, within any tradition, has more stages than such a view suggests. Some might be attracted to a two-stage view as follows. Stage one is that Situation S occurs and Bloggs knows about it. Stage two is that Bloggs applies his moral tradition to S and determines that what he is about to do is either morally required, morally prohibited, or (the most usual alternative) morally neutral. The real world is more complicated than this in at least three respects. One is that awareness has degrees. We can be dimly aware of all sorts of things which we neither reflect on nor treat as problematical. As an extreme example, take a driver's awareness of the road during a typical drive in the country. Some elements in our experience, in contrast, become salient. They really register on us; we really notice them. We may, as a result, treat them as problematic and reflect on them, although people who dislike reflection may not.

Second, even when a situation does register on us, it is not, as it were, transparent. There is not a full, equal light on all details of the situation, as each comes forward to announce itself. Even within a situation that really registers on us, some details will be much more salient than others. Furthermore, just what the details are may be a matter either of conscious interpretation or of what might be termed unconscious interpretation—the way the immediate presentation of a situation is structured by the bent of mind or expectations of the perceiver.

Third, it is of course not true that we judge all situations, or even all situations that really register on us, in relation to our morality. Not even Immanuel Kant lived like that. Not even J. J. C. Smart, who is often taken (and has taken himself) to be an act utilitarian, committed to a standard that applies to every human action, has lived like that. Smart uses the example of himself enthusiastically playing field hockey; his decisions on the field, he says, do not involve direct reference to the greatest good of the greatest number.[2] As he points out, it is better that they do not. What is involved here is not merely the importance of leaving room for spontaneity. This is a factor; much of life would lose its flavor if every step were accompanied by reflective demand for justification. But another factor is that it is simply impossible to treat everything one does as requiring a separate judgment that it is morally acceptable. Anyone who attempted to live in such a way would come close to paralysis. Highly moral and moralistic people take a large number of, but not all, elements of life as calling out for moral justification, or at least moral clearance. Most of us examine morally a rather smaller number of elements. No one subjects every particular action in her or his life to moral examination.

To sum this up: a moral tradition, whether or not it centers on rules of conduct, also includes the following. It provides training in moral significance, so that certain situations and actions register on anyone steeped in the tradition and can readily be seen as calling for reflection or moral judgment. It also will provide an interpretative scheme so that certain features of these situations and actions will seem salient, and will be perceived within the categories of the tradition.

One other complication in what moral traditions provide also should be mentioned. A tradition typically not only enables adherents to perceive when judgments of what ought to be done are called for, and guides them in making these judgments, but also provides a set of distinctions—or differentiations in weight and feel—within judgments of what ought to be done. One such distinction is that within the Western tradition between moral and other kinds of evaluative judgments, including ordinary practical judgments, aesthetic judgments, and judgments related to etiquette. Henry Rosemont and others have pointed out that this distinction does not occur within classical Chinese philosophy.[3] Neither does it occur within classical Greek philosophy. Let me concede this point. I will want, nevertheless, to continue to speak of the "moral" traditions associated with Confucian and Aristotelian ethics. The argument in support of this is that, even if there was not a category of the "moral" within these philosophies, our category of the moral fits fairly well the judgments Aristotle makes about certain kinds of actions, such as adultery, that he says are categorically wrong, and Confucian judgments about children who neglect or harm their parents.

Part of the point here is that a tradition may not assign equal weight to all transgressions. Eating with your fingers while smacking your lips is simply not on a par with murder. In our scheme we tend to treat as moral the issues that surround transgressions that we regard as serious. If another tradition regards certain actions both as categorically wrong and as serious transgressions, and subjects them to especially forceful blame, that is going to sound to us like morality, whether or not the culture marks something like our distinction with a classification term that we can translate as "morality."

It has come to seem to me that the picture is still more complicated than this. Consider Western moral traditions. Not only have there been distinctions between venal and venial sins, and between deadly and non-deadly sins, but also there have been more subtle differences between kinds of immorality which are treated as serious in different ways. Consider the case of someone who cheats investors out of their money, and that of a parent who entirely neglects and refuses to help his or her children. Both are serious transgressions, which elicit highly negative judgments. But the *kind* of immorality, and also our sense of what is lacking, differ between the two cases. We readily say that the dishonest financier has failed in a socially important way to play the game by the rules, and is immoral. I think that our abhorrence of the totally neglectful parent is in some sense moral; it certainly is as serious as our condemnation of the financier. But "immoral" is not the word we reach for, and the inadequacies of the two people seem very different.

Consider also a Confucian pair of cases. It has been suggested that

Confucius did not have anything like our concepts of choice and responsibility; but the truth may be, instead, that in his concentration on the
requirements of sagacity he had few opportunities to deploy these concepts.[4] One occasion was the case of Jan Ch'iu, who chose not to live up
to the education Confucius had given him, and whom Confucius held
responsible. "He is no follower of mine," Confucius said. ". . . You
May beat the drum and set upon him."[5] My suggestion is that Confucius treats the case of Jan Ch'iu differently from the way he would that
of someone who has no education or sense and whose very bad conduct
is only to be expected. Both are to be condemned, but not in the same
spirit.

A moral tradition need not be either unified or static. Some writers,
such as Alasdair MacIntyre, have spoke of a number of competing
Western traditions.[6] My sense is that these competing traditions have
some resemblances and are not entirely discrete. Also most people who
are not philosophers are not, I suspect, so neatly divisible into schools,
which suggests that it may not be so easy to individuate traditions
within a culture. All the same, MacIntyre is right in pointing out disunity related to competing schools. There also is disunity related to
competing models of what ethics principally concerns. If one thinks of
ethics primarily as telling us about commands made either by God or by
ideal moral legislators, then the subject of ethics would seem to be our
duties. If the model is rather a contractarian one, then rightness will
seem to be modeled on fairness. A model which has not been highly
developed in recent Western philosophy but which nevertheless has
some influence on ordinary people assimilates virtue to being fully
human. Any one of us may reach on different occasions for different
models. The parent who entirely neglects his or her children may seem
lacking in humanity, whereas the person who cheats investors out of
their money may be taken as unfair to those who were cheated or to
have neglected his or her duty.

Duty does not loom as large in moral discussions as it appears to have
done a hundred years ago, or in Kant's time. This is an illustration of
how moral traditions can change. In this instance the change appears to
be, as it were, from the bottom up. That is, the decline of duty does not
seem to be the result primarily of philosophical argument, or of any
intellectual movement. The form, as well as the content, of moral tradition responds to changes in the structure of society.

It should be clear from the brief account thus far that moral traditions
are enormously complicated, more like forms of life than like bits of
problem-solving software. Moral traditions carry with them both forms
of attention and areas of inattentiveness; they also involve interpretative
approaches to reality, so that two competing moral traditions can be like
two groups of people who insist, respectively, on seeing the duck-rabbit
as a duck (one group) or as a rabbit (the other group). Moral traditions

differ not only in how they notice and see what they condemn, and in what they condemn, but also in how they condemn it. It would be tempting to speak of every moral tradition as having its own voice, but the discussion of current Western attitudes to different forms of transgression suggests that a moral tradition can have more than one voice.

II

The idea of moral progress has suffered from the general opprobrium that has affected nineteenth-century ideas of progress (apart from technological progress). It is hard anyway to think of moral progress in a century in which Hitler and Pol Pot have flourished. Let me say first what I do *not* mean by moral progress, before developing the case that there is such a thing.

I do not mean, first, an improvement in actual behavior. People fall short of their ideals and moralities, or of the moralities available to them, in all sorts of ways; and I would not want to suggest that these phenomena have been becoming less pronounced. At the other extreme I do not mean that the available peaks of human perfection have become higher. It would be foolish to suggest that humanity now can do better than Confucius and Socrates; indeed it probably would be foolish to suggest that it now can do as well.

Let me instead focus on the stock of ways to think about moral issues that are readily available to cultivated people. There is some analogy to be made with the set of scientific theories available to university students of the sciences. These will not, on the one hand, represent the heights of ongoing scientific creativity. They are rather the received knowledge distilled, at least in part, from past creativity. This set of scientific theories will not necessarily correspond, on the other hand, to everyone's thinking about the world, or even to the thinking of every scientist. One might think of contemporary Western creationists, some of whom turn out to have Ph.D.s in geology, who reject important areas of established scientific knowledge. We can speak of something in the sciences as established knowledge if it has reached the point at which, we might say, the quality and the widespread awareness of the evidence or basis for it are such that there no longer is room for reasonable people to disagree about it. Estimates of the age of the planet earth arguably have reached this point. This does not mean that something like a formal deductive proof is available, and it certainly does not mean that there will be in fact no disagreement.

The idea of scientific progress includes the claim that more things can come to be known in such a way that there is no room for reasonable people to disagree about them. This is compatible with the possibility of future theoretical shifts so that what is known today may be known in a different form a hundred years from now. I propose that we view moral progress analogously. Here are three examples of moral knowledge which either has become established in the last one hundred and fifty years in the manner described, or which is in the process of becoming established: (1) Slavery is wrong. (2) Discrimination on the basis of race or religion is wrong. (3) Discrimination on the basis of gender is wrong.

These examples are compatible, in the way I have suggested, with the continued existence of virtual slavery in some parts of the world, with persistent warfare between different tribal groups, and with gross instances of racism and sexism. Nor would the wrongness of discrimination on the basis of religion be likely to win plebiscites in Northern Ireland or in various countries in the Middle East. The moral progress in these cases consists in the fact that not only do cultivated people, in various parts of the world, think that behavior of the indicated sorts is wrong, but that the justifications are so familiar that they can take it for granted. It has become received knowledge, not a polemical position. In the seventeenth century Sir Thomas Browne, in *Religio Medici,* argued against religious discrimination. There is a large step from this creative awareness to a situation in which educated people can be generally presumed to understand that religious discrimination is intolerable.

That there has been moral progress in the sense just characterized does not mean that there must continue to be moral progress, or that any shift in moral opinion must count as progress. Regress is always possible, probably more easily in morality than in scientific knowledge. It would be out of place here to rehearse the kinds of evidence and argument that can elevate something, such as the claim that slavery is wrong, from the status of moral opinion to that of moral knowledge. This is a large topic, which I have pursued in two books.[7] The process by which something becomes not only knowledge but established knowledge, presumed to be shared generally by appropriately educated people, calls for an analysis which is more sociological than philosophical. Let me merely suggest some parts of this analysis.

One facet of the process is a social closing of minds to possibilities. I will dwell on this, because it might be very counterintuitive. We all associate acquisition of knowledge with the opening of minds, and closed minds with ignorance. But it is arguable that personal perfectibility very often involves the closing off of possibilities, in that certain things (such as brutal or unjust actions) become unthinkable. At the extreme, a Confucian sage, say, would have no choices to make, in that a wide variety of unworthy actions would have ceased to be live options. Similarly, when something needs to be explained, a scientifically trained person usually can eliminate many of the alternatives that someone who is untrained might consider. She or he might refuse to consider magic as a possible explanation, and might also say something such as "Things do not simply vanish into thin air." Both moral and scientific educations involve narrowing of possibilities, although arguably someone who is a creative thinker in the sciences or in respect to moral matters might on occasions reverse the process, and might consider possibilities that the ordinary educated person would rule out of hand.

What accomplishes the social closing of minds to unacceptable possibilities? Consider a very recent bit of moral progress, the developed sense among cultivated people in many countries that discrimination on the basis of race or religion is totally unacceptable. For a long time some people have known this, but in a country such as America the process by which it became established knowledge was so quick that it is possible to get a clear view of how it took place. Part of the process was training in sensitivity. In a variety of media, including books, films, and television programs, people were encouraged to see life through the eyes of people of other races. This was an expansion of awareness, but it was accompanied by what might be described as brainwashing in a very good cause. Very young children in schools, and the population generally via the media, were indoctrinated with the idea that racism was outside the range of what was tolerable. The word "brainwashing" here should not be taken as derogatory. It refers to a process which, within limits and with proper objects, is highly necessary. One would not want to live in a society in which the great majority of people were not brainwashed at an early age to regard murder, torture, and random brutality as unthinkable.

Americans are so used to thinking of indoctrination programs as centrally directed, perhaps by a totalitarian government, that they may have difficulty in recognizing highly successful and pervasive programs that are not centrally directed. The anti-racism campaign of the last twenty five years is one example. An earlier example concerns law and order, the importance of deferring to law even when it does not seem to work very well, so that one does not "take the law into one's own hands." This is the central plot device of many a Western movie. I will return to this in the final section of this essay. Another, less attractive example is the systematic inculcation of habits and attitudes of deference in the "lower orders" of societies that have pronounced systems of social class. It will be taken as axiomatic that someone of a higher social rank is owed more in various kinds of cases, and respect for one's "betters" will be inculcated at a very early age.

A few remarks about racial and religious distinctions are in order. Even if there are stable and long-term differences between groups—itself a highly debatable proposition—discrimination is wrong, in part because it is wrong to prejudge an individual on the basis of membership in a group. Furthermore, to the extent that group identification remains important to many people, and since good morale may require conspicuous successes within a group, there is a strong case for affirmative action.[8] Also, there is no reason to suppose that differences, if any, between racial or religious groups will persist unchanged through time.

Increased opportunities or successes can bring about a change. It is arguable also that, often, when the cultural mainstream broadens, so that a group which has been outside is brought inside, there is an explosion of energy. This might help to account for the fact that most of the greatest English literature of the last hundred years has been written by Irish and Americans rather than by British authors, for the remarkable accomplishments of Jewish intellectuals during the same period, and for the increasing accomplishments now of women artists and scholars. One might mention also the contributions of black writers to American literature during the last fifty years, including *The Invisible Man,* in my opinion the best American novel of the period. The point is that accomplishments of various groups have responded, and will respond, to dynamics of social change.

The moral progress under discussion is *not* the result primarily of considerations such as these. Rather it reflects considerable friendly persuasion within a culture that certain thoughts are unthinkable, and perhaps also that related topics are to be avoided. Many kinds of comparison between racial or religious groups fall under this heading. There is some analogy with the extreme reluctance among many people, including many philosophers, to take up questions such as whether it imaginably ever could be justified to kill or torture an innocent person. Such issues have dogged discussions of utilitarianism, in that it looks very much as if many forms of utilitarianism yield answers of "Yes," so that utilitarians are in the position of advocating (in hypothetical cases) the unthinkable. Exceptionally sophisticated utilitarians, such as R. M. Hare, have devoted some effort to analyzing why what is in question is, and should be, unthinkable.[9] It is indeed very useful that we all regard murder and torture as unthinkable; even if it is true that there are imaginable cases in which they might have some justification, these cases never in fact come up. If we were to start to look for them (or if we relaxed our rigid opposition to the thought of them) the results might be disastrous. The best way to avoid slippery slopes is never to move, or even to look, in that direction.

III

We readily can imagine cases in which what is regarded within a culture as obvious is morally wrong, and what is regarded as unthinkable would be an advance. The classic recent discussion of this is Jonathan Bennett's.[10] Bennett suggests the operation of human sympathy as a corrective to moral prejudice, and this is a suggestion that Confucians would find congenial. My own view is that sympathy works well in cases of impairment of happiness, and less reliably well in those in which what is at stake is primarily dignity or fulfillment of potential; ethical theories that include a Kantian component can be most helpful in the latter. The point remains that moral traditions inevitably involve selective vision and sensitivity; and, despite the great advantages of this as compared to utter barbarism or unaligned mindlessness, we should worry about the possibility that we do not see or are insensitive to, something that is important.

A deeper one-sidedness is involved if our categories of ethical judgment lead us to reflect in more or less satisfactory ways about some kinds of problems while largely or entirely ignoring others. Let me illustrate this point by examining two sides to moral judgment, either of which could be emphasized within some moral traditions to the virtual exclusion of others. In pursuing this I do not mean to suggest that morality has only two sides. Indeed it might be useful to keep in mind the title of a book by Dorothy Emmet, the *Prism of Morality,* throughout the discussion. Nor do I mean to suggest that the distinction I make, which neatly separates two sides, is the only one with which we might possibly approach the subject.

One side is associated with an impersonal conception of justice or of considerations that resemble justice. It yields judgments of rights, protections, and entitlements, which one should recognize others to have regardless of one's relations to them or of what one thinks of them. The other is associated with the quality of one's particular involvement with other people or, perhaps, animals. It yields judgments that are not impersonal, in the sense that they may specify responsibilities or desiderata for one person that would not apply to others. To give an animal-oriented example of the two sides: Smith and Jones both have a responsibility, as a matter of something like justice, not to mistreat Smith's cat, but Smith has responsibilities to the cat that go beyond that and Jones does not.

Now in fact the word "justice" has an ordinary meaning that is much too narrow to do the job that I would like to have done here, or that many philosophers want it to do. If someone, with no provocation, beats you up, that is very wrong but it is not unjust, unless the person beating you up is a representative of a governmental body. The concept of fairness is even narrower. If a policeman beats you up, while this is unjust it is not unfair, unless you had won a contest in which the prize was not to be beat up, or it was not your turn among the prisoners to be beaten up. Words such as "justice" and "fairness" ordinarily are used within a narrow part of what morality is concerned with. What I want is a word with a much broader use, which I shortly will characterize. Because such a word is not available, I will appropriate the word "justice" for the purposes of this essay, using it in a specified technical (but broad) sense rather than in its ordinary meaning.

Let me suggest that it is highly useful that a society develop a repertoire of rights, protection, and entitlements that apply "irrespective of persons" and that typically have overriding force wherever they apply. I will use the word "justice" in relation to all of these. These may extend even to animals. Our obligation not to maltreat a dog has nothing to do with whether it is a nice dog or not, or whether we have been on friendly terms with it or not, although it should be added that maltreatment is even more shocking if it comes in the context of a history of friendly relations. There is no need to rehearse the range of rights, protection, and entitlements due to human beings; these are very often discussed. It should be emphasized that these not only apply irrespective of persons, but also that they typically fall out of very general formulations. One knows that, say, every human being is entitled to life, liberty, and the pursuit of happiness. Judgments of justice, in the extended sense in which I now am using the word, are distinctive both in the abilities required to make them and in the abilities that are not required. They require an ability to approach moral problems at a fairly high level of abstraction. They require also great steadfastness in applying principles or general rules despite temptations or distractions. They do not require, on the other hand, any special sensitivity to the special qualities of persons, since they apply irrespective of persons. Nor do they, insofar as they tend to use broad and familiar categories, require much sensitivity to special features of situations.

In some respects the development of this abstract, impersonal approach to justice is comparable to the development of modern physical science. Both are driven by a passion for generality and an image of an impersonal, objective knower. In both cases, a crucial element is the ruthless exclusion from notice of elements that do not fit the scheme. The color of the balls rolling down the inclined plane is irrelevant, as is the weather when objects are dropped from the Leaning Tower of Pisa, or the smell of nearby flowers. The moral theory which most closely parallels this is Kant's, in which rigorous insistence on the importance of those features in an action which correspond to what must be included in or excluded by universal law, or which fulfill or violate the requirement to treat other rational beings as ends and not merely as means, is accompanied by indifference (as regards morality) to all other features.

A moral tradition which centers on justice in this extended sense can be contrasted with one which centers on the importance of creating and maintaining a fulfilling and fully human network of relationships. This kind of tradition does not center on rights, protection, and entitlements; rather it centers on the concern we feel for our family and friends, and for people to whom we are sympathetic. Such a tradition will not be impersonal, in that the stage of human development of a person will always be a crucial factor in determining the options available to her or him, and in that it also will be the case that emphasis on personal relationships will lead to a strong sense of social place. Unlike a justice-centered moral tradition, this tradition, which I will call connectedness-centered, will not encourage reliance on abstractions or highly general procedures in order to decide what should be done. It will instead rely heavily on sensitivity to the projects, hopes, and suffering of others.

What I have just sketched are ideal types, and I do not mean to suggest either that Western traditions, even the one in which John Rawls is a major figure, are exactly like what has been characterized as a justice-centered tradition, or that the Confucian tradition is simply connectedness-centered. Confucian ethics has some very good things to say about justice. One might think of the "single thread" which runs through Confucius' thought.[11] It is impossible to read Mencius without a strong awareness of his very practical and down-to-earth concern with justice. Conversely Western moral traditions do seem to have some room for factors related to personal connectedness, although there is more room in consequentialist systems than in Kantian systems.

In the case of the West the picture is complicated by recent suggestions of gender differences in modes of ethical thought.[12] The depth of the differences is difficult to assess, partly because, as I am going to suggest, different modes of ethical thought are appropriate to different kinds of cases. If women engage in connectedness-centered thinking about cases of kind A, and men engage in justice-centered thinking about cases of kind B, it may be that both are adopting appropriate modes of thought; and it may be also that, as more women find themselves practically engaged with problems of kind B, and more men allow themselves to be engaged with problems of kind A, both kinds of thinking will be equally important to both women and men. In suggesting this, I am pursuing a line of thought associated with, among others, Kenneth Gergen, namely, that social generalizations often are time-bound.[13]

Let us return to the ideal types. To the extent that a tradition approaches the model of being connectedness-centered, one can expect certain strengths and weaknesses of it. One can expect a rich account of factors contributing to satisfying personal relationships, especially friendship and within a family. Political thought will avoid impersonality by construing both the state and the society along the lines of an extended family, so that personal relationships still matter and people are not supposed to be treated like numbers. These are important strengths. One weakness is that, in a society dominated by such a tradition, someone who in fact does not have the right sort of personal relationships can expect very little. There also will be some difficulty in knowing how to deal with strangers and outsiders.[14] One strategy might be to treat them as if they were within the network of personal relationships, but the pretence might be difficult to sustain.

The strengths and weaknesses to be expected of an entirely justice-centered tradition are very different. Such a tradition will be good in dealing with strangers and outsiders; after all, it will be said, they are just like anyone else, and fair is fair. A country governed by this attitude can be truly a land of opportunity. Not only will there be some degree of fairness to strangers, but, to the extent that the society approximates its ideals there will be dependable, impersonal administration of justice, thus making possible a high degree of stability and security. If people are governed by respect for the abstract ideals of law and order, rather than by a sense of the worthiness of people with whom they deal, or by any other kind of sensitivity, then everyone can know where she or he stands and business can be conducted in a rational way. Such a society might well be more prosperous than most and less subject to cataclysms of various kinds.

The major weakness of a justice-centered tradition will be the mirror image of that of the connectedness-centered tradition. Each will try to approach all situations in terms of its dominant model. One will interpret social justice in relation to the image of society as a giant family. Such an approach may work better in villages than among large urban populations. It may turn out to be difficult over a long period of time, also, to sustain the image of rivals, transients, and far-off peasants as really like members of one's family. The other will view personal relations in terms of duties and obligations of an impersonal sort that follow from abstract general rules, or from an attempt to assimilate all forms of personal commitment to promises. This is represented by the apocryphal Victorian who, nursing his or her sick spouse, murmurs, "I am only doing my duty." Such an ethics will have little or no room for what is done out of love; it is concerned with what one owes.

As the reader may gather, I doubt that either strategy can be successful for a long period of time. In any event, there is an alternative approach (alternative, that is, to assimilating all major matters of life within its rubric) available to a justice-centered tradition. It can draw a sharp distinction between the part of life that is governed by morality on the one hand and the rest of life on the other, and suggest that we treat these two parts of life very differently. An example is the distinction suggested by Kant's contrast between the categorical and hypothetical imperatives, or the one between morality and "expediency" outlined in paragraph 14 of chapter 5 of Mill's *Utilitarianism* and then redrawn more concretely in *On Liberty*. It is natural that the division between morality and other kinds of evaluative distinctions be a product of justice-centered traditions. We may refer loosely to what is on the other side of the distinction as private life. The distinction between the realm of morality on the one hand and private life on the other has great advantages and also great disadvantages. It makes possible, as Mill argues it should, a great sense of freedom in most of one's activities. Thus it is arguable that a justice-centered society will be likely not only to be more prosperous, stable, and secure, but also to have more personal liberty. The great disadvantage is that, once the distinction is made between the realm of morality and private life, it is not clear that ethics will have much to say about private life or that, if it does, anyone will listen. What results may approach an anarchy of private life. Paul Feyerabend has been quoted as remarking on the extraordinary contrast to be found in some scientists between, on the one hand, the meticulous insistence on standards in professional work and, on the other hand, the virtual absence of standards in personal relationships. A society in which there is an anarchy of private life will be one in which friendships and family relationships often do not go well. It suggests an image of a great many prosperous and free people, many of whom are also disconnected and lonely.

To return to the real world: it should be clear that I have been trying to suggest some faint resemblance between Confucian and Western moral traditions and the two ideal types under discussion, although the realities are much more complicated than the ideal types. What degree of resemblance there is suggests the following. Each tradition could learn a good deal from the other. Western moral traditions would gain enormously from the sophisticated and intricate insights developed in the Confucian analysis of personal relations. Confucians could gain from Western analyses of justice.

Part of the suggestion is that it might be possible for a moral tradition, if it is sufficiently flexible and tolerant of complexity, to have it both ways: to provide adequate and clear emphasis both on impersonal systems of justice and on the importance and peculiar requirements of personal relationships. This might seem a recommendation of double-vision. But, if the reader will forgive the optical metaphor, what I am recommending is bifocal ethics.

It is possible to distinguish between cases that best are approached within a justice tradition and those best approached from the standpoint of personal connectedness. This distinction can be made in a number of ways. A Kantian might very well begin with Kant's distinction between cases determinable by use of the categorical imperative and cases that instead call merely for hypothetical imperatives. There is noting drastically unusable about this distinction; where Kant is chiefly to be faulted is in his bland and jejune assumption that the latter could be lumped together under the pursuit of happiness, and (because not matters of principle) are not the concern of ethics. This blinded him to the significance of things that we really ought to do which are matters of love or friendship rather than matters of principle; his attempts, in a discussion of imperfect duties, to assimilate these to the side of life governed by the categorical imperative are in my view not entirely successful.[15] But it is possible for a Kantian to begin with something like Kant's distinction, and then to develop something like a Confucian account of how we ought to conduct ourselves in our relationships with others.

Something similar is possible for a consequentialist. It is often not realized that an insistence on making the world as good as is possible as an ethical standard can function as a way of justifying habits and systems of thought as well as individual actions, and that when it is used to justify habits and systems of thought it normally will be taken as an inappropriate standard for individual actions that are governed by the habits or systems of thought. Thus Mill, in *On Liberty,* argues that systems of rights are highly useful in a certain stage of social development, and that it is highly useful that we never calculate in individual cases the advantages and disadvantages of respecting rights. In much this way, a consequentialist could argue that it is highly useful to be governed by something like a Confucian view of personal relationships, and that to be governed entirely by such a view is never so much as to entertain the thought of opportunistic violations of standards for the sake of momentary advantages. Consequentialists also could adjudicate the boundary between the realm of impersonal justice and the private world in terms of the competing social utilities of alternative placements. Shifts of the boundary, as when nepotism came to be thought of as unacceptable, can be explained retrospectively in these terms.

This is all sketchy, but then discussions of the future of whole systems of thought are bound to be sketchy. The point remains that it is possible to combine a Western-style justice tradition with a very different kind of tradition, and that the best approach may be one in which different areas of life are guided by different traditions. I do not mean to suggest that there would be no difficulties or complications in this. In some areas the deliverances of justice-centered morality may have to be tempered by a connectedness-centered perspective, or vice versa. The activities of politics, with requirements of personal negotiation and compromise, may in some respects straddle any reasonable division between two realms of life. But there seems no reason to suppose that what I have called a bifocal ethics would be less equipped to deal with politics than any ethics we already have.

My recommendations have been addressed with the improvement of Western traditions chiefly in mind, although the argument has been that both Confucian and Western traditions could learn from another. The need to learn, though, may be more crucial for the West. This is because the assumption often made that the private world and the realm of justice are not only separate from but also sealed from one another may turn out not to be entirely true. If we ask where people, as it were, really live, the answer for virtually everyone is in the private world. Perhaps it is possible to maintain indefinitely a societal double life, in which sophisticated and demanding requirements of justice are usually met but in which, also, people often have impoverished and lonely private lives, sometimes marked by sloppiness and downright lack of standards in personal relationships. But it is hard to believe that impoverishment and sloppiness in one realm will not seep into the other. If people lack integrity in the most basic transactions of their lives, can we expect them to maintain it in the public realm? I do not mean to suggest that such questions can be answered a priori; it may be that for many the answer in fact is "Yes," that ethical compartmentalization works for them. But the questions suggest the possibility that development of bifocal systems of ethics may have more than theoretical or personal importance, and may in fact counteract forces leading to the erosion of Western traditions of justice.

Notes

My thanks to Diana Meyers and Loren Lomasky for helpful comments on a first version of this essay.

1. Cf. "Ethical Fallibility," *Ratio,* n.s., vol. 1 (1988); "Character and Ethical Theory," *Midwest Studies in Philosophy* 13 (1988).

2. Cf. J. J. C. Smart, "Benevolence As an Over-Riding Attitude," *Australasian Journal of Philosophy* 55 (1977).

3. Cf. Henry Rosemont, "Reply to Professor Fingarette," *Philosophy East & West* 28, no. 4 (October 1978): 515–516.

4. Cf. Herbert Fingarette, *Confucius—The Secular as Sacred* (New York: Harper & Row, 1972), chap. 2; and my "Confucius, Mencius, Hume, and Kant on Reason and Choice," in S. Biderman and B. Scharfstein, eds., *Rationality in Question* (Leiden: E. J. Brill, 1989).

5. *Analects of Confucius,* trans. by Arthur Waley (New York: Vintage Books, n.d.) 9:16, pp. 156–157. See also 6:10, p. 118.

6. *Whose Justice? Which Rationality?* (Notre Dame: University of Notre Dame Press, 1988).

7. *Ethical Knowledge* (London: George Allen & Unwin, 1970), and *Foundations of Morality* (London: George Allen & Unwin, 1983).

8. Cf. my "Relations Between the Sexes: Timely vs. Timeless Principles," *San Diego Law Review,* 1989.

9. R. M. Hare, *Moral Thinking* (Oxford: Clarendon Press, 1981).

10. "The conscience of Huckleberry Finn," *Philosophy* 49 (1974).

11. Cf. *Analects of Confucius* 4:15; Herbert Fingarette, "Following the 'One Thread' of the *Analects,*" *Journal of American Academy of Religion* 47 (1979).

12. Cf. Carol Gilligan, *In a Different Voice* (Cambridge: Harvard University Press, 1982), and also the essays in Eva Kittay and Diana Meyers, eds., *Women and Moral Theory* (Totowa, New Jersey: Rowman & Littlefield, 1987). Diana Meyers has pointed out to me that Viriginia Held's essay in this collection, in particular, anticipates my argument that moralities should include more than one focus and, consequently, different ways of approaching different domains of moral activity. See also Virginia Held, *Rights and Goods: Justifying Social Action* (New York: Free Press, Macmillan, 1984).

13. Cf. Kenneth J. Gergen, *Toward Transformation in Social Knowledge* (New

York: Springer-Verlag, 1982). See also Linda Nicholson, "Women, Morality, and History," *Social Research* 50 (1983).

14. Cf. David L. Hall and Roger T. Ames, *Thinking Through Confucius* (Albany: SUNY Press, 1987), pp. 308–310. See also Derk Bodde, *Peking Diary* (New York: Fawcett Premier Paperback, 1967), pp. 33–34.

15. For more sympathetic discussions, see Thomas E. Hill, Jr., "Kant on Imperfect Duty and Supererogation," *Kant-Studien* 62 (1971); Barbara Herman, "The Practice of Moral Judgment," *Journal of Philosophy* 82 (1985); and Marcia Baron, "Kantian Ethics and Supererogation," *Journal of Philosophy* 84 (1987).

Culture and the Aesthetic

ARTHUR C. DANTO

THE SHAPE OF ARTISTIC PASTS,
EAST AND WEST

In the Robert Ellsworth Collection of Nineteenth and Twentieth Century Chinese Art, at the Metropolitan Museum in New York, there is an affecting work by Wan Shang-lin (1739–1813), who is, as a landscape painter, said in the neutral prose of this collection's spectacular catalog, "to have been influenced by Ni Tsan (1301–1374)."[1] The image on Wan's scroll is of a monk in a somewhat austere landscape, identified as Lung-men; but as we know from the inscription, the image itself is less about its pictorial subject—the Lung-men monk—than it is about a painting of that subject by Ni Tsan, which Wan may or may not have seen. It is intended for an audience which in effect can compare Wan's image with a remembered or imagined original, or in any case knows enough about the work of Ni Tsan to be able to make comparisons. The inscription itself is inscribed with a vigor singular in contrast to the rather pale and diffident image composed of trees, rocks, and the isolated itinerant; and though in no sense a student of calligraphy, I feel confident that the difference in stylistic address is intentional and meant to be appreciated as such: the disparity between writing and drawing exhibits that difference in affect between memory and waking perception which Hume identifies as a gradedness in vivacity.[2] There is a tentative fadedness in the image, as if it were dimly recalled. This interpretation must of course be mooted by the fact that Ni Tsan's own style, in which strokes have the watery feel of washes, was itself intended to leave unresolved the question of whether the landscapes he was so fond of painting were themselves perceived or dreamt. They are almost languorous in consequence of this mood, which seeks to make as vivid as the subject allows the palpable undecidability between illusion and reality, after all the questions a monk might himself raise regarding the landscape through which he makes his meditative transit.

Here is a poem à propos by Ni Tsan himself:

> When I first learned to use a brush,
> Seeing an object I tried to capture its likeness.

Whenever I traveled, in country or town,
I sketched object after object, keeping them in my painting basket.
I ask my master Fang I,
What is illusion, what real?
From the inkwell, I take some inkdrops,
To lodge in my painting a boundless feeling of Spring.[3]

Let us now turn to Wan Shang-lin's inscription, which in a certain sense instructs us as to how the subjacent image is to be appreciated, and which connects it and its original, as it connects Wan and Ni Tsan, in a complex artistic network:

I have seen two paintings of the Lung-men monk by Ni Kao-shih [Ni Tsan]. One belongs to Yao Hua tao-jen and one to the governor of Yao-chou. Both have some brushwork of excellent quality, but neither can be judged with certainty as genuine. For eight or nine years, these two paintings have been puzzling me. Today is the sixth day of the ninth month, 1800, one day before the results of [the] examination are to be published. We are gathered at the I t'ing Studio. I have been doing some sketches of hermits and suddenly the paintings came to mind. So, from memory, I have done this copy. If it has some similarities, it is as Tso-chan [Su Tung-p'o] says, "similarity in surface only." I feel embarrassed [for the quality of my work].[4]

We may infer a great deal regarding the structure of the Chinese artist's world from this. There were of course no museums in our form of that crucial institution, and certainly none in which artworks from various traditions hang cheek-by-jowl under the same accommodating roof as in the paradigmatic encyclopedic museum we assume to be the norm, but it would have been common knowledge in which collections works were to be found; and the assumption is that these could be studied by scholar artists. It is clear that there were criteria of connoisseurship, as there always are when there is the practice of collecting, and where the issue of genuineness has some importance. We must not suppose that genuineness connotes authenticity, at least in the sense in which imitation connotes inauthenticity; it is no criticism of Wan Shang-lin's painting *that* it is an imitation, but only one *as* it is, as an imitation, good or bad. After all, Wan's painting was preserved, I think, not unlike the way in which we preserve copies by Degas of Poussin, because Degas achieved an independent stature, and anything from his hand has meaning and certainly value in even the crassest sense of that term. I suspect that Wan's painting would have value even if he did little else beyond imitations of Ni Tsan.

There was an important practice of imitating Ni Tsan, as the existence of two copies of the same work in known collections perhaps testifies, even though, or perhaps possibly because, as Wen Fong writes, Ni Tsan was inimitable. According to Wen Fong, the artist Shen Chou

(1427–1509) "nurtured a life-long ambition to imitate Ni Tsan, yet, according to one story, every time he applied his brush to paper his teacher would shout, 'No, No, you have overdone it again.' "[5] So for half a millennium there can be traced a suite of paintings in the style of Ni Tsan, some of them, just as Wan Shang-lin observes, possessing brushwork excellent enough that the question of genuineness can be at least raised. So the bland art-historical commonplace "influenced by Ni Tsan" scarcely serves to explain the complicated relationship in which the members of this history stand to one another, or to Ni Tsan himself. But neither do the words "imitated by Ni Tsan" altogether capture as a description the action glossed by Wan Shang-lin in his own inscription.

Here I can but speculate on a tradition to which I am in every essential respect an alien, but at the very least we can say that these imitations were not intended to deceive anyone, or to cause in them false beliefs about the provenance of the work. Something rather more like what Aristotle must have had in mind in the *Poetics* defined this practice: "It is natural for all to delight in works of imitation."[6] Now in truth, though irrelevant to this tradition, no one the least familiar with Ni Tsan's work could be taken in by this imitation. This is not simply because the authority of Ni Tsan's brushwork is absent, even if all the standard motifs are there: the paired trees, for example, the water, and the rocks. Something else is absent, or, if you like, present, in this painting which could not have been present in the original; what is absent is a quality with which this presence is incompatible. Wan has his monk facing a cliff, which situates him in a kind of enclosure, almost as though he had encountered an obstacle, whatever this may mean in the trackless atmosphere of monastic reality. The paintings of Ni Tsan are marked by their abstract openness, their "boundless feeling"; the empty paper becomes a kind of empty, dreamful space from which the possibility of horizons has been subtracted. I do not know whether this emptiness was invisible to the Chinese artists who imitated Ni Tsan or not. There are of course always things that reveal the copyist, things he puts in without necessarily being conscious of doing so, because what is in the original just makes no sense to him and he spontaneously compensates. Leo Steinberg, from whom I learned the revelatory utility of copies, points out that in *The Last Supper,* Christ is shown virtually without shoulders, essential, in Steinberg's view, to the larger compositional effect of the work, but anatomically impossible, so that copies of that work almost invariably "correct" the drawing; and in late copies indeed Christ has the shoulders of a football hero.[7] Possibly Wan Shang-lin, who, remember, was working from memory, felt there had to be "something there," and so unconsciously "corrected" his master, and in fact transformed the work in an almost metaphysical way. Or there may be another answer. Imitating Ni Tsan may have so concentrated on brushwork and motif that it had become impossible to see the other components of the work, or to see the work in any other way. This can happen with work which is highly (forgive the word) "influential." Try to imagine (I take the example from Michael Baxandall[8]) how Cezanne would look if Cubism had never been invented. The meaning of Cezanne to counterfactual artistic traditions in possible other worlds is tantalizingly inaccessible. Suppose the Chinese artist admired the spatialities in Ni Tsan; then the quality of his lines might have become almost irrelevant, and someone could have been complimented on the success of an imitation that someone fixated on lines could hardly so much as see as such at all. But that, of course, was not the tradition. In the tradition that unites Ni Tsan and Wan Shang-lin, the brushwork counts for everything. And we have after all to remember that not until later in the nineteenth century than 1800, after photography was introduced into China, was exact resemblance ever an ideal. There was never in Chinese painting the defining ambition of Western art to dupe birds; at most one would want the vitality of one's brushwork to match the vitality of one's subject. So it would be enough, perhaps, for something to be an imitation of Ni Tsan that it should do this, and within these limits the imitator had the freedom to do what he or she wished; it would no more be expected that no one could tell the difference between Wan and Ni Tsan than that no one could tell the difference between the painting of a tree and the tree itself.

"When every boulder or rock shows free and untrammeled inkstrokes, then the painting will have a scholar's air. If it is too laborious, the painting will resemble the work of a craftsman."[9] So wrote Ni Tsan. Here we can begin to see the extreme difficulty, one would almost say the impossibility, of imitation as the Chinese envision it, or at least its challenge. One must paint as the Master painted and *at the same time* be free and untrammeled. The imitation cannot be outward indiscernability; rather the work must flow forth from the same internal resources, and painting in the style of Ni Tsan in consequence becomes a form of spiritual exercise. We get a whiff of this possibility in our own culture, of course, in the instruction of the Guardians in Plato's *Republic,* though in the reverse direction: Plato worries that we will become what we imitate, and so we must have morally acceptable models. On my view, the Chinese thought was that we can imitate *only* if we in fact become like our model, however this is to be achieved. Outward similarities are what we might expect from a craftsman. It is the internal similarities that count. By 1800, Ni Tsan had become a legend and in a sense an imperative. Stories were told of him as a noble recluse, the embodiment of great virtues: purity, courage, equanimity in the face of hardship, a man for whom vulgarity was the evil to avoid. Ni Tsan was like one of the Sage Kings! So he was constantly reinvented, cited as a precursor, celebrated as a hero. In imitating Ni Tsan one was making a moral stand, creating a narrative for one's life, filling the shoes of greatness.

"Influenced by Ni Tsan!" That would be like reading in a life of Saint Paul "influenced by Jesus Christ."

The philosophical shape of art history in China differed so from that of art history in the West that Wan Shang-lin's narrative simply would not have been available for a Western painter of any significance; he could not have represented himself as situated in the kind of history in which Wan felt himself at home. We are after all speaking of a stretch of historical time that corresponds almost precisely to that which takes us from Giotto to Jacques-Louis David, hence a period of periods growing out of and transcending one another in a way that pointed a progressive vector. We have the three Vasarian cycles, anchored in Giotto, Masaccio, and Raphael: Mannerism; the Baroque, in which the church was able to call upon painters and sculptors and even architects to achieve illusory feats of which even a master like Masaccio would have been incapable; and we have the long age of the academies in which, by 1800, the state now rather than the church was asking that artists articulate the values of the revolution and define the meaning of citizenship again in ways inaccessible to art near the beginning of this period. Painting was the progressive discipline par excellence, and no one who took himself seriously as a painter would have wished to have been born at an earlier time, or would seek through imitation to reenact the works of earlier masters. To be sure, the Renaissance defined itself through a narrative that connected it with Greece and Rome, but this required a representation of the intervening time as merely dark ages, a time of lost skills that had to be rediscovered and of ignorance that had to be driven away, a long descent into shadows from peak to peak of light. The next time something like this occurred was in the Pre-Raphaelite movement in England, where again the effort, audacious in conception when we think of the actual gifts of its major practitioners, was to dismiss as a kind of aberration everything from Raphael down, to make a new beginning, returning to the masters in an effort to relearn visual truth. Between Wan Shang-lin and Ni Tsan was the hapless Shen Chou; the painters of the Lung-men monk in the two versions known to Wan, if these were not (as very likely they were not) by Ni Tsan himself; and then the many others who sought to preempt for their own life and work the style of Ni Tsan. None of these felt either that he was making a new beginning or that between himself and the master was a dark wood in which the art of painting wandered or languished. Wan's was a vectorless history. Past and future were so of a piece that there was no conceptual room for modernity, and the concept of influence had to mean something different from what it would to a Western artist, one, say, who copied a predecessor, not caring about similarity, not matching himself against his model, but simply learning how was something done, in order, miming the structure of art history itself, to internalize and go beyond what came before.

Michael Baxandall writes: " 'Influence' is the curse of art criticism primarily because of its wrong-headed prejudice about who is the agent and who the patient; it seems to reverse the active/passive relation which the historical actor experiences:

> If one says that X influenced Y it does seem that one is saying that X did something to Y. But in the consideration of good pictures and painters, the second is always the more lively reality. If we think of Y rather than X as the agent, the vocabulary is much richer and more diversified; draw on, resort to, avail oneself of, appropriate from, have recourse to, adapt, misunderstand, refer to, pick up, take on, engage with, react to, quote, differentiate oneself from, assimilate oneself to, assimilate, align oneself with, copy, address, paraphrase, absorb, make a variation on, revive, continue, remodel, ape, emulate, travesty, parody, extract from, distort, attend to, resist, simplify, reconstitute, elaborate on, develop, face up to, master, subvert, perpetuate, reduce, promote, respond to, transform, tackle. Most of these relations just cannot be stated the other way round—in terms of X acting on Y rather than Y on X.[10]

Raphael is often described as the most influential artist who ever lived, chiefly, I think, because his compositional strategies entered the curriculum and became the way artists in academies were taught to compose well into the nineteenth century. But very few of the artists so influenced were so influenced in the way in which Wan was influenced by Ni Tsan. There were, of course, artists who sought in a certain sense to paint like Raphael, say as Benjamin West did in portraying his family in *tondo* format based upon Raphael's *Madonna della sedia*. But even in that case, there is a metaphorical reference being made, and a different order of rhetoric transacted than anything I find in Wan Shang-lin.

I think we cannot too heavily stress the fact that, without having necessarily to affirm quite so voluntarist a view of our relationship to the past as we find in Sartre, who says such dramatic things as that we choose to be born, the past is very much a function of the present, in the sense that what causes us to act as we do is not so much the things that influence us, but the representations of the past that define us as artists, and through which, say, Ni Tsan was constituted the "influence" through which Wan Shang-lin painted. Historical explanations accordingly do not carry us, as from cause to effect, from the influence to the influenced, but rather must account for the representation, the complex of beliefs, feelings, and values, through which influence and influenced arise together as an historical unit. This may be the deep reason why we might see in Ni Tsan things to which those for whom he was an influence were necessarily blind, and why, in a certain sense, the past yields facets for our admiration to which those contemporary with it, or more directly influenced by it than we, are blind. Monet was constituted a predecessor by the Abstract Expressionists by virtue of certain features of the Water Lily paintings becoming salient in the retrospective light of scale, all-overness, and freedom of brushing that could not have meant to Monet or his contemporaries what they came to mean for artists for whom Pollock opened up the past. Or think, for just these same reasons, how Fragonard's *Figures de Fantaisie* were so greatly admired by artists in New York who visited the great Fragonard exhibition of 1988 for whom *The Progress of Love,* unquestionably his masterpiece, should become both an influence and a meaningful, because active, past. Possibly it is the mark of Post-Modernism that anything can become an influence at any time, a disordered past corresponding to a disordered present and future.

Since Vasari, to be an artist in the West has been to have internalized a narrative which determines the way we can be influenced by the past. The difference between Western and Chinese artists will then be a difference in lived narratives and modes of available influence. Modernism, alike in China and the West, meant the dismantling of these narratives and a reconstitution of our relationship to the past. To this I now turn.

Wan Shang-lin lived in fortunate times, in that he could practice an art against a tradition that had not radically changed for five centuries. He could represent his work as simply seeking what the masters sought, imitation being as good a means as any. His contemporaries in the West, too, lived in fortunate times, in the sense at least that they understood themselves as belonging to a history that they understood what it meant to continue. Not long after 1800 in France and in most of the other countries of Europe, the cosmopolitan museum appeared—the Louvre, the Brera, the Rijksmuseum, the Prado, and the Kunsthistorisches Museum were founded within a few years of one another—in which artists could study the masterpieces of their tradition. As late as the Impressionists, artists were in the spirit of wholeness with their tradition. The Impressionists in particular saw their task very little differently than Vasari did, as the conquest of visual appearances, of arranging colors across flat surfaces in such a way as to affect the retina as it would be affected by some scene in the real world to which the painterly array corresponded. They felt themselves closer to visual truth than their predecessors, hence as continuing a tradition to which they belonged. Their discoveries regarding the colors of shadows belonged to the same progress as linear perspective, aerial perspective, chiaroscuro. They craved academic recognition. Even Rousseau, who saw himself as the great master of the modern, aspired to the *Légion d'honneur.* Modernism came about when this entire tradition was called into question by artists who no longer felt themselves to belong to it. And something of the same sort happened in China over much the same period. To be modern is to perceive the past as the locus of only negative messages, of things not to do, of ways not to be. I think that modernity begins with the loss of belief in the defining narrative of one's own culture. When that narrative is strong and taken simply as the way things are, it is almost impossible to be influenced by another culture. After all, works of art were imported into the West from the first establishment of mercantile routes; Chinese porcelains appear in the Dutch still lifes of the seventeenth century, but merely as objects to hold fruit, though of course there was a demand for pottery in the Chinese style, as we know from the fact that it was broadly imitated around 1700 by the potters of Delft. There can be a great deal of such importation and imitation without the premises on which cultural complacency rests being greatly shaken. Who can forget the atmosphere of exotisme/erotisme of Odette's drawing room, with its Japanese lanterns and Chinese pots, its screens and fans and cushions of Japanese silks, the innumerable lamps made of porcelain vases (and some Turkish beads), though the marvelous lantern, suspended by a silken cord, was lit from inside by a gas jet "so that her visitors should not have to complain of the want of any of the latest comforts of Western civilization," as Proust writes archly.[11] The superiority of Western Civilization was never doubted, and one of the premises of Victorian anthropology was in effect that there is a moral direction in history as there is in evolution, that societies and species evolve toward optimality, and that Western Europe was history's masterpiece just as *Homo sapiens* was Nature's. The superiority of Chinese civilization was no less an axiom for those who lived it. The relationship to the outside would be fundamentally one of curiosity. The outside was the object of curiosity in the double sense of embodying strangeness, as in "curio," and as something to understand as an object of scientific curiosity.

The outside in neither sense was something we might aspire to as a form of life; Kant, who must have learned about the South Seas from Captain Cook's *Voyages,* sees them as places where lives of extreme pleasure and indolence can be lead, but not, he argues, lives we can rationally will for ourselves. Nor could we rationally will to live the lives ethnographers began to explore throughout the nineteenth century. But the presumption was that these were like living fossils, stages through which we advanced; and a complex narrative was assumed in which the savages of Africa and Oceania were ourselves seen through the wrong end of the telescope of social evolution just as they, looking through the right end, could see themselves as us. We would be the goal to which it was the White Man's Burden to conduct them, though there was an empirical question, I suppose, as to whether their stage of social development did not also mark a correlative stage of intellectual development, so that they could not master the form of life toward which they could merely evolve, and our task was that of shepherds, giving them some skills useful to them (and economically valuable to us). The African who aspires to a European form of life would be essentially an object of comedy, an attitude, I think, that lasted surprisingly late, well into the 1950s, in such novels as Joyce Cary's *Mister Johnson*. Indeed the Other in Western Art—whether the pygmy, as even in the paintings of Pompei, the Hottentot, or the Chinese in eighteenth-century paintings of monkeys doing such things as painting pictures or playing instruments or of children conducting flirtations—was very largely comical, an occasion for reflecting on our own superiority, as when we watch primates doing nearly human things in the zoo. Parallels are to be found in Chinese art as well.

For me, the deep change, and indeed the beginning of modernism, begins in the West when Japanese prints became objects not of curiosity but of influence. Monet collected Japanese prints, as Matisse and Derain collected African masks and figures. But Van Gogh and Gauguin decided to constitute the masters of the Ukiyoe print as their predecessors, as Picasso determined a tradition in the Ethnographic Museum of the Palais de Trocadero to be the relevant past for the Demoiselles d'Avignon. It was, in the case of Japanese art, not simply that these stopped being objects of charm and curiosity and exoticism, connoting, as in Odette's overheated interior, pleasures forbidden by the moral world embodied in the bourgeois decor she was anxious, as a high-class courtesan, to put at a distance; it was that these prints showed the right way to represent in art, and if these were right, an entire artistic tradition was wrong and an entire progress was beside the point. Part of this had to do with the treatment of space, part with the ideal of an illusion that three-dimensional space, whose conquest was the glory of Western art, made possible. Gauguin drew everything toward the surface, rejected chiaroscuro, flattened his forms by bounding them with heavy lines—though like Odette, who took it for granted that she should use gas to illuminate her lantern. Gauguin benefited from the easy availability of manufactured pigments to get colors in a relatively pure state, defined as "coming from the tube." (It was by and large chemical pigments that finished off the Japanese print.) In desituating his own art from his own tradition, accepting as influences the Japanese masters, Gauguin simultaneously was engaged in a piece of cultural criticism; he explicitly said, when he considered relocating to Tonkin, that "The West is rotten." I cannot here discuss the reverse impact of Western representational strategies on China, but the Ellsworth collection presents us with an artworld under powerful transformation, corresponding, I suppose, to the immense social and economic changes China was undergoing in the same period, but with the unmistakable truth that when the Chinese artist allowed himself to employ Western strategies, aiming at likenesses using illusory space and chiaroscuro, exploiting shadows and illuminational sources, altering the canon of acceptable subjects, behaving in ways Ni Tsan would certainly dismiss as "vulgar," this, too, was an act of cultural criticism, a calling into question of an axiom of cultural supremacy. My own first impression on walking through the Ellsworth collection was that in some mysterious way Chinese art had begun to look *modern,* as if Modernism were a style of historical dismissal, as, of course, it is. Chinese and Western art in the nineteenth and early twentieth centuries are almost locked in that kind of ironic relationship we find in a famous story of O. Henry, where each character sacrifices what the other is anxious to acquire, where the comical denouement would consist in the Chinese proudly displaying a work in faultless perspective to a Western artist who has achieved a perfect oriental flatness.

There have been three strikingly different narrational moments in Western history, moments in which the present means something different because the past to which it is related means something different. The first of course was the Renaissance, which is a narrative of recovery, a plot of losing and finding. Here the deep historic question is why was it lost and how was it found again. Gibbon's answer, "Barbarism and Christianity," is to a question which presupposes this sort of narrative, though of course it has in its own form something of a Christian cadence of paradise, fall, and redemption to paradise, and I am not certain that the narrative would have insinuated itself in the minds of historical theorists were it not for the concept of the fall. The narrative, of course, was over; once risen we are never to fall again. So I suppose in an important sense history itself was over, and we pass into an age of academies.

The second was the Enlightenment, which, after all, furnished the logical shape of what came to be Victorian anthropology. It was, in Kant's powerful and moving expression, "Mankind's coming of age."[12] History was a vectored progress marked by growth and stages. If contemporary culture really is mature, and superior, as adults are superior to children—rational, master of our own lives, our growth behind us— then either we can say that history is over, or that we have reached a stage beyond which we can only imagine things like the Superman; for Nietzsche but continued the narrative, agreeing in large measure with its logic, but dismissing the complacency of regarding *Homo sapiens europanensis* as the apex. Zarathustra is there to help us onto the next thing, as those who felt the White Man's Burden undertook the obligation to bring the stragglers abreast of us in the confidence that this was the last redeeming stage of history, what made it all worth while.

The third was Modernism, which in my view begins in the mid-1880s with Van Gogh and Gauguin, who repudiated the entirety of their own artistic pasts and sought their influences elsewhere, in Japan or Egypt or Polynesia, the art of which was, in Gauguin's view, finally more rational, more "cerebral," than that with which it had spontaneously been contrasted. Both of them undertook to enact their beliefs by dramatic dislocation; Vincent went to Arles because he was looking for a reality whose visual representations would be like Japanese prints, and

Gauguin went to Tahiti, where he had to carve his own Polynesian idols. The historical problem of modernity, for me, is what happened to account for the representation of their own past as less relevant to them than the imagined past of other cultures; what accounts for the profound shift in self-evaluation between the Crystal Palace Exhibition of 1850 and the Exposition Universelle of 1889. The philosophical problem is the logical form of such explanations and the analysis of historical causation when the effect is narrative representations which may or may not be true. Wan Shang-li would still be correctly described as influenced by Ni Tsan even if Ni Tsan did not exist, as Gauguin was influenced by an art that it was one of the profounder disappointments of his voyage out to discover did not exist. It is as though we had effects without causes.

I have neither an historical explanation of the modernist narrative to offer, nor a philosophical analysis of the logic of such historical explanations. But I do want to say something about how modernism in art realized itself. Political circumstance, for better or worse, aborted this development in China, as it did in the Soviet Union and as it would have done in Germany had Nazism, with its strong views in regard to modernism as *entarrete Kunst,* triumphed.

When Braque and Picasso were coinventing Cubism, Braque afterward wrote that they stopped going to museums. Braque had haunted the Egyptian collections of the Louvre when he arrived in Paris in 1902, and I have too often thought of Picasso at the Trocadero. There is a story about Braque driving with his wife through Italy, stopping in front of a museum, and saying, "Marcelle, you go in and look around and tell me what's good in there."[13] He was anxious not to spoil his eye with old painting, Francoise Gilot tells us, and nothing could more eloquently express the attitude toward the past that is proper to the modernist narrative.[14] No one, inevitably, puts it better than Picasso:

> Beginning with Van Gogh, however great we may be, we are all, in a measure, autodidacts—you might almost say primitive painters. Painters no longer live within a tradition and so each one of us must recreate an entire language. Every painter of our times is fully authorized to recreate that language from A to Z. No criterion can be applied to him *a priori* since we don't believe in rigid standards any longer. In a certain sense, that's a liberation, but at the same time it's an enormous limitation, because when the individuality of the artist begins to express itself, what the artist gains in liberty he loses in the way of order, and when you're no longer able to attach yourself to an order, basically that's very bad.[15]

You can look at this in two ways. One is a way recommended by Ernst Gombrich in his influential history of art, where he concludes by saying, "There is no such thing as art, there are only the individual artists." Or you can say that the philosophical question of the nature of art became urgent, all the more so in that the connection with the past has been broken, and all you are left with is a kind of negative aesthetics: not this, not that. One response to this has been the creation of a modernist aesthetic, which is essentially ahistorical. Formalist analysis cuts across all times and all cultures, making in effect every museum a Museum of Modern Art. All art exists for display and formal delectation, across an aesthetic distance. All works of art—the Dogon figures, the watercolors of Wan Shang-lin, the works of Picasso—stand outside life, in a space of their own, metaphorically embodied in the plexiglass display case, the bare white gallery, the aluminum frame. When one seeks a deeper connection between art and life than this, modernism is over. That is our present situation. The effort to reconnect life through reconnecting with the past, as in the referential strategies of Post-Modernism, is pathetic. Formalism is finally unsatisfying, and the need for a philosophy of art under which art is responsive to human ends is a matter of absolute priority. It is the mark of living in the posthistorical period that we face the future without a narrative of the present.

Notes

1. Robert Hatfield Ellsworth, *Later Chinese Painting and Calligraphy 1800-1950* (New York: Random House, 1986), vol. 1, p. 74.

2. ". . . the difference betwixt [the memory] and imagination lies in its superior force and vivacity." David Hume, *A Treatise on Human Nature,* part 3, sec. v.

3. Wen Fong, *Images of the Mind* (Princeton, New Jersey: The Art Museum, Princeton University, 1984), p. 120.

4. Ellsworth, op. cit., p. 74.

5. Wen Fong, p. 126.

6. Aristotle, *Poetics,* 1448[b], 8-9.

7. Leo Steinberg, "Leonardo's *Last Supper,*" *The Art Bulletin* 36, no. 4 (1973):297-410, eps. 397.

8. Michael Baxandall, *Patterns of Intention* (New Haven: Yale University Press, 1985), p. 58.

9. Wen Fong, op. cit., p. 123.

10. Baxandall, op. cit., pp. 58-59.

11. Marcel Proust, *Swann's Way,* trans. by C. K. Scott-Moncrieff in *Remembrance of Things Past* (New York: Random House, 1934), p. 168.

12. Immanuel Kant, *Perpetual Peace.* Author's translation.

13. Francoise Gilot and Carlton Lake, *Life with Picasso* (New York: McGraw-Hill, 1964), p. 266.

14. Ibid., p. 69.

15. Ernst Gombrich, *The Story of Art* (London: Pantheon, 1972), p. 446.

MEGUMI SAKABE

SURREALISTIC DISTORTION OF LANDSCAPE AND THE REASON OF THE MILIEU

I

In his recent book, *Le sauvage et l'artifice—Les Japonais devant la nature* (Gallimard, 1986), Augustin Berque, a French specialist in human geography and Japanology, characterizes the paradoxical situation in which the Japanese nowadays find themselves with respect to their attitudes toward nature. He points out that Japan was by far the most polluted country in the world during the period of "High Growth" in its economy, from 1965 to 1975. This growth was accompanied by the destruction of the landscape through rapid development by large (sometimes multinational) enterprises. For example: in a project undertaken by the petrochemical megalocomplex on Shibushi Bay in Kyushu, the prefecture of Kagoshima—under the very slogan of "protecting" nature—planned the total destruction, by reclamation, of a portion of the littoral landscape that had been recognized as so remarkable that a part of it had already been designated for special preservation. "At this degree of distortion of the 'médiance' (man-milieu relationship)," says Berque, *"the inversion of the relation of the society to the place came close to surrealism:* the functionalization of the territory, demanded by an economic need, presupposed the utter destruction of all the elements of nature in that territory."[1]

This is really black humor: in this scene of a coastline that was polluted, reclaimed, and totally embanked, "surrealism" became a "reality." Of course, this was not the result of any artistic intent but rather the result of the motivation to exploit nature for the purposes of industrialization through the application of high technology.

How different this situation is—and how ironic—when compared with that period during which "Japonism" had such an influence on the French Impressionist movement at the end of the nineteenth century! Undeniably, the dialogue between the East and the West has entered a new phase, in which the "deep structure" of the respective cultures, a structure which until now does not seem to have been fully disclosed, has inevitably been called into question.

For the moment, confining ourselves to the subject of the problems of Japan, what can or should we think concerning the paradoxical attitudes toward nature of the Japanese today? There is, on the one hand, a well-known tradition of intense attachment or refined sensibility with regard to nature, manifested in the literature and art of Japan from its beginnings. On the other hand, there is what might be called a contemporary over-functionalization of the land and the landscape, "demanded by an economic need," which sometimes even goes to the extreme, that is, "the utter destruction of all the elements of nature in that territory." Can we, as many specialists in cultural problems have done, attribute the latter attitude to the "bad" influence of Western culture culminating in modern technology? Or, as Berque says, are the two attitudes mentioned above just two sides of the same coin?

Pointing out the specific feature of the Japanese notion of nature and the natural (*shizen* = of itself), and its inevitable influence on the attitude that Japanese administrative authorities assume toward the development of land for industrial use, Berque argues as follows:

> In this affair, therefore, it is just [such a] high estimation of the natural and the becoming of oneself [*Nari*] that brought about the destruction of nature and being [*Ari*]. The ecological crisis brought about by "High Growth" reveals a crisis which is more profound: the crisis of the very principle of nature, [and,] therefore, inseparably, that of the principle of culture, in human beings as well as in the landscape. It is just what was expressed in the embarrassment which all Japanese felt at that time. [2]

Is there any way out of this paradoxical situation? Does there remain any chance of success in finding a way to the re-naturalization of culture, or, in other words, to the reintegration of nature into culture? Berque suggests that, in order to break out of the dead end in which the Japanese now find themselves, it will be necessary for them to learn at least something of the "reflective" element of the Western "logos."

One may discern here the germ of a possible dialogue between the East and the West in a new phase of their relationship. But, to enter into this sort of dialogue, there must be some modification, not to say "deconstruction," of the conceptual materials which each side possesses at present. What would the modifications be for the respective sides in this dialogue? And what influence would those modifications exert on the way in which Easterners or Westerners concern themselves with their own cultural tradition or history of culture?

Allowing my discussion to take its cue from the questions above, I shall treat the following series of problems: (1) the concept of *fūdo* of Watsuji Tetsurō (1889–1960), and the attempt by Berque to develop it further and introduce it into the conceptual materials of Western thought; (2) a new phase of thinking about the notions of "subject" and "nature," and a consideration and rehabilitation of the notion of "logos"; (3) the reevaluation of some aspects of Japanese cultural history which have hitherto been somewhat neglected; (4) the prospects for a new phase of the dialogue and a new aspect of "logos," especially in the dimension of the interrelationship between "symbolic praxis" and reality.

II

Berque's *Le sauvage et l'artifice* was written at least in part as an attempt to develop further the notion of *fūdo* presented by Watsuji Tetsurō in his *Fūdo, an Anthropological Study* (1935), so that it could be applied to the problem of the present-day attitude of the Japanese toward nature.

In order to avoid being caught in the subject-object dualism that dominates modern Western thinking, Berque uses the word "milieu" instead of "climate" to translate *fūdo*. *Fūdo* (literally *fū*, the air, or wind, and *do*, the soil, the land, a region) originally refers to the elements or elemental features among which the inhabitants of a region live. It is, therefore, not confined to the so-called geographical and meteorological features of the environment, which can be treated objectively, but rather denotes the environmental features as "lived through," "experienced," and "interpreted" by its "inhabitants." In other words, *fūdo* means, originally and principally, the concrete and regional human *Umwelt*, or the totality of the human-environment relationships of a region.

It is noteworthy that in introducing this translation of "milieu" for *fūdo*, Berque was considerably influenced by the method of phenomenological or "humanistic" geography, which has been flourishing since the middle of the 1970s. And, more generally, he was equally influenced by some contemporary thinkers who tried to surmount the dualism of subject and object—thinkers such as Mikel Dufrenne, Jean Piaget, Gilbert Durand, and Gilles Deleuze.

In the second part of his book, entitled "The Reason of the Milieu" or "Savage Nature, Constructed Nature," starting from the definition of the milieu as the "relationship of a society to space and nature," Berque presents a system of some related notions or terminologies (some of which are newly forged by himself), making clear the conceptual framework around the core notion of *fūdo* and rendering it operable in concrete circumstances and research.

The following are some important notions elucidated by Berque:

1. *Mesology (mesologic):* the theory of milieu, which is not limited to the natural environment as in the case of ecology but embraces as well the dimensions "lived through" and "made sense of" by persons.

2. *Médiance:* the dimension or attributive character of the milieus; the sense or meaning of a milieu (at least partially given by persons collectively or individually).

3. *Choresie (choresic):* the dimension of the similar and the referential; the decomposition of the "topical" reality (of the geographical place) and recomposition of its elements in the systems of signification which permit one to communicate, that is, to represent partially the reality outside of its place of presence. (From the Greek *chorein,* to retire, displace, comprehend.)

4. *Trajectivity (trajection, traject):* the dimension of the praxes out of which the milieus arise; the dynamic combination of two or more referentials: subjective/objective, natural/cultural, collective/individual . . . ; the combination of metaphor with causality, of projection and consecution, of contingent and determined; the combination of the "choretic" and the "topical"—which can include material displacements.

In developing this system Berque intends, under an impulse issuing from phenomenology, to make clear and render operable a conceptual framework that is free from the rigid dualisms of subject and object, the natural and the cultural, the collective and the individual, human beings and the environment, and so forth. At the same time, he aims to free himself definitively from the geographical or environmental determinism (or "aerial imaginarism") into which the discussions of "climate" have very often fallen since the latter half of the nineteenth century.

Berque argues that even Watsuji in his concrete analysis of the *fūdo* of various regions of the world (deserts, grasslands, and so forth) often lapsed into geographical determinism. Berque therefore aims to clarify and develop the notion of *fūdo* further, defending it against the (often unconscious) invasion of geographical determinism, so as to make it operable, for the present purpose, in considering the attitudes of the Japanese toward nature.

One might also characterize what Berque intends here in his book as a continuation of the dialogue between the East and the West inaugurated by Watsuji half a century ago. In his analysis of *fūdo,* starting from his own experiences of various "milieus" lived through in his voyage from Japan to Europe via the Indian Ocean and the Suez Canal, Watsuji tried to focus his attention on the geographical features "experienced" by the inhabitants of a region, which are neither simply objective nor simply subjective, but partake of both of these qualifications. It was mainly under the influence of the phenomenological hermeneutics of Heidegger that he undertook such an attempt.

One of his main aims, Watsuji declares in the preface of his book, is to discover some of the characteristic features of human existence with respect to space, which, he thinks, in spite of their equal importance with temporal features, are unduly neglected by Heidegger in *Sein und Zeit*. He says also that *fūdo* is to the life of the community what the body is to the life of the individual human being. Considerations of *fūdo* may thus be regarded as being parallel with those of the body "lived through" or "interpreted" by individual human beings.

Besides the influence of Heidegger, the idea of the science of *fūdo* clearly shows some influence of Herder's idea of "climatology," from which Watsuji derived his own theory of *fūdo* and developed it further. One might, therefore, find in Watsuji's book at least some traces of the cultural pluralism of Herder, who, remarkably free from the ethnocentrism of European culture, puts equal weight on every culture in every region of the earth and in all periods of human history.

III

In any philosophical attempt to surmount the modern dualism of subject and object, it may be essential to revise thoroughly the notion of the subject as well as that of the object, insofar as they are conceived, respectively, in the frameworks of (1) anthropocentrism and (2) objectivism (in the sense that nature is regarded exclusively as an object of human manipulation). In several other works, in addition to *fūdo* (especially in *Ningen no gaku toshite no rinrigaku*, "Ethics as the Study of *Ningen*"), Watsuji pursues the same critique of the dualism of subject and object, with special emphasis on the revision of the notion of subject, again under the influence of Heidegger's methodology.

In accordance with the tradition of Buddhist thought, as well as through hermeneutic analysis of some Japanese words concerning intersubjectivity, Watsuji tries to present a "nonsubjectivist" view of intersubjectivity or of the intersubjective field ("nonsubjectivist" in the sense of the Cartesian subject).

The word *ningen* means, in ordinary Japanese usage, an individual human being, while in the original Chinese usage *ningen* means in between *(gen)* human beings *(nin)*, that is, society or the human world. Watsuji understands this change of meaning as made possible by the fact that, in Japanese, the same word *hito (nin)* signifies both "human being" and "other human being." There is an implicit understanding that a human being can never be a human being without being situated beforehand in a relation to others, or, in other words, in the field of "in-between," or "between-ness" (the *gara* of *aidagara* means way of being, feature). The totality of relationships or the field of relationships *(aidagara)* is in the tradition of Japanese thinking. It is, in fact, logically, and perhaps even ontologically, prior to the so-called individual subject. Through this procedure of the dissolution of the individual subject into the field of between-ness, Watsuji tries to develop his own system of ethics.

There are, however, some problems in this attempt of his.

1. The priority of "between-ness" or the intersubjective field over the individual subject entails, almost as its logical consequence, a tendency to conformism or even totalitarianism, to the suppression of the active manifestation of individuality or the rights of individuals. One can discern such a tendency in the dialectical relationship (of a somewhat Hegelian hue) between the totality of "between-ness" and the individual subject presented in Watsuji's ethical writings. As pointed out by Berque and many other specialists in Japanese culture, there is in the Japanese mentality, as represented typically by Watsuji, a certain tolerance toward totalitarian tendencies. In fact, toward the end of World War II, Watsuji fell prey to just such tendencies.

2. In spite of the dissolution of the individual subject into the field of between-ness and his detailed and subtle investigation into the structure of that field, the dimension of "nature" is almost totally overlooked by Watsuji. Although he tried in the third volume of his "Ethics," published after World War II (1949), to integrate into his system the earlier discussion of *fūdo* along the lines of Herder's cultural pluralism, he still did not seem to be able to free himself from a Hegelian vision of the linear development of human history.

One might see the exclusion of nature from the scope of Watsuji's consideration of "between-ness" as the counterpart of his tendency toward geographical determinism in *fūdo* as mentioned in the preceding section. Thus, after all, in spite of his declared attempt to overcome modern European subjectivism or the dualism of subject and object, Watsuji was unable to free himself entirely from these tendencies, which, at least until very recent times, have dominated many fields of scientific thinking. Accordingly, if one is to refine and develop further the lines of thinking inaugurated by Watsuji, it will be absolutely necessary to undertake a fundamental reconsideration of the notions of subject (including intersubjective subject as "between-ness" and so forth) and object (including nature) and finally the interrelationship between the two.

It is just on this point that Berque attempts a breakthrough of his own. What is remarkable and even surprising in Berque's attempt is that, taking advantage of his position as cultural geographer, he dares to expand the very notion of subject beyond all human subjects and the notion of intersubjectivity to "nature" itself. Wiping away all the traces of object or objectivity from it, Berque defines or redefines afresh the notion of nature insofar as it is the ultimate subject. Nature, as Berque defines it, is *"that which, in the world, has no sense whatever either by virtue of or for human beings, but rather has a sense within and around human beings."*[3]

"Having no sense either by virtue of or for human beings" means "having no sense either subjectively or objectively." And "having a sense within and around human beings" will mean that nature is regarded here rather as (1) natural desire in human beings and (2) the

nature-landscape around human beings, both of which remain, by definition, in the domain of the unconscious (or subconscious) and the
domain of invisibility or quasi-visibility.

This definition of nature as the ultimate subject (which seems to me
to be influenced by Lacan's notion of subject) is in any case completely
free of the kind of objectivism dominant in the tradition of modern science. Nature is reduced here to a "residue," which remains mostly hidden but sometimes reveals itself, symbolically (and especially at some
"critical" moment, in the widest sense of the word) through the fissure
between the subjective and the objective.

Berque writes about the manifestation of nature by the "aesthetics of
incompleteness," as represented typically in the Japanese notion of *ma*
(interval, distance—the same *kanji* as *aida*):

> In the aesthetics of incompleteness, the subject/addresser takes it for
> granted that the other will intervene to complete the message. In other
> words, abdicating the autarchy of the subject, he or she commits to the
> community the task of accomplishing the work by conferring upon it a col-
> lective sense into which his or her proper subjectivity fuses itself. In any
> case, to the extent that the addresser-subject incarnates his or her culture,
> to the extent that, through him or her, the culture speaks as a greater sub-
> ject, this abdication means that there appears here a still greater subject,
> other than culture: that is, necessarily, nature.
>
> In the moment of enunciation, then, the ego of the addresser falls silent, so
> as to let speak another subject of another dimension: the matrical field
> which envelops his or her individuality. This mechanism implies a strong
> homogeneity between the addresser and the field from which he or she
> issues; otherwise, all messages would lapse into incoherence, and all works
> would dissolve into meaninglessness.[4]

Nature as a "residue," mostly hidden, but sometimes revealing itself
through the fissure between the subjective and the objective, and by the
aid of the symbolic praxis of the individual subject issuing from the
matrical field of the community—such a notion as the final and unique
subject of all appears to occupy the place once taken, for example, by
the hidden God, or the Heideggerian Being.

If nature is redefined in this way, what is or what can be the possible
relationship of nature to the reflective element of thinking or to reason
in the widest sense of the word?

Berque claims the indispensability of such an element, as is represented in the East by *ri,* or in the West by "logos":

> Like all other societies, Japanese society needs the *ri* in order to think and
> to act, as well as the *ba* (field) to feel and to exist in. It needs, like all
> societies, not only to distinguish subject from object, to hierarchize causes
> and consequences, so as to work upon nature; but also to unite them "tra-
> jectively," to transpose them metaphorically, so as to "live" its nature and

gain access to its sense. Like every society, it needs the internal force of each person no less than the external force of the community. To insist exclusively on the "milieu" to the neglect of the person is nothing but a sterile inversion of the occidental paradigm, a dangerous caricature of the characteristic milieu (médiance) of Nippon.

The subject may wander from the person to his or her surroundings, and from culture to nature; the intrinsic forces of the milieu of Nippon may animate the meteorological elements, the mountains and the waters, the trees and the plants for the welfare of all. Well and good! but may the individual consciousness not abandon its reflectiveness at the same time, this being the ultimate guarantee of reason and freedom![5]

Reflectiveness (*réflexivité*) is the ultimate guarantee (*gage*) of reason and freedom. This reflectiveness operates by transversing, so to speak, vertically the horizontal parallelism of the dimensions of subject-object, and mediates between the depth of the latency and the symbolic manifestation of nature. Reflectiveness is, on the one hand, deeply rooted in the dimension of the silent and unconscious latency of nature, and, on the other, as a "tangent" or "differential," symbolically expressive of the activity of this latent nature coming up vertically through a point in a horizontal dimension called "reality" or "real world."

Such "reflectiveness" would be, I think, in the Western tradition of thinking, more like the reason of Leibniz or Nicolaus Cusanus than like that of Descartes or Kant. (In fact, Berque mentions the notion of "complicatio-explicatio" of Nicolaus Cusanus and Bruno.) In any case, what is certain is that, by this "explicative" or "differential" (or "projective" or "topological" reason), one could trace the way in which the "surrealist" expression comes out from or through the dimension of "reality."

Here, I hope it will be possible for Westerners to ascertain the point from which the dialogue might be fruitfully carried on between the East and the West in a new phase of their interrelationship.

IV

Once the point of view of nature as subject or subject as nature mentioned above is attained, it will entail some change, also on the part of the East or more especially of Japan, concerning the general view of cultural history and the evaluations of figures or schools therein. In fact, Berque presents some extremely interesting views about several aspects of Japanese cultural history.

First example: Berque writes about a possible reevaluation of the style inaugurated by the tea master Furuta Oribe (1543–1615). Oribe, in remarkable contrast to his predecessor and master Rikyū, who always respected the "natural" elements in landscape gardening and was consequently regarded as orthodox, liked to put the artificial right in the midst of the natural. For example, he employed cut stones as well as natural stones to make a garden path.

Here is what Berque says about Oribe's style of gardening:

The offhandedness with which Oribe combines here the straight and the curved is, certainly, a mark of "irrespect" toward the order of nature; but also toward the order of culture, which would have an inclination to a higher degree of homogeneity and regularity (whether of "natural" stones, or of cut stones). The co-presence of the two styles of stone arrangement, denying the fulfillment of neither of these two orders, *produces an effect of splitting of the ordinary sense* (the irregular side of the grand paving stone has in effect the air of splitting!).

I will pay attention to the close relationship between this splitting and the above mentioned "evocation of the natural." For, Oribe, though in sharp antithesis to Rikyū, is not a mere mannerist; for, trying to systematize the apparent contingency of nature, he attains a brilliant success *in splitting culture, and hence in rendering passage to the sense of nature*—in thus giving birth to nature. In the pavement of the Ennan [a garden in Kyoto], there appears something of itself, which disarranges the extrinsic orders. Does one define nature otherwise?[6]

Berque comments also on the orthodox evaluation of the "Rikyū-esque" style that arose in the first half of the Edo period:

In addition, I do not think that it is chance if the [Back to Rikyū]—i.e. to the [natural]—, which will mark subsequent decades, coincides with the steps taken under the police order of the Tokugawa regime: striving to found itself in nature, such an order could no longer admit such dividing of orders as Oribe had brought forth. The [natural] style was better suited to it—but this time it was deprived of the creativity of Rikyū, it was dena-turalized because it was more closely subordinated to the usage (which I have called, a little too strongly, "The referential"). To the very extent that the society takes nature as a paradigm—a model which culture repro-duces—true nature cannot in fact be expressed other than by a creative leap vis-à-vis this paradigm. In other words, in the context where culture exalts the natural, nature is not just to do the natural.[7]

Second example: Berque holds in high esteem the poetics of Fujitani Mitsue (1768–1832), who was quite an isolated figure in the tradition of the Kokugaku school and has thus been regarded as manifestly nonor-thodox:

Mitsue professed that this side of the opposition of the *ri* (principle, order, reason) and the *yoku* (desire) works the "motive of life" *(inochi no gendō)*, which unifies nature. This latent motive is the "grand Desire" *(dai yoku)* which integrates us into the cosmos—Bergson might have called it The "élan vital," and Lévi-Strauss "vouloir obscur". . . . In order to redis-cover this fundamental motive, one must distinguish between the "latent way" *(yūro)*, which is that of *yoku*, and the "patent way" *(kenro)*, which is that of *ri*. Neo-confucianism is committed only to the latter, being different from Shintoism (here Mitsue opposes the "way of men" with the "way of the gods"). What one must do is to take the way of the gods, namely, to give way to *yoku* in its latency, while in its patency, one should try to reflect on this course in terms of *ri*. Thereupon, Mitsue founded his theory of the "spirit of words" *(kotodama)* and his poetics. His poetics gives a central role to the "inversion of words" *(tōgo)*, which consists, so as to express more effectively, in saying the "reverse" of what one thinks. It is not a simple inversion on the verbal level (white/black, etc.), but a true change of dimension: to pass from the word, which is the obverse, to the spirit, which is the reverse, so as to surmount the pillory of words which "kill the gods." "The gods are present in the moment of inversion, and are nothing other than the spirits of words."[8]

The following is another comment of Berque on the poetics of Mitsue, which one might regard as a sort of "negative theology" in the tradition of Japanese culture:

By a deconstructive recurrence to itself, culture can give way to a sense which proper sense blockades. This latent sense, which might be called *kami* (gods) or "nature" (or also "unconscious," "dream," etc.), would not reveal itself without paying the price of uncovering (the Greek would perhaps say *alètheia*), or "dislocation," of the logos, which, for the moment, disavows reason. But, for the moment only, because reason soon recovers the space which it had left vacant, whether by "collection" (incorporating the new sense into its proper constructions [as Kuhn defines it]), or by obliteration (forgetting or obstructing the new sense).

The example of the inversion of the word shows us that Japanese literature could *deliberately dislocate the word, establish the vacancies of the cultural sense so as to let rise the sap of the more profound sense of nature.* In so doing, it followed the tendency defined above; for this influence, which was voluntarily sought, in turn nourished the literature (the culture) itself. Surrealism did the same thing (in terms, evidently, of our proper culture).[9]

V

"At this degree of distortion of the 'médiance' (human-milieu relationship), the inversion of the relation of the society to the place came close to surrealism: the functionalization of territory, demanded by an economic need, presupposed the utter destruction of all the elements of the nature in that territory."

The preceding, already quoted at the beginning of this essay, was Berque's comment on the project of the petrochemical megalocomplex on Shibushi Bay in Kyushu during a period of "High Growth" in the Japanese economy. Berque continues as follows: "A reaction could not but be forthcoming—in the form of a 'residential protest' movement."

Berque indicates thus the indispensable role played by residential protest in stopping this destruction of the environment by "High Growth":

Now, before the residential protest movement was mounted in opposition to the devastation which the environment was suffering, and thereby blocked, de facto, the mechanisms of "High Growth," no brake of an internal nature (that is to say, coming from a rational inquiry into the "why" of the things that were happening) restrained the persons responsible for this devastation. Quite to the contrary, the book that Tanaka Kakuei published just before his accession to the post of Prime Minister in 1972: *Nihon Retto Kaizoron* (Remodeling the Archipelago), a veritable swan song of the official ideology of High Growth, proposed doing even more and even faster what had been done up until then.[10]

Unmistakably, Berque sees here in residential protest a manifestation of the "reason of the milieu" ("la raison du milieu": a sort of "wisdom of the earth") against the reason of the technocrats. This "reason of the milieu", which is expressed as the voice of nature, is a response to the image of environmental distruction as surrealist distortion. This response itself manifests a surrealistic coloring in the primal outcry of the local residents. Here, in this (vertical) dialogue in an extreme situation, the "reason of the milieu" reveals a dimension that is neither subjective nor objective, but just "trajective" or transverse. It expresses itself through a symbol which serves as a differential indicating a tangent to the so-called real world in which we live. Here, in this dimension, a surrealistic expression will signify or symbolize a crisis that we actually confront as well as a hope of escaping therefrom. (One might recall here the tableaux of the A-bomb by the Marukis or "Guernica" by Picasso.)

This "reason of the milieu," which, by virtue of its being Janus-faced and transcending all the horizontal dimensions of the real world, could serve as a mediator between symbolic praxis and reality. It will also surely serve, I hope, as an indispensable mediator of the dialogue between the East and the West. By way of this "reason of the milieu," the crisis and the hope, the reason and the counter-reason, and the ratio and the inverse ratio will coincide with each other. The useless will prove itself, paradoxically, as in Lao Tzu and Chuang Tsu, to be most useful and valuable.

Notes

1. Augustin Berque, *La sauvage et l'artifice—Les Japonais devant la nature* (Gallimard, 1986), p. 239; my translation and my emphasis.

2. Ibid., p. 212.

3. Ibid., p. 287; my emphasis.

4. Ibid., pp. 258–259.

5. Ibid., pp. 281–282.

6. Ibid., pp. 201–202; my emphasis.

7. Ibid., p. 202.

8. Ibid., pp. 187–188.

9. Ibid., p. 189; my emphasis.

10. Ibid., p. 211.

RICHARD WOLLHEIM

WHY ART CHANGES

I

In this essay I should like to consider whether there is anything in the nature of a general answer to the perennial question, Why does art change? By a general answer I mean one that does not rely on special or unique circumstances like military or natural disaster, or even the presence on the artistic scene of an exceptionally powerful artistic personality: though one thing that we might expect of a general answer, as I conceive of it, is that it should explain why the artistic scene is as reactive as it all but invariably is to strong personalities of an innovatory kind.

Two kinds of general answer I shall initially foreswear. Both have had their advocates. Indeed by far the greater number of those who have attempted our question have settled for an answer of the one or other of these two kinds. The first kind of answer has it that artistic change is fundamentally artistic *progress* in that, when art changes its overall appearance, this is because some one aim of art is thereby more effectively realized. The most famous advocate of this view in Western culture was Giorgio Vasari in his monumental *Lives of the Painters,* who saw in the story of Italian art the successive conquest of appearances. The second kind of answer has it that artistic change of a deep kind corresponds to changes in perception: not necessarily to changes in the underlying mechanisms of perception or in the nature of the visual field —though the view is often presented in a way that is regrettably imprecise on this point—but perhaps only to changes in the emphasis that the artist puts upon, or in the attention that he gives to, different organizing features of the visual field, which itself remains constant. The great German-speaking art historians of the turn of the century, such as Heinrich Wölfflin and Alois Riegl, are the best-known advocates of this view. Neither kind of answer seems to me plausible, and both present additional problems of interpretation.

As the thinkers I have quoted suggest, I shall, in proposing an answer to the question, frame it solely for the visual arts. I believe that analogous answers can be worked out for the other arts, but I shall not, in this essay, even try to show how this might be done. Another restriction under which this essay labors is that the answer it gives is formulated solely with Western culture in mind. To some this will seem straight off a grave deficiency. I think not: and that is because I believe that, in issues like this, it is only when we are provided with an answer that is well-formulated for a given context that we can begin to judge whether its application is likely to be dependent on, hence limited to, that context, or whether it is wider, indeed universal, in its scope. An analogy that impresses me is the nature of language, and the dispute over its universality. For the view that all languages have a common structure was not a view that could claim cogency until someone produced a well-formulated structural account of one natural language. With such an account available it then became easier to discuss whether all the structure with which it credited the pilot language was attributable to purely local or to universal factors, and at the same time the question of how to identify what would be the parallel structural features (once we believe there are such things) in other languages became an amenable question.

II

One reason why it might be thought that the answer that I shall give has a good chance of possessing, if not universality, then at least a broad application, is that my answer is grounded in the nature of pictorial content or (as I shall say) pictorial "meaning": it derives, as you will see, from how pictures gain meaning. It seems to be a reasonable assumption that pictures gain meaning in a way that is transcultural. After all, how they gain meaning is part of what leads us to think of them as pictures. So, if pictures are transcultural, pictorial meaning (or how it arises) is transcultural, and, if pictorial meaning is transcultural, then (if I am right) why artistic change occurs is transcultural.

The first and most fundamental thing to be said about pictorial meaning is that it arises in a quite different way from the way in which linguistic meaning comes about. One reason why this is a fundamental thing to say is that it goes against a whole lot of theories on the subject, which are currently in favor, and which may be identified through their resolve to assimilate pictorial to linguistic meaning. These theories include structuralism, hermeneutics, semiotics (when this is conceived of as offering a unified view or a homogeneous account of all signs), and probably poststructuralism. They reveal the tendency that leads me to group them together in their common practice of talking of "reading" pictures: something which I am convinced we do not do. We look at them, we see them, our eyes interpret them.

The most perspicuous way of showing the difference between linguistic and pictorial meaning is to concentrate on one form of pictorial meaning: representational meaning, or the capacity that a flat surface has to produce the sense—the sense, not the illusion—of objects in depth. (It is a derivative feature of the difference between linguistic and pictorial meaning that, whereas there is only one form of linguistic meaning, or that which semantics studies, there are several different forms of pictorial meaning, for example, representational, expressive, metaphorical.)

I turn, then, to the ways in which representational meaning differs from linguistic meaning. I shall use as my example the picture of a bison contrasted with the word "bison." Imagine, if you will, the two, picture and word, side by side, and then set over against them an actual bison.

In the first place, there is a difference in the role played by experience in the two cases. With the word—as, of course, also with the picture—we need experience epistemically, that is, we need experience in order to discover what word, what picture, is there. But in the case of the word, that is all there is for experience to do: once we have found out what word it is, no further purpose is served by further experience of the word. We cannot stare ourselves into an understanding of the word, whereas something like that is just what we do in the case of the picture. By looking at the picture, we can, other things being equal, find out what the picture means: in standard cases the meaning of the picture is given in the experience of it. By contrast, once we know what the word is, what we further need to know, in order to discover what it means, is something in the nature of a rule, or a convention, linking the word to some part of the world: something of the sort that has made it seem plausible to many thinkers to say that language in its relation to the world is arbitrary.

A closely connected point, which any account of pictorial representation overlooks to its total detriment, is that we can—can and *do*—learn, by looking at pictures of things, what the things pictured look like, even when we have never seen the things in actuality. The two points are related. They are related in this way: If, as the first point has it, we can find out what pictures mean by looking at them, it does not follow that we can always *say* what they mean, or put a word to what they represent. Indeed, with abstract pictures we can go very little way in this direction: we can say only such things as that they represent large or amorphous shapes. However, when we do learn to put a word to what some picture represents, then, because of the first point, we know what the sort of thing to which the word applies looks like; that is, the second point is established.

Second, there is a crucial element of transfer in our understanding of what pictures mean. By "transfer," I have this in mind: Given that other things are equal, and that we can grasp what the picture of a bison means, then there is every reason to think that we shall be able, when shown it, to grasp what the picture of, say, a hippopotamus means; that is to say, if we know what a hippopotamus looks like, we shall be able to recognize it as the picture of, say, a hippopotamus, and if we do not know what a hippopotamus looks like, we shall be able to learn this from looking at the picture. However, there is no analogous transfer in the case of language. Suppose we were foreigners to the English language; then it would be groundless to think that the fact that we had grasped what the word "bison" means would in any way advance our chances, on first hearing it, of understanding what the word "hippopotamus" means. Learning each word is a distinct cognitive achievement: we cannot, it is true, learn a language a word at a time, but for each word that we learn, there is no other word, there is no other group of words, that we thereby learn or are likely to understand.

In the preceding argument the phrase "other things being equal" might seem to require clarification. Indeed, does it not beg the question? For it might be contended that other things *are* equal, or that representation can be grasped, only when a set of rules or conventions has been learned and internalized. I do not believe this, and in using the phrase "other things being equal," I was acknowledging the existence of those anthropologists, in many cases ideologically inspired, who have claimed that the capacity to grasp representation, or what I call seeing-in, to which I shall turn in a few minutes, though present in some cultures or amongst some races, is absent from others. None of the evidence produced by these anthropologists in fact supports such a conclusion, though it does something to suggest a far weaker hypothesis: namely, that in cultures where certain comparatively subtle cues to indicate represented depth are traditionally absent, representations that depend on such cues will, when introduced to members of the culture, initially not be seen as such. In talking of other things being equal, I was, then, making the point that this kind of complication was not present.

Third, the kind of experience that we draw upon in order to discover what a picture means is continuous with our ordinary experience of the world. Reading is not: it invokes a special skill, not an enlarged perceptual capacity. However, this last point about the connection between experience as it enters into the understanding of pictures and our normal experience of the world is, it must be recognized, a quite generalized point as far as pictorial understanding is concerned. It is not confined to what I have so far been talking about: that is, representational meaning. It holds for every form of pictorial meaning, each form either drawing on different experiential or perceptual capacities or, if not that, drawing on the same capacities as other forms but doing so differently. In *Painting as an Art,*[1] I attempted to show this in detail for all the various forms of pictorial meaning that I there distinguished. In this essay I shall briefly show for just two forms of pictorial meaning—indeed the two forms that I take to be basic—how the connection holds. I shall do so for representational and for expressive meaning.

In the case of representational meaning, the picture, if it is to disclose its meaning, must engage with a perceptual capacity that we have, probably innately, which I call "seeing-in." Seeing-in is triggered off by the presence within the visual field of a differentiated surface—not every differentiated surface will do, but I doubt if it is possible to say anything informative about what kind of differentiation qualifies—and, when seeing-in is activated, there occurs an experience that has two aspects to it. The subject simultaneously is observant of the differentiated surface as such *and* is aware of something absent in front of, or sometimes behind, something else. This capacity precedes representational art both logically and historically: logically, in that we can see things in surfaces that neither are nor are believed by us to be representations—for example, stained walls, frosted panes of glass, clouds, the bark of trees—and historically, in that our remotest ancestors surely engaged in such exercises long before they thought to decorate the caves they lived in with the images of the animals they hunted.

In the case of expressive meaning, we find structurally a similar situation. The expressive picture, if it is to disclose its meaning, must engage with a specific perceptual capacity that we have, which again precedes the form of pictorial meaning it explains—in this case, expression in art—both logically and historically. I call this capacity "expressive perception," and expressive perception occurs when, say, looking out across a broad estuary with many fingers of water oozing their way out towards the sea, and flat salt-marshes, and low-flying birds, we find the scene melancholy and the sadness starts to penetrate us, or when we catch sight of a small Alpine village at the foot of snowclad mountains, the large timbered barns and the steeple of the church breaking through the apple blossoms, and we find the scene happy and our spirits rise. Finding a scene melancholy or happy through looking at it are cases of expressively perceiving in a certain way, and this capacity, too—as indeed the examples show—precedes expressive art both logically and historically.

III

In one important respect, the account I have just offered of the interaction between pictorial understanding and perceptual capacity and of how the latter contributes to the former, is deficient: an element is missing, and this omission can totally vitiate the account. For I have so far spoken as if any experience, provided only that it is of the right perceptual kind, will serve to give the meaning of the picture: I have spoken as if, for instance, a given representational picture represents whatever anyone can see in it. Such a view is not what I am proposing and it is altogether wrong. The representational meaning of a picture is given only by what can be *correctly* seen in it, and what is correctly seen in a picture is a matter of what can be seen in it *and* accords with the fulfilled intentions of the artist. Similarly the expressive meaning of a picture is given by what can be expressively perceived in it *and* accords with the fulfilled intentions of the artist. A fully articulated account of pictorial meaning, generalized for all forms of meaning, will show that, for every picture, its meaning depends upon a triad of factors; they are (a) the fulfilled intentions of the artist, which cause him to produce (b) a surface marked in a certain way, which in turn causes (c) a certain experience in the mind of a suitably sensitive, suitably informed, spectator.

IV

One problem to which the broad account of pictorial meaning that I have just been offering gives rise is this: What is the proper relationship between the first and the third of these factors? Or: Within what limits will the artist want the experience that the spectator has on looking at the surface as he, the artist, has marked it, to fall, if he is to feel that his intention has been fulfilled? The truth of the matter is that there is no general answer to this question, and in this respect the example of representational painting, which is useful in so many ways, may prove misleading: it may encourage us to oversimplify the issue. For it is inviting to think that, if, say, an artist wants to represent a bison, there is a neatly circumscribed range of experiences within which that experience which the spectator has on looking at the marked surface must fall if the artist's intention is to be fulfilled, and the picture is in consequence to represent a bison. However, even within representation this way of conceiving the issue can come to seem inadequate. For so far we have been concentrating narrowly on what has been called, not totally perspicuously, the *what* of representation. Once, however, we broaden our range and consider what may contrastingly be called the *how* of representation, the issue starts to look different. For now suppose that what interests the artist is not a mere matter of representing a bison, but is a concern with representing the bison in a certain way: as, for instance, aggressive, or lordly, or ruminative. I suggest that it will no longer seem quite so obvious what experiences the artist should want to induce in the mind of the spectator, hence it will not seem quite so easy for him to know how he should mark the surface.

However, as we turn from representational meaning to expressive meaning, the question of how the spectator's experience should relate to the artist's intention if the artist's intention is to succeed, or (the same thing) if the spectator's experience is to capture the meaning of the picture, will get more evidently problematic. With expressive meaning the artist could never find it plausible to think that there was a class of experiences delimited in advance of his making his picture, out of which he must pick one to induce in the mind of the spectator by the way he marks the surface, if his intention is to be fulfilled. No, it must be evident to him that the only way in which he could form a view about which experience went with his present intention was through a process of trial and error. The matching of experience to intention is essentially improvisatory. And one further reason why a consideration of expressive meaning forces this upon us—though, in fact, a more thoughtful consideration of representational meaning could have led us to the same conclusion—is that by the time we come to expressive meaning we evidently cannot make do with the narrow conception of intention that the literature of aesthetics encourages. Intention, if it is to fill the role in an account of pictorial meaning that I have assigned to it, must include a whole range of psychological factors in the artist's head, provided only that they are causally active in the making of the picture. They will include desires, beliefs, emotions, phantasies, memories, hopes, as well as what we should more narrowly call intentions. But with this broader view of intention before us, the question returns with more urgency: How, or by what process, is the artist able to use trial and error to match the experience that he hopes the marked surface will induce in the spectator to the intention that is meanwhile causing him to mark the surface?

In *Painting as an Art* I made a suggestion, which was intended to do two things in one. It was intended to give us a better conceptualization of the issue, and also to allow us some insight into how the issue is dealt with in practice. The suggestion was that we should first recognize that, when we talk in this context of a spectator, we are talking not of a person or of a class of persons but of a role: a role filled by someone who can and will fill other roles. Having done this, we must then realize that the crucial application of this point is that the artist, the person who fills the role of artist, must also fill the role of spectator. It is important to see why he has to do this. He assumes the role of spectator not, as any one of the rest of us might, so as to find out what he had made, but so as to make it. What he makes he makes with—that is, he makes partly with —his eyes. A useful analogy would be this: the artist uses his eyes in the way in which the driver of a car—not in the way in which the passenger in the car—uses his. The driver, the adequate driver, does not use his eyes to see where he has driven: he uses his eyes to drive. If the artist uses his eyes to paint, one of the uses to which he puts his eyes is to see, as he marks the surface, whether the marked surface that results is likely to produce in the mind of a spectator an experience that is adequately attuned to the intention that exists in his own, in the artist's, mind and that is causing him to mark the surface as he does. An additional use, a further and intimately related use, to which the artist also puts his eyes, is to gain an ever-sharpened idea of just what it is for an experience to be attuned to an intention: something on which he is likely to feel that he can never know enough.

V

If you have been patient enough to follow me this far, you are in for a pleasant surprise. Let me tell you that we are now moving into the area in which it will be possible for me to answer my question, "Why does art change?" In other words, the basic materials are present.

For, as I see things, the fundamental reason for overall artistic change lies within the essentially improvisatory nature of the fit of the spectator's experience to the artist's intention. My claim is this: if an artist or, more forcefully, a succession of artists were repeatedly to induce the same experience in order to convey the same intention, this procedure would eventually result in failure. By talking of failure, what I have in mind is that, though the spectator might continue to recognize the intention that had motivated the succession of artists, this recognition would cease to be experiential, it would become purely cognitive. The spectator would no longer have the kind of experience in which meaning can be grasped. In this way, the artist, or succession of artists, would cease to make meaningful pictures: even though it might be evident what meaning the pictures would have had if they had had any.

At first this suggestion might seem artificial. Why should success, reiterated, spell failure? And if, after a while this might seem, like so many questions in philosophy, a real killer of a question only so long as we lose all contact with the subject matter it is putatively about—in this case, art—nevertheless the position itself, *my* position, might seem to create its own special problem. For we might wonder why it is that if, as spectators, we can become fatigued with a certain artistic solution once this is over-employed by a succession of artists, we do not become similarly fatigued with the solution in its original version once we have had a succession of encounters with it, or have been over-exposed to it.

In point of fact this last problem is not one that is conjured into existence by my position. It is a deep problem, and one whose existence all those seriously interested in the arts have to be ready to concede. It has proved fatal to the various attempts to apply communication theory, and the associated notion of redundancy, to the arts and to our perception of them. I think that a resolution of this problem requires that we give proper weight to the broad historical framework through which the spectator has to perceive the work of art. Without such a framework many of the properties for which we admire works of art—originality, ingenuity, spontaneity, freedom, independence—just will not adhere to them. They will fall off, like recycled stamps.

However, artificiality is a serious charge. Can it really be the case that something seemingly so profound as that art has a history—for that, after all, is the issue with which we are dealing—can be explained in terms of something seemingly so fortuitous as fatigue? If artificiality does attach to my suggestion—and I should like to make the point that, when we are dealing with a phenomenon essentially experiential as we have seen the visual arts to be, it is inappropriate to be absolutely certain that fatigue is an irrelevant reaction—then I believe that we have at our disposal a way of dissolving it. What we need to do is to reintroduce an idea I have already proposed: that, whenever we think about the spectator, we should recognize that this is a *role;* further, that it is a role that the artist can, indeed must, also adopt. The artist's adoption of the role of spectator is, I have suggested, crucial to his being, to his working as, an artist. So let us now build the idea of the artist as spectator, or of the spectator inside the artist, into my suggestion that it is the weariness of the spectator with old ways of matching experience to intention that motivates change in the arts. As soon as we do so, the suggestion rather radically alters character. It loses artificiality. For it no longer depicts change in the arts as led from the outside: it restores our intuitive conception of it as driven from the inside. It arises from something that occurs in the artist's head as he fixes his eyes upon the surface which his hand is in the art of marking. And what drives it is not something superficial; what drives change is nothing less than the artist's concern to preserve for his art its claim to meaning.

VI

It would be wrong to put forward an account of artistic change even as schematic as this without giving any indication of what the countervailing forces, or the forces adverse to change, might be.

Within the very delimited domain which is my primary or initial concern—the visual arts of Western culture—the most manifest countervailing force is that of style. By "style" I mean style in its primary usage, or "individual style." Individual style may be contrasted with what I call "general style": a term that I use to cover period style, and school style, as well as the great recurrent, historical styles, such as classicism and (as some art historians use the term) the baroque. Now there is nothing in the nature of things that corresponds to general style: invoking a general style is in effect just a way of classifying together a mass of material that seems, at any rate at a given moment, to be susceptible of common description. However, there is something real that corresponds to individual style. In those artists who have achieved an individual style—and it is distinctive of my view that this is an achievement, hence not to be automatically attributed to all—style is a highly complex and well-structured disposition that accounts for not uniformity of output but something far more elusive, which is the commonality of a single artist's response to different tasks or problems. In the visual arts, individual style has a special significance, and it has so for the often overlooked reason that in these arts style is a modification of the psychomotor system. The same is not true of the other arts, or, more precisely, it is true of all of them to a lesser degree, and of some of them not at all.

If the foregoing account of individual style is true, and if style is, in turn, as significant a factor in the development of the visual arts as this account suggests, then there will be something in the nature of a dialectical relationship or tension between style and the factor that I have identified as fatigue. One way of putting this would be to say that characteristically old style delays change, but new style, when it appears on the scene, has the potential to accelerate it.

VII

Some might think that this account holds true only of the modern age, others that it holds true only of Western culture. Both groups of critics might be right—though, I have to say, I would be surprised. But the broad theoretical *caveat* I want to introduce is this: that it is crucial to recognize that my suggestion has no quantitative aspect. It neither asserts nor implies anything about, say, the particular period of time within which the spectator will find similar experiences fatiguing, or about the particular degree of similarity between experiences that will cause him to find them fatiguing, or about the particular degree of dissimilarity that he will expect of new experiences if they are to restore meaning to art. I very deliberately did not introduce this kind of consideration into my account. Such considerations certainly seem to be culturally or historically relative. What is acceptable repetition in one culture will not seem so in another; what calls for innovation at one moment of history will be readily tolerated at another; and what will seem an appropriate response by the artist to either kind of situation in one place, at one time, will seem excessively brash, or gratuitously muted, in different circumstances.

My suggestion is that, if the broad account I offer seems promising, what we should aim to do is to combine it with a number of different time frames, see if any of these distort its essential features, and, if we find that they do not, then try them out as offering suitably varied accounts of artistic change for different societies, different periods. In this way it might ultimately prove plausible to offer a qualitatively similar account of the development of the visual arts in Western and Eastern cultures, despite the enormous surface differences that exist, over which relativists have always gloated and always will.

Note

1. A number of the ideas deployed in this essay are to be found in Richard Wollheim, *Painting as an Art,* the 1984 Andrew W. Mellon Lectures in the Fine Arts (Princeton, 1987), where they are in certain cases argued for in greater detail.

Culture and the Religious

FREDERICK J. STRENG

THE TRANSCENDENTAL IN
A COMPARATIVE CONTEXT

Despite the often noted secularity in our modern, technology-domi-nated society, a concern for the transcendental in human experience remains.[1] We continue to seek resources for well-being beyond those determined by economically and politically powerful social groups, and ways of knowing that transcend our own private perceptions. In new ways we continue to ask longstanding philosophical questions on how do we get beyond personal subjectivity and cultural-social bias.

In recognizing that the human awareness of the transcendental is found in the past and present I want also to acknowledge from the beginning the cultural and historical contextuality of this presentation. This philosophical analysis assumes the value of analytic reflection, and the significance of understanding ourselves and our social-physical environment. Later I will indicate diverse modes of awareness by which people have apprehended the transcendental, and point out that a con-cern for meaning is only one mode in which the transcendental is known. However, I use procedures of analogical comparison, and appeals to historical-cultural forms in this essay in an attempt to "make sense" of my being-in-existence. Thus, this presentation uses a mode of consciousness focused on meaning in order to communicate something about the transcendental.

A second reflection on contextuality regards the qualifying phrase "in a comparative context" found in the title. My presentation is focused through the lenses of similarity and difference. On the one hand, there is the distinctiveness, the particularity, found in historical conditions; on the other, there is the assumption that there is some continuity, at least some partial identity, among the experiences of the transcendental. This assumption about the continuity does not automatically require a com-mitment to finding a universal essence at the heart of all the forms of transcendental awareness. It only predisposes the investigator to formu-late analogies between those aspects of phenomena that have similar form, and to seek deeper conditioning structures or patterns within similar forms by which to compare and contrast groups or types of phenomena. By considering the meaning of the transcendental as found in its diverse variety we force ourselves to confront "the other" in two senses. First, we respond to other people in their particular (and different) physical and social expression; second, we engage different dimensions of that experienced reality which other people regard as transcending themselves.

A comparative study has a unique capability for raising questions about the meaning of human expressions in that it heightens one's sensitivity to one's own mind-set, which, however, need not be frozen into early childhood patterns or cultural habits. In the confrontation with the "otherness" of alternative positions, we find ourselves in an ambiguous position. We look at the diverse expressions of the transcendental from our own historically conditioned standpoint, which provides a structure for experiencing our own freedom and integration of relationships with others; at the same time we acknowledge the importance of the differences found in the alternative positions as necessary for our own self-transcendence. It is this ambiguity found in the embeddedness of transcendental awareness in specific conditions of value-formation to which I want to address my remarks. By briefly exploring aspects of this issue we can at least identify some problem areas which appear when we take seriously both the conditionedness of any expression of the transcendental (including one's own) and the cross-cultural general human effort to gain some self-transcendence. The three aspects are (1) the procedural significance of taking cultural-historical particularity seriously, (2) the recognition of different modes of human awareness in expressing the transcendental, and (3) suggestions about the character of self-transcending awareness in a comparative context.

I

When we consider the transcendental in a comparative context we are doing a certain kind of thinking. We form ideas in response to tangible objects, such as other culturally defined concepts, practices, and expressed attitudes. As specific objects, social forms are limited by historical-cultural conditions. At the same time, when the object is an expression of the transcendental, we recognize that these determinate images and symbols have multiple levels of meaning. They may refer to political, psychological, and philosophical contexts simultaneously. By focusing on these cultural objects we understand these expressions as objects external to our own subjectivity. They are part of our environment. We give then value—without judging their validity according to our implicit standards—as conditioned expressions of a human environment that extends beyond our own conditioned awareness. This kind of thinking recognizes and values the distinctiveness of other people in that the distinctiveness is seen as a specific variation in a general human situation of conditionedness; the difference between "them" and "us" is not necessarily that they have made a mistake in using a language, images, or practices different from our own. By being there, these expressions are recognized as valuable in the subjectivity of others, and at the same time valuable to our subjectivity as part of our social environment.

To understand what someone means by appealing to self-transcendent consciousness requires the location of specific ideas, feelings, and actions within systems of interrelated data. Such systems contain implicitly normative rules, or patterns of psychological-mental and physical-social action, which determine what can and cannot be integrated into a system of meaning. With regard to philosophical and religious expressions of the transcendental, these structures include language learning, social patterning, and value-forming procedures such as meditation, analytical reflection, or ritual. The variations within human experience take on the formidable character of identity and self-transcendence. Alternate historical-cultural expressions of the transcendental in our global social environment, then, are not just variations of a single human procedure of transcendental awareness, but incommensurable alternatives whose understanding requires an imaginative and emotional shift from one orientation, one normative procedure, to another. In order to take the comparative context of our task seriously, then, we must recognize the significance of the diverse normative procedures—not simply the conclusions—of different expressions of the transcendental.

Before moving on to the recognition of a continuity—thus, some comparability—between incommensurable approaches to the transcendental, I want to comment on two recent statements by philosophers who recognize a fundamental pluralism in human approaches to truth and reality. The first is Walter Watson's analysis in his book *The Architectonics of Meaning*.[2] In his book Watson attempts to show that at the core of different philosophical systems there are different principles which determine what counts as facts (reality) in human reflective experience. Each principle contains unacknowledged value judgments, but presumes that it is grounded in "conditions of knowing that are the same for all."[3] Thus, critiques of other philosophies *require* translating the others' claims into terms that fit into one's own conditions for knowing, and thus are not critiques of what has been asserted within their own procedures of knowing. Truth, then, "admits of more than one formulation";[4] at fundamental levels of orientation to life the difference in approaches does not allow for systems of thought to agree fully. However, they can be compared within the context of one system or another as long as we remember that we can use only one system at a time.[5] This assessment of our situation in comparative philosophy is correct, it seems to me; thus, it becomes important to recognize the particularity of the comparative approach one takes.

The second point that I want to consider is found in Raimondo Panikkar's essay "What Is Comparative Philosophy Comparing?"[6] There he recognizes that despite the fact that the encounter with another orientation stretches one's conceptual formulations, and one can affirm that there are very different ways of reaching intelligibility, still a person does not stand exactly in the place of another person. This raises the issue of the possibility to know in a transcendental manner what is beyond the limits of one's own framework of intelligibility. He argues:

> Pluralism is not concerned with multiplicity or diversity as such, but with the incommensurability of human constructs on homologous issues. The problem of pluralism touches the limits of the intelligible (not just for us but in itself). . . . It touches the shores of the ineffable and thus of silence.[7]

In answer to the question posed in his title, then, he suggests that comparative philosophy is an exchange of myths, even when we extend the horizon of our own myth, and its inherent structural procedure, to include the assertions of other myths. In a summary statement, he notes:

> Comparative philosophy, qua philosophy, makes us aware of our own myth by introducing us to the myth of others and by this fact changes our own horizon. . . . It saves us from falling into the fallacy of believing that all the others live in myths except us.[8]

Here, again, is a recognition that we and others must take a position on "homologous issues" which is conditioned by the peculiarity of standing in one place rather than another. By affirming this, we acknowledge both the possibilities and limits of our own procedure for intelligibility. To know this, of course, is no small disclosure, especially when we consider the issues of "the transcendental." By recognizing the particularity not only of the subject of understanding, but also the particularity of our own approach, we acknowledge the need to engage other orientations cross-culturally and to provide a self-critical perception of limits and possibilities of any approach to a comparative topic.

What, then, is the particular approach in this comparative study of the transcendental? The principle of correlation between divergent expressions is that of analogies, homologous experiences, and similar behavior. This analogical procedure requires identifying human expressions that have a similar meaning for the participants as an investigator moves from one locus of experience to another. Comparisons are made by a perception of a common significance in two (or more) cultural data, and identifying that continuity of significance by a general class term. Analogies are conceptual lenses through which specific terms and practices within one cultural context are seen to have meanings similar to those terms and practices from another cultural context even if there is not etymological or precise morphological identity.

The procedure here will not focus on identifying linguistic correlates for the term "transcendental." Rather, we will attempt to identify analogous existential contexts in which many different concepts are used to indicate the normative procedure by which people live in self-transcending awareness. That is, we will identify and describe in the second part of this presentation several modes of human awareness in which self-transcendence functions. These modes of transcendental awareness are seen as expressions of a complex of presuppositions and social-institutional practices arising within specific cultural expressions, but which have cross-cultural similarities defined by common value-creating structures. These structures identify the complex of assumptions about the nature of knowing and practices for cultivating transcendent awareness in which particular concepts and procedures for self-transcendence are embedded.

The particular approach to this comparative study arises out of a concern for the practical significance of the transcendental. It focuses on the existential judgment found in different cultures regarding the power of self-transcending awareness to effect personal and social well-being. It requires examination of ritual, experiential, and ethical forms of transcendental awareness, as well as its reflective and conceptual articulation. Such an approach requires a shift from an analysis of symbolic representations and concepts about the transcendental in themselves to an exploration of the modes of human life in which the power of the transcendental is recognized as an effective means of fulfillment. Thus, various kinds of practice, such as religious worship, ethical obligation, and spiritual meditation are recognized as important contexts in which to understand the meaning of the transcendental.

By placing the issue of the transcendental in the context of lived experience, I am not suggesting that its nature is reduced to social fabrication. In the final section we will consider some implications of the variety of modes of self-transcendent awareness for the character of the transcendental. My point here is to affirm the need to place the issue of transcendental knowing in the context of lived experience as found in different cultural contexts. By focusing on this issue in terms of its effective power as perceived by its advocates we can understand the different ways that the transcendental is known and expressed. Indeed, it is perceived as a power to transform life because it expresses an often hidden reality ("spirits," or the spiritual reality), which provides deep meaning or superlative value, and is, as well, perceived as a determinative force (or forces), which must be taken into account if one is to live well in this life and after. As a force, the transcendental confronts human beings in their experiences of suffering, death, and evil as well as in exalted experiences of awe, wonder, and peace. In the next section we will look at different manifestations of transcendental awareness, which presume diverse modes of apprehension through which the transcendental is known and actualized.

II

A recurring theme in several recent books on "transcendence" is the diversity of its forms and meanings.[9] Nevertheless, the discussion typically and necessarily engages two complementary dimensions of the transcendental: (1) its ontological character and (2) the way or procedure for knowing and effectively actualizing this reality in daily living.

In the following discussion the descriptive focus is on different modes of actualizing the transcendental; however, a mode of awareness is not regarded by its proponents as an indication of some purely subjective perception of a mutually exclusive object. Rather, the transcendental reality is recognized by the advocates of any mode of awareness as the power which makes the apprehension and practical effect possible. Because the transcendental has to do with reality that is often hidden but very powerful for implementing a superior value in self-awareness, it is not experienced as totally separate from the mode of awareness of the knower/practitioner. The awareness of transcendence, in this study, is itself seen as a constituent of the participant's perceived state of being. In many historical expressions of the transcendental, two or three of these different modes of transcendental awareness are combined; but in other expressions, claims are made which emphasize one or another mode as distinct and normative in themselves. By focusing on examples which express modal differences, we can note how expressions of the transcendental which have diverse cultural-historical forms participate in the same procedure or mode of awareness.

We should also note that by concentrating on the different modes for apprehending the transcendental I cannot—due to space limitations— provide detailed analyses of the specific cultural-historical contexts in which the examples are found. The claim here is only that the examples have sufficient similarity to be included in the analogous concepts of distinct "modes of awareness," which indicate valorizing (or norm-producing) structures by which the transcendental is apprehended and expressed. The four structures which we will briefly describe are those which identify the transcendental reality with (1) symbolic meaning, (2) feeling, (3) moral social action, and (4) aesthetic sensitivity.

The first mode of apprehending the transcendental is a dominant one in Western philosophy and religion. It is the use, and analysis, of symbolic meaning expressed in words, concrete imagery, and gestures. In this mode the practitioner identifies the deepest sense of his/her being with meaning, and seeks to overcome the limitation of subjectivity by symbolic and conceptual knowledge of what there is. For example, the late Christian theologian Paul Tillich identified the deepest human consciousness with a struggle for fulfillment of meaning. His identification of ultimate reality with the pursuit of meaning is made clear when he claims:

> Meaning is the common characteristic and the ultimate unity of the theoretical and the practical sphere of spirit, of scientific and aesthetic, of legal and social structures. The spiritual reality in which the spirit-bearing forces (Gestalt) live and create is a meaning-reality [*Sinnwirklichkeit*].[10]

In this mode of apprehension hermeneutics has an ontological character; construction of meaning is an activity that underlies all human activities and expresses what human beings are.

In this mode of transcendental apprehension, the transcendental is depicted as the source of revelation, expressed in sacred words and ancient stories or myths which tell symbolically the origin of life. The sacredness of such special primordial "words" as the Bible, the Qur'an, and the Veda Saṃhitā, is defined, according to their followers, by their sense of the "otherness"—the transhuman, eternal, or divine character —of these words. At the same time, it is precisely these words, in distinction to others, through which the self-transcending truth is known. An important philosophical dimension of this mode of apprehending the transcendental through words is brought out by the Christian theologian Robert Scharlemenn in his book *The Being of God*. Here he analyzes the sense of the phrase "God is the word," asserting that some words or propositions present both the human sense of reality and its meaning at the same time.[11] Examples are "I," "this," "here," and "now." Likewise, "god" is such a term, which in its usage instantiates by presenting (donating), and not only interpreting, a transcendental thinking. The use of the term "god" is different from abstractions of subjectivity and objectivity as such, however, because it is used, says Scharlemann, "in the interest of a realm in which the division of subjects and objects no longer applies."[12] He argues:

> God is the unity of thinking and being, but this is perceptible only in the word that names it. To think of God is to think of the thought that is independent of us and others.[13]

Following this line of thinking, the term "god," and all names of god, plus divine actions and declarations, are indicators and instantiators of the transcendental, which is a negation of the finality of either subject or object, each of which then becomes a signification of a context that is beyond themselves.

In this mode of awareness the central issue is to recognize *which* primordial (sacred) word or name of god, *which* sacred scripture, *which* incantation or invocation is the signifier-cum-instantiator of the ultimate limit and possibility in which any particular form has meaning. It is also not surprising to find generation after generation within theistic communities, such as Jews, Christians, Muslims, and Sri Vaishnavas in Hinduism, spending immense effort to interpret and distinguish between better and worse understandings of that primordial word manifested in their stories, declarations, or chants.

When meaning is identified with being-in-existence, not only words, but also visual images and symbolic bodily actions become the means for instantiating the transcendental. In Judaism, where the true sacred name of God is unutterable because of its "otherness," ritual study of the Torah provides a bodily expression of engagement with the Holy One. Likewise, remembrance of sacred times, such as the Passover or the Sabbath, shapes in concrete ways the observant Jews' sense of the transcendental. E. M. Zuesse describes the transforming power of Jewish ritual when he writes:

> Submission to a ritual universe requires acceptance of a center outside the self; every act involves this "centering" transformative dynamic, thus sedimenting in the preconscious as well as conscious level the experience of otherness.[14]

Similarly, the Christian sacred ritual of the Eucharist as understood by Roman Catholicism symbolically repeats divine action in the world through Christ's sacrifice, and believers thereby have their meaning-world instantiated. Likewise, many tribal communities, in their initiations as adult members of a society, and in ritual and symbolic identifications with their ancestors and spirit beings, experience "an incipient transcendence" in the routines of daily living.[15]

Limitations of space here prevent an extensive elaboration of the three remaining modes of transcendent awareness. I will, however, try to indicate in a preliminary way the diverse grounds of awareness in order to make a case for disallowing an identification of the nature of the transcendental with only one or another mode of awareness and then universalizing that mode for all expressions of transcendent awareness. The second mode of awareness that I will briefly describe is that which identifies the reality of being-in-existence with feelings. In the past the personal experience of the sublime, the numinous, the "wholly other," typified in Rudolph Otto's analysis of the *tremendum mysterium et fascinans,* has been regarded as the core of transcendental awareness.[16] Here the emphasis is on wonder or awe, which combines the exuberance of sensing infinite possibilities with the knowledge that human beings are limited most profoundly by forces of which they are often unaware. The experience can be a dramatic, overpowering one in which a person experiences ecstasy; or it can be one of quiet comfort, or reverence, in which one senses the unknown depth of existence. While such a feeling reorders the priorities of living, the core awareness is not so much the instantiation of meaning given in the primordial word, but the sense that before the transcendent presence one forgets where one is. Eliot Deutsch has captured this awareness in his discussion on religious knowing when he writes:

> In knowing religiously there is the transformation of ordinary knowing in virtue of the realization, in loving, insightful wonderment, of that which is incommensurable with . . . ordinary knowing.[17]

This awareness, while located in radical subjectivity, gives up the ego-centered subjectivity that the "I" makes judgments about this experience within a larger rational framework. It is that sensitivity in many theistic traditions of the absolute sovereignty of God: "to God alone be glory." For example, the Muslim theologian Al-Nasafi declares the utter mystery of God, which is beyond all attempts at understanding, when he says of God:

> He is not an attribute, nor a body, nor an essence, nor a thing formed, nor a thing bounded, nor a thing numbered. . . . He is not described by *mahiya* [whatness], nor by *kafiyyah* [howness]. . . . There is nothing that resembles him.[18]

In this feeling-mode of transcendent awareness, worship, as a deep experience of the transcendent presence, becomes a unique and extraordinary way of knowing. Devotion, as a distinctive personal communion, a yearning for the divine presence and an overwhelming joy feeling that presence, is regarded as superior to any kind of reflection that acknowledges the transcendent as a universal ground of existence; likewise, it supercedes any silent meditation or yoga which eliminates all form. Such a way is exemplified in the unbounded affection for "the supreme person" which the Hindu theologian Rāmānuja describes for the wise ones (*jñānīs*). "These supreme devotees," comments John Carman in his study *The Theology of Rāmānuja*, "worship God from the sheer joy of experiencing Him in devotion and also with the consciousness that they are His sésas and are therefore obligated to render Him all that a servant should do for his master."[19] This way of transcendent awareness, then, denies that the reality of the transcendental is knowable by human reflection, and requires a radically different experiential sensitivity originating from another source beyond the horizon of symbolic or conceptual knowing.

The third mode of awareness that we will consider, by contrast, assumes that our being-in-existence is most deeply perceived in everyday moral actions. The transcendental is known in and through physical and social relationships; it is radically immanent. The rhythm and order found in nature and appropriate social relationships provide one with a comprehensive sense of the implicitly dynamic that transcends all particular forms, yet is found expressed in them. Thus, the transcendental is not a "wholly other" which is experienced internally through devotion; nor is it a sacred order and power manifested in symbols, sacraments, and the special use of words; it is a cosmic order, a set of relationships between all things, which provides the ultimate context in which particular actualizations of existence are possible.

This expression of the transcendental is found exemplified in the Chinese "Literati Tradition" ("Confucianism"), where the Tao is said to be immediately present in one's experience if a person is aware of one's proper place in the implicit harmony of things. In a statement credited to K'ung Tzu, we read:

> The Master said, "The *tao* is not far from man. If what one takes to be the *tao* is far from man, it cannot be considered [the true] *tao*."[20]

This principle of regularity present in everyday existence, however, is not an unchanging static order since internal to it there is movement or change. While this dynamic harmony has an inner tendency to bring about abundance and renewal, claim the advocates, the objects and events of existence have an openness, or freedom, to interact in ways that may or may not lead to their actualization, and which in human events require moral choices. The most profound moral choices manifest this immanent-transcendent dynamic harmony; so the concern for personal virtues such as sincerity *(ch'eng)* or humanness *(jen)* are not simply advocated for their social (instrumental) value. In his analysis of the *Chung-yung*, Tu Wei-ming affirms that it is precisely in the claim that human nature is imparted by Heaven "that morality in *Chung-yung* can be said to have a transcendent anchorage."[21] He continues:

> Actually, *Chung-yung* maintains that common human experience itself embodies the ultimate ground of morality, and thus provides the theoretical basis for actualizing the unity of Heaven and man in the lives of ordinary people.[22]

Another twentieth-century Chinese scholar, T'ang Chün-i, has described the awareness of the transcendental in life as the actualization of *jen*. He writes:

> At their early stage, infinity and transcendence are like a bud—a bud of "the will to create," a bud of creativity which spontaneously permeates our "human heart" in its immediacy. This is called "the seed of earnest *jen*." . . . It is embodied directly in our natural life and physical constitution, as a master of them, transforming our physical constitution into a subject of morality sustained and beautified by its creativity.[23]

For T'ang, as for Tu, the capacity for true morality, which makes human life worthwhile at all, is found in an ultimate context that transcends any individual or community purpose, but which must be actualized in physical, social, and personal events.

Another important expression of the transcendental in social action is found in the classical orthodox Brahmanical understanding of *dharma* (law, truth). In the early text *Taittirīya Āraṇyaka* (10.79) we find:

Dharma is the foundation of the whole universe. In this world people go unto a person who is best versed in dharma for guidance. By means of dharma one drives away evil. Upon dharma everything good is founded. Therefore, dharma is called the highest good. [24]

In his discussion of the traditional Hindu law books, T. R. V. Sastri points out that the *sanātana dharma* (which he translates as "perennial religion") applies to daily life and behavior in an all-embracing way; however, it should not be thought of as unchanged or never modified. [25] Rather, there are many different kinds of obligations and duties according to one's nature (birth) and particular circumstances, as well as different levels of fulfillment. While the performance of one's dharma as an expression of one's place in the cosmic order may require continual attention to interpreting sacred texts, the actual doing of one's duty— obedience to the eternal law—is the mode of actualizing the nature of the universe. As the *Manu Smṛti* (II.14) states:

For the man who obeys the law prescribed in the revealed texts and in the sacred tradition, gains fame in this (world) and after death unsurpassable bliss. [26]

By one's action (karma) in everyday social living, a person is participating in the transcendental. [27]

The fourth, and last, mode of transcendent awareness which we will briefly note is one which identifies an aesthetic sensitivity (for the lack of a better term) with reality. The core assumption here is that the quality of consciousness of the knower is as much a condition for the presentation of the transcendental reality as the object of knowledge. It stresses the importance of the freedom from a conventional subject-object mode of knowing in the awareness of that which is both beyond and within conditioned existence. It is a freedom which recognizes not only the power to construct and reconstruct our experienced world, but also the freedom to desist from such construction in special meditative awareness, which frees one from attachment to the constructions necessary for everyday living. This mode of awareness is typified in the knowledge of Brahman *(Brahmavidyā)* and yogic *Nirvīja-samādhi* in Hinduism (as well as in the realization of *nirvāṇa* and the perfection of wisdom, *prajñā-pāramitā*, in Buddhism, though space limitations prevent their description).

A prime example of this mode of transcendental awareness in the Hindu Upaniṣads is found in the *Bṛhadāraṇyaka Upaniṣad*. The diversity of what is seen in the conventional empirical world, in dreams, in language, and in symbols is unified in the "universal self" (IV.3.7) and is likened to deep sleep or the experience of sexual union, insofar as a separate ego-consciousness disappears. The *Bṛhadāraṇyaka Upaniṣad* IV.3, verses 21 and 23 describe it:

> Now when, asleep, he desires no desire and sees no dream, even this is his form (aspect, practically "state") that desires (only) the Self, that has attained desires, that has no desires. Just as a man who is embraced by a beloved woman knows nothing outer or inner, even so this bodily Self (atman), when it is embraced by the Self-consisting-of-intelligence, knows neither outer nor inner.

> If, then, he does not see—though seeing (having the power of sight), he sees no object of sight, since it (or he?) is indestructible. But there is not, then, any second thing, other and separate from him, which he might see.[28]

This Self, which is the unity of empirical objects, of being *(sat)* and non-being *(asat),* is later (IV.4.5) identified with Brahman, indicating that this Self is both the individual who transcends ego-identification and the transcendental reality which cannot be located simply in the subjective transcending awareness.[29]

A similar demand to shift from conventional perceptions of objects to a mode of contemplation beyond the fluctuations of the mind is found in the Yoga philosophy of Patañjali. Based on an assumption that there are different levels of consciousness, here the key issue in knowing the transcendental reality is the ability to still the modifications of the mind; without this effort the core of one's being, the Seer *(puruṣa)* is hidden within mental-emotional images constructed by one's conditioned ego. The *Yoga Sūtras* (I.2–4) declare:

> Yoga is the suppression of the modifications of the mind (2)
> Then the Seer abides in itself. (3)
> At other times the seer appears to assume the form of the modifications of the mind. (4)[30]

The ability to get beyond the habitual states of knowing, characterized by restlessness and distraction, but also by moments of concentration, requires a "balanced insight" into the distinction between the pure Self *(puruṣa)* and the quieted mind fixed in one-pointedness *(buddhi).* Anything manifested even by the most subtle mental concentration is limited and transient. True liberation is the realization of "the Seer" or pure self without modification by the most subtle mental fluctuations.[31] While the Sāṃkhya-Yoga metaphysics is regarded as dualistic—in its distinction between *puruṣa* and *prakṛti*—and the Upaniṣadic expression given above is nondualistic *(advaita),* both require a mode of apprehension that negates the kind of knowing which considers the subject-object dichotomy to be a necessary condition of knowledge; both reject mental or physical action as a necessary condition for realizing the transcendental reality in life.

III

An examination of different modes of transcendent awareness forces us to recognize not only different understandings of the transcendental, but also different evaluative procedures which are embedded in these different understandings. We are forced to ask *how* we come to an apprehension of that which transcends both our subjective awareness and our communal opinion regarding the nature of the transcendental. Such an analysis highlights the difference between a concept of the transcendental and the complex of human experiences in which the transcendental is known. By recognizing that the identification of the transcendental with meaning in a linguistic and symbolic context is only one mode of self-transcendent awareness we can acknowledge the limitations, as well as the power, of the assumptions which are implicit in comparative questions of meaning. Nevertheless, the transcendental concepts—for example, god, tao, brahman, spirit—are important indicators of a context of awareness—an awareness that one's existence and one's communal frame of reference are located in an often hidden, more comprehensive, and more powerful context. They indicate an ontological referent beyond, while including, one's psychosocial experience; but they also reflect particular modes of experience which result from different valorizing processes. While all of the modes of transcendental awareness acknowledge the limits of conventional horizons of knowledge, and claim to provide the means to overcome the self-deceptions inherent in these limits, they indicate different procedures in life practices whereby a person actualizes the transcendental.

By focusing our comparative study of the transcendental on the procedures of transcendent awareness in life practices we highlight the significance of the advocates' claims for particular modes of apprehension. We acknowledge the advocates' disposition for valorizing their lived experience in a particular way. As the first section of this presentation tried to make clear, a comparative study emphasizes the distinctiveness of approaches to transcendental awareness, and seeks to avoid any unreflective acceptance of one approach over another. Thus the significance granted to one advocate's approach is juxtaposed with the significance of another. Different approaches, then, manifest different descriptions of the transcendental in light of different valorizing procedures, despite the common claims for expressing the "otherness" of the transcendental and the power for transforming the participants in their life experiences. This study suggests that the self-transcending quality of participating in "otherness" is not removed from the actuality of the relative and particular processes which make the particular mode of transcendent awareness available to the participant.

In the context of this comparative study, then, the nature of the transcendental is the value-granting awareness of the self-transcending reality on which all beings, in this world or any possible other one, depend for their well-being. It is the implicit structure of personal subjectivity and social action which is the normative basis for actualizing a self-transcending freedom, value, and order. Thus, it is not simply a concept of unrestricted "otherness," nor a historical-cultural construction (that is, simply a product of a particular time and place). While any expression of the transcendental is conditioned by historical and psychosocial processes, internal to the transcendental awareness is the recognition that the reality one participates in must, of necessity, extend beyond one's particular conditioning processes.

What is often not recognized, and what this comparative study indicates, is that the procedure for actualizing the transcending awareness itself cannot be identified with the transcendental. The social-institutional structures which have historically provided the normative processes for self-transcending awareness have often been approved by their advocates as the only procedure for attaining such an awareness. Due to the implicit normative character of the procedures which have been effective—assuming, as I do, the significance of the advocates' claims—this is not surprising. Nevertheless, it is precisely a cross-cultural comparative analysis which shows the limits, as well as the possibilities, of any culturally determined formulation of any particular mode of apprehension. Unless we recognize an indefinite openness of meaning, nature, and purpose in that self-transcending reality, we will continue to identify that which is beyond our own particular subjective or social stance with a particular mode of self-transcending awareness, namely, those implicit normative structures by which *we* seek self-transcendence.

When we explore alternate modes of transcendent consciousness we are faced with the possibility that the procedures of our own self-transcending consciousness are not the only processes by which everyone in every cultural context must transcend a personal and cultural world. Rather, we recognize that simultaneously we signify, and grant value to, an incalculable freedom and ordering process expressed through a specific mode of consciousness. At the same time, we deny that this signification and mode of valorization encompasses completely the meaning and value of such freedom and order. Such an approach to the issue of transcendent awareness in the human experience affirms that the transcendental is not simply "the hidden," or the "beyond" outside the conventional experiences, but is a factor in the experiencing processes themselves; it requires acknowledging quite different ways by which the creative and constructive power of human experience can apprehend the simultaneous affirmation and rejection of the limit of experienced life.

The approach taken here suggests that at least one aspect of the hermeneutical context in which one can make sense out of the multiplicity and incommensurability of ways to know and express the transcendental is to acknowledge the ambiguity inherent in the experience of "limit." The limit of human experience is both the terminal horizon of one's experience and that which is beyond this end point—the context in which a particular something exists. Thus the self-transcending consciousness explores what is simultaneously limited and unlimited, what is particular as the object of some mode of consciousness and an unlimited capacity for creative reconstruction and imaginal deconstruction. It is then not surprising that the transcendental is signified by such notions as "mystery," "freedom," "power," and "infinite order" because the experiences that these terms signify reflect the capacity for all forming-activity plus the power for freeing one's awareness of form; they indicate the immediate center of any individual experience plus the limit of self-awareness where "the other" begins; they express the constant foundation for all possibilities and the dynamic transforming power that manifests only the best of all possibilities.

What is it, then, that we learn from an attempt to understand the transcendental in a comparative context? One thing is that because the transcendental is not simply an important concept, an unusual experience, or a cosmic demand for particular action, we must rephrase our traditional questions about it. The particular expressions of transcendental awareness result from various definitions of the knower, knowing, and the known, and from different procedures for valuation and foci of signification. When we take seriously the embeddedness of transcendent awareness in cultural expressions, we find no transcendent, archemedian object or process that is self-evident for all people.

Likewise, we learn that the procedure itself for understanding the transcendental involves both personal subjective and cultural assumptions, which condition any description of transcendental experiences and valorizing processes. The particularity and incommensurability of basic valorizing procedures for claiming validity of transcendental awareness provide no guarantee of surety in these claims; they, rather, call for a sensitivity of, and an openness toward, different means for securing these claims. They suggest that no single mode of transcendent apprehension can fully appropriate the "otherness" which is part of the inherent ambiguity of existence. This is to say that the *capacity* for freedom and order is not simply a product of a particular historical context —in prehistory, traditional society, or modern (postmodern) times— though it is given particular expression in different temporal and cultural situations.

What we can learn apropos of our contemporary situation, informed as it is by a plurality of incommensurable procedures for transcendental awareness, is the need for dialogue between people who have these divergent evaluative procedures. If the characterization for the continuing need of self- and communal-transcendental awareness given in this presentation is accurate, contemporary people need to explore the "otherness" in which they already participate by engaging that capacity as found in a comparable expression of others. Indeed, there is a danger in recognizing the incommensurability of procedures for transcendental awareness, namely, a pernicious kind of relativism that emphasizes the isolation between groups who hold different valorization procedures. Such relativism suggests that one group of people is automatically restricted to those of its own procedures that are found effective for achieving their goals. This position fails, however, to recognize the capacity found within the self-transcendental awareness to re-learn, to re-structure their sensitivities. Just as importantly, it fails to take the character of self-transcendence seriously in its engagement with "otherness."

The self-transcending ordering of life requires a reaching out to others by way of implementing the interconnection with others as part of a self-transcending awareness. This requires a shift in thinking about the transcendental from an exclusivist position to one which recognizes a "family" or "federation" model of interaction. While fully acknowledging one's own particularity in approaching the transcendental, and without requiring full consensus on the procedures for knowing the transcendental, a self-transcending awareness today requires an engagement with others to locate at least a partial set of workable rules for finding meaning and freedom in an acknowledged ambiguous human experience. We and other people must make some practical decisions on how to live with each other in light of some commonalities and some differences in procedures for attaining well-being. We are required to live in a tension—which hopefully will not be debilitating—between our own procedures and cultural constructs of self-transcending awareness and a recognition of the "otherness" in which we also, at least partially, participate. The awareness of the transcendental in a comparative context, then, includes a redefinition of ourselves: selves which become themselves by acknowledging and affirming the "otherness" of others.

Notes

1. The term "transcendental" is used in this essay as an adjectival indicator for a variety of personal and social experiences or sensitivities. It is not intended to affirm any specific Western philosophical position, e.g., a Kantian perspective, nor a specific Eastern view, e.g., a popular contemporary interpretation of the Advaita Vedānta position.

2. Walter Watson, *The Architectonics of Meaning* (Albany: SUNY Press, 1985).

3. Ibid., p. xii.

4. Ibid., p. ix.

5. Ibid., p. 10.

6. Raimondo Panikkar, "What Is Comparative Philosophy Comparing?" in

Interpreting Across Boundaries: New Essays in Comparative Philosophy, ed. G. J. Larson and E. Deutsch (Princeton, New Jersey: Princeton University Press, 1988), pp. 116–136.

7. Ibid., p. 130.

8. Ibid., p. 134.

9. *Transcendence,* ed. H. W. Richardson and D. R. Cutler (Boston: Beacon Press, 1969); *Transcendence and the Sacred,* ed. A. M. Olson and L. S. Rouner (Notre Dame: University of Notre Dame Press, 1981); *Ways of Transcendence,* ed. E. Dowdy (Bedford Park, South Australia: Australian Association for Study of Religions, 1982).

10. Paul Tillich, *What is Religion?* ed. and with Introduction by James Luther Adams (New York: Harper & Row, 1969), pp. 56–57.

11. Robert Scharlemann, *The Being of God* (New York: Seabury Press, 1981), p. 158.

12. Ibid., p. 162.

13. Ibid., p. 170.

14. E. M. Zuesse, in *Ways of Transcendence,* p. 31.

15. See H. Deakin, "Some Thoughts on Transcendence in Tribal Societies," in Dowdy, *Ways of Transcendence,* pp. 95–109; and F. J. Streng, "Creation of Community Through Sacred Symbols," in *Understanding Religious Life,* 3d ed. (Belmont, California: Wadsworth Publishing Co., 1985), pp. 43–62.

16. Rudolph Otto, *The Idea of the Holy* (Oxford: Oxford University Press, 1958; first published 1932).

17. Eliot Deutsch, "Knowing Religiously," in *Knowing Religiously,* ed. L. S. Rouner (Notre Dame, Indiana: University of Notre Dame Press, 1985), p. 27.

18. Al-Nasafi, in *The House of Islam,* ed. K. Cragg and R. Speight (Belmont, California: Wadsworth Publishing Co., 1988), p. 15.

19. John Carman, *The Theology of Rāmānuja* (New Haven: Yale University Press, 1974), p. 190. For other examples of this mode of awareness see Streng, *Understanding Religious Life,* chap. 2.

20. K'ung Tzu, *Chung Yung* XIII.1, in L. G. Thompson, *Chinese Religion,* 4th ed. (Belmont, California: Wadsworth Publishing Co., 1989), p. 6.

21. Tu Wei-ming, *Centrality and Commonality: An Essay on Chung-Yung,* Monograph no. 3 of the Society for Asian and Comparative Philosophy (Honolulu: University of Hawaii Press, 1976), p. 104.

22. Ibid., p. 104.

23. T'ang Chün-i, "Religious Beliefs and Modern Chinese Culture, Part II: The Religious Spirit of Confucianism," *Chinese Studies in Philosophy* 5, no. 1 (Fall 1973): 60. For an analysis of the differences between three contemporary philosophical positions on reality see F. J. Streng, "Three Approaches to Authentic Existence: Christian, Confucian and Buddhist," *Philosophy East & West* 32, no. 4 (October 1982): 371–392.

24. Translated by R. N. Dandekar, found in *Sources of Indian Tradition,* ed. Wm. Theodore de Bary (New York: Columbia University Press, 1958), pp. 220–221.

25. T. R. V. Sastri, "The Smṛitis: Their Outlook and Ideals," in *The Cultural Heritage of India*, ed. C. P. Ramaswami Aiyar (Calcutta: Ramakrishna Mission Institute of Culture, 1962), vol. 2, pp. 314–315.

26. *The Laws of Manu*, trans. by G. Buhler (Delhi: Motilal Banarsidass, 1964; first published 1886), p. 31.

27. For further discussion and examples from Eastern and Western sources regarding this mode of transcendent awareness in everyday action see Streng, *Understanding Religious Life*, chap. 4, "Living in Harmony with Cosmic Law"; and *Ways of Being Religious*, ed. F. J. Streng, C. L. Lloyd, Jr., and J. T. Allen (Englewood Cliffs: Prentice-Hall, Inc., 1973), chap. 3, "Living Harmoniously through Conformity to the Cosmic Law."

28. E. Deutsch and J. A. B. van Buitenen, *A Source Book of Advaita Vedānta* (Honolulu: University of Hawaii Press, 1971), pp. 27–28.

29. For an analysis of some basic hermeneutical issues in understanding the Upaniṣadic portrayal of "being" *(sat)*, see W. Halbfass, "On Being and What There Is: Indian Perspectives on the Question of Being," in *The Question of Being: East-West Perspectives*, ed. by M. Sprung (University Park, Pennsylvania: Pennsylvania State University Press, 1968), pp. 95–109.

30. Translated by P. N. Mukerji in Swāmi Hariharānanda Āraṇya, *Yoga Philosophy of Patañjali* (Albany: SUNY Press, 1983; first published in 1963), pp. 6, 11, and 12.

31. For the distinction between *samprajñāta-yoga* and *asamprajñāta-yoga* (including *viveka-khyati*), and the distinction of the latter from the permanent state of liberation *(kaivalya)*, see Araṇya, *Yoga Philosophy of Patañjali*, pp. 6–10.

REFLECTIONS ON RELIGIOUS
PLURALISM IN THE INDIAN CONTEXT

Some Theoretical Considerations Concerning Pluralism and Relativism

The question is often raised: if pluralism in aesthetic and religious judgment is considered legitimate, especially in cross-cultural contexts, how can a pernicious relativism be avoided? There are two points here that should give us pause, the notion of "religious judgment" and the concept of "pernicious relativism." I am not at all sure that religious judgment provides as large a set of instances of religious language as has commonly been thought to be the case. I have gone into this question elsewhere[1] and only give an indication of the kind of thing I refer to here. If the Rabbi says "You ought to keep a *kosher* kitchen," then he is clearly prescribing. But if I say "Breathe on me breath of God," it is not so easy to say exactly what I am doing. I am certainly not ordering the deity. The language of hymns and songs, of scripture and spiritual teachings exhibits a mind-boggling variety—and this variety includes much that is nonjudgmental. Doctrinal statements *appear* to be cast in judgmental form. But what about, say, *"Om"?* This is technically a syllable having mantric significance and power and probably is not to be regarded as a "word" in the strict sense. We would probably have to stretch our demarcations of religious language in order to bring it in, and yet to omit it would amount to leaving out a "potent" element in the Indian terminological basket. The number of doctrinal statements that can be extracted out of Hindu religious terminology (I deliberately do not say "discourse" because this word again seems to me to have a particular set of connotations)—and let us keep to Hinduism—may not be all that many and this does not in any way amount to a deprivation.[2] In short, in reflecting on religious pluralism in the Indian context I shall not cast my net particularly on "religious judgments."

I turn next to the idea of "pernicious relativism." Relativism is a position which has been held especially with reference either to what is "right" or to what is "true," the former giving rise to ethical relativism and the latter to cognitive relativism. The phrase "religious relativism" has been somewhat neutral between these two, some users being worried about the diversity of ethical precepts in different religions (something always underplayed by "universalists") and others being disturbed by the diversity of truth claims. At first sight the former has a more pragmatic air about it than the latter in the sense that what is enjoined or forbidden has prima facie a more immediate bearing on what we do than "beliefs" purporting to reflect "the truth." Anthropologists, rather unfairly, I think, have been credited (or discredited) with providing grist for relativisms of various kinds. It is all to the good, in my view, if it is recognized that rationality, truth, rightness and wrongness, and so on are all concepts that come in multifarious cultural garbs.

Let us assume that relativism, whether ethical or cognitive (and the link or otherwise between these needs looking into) stands for firstly, "right/true means right/true for me or for my society"; secondly, "this rightness/truth is to be understood functionally"; and thirdly, "it is therefore wrong for me/my society to judge/criticize/condemn/interfere with the functioning of such ethical/cognitive stances as may be evidenced in other individuals/societies through verbal and nonverbal behavior." Some philosophers have maintained that in the third of these a switch is made to a nonrelative use of the terms right/wrong and that this switch is unwarranted given the use of right/true in the first position taken. But do we not often apply precisely this kind of mix of absolutism and relativism? Second example: "One should always be kind" but "Sometimes it is kinder to be unkind. It was kinder to let him believe that there was no hope of a recovery." It may be objected that this illustrates a case of apparent unkindness which was actually a case of kindness. But all I want to say here is that inconsistent absolutism and inconsistent relativism are precisely the points of view that obtain in the actual world.

The other matter that can be raised is that criticism is not only something we turn on others but often as well direct on ourselves. The other person may indeed sometimes rebuke us for excessive self-criticism and this on various grounds: "Be kind to yourself," "Don't goad yourself." Assessment, whether by ourselves or others, can be in various tones of voice, and in any case nothing that is human can be made from a *sub specie aeternitatis* standpoint. Advances in moral sensitivity and religious insight (I beg the question what "advance" means here) very often occur through a fine honing which may come about through self-criticism or the criticism of others. Indeed the word "criticism" may be too strong. It is often the juxtaposition of the familiar with the "other" which brings about change. If constant reassessment goes on, as I think it does and should, the polarity between absolutism and relativism assumed to obtain by philosophers may in fact hardly obtain in the real world. Another way of putting it is to say that relativity is inevitable, and relativism is not. When pressed as to the difference, I would say something like this: to admit relativity is to admit the partiality of all finite points of view and not to bewail this; to concede relativism is to admit partiality and to lament it. The self-confessed relativist is usually pushed into this regret by the absolutist. There is, of course, another sort of relativist who is tough-minded about his relativism. Such a position involves maintaining that the values/institutions and so forth of each culture are self-validating and that there the matter ends. At any rate the terms relativism and absolutism can only survive in tandem.

I do not think the term "relativity," however, is subject to any such qualification, and I believe that a recognition of diverse cultural baskets, between which family resemblances may or may not obtain, *does* involve an admission of relativity. Since some of the points of view in these baskets are incompatible with each other, aggregating their fragmentariness will not produce a whole (this position is taken by some, however) but further underline their diversity under the capacious umbrella of what being human can encompass. In short, I am not at all sure that relativism can be pernicious. If relativism involved saying that *no* evaluation, whether self-evaluation or otherwise, is possible, this would be wrong-headed rather than pernicious. And, as far as relativity is concerned, I do not think the admission of it lends itself to the charge of being pernicious. Nobody can see an elephant from every point of view simultaneously, no matter how good his vision might be. Phenomenalism comes to the rescue, perhaps, but not entirely. The plurality of points of view to a large extent has to be taken on trust since we are familiar largely with our own.

Let us see what the resources of phenomenalism can provide in this regard, transferring what properly belongs to a particular analysis of perception to the religious field. This amounts to the following kind of use of hypothetical language: "If I were a Muslim I would spread my prayer mat at this time of the day." Or "If I were the lady of the house down the road I would bring a glass of water out into the garden early in the morning and make an oblation to my ancestors." But, whereas it is perfectly possible for me to look at the table from this or that place, and no position is *ipso facto* excluded from my view, is this the case with the hypothetical religious stances mentioned just now? John Hick uses an argument of a similar kind to point up the geographical contingency of our religious allegiance. But the whole point of the phenomenalist theory is, unless I am much mistaken, that there is a kind of continuum of hypothetical positions. If there were a radical discontinuity between them we would refer to "another object" which is not this one that I am looking at now. This discontinuity is precisely what we recognize when we note that X does this and X does that—neither of which we do. I do not believe that the alternatives have the sort of "availability" some people reckon they have and I am skeptical about this availability precisely because of the separate historical roots that our respective traditions have.

Let us next take the case of a member of an obscure sect who says to me "How can anyone not see that?" and who would, I suppose, be described as an absolutist by most philosophers. What I mainly noticed about this position when I encountered it was that it revealed on the part of the speaker a kind of "block" rather than a conviction of the other's wickedness/ignorance/being wrong, and so forth. But to notice this kind of block provides a caveat. The caveat is as follows: religious standpoints are not disinterested and this is at least one major way of distinguishing them, say, from perceptual perspectives. But religious standpoints are not unique in not being disinterested. They share this characteristic, for example, with political and ethical stances and the judgments that stem from them. Although the phrase "blind faith" is commonly used by critics of religion, the kind of phenomena to which oblique reference is thereby made are also found outside religion. For example, the insider/outsider distinction can be quite sharp in the domain of political allegiance.

The pebble I would like to drop into the pool of discussion at this point is the question whether religious plurality is more challenging than the other sorts of plurality which everyday experience, and the more specialized data provided by cultural anthropologists, furnish us with. What are those who speak in terms of challenge referring to? Here are some possible answers:

1. The Christian feels challenged by the sight of the Buddhist "measuring" his full length round the stupa at Sarnath on the ground that "His religion costs him something. What does ours cost us?"
2. The theologian might feel challenged by what he sees as rival truth claims, and some of these might come from *within* his own tradition.
3. There might be a sense of offence that others are "outside the fold," leading to a challenge to convert.
4. The challenge to find some deeper unity could arise from several sources, for example, the need for peace, the desire to globalize or universalize, from theologizing, or from some rather more philosophical consideration of a monistic kind. In other words, it is not patent that the challenge should be regarded in one way. In some historical contexts the relevant word might be "threat" rather than "challenge" where certain communities have faced the possibility of annihilation by those of a persuasion different from their own. There are still parts of the world where the whole question presents itself in terms of survival.

It is time I turned to what is the theme of this essay, religious plurality, specifically in the Indian context, or I should rather say, in the context of Hinduism. The thicket of considerations I have mentioned so far "fence" the area, or at least it was with this consideration that I have proceeded in this rather roundabout manner.

Religious Plurality and Hinduism

It is usually the case in the collective sphere and where collectivities coexist (I use this word in a factual sense and not with the evaluative connotation often used in India) that the presence of "others" serves to promote a sharpening of self-definition and "in-gathering," a focusing of identity. A comment made by the late Professor J. L. Mehta is significant in this connection. He writes of the Indian cultural tradition that "It has at no time *defined itself* in relation to the other, nor acknowledged the other in its unassimilable otherness, nor in consequence occupied itself with the problem of relationship as it arises in any concrete encounter with the other."[3] Religious plurality, on such a view, does not present itself as a problem to the Hindu, but something which in India has always been primarily a *fact,* a matter which poses adjustment at the behavioral level rather than provokes intellectual exchange of ideas in the realm of theorizing. Whether this has been an advantage or not I am unable to say. Successive waves of invaders entered the Indian subcontinent and the Hindus reacted in diverse ways, the Hindu community itself, we must not forget, being highly differentiated. The two major strategies were: (1) assimilation and (2) the water-tight compartment response. Sometimes one can detect both going along together, paradoxical though this may seem. What I mean is that certain cultural traits were sometimes assimilated along with a this-far-no-farther reaction to the rest of the cultural complex. Hindu society has in this respect shown both openness and accommodation as well as resistance.

Hindu philosophical life has traditionally been associated with disputation about matters of theory, especially focusing on whether or not systems or particular tenets were in line with the canonical literature. A system such as Advaita Vedānta has acquired the status of religion, whereas one could not conceive of Platonism or Aristotelianism becoming such. It is also interesting to note that within the philosophical systems the issue of God's existence or non-existence never had pride of place, the question of how bondage was to be overcome being deemed far more important. The majority of the systems are not theistic. And yet nontheism was by no means thought to be incompatible with a religious outlook.

The rise of cults as a phenomenon in Hindu religious life hardly promoted dialogue, since it had always been recognized that there are many paths to the Divine and that each must find the way which suits him or her best. This occasions neither dispute nor dialogue but a "letting-be" which should not be confused with the "X likes marmalade/Y likes jam" invoked by the emotivist. The former is based on an ontologically grounded admission of a plurality of valid paths, and the latter on the theory that metaphysical/ethical/religious preferences are mere expressions of personal feelings.

Hinduism includes the *iṣṭādevata* (favorite god) idea. This is the particular form which henotheism takes in India, the validity of all allegiances being taken to be perfectly compatible with individual allegiance to a particular deity, the latter being regarded as a manifestation of a more general principle. What is perhaps even more interesting, in contrast to the commitment models in the Semitic group of religions, is the phenomenon of multiple allegiance.[4] This is based on the idea that various sources of enlightenment and consolation are open to man and availing of one source does not preclude availing of another. For example, one may combine attendance at discourses on the *Gītā* in the local park with participation in Durga Pūjā and visits to Sri Aurobindo's ashram at Pondicherry. Such "latitudinarianism" enlarges a man's social circle without necessarily giving rise to dialogic situations. If the nearest to God-talk be the question-and-answer sessions in parks in the early morning, one can see how scarcely dialogic these sessions are.[5] The inquirer seeks an answer and gets it. The *guru/shishya* (teacher/ pupil) encounters of the philosophical schools in ancient times were, perhaps (how can one guess?), more genuinely dialogic. In the Indian situation there is room for a tolerant noting that others are offering obeisance elsewhere without thereby being provoked to exchange of thoughts. Moreover, the coexistence of diverse forms of observance has always been in the context of common rites of passage, places of pilgrimage, and various ritual observances governed by brahminical ruling over the centuries. Differences are not correlated with "rival truth claims" and are even regarded as "not mattering," that is, the differences do not surface in a sense that "I am right and you are wrong." It can also be mentioned that cultic observance of a particularistic kind has gone, along with belief in *Bhagwan* (literally, God), without any incongruity being felt. Another word in common use is *paramātma* (literally, the supreme soul). All this is based on the presupposition of the infinity of the Divine, something which provides ontological warrant for the diversity of ways of approaching Him/It. It can be seen that the notion of commitment sits uneasily in such a way of thinking. And it is the idea of commitment and the assumption that commitment and belief are inseparable that has made the whole project of interreligious dialogue challenging. The points detailed so far have concerned the way in which diversity is tackled *within* what the Indian theologian Devanandan calls "the Indian family of religions."

When we come to the relation of Hindus to communities outside the Hindu fold we find here, too, a largely behavioral adjustment. Hindus in north India often prefer to have their family weddings solemnized in *gurdwaras* (Sikh temples), for Guru Nanak, the founder of the Sikh faith, is much revered by all communities. Hindus and Muslims visit the shrines of saints and pirs alike. Muslim workmen in some parts of India make the idols used in Hindu worship. Again, the musicians who accompany dancers of classical dance forms (which usually have themes from Hindu mythology) are commonly Muslim. There is also another phenomenon which could be classified under the general heading of "secularization" if we are considering Hindu religious behavior. Seasonal village fairs still provide important markets for local craftsmanship and industry and help to connect the economic life of diverse communities with religious concerns. Pushkar Fair, which takes place in Rajasthan around the time of the full moon in November, has a religious focus in a temple consecrated to Brahma, the earliest deity in the Hindu trinity. But who is to say which predominates, the occasion for religious ritual or the economic significance of the large cattle fair which takes place at the same time. An equally intriguing case is that of the Kathak dance form which originated as a temple ritual around the myths and legends about Radha and Krishna. But it came to its height in the nineteenth-century courts of the nawabs of Oudh who were, of course, Muslims. Can we say that aesthetic considerations overrode the religious? This would be too simplistic. What is perhaps more the case is that if the religious elements in cultural patterns in India pervade them in a subtle manner it is no less the case that the economic and the social and the aesthetic pervade whatever be commonly recognized as "religious." The appropriate language is not that of encounter or dialogue so much as that of mutual adjustment and sometimes integration.

Hinduism, being a noninstitutionalized religion, is free of dogma. As a concomitant of this there is, for example, no word for "heretic" in Sanskrit. The nonorthodox, that is, one who does not accept the authority of the Vedas, is in a different category. His views are not anathema. What we do find, however, in different periods of the Indian history of ideas, is a sequence of philosophical concepts which are often vaguely formulated and more commonly just invoked, and which in sedimented fashion, have become part of the ethos of the country (if the woolly but useful term "ethos" be allowed). One of the earliest of these is the concept of *unity*, which was probably born out of a cosmic consciousness which was part and parcel of an agricultural way of life. Its most abstract formulation is the *Brahman-ātman* equation of the Upaniṣads (expressed in the aphorism *tat tvam asi*—"thou art that"). This should presumably extend to everyone wherever they may be. Although one might imagine that a highly humanistic philosophy would evolve from a world view of the unity of all souls deriving from a metaphysic of identity, it was not until Swami Vivekananda that this implication was drawn out. Lofty though the Upaniṣadic metaphysic may be, no dialogic possibility can be read from it, but only the conception of realization of the unity of humankind at a level which we are not commonly aware of in everyday life. Swami Vivekananda saw its potential as a consciousness-raising, even conscience-raising, concept (to use contemporary language) and, to his credit, advocated a program of action which would concretize its intent.

Philosophical appeal to the idea of unity apart, there is another purely epistemological gambit which these days is sometimes cited as a characteristically Hindu way of coping with diversity; I refer to the gambit of initial refutation of the point of view of the opponent *(pūrvapakṣin)* before proceeding to the exposition of one's own view. One way of looking at this is to applaud it for recognition of "otherness" in the first place and then give equal applause for sugaring the pill of pointing out the error of the other's view by granting it partial truth. The sting of tracking this down to ignorance is removed by the admission that *all* are subject to ignorance. Presumably some views are more erroneous than others and why there should be error at all is not something for which any answer can be given. But one can take the *pūrvapakṣin* approach in various other ways, of which these are some. Toppling the other person's point of view first could be taken as a sign of discourtesy rather than tolerance. Or, alternatively, if all standpoints are taken to be defective in some manner or other, the exercise of argument may seem rather futile. Above all, the exercise takes on an *artificial* air, remaining, as it seems to do, at the mere level of debate. In fact, the technique seems to have been prevalent particularly where *epistemological* issues were concerned.

As far as religion is concerned there is another part of Hindu tradition which positively discourages debate/argument and this is the communication of teaching from the guru to the pupil, in a form specific to the needs of the pupil, with various pupils being instructed in separate ways. One might throw in an oblique reflection here. A great part of Hindu prescription in the *Dharmaśāstras* concerns, basically, the avoidance of conflict. *Lokasaṃgraha* could almost be said to be defined by a kind of prosperity that was free of conflict and did not invite it. A prosperous society of this type would have to be strictly ordered and virtually closed to threatening/tantalizing influences from the outside. Intellectual venturing therefore had to be within well-understood bounds. The concept of *svadharma* (one's own law or duty) in this context exerts a tempering or limiting influence (depending one how one views it) on the scope of verbal interchange. If doing another's duty offends against the *svadharma* principle, and can bring danger, then presumably entertaining another's point of view also carries the possibility of danger. *Parādharma* is not sinful, it is important to note, but is likely to bring about social disharmony and is therefore bad. Over the centuries it was found that in order to neutralize alien influences and virtually rob them of their sting no method is as effective as that of assimilation, for diversity ceases to be diverse and the original tradition can henceforth claim the merit of already having the new element.

Now let us take the concept of the fragmentariness of the truth, which underpins metaphysically the *iṣṭādevata* idea and in Jainism provides a ground for radical pluralism and belief in nonviolence, and see which way it leads. While this could make for a sense of the complementariness of diverse visions and an appreciation of others' points of view, in fact other elements in the Indian world view have pulled in rather a different direction. To give an example, if one adheres to a theory of separate karmic lines, this goes along with stressing the individuality of *svadharma* (individual personal destiny) and therefore suggesting the nonrelevance of others' insights to one's own personal path. As far as religious affiliation is concerned, the *karma* theory reinforces radical diversity, since a switching of causal lines is ruled out. Thanks to past causal efficacies we have no alternative but to be as we are, religiously.

Let us move on to another characteristic which is deeply embedded in the Hindu ethos, the sense of life as a continuum extending beyond the bounds of humanity to the animal kingdom, and beyond the present generation to past and future generations. Gandhi took issue with the utilitarians not only because of their espousal of the majority principle, which left out of account the minorities, but because they conceived of welfare only in human terms. In effect this sense of a continuum finds voice in an awareness of *heritage*. It is, in other words, not something which intrinsically makes for a curiosity about "otherness." It is necessary to note, too, that, by and large, in cultures where "otherness" has been experienced through conquest or economic infiltration this in itself is a strong disincentive to dialogue. The culture which is invaded naturally reacts in a defensive manner so as to preserve its own identity. Hindu society has carefully safeguarded itself against "the other' by a network of taboos regarding pollution which only began to break down with the attraction of economic betterment. I offer only one example. When the Bata Company first established their factory in Bengal, an anthropologist, who was collecting data about the caste composition of the workers, found a large number of Brahmins working there. On asking one of them how this could be reconciled with his Brahminical status he was told "The machine handles the leather. I handle the machine." As the century approaches its final decade no such apologia would probably be given today. *Lokasaṃgraha* means prosperity; whatever brings about prosperity is acceptable. This example illustrates the continuity over centuries of the Hindu legitimizing of the practices which lead to prosperity. Oddly enough, Hindu society has also legitimized just the opposite as well, practices which lead to poverty, the whole renunciatory style of life amounting to just this. Contradictions do not invite sublation but acceptance as facts of life.

We have, however, yet to take into account the impact of certain nineteenth- and twentieth-century phenomena on the Hindu perception of religious diversity, for, while what happened reinforced many of the traits sketched above, new factors broke up the old rural economy with which traditional Hinduism, for all its inner diversity, had been for generations inextricably linked. For reasons of time and space, I shall make brief reference to only three thinkers (there are of course many more, to say nothing of the movements founded by various reformers)—namely Raja Rammohun Roy, Gandhi, and Radhakrishnan. Raja Rammohun Roy is the first of these chronologically and, apart from the usual way of situating him within the context of the Brahmo Samaj, it is worthwhile seeing how his contemporaries viewed him. His friendship with Unitarians was well known. Also well known were the things he denounced: for example, idolatry and atheism. It is rather less easy to pin down exactly where he stood vis-à-vis the pluralist environment in which he himself lived. Kissory Chand Mitter wrote that the *Tohufut-ul-Mowahedeen* (published in Persian in 1803) "discloses his belief in the unity of the Deity, His infinite power and infinite goodness, and in the immortality of the soul."[6] The constant references to the "One True God," brotherhood and equality, all show a strong Islamic influence. The Raja's own familiarity with Persian, his style of dress, and the social circles in which he moved confirm the importance of this influence. In Bengal this occasioned less alarm than it might have done elsewhere. If it was his Unitarian friends that disposed him to go against the Trinity, it must have been his Muslim associates that reinforced his dislike of idolatry.

Hindus saw him each in their own light. Bipin Chandra Pal spoke of him as a believer in *nirguṇa-Brahman* (distinctionless Reality), reading into his writings a penchant for an impersonal absolute which could scarcely have provided a focus of Brahmo Samaj *upāsana* (practice). Members of the Hindu Theophilanthropic Society in the 1830s were delighted that the Raja castigated skeptics even though the latter's rejection of superstition brought them far closer to him in point of view than to the "average Hindu." His contemporaries seem to have been worried about his critique of tradition, his apparent rapprochement with Christians and Muslims, and the critical way in which he regarded the rituals and observances which have always for the Hindus remained at the core of their form of life. If he alarmed his fellow Hindus he did not greatly please his non-Hindu friends either. His rejection of Christology could not but dismay all non-Unitarian Christian missionaries. His impatience with miracles and anything that savored of myth once more disposed him towards Muslims, and among them especially the rationalist Mu'tazilah, those who called themselves *"ahl al-tawhid wa al-ad"* (people of unity and justice).

The Raja's attitude to religious pluralism needs to be understood, it seems to me, both as an outcome of his travels, for he seems to have found people "agreeing generally" about the notion of one Being, and in relation to his near-futuristic sense that a new age would recognize each religion as *the* truth specially and ethnically expressed. The booklet called *The Universal Religion,* published in 1829, looked forward to the convergence of the historic religions to a center which was the ideal of "Universal Religion." As a reformer he believed this convergence would be promoted by the pruning and purifying of each tradition so that superstition, prejudice, and *tamasic* ritual would be minimized. When pressed as to how the extremes of "abstract universalism"[7] and idolatry were to be avoided, the Raja identified himself with what was common to almost all reformist Hindus then and since, namely, reliance on ethical precept as a means of securing peace and happiness. The latter goals of course neatly tie up Hindu *abhyūdaya* and Utilitarian welfare. The "purer form of religion" to which he looked would both highlight a belief in one God and promote service to humanity. This was a program for the future, no doubt.

Raja Rammohun Roy's approach to religious pluralism, rooted in his own position in space and time as it was, brings to my mind the comment of a philosopher from another continent and who philosophizes a century and a half later. A few years ago, H. D. Lewis made the following comment: "We need the varieties as well as different ways of closing the gaps where possible."[8] The Raja recognized the discreteness of separate historic traditions but thought that the gaps between communities could be bridged by each putting his own house in order (a phrase Gandhi used a century later) and by concentration on both the ethical core of each religion and the worship of the "One True God." The bridges constructed by the Raja included his scholarly work as a translator of classical texts as well as his role as a demythologizer. The latter involved not only a going back to roots but owed a lot to cross-fertilization. Moreover, he shared two vital beliefs with those who speak of crossing the Rubicon of separation today, namely, a conviction that a transcendent mystery lay behind *all* religious traditions, and that religious *praxis* (which he interpreted in an ethical rather than a ritualistic manner) must serve the betterment of the everyday life of humankind. The Raja's recognition that the intolerable must be avoided and the multiplicity of religious experiences be recognized has a very contemporary ring to it. If scholarship and a reformist temper provide the key to Raja Rammohun Roy's response to religious pluralism, it was the day to day experience of living in a religiously plural environment and especially an awareness of the potential for conflict that this contained which shaped Gandhi's response.

His first biographer, Joseph J. Doke, refers to Gandhi's sympathies being so wide that he seemed to have reached a point where the formulas of sects had no meaning for him. Gandhi was not interested in rival truth claims because he understood truth very differently. It was treated by him in three ways, as I have considered elsewhere,[9] ontologically as *sat* ("truth" or "reality"), existentially (almost à la Tillich in the sense of being "seized" by), and empirically through exploration and discovery. But because it was his habit never to separate religion from economics, politics and all that concerned both the individual and society, this provided for him multiple entry points into the lives of people outside the Hindu community. He never ceased to add to his scholarly base in the study of other religions, something embarked on in London and which continued to the end of his days. This study was not undertaken through mere curiosity but came from a desire to learn more about what "mattered" to his friends. The business acumen and honesty of the Muslim merchants brought them close to one who immediately recognized their "bania" virtues. His behavior in a religiously plural world can be seen in the light of his commonsense realization that people belonging to different communities do not encounter each other in theologically charged contexts but in day-to-day living. The daily round and common task sometimes provides occasions for friction, as he found during his leadership of the nationalist movement. There were mainly two prescriptions for that, dealing with the economic problems which invariably lay beneath the friction of groups, and bringing diverse elements together in the service of a common cause. In this way Gandhi developed a sense of when the "religious" elements in a situation provided the clue to action, and when other elements (especially the economic) needed dealing with. An example of the former is found in his comforting a Muslim woman demented by grief at the killing of her son by the words "Allah gave him to you and it was His will to take him from you," a message which immediately got through to her in her grief. In East Bengal one day an explosive situation was defused by his pointing out that the problem that faced those that lived there was economic and not communal (in the Indian sense of that term) since 80 percent of the land was owned by 20 percent of the population.

Like other Indians from Rammohun Roy onwards, Gandhi was inclined to set store by the common ethical values which seemed to go along with diverse religious beliefs. But he was too realistic to rely on what is after all a somewhat theoretical point, since a centuries-long lip service to a host of ethical precepts has not prevented violence from dogging the entire history of humankind. Gandhi therefore cast about for new experiments in living, consciously bringing together people of different communities in these experiments. The common observance of festivals, avoidance of food that gave offence to others, attempting to *value* what others valued, instituting a common prayer meeting for all—these were some of the ways in which Gandhi responded to a religiously plural situation. On his return to India all these experiments fitted under a larger umbrella, that of nationalism.

Gandhi, it seems to me, had an uncanny awareness of the *barriers* to interreligious understanding. Of these barriers, which he himself had come up against, I mention just a few—doctrine, ritual, specific practices, and situations seen as provocative. The doctrine of the Incarnation, ritual in temples to which Harijans were denied entrance, practices regarding the slaughter of animals, the playing of music in front of mosques—all these were occasions of "offence" to some community or other. These examples bring out the inadequacy of injunctions about tolerance, equality, or underlying unity, for these worthy concepts are all abstractions and therefore lack the power to defuse the inherent violence which Gandhi found so very near the surface in the pluralist societies he was familiar with.

Gandhi was too much of a realist to set much store by either an original Alpha ground or an Omega point of ultimate convergence. Common imperfections, he believed, were balanced by common positive powers for good. His own methods of cultivating the latter were the self-purification of the individual and the practical experience of constructive work. Rapport with those of other faiths, he thought, could not be attained by dialogue per se, nor in any case could it be made a specific object of search. In this, I believe, his instinct was on the right lines. It is in the context of *work* that we are in contact with "others" whether they be of other faiths or of our own. Gandhi's idiosyncratic use of the distinction between masses and classes might be recalled in this connection. Like Mao, he understood "masses" to mean the peasantry. He had found that there may well be more in common, say, between a Hindu and Muslim villager than between either of these and a member of the upper classes. Amity these days is associated by anthropologists with kinship groups, but amity also comes about between those of different kin and different religious allegiances. It is out of such rock-bottom amity that sometimes in spite of, and more rarely *because of,* different religious allegiances, a fraternal association can be built up. In the meantime no one has a right to interfere with the fragmentary vision of others, for our own vision is no less fragmentary. This is the content that Gandhi gives to the concept of the *validity* of various religious paths. The validity stems from our common humanity and our common imperfection. The nonviolent man is the one who has understood this validity. The sacred cannot be avoided since the demarcation of sacred and profane is as foreign to the Hindu way of thinking as it is to the Muslim. Gandhi finds this not a drawback but a source of strength. But it can only be such if social and economic injustice is tackled first.

The comment just made about the sacred and the profane can provide an introduction to Radhakrishnan's thinking about religious pluralism, for he would not have agreed with it. In 1939 he wrote:

Real religion can exist without a definite conception of the deity but not without a distinction between the spiritual and the profane. . . .

> Religion is not so much a revelation to be attained by us in faith as an effort to unveil the deepest layers of man's being and get into enduring contact with them.[10]

In contrast with what we found in Gandhi, Radhakrishnan's writings have a strictly philosophical perspective in favor of which he used to cite well-known passages from the *Ṛgveda,* the Upaniṣads, and the *Gītā.* The quotation above throws interesting light on some of the issues. Radhakrishnan's distinction between the spiritual and the profane (note: not *sacred* versus profane) is linked with the Śaṅkarite distinction between the *vyavahārika* (practical level) and the *paramārthika* (ultimate level). The various expressions of truth to be found in diverse religious traditions are at the former level. The goal, however, is not the path but what lies beyond the path. This can, in contrast, be set alongside Gandhi's stress on the continuity of means and ends, which sees the *vyavahārika* as precisely the arena where the spiritual battle occurs, and where also, of course, our relations with those of other faiths take place. To see the religious quest as "an effort to unveil the deepest layers of man's being" recalls the *mahāvākya* (great saying) of the Upaniṣads, but also recalls the language of a purely clinical discipline, namely, depth psychology. The method of cultivation of inwardness common to both the *ātman* and *anātta* (no-self) traditions is reckoned to take us beyond "otherness," so it can hardly provide us with that *appreciation* of otherness which we are seeking.

One special difficulty in interpreting Radhakrishnan's line of thinking is that his writings and speeches veer beyond what is strictly philosophical and toward what is more popular. Speaking philosophically he refers to "different religions not as incompatibles but as complementaries, and so indispensable to each other for the realization of the common end."[11] Addressing a Japanese audience decades later he said, "All the religions of mankind under the stress of modern thought are moving forward to a realization of the spirit of religion, reaching forth to the fundamental and lasting verities of truth and love."[12] In his public pronouncements his focus was, not unnaturally, on peace. At times he was confident that religion was gradually being purged of "superstition, ritualism and obscurantism" and at others said that this is what *ought* to be the case. While public pronouncements may serve to give a positive and optimistic orientation to thinking and project a healthy image abroad, the philosophical issues must be given due attention.

The validity of religion, for Radhakrishnan, seems to have an instrumental value: its instrumentality in achieving "realization," a word commonly used by Vedāntins when they express themselves in English. Now, if the various traditions cloud the truth in the very process of diversifying it, it follows that the aspirant for such realization will find in religion as ordinarily understood not so much a path as something to be transcended. And if the path is to be eventually left behind we can scarcely find herein the motive for exploring, however sympathetically, the path of another. The target is the "realization" of spirit and not the rapport between one human being and another. It is perhaps difficult for any form of idealistic monism or nondualism to grant adequate status to plurality. Furthermore, the target is an experience, albeit of a highly rarefied kind, and which has no necessary bearing on our relations with our fellows. In any case, if the Real is neither personal or impersonal, this is yet another reason why it can scarcely have any bearing on the life of human beings.

But there are other strands in Radhakrishnan's thought. It was noted earlier that both Rammohun Roy and Gandhi attached importance to the idea of reforming the tradition, putting one's house in order. Radhakrishnan also spoke in these terms. For example, he wrote: "We can so transform the religion to which we belong as to make it approximate to the religion of the spirit. I am persuaded that every religion has possibilities of such transformation."[13] There is an addendum written elsewhere that if such transformations do not occur in the religions we know, "we may anticipate a better one."[14] Perhaps indeed it was the latter that he was at bottom advocating, "the religion of the spirit," maintaining that it had an ancient lineage in the wisdom of the sages.

The problem is that religion so conceived seems indistinguishable from the kind of mysticism that takes flight from the actual world, including the people in it. It must be conceded that Radhakrishnan's utopian thinking on the above lines, however, coexists with much that uses a language more geared to the facts of plurality, namely, "meeting," "friendship," and "fellowship." His hardcore philosophical work, however, continues to speak of a unity, whether originary or otherwise, with which plurality can hardly be reconciled, for philosophies of plurality take their stand on the primacy of the particular. In this case, the particularity concerned is both that of the diverse religious traditions in all their specificity and the particular individuals who have allegiance to them.

A sense of history predisposes one to take plurality seriously, for although the metaphor of diverse paths can suggest a single destination, it can with equal facility suggest diverse destinations. To understand the other as sympathetically and seriously as possible, to avoid conflict and promote concord, to awaken common involvement in the struggle for justice, are targets which are enough to get on with. Recalling whence we have come in this discussion, the question is still open whether the *study* of religion can be as disinterested as we usually think it should be. The *relationship* with individuals who profess different faiths quite clearly cannot be disinterested. If it is a caring relationship, then the gulf experienced between the insider and outsider can narrow. The nature of the further shore becomes clear only as the journey continues.

Notes

1. Margaret Chatterjee, "Does the Analysis of Religious Language Rest on a Mistake?" *Religious Studies,* vol. 10, pp. 469–478.

2. I do not think that what the Indian sociologist Veena Das calls the "semiticization of Hinduism" is actually taking place. Hindus have never been worried about their absence of creeds. The present proliferation of gurus is not at all concerned with creeds and it is this proliferation plus politicization (no connection between the two) that are the two chief characteristics of the present Indian "religious scene."

3. J. L. Mehta, *The World's Religious Traditions,* essays presented to Wilfred Cantwell Smith, edited by Frank Whaling (Edinburgh: T. T. Clark, 1984).

4. Margaret Chatterjee, "The Concept of Multiple Allegiance," in *The Religious Spectrum* (Delhi: Allied Publishers, 1984), chap. 6.

5. The person conducting such sessions is likely to be someone learned in the scriptures or epics, but not a priest.

6. *Calcutta Review* (December, 1945).

7. A phrase used by Bipin Chandra Pal in 1901.

8. H. D. Lewis, in an interview by Janusz Kuczynski, published in *Dialectics and Humanism* 4 (1987): 14.

9. Margaret Chatterjee, *Gandhi's Religious Thought* (London: Macmillan & Co./Notre Dame University Press, 1983).

10. Radhakrishnan, *Eastern Religions and Western Thought* (Oxford: Clarendon Press, 1939), pp. 19, 21.

11. Radhadkrishnan, *The Hindu View of Life* (London: George Allen & Unwin, 1927), p. 43.

12. Radhakrishnan, at the International Congress of World Fellowship of Faiths (Tokyo), October, 1956.

13. Radhakrishnan, *Recovery of Faith* (New York: Harper/World Perspectives, 1955), p. 204.

14. Radhakrishnan, *East and West in Religion* (London: Allen & Unwin, 1958), p. 19.

LENN E. GOODMAN

THREE ENDURING ACHIEVEMENTS
OF ISLAMIC PHILOSOPHY

A few years ago our Philosophy Department had a visit from the chairman of a sister department in an Islamic country. The visitor was warmly welcomed and invited to speak in our departmental colloquium and at the East-West Center, where the hope was that he could speak as a representative of the philosophies of the Islamic world. But this expectation embarrassed our visitor. He was grey haired and Oxbridge educated, wore chino slacks, a blue blazer, and paisley necktie. During his visit he confided in me that the embarrassment he felt was not confined to this visit. At home, too, he was hearing requests for Islamic approaches to philosophy in the department he chaired. Were these requests expressions of the new sense of ethnicity and traditionalism felt in many contexts around the world at the time? Were they expressions of the resurgent militancy and confidence of Islam? "What do they want from me," my visitor asked when we were alone, "—to use examples about Zayd and Amr instead of Smith and Jones? To start off each paper I write and each lecture I give with a *bassmallah?* To teach Shariati and Mawdudi?"

The difficulties of the situation are not to be minimized. But perhaps some of the impetus behind the pressures my colleague was feeling was from legitimate if inchoate expressions of an unsatisfied hunger for knowledge about the large but almost legendary achievements of classical Islamic philosophy. Every well-trained student in the history of philosophy knows that between the great figures of antiquity and the founders of modern philosophy in Europe, "the Arabs"—in fact, Muslim philosophers of many backgrounds, writing in Arabic—brought to the West a new knowledge of the disciplines of philosophy, mathematics, astronomy, and medicine. Few students know whether such figures as Avicenna or Averroes made any large or lasting original contribution to philosophy or merely served as a bridge to be crossed and left behind, transmitting, perhaps, a somewhat confused impression, say, of Aristotle, which remained to be corrected in the Renaissance and the Enlightenment.

Part of the problem is that the relevance of Aristotle himself or of his predecessors and successors remains somewhat obscure to philosophers both of the East and of the West. If the past is no more than prologue, and ancient or medieval philosophy is important only as an exercise for undergraduates or a series of trenchant challenges accompanied by fumbling answers to questions more adequately posed or more correctly dismissed by our contemporaries, then philosophy does not really need its past, and changing Smith and Jones to Zayd and Amr will be as Islamic as it gets.

At the risk of seeming impertinent, I offered a suggestion. My colleague's nation, after all, has undergone decades of constitutional turmoil in search of a polity that would preserve Islamic principles and values yet cast them in a modern recension. What modernity requires or implies is as much subject to argument as is the proper content of Islam. But it occurred to me that al-Fārābī in the tenth century confronted many problems analogous to this one, as a result of his profound encounter with Greek philosophy. He worked out a philosophy of culture in the context of an Islamic society that had already passed through three centuries of religious, political, and intellectual crises and that was undergoing dramatic alterations even as he wrote. I asked my visitor what he thought of teaching al-Fārābī or Ibn Khaldūn. Both were social thinkers of world historical stature who in different but related ways had addressed the question of an Islamic polity. My visitor was unfamiliar with either and was very surprised that I imagined that medieval thinkers might contribute to social discourse in the last years of the twentieth century.

Certainly one can cross the sea without knowing much about its floor or the creatures that swim beneath its surface. But philosophers, still imbued with the conceptual radicalism of the Socratic tradition, like to believe that they do not ignore foundations, even when they adopt the Cartesian/Humean style of addressing issues as though no one had ever addressed them before. Contemporary philosophers often associate that style with the clean sweep of conceptual radicalism, imagining that there can be no issues or agendas on the table but the ones they lay there and ignoring—as no professional gambler would do—the question of what may be under the table. Everyone admires originality, but one of the uses of the past, and of comparative philosophy on a broader scale, is to allow us to distinguish genuine originality from mere ignorance or lack of penetration into the outcomes of our views. The broader our repertoire, the more clearly and critically we can see how the typology of philosophic problematics and proposed solutions breaks down or hangs together, and the more genuinely critical (which means self-critical) our thinking can become. This, I think, is the central goal of comparative studies in philosophy—not the paradoxical goal of penetrating the inscrutable,[1] or the perverse one of rendering the exotic banal, but the properly philosophic goal of broadening our dialogical milieu to include all of the best thinkers whose ideas can modify or inform our own. Such engagement can have at least three outcomes: (a) by growing more familiar with the full repertoire of philosophic thinking we come to see disparate positions not as isolated doxographic data but as integrated and rational responses, of varying degrees of critical sophistication and synthetic comprehensiveness, to specific intellectual problems; at the same time (b) what once looked novel, outlandish, or unprecedented is now seen to have an ancestry and a living kinship with families of related discussions, whether by common descent or by analogy of response to the universal human condition. As Spinoza teaches us, the outcome of our supposing a thing to have nothing in common with anything else is amazement, but understanding grows from recognition of the relations among things. (c) Once we understand the conceptual affinities of philosophical ideas, we see that the achievements of philosophers are cumulative, just as the problematics of philosophy are perennial. We can then see most clearly why it is that the thinkers of the past and of many and diverse cultures have something to tell us from which we can learn and by which we can hope in some measure to overcome the merely sophomoric kind of originality.

The crisis of modernity itself is not a new phenomenon—the philosophers who wrote in Arabic, whom we call medieval, called themselves modern (*muta'akhirūn,* latter day thinkers) and meant by that to express their sense of difference from the ancients. They, like us, confronted problems of critical appropriation. Yet, while their identity as moderns set them apart from the past, they had another identity that placed them in communication with a past which they could regard as their own, no matter how archaic its terms or widespread its roots. For all were linked by culture and tradition to a scriptural foundation, whose themes they hoped to appropriate, but whose idiom was decidedly not their own. In recognition of their common intellectual ideal and the common roots of the heritage that was articulated in their diverse communities of faith, they called one another *muḥaqqiqūn,* adherents of the same highest truth. They borrowed freely from one another's arguments and expressed respect for the theological values that led close adversaries to conclusions at variance with their own. Differences of language, culture, or confession meant much less to them than did affinities of problematic which might lead to a clue or a usable argument. So they translated, wrote commentaries, critiqued, and pirated one another's ideas systematically and wholesale, forming a literature that reads as though it were a single ongoing dialogue across the confessional boundaries and down the generations.

One use of the past lies in the recognition that the glory days of philosophy in the Islamic milieu were the days when Islamic civilization and culture were actively and eagerly assimilating alien materials. The decline of Islamic civilization coincides with the ending of that openness. Yet even without the threat of reaction based on suspicion as to where philosophy came from, whose mind it had been in, and where it might lead, the mainstream tradition of open and explicit, humanistic philosophy all but died out in the Islamic world as a result of its own internal quest for rigor. The drive to make philosophy a science ossifies and desiccates, formalizes and scholasticizes inquiry so severely that by the time of Ibn Rushd philosophy was presenting itself as a kind of closed circle. We can recognize analogues among our own coteries of philosophers who confine their universe of discourse to one another's theories, to the neglect of the far more rambunctious realm of human experience and values at large. Part of the profit of the past for us might lie in our understanding of the self-marginalization of philosophy as a result of the self-imposed parochialism of earlier generations of formalists.

This essay is an appreciation of three lines of thought developed by medieval Muslim philosophers who hold continuing relevance for us: (1) al-Fārābī's theory of culture and religion, which grows out of Platonic reflections on the scripture and history of Islam and is developed further, not only by other Muslim thinkers like the Ikhwān al-Ṣafā', Ibn Ṭufayl, and Ibn Khaldūn, but also by non-Muslims like Maimonides, as a means of enhancing their understanding of the phenomena of religion, prophecy, politics, and ideology; (2) Ibn Sīnā's account of being, a brilliant synthesis of Aristotelian and scriptural metaphysics that uses the insights of modal logic to provide a subtle and still accessible framework for addressing the problems of necessity and contingency; and (3) al-Ghazālī's celebrated critique of causality, which affords us not only a means of addressing the issues of creation and eternity, voluntarism, and intellectualism, but also an entrée into the issues of rationalism and empiricism.

1. Al-Fārābī on Religion and Culture

In what proves to be an extended meditation on Plato's thesis that philosophers should be kings or that kings somehow should acquire the insight of philosophers (*Republic* V.473d; cf. VI.484d), and on Aristotle's related thesis that the man of practical wisdom (*phronesis*) must have not only the ability to choose means judiciously, as conducive to his ends, but also wisdom in the choice of ends—"that a man cannot have practical wisdom unless he is good" (*Nicomachaean Ethics* VI.12.1144a.36; VI.5; VII.10; *Rhetoric* I.6, 1362a.16–21)—al-Fārābī argues that the true legislator *is* a philosopher, since only a philosopher has the insight needed to legislate wisely, and that the true philosopher is a legislator, since legislation in behalf of the common good is the ultimate perfection or fulfillment of the philosopher's role. A ruler who lacks philosophy will fail for want of understanding of the general conditions of human felicity and the particular conditions of felicity in the diverse nations of humanity. A would-be philosopher who does not legislate is a mere armchair theorist—for theory itself cannot be perfected without its implementation. True, a society that fails to avail itself of the philosopher in its midst has only itself to blame—that philosopher remains the rightful *imām* all the same. But one who develops theory in the abstract, without being able to communicate it to the populace and thereby implement it, is a false philosopher—not a counterfeit like the intellectual who fails of the truth and legislates against the common interest, but an unfulfilled intellectual, who does not achieve the full practical fruits of philosophic insight, either failing to extend what knowledge he has into the governance of his own existence, or failing to effectuate his understanding by introducing it to others "in the measure of their capacity." Such people come to regard philosophy itself as useless.[2]

The philosopher, al-Fārābī argues (cf. *Republic* VI.485–486, and *Nicomachaean Ethics* VI.10.1142b.20–22), will have all the virtues. For without them he will be unable to act upon, implement and institute his insights. He is the true ruler—prince, philosopher and *imām*.[3] He rules legitimately because of the integration in him of the moral and intellectual virtues, which is the same as to say that he rules legitimately because of his capacity to integrate the society he governs, bringing its beliefs and practices into line with the requirements of goodness and truth and into harmony with each other. "Therefore, the prince occupies his place by nature and not merely by will." And his subordinates, too, govern and administer because of their particular virtues, and only secondarily because they are chosen or because they choose to do so.[4]

To implement or institute his insights, the prince relies on instruction by way of language and on enculturation by way of habit. Instruction may use argument or symbols, which translate pure ideas into a vocabulary of related images for the benefit of the masses, who cannot think conceptually (cf. *Republic* VI.494a). Enculturation aims at the formation of character, arousing resolution, discipline, and enthusiasm, which lead individuals to act as though "enraptured"—spontaneously performing right actions on the basis of the virtue they have acquired. In the well-ordered society, philosophy and religion support one another in securing the common good. But philosophy uses concepts where religion relies on beliefs: "In everything of which philosophy gives an account based on intellectual apprehension or conception, religion gives an account based on imagination. In everything demonstrated by philosophy religion employs persuasion."[5] Some of the symbols used in instilling the beliefs that correspond to true ideas are universal, but some are best suited to the needs and outlooks of particular nations.[6] Presumably, the same might be said of habits and virtues. Are there habits which should be enculturated in the philosopher? Indeed there are, since the philosopher will require all the virtues, and above all, the intellectual habit, which will enable him to rule.[7] But philosophy is more universal than religion, since it does not rely for its discoveries on the particularities of local symbolism, which may be quite parochial.

Adapting Aristotle's remarks about the natural supremacy of the civilized (*Politics* I.8.1256b.20–25), al-Fārābī is able to claim that a legitimate ruler will have military as well as pacific virtues.[8] Indeed he justifies aggressive warfare "to conquer the nations and cities that do not submit to doing what will procure them that happiness which man is made to acquire. . . . The warrior who pursues this purpose is the just warrior, and the warfare that pursues this purpose is just and virtuous warfare."[9] One of the detriments of the Platonic and Aristotelian insistence on a sharp distinction between subjective and objective happiness is that it becomes possible, as in al-Fārābī's argument here, to infer that men can be forced to a state in which their maximal felicity is possible. Al-Fārābī recognizes the analogy with parental responsibility; but, unlike our liberal tradition, he argues that a ruler's power and responsibility for forming the characters of his subjects (and potential subjects!) must be greater and not less than that of a father in forming the character of his children.[10]

By the same token, though, the argument does not entail and indeed does not allow mere military self-assertion: it justifies offensive warfare *only* in behalf of civilizing ends. So it covers the Islamic institution of *jihād* in a generic way (just as Aristotle justified the Greek institution of slavery in a generic way) that includes "civilizing" wars by others as well as by one's own, but excludes false or spurious Islamic wars that may be only nominally or notionally fought in behalf of a civilization-bearing mission. Further, in keeping with the Quranic (2:256) principle of "no compulsion in faith," al-Fārābī's argument allows for the implementation only of ethos-forming institutions, not for the enforcement of dogmas. For the acceptance of ideas depends entirely on demonstration or persuasion.[11] The separateness of the cognitive from the ethical sphere protects the former from claims made in the name of the latter.

Legislative institutions in general and symbol systems in particular vary in their universality of appeal and effectiveness *over time* as well as across cultures. The best are those with wide applicability that can guide nations without much change of goal "except over long periods." Some suasions are of only temporary or immediate value; others should be recorded for posterity.[12] Al-Fārābī stops short of saying that any mere institution or set of words, as opposed to ideas, deserves or is capable of permanence. And the reason for this striking qualification to the Islamic doctrine of the eternity of the Qur'ān is plain: Where Aristotle had argued that law issues from practical wisdom and intelligence (*Nicomachaean Ethics* X.9.1180a.22), al-Fārābī sees that the schematism that brings laws into the realm of the doable good without bringing norms down to the level of unique, particular situations (the proper sphere of practical wisdom) is the work of imagination. Given al-Fārābī's striking articulation of Plato's division (for example, *Republic* VI.477–478) between knowledge and opinion, we can understand better the title of al-Fārābī's famous work, *Mabādi' ārā' ahlu-'l-madīnatu-'l-fāḍila.* This does not mean "On the Perfect State," or "The Virtuous City," or "The Ideas of the Inhabitants of the Excellent State," or even, as Walzer attempted to render it literally: "The Principles [that is, essential features] of the Views of the Citizens of the Best State"[13]—as though 'Principles' were to be taken attributively, to yield "Principal Views"—and as though the Arabic title contained reference to the idea of citizenship. Rather we can render precisely: *The Principles behind the Beliefs of the People of the Preeminent Society*—that is, the conceptual foundations of their beliefs, with 'beliefs' or 'opinions' taken in Plato's sense, as set apart from knowledge. These principles (rather than any notions that al-Fārābī would call beliefs) are what is actually discussed in the *Ārā'.* They are what the legislator must know if he is to use his faculty of imagination to clothe philosophic ideas in concrete imagery and flesh out philosophic values in ethos-building practices like those of civil and criminal law, moral and ritual obligations, and supererogatory prescriptions.

Al-Fārābī departs strikingly from Plato (*Republic* VII.519e) in holding that the assumption of political responsibilities is not a sacrifice of the higher for the lesser good but a fulfillment of the philosopher's true nature, without which he is frustrated as a philosopher, debarred from *philosophical* fulfillment.[14] Rhetorical persuasion and social legislation are the proper work of philosophers, and the poetry Plato had both feared and praised for its power over the human heart can be found doing its persuasive work in scripture. Religion, al-Fārābī explains, is founded on similitudes, poetic images that body forth the unseen in tacit metaphors that refer overtly to the sensory. Religion symbolizes the ultimate realities—God and the incorporeal beings that mediate between God and nature—as political figures, their actions as edicts (cf. Aristotle, *Politics* I.2.1252b.24–27). Religions represent the hierarchy of beings in terms of spatial or temporal rank and order, the powers of nature as though they were the faculties of a man, prime matter as water or the abyss, nothingness as darkness, happiness as the ends that the vulgar imagine to comprise it.[15]

The scriptural accounts of "whither and whence" are true in that they point the way to truth, in much the way that the natural world is real insofar as it portends a higher reality.[16] But the cosmogonic stories of the world's religions—pointedly, paradigmatically, including Islam— are symbolic representations of the truth known to philosophers: that the world's dependence upon God is eternal, not the outcome of a single temporal event. The governance of God is not an anthropomorphic superintendence but an immanent provision of powers and forces to the natural species of things, via the incorporeal agency of the Active Intellect ("which is what ought to be understood as the 'Faithful Spirit,' or 'Holy Spirit'" of religious parlance, "mediating between God and a man who is inspired by revelation").[17] And the judgment of God is not executed in the corporeal and sensual terms that scriptures represent it, the "promise and threat" of Quranic parlance. Such rhetoric is intended to impress and exact obedience from the masses, who have little access to notions beyond those which their senses present to them. Philosophy is prior to religion, al-Fārābī argues, both in time and in content. It contains the true meanings of religious symbols and should be relied upon by those who raise their heads sufficiently from what they are told, to contemplate notions beyond the apparent. Behind the surface elitism of al-Fārābī's disparaging remarks about the masses (an attitude shared by all the Muslim philosophers except al-Rāzī), we sense a powerful and inviting empowerment of the reader, who is brought into the elite by being awakened to the awareness of higher, conceptual meanings that open up before him as he reads. For, as al-Fārābī tells us, there are many who can follow a philosophical argument although they cannot construct one.

Modern and postmodern sensibilities may feel impatience with al-Fārābī's notions, perhaps even with his impatience toward literalism, fideism, and fundamentalism. Pascal, for one, has turned the tables on al-Fārābī's Platonizing rationalism by setting forth in post-Cartesian epistemic terms the pietistic claim that the heart hath reasons which the reason knoweth not; and William James, for another, has founded a willful, American, practical-sounding philosophy upon just this principle. Pascal was not quite as innocent as al-Fārābī of the avenues of connection, which lie through the channels of the heart, by which the cognitive and the practical spheres are linked, so that "masses and holy water" may pave a path for faith, even though assent may seem to wait for argument or persuasion. For culture, especially religious culture, is not merely a matter of character, to which convictions are irrelevant. And symbols in the form of rituals can act upon belief as well as or better than persuasion—so that there is force in faith, as Muḥammad saw when he tried wisely to restrain it, even as he went about creating the institutions which would implement it by exactly the methods that Aristotle had said are used in the formation of character: pleasures and pains, promises and threats, exhortations (especially of adolescents), and the setting of examples. As the hadīth so prominently quoted by al-Ghazālī rightly says: "Every child born is born in a state of nature, and its parents make it a Jew, a Christian, or a Magian."

When I say that al-Fārābī's account of culture and religion has an enduring value today, I do not mean that we can somehow put on al-

Fārābī's legendary fur hat and Central Asian cloak or try to dance to the music he is said to have loved and performed so well.[18] Even without the aid of deconstructionist hermeneutics we can savor al-Fārābī's appreciation of the projective character of political imagery in religious discourse. But we can also apply al-Fārābī's observation to his own system: how far has the philosopher departed from political projections, when the metaphysical scheme of hypostases he puts forward as the truth is still grounded in the idea of an ontic hierarchy based on the imparting of powers and receiving of recognition that parallels the feudal delegation of authority and receiving of fealty? We still see here the political architectonic of al-Fārābī's time, that applied not only in Europe or the Middle East, but even in the *daimyo* culture of Japan.

In al-Fārābī's political thought proper, as in that of Aristotle, there is a tension that grows profound in the measure of the philosopher's awareness of its presence in his thought, a tension between the kind of explanation that exposes and critiques and the kind that justifies and legitimates. When al-Fārābī speaks of the philosopher as the *imām* and legislator, he can mean that the philosopher is the rightful ruler, as he does when he treats all others as usurpers, implying a radical, Platonic critique of all political institutions that fall short of true philosophy; or he can ascribe legitimacy to existing regimes, insofar as their possession of authority and effective exercise of legislative functions must rest upon a philosophic base, as he does when he says, in a more Aristotelian vein, that the prince and all his delegates hold authority by nature and not simply by will. The ambivalence of conceptual radicalism and the ambiguity of its dicta about actual regimes run all the way back to the Sophists—to Thrasymachus' power to turn his analysis of justice as the interest of the stronger to either side of an argument about the status quo, making of it a radical critique of self-serving by the powers that be, or an unyielding, Machiavellian rationale of all that is done, has been done, or might be done, so long as there is the power to do it. Moderate thinkers like Aristotle and Locke drink from both sides of the cup: legitimating authority by its power but cautioning would-be tyrants with a Platonic warning as to the self-undermining character of the abuse of power. More radical thinkers, like Hobbes or Hegel seem more prone to the ambivalence latent in their radicalism: they can at once justify more earnestly and warn more gravely. In the most radical—a Mao or Mussolini, a Lenin or Gentile—the ambivalence becomes schizoid, tolerating and justifying everything and nothing.

Al-Fārābī participates in one of the more moderate forms of this ambivalence and is not the philosopher to help us to resolve it. Yet the very fact that he looks at such Islamic institutions as *jihād* and the Qur'ān through the eyes of Plato and of Aristotle makes his efforts at conceptual appropriation far more perceptive and interesting than they would be had he simply followed the advice of our cultural relativists and studied those institutions from within, not departing from the repertoire of the categories they generate. We cannot say that Aristotle or Plato somehow have an edge on objectivity, so that their prejudices amount to reason and the reasonings of others, outside their ambit, are mere prejudices. It is the power of the tools of Socratic analysis, Platonic dialectic, and Aristotelian logic that makes Greek thinking no longer merely Greek but universal; and it is because of that universality that we can expose even Greek prejudices as prejudices. But we can say that the very alien .ess of Greek conceptual devices to the givens and imponderables of Islam sets those givens and imponderables in a clearer and more critical light. Quranic imagery can be both appreciated and criticized when it is recognized as imagery. It can only be marveled at when confined to its own terms. *Jihād* can be assayed, globally or (perhaps more relevantly) in concrete deliberative instances, when its rationale is voiced in conceptual terms. Without such conceptualization its legitimacy or illegitimacy, globally or concretely, remains opaque.

The contrast between a philosopher like al-Fārābī and an ideologue like Abu-'l-Ala Mawdudi (ca. 1903–1979) makes clear just what opacity means here and how al-Fārābī's clarity and ambivalence are counterparts of one another. For it is the contrast of a conceptual ideal with empirical reality that opens up the question of the adequacy of either to the other—the adequacy of an ideal to the empirical given in what purports to be science, and the adequacy of a given to the ideal in what purports to be statesmanship. Mawdudi, in reaction to what he perceived as the decadence and febrility of the West, of democracy, of liberalism, secularism, and humanism, sought to reaffirm the sovereignty of God, the comprehensiveness and perfection of the *Sharia,* and the delegation of "all administrative matters and all questions about which no explicit injunction is to be found in the *Sharia*" to "the consensus among the Muslims . . . capable and qualified to give a sound opinion on matters of Islamic law."[19] This is not the place to discuss Mawdudi's rationalizations for the nonparticipatory citizenship he reserves for *dhimmis,* or to explore the mode of consciousness involved in putting forward clericalism as the purest (and safest) form of democracy or confining popular and representative democracy to the execution of God's will. What is important to us here, conceptually, is that Mawdudi has left that will opaque to analysis and all purported expressions of it opaque to critique.

In al-Fārābī's frame of discourse, the use of alien categories has opened up a space in which critical thinking can operate. One can ask about the adequacy of Quranic symbols in representing what they may portend and about the adequacy of various interpretations of those symbols. One can ask about the legitimacy of any campaign that purports to pursue the path of God. The alien categories call forth a deliberative and speculative objectifying of the given or proposed, allowing it to be treated as one's own. Confinement of the same symbols and institutions within their own terms brackets them within the bonds of referential opacity and renders them ultimately other, inscrutable, to be appropriated or rejected purely on the basis of impulse. If Muslims today ought to study al-Fārābī, it is not because he is "their own"—as though Muslims could understand only what issues from within their own "world." Rather, they should study al-Fārābī because he brings to seemingly familiar experiences and institutions an outlook alien enough to allow the all too familiar habits and symbols to be cross-lighted and appear somewhat alien. For it is only in some such cross-light that critical consciousness is possible, and it is only through critical consciousness that the habitual or the symbolic becomes actively and intellectually appropriable as our own.

2. Ibn Sīnā on Being and Necessity

The Muslim philosophers of the Middle Ages received two conflicting accounts of being, both ancient and with high claims to authority. By Aristotle's account, being is determinacy. The notion that Aristotle simply concretizes the subject term of a categorical judgment to generate the notion of a substance is a crude misrepresentation. On the contrary, for Aristotle, whatever is a *this* or a *such*—above all, whatever holds together and *functions* in a unified, coherent pattern—has the definiteness that Aristotle requires and expects of a substance. It is not the case that Aristotle simply expects nature to abide by laws; on the contrary, it is those things that do abide by laws or patterns, always or for the most part, that are identified as substances—those among them, that is, that exist in themselves and do not exist *in* or *of* other things, as is indicated but not definitively established by the common usages of language. For we say 'the color of the horse', not 'the horse of the color'.

Aristotle found substance by searching for constancy and stability—persistence through change and definiteness of identity and character. He was looking for that *being* of which the Parmenidean dicta were true: what did not change, come to be, or pass away, but was one and self-same in some sense acceptable to logic and tolerant of the legitimacy of phenomena. So it is not surprising that species, essence, or Aristotelian form, as the locus of determinacy in the Aristotelian universe, should take the palm as the most promising claimant to the title of substance. For form/species is the object of scientific knowledge and the subject of universal and necessary, changeless predication. Nor is it surprising that the runners-up, the candidates that meet at least some of the criteria of substantiality, should be the concrete particular (as the unchanging substrate of all changes short of coming to be and passing away, substrate of the accidents, referent of all other categories, and unit of arithmetic identity in the realm of multiplicity and change) and matter (as the ultimate, notional substrate of change and predication, ground of arithmetic unity and individuation, and basis of potentiality).

Invariance was the grail sought from the time of Parmenides, and Aristotle departed most strikingly from Plato not in denying the reality of Plato's forms but in finding their invariance within the world of change. But the outcome of Aristotle's search for substance was the discovery of every aspect of constancy that could be found in nature and the projection of the categories of that constancy beyond nature on a metaphysical scale. So time and space and change were all continua, and therefore became eternal; causality was discovered in regularity, and therefore became necessary; and substance, whether found in species, form, matter, or even the mind of individuals, was eternal. Like the presocratics, Aristotle expected and found the ultimate principle of being to be divine. And, like the first principles of the presocratics, his divinity was at its most effective as a principle of explanation when it acted immanently, *through* rather than *upon* things like a deus ex machina in a bad play, whose doings were not organic to the action and the characters of the participants in the drama. Its identity was compact with theirs, for it was their rational principle and form, and as such was their very being—the "what-it-was-for-a-thing-to-be" that thing.

In the alternative, scriptural tradition stemming from the Torah and preserved for Muslims in the Qur'ān, the kind of compactness of being with its first principle that Aristotle found in all natural kinds was reserved to God, one and transcendent, regnant, as Quranic language puts it, over all. Only God is eternal and everlasting; nothing in the world is. Nature's light is not its own but is commanded into being by the creative word of God. Man's life is not his own, but breathed into him by God. The species of things are not eternal, nor are the succession of day and night, the elevation of the heavens, or the separation of land from water. All is the work of God. Heaven and earth were created by God, and nothing in nature needed be determined as it was. What God imparts to being is not eternal and inalienable wisdom, implicit in the very natures of things, as in Aristotle's thesis of the intrinsic wisdom of means and ends, that shows the eternal identity of each species and renders nature intelligible, but the transcendent bounty and grace that provides extrinsically for the needs of all beings beyond what they unaided could provide and renders nature good.

The contrasting theologies of wisdom and grace have corollaries that bring them into conflict. For the creationist metaphysic of grace is one of contingency, based on abstraction of the empiric characters of things: God need not have made this being so, need not have provided this. Generalized, this abstraction becomes the contingency of being, the nonnecessity of creation. As for the intellectualist metaphysic of wisdom, which leads Aristotle to say, in his immanentist language, that nature does nothing in vain, it leads to the necessity of all true beings—

the eternity of matter, form, species, minds, and the celestial bodies that form what are later called the "principal parts" of the cosmos. Being is necessary by its nature, and the task of science is to discover in specific and in general terms the grounds of that necessity. In so doing the philosopher discovers and makes his own the wisdom of nature, which is divine.

Scriptural metaphysics was not, like Aristotle's, developed as a system (although scriptural morals and legal expectations were). But the models of the abstract systems of philosophers allowed the *mutakallimūn*, the dialectical theologians of Islam, to make good the deficiency many times over—and in the process to crystallize the metaphysics of Aristotle and his followers as a countertype to the metaphysics of scripture. So there emerge, as a product of the labors of the *kalām* and of the successors of Aristotle, two rival systems: a metaphysics of eternity and necessity, and a metaphysics of contingency and creation.

Following the lead of Aristotle and of Parmenides before him, and responding to the seeming mythicism of monotheistic accounts of creation, neoplatonic philosophers like Proclus and Simplicius develop a polemical eternalism that argues for the eternity of the cosmic order on metaphysical, theological, and even logical grounds. Their elenchus in behalf of eternity is met on their own grounds by monotheists like the Christian Philoponus in the sixth century, the Muslim al-Kindī in the ninth, and the Jews Isaac Israeli and Saadiah Gaon in the early tenth century. But the response of the *kalām* in the early centuries of Islam, drawing on now lost traditions and on their own dialectical creativity, was far more radical. At its extreme, the occasionalist atomists of the *mutakallimūn* assigned the idea of being only to the immediate datum: anything more would be another given, radically dependent, like the first on the free act of God. To infer from one given to another was to presume upon the grace of God. So a finite being was an atom of duration no longer than an instant and of extension, either nil (since to be extended beyond a single point would require an additional bestowal of being on God's part) or minimal, the merest minimum entailed in the initial given. All characteristics were "accidents," and the only relations among things were relations of aggregation—that is, collocation of atoms—and succession. For if there were essential attributes in things or true causal relations among them, on a "horizontal" plane there would be creativity or power in creation, and God's power and creative act would not be absolute.

The idea of nature, the notion of dispositions or potentiality, free will, or any independent or self-directed action became highly problematic on such a scheme, and the *kalām* itself became highly fissured with dissensions and convoluted with distinctions and equivocations in efforts to determine just how far and in what direction to go in preserving or qualifying the logic of the extreme position.[20] But what is important to us is that the orienting logic was the logic of contingency, drawn up in conscious opposition to the Aristotelian eternalism and essentialism and founded on the centrality of God's creative act, recognition of the absolute dependence of all finite being, every fact and act upon the immediate pleasure of God.

Science, on such a scheme, became at best the awareness God allowed or implanted as to the usual and accustomed (but by no means necessary) course of his actions. And ethics, too, were threatened. For many *mutakallimūn* by the tenth century were reasoning that if God's pleasure was the ultimate given, it was not for man to judge God's acts. They were good and just by definition, and even predestination was no detriment to their absolute justice: God might command us to obey and then punish us for doing so, if He so pleased. For "there is no injustice to a chattel." And we are all God's chattels.[21]

The achievement of Ibn Sīnā to which I want to call attention is his creation of a synthesis between the two radically opposed accounts of being I have sketched—the metaphysics of being as an eternal given bearing within itself its logic and its law, and the metaphysics of radically contingent being, receiving its all from above. Both positions are extreme, polarized by centuries of polemic, resting on rival sets of premises, tacit and explicit, and canonizing in each case a cosmology that seeks to recognize the fundamental moral and metaphysical truths about the world but finds them in radically opposing crystallizations of the values in existence. For where Aristotle finds divinity and wisdom in the necessity each kind bears within itself, the *kalām* points to a transcendent Deity, found not by uncovering the seeds of eternity in finite things but by recognizing the radical contingency of all that is finite and acknowledging the absolute emptiness of the world without the divine creative act.[22]

The key to Ibn Sīnā's synthesis is a single phrase, based on his own appreciation of the source of the divergence between scriptural and Aristotelian cosmology, and thus between the rival schemes of metaphysics. The phrase is *considered in itself.* Considered in itself, each finite thing is radically contingent. It does not contain the conditions of its own existence; and, considered in itself, it need not exist. Its causes give it being, and it is by abstracting from those causes that we can regard each finite being, or the world as a whole, as radically contingent. But, considered in relation to its causes, not as something that in the abstract might never have existed, but as something concretely given before us, with a determinate character, the same conditionedness that required us to admit its contingency now requires us to admit its necessity: considered in relation to its causes, this finite being *must* exist, in the very Aristotelian sense that it *does* exist, and must have the nature that it has in that its causes gave it that nature. This is not an argument that even the most radical occasionalist of the *kalām* can afford to dismiss. For although *kalām* occasionalism is founded on the complete subordination or rather extinction or eclipse of horizontal causality in favor of the "vertical" causality of the divine creative act, no *mutakallim* will deny causality itself, lest he lose the nexus of reason between finite beings and the absolute act of God, who is their condition. No *mutakallim* will deny the nexus between determinacy and a determiner, for the central theme of the *kalām* is that God establishes all determinacy in things, down to the determination of existence over nonexistence.[23]

Following a distinction that Aristotle makes between the question of what a thing is and the question of whether such a thing exists, Ibn Sīnā, then, can draw up a famous distinction of his own, the distinction between essence and existence, which will enable him to find a truth in both the metaphysics of Aristotle and the rival metaphysics of creation. This will not be simply a matter of calling creation a mythic symbol of emanation, as the Farabian philosophy would do, but of assigning to each of the rival views its due measure of truth. All finite beings, Ibn Sīnā argues, are contingent, inasmuch as we can abstract from whatever assumptions we make when we assume their existence. Existence, then, is a separate notion, over and above the essence of a thing. It is not, as Aristotle supposed, identical with the very essence of each thing, so that for a thing to be is for it to be the kind of thing it is. On the contrary, Aristotle's own distinction of what from whether shows that this cannot be so, and Ibn Sīnā has only to expand that distinction from the realm of particulars, where Aristotle introduces it, across the realm of species (which Aristotle would not allow it to traverse)[24] and onto the cosmos at large, which is, despite Aristotle's views as to its necessity and divinity, a finite thing by his own account, and therefore, as Ibn Sīnā reasons, itself contingent.

All contingent beings require a cause to determine their natures—that is, to set the bounds of their contingency—and to determine their existence over nonexistence, if they are to exist. So, if there is a finite being—myself or any object of perception or appearance—it is contingent and requires not merely a cause but (since there can be no infinite regress of causes) a necessary being as the counterpart of its contingency and ground of its determinacy. The necessary being has no (external) cause but contains within itself the conditions of its existence. Here essence and existence, then, *are* one. Here we have the kind of radical simplicity, the subsumption of the attributes of God within His identity, that the early radicals of the *kalām* had insisted on in their polemics with Christian theologians, who had sought to make God's attributes into hypostases emblematic of the trinity. More importantly for philosophy, we have the roots of the ontological argument. Ibn Sīnā did not utter it, but the concept of a necessary being, as Kant insisted, is what makes the contingency argument possible. And the ontological argument was not possible before Ibn Sīnā had created a third major option in metaphysics, beyond and yet incorporating both the contingency of the *kalām* and the essentialist eternalism of Aristotle. For in Aristotle's metaphysics, necessity of being was found not just in the highest god, Intelligence, but also in the spheres and their intelligences, the species of natural being, and the cosmos as a whole. An equivalent of the ontological argument could be offered, and in a way was offered, with respect to all of these. Necessity of existence, fusing essence and existence, was not unique to a single God.

Ibn Sīnā's cosmos, by contrast with Aristotle's, was contingent. But, by contrast with the cosmos of the *kalām,* its contingency did not negate natural necessity, or the efficacy of natural causes and potentialities, including human actions and dispositions. Ibn Sīnā's scheme did not impugn the authority of science or the reliability of human moral judgment, even as applied to life and the act of creation itself. Finite things were contingent in themselves but necessary with reference to their causes and ultimately to God, who is the Cause of causes. Thus the natural order retains its integrity and the continuity of its categories—time, space, causality, the wholeness of the human intelligence and moral sense—within the rationality of God's plan. God's wisdom guarantees that integrity and continuity, while the integrity and continuity discoverable within the world argue God's superintendant wisdom and outpouring benevolence.

For many later thinkers, what was most striking in Ibn Sīnā's metaphysics was the concession of temporal creation to the arguments of the Aristotelians. The continuities of time and causality were allowed to overspill the finite cosmos into eternity. But even those who blamed Ibn Sīnā and al-Fārābī for conceding the eternity of the world and making the seeming automatism of emanation the ultimate meaning of creation adopted both the emanative scheme of the neoplatonists and the distinctive Avicennan solution to the question of the world's relationship to God. Both al-Ghazālī and Maimonides, for example, reinstate creation but within an emanative universe; both allow—and Maimonides insists upon—the integrity of causal bonds and independent valuative judgments within the natural realm of finite being. And both make the necessities, values, and categories of nature relative to nature's ordained scheme, rather than the absolute requirements of disembodied, decontextualized reason or logic, as their predecessors in philosophy had been inclined to do. Although Ibn Sīnā does not make quite the same journey, it is his creative synthesis in metaphysics which makes their achievement possible. For it is he who reinstates the Platonic recognition that all necessities in nature, in the realm of becoming, are relative, not absolute.

It is a common canard against the God of rationalism, the God of the philosophers, as it is sometimes disparagingly called, that He is cold, unavailable to the human heart, and unavailing to human needs. But the work of Ibn Sīnā shows us a God of reason that can serve at once as the guarantor of science and the integrity of nature, the ultimate source of all our understanding, the summit of all goodness and generosity, and the focal point of devotion. It is a modern heresy, very much the work of the consumerist philosophy of William James and his ilk, that God may *or must* be designed somehow around human "needs" and wishes. No classical or medieval philosopher committed to the idea of a Creator, Author, or Ground of existence could utter such a claim without wholly turning his world upside down. As Saadiah Gaon says in his trenchant confrontation with the problem of evil in the context of the Book of Job: "Wisdom is not identical with what creatures yearn for, nor is the right course of action that which human beings are pleased with. . . . The proper object of concern is not whether the decrees of the Allwise gladden His creatures or grieve them. For what is agreeable to them is not the standard of His wisdom. Rather, His wisdom is the standard for them."[25] Few monotheist philosophers in the Middle Ages, regardless of their confessional allegiance or sectarian outlook, would have dissented from that proposition.

Consider now the theism of Ali Shariati (1933–1977), the outspoken non-mullah who has been called the ideologue of the Iranian revolution.[26] Shariati does not speak from the common identity of the *muhaqqiqūn* but more narrowly as a Muslim. Islam, he argues, by giving the old monotheistic idea, *al-tawhīd,* a new "degree of signification," gives it a whole new meaning. Shariati turns al-Fārābī on his head: It is not the truths of reason but the symbols through which they are expressed that are now eternal and universal. We are not told how what is contextualized culturally and articulated in the idiom of a particular language and tradition somehow becomes more universal than the ideas it expresses, but the general drift becomes clear when the new meaning of monotheism is spelled out: It "gives man certainty and a sense of security and inner tranquility; it also makes him responsible for the welfare of his own self and the society in which he lives . . . . *tawhīd* embodies all the manifestations of religious faith in the spiritual as well as material life of man." It eliminates greed, fear, and ignorance— which are the causes of all corruption, distortion, and immorality.[27] What we see here is not a critical response to the problems of faith, but an attempt to find the contours and the content of faith by touching all the bases, addressing all the constituencies, and promising attention to all "needs": moral, spiritual and material, individual and social: "Thus Shariati points out that when he takes the question of belief in One God seriously, it is not in order to engage in theological or philosophical argument about it; more correctly, it is an attempt to comprehend the spirit of history and existing sentiments regarding this affirmation in every age." Yet Shariati's historicism is not quite as catholic as, say, Condorcet's. He is the enemy of the *akhunds,* or popular preachers of

Iran, if they were tools of the colonialists; and he is the enemy of all Safavid history, although it was the Safavid, dervish dynasty, beginning with their rise to power in 1500, who made Iran so thoroughly the Shi'ite country that it is today. Like Mawdudi, Shariati sets forth the image of a small patch of sacred history soon after the death of the Prophet, as a screen on which to project his positive social ideal. But for Mawdudi this is the romanticized reign of the four *rāshidūn* khalifs; for Shariati, it is the regime of Ali and his immediate descendants and followers. Patrice Lumumba can be entered into the pantheon of martyrs, but many a Sunni saint cannot.

By engaging in a disciplined inquiry that Shariati seems inclined to dismiss as mere logic chopping, Ibn Sīnā succeeds, even if only glancingly, in touching the heart of what Islamic, Christian, and Jewish scripture affirms as to the ultimate reality and unity of the Creator of heaven and earth. And he unites that affirmation in a single synthetic theory with a rival thesis that was similarly motivated but diametrically opposed to it in its conceptual articulation, emphases, and values. Shariati, by contrast, using a method designed to reach the bedrock of authenticity and "to comprehend the spirit of history," fails to make contact with his Persian countryman of less than fifty generations past and reduces the faith of his living countrymen and his fathers to a kind of cosmic security blanket, designed and marketed to meet the needs of all constituencies—religious, moral or political, social or economic, and sacred or profane.

3. Al-Ghazālī and the Critique of Causality

"The connection between what is familiarly held to be a cause," al-Ghazālī writes, "and what is held to be its effect is not a necessary one in our view." For the two are distinct and neither implies the existence of the other.[28] Al-Ghazālī does not say that natural events do not cause one another, despite the tendency of later philosophic critics, both in his time and in our own, to assimilate his position to that of his theological predecessor al-Ash'arī, and to assimilate al-Ash'arī's severe curtailment of the idea of dispositions or capacities to the most radical occasionalism of the *kalām,* a position which al-Ghazālī explicitly rejected and which al-Ash'arī himself had labored carefully, creatively, and critically to transcend.[29] Unlike the *mutakallimūn,* whom he, like al-Fārābī, assigned the role of defending the faith of the philosophically unsophisticated, al-Ghazālī did not reject the Aristotelian idea that things have definite characters of their own. He allowed that it was contradictory to affirm the particular while denying its governing general predicate, and thus allowed that two like bits of matter will behave identically in identical circumstances.[30] But he could rely on God, as the emanative source of forms, to provide being itself (since being *is* form) and thus to create. And he could rely on God again, as a volitional agent, to provide the extraordinary differentia that would alter natures suitably to allow miracles. For there really was no difference in principle, as the Qur'ān itself (36:79) had argued, between, say, God's creative imparting of life to the inanimate and the crucially miraculous restoration of life to the dead.[31] In accounting for natural events, the theistic philosophers, *muḥaqqiqūn*, "admit that these temporal events emerge by emanation *(tufīḍu)* from their principles *(mabādī'*, that is, their *archai.*)"[32] So what is needed to protect the possibility of miracles or creation is not repeated interventions but a continuous emanative activity of God.

Al-Ghazālī's approach is a reminder to the philosophical adherents of emanation that by their own account all being and definition stem from God (by way of formal principles) and an insistence (pace the philosophers) on the volitional character of God's emanative act.[33] For without a free act of will, al-Ghazālī argued, divine simplicity could never produce the multiplicity and change known in nature, or make the many determinations that differentiate the actual from the possible. Al-Ghazālī's Neoplatonic adversaries are aware of the difficulty of deriving multiplicity and change from simplicity and invariance. Both al-Fārābī and Ibn Sīnā offer elaborate accounts of the emergence of incorporeal intelligences from the One and of the uncreated and incorruptible spheres from the intelligences. But the accounts are unconvincing, and the persistence of such accounts throughout the history of medieval Neoplatonism testifies only to the persistence of the problem and the ingenuity of the generations of philosophers who sought to solve it. Those Neoplatonists most loyal to the rigorous demands of the tradition relied on the Neoplatonists' notion of matter, particularly of a primal intellectual matter, to serve as a principle of otherness and differentiation from the very outset of emanation. But this solution seemed either to sunder the divine nature or to alienate from God some or ultimately all of nature, placing it beyond God's control. So those Neoplatonizing thinkers whose loyalties lay closer to the scriptural traditions—al-Ghazālī, Maimonides, the Kabbalists, and many Christian thinkers—relied on God's will, acting from the simplicity and self-sameness of God's nature, to impart existence, differentiate creation, and assign the determinate natures which things have, but need not always have had, as if by a necessity of logic.[34]

The insistence by committed monotheists on preserving the volitional character of divine creation serves not only to secure some measure of the reality of the God of tradition against reduction to a mere logical notion or rotary engine energizing the spheres but also allows the projection of a far richer and more open conception of the universe than the determinist intellectualism of accredited, eternalist heirs of Greek Neoplatonic Aristotelianism could afford: it preserves, to begin with, the syntheticity of the judgment that God's work is good. This does not collapse into a mere tautologous recognition of God's authorship but remains as an autonomous valuation of the worth of life and the beauty and goodness of creation, bespeaking acts and choices of God which might have been otherwise, and which tell us, being as they are, not only about God's nature but about God's grace.[35]

Second, there is the necessity of empiricism. Aristotelian science explains by discovering why things *must be* as they are. In the advanced and rigorous systems of the Neoplatonic Aristotelians all determinacy is determined, not only by the locking in of all events within the seamless boundaries of material engagement—with a cause before and an outcome behind each temporal moment and no spatial discontinuities to allow gaps for chance (as in Epicureanism)—but also by the essential natures of things, which are eternal, and whose necessities are necessities of logic. These essential natures are the mediating causal principles (*mabādī'*) mentioned by al-Ghazālī in his allusion to the vertical dimension of causality in the philosophy of the Neoplatonists. What their presence reflects is the fact that vertical causality in the Neoplatonic cosmos is a matter of logical implication: effects "follow from" their causes, the first principles, in the same sense that theorems in geometry follow from their axioms. The divine principles stemming from God and reaching the world through the Active Intellect, in its capacity as Bestower of Forms, specify the natures of things from the most universal form of goodness down to the sheer particularity of the members of each species, whose interactions with one another necessitate even the "accidental" characteristics of each item and event in nature. God knows the world a priori and of necessity, by understanding and containing the principles from which all facts follow. Human science is the endeavor to capture some measure of that necessity. But if science were complete it would know every fact and why it was so: it would know why whatever exists must exist as the final row of stitches in the emanative net of implications, spun out from the incorporeal and anchored in matter, the ultimate condition of otherness. For universality must reach specificity and particularity for differentiation to be complete. And a perfect science would know why it is that whatever does not exist and will never exist cannot exist, since it will understand how it is that nature affords it no room.[36]

Al-Ghazālī's theistic voluntarism, taken up by Maimonides, leaves a much more open universe: actuality does not exhaust the realm of possibility. For there is no logical contradiction in denying what is in fact the case, and logic, al-Ghazālī insists, no surrogate of logic, sets the only real boundaries to possibility. Here al-Ghazālī follows Ibn Sīnā's moderated version of the contingency doctrine of the *kalām*. But he uses the teaching against Ibn Sīnā's own conclusion: if it is true that we can without internal contradiction posit that the world need not have been, or that any given thing might have been radically other than as it is, so that the world and all things in it are genuinely contingent, it follows not only that we cannot regard all things as necessary absolutely but also that the future is genuinely open, that no merely a priori understanding, no matter how complete, could ever tell us what the world will be like. We must study the world a posteriori, not merely because our knowledge of its "principles" is limited but because even God knows all particulars, not by way of their universals, nor simply because what is follows from and corresponds to His wisdom, but because He freely chooses what things to create. And if there is a system of nature and there are real interdependencies among the essences of things, that system, too, including time and space, is part of what God has chosen, and those interdependencies are products not of logic but of God's act.[37]

Al-Ghazālī founds a modest, almost reticent accommodation of natural science and autonomous human valuation upon this reasoning. Maimonides goes further, building upon the foundations al-Ghazālī laid, to erect a vigorous defense of scientific naturalism, human freedom, and autonomous moral judgment. In both cases we can see the conceptual affinities of the ideas of creation and divine freedom on the one hand with the ideas of empiricism, the open and emergent future, and the integrity of the human person as a speculative and valuative subject.

Al-Ghazālī represents temporality as the product not merely of an eternal will but of an eternal plan. He is no process theologian, treating God Himself as the emergent outcome of creativity. But neither does al-Ghazālī's God merely "consult" the eternal forms, as Plato's Demiurge does. A craftsman God, as I have argued elsewhere,[38] works to plan and with preexistent materials that are in some measure recalcitrant. But a Creator God, like a creative artist, is responsible for His own materials, and the chosen end is itself a product of the activity, completed only in the execution—like the pattern of history, or the law, or humanity itself. In that measure, divine creativity is participatory. It is not what it will be until the object of creation has had its say. These thoughts extrapolate far beyond al-Ghazālī's original intentions in taking up the cause of creation where Philo, Philoponus, al-Kindī, and Israeli had laid it down. The trajectory of further developments runs a still uncompleted course from al-Ghazālī to Maimonides to Thomas, to Spinoza, Bergson, and the present. The seeds of this development, which leads to Spinoza's idea of the conatus, Bergson's account of freedom and his cleansing idea of the open society, and David Burrell and Joseph Incandela's recent proposals that the proper model of divine knowledge is practical rather than speculative,[39] are embedded in the Talmudic idea (Mishnah Sanhedrin 4.5) that the persons who issue from God's "mold" are not identical but unique. They are enshrined as well in the medieval image of the cosmos as an organism rather than a machine.[40]

But they are fostered by al-Ghazālī's trenchant defense of scriptural creation as more than a mere myth, a defense taken over from earlier *muḥaqqiqūn* and left enhanced and enriched for others. For in creationism God's purpose is seen as constituted within and through His work rather than outside, before, or beyond it.

Once again, if we compare a contemporary leader of Islamic thought with the achievement of his medieval forebears, there can only be disappointment with the failure of the twentieth-century figure to rise above ideology and appropriate from his own heritage that intellectual scope and spirit of catholicity which al-Ghazālī tells us made him "thirst from an early age to apprehend the true natures of things" and scorn to rely on blind faith in authority *(taqlīd).*[41] Sayyid Quṭb (1906–1966) was a leader of the Ikhwān al-Muslimīn in Egypt, the group that inspired the assassination of Anwar Sadat. He was deeply influenced by Mawdudi and exercised in turn an important influence on Shariati. His writings, including a widely diffused and excerpted thirty-volume commentary on the Qur'ān, have influenced Muslims throughout the world, including Black Muslims in the United States. Like al-Fārābī, Quṭb was very much a political writer, but unlike Ibn Sīnā he never held political office and his program for the Islamic polity, the *'umma,* was largely formed not by conceptual desiderata but by his rejection of the British stance in the Middle East during the Second World War and his experience of alienation and culture shock as a student in Washington D.C. and California—specifically, in witnessing the widespread American (and Soviet) support for the establishment of the State of Israel. He took refuge in Islam from his former faith in Western-style liberalism or nationalism. But his Islam was not the lambent faith of al-Ghazālī, who saw absolute trust in God as the highest expression of Islamic surrender to God's will.[42] The spiritual humility of the al-Ghazālī who opposed Aristotle for saying that there is a proper mean in pride and held that utter humility is the optimum for man is replaced with a truculent triumphalism which appeals to Western guilt over colonialist, neocolonialist, and purportedly colonialist adventures, yet simultaneously demands control of the world in the name of the religion of submission:

> Truth and falsehood cannot coexist on earth. When Islam makes a general declaration to establish the lordship of God on earth and to liberate humanity from the worship of other creatures, it is contested by those who have usurped God's sovereignty on earth. They will never make peace. Then [Islam] goes forth destroying them to free humans from their power. . . . [T]he liberating struggle of jihad does not cease until all religion belongs to God.[43]

Quṭb's political application of religious ideas has been compared to the ideas of Latin American and Afro-American liberation theology.[44] In many ways the rhetoric is similar. But the claims remain distinctive, not

in their stridency or urgency but in the totality of their demand for domination. For Qutb, like Mawdudi, believes that all human sovereignty
is usurpation—but faithful Muslims are nonetheless qualified to exercise the sovereignty of God over their fellow humans. The Sufi idea that
the *greater* jihad is the fight for self-mastery is lost sight of here, as is the
worry of the Ikhwān al-Ṣafā'[45] that worldly authority corrupts religion
and debases it into subordination to its *younger* sibling, politics:

> This religion is a universal declaration of human liberation on earth from
> bondage to other men or to human desires. . . . To declare God's sover-
> eignty means comprehensive revolution against human governance in all
> its perceptions, forms, systems and conditions and total defiance against
> every condition on earth in which humans are sovereign. . . . This decla-
> ration means the extraction of God's usurped sovereignty and its restora-
> tion to Him.[46]

To be sure, the Qur'ān tells us that there is no compulsion in religion,
but Qutb wrings a qualification from this categorical norm by juxtapos-
ing the obligation to combat those who oppose the way of Islam by
force. He thus interprets the mission of Islam as the militant and military destruction of all secular authority, all who actively resist the dominance of Islam—as, for example, by legislating laws.

It might be thought that such theocratic claims to universal authority
are common to all scriptural monotheistic faiths. But Christianity,
despite the temptations of triumphalism, preserves its early fear of secular power; and the Hebrew Bible, despite its many universal claims to
allegiance, insists that the law is on earth, to be interpreted and appropriated or rejected by men.[47] Islam, too, despite its many historic
phases of aggressive militancy, does not universally interpret itself as
engaged in a struggle for world domination. As Fazlur Rahman wrote:
it is historically unacceptable, as some modern Muslim apologists have
done, to pretend that the expansionist *jihād* of early Islam was purely
defensive, but "it is only the fanatic Khārijites who have declared *jihād*
to be one of the 'pillars of the Faith':

> Other schools have played it down for the obvious reason that the expan-
> sion of Islam had already occurred much too swiftly in proportion to the
> internal consolidation of the Community in the Faith. Every virile and
> expansive ideology has, at a stage, to ask itself the question as to what are
> its terms of coexistence, if any, with other systems, and how far it may
> employ methods of direct expansion. In our own age, Communism, in its
> Russian and Chinese versions, is faced with the same problems and
> choices.[48]

To acknowledge that there may be spatial or temporal boundaries even
to the idea of Islam is to recognize the distinction between generic *islām*,
subservience to the will of God, and institutional Islam, a specific concrete mode of articulating an awareness of such subservience. It is to

recognize that there are limits in all human ideas and all human articulations of ideas, regardless of how universal they may be. It is to recognize with al-Fārābī that not every system is ideally suited for every people and environment. But that is an admission that Qutb is not prepared to make: Unless all alternative modes of awareness and all alternative modes of articulating revelation are subordinated to Islam, he assumes that the legitimacy and authenticity of Islamic revelation and tradition have been impugned—and, indeed, injured.

Al-Ghazālī's critique of causality, like Sayyid Qutb's polemic in behalf of Islam, is an affirmation of divine sovereignty undertaken in the name of liberating the human spirit from dependence on all things less than God. Like Qutb, al-Ghazālī finds a practical significance in this theme, but he does not interpret it so largely in terms of world hegemony. It is because al-Ghazālī understands the central issue of the prior Islamic critiques of causality among the schools of kalām that he can leave behind the kalām atomism and occasionalism and yet preserve the Islamic theme that there is no power and no strength but in God. One who fully recognizes God's sovereignty is one whose hope and fear rest in none but God, who has severed the bonds of dependency upon earthly things. Such a person has achieved the true dependence upon God (tawakkul) which is the practical expression of the highest phase of monotheism, where God is seen in all things. When one sees God in all things, one need not deny the reality of things distinct from God (as men are distinct from one another and from God, al-Ghazālī argues, by the differences in their histories and the contents of their consciousnesses) and one need not deny the efficacy of proximate causes. Al-Ghazālī denies only their necessity. He preserves what is of moment spiritually and metaphysically in the Islamic discontent with proximate causes not by denying that winds blow across the seas or that ships are what sail upon them (that would be to deny the Quranic appreciation— 2:164, 14:32, 16:14—of God's providing the seas for navigation) but by only by affirming the dependence of those causes upon God. To say "if only . . ." or "had it not been for . . .", he can still write, following the pietist tradition of Islam, is of a piece with polytheism—because it places our hope or fear elsewhere than in God. Proximate causes act not by a power of their own but by a borrowed power. That was the theme that Ibn Sīnā's doctrine of contingency also sought to vindicate by way of argument. And it was also what the Qur'ān itself said (17:66, 22:65) of the sailing of ships upon the seas. To deny the presence or the action of wind or waves would be to trivialize God's act. But to ignore or negate the moral and political personhood or spiritual subjecthood of others is the same affront. Al-Ghazālī does not deny the action of the pen or the hand, but only that they act alone. What radical monotheism calls for, he reasons, is only that we affirm, as he does, following the Neoplatonists, that the powers and strengths, characters and disposi tions of things come to them from Above.[49] If the recognition of such a claim issues an imperative, the force of that imperative is upon the self —that it seek self-mastery and self-perfection, and in regard to others it authentically evokes only the imperative to recognize their God-given subjecthood.

The morally sensitive person is not the one who feels his own injuries most sharply and voices his own grievances most tellingly, but the one whose sensibilities are most catholic and who is most able to conceive and articulate the joys and pains of all, himself included, in a system of mutual recognitions and respect. By the same dialectic, it is a distinctive feature of a world religion, of which Islam is surely one, that it relates its adherents not only to the natural cosmos but also to a social world in which their own constructions have a part but not the only part; and it is a distinctive feature of a sect that its claims but not its sensibilities are universal. Qutb's curious articulation of the idea of liberation, which seeks to impose on others what they would regard in the same oppressive terms as what he and allied liberators seek to destroy, lacks that elemental tact which is the root of ethical teaching in Islam, as in all world religions worthy of the name. Qutb casts Islam in the role of a sect or faction untrue to its original prophetic spirit. The rhetoric is Islamic, but the intentions are all too transparent and all too human. For, contrary to what Shariati supposed, it is not words or symbols but ideas and values that are universal—as al-Fārābī, among others of the thinkers of Islam, clearly and cogently proposed.

* * *

Walking across our beautiful campus once, around this time of year, I fell into step with a colleague formerly associated with the East-West Center. When he heard that I was a member of the Philosophy Department, he asked about my specialty, and I told him of my interest in Jewish and Islamic philosophy. "Oh," he said, "you're one of those absolutists. . . ." He was in retirement and had been taking courses at the university. What he had learned was that universalist ideologies cause bloodshed; to believe in an absolute was to be some sort of absolutist. Foundationalism was fundamentalism in disguise, and to expect cumulative achievements in philosophy or any convergence toward common understanding in science or shared standards of appreciation in the arts seemed tantamount to fascism—since what is held to be true or valid or valuable will inevitably be promulgated through the captive media and then enforced by dint of arms. My colleague evidently did not know what the Ikhwān al-Ṣafā', the Sincere Brethren of Basra, said a thousand years ago: that it isn't religion or philosophy that lead men to slay one another, but religion's younger and usurping brother politics, that the slaying called for by the religions of the world is the slaying of the ego in acts of self-sacrifice and spiritual quest.[50] My colleague did not know that in the realm of the mind for two persons to claim the same territory need not make them enemies but can make them allies. He certainly did not know of the historic and centuries-long intellectual collaboration between Islamic and Jewish philosophy and might have been surprised to learn of philosophers in Tel Aviv studying and publishing Islamic texts in search of the insights they contain, or of the work of Dr. Mehdi Mohaghegh, a delegate to this conference, publishing a medieval Arabic commentary on Maimonides in Iran.

Walking across our campus this summer, with the rainbow shower trees once again in bloom, their uniquely beautiful blossoms a hybrid of species from two continents, Africa and South America, I met many colleagues who saw the announced topic of this essay and asked me what *are* the three enduring achievements of Islamic philosophy—as though there were just three. In the time allotted I could give only a sampling of the riches of one tradition. Had I known how much reference there would be here to the overworked idea of incommensurability and to the false exoticism and invidious essentialism it fosters, I might have chosen to stress even further than I have those cases where Jewish and Islamic formal philosophies have complemented and aided one another's discoveries.[51] Given sufficient time, one might, in the manner of the medieval Hebrew poets, suggest the comprehensiveness of the cross-cultural collaboration by grouping themes not in a trinity but acrostically, in multiple alphabets. But even without such an agenda, the cases I have chosen reveal both the possibility of gaining ground in philosophy and the collaborative nature of that project. The Ikhwān al-Ṣafā' describe their ideal man as: "Persian by breeding, Arabian in faith, Hanafite [that is, moderate] in his Islam, Iraqi in culture, Hebrew in lore, Christian in manners, Damascene in piety, Greek in the sciences, Indian in contemplation, Sufi in intimations, regal in character, masterful in thought, and divine in insight." As the Qur'ān (24:35) puts it, "God is the light of heaven and earth. The symbol of His light is a niche that holds a lamp, a lamp enclosed by glass, a glass that gleams as though it were a star, fed from a blessed olive tree neither of the East nor of the West, whose oil all but gives light even when untouched by flame—light upon light."

Notes

1. See my essay "Six Dogmas of Relativism," in M. Dascal and L. Olive, eds., *Cultural Relativism and Philosophy* (Leiden: Brill, 1991).

2. See al-Fārābī, *Fī taḥṣīl al-ṣaʿādah*, "On the Attainment of Happiness," trans. by M. Mahdi, in *Alfarabi's Philosophy of Plato and Aristotle* (Ithaca: Cornell University Press, 1962), pp. 45–49 and 39. In the *Republic* VI.495, Plato worries that the philosophically talented will forsake philosophy as they mature, leaving her "forlorn and unwed." They themselves "live an unreal and alien

life, while other unworthy wooers rush in and defile her. . . ." He calls the weakling pretenders to philosophy manikins and adds an almost Dickensian vignette "of a little bald headed tinker who has made money and just been freed from bonds and had a bath and is wearing a new garment and has got himself up like a bridegroom and is about to marry his master's daughter who has fallen into poverty and abandonment." The alien life of the philosopher beguiled away from philosophy is in his loss and the loss to society of the chance of his leadership (for which he had shown his propensity even in boyhood). The perversion in entrusting philosophy to the "manikin" is that he has no capability for leadership but squanders what intellect he has in making philosophy a cunning little craft deserving of its reputation as mere jargon mongering.

3. Plato uses the same sort of language about the true pilot at *Republic* VI.488e.

4. Mahdi, *Alfarabi's Philosophy,* pp. 29–34.

5. Ibid., p. 44 with 29–37.

6. Ibid., p. 36.

7. Ibid., pp. 28–30.

8. Ibid., p. 40.

9. Ibid., p. 37. Cf. the discussion in Joel Kraemer, "On Maimonides' Messianic Posture," in I. Twersky, ed., *Studies in Medieval Jewish History and Literature,* vol. 2 (Cambridge: Harvard University Press, 1984), pp. 109–142; Charles Butterworth, "Al-Fārābī's Statecraft: War and the Well-Ordered Regime," in J. T. Johnson and J. Kelsay, eds., *The Justification and Limitations of War in Western and Islamic Religious and Cultural Traditions* (forthcoming).

10. Mahdi, *Alfarabi's Philosophy,* pp. 36–37.

11. Ibid., p. 44.

12. Ibid., pp. 29–30, 38–39.

13. See his *Al-Fārābī on the Perfect State* (Oxford: Oxford University Press, 1985), p. 1. The bracketed explanation is Walzer's.

14. Mahdi, *Alfarabi's Philosophy,* pp. 45–47.

15. Ibid., p. 45; cf. Maimonides, *Guide to the Perplexed* I.20, 26, 36, 46, 47, 57, and my *Rambam* (New York: Viking, 1976), pp. 52–119.

16. See *Arā'* 279 and my discussion in "Jewish and Islamic Philosophy of Language," in K. Lorenz, ed., *Handbuch Sprachphilosophie* (Berlin: De Gruyter, 1991), 1.2.2.3.

17. *Arā'* 53. Cf. Maimonides, *Guide* II.6, and my discussion in L. E. Goodman, ed., *Studies in Neoplatonism and Jewish Thought* (Albany: SUNY Press, 1991).

18. See S. H. Nasr, *Three Muslim Sages* (Cambridge: Harvard University Press, 1964), p. 16, for these traditions.

19. Abu 'l-Ala al-Mawdudi, *Islamic Law and Constitution,* ed. and trans. by Kurshid Ahmad (Lahore: Islamic Publications, 1967), p. 148, and the discussion in Charles Adams, "Mawdudi and the Islamic State," in John Esposito, ed., *Voices of Resurgent Islam* (New York: Oxford University Press, 1983), pp. 99–133.

20. Al-Ghazālī's teacher, al-Juwaynī, for example had (prophetic) reser-

vations about radical atomism: if atoms could get along without accidents, he reasoned, perhaps they could get along without God.

21. See al-Ash'arī, *Kitāb al-Luma'*, ed. R. J. McCarthy (Beirut: Catholic Press, 1953), p. 99 and appendix 4. See also al-Ash'arī's *Kitāb al-Ibāna 'an Uṣūl al-Diyāna*, trans., Klein, pp. 106 ff.; A. J. Wensinck, *The Muslim Creed* (London: Cass, 1965; first ed., 1932) chap. 5.

22. Cf. al-Juwaynī, *Kitāb al-'Irshād*, ed. by Luciani, p. 2.

23. Thus al-Juwaynī calls God "the Cause of causes." This language, which al-Ghazālī echoes, is vacuous if causes are unreal. See *K. al-Irshād*, ed. by Luciani, p. 84; al-Ghazālī, *Iḥyā'* XXXV.1, 4.187.

24. Remember that all species in Aristotle are eternal and unchanging and that the universal quantifier in a syllogism bears existential import, whereas a proposition that will never be true must be classified, according to Aristotle, as impossible.

25. *The Book of Theodicy: Translation and Commentary on the Book of Job*, trans. with commentary by L. E. Goodman (New Haven: Yale University Press, 1988), pp. 126–127.

26. See Abdulaziz Sachedina, "Ali Shariati: Ideologue of the Iranian Revolution," in Esposito, *Voices*, pp. 191–217.

27. Sachedina, "Ali Shariati," p. 200.

28. *Tahāfut al-Falāsifa*, Physical Sciences, First Discussion, ed. by M. Bouyges (Beirut: Catholic Press, 1962), p. 195. This edition will be cited by page below as *TF* along with the corresponding passages in Bouyges' edition of Ibn Rushd's *Tahafut al-Tahāfut* (Beirut: Catholic Press, 1930), cited by page as *TT*. Van Den Bergh's translation, *The Incoherence of the Incoherence* (London: Luzac, 1954), is keyed to Bouyges.

29. See my article "Did al-Ghazālī Deny Causality," *Studia Islamica* 47 (1978): 83–120, and "Ordinary and Extraordinary Language in Medieval Jewish and Islamic Philosophy," *Manuscrito* 11 (1988), n. 31.

30. *TF*, pp. 203 and 200= *TT*, pp. 536 and 533.

31. See al-Ghazālī's *Risālah fī-'istiḥsān al-Khawḍ fī 'Ilm al-Kalām* in McCarthy, ed., *Kitāb al-Luma'*, p. 90; English trans., 123–125.

32. *TF*, p. 197 = *TT*, p. 525.

33. This last was the key issue in al-Ghazālī's defense of creation in the First Discussion of the *TF*, as Maimonides was keenly aware. See *TF*, p. 57 = *TT*, p. 35.

34. See the essays by John Dillon, Carl Mathis, Arthur Hyman, Bernard McGinn, David Novak, and Steven Katz in my *Neoplatonism and Jewish Thought*.

35. See Eric Ormsby, *Theodicy in Islamic Thought: The Dispute over al-Ghazālī's 'Best of all Possible Worlds'* (Princeton: Princeton University Press, 1984), for the price al-Ghazālī's paid in terms of his reputation for the effort to sustain some measure of independent human valuation of nature, as natural theology requires.

36. See Aristotle *De Caelo* I.10–12, and *Physics* III.4.203b.30.

37. Cf. e.g. Philo, *De Opificio Mundi* xvi.52. For the notion that what is natu-

ral may be judged relative to specific patterns within nature or relative to the larger pattern or tendency of nature, see the discussion of Philoponus in S. Sambursky, *The Physical World of Late Antiquity* (London: Routledge & Kegan Paul, 1962), pp. 93–96.

38. See my "Three Meanings of the Idea of Creation," in B. McGinn and D. Burrell, *God and Creation* (Notre Dame: Notre Dame University Press, 1989).

39. See his essay in L. E. Goodman, *Neoplatonism and Jewish Thought,* and Joseph Incandela, *God's Practical Knowledge and Situated Human Freedom,* (Ph.D. thesis, Princeton University, 1986).

40. For al-Ghazālī's use of the macrocosm as organism idea, see his *Ma'ārij al-Quds,* 179–196.

41. Al-Munqidh Min al-Ḍalāl, ed. by Farid Jabre (Beirut: Commission Internationale pour la Traduction des Chefs-d'Oeuvre, 1959), pp. 10–11; trans. in *The Faith and Practice of al-Ghazālī,* by William Montgomery Watt (London: George Allen & Unwin, 1963; 1953), pp. 20–21.

42. *Iḥyā'* XXXV.

43. Qutb quoted in Yvonne Haddad, "Sayyid Qutb: Ideologue of Islamic Revival," in Esposito, *Voices,* p. 82.

44. Haddad, "Sayyid Qutb," p. 81.

45. See my *Case of the Animals vs Man* (Boston: Twayne, 1978), pp. 193–196.

46. Haddad, "Sayyid Qutb," p. 81.

47. Deuteronomy 30:12; cf. P. Sanhedrin 22a, B. Baba Metzia 59b: "Even a voice from heaven proves nothing; the law of Sinai commands us to decide according to the majority" (Exodus 23:2); B. Yevamot 40a; B. Gittin 10b; Tosefta Sota, 15.10. God is said to rejoice at scholars getting the better of an argument and using the principles of the Law to depart from its apparent dicta.

48. *Islam* (Garden City, New York: Doubleday, 1968; first ed., 1966), p. 34.

49. See *'Iḥyā'* XXXV, bayān 2 (Cairo, 1312 A.H.), 4.188–191, following Makki, *Qūt al-Qulūb* II.1 (Cairo, 1310 A.H.), 2.4.

50. See *The Case of the Animals vs Man,* pp. 194–195.

51. See L. E. Goodman, "Crosspollinations: Philosophically Fruitful Exchanges between Jewish and Islamic Thought," in D. Lassner, ed., *The Jews of Islamic Lands* (Detroit: Wayne State University Press, forthcoming).

TWO DIMENSIONS OF RELIGION: REFLECTIONS BASED ON INDIAN SPIRITUAL EXPERIENCE AND PHILOSOPHICAL TRADITIONS

The challenge of modernity to traditional culture addresses itself with special force to religion. If science and humanism may be said to determine the basic values of modernity, religion has generally stood for a divinely revealed tradition. For the modern mind culture is a purely human enterprise which moves into the future in a tentative, experimental manner. For religion, on the other hand, man must seek to follow what God has revealed to him in the past. The two attitudes, thus, appear to be plainly contradictory.

Although this sense of contradiction has been borrowed from the West by some modern Indian thinkers, authors, and statesmen, most of the savants and philosophers from Ram Mohan Roy to Gandhi and Radhakrishnan have thought differently. They have looked upon modernity itself as a restoration (uddhāra) of tradition to its original purity. Defining religion in terms of pure spirituality they have distinguished its perennial dimension (sanātana-dharma) from its epochal manifestation (yuga-dharma). They have not found any essential contradiction between religion and science or religious law and social reform. Nor have they seen any reason for social conflict in the diversity of religion.

The present essay is an attempt to present and examine the immanent dialectic and axiology of this attitude towards religion and culture in the light of the philosophical and spiritual heritage of the nondualistic tradition of Advaita Vedānta and Mahāyāna Buddhism.

The problem of culture and modernity is either the problem of relating two historical phases of culture, past and present, or that of relating the ideal dimension of culture with the contemporary phase of its historical development. It is sometimes assumed that past culture, along with religion as a means of social security and welfare, will be rendered obsolete by the growth of technology, as were Paleolithic cultures by the advancement of civilization. On the other hand, it is arguable that technology does not alter the basic existential situation of man as a conscious being facing the certainty of death. From remote antiquity this is the situation with which religion has been primarily concerned, seeking to give assurance *(niyāma, abhaya)* in the face of anxiety and dread. Indeed, history itself inculcates *vanitas vanitatum,* as Vidyāraṇya, a Vedāntin, points out.[1]

Although it primarily concerns man as an individual person, a religion is at the same time a historically given tradition of a distinctive kind of value-seeking *(paramārtha-marga).* Like art, religion seeks an ideal and infinite value *(artha),* and its seeking is creative. Although creativity as free self-determination and expression is common to art and religion, creativity is primarily imaginative in art while in religion it claims to spring from the whole person rooted in its sense of reality. As Radhakrishnan notes, religion is "The reaction of the whole man to the whole reality."[2] The truth claims of religion in general, or of particular religions, have never been uncontroverted, but these controversies really reflect the inner dialectical tensions of the cultural ensemble itself of which faith and reason constitute inevitable dimensions in varying patterns of relationship.

Religion is given to us not only indirectly through its surviving records but also directly through our participation in its inwardness.[3] These two ways of apprehending religion are as different as is the reconstruction of another's ideas and experiences from one's own experiences. The historical awareness of religion is not the awareness of the object of religious awareness but of the description recorded of it subsequently through reflection and symbolization. What we reach through history is the reconstruction of empirical responses—intellectual, emotional, or practical—to the primary religious experience. On the other hand, in our participation in religious experience we gain immediate access to a distinctive kind of value ultimately realizable as spiritual freedom.[4] The historical awareness of religion remains neutral about its authenticity but necessarily perceives it within a context of human action constituting social causes and consequences. It also implies the imaginative participation of a neutral observer who reads the meaning of expressive symbols embedded in the historical records. Direct participation, on the other hand, carries the self-authenticating experience of value. If the historical awareness suffers from indirectness, distance, and uncertainty, direct participation suffers from being fragmentary, subjective, and uncritical. The study of religion exclusively from historical records tends to merge religious into social history, and the agnosticism latent in the scientific historical attitude promotes a relativistic, even skeptical point of view towards religious faith and its objects. Exclusive dependence on religious participation, on the other hand, tends to encourage the error of intolerance, which fails to see an experience different from one's own as having claims to equal authenticity. It is also difficult for direct participants to realize that their experience is an event in a context which includes their structured subjectivity, a particular symbolic tradition in which they share, and a complex of social factors.

These two ways of apprehending religion, through historical reconstruction or through direct participation, are distinct but connected and even complementary. Direct participation normally requires the mediation of a symbolic and institutional tradition. This is as true of the ordinary man today as of the great seers and prophets of the past. When Buddha set out on his spiritual quest, he was in the first instance inspired by the sight of ascetics in Kapilavastu and later instructed by them.[5] Even though he ultimately discovered a path of his own and had a unique experience, his description of the path and of his experience show that these could not have been totally unconnected with earlier tradition.[6] In fact, he himself claimed to have rediscovered an ancient truth seen by past seers and prophets.[7] The Upaniṣadic seers had similarly declared that spiritual knowledge must be had from a teacher.[8] Religious experience, thus, normally seems to presuppose tradition and issues into one. Religious belief and practice normally tend to follow some preestablished tradition. Even when they ostensibly break from tradition they appear to derive many of their elements from one or more past traditions.

This connection of religious experience with tradition is not fortuitous. Religious experience has been traditionally held to arise normally from religious faith and practice. The Buddha included faith among the Five Spiritual Powers. The *Yogasūtras* mention faith as the first means to *yoga*.[9] The *Gītā* says that those who have faith attain to knowledge.[10] Initiation into the tradition is, in fact, generally regarded as the beginning of spiritual life. Religious practice, too, involves the use of traditional symbols and prescribed actions. Religious experience, again, demands to be understood and related to the thought and institutions determining common life. This, again, requires the help of traditional ideas and symbols even though one may disagree with them in some respects. Experience and tradition, thus, appear to be inseparable.

Now tradition is the primary mode of history, that is, the mode by which culture subsists in time. The awareness of religious tradition is, thus, necessarily an awareness of history, even though this awareness may not be critical or objective. Religious experience could, as a result, be said to belong to a historical tradition in which it arises and finds its concrete existence. At the same time, the critical awareness of this tradition is hardly possible without the imaginative recreation of its focal religious experience, and that presupposes a basic acquaintance with religious life. It follows from this that while religious experience presupposes the recapitulation of a historical tradition in some sense, that history in turn finds its central focus in experience.

To these two modes of apprehension, then, correspond two distinct but interconnected dimensions of religion, namely, its inwardness accessible to experience alone and its external and historical expression in terms of social and cultural forms. With respect to human subjectivity, religion may be described as inner or spiritual illumination, while corresponding to man's objective being, social and natural, religion may be seen expressed in social and symbolic forms. Concrete religious life reflects the transcendental unity as well as the empirical duality of human nature. Man's awareness of his subjective existence enables him to distinguish it from mere natural or animal existence and gives him intimations of freedom and dread as well as the sense of obligation and commitment. The emergence of religious faith transmutes this existential awareness by intimating the reality of a supernatural order and imbuing it with the hope of immortal life and assurance in the face of death. This change in inner awareness expresses itself diversely in the social context. It changes the awareness of other persons and the meaning of familiar acts, and this change is reflected in the creation of new norms and symbols. The glimmering of spiritual awareness in the loneliness of subjective being, however, does not at once alter the habitual representations of natural and social objects so that the two kinds of representations remain mixed up. Similarly the working of moral awareness at the interpersonal level remains fixed with the habitual perceptions and patterns of the biosocial world. The association of introverting spiritual awareness with the extroverting awareness of the senses tends to generate tension just as is done by the association of moral consciousness with a social structure based on egoistic and instinctive tendencies. As the seeking for authentic or spiritual being, religion has a timeless dimension. As the social and cultural expression of this seeking, religion has an inevitably historical dimension involved in change and transformation. Compounded of mutually superimposed subjectivity and objectivity, human self-consciousness is subject to contradictory pulls.[11] The true Self or authentic being is obscured by inauthentic images and its autonomy is lost in the heteronomy belonging to the representations of Nature. The struggle of authentic and inauthentic self-awareness is, thus, perpetual in human life. It has been diversely pictured in religious tradition. Its pervasive description in the Indian tradition has been in terms of Wisdom and Folly, or, rather, Vision and Delusion, *vidyā, avidyā*.[12] The same duality and tension of human self-awareness expresses itself at the practical and social level in terms of moral perceptions and conflict. Instincts and reason, egoism and altruism, interests and values form the complex fabric of social existence. The really moral as distinguished from the purely utilitarian aspect of the social order may be said to derive from its vision of authentic existence. The particular content of this socioethical world, however, depends as much on the character of its foundational vision as on the conditions of civilization obtaining in that particular society.

While vision constitutes the timeless essence of religion, it presupposes a systematic practice which in turn presupposes a doctrinal system, a moral code, and a social organization which would facilitate it. The social ethics in which a religion expresses itself practically may be said to constitute its changing historical body.

It might be objected that this characterization of religion as a timeless vision expressing itself in an evolving social ethic is at once too wide and too narrow, since its inclusion of vision would exclude primitive religions while it would at the same time include those nonreligious modern societies which do have a secular vision and corresponding social ethic. Now as far as primitive religions are concerned, it is difficult to reach their inner content with any degree of certainty. Of the actual religions of prehistoric times there are no adequate remains or records. As for the surviving primitive religions, much of their documentation suffers from lack of sympathy *ab initio*. Their observers unfortunately either believed that spiritual religion could hardly have existed before a specific historical revelation, or they tended to confuse primitive religion with primitive civilization. If we turn from the documentation of travelers, missionaries, or anthropologists to ancient records in India, we find that Tantricism includes and sanctifies a good deal of what was undoubtedly a part of primitive religious ideas and practices. The Buddhist *Sādhana-mālā* contains many examples of this. The fact is that vision or *vidyā* in the context of religion should not be understood to mean an intellectual or rational overview or insight. It has rather a mystical or occult sense and means the immediate or intuitive apprehension in a state of concentrated absorption that is reached as the culmination of religious practices. All such visions are not the same although they share a common dimension, namely, of producing a sense of having gained access to a principle transcending the natural order, often as a principle of awesome power and majesty called Deity or *devatā*. This would serve to distinguish religious vision from any secular view. Religious vision is neither fantasy nor a rational view but an intuitive, supernormal experience.[13] Religious ethic, as understood in the Indian tradition, is similarly not the outcome of the rational calculation of interests and utilities or mere consensus, but grounded in the purity and elevation of the heart *(citta-śuddhi)* and the disinterested recognition of a higher law *(dharma)*. The fact is that moral consciousness as such is an integral part of religion. It is a form of disinterested willing accompanied by the higher emotions or *kuśala-hetus*. Its subject is the person endowed with rational discrimination and its object is the ideal self glimpsed in terms of its perfections and law. The translation of moral consciousness into concrete social or practical norms, however, required its interpretation in terms of specific classes of subjects and objects as given in specific situations. Neither can these situations be concretely universal or recurrent, nor can the moral consciousness be translated into a code unambiguously or infallibly. The fact is that such codes can only be worked out by a faculty which supplements morality and mediates between the general ideal and the detailed real. It may be said that insofar as a system of social norms may be taken to be expressive of pure moral consciousness, it may be identified with religious ethic. A good deal of social ethics, however, which is concerned with norms relating to empirical ends and means, would remain outside it.

It needs to be clearly realized that religion and irreligion may both claim or appear to be what they are not. A person or group may hold orthodox religious doctrines and practice religious rites without being really religious just as a person or society which denies religion may yet give high place to idealistic moral principles and thus be religious in practice. For example, although the modern ideals of liberty and equality, social justice or human rights, have arisen in the wake of rational humanism in nonreligious contexts, their essential spirituality or morality cannot be questioned. The modern care for the insane or the prevention of cruelty to animals is another illustration of genuine higher emotions without any reference to religious beliefs. On the other hand, it is obvious that in earlier ages, although religious and moral consciousness apprehended some of these values in the abstract, it was unable to give them an adequate social expression. Modern psyche, thus, cannot be considered irreligious since its practical idealism and humanism are deeply moral and hence essentially religious.

Against this must be placed the common assumption of historians and social scientists that modern civilization is not only secular but in important respects antireligious. Gibbon had claimed this in the pages of his *Decline and Fall of the Roman Empire,* where he described "The triumph of barbarism and religion." The irony of Gibbon may be said to be borne out by the fact that the modern advance of civilization has been apparently paralleled by the retreat of religion:

> The Sea of faith
> Was once, too, at the full . . .
> But now I only hear
> Its melancholy, long, withdrawing roar.
>   (Mathew Arnold, "Dover Beach")

History and anthropology both attest to the fact that while religion has been since prehistoric times the prime determinant of social and cultural forms, it has now been increasingly deprived of this role. There is indeed an influential modern opinion which regards religion as no more than a dated historical formation which cannot be expected to give any knowledge of reality or any guidance in matters of social behavior, organization, or policy. This view of the antagonism of modernity to religion would be supported by the opinion of those who find modern civilization characterized by materialism and worldliness or, on the other hand, by the opinions of those who regard religion as nothing more than a subjective attitude, an illusion, or a mere ideology.

In this gross form the opposition of modern to religious values will perhaps be discounted by thoughtful persons. It is true that religion has increasingly ceased to organize society in modern times but modern society is not on that account less expressive of moral values. Love and pity, selflessness and justice, are as much modern as ancient. Indeed, they have found better institutional realization now than ever before. As for worldliness and violence, or egoism, individual or collective, these have plagued mankind from ancient times. There is no substantial reason, then, for opposing modernity to religion in its practical or moral aspect. There is no doubt that the traditional social codes of religions are now largely dated but that only means that older lawgivers, even when religious prophets or seers, could not rise above the limitation of their times. Indeed there is a reason why no social code capable of detailed practical guidance can ever be universal. Morality is rooted in the heart and expresses itself primarily in terms of volition characterized by selflessness and motivated by the higher emotions. In its primary form moral consciousness does not contain any detailed practical prescriptions but merely a general direction for the realization of an ideal end. While this consciousness is universal as are the basic ideal ends apprehended in different religious traditions, they cannot be converted into any practical code without reference to some particular social reality. For example, the ancient Indian ideal of nonpossession or *aparigraha* may claim universal validity but the institutions and laws of mendicancy do not enjoy the same status, and in any case they have varied in different religious traditions and ages. Charity, again, is universally admitted as a moral ideal in all religions. The modern welfare state seeks to alleviate poverty in a different but more efficient manner. Peace and nonviolence have a high place in all religions and yet no religion has seriously outlawed war or found an alternative to the state which is essentially coercive. In this respect there has been no change in modern times except that the growth in the power of the state has made its action more effective and wars more fearful.

This distinction between universal moral principles and the codes of social ethics is clearly made in the Indian tradition. Universal moral principles are called *sādhārana dharma* which is distinguished from *varṇāśrama dharma*. The universal principles are held to be absolute and obligatory on all persons at all times while the norms of the social code are relative to one's position and role within a specific social order. The *Yoga-sūtras* list the universal principles thus: Nonviolence, Truth, Nonstealing, Chastity, Nonpossession, Purity, Contentment, Austerity, Study, and Piety.[14] Manu lists the ten great features of *dharma* as Fortitude, Forgiveness, Self-control, Nonstealing, Purity, Control of the Senses, Reason, Self-knowledge, Truth, and Absence of Anger.[15] These and other such lists are elaborations of a single fundamental principle. The *Mahābhārata* states that the essence of virtue is doing good to others, the essence of sin injuring them. The *Gītā* similarly defines morality in terms of not doing to others what one would not like to be done to oneself. It also defines right action by the disinterested performance of duty.[16] The *Yogabhāsya* says that all the virtues are only contributory to the perfection of nonviolence.[17] Buddhist philosophers have explained that morality is nothing but good will *(kuśala-cetana)* and its exercise. The goodness of the will depends on its motivation *(hetu)*. If the will is not defiled by self-interest, hatred, and irrationality but is associated with disinterested love and reason, then it is good will. Beginning with nonviolence, moral life finds its perfection in compassion. That despite sectarian differences there is a core of common moral principles in all religious traditions was clearly announced by Aśoka, who declared that although sects and schools differ, they all seek the same thing, namely, self-discipline and the purity of the heart.[18] This vision of the ideal unity of religions *(samavāya)* remains the basis of religious toleration.

It is well known that Aśoka characterizes *dharma* only by its moral attitude without any reference to metaphysical or theological doctrines. This has puzzled many modern investigators. But the fact is that Aśoka merely follows the Buddha, who had preached a moral way without reference to any speculative views or *ditthis,* metaphysical or theological.[19] He definitely discouraged metaphysical speculation. For him the spiritual experience is essentially self-authenticating and truth a matter of personal realization *(pratyātmavedanīya)*. The end of the spiritual path is simple freedom from the passions, for oneself and for all others.

Now many religious traditions derive moral obligations from the scriptures or divine commandments or some given social or ecclesiastical tradition. Brahmanical works regard the Vedas as the ultimate source of *dharma,* though they also regard tradition, example, and conscience, too, as supplementary sources. Apart from conscience or the example of authentic persons, the other sources are really required for deriving concrete social and ritual duties. This concrete social ethic of traditional religion or its scriptural authority was not accepted by the Buddhists or the Jainas or many of the medieval saints or modern social religious reformers. This attitude of emphasizing a universal morality and rejecting the authority of the traditional socioreligious ethic was an ancient attitude which gained power as a social force after the introduction of modernity. The contemporary Indian attitude does not regard secular, modern values as being opposed to spiritual religion but only to diehard and fanatical traditions that regard religious law as the basis of social and political identity. This attitude in contemporary India derives immediately from Nehru and Gandhi, behind whom stand the great religious and social reformers of nineteenth-century India. They discounted any basic contradiction between the values of liberal modernity

and those of spiritual religion. They argued that general religious tolerance and synthesis as well as the neutrality of the state in religious matters were pervasive features of the age-old tradition of India, that the
social inequality current in the caste system was inauthentic and the
result of historical corruption, that individual freedom and social equality were in line with ancient spiritual ideas, and that far from there
being any conflict between religious faith and science, there was every
reason for supposing that the two were in perfect harmony—so much so
that the progress of science could well be used to confirm religious faith.
Raja Ram Mohan Roy virtually founded a new comparative study of
religions on the assumption of their fundamental unity. Rāmakrishna
Paramahaṃsa confirmed this idea on the basis of his own remarkable
personal experiences. Gandhi and Vinoba have illustrated the idea in
practice. Dr. Bhagwan Das and Radhakrishnan gave it theoretical support. The basic assumption in this way of thinking is that what is essential to the religious tradition may be perennially recognized and interpreted rationally. What is merely the product of a particular age of
social history and civilization must be regarded as accidental and dis-
pensable. This distinction between the perennial and historical dimensions of religion enables the reconciliation of its continuity with change
as it is reformed and updated.

It may be argued that this is too facile a reconciliation because it disregards some important religious values. Religious practice is not simply moral but also includes prayer, worship, and ritual, which require
the virtues of obedience, piety, and devotion. Besides practice, religion
also has the aspect of doctrinal belief or faith. The zealous propagation
of one's faith, the struggle against its enemies, and the fight to establish
a society and state exclusively on its basis have also been sometimes
regarded as religious duties. In all these respects religious traditions are
not only different but antagonistic. They are also in these respects hostile to the modern values of rationalism and secularism. Religions also
give the impression of providing supernatural means (*alaukika sādhana*)
for the realization of such secular ends as security, welfare, and satisfaction. As such they appear to be a wishful or magical alternative to scientific technology or social action.

Now as for prayer, worship, and ritual they are nothing but the invocation of symbols for directing the mind to the object of faith. In other
words they are really a recollecting of faith or a strengthening of it.
Insofar as faith centers on God, devotion would arise naturally from the
depth of faith. It would then seem that the crucial fact to be considered
is the nature and content of faith. The old Indian word for faith is
śraddhā which means placing one's heart in something. It originally
denoted the attitude of heartfelt enthusiasm toward the practice of spiritual life and the source of its guidance. In the context of a personal spiritual relationship with the Master it strengthened receptivity and

unflagging zeal in religious practice. According to the ancient formula, from faith or trustful receptivity follows zealous and unflagging effort, from effort comes recollection, from recollection concentration, and from concentration vision or intuitive knowledge. The real content of faith becomes a matter of knowledge only at this stage. The content of faith as belief at the outset is a verbalized and discursive opinion. As such it is incapable of representing spiritual truth in its wholeness, transcendence, or infinity. It can only attempt to communicate the truth in a negative, analogical, metaphorical, or symbolic manner.[20] Faith as doctrine is merely the finger pointing to the moon, and there could be numerous alternative pointers depending on who is to be enlightened. The Buddha, thus, laid down that what is important in the teaching is the meaning, not the words, and the meaning can be properly understood only through personal realization. Until such realization, the doctrine is nothing but the indication of a practical path. Such an intellectual understanding of the path is styled the Right View or *samyak dṛṣṭi,* but it is still a *dṛṣṭi* or view, and ultimately all views must be abandoned. For the beginner it is only a first step to climbing toward the mansion of wisdom. He must not, however, hold to it as a speculative view but only as practical guidance. Else he would be like the child catching the finger while seeking the moon or like the fool who is afraid to abandon the raft even on reaching the other shore. The Buddhists believe that the Master taught different doctrines to different disciples in accordance with their capacity and predispositions. All the doctrines merely express his skill in means. The Buddha indeed ridiculed those who fought for their different religious doctrines. He compared them to the Seven Blind Men who disputed the nature of the elephant on the basis of their fragmentary experiences.[21] Being beyond words and concepts, spiritual truth cannot be described in its essence. Only the practical path to its realization may be indicated, and that, too, must vary from individual to individual.

In the Upaniṣads similarly a distinction is made between *paravidyā* and *aparavidyā,* higher learning and lower learning.[22] All the arts and sciences including the scriptures and the sacred lore are included in the lower learning. When the sage Nārada goes to Sanat Kumara and complains that despite all his learning he could not attain to freedom from sorrow, the latter explained that nothing but the Infinite could satisfy the human spirit.[23] The lower learning concerned with the finite is ultimately no more than ignorance or *avidyā.* Śaṅkara declares that all the scriptures, as also all the rational means of knowledge, presuppose the false egoistic self-consciousness arising from the mutual superimposition of the Self and the Nonself. Consequently all empirical and logical knowledge including scriptural knowledge is within a radical or transcendental illusion.[24]

Insofar as faith has cognitive meaning, it falls within the working of innate ignorance or *avidyā,* but it is part of the practical path that leads to the higher immediacy of *prajñā* or *paravidyā.* It is a common assumption in the Indian tradition that man is subject to a primordial or original ignorance which gives him a bodily self-awareness and causes attachment to the objects and pleasures of sense experience. The Buddhists argue that sensuous immediacy as well as intellectual constructions both obscure the real nature of things, which can be realized only in terms of a synoptic vision such as Buddha had when he became enlightened. The force of existential suffering and human bondage is rooted in illusion, and freedom belongs to the eternal nature of the "self" or the noumenal ground of empirical existence *(dharmatā),* which is revealed in the culminating vision of spiritual *praxis* or *sādhana.* In view of the eternal or *nityasiddha* nature of spiritual reality and its inalienable self-illumination, spiritual *praxis* or *sādhana* must itself be in an ultimate sense illusory. It would be like an element in the dream which serves to wake up the dreamer, illusory but serviceable pragmatically.[25] Similar is the status of scriptures and their dogmatics. They have a relevance in the context of spiritual practice. Their pragmatic truth, *sāmvṛta* or *vyāvahārika,* as it has been called, presupposes a specific context, personal or social.

If the empirical existence of man is marked by suffering and bondage owing to the delusive effect of his spiritual ignorance, spiritual illumination reveals an eternal reality where no duality or limitation obtains. Since the subject-object distinction is said not to obtain here, it is obviously difficult to interpret it. It has been interpreted in Vedānta as self-knowledge on account of its being nonobjective immediate awareness. It has been interpreted in Buddhism as Emptiness on account of its absence of determination. It has also been interpreted as the revelation of Divinity since it may be construed as the unique ground from which all subjects and objects seem to emerge.[26] The fact is that these interpretations represent the working of speculative reason and are not adequate to nondual experience. Indeed the very use of the word experience is questionable. All experience appears relative to particular subjects and objects. It is a transient event in time and subject to error. In its immediacy it is too vague to constitute worthwhile knowledge. As the basis of judgmental knowledge it needs the relational constructions of the intellect. If experience or knowledge is taken in this ordinary sense, spiritual vision is certainly neither "experience" nor "knowledge" because its prerequisite is the suspension of the normal faculties of perception and thought, namely, the senses and the intellect. It is the faith of the Buddhist and the Vedāntic mystic that beyond the empirical existence and consciousness of man there is a timeless principle which cannot be determined by the categories of thought but may be revealed in a nondual awareness. Despite different metaphysical standpoints and religious attitudes most Indian schools of thought have accepted the reality of a suprarational intuitive knowledge which is free from the possibility of error. This kind of knowledge is free from images and concepts, words and relations. It represents the natural luminosity of consciousness, which is infinite at its highest. Different systems of Yoga seek to develop the methodology of restoring consciousness to its original or ideal condition. although theories differ, the practice of Yoga has a remarkable uniformity.

It is the belief in Yoga and the possibility of direct spiritual knowledge born of it which has remained the bedrock of religious faith in India. It is the possession of such knowledge which is held to give authenticity to the religious teacher who must also naturally exemplify the moral ideal of the free person.[27] In different ages of social and cultural crises from the sixth century B.C. to the early twentieth century there have been successive waves of such authentic teachers. From Buddha and Mahāvīra, Nāgārjuna, and Śaṅkara to Nanak, Kabir, and Chaitanya, and to Rāmakrishna Paramahaṃsa, Ramana Maharsi, and Sri Aurobindo in our own times there has been a long succession of such teachers who could say, like Rāmakrishna, that they had personal and direct knowledge of the spiritual verities that they talked about. Narendra, who became Vivekananda, later declared that Yoga provides religion with its scientific basis.[28]

We might consider an alternative view of the nature and authenticity of religion at this stage. On this view religion is nothing if not the love of God who reveals Himself to some seer or prophet or incarnates Himself to save man from sin and evil and opens for him the way to eternal life and blessedness. God, the scriptures, the prophet or the incarnation, and faith constitute the four pillars on which the edifice of religion is reared. The first three being already given, the task of the religious man is to believe and conform to what God has revealed in the scriptures through the prophet or incarnation. All higher religions appear to believe that they have originated from a foundational revelation which represents an encounter between human reality in time and a superhuman reality beyond time. Concretely this revelation means to each tradition a set of literary texts or scriptures held to be authoritative. Although different religious traditions conceive revelation and scriptures differently, all of them face a similar predicament. As soon as revelation is identified with a literary text, it acquires the character of a historic cultural document of which the *meaning* can only be understood in terms of the *context* of a specific stage in the development of human reality, social as well as individual. The question of its *truth* is similarly complicated by the fact that while the authority of the revelation derives from the timeless superhuman reality, revelation itself appears to be an experience occurring to a particular human being in a particular situation. Will not revelation be affected by the limitations and fallibility of its recipient? The fact that for a specific tradition revelation is available only in a specific linguistic expression makes the question especially pertinent. Language is a historically determined social phenomenon and the scriptures must represent its use by a human individual in accordance with current usage and his own habits of thought and expression. It would be a natural temptation to think of the scriptures as the literary work of their human authors rather than of God. Perhaps they could be revealed in the same sense in which poetry is inspired. This is the common approach of modern rationalists, historians, and anthropologists towards ancient scriptures except that some of them might make an exception of the scriptures of the faith to which they themselves belong. Unfortunately this approach misses the very category of the religious by reducing its expressions to mere social facts.

It is only after premising that religion is a distinct and autonomous dimension of human experience that the problem of relating it to the changing history of society and culture as a whole arises. That revelation as expressed in scriptural records has a necessary sociohistorical aspect has been argued above. That the scriptures express eternal and supernatural truth in an infallible manner is an article of faith on which the authenticity of the religious tradition depends. How is the plain historicity of the scriptures to be reconciled with their claim to timeless authority?

Among Brahmanical thinkers the Vedas were accepted as the scriptures of prime authority, though the nature of the Vedas was diversely conceived in different schools. The most orthodox were the Mīmāṃsakas, who held that the Vedas constitute a literal, eternal, and impersonal revelation.[29] The Veda consists of letters, words, and sentences in a unique order. This literal set has subsisted through all time and it has done so in a self-subsistent and impersonal manner. The Veda is revealed as word, word as uncreated and superhuman, eternally subsisting but known among men through an unbroken and immemorial tradition. Not being the words spoken by any person, the Veda is free from the possibility of prejudice and error.

The obvious difficulties in this defense of the Veda as eternal and infallible word were pointed out by other schools. Words, being sequences of perishing sounds, are ephemeral. Their power of signification, too, is conventional and dependent on social usage. What language does is to communicate human intents and purposes. Being an example of linguistic usage the Vedas could hardly be eternal and superhuman. The Vedas, indeed, themselves refer to their earlier and later human authors who claim to be poets. They also refer to various historical persons and places. The ideas they express are sometimes irrational and not always in good taste.

In reply to such criticism the Mīmāṃsakas defended their position by distinguishing words from the sounds which express them. Articulate sounds are doubtless perishable but they are manifestations of ideal sound-units represented as letters. These can be recognized as identical in varying sounds. Actual sounds and these ideal phonemes or *varṇas* may be compared to the sign-vehicle and the sign. The words are sequences of such ideal sound units or letters. Nor can language be regarded as a human creation because men are known always to have used language and never to have created it. If someone had no access to language he would grow up dumb. Language is learnt as a standard preexisting pattern of signs and meanings, not as an exercise in new and arbitrary creation. The use of language seeks to conform to a given standard which education seeks to maintain. Deviations from it indeed produce linguistic corruptions. Even though these corrupt languages may become socially current it does not mean that the original language ceases to subsist in its ideal form.

Nor, again, is it right to think of language primarily as the expression of human intentions. A sentence expresses a meaning which follows from the sentence itself, not from a person. These meanings are merely sentential intentions. The Mīmāṃsakas deny that Vedic sentences contain any proper names referring to human beings or historical places. The Vedas primarily consist of universal or hypothetical propositions of an injunctive nature. What they reveal are eternal norms of action. The so-called human authors of the Vedas are only the seers to whom its vision became available. The Mīmāṃsaka view of the Vedas, thus, excludes all empirical facts from its primary content which consists of transcendent values and connected norms. Since man cannot attain to any knowledge of transcendent truths himself, the Vedic scriptures are the sole source from which he can gain guidance with respect to norms and values, which go beyond natural instincts and experiences.

For orthodox Vedicism, then, the Vedas as scripture are the eternal and impersonal word from which alone man can gain a knowledge of religion, which consists in the performance of duties enjoined in the scriptures. There is no reference to God in this view, and mysticism of all kinds is rejected.

The Naiyāyikas or Logicians, on the other hand, regard the Vedic scriptures as the word of God, who is conceived as the supreme person. The Vedas, thus, become the revelation of the eternal wisdom of God for the ultimate good of man. The grace of God is responsible for this revelation to the seers. This idea of God as revealing the scriptures out of His grace is repeated in the various Agamic sects in different ways. These views have a certain similarity to those current in the Higher Religions of Semitic origin except that in none of these Indian views is revelation a unique historic event. It is either timeless or recurrent.

In contradistinction to the Vedic or Āgamic views, which define the scriptures either as the word of God or as the eternal and nonpersonal word, the non-Vedic Indian faiths regard the scriptures to be the recorded teachings of some perfected or enlightened man, someone who has reached authenticity and attained to freedom. The Jainas believe that the canon has suffered a good deal of loss in the course of time, but they also believe that the basic principles of the faith have been preserved traditionally. Besides, Jaina saints and Masters claim to have personally realized them from time to time. The tradition of Jaina faith thus becomes a living tradition of spirituality which is capable of self-authentication. Nevertheless the tradition remains remarkably conservative, not so much because it holds fast wholly and literally to some ancient texts but because it firmly maintains some ancient principles in theory and practice. This conservatism, however, is confined to the life of the Jaina ascetics, but does not affect the adaptability of the Jaina lay community.

The Buddhist view of the scriptures is quite distinctive. The scriptures were generally accepted to be the words of the Buddha, but whether a text attributed to the Buddha was really authentic needed to be examined. The ancient criterion in effect was that the text should be found in the canon as authorized in the First Council. Unfortunately, after the Second Council and the growth of the Eighteen Sects, different versions of the canon itself came to be current. The old sects then stuck to accepting only their own versions as correct, rejecting the other versions as inauthentic. The Mahāyānists went further to devise a rational test. The authenticity of the text must be judged from its conformity to the true nature of things or *dharmatā*. The words of the Buddha were identified with words expressive of eternal verities. Since identities are reversible, any expression of spiritual truth could therefore be deemed to be the words of the Buddha. This effectively replaces the concept of scriptural authority by that of rational authority. At the same time it would certainly tend to dilute the reliance on merely old texts. The Mahāyana certainly produced a vast amount of new *sūtras* attributed to the Buddha. A distinction was also made between the texts to be understood in their plain sense or in their hidden sense. The notion of a secret or mystical tradition was also formulated. The situation was further complicated by the fact that, from the beginning, the Buddha refused to have his own words canonized. He wanted everyone to understand his meaning and remember it in his own speech and he spoke to everyone in the specific context of his individual needs and disposition. The initial divergence of remembered words which this situation must have produced could never be completely eliminated by the Ecumenical Councils because none of them was attended by all the parties. While a vast mass of canonical literature thus proliferated, another view tended to gain ground that spiritual truth is inaccessible except to a mystical vision. It is true that the Buddha had always emphasized the need for personal experience, but most Buddhists believed that the Buddha had used words as an expedient. But was it really possible that the Buddha, ever absorbed in the vision of spiritual truth, could have used words? The view, therefore, was advanced that the Buddha had in reality never spoken. The real Buddha, indeed, can never speak, though he may appear to do so as an expedient.

Buddhist logic tended to support the mystical tendency of Buddhist thought. Word and thought are inseparably joined together in a single process of conceptual construction designed to enable man to act successfully in the situation in which he finds himself. Meanings are not to be identified with reality but are only ideal constructs and their validity or usefulness is only pragmatic. Words may, then, be seen as sign-constructions with an essential element of arbitrariness arising from the historical conditioning of the minds to which they relate, that is, to their habitual tendencies, ideas, and purposive activities. The significance of words rests on the knowledge and character of the person who uses them and the context in which they are used. They can, however, only have a relative and pragmatic meaning. They can never communicate the noumenal nature of reality or spiritual truth.

On this mystical view of "revelation," there cannot be any such thing as a unique revelation. Revelation exists only as an inward vision, but the vision is theoretically attainable by everyone. The Buddha as a human individual thus ceases to be of importance. The truth itself, of which the realization makes one the Buddha, becomes the real Buddha. The essence of Buddhahood is *bodhi* or intuitive vision, where "the mind becomes non-mind."

Revelation may, thus, be seen to have two distinct but connected meanings. It may mean a definite verbalized message recorded in scriptural texts or it may mean inner illumination or inspiration. Both these meanings are connected because without the scriptural record revelation would not found a tradition, and without being regarded as inspired it would lack authenticity and again fail to found a tradition. Whether the scriptures are regarded as the eternal word or as the word of God or as the words of an enlightened or inspired person, in every case, they are the manifestation of eternal knowledge which could happen through the medium of many persons. In no case is the revealed scripture a unique historical event. In every case, however, we have a fixed literary text or texts from a past age of which the understanding and authority have to contend with changed linguistic, social, and intellectual conditions. Since the scriptures invariably speak in a past tongue and idiom within a context where the sociohistorical parameters have undergone change, they cannot be understood without a process of interpretation, linguistic, intellectual, and contextual. This process involves the decoding of archaic words, idioms, and symbols and the rediscovery of the essential context in its universal aspect. It is the recovery of the symbolic meanings and the recreation of the original but essential context that present problems of which the form changes with time. During the long historical ages of the religious tradition in India several devices were developed consciously or unconsciously to maintain the intelligibility and relevance of scriptural texts. In the first place, the scriptures themselves were allowed to grow for a considerable time. Whether Vedic, Buddhist, or Jaina, the scriptures constituted in their earliest form a growing oral tradition where the interpretative understanding of successive generations of students could not be wholly kept out of the original text. In the case of Vedic literature it grew over centuries and the seers were distinguished as earlier and later. Even the *Brāhmaṇa* literature, which described ritual, was accepted as part of the revealed scripture. In this literature verses from the ancient hymns are quoted and applied to suit a developed ritualistic context. The *Āraṇyakas* and the *Upaniṣads* were also counted as *śruti* although they were much later and include philosophical debates in historical time and place. It is the *Upaniṣads* that have remained the core of Vedic revelation for Vedānta, which is philosophical Hinduism *par excellence*. On the other hand, the priestly class strove to maintain the ritualistic tradition and emphasized the authority of the *Brāhmaṇas*. Apart from the careful study of the ancient language through the sciences of grammar, etymology, and lexicography, a whole science of exegesis called *Mīmāṃsā* was developed for the purpose. Side by side with the canons of contextual interpretation, the commentators also used selective emphasis on different sections of the scriptures as an important method of adapting them to the changing tendencies of later ages.

In the early post-Vedic age a series of systematic formulations were made on the basis of the earlier sacred literature as well as new philosophical and spiritual tendencies. These were called *smṛti* or tradition in distinction to *śruti* or revelation. In practice the guidance of the *smṛti* was accepted for the elucidation of the *śruti*. These *smṛti* works continued to grow for centuries and were not subject to the same careful textual check as the *śruti*. As a result, *smṛti* works, especially the *Purāṇas*, contain many apocryphal works, and except for modern historical criticism there is no way of distinguishing the genuine from the apocryphal. The result was that a millennium during which the revealed scriptures of *śruti* continued to be created was succeeded by another during which grew up the *smṛti* works embodying the sacred tradition. For all practical purposes the scriptures meant the *śruti* plus the *smṛti*, the two together constituting a vast literature which summed up the historical development of more than two millennia.

As schools and sects proliferated after the classical age, the masters or *ācāryas* who founded them or propagated their cause composed commentaries on selected scriptural texts. These commentaries, which adapt old texts to new ideas and customs, served in effect to continue the process of silent modification which the *smṛtis* had already carried a long way. The other side of this process was, of course, the conservative continuance of archaic ideas and institutions.

By the side of this interpretative adaptation and continuation there was also a more radical tendency, which rejected ancient scriptures and appealed to reason or personal experience or to new and alternative scriptures. This can be illustrated by the Bhāgavatas or the Pāśupatas, the Buddhists or some of the medieval sects and saints. The methods traditionally used to adapt the scriptures to altered needs, thus, included the following: accepting the work of new seers as scriptures or attributing new scriptures to old authors, supplementing the revealed scriptures or *śruti* by works embodying the authoritative tradition of *smṛti,* developing an elaborate science of interpretation, understanding scriptural texts in the light of commentaries, even rejecting the old scriptures on the basis of personal experience the record of which tends to acquire a nearly scriptural authority. Some of the devices used in interpretative adaptation are: selective textual emphasis, appeal to etymological, metaphorical, or symbolic meanings, delimitation of the application of the text to some specific meanings, delimitation of the application of the text to some specific context, determining an order of priority between alternative texts, and distinguishing between alternative points of view from which the texts could be evaluated.

It would be obvious that the continuity of the religious tradition in India has been in and through changes. Concepts and doctrines, symbols and institutions, have changed, but some of the basic values and the method of realizing them have remained the same. Perhaps the focal point of these values may be said to be the freedom of the self and the method of realizing it as Yoga. "This is the highest duty or *dharma,* namely, attaining to the vision of the self through Yoga." The most obvious fact about the self is that it is self-evident and undeniable even though its nature may be disputed. The Vedānta held the self to be the only reality, essentially transcendent. At the other end of the scale were the materialists for whom the living body was the only self. Others identified the self with the soul or individual spiritual principle capable of knowing and willing essentially or *per accidens.* Such a soul was often felt to require the complementary concept of God where it would find its fulfillment. The *Upaniṣads,* however, declared one should worship the self through contemplation. The self is, indeed, the real divinity within. Even for the theistic dualists the individual soul must realize its spiritual nature before it can genuinely turn away from the world towards God. The Buddhists deny the self in the sense of an individual soul but they reject materialism also and believe that unless one sheds Everyman's false notion of the self, one cannot be free from suffering. Thus despite theological and metaphysical differences there is an agreement on all sides that enlightenment about the self is the highest end or at least a *sine qua non* for it, and that this end cannot be attained without getting rid of a false notion of the self. An innate delusion pertaining to the self is the original cause of human suffering. This delusion consists in identifying the self with some natural or social object. All the schools are agreed that the physical body or the social relations and roles to which the ego is attached do not constitute the true self. The sense of self in such objects is the basic cause of suffering. Even the mind and its states and processes fall within the nonself because they, too, are ephemeral events and objects. Objectivity and finitude, transience and dependence, these are the characteristics of the nonself, of what cannot be the self since the very notion of the self requires it to be for itself subjectively and timelessly. Even without agreeing about the nature of the self, all the schools are agreed that the attachment of the ego to the nonself must be eradicated. This removal of *avidyā* is the precondition of the freedom of the self.

Now freedom has an empirical and a transcendental meaning. Empirically, freedom means *kartṛtva,* the power of the self to act by itself without the constraint of another. Freedom in this sense is the presupposition of moral responsibility. Transcendentally, freedom refers to *mukti,* the very being of the self by itself. The two meanings are connected, the first being initial and instrumental, the second final and essential. As soon as self-conscious choice *(sankalpa, cetanā)* emerges, action moves from the instinctive *(pravṛtti)* to the moral plane *(karman).* It is the sense of the ubiquity of existential suffering in the life of action and experience which leads to the search for spiritual freedom. It means in the first place freedom from suffering where suffering is not simply pain but the tears which attach to things by virtue of their mortality. In the second place, it is the eradication of external constraints or heteronomy. Freedom in this second sense is a precondition of the elimination of suffering and cannot be achieved without detachment from temporal objects, physical, social, or psychic. Since human existence was traditionally conceived as a cycle of birth and death interspersed with experience or suffering, the freedom of the self could be described as freedom from this cycle or *saṁsāra.* Freedom or *mukti,* thus, means freedom from ignorance about the self, that is, *avidyā,* freedom from the passions or *kleśa,* freedom from suffering or *duḥkha,* and finally freedom from death and time. The Buddhists, the Jainas, and the Yogins also conceive the ideal of freedom from all limitations to knowledge, while the Siddhas seek freedom from all natural limitations. Such freedom would be possible only if the self were an eternal and spiritual principle with inherent knowledge and power. For the Advaitins the self is universal and self-sufficient. Its freedom is its essence and is nothing but its infinity. Its realization is no more than the dispelling of an illusion and requires no real action or change for the real self does not act. When duality and time are held to be real and a distinction is made between the self and God, the freedom of the self becomes the freedom of willing or choosing its object, while in God it becomes the power of creating at will. If the self is endowed with a real will its freedom must imply the power of choosing effectively, and that presupposes right knowledge.

While in Advaita right knowledge manifests the eternal freedom of the self, in the theistic systems it turns the soul towards God making the real love of God possible. The soul is freed from the world and surrenders its will to the infinite freedom of God.

The freedom which is presupposed in moral action belongs to the self as an embodied rational and social person who is both a subject and an object. This freedom is at least partly illusory because insofar as the self is constituted as an object, it assumes corresponding limitations and departs from its own real nature. For this reason religious traditions in India are agreed that moral freedom in temporal life is only a stepping stone to spiritual freedom in eternity. It should not, however, be supposed that this attitude totally neglected the social institutionalization of freedom. It was realized that the practice of moral and spiritual life does require a congenial social, economic, and political order. The Dharma-śāstra took up the task of regulating society to facilitate moral and religious life. The Nītiśāstra sought to lay down prudential principles of economic and political policy. Religious freedom was well recognized, and so was a good deal of autonomy in relation to ethnic, regional, occupational, or religious groups. The state was expected to look after the general conditions of welfare. Gradually, however, the Dharma-śāstra became an overconservative and reactionary system of iniquitous laws and superstitious ritual and the Nītiśāstra increasingly irrelevant.

To sum up: freedom was not conceived primarily as privacy or as opposition to authority, or as the securing of rights or powers. It was conceived as the pursuit of ideal life whether through conformity to moral and religious law, or through detachment from the world, or through the love of God or the attainment of self-knowledge. Despite the accent of this attitude on resignation it was not, however, inconsistent with the struggle for traditional rights as a matter of duty or with the reform of the existing order for the sake of its original ideals. From Ram Mohan Roy to Mahatma Gandhi, liberal reformers thus did not feel that they were arguing against the original ideas of the socioethical tradition. Modern social and political ideas, liberal or socialist, have not been felt as antagonistic to the genuine moral and spiritual ideals of the ancient tradition. Nor has science been felt to be a danger to religious faith. On the contrary, there has been a renewed emphasis on the testability of spiritual truth through personal experience and a growing distaste for mere faith or dogma. Yoga in its various aspects has been generally upheld as the genuine science of spiritual life. Underlying the historical diversities of beliefs and practices one could perhaps see in terms of spiritual experience a perennial and universal order of truth in religion. Its expression and interpretation in terms of specific social and cultural contexts, however, produces historically divergent and changing forms of religion which would be naturally subject to revision.

Notes

1. *Pañcadaśī,* 7, 23.

2. Radhakrishnan, *The Idealist View of Life* (London: Allen & Unwin, 1957), p. 88.

3. The success of the nonparticipant observer in appropriating religion depends on the degree to which he has access to the psyche behind the behavior; and that implies instruction about the meaning of religious acts. The role of such instruction is parallel to that of historical records or symbols. Traditionally, one is initiated into religious life through "instruction," which may take the form of a symbolic act.

4. Freedom or *mukti* is the pervasive Indian description of the supreme goal of spiritual life, though happiness here and hereafter is also admitted as a subordinate goal, especially in the context of ritualistic religion. The experience of purity, vitality, wonder, sublimity, dread, etc. have also been mentioned in different contexts.

5. Cf. G. C. Pande, *Studies in the Origins of Buddhism,* 3d ed. (Allahabad: University of Allahabad, 1957), pp. 373 ff.

6. Ibid., pp. 512 ff.

7. *Majjhima* (PTS) III.4–6.

8. *Chāndogya Upaniṣad* VI.14.

9. *Yogasūtra* I.20.

10. *Bhagavadgītā* IV.39.

11. See Śaṁkara's Introduction to his *Brahmasūtrabhāṣya.*

12. See, for example, *Kaṭha Upaniṣad* I.2.4.

13. See S. Radhakrishnan, *The Idealist View of Life,* pp. 92 f.

14. *Yogasūtras* II.30–32.

15. *Manusmṛti* VI.92.

16. *Gītā* VI.32; II.47.

17. *Yogabhāṣya* ad *Yogasūtras* II.30.

18. Cf. D. C. Sircar, *Select Inscriptions* (Calcutta: University of Calcutta, 1965), vol. 1, p. 27.

19. See S. N. Dube, "Religious Convictions of Aśoka," *Rajasthan University Studies* (Jaipur: 1965–1966), *Le Traite de la Grande Vertu de Sagesse (Mahāprajñā-pāramitāśāstra,* trans. by E. Lamotte), vol. 1, pp. 40–41.

20. The nature of religious language and the problem of communicating spiritual truth have been much debated. There was a strong tradition in Advaita as well as Mahāyāna that spiritual truth defies linguistic expression. Also the role of language was often said to be merely negative, and in any case indirect or metaphorical. *Naiṣkarmyasiddhi* III.63–85; *Vedānta-Paribhāṣā* IV; Cf. K. S. Murty, *Reason and Revelation in Advaita Vedānta* (Waltair: Andhra University, 1959), pp. 53 ff.

21. *Udāna* 6.3.

22. *Muṇḍaka Upaniṣad* I.1.3–5.

23. *Chāndogya Upaniṣad* VII.

24. Śaṅkara, Introduction to *Brahmasūtrabhāṣya*.

25. Cf. Nāgārjuna, *Mādhyamaka* XVII.31; *Bodhicaryāvatāra* 9.9 ff.

26. This is explicit in the monistic theists like the Kasmira Saivas or the Viśi-ṣṭādvaitins.

27. This is best portrayed in the *Gītā* II.55 ff.

28. Vivekananda, *Complete Works,* vol. 7 p. 427 ff.; cf. Ranganathananda, *Swami Vivekananda's Synthesis of Science and Religion* (1987).

29. Jaimini, *Mīmāṃsāsūtras* 1.1.5 ff.

Culture and the Political

GRAHAM PARKES

BETWEEN NATIONALISM AND NOMADISM: WONDERING ABOUT THE LANGUAGES OF PHILOSOPHY

I think nationalism is OK in practice but lethal in theory.
Werner J. Dannhauser

A salient feature of the context in which the following remarks about nationalism and philosophical language were first uttered was this: that most cross-cultural dialogue is conducted in a single language, English, while the majority of philosophers are accustomed to thinking and conversing and writing about philosophy in their different native tongues. Although English is a fine language distinguished by the vastness of its vocabulary, a tongue quickened by the most vital poets, it has never been seriously proposed as the optimal medium for philosophical thought. That is a distinction that has been claimed by several of the native tongues (or their ancestors) of our visitors from abroad—such as Sanskrit, Chinese, and Japanese, or else European languages with roots closer than English to Latin as well as to ancient Greek, womb of the very idea of *philosophia*. This is not to imply that the Anglophone bias necessarily vitiates the exchange of thoughts; but the torque it imparts to dialogues between traditions embodied in other (especially non-Indo-European) languages is easy to underestimate.

The initial impulse for the reflections that follow came from a difference of opinion among scholars in this country concerned with the study of Japanese philosophy, and of the philosophy of the so-called Kyoto School in particular. Some Japanologists here have followed the lead of certain Marxist thinkers in Japan by invoking a number of nationalistic and right-wing texts written during the 1930s and 1940s by the leading Japanese thinkers of the time (Nishida Kitarō, Tanabe Hajime, Watsuji Tetsurō, and Nishitani Keiji), in order to say that the connections between the thought of the Kyoto School and various patriotic political positions are so close as to negate its status *as philosophy*. If a school of philosophical thought generates claims concerning the unique superiority of a particular nation, so the argument goes, it forfeits its claim to be philosophy, which is meant to address the human condition on a universal plane, and is reduced to the status of mere nationalist ideology.[1] Given that such chauvinist claims are frequently accompanied by the proposition of one's national language as being the best medium for philosophical thought, it might be worthwhile to reflect more generally on the nature of *language* as the medium of philosophical activity. (There may of course be practical situations in which nationalistic sentiment is a salutary thing; but in a century that has seen several upsurges lead to dire consequences, and at a time when nationalism again threatens to disturb the peace in a number of regions, it is well to cultivate a suspicious eye for the phenomenon in theory. And I suggest that as philosophers we would do well to think about its relationship to the language of philosophy in particular.)

In this spirit, I will focus on aspects of the work of two thinkers from Germany and two from Japan. After a brief consideration of some remarks of Nietzsche's about language's relation to philosophy, I shall pursue the theme through several texts penned by Heidegger in the twenties and thirties (whose prominence in the news this year does not, sadly, derive solely from its being the centenary of his birth). From the Japanese side, I shall introduce some aspects of the work of Professor Nishitani Keiji, who has been one of the philosophically most nomadic thinkers of the century, and of a far-ranging thinker from the University of Tokyo, Professor Sakabe Megumi.[2]

I

Nationalism is a modern phenomenon which came to the fore toward the end of the eighteenth century, and a recent writer on the topic has seen it as a cultural system that emerged with the decline of two kinds of cultural systems which preceded it, "the religious community" and "the dynastic realm."[3] To the extent that a large part of the meaning of people's existence formerly came from their being adherents of a certain religion, or members or subjects of a certain dynastic family, one might well expect the decline of the power of these institutions to be accompanied by an increase in nihilism. The suspicion that nationalism is often largely a response to nihilism is one worth entertaining as we proceed.

In *Beyond Good and Evil* (his first published work to mention "nihilism"), Nietzsche warns, several decades before Wittgenstein, of the seductive effect of certain forms of "grammar" upon our way of thinking about the world—and even of experiencing it. In the book's first section, he adduces the sentence "I think" as a case in which the tendency to be seduced by language is especially strong.[4] Just because there is thinking going on, there is no reason to conclude, as Descartes did, that there exists an "I" that is doing it. Even to say "*Es* denkt," "it thinks," is to say too much, to infer according to the following "habit of grammar": "thinking is an activity, to every activity there belongs one who acts, consequently . . ." (*BGE* 17). One might suppose that thinkers thinking in a language such as Japanese, which doesn't say "I think" or even "*it* thinks," but simply "thinks" or "thinking is going on," will be less inclined to posit an agent or subject as the productive cause of every mental activity. Such a surmise is encouraged by Nietzsche's contention that the singular "family resemblance" (another of Wittgenstein's ideas anticipated) between "Indian, Greek, and German philosophizing" arises from "the common philosophy of grammar" that comes with affinities among languages (*BGE* 20). His conclusion is that

> Philosophers in the domain of the Ural-Altaic languages (in which the concept of the subject is most poorly developed) will most probably look "into the world" differently and be found on different paths from Indo-Germans or Muslims.[5]

In remarking on "the spell of particular grammatical functions" in this way, Nietzsche is not engaging in any kind of competitive philology by suggesting that a strong sense of the subject makes for more powerful thinking. The epithet "most poorly developed" is rather to be taken in a neutrally descriptive sense; and since the context is the culmination of a series of devastating attacks on precisely "the concept of the subject," the implication is that a weak concept of the subject would likely conduce to some quite robust philosophizing. He can also be read as drawing attention to a source of potential misunderstanding between philosophers engaged in dialogue across traditions ensconced in widely disparate language families.

Nietzsche's thinking in general perpetrates a relentless attack on all the ideals that have supported the Western philosophical and religious traditions, such that even his detractors have to admire the resoluteness of his confrontation with the nihilism ushered in by their collapse. While he was for much of his actual life homeless and literally stateless, it is on the existential level that Nietzsche most commends the condition. In an aphorism of *The Gay Science* entitled "We Homeless Ones" he writes: "We children of the future, how *could* we be at home in this today! We feel disfavor for all ideals that might lead one to feel at home in this fragile, fragmented time of transition . . ." (*GS* 377). Fifty years later, in Heidegger's *Being and Time* (*Sein und Zeit*), the impact of the death of God and the demise of all idols is registered in the experience of *Angst*, which shatters whatever meanings have been spun across the abyss of nonbeing, so that the world becomes brittle *hinfällig*, liable to collapse at any moment, and so no longer providing a familiar environ in which one can feel at home (*SZ* §40).

Excoriating the dissimulations of *das Man* that would cover up the abyss with superficial platitudes and promote an understanding of our being which is concerned to have us feel at home in a world of familiar things, Heidegger argues that the most primordial human condition is one of *Unheimlichkeit,* a strange and uncanny state of being not-at-home in the world, *"Nicht-zuhause-sein."* Just as Nietzsche as the herald of European nihilism had encouraged his readers to confront the abyss of meaninglessness with an unwavering gaze, so Heidegger advocated resoluteness in the face of the void and courage in the engagement with the *Angst* that discloses the nothingness of death.

This kind of existential stance is maintained in the works Heidegger published at the close of the twenties; but in the early thirties, around the time he began to take up the question of nihilism, a new element is introduced into his thinking having to do with "spirit" *(Geist)* and the nation *(das Volk).* In *Being and Time* the questioning of Being was undertaken at a level much deeper than that of peoples or nations, and the existential analytic treated simply of *Dasein,* "being-here," "being-there," understood as a more general term even than "human being." But in the infamous Rectorship Address of 1933, *Dasein* is qualified by the compound adjective *geistig-volklich.*[6] Heidegger invokes the specter of nihilism by way of Nietzsche's saying "God is dead," but his response is articulated entirely within the context of "the forces of earth and blood" and "the spiritual mission of the German people."[7] We appear to have slipped up an ontological level or two from the level of pure "being there."

It might be argued that the rhetoric of Heidegger's speech must be taken in its very peculiar context. Be that as it may, this kind of language persists for a couple of years and into a strictly scholarly context in which it is even more disconcerting. In 1935 Heidegger gave a course at Freiburg entitled "Introduction to Metaphysics," and the published version of these lectures contains some of his existentially most forceful writing.[8] The first chapter, "The Basic Question of Metaphysics," poses that question at the very outset: "Why is there anything at all, and not rather nothing?" and Heidegger goes on to engage it in his finest existential style. As in the Rectorship Address two years earlier, Nietzsche is in the background, and is cited more frequently. The totality of what-is still "trembles" and "vibrates" as beings hover over the abyss of nonbeing, and again the specter of nihilism shimmers behind it all (pp. 23-31; 18-24).

Heidegger reminds us that in asking the question "Why is there anything at all?" we always "stand in a tradition," since "philosophy has always asked about the ground of the things that are" (pp. 24; 18). Among the things-that-are that he goes on to list in the course of trying to distinguish the Being of beings from the beings themselves, Heidegger mentions the Japanese (pp. 76; 58), along with a symphony concert in Tokyo (pp. 29; 38). The reader may thus be excused for supposing that a thinker from that tradition—the medieval Zen master Dōgen, for example—might count among those who have posed the fundamental question of philosophy, or "asked about the ground of the things that are." One would be all the more inclined to suppose this since, for all his reclusiveness in the Black Forest, Heidegger was probably the least isolated of any of his colleagues from other philosophical traditions, thanks to a steady stream of philosophers from China and Japan who had been coming to Marburg and Freiburg to study with him since the early twenties.[9] Nor would it be unreasonable to expect that a thinker or two from the Chinese Taoist tradition might be included in the fold of fundamental questioners, since at least five years before he gave these lectures Heidegger appears to have been familiar with Martin Buber's edition of the *Zhuang Zi*.[10]

However, Being itself soon gets associated with "the spiritual fate of the West" (pp. 37; 28), and before we know it Europe has been placed in the center, "between Russia and America," and "the German people" granted the status of "the metaphysical people" and placed "in the middle" of this center (pp. 37–38; 28–29). The world is collapsing all around, the totality of beings is shaken to the core by shock-waves of nothingness, and Heidegger's hypercentrism has his audience take refuge in a particular region of the earth. He claims that the asking of the question "How does it stand with Being?" moves one "into a landscape" and prompts the realization that the task is to "regain *Bodenständigkeit*"—to find a footing with which to take a stand on a specific piece of soil. (A far cry, this, from Nietzsche's exhortations to the light-footedness of the wandering dance.)

Even the most ardent admirers of the tradition from Leibniz to Husserl and Heidegger himself deserve to be offered some *philosophical* (rather than socio-biological-political) ground for this privileging of the German *Volk*—something beyond a steady output and an outstanding track record. And indeed such a ground is indicated at the end of the book's first chapter, where the contemporary misrelation to language is said to arise from a faulty relationship with Being itself. Thus the question of Being turns out to be inextricably entwined with the question of language (pp. 51; 39). And while the succeeding three sections contain some of Heidegger's finest reflections on this question in the context of early Greek thought, they start off on the wrong foot, for some of us, with the pronouncement to the effect that ancient Greek "is, along with the German language, at once the most powerful and most spiritual language (with regard to the possibility of thinking)" (pp. 57; 43).

We can surely grant that all thinking moves within the flow of a tradition and in the medium of a particular language, and yet wonder what it is about Greek and German that makes them the "most spiritual" of languages, if spirit is (as Heidegger has said several times that it is) "primordially attuned, knowing, and resolute openness to the presencing of Being." If language is (as he will say later) "the house of Being," how can Heidegger be so sure that it contains only two mansions?

II

If we look at the history of Japanese ideas about language over the past two centuries, we find at the outset a linguistic chauvinism that makes Heidegger's look rather modest. A number of forces and tensions developed in the course of the Edo period in Japan which led to a cultural crisis, one manifestation of which was a violent reaction against the centuries-old influence of Chinese culture. A salient feature of Tokugawa "nativism" (kokugaku), an intellectual movement that began in the early eighteenth century, was a theory of language based on the premise that the original Japanese language (Yamato kotoba) was superior to all others by virtue of its divine origin.[11] Some formidable intellects thought this way, and some otherwise profound linguistic theories were developed by the kokugaku thinkers. But while elements of a similar linguistic chauvinism appear in the nationalistic writings of several major figures in early twentieth-century Japanese philosophy, they are conspicuously absent from the work of Nishitani Keiji—an absence whose ground is worth considering.

One reason is that Nishitani is probably the most cosmopolitan thinker of his generation, but it also has to do with the thinking he has devoted to the problem of nihilism. In 1949 he delivered a series of talks on the topic, which were subsequently published as a book.[12] After a discussion of the history of European nihilism focusing primarily on Nietzsche and Heidegger, Nishitani goes on to inquire into the significance of nihilism in the Japanese context, in a chapter entitled "The Meaning of Nihilism for Japan." He points out that in the case of Japan the crisis of nihilism was in an important sense "compounded" in comparison with the situation in Europe. The indiscriminate importation of Western culture and technology dictated by the Meiji Restoration served to cut succeeding generations off from their own cultural heritage. The resultant nihilism was aggravated by the fact that these imports already harbored the "virus" of European nihilism, which was then able to proliferate in the void left by the loss of traditional values. As a good Nietzschean, Nishitani realizes that an abyss of such immense dimensions affords the possibility of renewal, and that if one stays with the current of nihilism long enough a situation will emerge conducive to a *recreation* of value.

Nishitani also follows Nietzsche's suggestion that after such a break a new kind of responsibility to the ancestors arises, and that a creation of new values necessitates a reappropriation of certain elements from the tradition. In this context he speaks of the loss of "spiritual foundation" on the part of the Japanese, and of the necessity to regain a connection with the Japanese "spirit." But this is to be done from the position of having already assimilated the European intellectual and cultural tradition—and is not, as some purists of the time would have had it, a matter of purging the culture of all foreign elements. While Nishitani recommends a reappropriation of the Buddhist idea of the field of emptiness *(kū)*, for example, he stresses that this idea, too, must be rethought into a modern context. There is no talk of the superiority of the Japanese language, but rather a branding as superficial of nationalistic reactions to the loss of a sense of self brought about by the nihilistic crisis. Indeed, there is a strong implication that an outbreak of nationalism is precisely a symptom of an inadequate response to a nihilistic condition, a sign that one has not let oneself down far enough into the depths of the self that are opened up by the experience of nihilism. From this perspective, the nationalistic response of Heidegger's Rectoral Address would be a slip into superficiality in comparison with the story in *Being and Time* in which, when *Dasein* returned from the chastening experience of *Angst*, "naked" in its being thrown into *Unheimlichkeit,* no national costume was worn (*SZ* §68b).

Before returning to this issue in conclusion, let us turn to Professor Sakabe, who is distinguished among his contemporaries in Japan by the fact that he combines a comprehensive understanding of the Western philosophical tradition with a strong interest in the major Japanese thinkers of the past two hundred years. A book published in 1976, *Kamen no kaishakugaku (Hermeneutics of the Mask),* contains an essay entitled "Toward the Future of Thinking in Japanese: Logic and Thought in Japanese and Western Languages," which is eminently pertinent to reflections on the enterprise of comparative philosophy in general. As mentioned earlier, several of the "nativist" thinkers in Japan held that the "spirit of the Japanese language" *(kotodama)* was superior to all others. But with the influx of Western ideas after the Meiji Restoration, the prevailing opinion changed from one for which Japanese has a quite unique *logos* to one portraying it as a hopelessly *illogical* language, characterized by such vagueness and ambiguity as to render it a virtually impossible medium in which to engage in rational thought.[13] Drawing on the work of the preeminent linguists of this century in Japan (Tokieda Motoki and Mikami Akira), Sakabe demonstrates that while Japanese is less suited than Indo-European languages to certain types of logical thinking, there are some areas of inquiry in which it appears to facilitate philosophical thought better than its Western counterparts.

One of the grounds for this assertion is the emphasis Japanese places on predication, and the corresponding omission of the subject or its inclusion in the predicate (which brings us back to the Nietzschean theme with which we started). Lacking any equivalent to the Greek notion of *hypokeimenon* or the Latin *subjectum,* Japanese is—as Nietzsche intuited—less likely than Indo-European languages to lead its speakers to posit a substance underlying the properties of a thing or a subject holding together the mental states of a person. (This is a major reason why Buddhist ideas lent themselves so easily to expression and adaptation in Japanese.) When this lack is conjoined with the lack of an "existence-verb" functioning as a copula, the presence of which in Indo-European languages tends to lead to metaphysical hypostatization and abstract ontologizings, the result is a language designed to keep its speakers on the edge (as the very word for "language"—*kotoba* or *koto no ha*—suggests).[14]

In contrast to the case of "subject-oriented" and predominantly conceptual languages, meaning in Japanese is far more situation- and discourse-dependent, and thus more informed by *différance* (in the sense of Saussure as reinscribed by Derrida) than Indo-European languages. Sakabe argues that one effect of this "differential" structure is that someone thinking in Japanese is less likely to drift away from the ever-changing flux of finite existence; or, once drifted away, is more likely in thinking to be brought back by the language itself to "the realities of time and death." A full appreciation of the poetic qualities of Japanese may, he suggests (in terms reminiscent of Nietzsche and Heidegger at their best), "release our thinking into the infinite multiplicity of metaphors that sink away into silence, or the space of the infinitely overlapping masks of the world behind which one can never reach the real face."

Modern Japanese philosophy has traditionally meant "Western philosophy," having originated around the turn of the century with the translation into Sino-Japanese compounds of the major philosophical vocabularies of Greek, Latin, German, French, and English. In the introductory section of his most recent book, *Kagami no naka no Nihongo* (*Japanese Language [Reflected] in Mirrors*), Sakabe talks about his program for exploring the possibilities of thinking and writing philosophically in the medium of indigenous Japanese terms.[15] Following the lead of such thinkers as Watsuji Tetsurō and Kuki Shūzō, he is concerned to reappropriate some of the vocabulary of *Yamato kotoba* for contemporary philosophical reflection—yet while avoiding his predecessors' divagations into linguistic chauvinism. Sakabe's earlier essays display an erudite command of poststructuralist and deconstructionist strategies in their explication of the complexities of such terms as *omote* ("mask"), *kage* ("shadow"), *shirushi* ("trace"), and *utsushi* ("image"), and of the implications for contemporary philosophical discourse of their multiple and shifting meanings, especially in the realms of aesthetics and poetics.

All these terms exhibit a basic duality in their meanings, and their inherent ambiguities lend themselves to some illuminating philosophical elaboration, only a rough sketch of which can be offered here. *Omote* means "face," or "front"—but also the "mask" which conceals the face, and a "surface" which covers a depth beneath it. Any attempts to determine a univocal meaning of this word (or any of the others) in terms of a structure of appearance versus an underlying reality are frustrated by an interchangeability that is "built into" to the language. *Kage* means "shadow"—but also "light" and "reflection" in the sense of the image produced by reflected light. Sakabe remarks on the similarity with Plato's idea of "images" as opposed to "real things," but shows that the way the Japanese term works makes the "other" of the self turn out to be the "same." From a consideration of the ways in which such words as *tsukikage,* meaning "moonbeam," *hokage,* meaning "firelight," and *hitokage* (literally, "person-shadow"), meaning "[human] figure" denote actual presences, Sakabe concludes that in a sense, "Nothing exists except *kage.*" The philosophical grammar of *utsushi* is related, insofar as its meanings range from a complex involving "reflection," "appearance," and "copy" to connotations of transference, change, and flux. The related verb and noun have to do with the idea of "projection" as it concerns the day-world of consciousness as opposed to the dream-world and the realm of madness—the priorities between which nevertheless remain inherently undecidable. *Shirushi* exhibits a peculiar temporal ambiguity between its referring to future and past events. On the one hand it means "sign," "omen," or "symptom," and on the other "effect" or "trace." Its complex functioning within all three temporal horizons is reinforced by its connections with the verb *shiru,* "to know" (which has the interesting Nietzschean connotations of "to master," "to dominate").

What is distinctive about Sakabe's treatment is that insofar as he explicitly warns against the dangers of extolling the uniqueness of Japanese culture when dealing with such issues, he is able to emphasize the distinctive nature of these ancient words without lapsing into ethnocentric ideology. A strong advocate of cultural pluralism, he shuns linguistic purism and argues that Japanese thinking can retain and enhance its vitality only if the language continues to absorb and incorporate foreign elements. But the primary thesis is that Japanese philosophy will wane if it thinks only in terms translated from European languages and ignores the roots of its own medium.

III

At the end of a series of three lectures delivered in 1940, later published under the title "Patriotism and Nationalism," the Dutch intellectual historian Johan Huizinga characterizes nationalism as "a mental and historical phenomenon" in terms that are also relevant to its manifestations in philosophy:

> Every cultured and right-minded person has a particular affection of a few nations other than his own, nations whose land he knows and whose spirit he loves. Summon up an image of such a nation, and enjoy it . . . in a

[composite] view. You perceive the beauty of its art, the vigorous forms of its life, you experience the perturbations of its history, you see the enchanting panorama of its landscapes, taste the wisdom of its words, hear the sound of its immortal music, you experience the clarity of its language, the depth of its thought, you smell the scent of its wines . . . you feel that altogether, stamped with the ineradicable mark of that one specific nationality that is not yours. All of this is alien to you—and tremendously precious as a wealth and luxury in your life.[16]

This is where the nomadism, finally, comes in. If, in the face of an attack of nihilism one declines to take a stand on the literal ground of one's home—"The meaning of my life is to be a Scot, or a Japanese, or a German, or whatever"—as a metaphorical ground for thought and culture, and can find instead a footing in some other languages and cultures as well, the nihilism may overcome itself without a back-lapse into nationalistic posturing.

Huizinga's recommendation is a vivid exemplification of the nomadism Nietzsche prescribed as an antidote to nationalism as "the sickness of the century."[17] The contrasts with Heidegger on this issue are striking, on both the literal and metaphorical planes. While Nietzsche was for the greater part of his career actually nomadic, Heidegger spent most of his life solidly *bodenständig* in the Black Forest. And while, intellectually, Heidegger would leave the German tradition only to go back to ancient Greece, Nietzsche constantly engaged in and recommended to others the practice of intellectual nomadism.[18] An aphorism from 1879 entitled "Where one must travel to" begins as follows:

Direct self-observation is not nearly sufficient for us to know ourselves: we require history, for the past continues to flow within us in a hundred waves; we ourselves are, indeed, nothing but that which at every moment we experience of this continued flowing. . . . To understand history . . . we have to *travel* . . . to other nations . . . and especially to where human beings have taken off the garb of Europe or have not yet put it on.

The prescription is explicitly deliteralized as the passage continues:

But there exists a *subtler* art and object of travel which does not always require us to move from place to place. . . . He who, after long practice in this art of travel, has become a hundred-eyed Argos . . . will rediscover the adventurous travels of his ego . . . in Egypt and Greece, Byzantium and Rome, France and Germany . . . in the Renaissance and the Reformation, at home and abroad, indeed in the sea, the forests, in the plants and in the mountains. Thus self-knowledge will become knowledge of everything [*All-Erkenntniss*] with regard to all that is past. . . .[19]

While Nietzsche generally thinks of the flow of the past as happening "in the blood" in the narrower sense, the global scope of the last sentence cited surely militates against excluding India, China, and Japan from the grand tour.

When it comes to talking on the other side of the abyss of nihilism, each language that has sustained philosophical reflection holds its own joys for the thinker who thinks in its medium. One might consider the way the middle voice of the verb in ancient Greek can work to give the sense of an occurrence "between active and passive"; the play of images in classical Chinese which produces models rather than concepts;[20] the features of Japanese discussed by Sakabe and others that let one think things extraordinarily; the myriad homophonous words and phrases in French that have allowed someone like Derrida to elaborate something like deconstruction; and the way so many words in German, at the hands of thinkers such as Hegel and Heidegger, can be broken up into their basic components and then reassembled into productive compounds. (It is tempting with respect to this last to warn against the dangers of "Lego"-centrism).

There is no need, then, to posit any one of these major languages as the best, the most thought-promoting, or whatever. More enlightening is to try to appreciate the different idioms of alien tongues for what they allow one to do philosophically, what they enable the thinker to say and what not. Benefits accrue from this attempt even short of a comprehensive acquaintance with the language; the ability to use a dictionary together with some basic knowledge of how the language works will do much to enhance an appreciation for alien textualities. The practice of linguistic nomadism may thus impart to the course of our thinking a broader range and a more comprehensive subtlety.

Notes

Part of the research for this essay was generously funded by the Japan Studies Endowment at the University of Hawaii, through a grant from the Japanese government.

1. I have discussed one aspect of this issue in "Nihilism and Nationalism: Nishitani Keiji's Prescription for Recovering from One with Contracting the Other," forthcoming in a volume on modern Japanese philosophy, edited by T. P. Kasulis and William R. LaFleur.

2. Professor Sakabe's contribution to this volume touches lightly at a few points on some of the themes of the present essay.

3. Benedict Anderson, *Imagined Communities: Reflections on the Origin and Spread of Nationalism* (London: Verso Editions, 1983), pp. 19–20.

4. *Beyond Good and Evil*, aphorism 16 (henceforth "BGE" followed by the aphorism number). Nietzsche is not proposing something as strong as the Sapir/Whorf thesis of linguistic determinism but the more defensible proposition that one's language conditions in some important ways experience of and reflections about the world.

5. Japanese belongs to the Ural-Altaic family, though Nietzsche does not say this.

6. Martin Heidegger, "The Self-Assertion of the German University," trans.

by Karsten Harries, *Review of Metaphysics* 38 (March 1985): 474. Jacques Derrida offers an illuminating reading of Heidegger's use of the term *Geist* and its cognates in the Rectoral Address, and elsewhere, in *Of Spirit* (Chicago: University of Chicago Press, 1989), especially chap. 5. An intelligent setting in the context of the Address is to be found in Hans Sluga, "Metadiscourse: German Philosophy and National Socialism," *Social Research* 56, no.4 (Winter 1989).

7. "The Self-Assertion of the German University," pp. 475–476.

8. Martin Heidegger, *Einführung in die Metaphysik* (Tübingen: Niemeyer, 1953), pp. 37–38; *An Introduction to Metaphysics,* trans. by Ralph Manheim (New Haven and London: Yale University Press, 1959), pp. 49–50. For the next few paragraphs these editions will be cited in the body of the text, in this order, simply by the page numbers.

9. Among the Japanese were four of the greatest thinkers of the first half of the century: Tanabe Hajime, who came in 1922, Miki Kiyoshi (1923), Kuki Shūzō (1925), and Watsuji Tetsurō (1927). For the fuller story, see Yuasa Yasuo, "The Encounter of Modern Japanese Philosophy with Heidegger," *Heidegger and Asian Thought,* ed. by Graham Parkes (Honolulu: University of Hawaii Press, 1987). Nishitani Keiji was to arrive in Freiburg the year after Heidegger had given the "Introduction to Metaphysics" lectures. I examine the issue of Heidegger's acquaintance with Asian thought through contact with philosophical visitors from China and Japan, as well as through extant German translations of Asian texts, in "Heidegger and Asian Thought: How Much Did He Know, and When Did He Know It?" in *Heidegger: Critical Assessments,* ed. by Christopher Macann (London: Routledge, forthcoming). For an account of Nietzsche's impact in Japan, see my essay "The Early Reception of Nietzsche's Philosophy in Japan," in Graham Parkes, ed., *Nietzsche and Asian Thought* (Chicago: University of Chicago Press, 1991).

10. See Otto Pöggeler, "West-East Dialogue: Heidegger and Lao-tzu," and also the editor's contribution, "Thoughts on the Way: Being and Time via Lao-Chuang," in *Heidegger and Asian Thought.*

11. See H. D. Harootunian, *Things Seen and Unseen: Discourse and Ideology in Tokugawa Nativism* (Chicago: University of Chicago Press, 1988), especially chaps. 1 and 2. Other languages—Arabic, Hebrew, Sanskrit, and Latin—have of course imagined themselves as divine scripts or sounds emanating from a higher order of reality. (See also the contribution of Thomas Kasulis to the present volume.)

12. Keiji Nishitani, *Nihirizumu* (Tokyo: 1949); *The Self-Overcoming of Nihilism,* trans. by Graham Parkes with Setsuko Aihara (Albany: SUNY Press, 1990).

13. Nishitani writes tellingly about the "inferiority complexes" of many Japanese intellectuals during this period (*The Self-Overcoming of Nihilism,* chap. 9, sec. 2).

14. Of relevance to this issue is the impressive comparative study of Jean-Paul Reding, *Les fondements philosophiques de la rhetorique chez les sophistes grecs et chez les sophistes chinois* (New York: Peter Lang, 1985), some of which has been excerpted and translated in "Greek and Chinese Categories: A Reexamination

of the Problem of Linguistic Relativism," *Philosophy East and West* 36, no. 4 (October 1986). For a contrasting—and equally impressive—view, see Appendix 2 of A. C. Graham, *Disputers of the Tao* (La Salle, Illinois: Open Court, 1989).

15. "Conversation with the Editor," in *Kagami no naka no Nihongo* (Tokyo: Chikuma, 1989). The *Kagami* ("mirrors") of the title refers to the other languages in which Sakabe has written and presented papers on this topic over the past decade or so, primarily to audiences in Europe.

16. One is fruitfully reminded of Jacques Derrida's discussion of the systematic ambiguity of the term *pharmakon* in Plato's texts ("Plato's Pharmacy," in *Dissemination* [Chicago: University of Chicago Press, 1981]), as well as of Freud's essay "On the Antithetical Meaning of Primal Words."

17. *Human, All Too Human* II.2, 87; see also *HA* I.475 and II.2, 215 and 292. Other spectacular attacks on nationalism can be found in *The Gay Science* 377, *BGE* 242, 256, 268, and *Ecce Homo*, "The Case of Wagner," par. 2.

18. For an exposition of Nietzsche's nomadism as a hermeneutical strategy, see Eberhard Scheiffele, "Questioning One's 'Own' from the Perspective of the Foreign," in *Nietzsche and Asian Thought,* ed. by Graham Parkes (1990).

19. *Human, All Too Human* II.1, 223 (translation slightly modified).

20. See the essay by Roger T. Ames in this volume.

AZIZ AL-AZMEH

THE DISCOURSE OF CULTURAL AUTHENTICITY: ISLAMIST REVIVALISM AND ENLIGHTENMENT UNIVERSALISM

I take it as an accomplished fact that modern history is characterized by the globalization of the Western order. Despite protests of a bewildering variety against this accomplished fact, it remains incontestable, especially as, with few exceptions of an isolated and purely local nature, these protests have taken place either in the name of ideologies of Western provenance—such as national independence and popular sovereignty—or substantially in terms of these ideologies, albeit symbolically beholden to a different local or specific repertory, such as the Iranian regime of the Ayatollahs. The validation of universalism does not arise from some transcendental or immanent criterion, but quite simply from affirming the rationality of the real.

The reasons for this are manifest: the conditions of Western economic and political conquest and hegemony in the modern age have engendered, for good or for ill, correlative conditions of equally real ideological and cultural hegemony. The East—and I only use this term for convenience—has been heavily impregnated with novel categories of thought, methods of education, contents of knowledge, forms of discourse and communication, aesthetic norms, and ideological positions. It has become impossible to speak with sole reference to traditional texts and without reference to Western notions.

There is nothing particularly mysterious about this irreversible state of affairs, and the conditions for cross-cultural knowledge are not distinct from the conditions of knowledge in general. A cross-cultural epistemology is neither possible nor desirable. Knowledge is always of an object, and in this view the quiddity of other cultures is not substantially distinct from the objectness of any other object of knowledge—knowledge being empirical, aesthetic, historical, and its objects therefore being appropriate for these modes of apprehension and reason. Culture is a very coy object and is a term rather thoughtlessly applied to objects poorly apprehended or regarded as somewhat exotic and quaint.

One would therefore be better advised to speak of a universal civilization comprising a manifold of historical formations—the European, the Arab, the Indian. Each of these is highly differentiated, but these differences, or the cluster of such differences, are globally articulated and unified by the economic, political, cultural, and ideological facts of dominance. Each historical unit is, moreover, multivocal, and Europe of course is no exception to this, despite the claims that are made on behalf of a triumphalist Hegelianism, somewhat impoverished by the elimination from it of history.

In this light, the notion of incommensurability and its cognates appears quite absurd, not only because historical units are not analogous to paradigms and apprehension is not analogous to translation. Neither are they homogeneous, self-enclosed, and entirely self-referential entities, as would be required by the assumption of univocal irreducibility. The consequences of such assumptions exceed the simple elision of history and lead to a barren and naive relativist temptation with at best a patronizing rhetoric of intercultural etiquette dressed up as a philosophical hermeneutic. More perniciously it leads to the absolute relativism that underlies apartheid and the culturalist pretensions of some political groups such as those that came to prominence with the conjuration of the Salman Rushdie affair.

This compulsory universalism can be illustrated with a particular case made all the more poignant because it is an advocacy of exclusivism and of incommensurable distinction. I have indicated that Europe has everywhere spawned ideological and cultural phenomena as diverse as her own. What appears in the East under the guise of traditionalism is normally an apologetic or a radically reformist discourse whose terms of articulation and criteria of validation are by no means traditional—traditions do not validate themselves. They are idioms. There are indeed deliberate archaisms and medievalisms that may appear in direct continuity with the past. Among these I would class the cultivation, for the purposes other than recondite antiquarianism and historical research, of such matters as the magnificently ornate re-paganized Neoplatonism in vogue in Iran. This naturally evokes a chilling sense of the Gothic, but could with some effort be made comprehensible in historical conditions overdetermined by European modernity. For it is a fact of the modern history of the Arab World, or of Iran and other countries with Muslim majorities—and it should be strongly emphasized that Islam is not a culture, but a religion living amidst very diverse cultures and thus a very multiform entity—that the predominant literate discourses in social and political life are local adaptations of Enlightenment and post-Enlightenment traditions, such as Marxism, naturalism, liberalism, and nationalism.

In what follows, an attempt will be made to anatomize a notion of much potency in modern Arab social and political thought: it is hoped that a paradigm that will make comparable other exclusivist ideologies increasingly at work in the world, such as right-wing Hindu communalism, Zionist fundamentalism both secular and religious, and much else, will become explicit.

I

In common with other subaltern nationalisms, as with defensive, retrenching nationalisms and with populist ideologies, the notion of authenticity is widely used both in formal discourse on matters political and social and in the interstices of casual comment. The notion of authenticity is not so much a determinate concept as it is a node of associations and interpellations, a trope by means of which the historical world is reduced to a particular order, and a token which marks off social and political groups and forges and reconstitutes historical identities. In these senses the notion of authenticity has analogues elsewhere, doubtless officiated under different names.

Asala is the Arabic term for authenticity. Lexically, it indicates salutary moral qualities like loyalty, nobility, and a sense of commitment to a specific social group or a set of values. It also indicates a sense of *sui generis* originality; and in association with the senses previously mentioned, *asala* specifically refers to genealogical standing: noble or at least respectable descent for humans, and the status of equine aristocrats. Combined together and transferred to an attribute of historical collectivities, Arab, Muslim, or other, *asala* becomes a central notion in a romantic conception of history which calls forth features commonly associated with such a conception. Of primary importance among these features is a vitalist concept of nationalism and of politics, replete with biological metaphor and, occasionally, a sentimentalist populism.

Ultimately, therefore, the notion of authenticity is predicated on the notion of a historical subject which is at once self-sufficient and self-evident. Its discourse is consequently an essentialist discourse, much like the reverse it finds in orientalism, in discourses on the primitive, and in other discourses on cultural otherness.[1] In common with these discourses, the discourse on authenticity postulates a historical subject which is self-identical, essentially in continuity over time, and positing itself in essential distinction from other historical subjects. For the viability of a historical subject such as this, it is essential that its integrity must be maintained against a manifest backdrop of change of a very rapid and profound nature. It therefore follows that change should be conceived as contingent, impelled by inessential matters like external interference or internal subversion, the effects of which can only be faced with a reassertion of the essence of historical subjectivity. History therefore becomes an alternance in a continuity of decadence and health, and historiographical practice comes to consist in the writing of history as a form of classification of events under the two categories of intrinsic and extrinsic, the authentic and the imputed, the essential and the accidental.

It is therefore not fortuitous or haphazard that the title under whose name this discourse (and its political implications) is officiated should be revivalism, *nahda,* in line with similar historical and ideological experiences of which the *Risorgimento* readily comes to mind. For this entire ideological trope can be described as one of ontological irredentism, it being the attempt to retrieve an essence that the vicissitudes of time and the designs of enemies, rather than change of any intrinsic nature, had caused to atrophy. The counterpart of this was that the degraded conditions of today are mere corruptions of the original cultural essence, the retrieval of which is only possible by a return to the pristine beginnings which reside in the early years of Islam, the teachings of the book of God, the Koran, and the example of the Prophet Muhammad. It must be added at the outset, however, that though revivalism was initially Islamist, and has tended to don the Islamist cloak in the very recent past, it received its most thorough grounding in the context of secular Arab nationalist ideology, which regarded Islam as but one moment of Arab glory, albeit an important one.

In historical terms, this constellation of notions came into currency in the second half of the nineteenth century, first with the Young Ottomans in Istanbul, and particularly Namik Kemal (1840–1888), and shortly thereafter in the writings of the remarkable Jamāl al-Dīn al-Afghānī (1839–1897). Afghānī was not a profound thinker, but a very potent speaker and charismatic conspirator. His careers in Istanbul, Tehran, Kabul, Hyderabad, Calcutta, Cairo, London, Paris, and St. Petersburg have left an important imprint on pan-Islamism in the Arab World, which, in certain respects at his time, can be regarded as a form of protonationalism.[2] Afghānī left a body of miscellaneous writings, most notably his polemic against the pro-British Indian Muslim reformer Sir Syed Ahmad Khan (1817–1898),[3] with whose ideas, it must be stressed, he was not really at variance. He inspired the journal *Al-ʿUrwa al-Wuthqā,* a collaborative body of political, cultural, and reformist writing published in Paris in 1882–1883 with his then disciple, Muḥammad ʿAbduh (1849–1905), who was later to become the Arab World's foremost and most subtle Muslim reformist.[4] A section of ʿAbduh's writings are in tune with the general theses of Afghānī, but are far more finely tuned and retain none of Afghānī's occasional crudeness of conception, and ʿAbduh's disciples number some of the Arab World's foremost Muslim reformist and nationalist leaders in the early part of this century. This same constellation of notions was channeled into the mainstream of Arab political and social thought through the nationalism which was later to become Turkish nationalism exemplified in Zia Gökalp (1875–1924) and the Arab nationalism of his erstwhile associate, Satiʿ al-Husri (1880–1968),[5] although Husri was not a romantic revivalist and populist like Gökalp, and romantic revivalism was only to enter the Arab nationalism between the wars, a process to which Husri, though at the peak of his career, was far too sober a positivist sociologist and educationist to contribute.

Before describing the anatomy of the notion of authenticity, it will be well to make a number of further historical specifications. It was rare after Afghānī for Islamist revivalism to take the romantic form until very recently; its revivalism was concentrated on the revivification of a utopia which consisted of a clear set of precedents of a social, legal, and moral order unconnected with an elaborate notion of history. It was only when Islamism associated itself with nationalism—the prevalent ideological impulse in the Arab World—and assimilated it in such a way that Islamism became a viable medium for the articulation of national-ism, that Islamism became romantic and returned to the tropes of Jamāl al-Dīn al-Afghānī, who is idolized by today's Islamists. Finally, it must be stressed that it is extremely difficult to study precisely how Afghānī or his acolytes became romantic. The notion of authenticity, which will be described presently, lies at the intersection of a number of concepts that are foreign to classical Islamic thought, which constituted the core of Afghānī's education. It is well known that the highlights of European thought were becoming quite familiar in Cairo, Istanbul, and elsewhere from the early part of the nineteenth century and that they contributed to the formation of Young Ottoman thought.[6] But I believe it to be impossible philologically to trace European influence from such quarters of paramount importance for the notion of authenticity as Herder and the German historical school of law associated with Savigny and others at any time before about 1930, although some French think-ers in a roughly similar vein, such as Gustave Le Bon, were fairly well known.[7] If influence there was, it would most probably have come orally or implicitly in the body of occasional writing such as journalism; it is also very important to study the social and political conditions under which romantic nationalism (or proto-nationalism) could grow spontaneously.

II

The nation for Afghānī is akin to a body—and although he changed his mind over what constituted a nation, in the final analysis he devalued ties of ethnicity and, to a lesser extent, of language to the advantage of the bond of religion.[8] A nation consists of estates analogous to parts of a body, or of individuals whose organic unity is that of the parts of a vital organism. This organism is infused with a vital force like that which permeates its individual organs, and the power of this individual vitality is directly proportional to that in the whole organism.[9]

This organismic, vitalist paradigm has its major notions—if not its object, a sociopolitical order—in medieval Islamic natural philosophy. Equally important is that it naturally invites comparison with Herder's notion of *kräfte* as inner sources of vitality and dynamic principles for the continued existence of nations; the question as to whether Herder's romanticism is medieval in its conceptual inspiration is irrelevant to its modernity and to the vital part it played in nineteenth and twentieth-century ideological tendencies; though Afghānī's ideas initially were shaped in Iranian seminaries, they were received in Calcutta, Cairo, Istanbul, and Paris, where they were filtered through contemporary social and political categories. Also like Herder's, Afghānī's paradigm concretizes this vital principle for the unity and cohesion of bodies national in culturalist terms and, like Herder's emphasis on *Bildung,* finds in civic and moral education the key to the maintenance and resuscitation of national glory. The vital spirit in empirical terms is a yearning in the hearts of men for glory and a leaning towards the consummate realization of values. And this vital spirit is operative only when it impels bodies national with a desire for excellence and distinction in wealth as well as glory and might *('izz).* [10]

In situations of conflict brought about by pervasive Western interference in the Middle East, this perspective was not unnaturally invested with a social Darwinist stance. It is well to bear in mind that the "conflict theory" of political sociology was emerging in Germany at about the same time—proponents of this theory, as well as Afghānī, were keenly interested in Ibn Khaldūn's theory of the power of state, which they used in the construction of a nationalist romanticism. [11] The struggle for existence, Afghānī tells us, pervades human history no less than in the animal kingdom and inanimate nature. The reason for this is that "might is the visible aspect of life and of continued existence . . . and might is never triumphant and concrete except when it weakens and subjugates others." As illustration, Afghānī cites the powers of nations, and specifically the subjugation of the Ottoman Empire by the European powers. [12]

What, in this perspective, is history? And what does the passage of time yield? It can be noted that the subject of history is the body national. Each body national, as in Herder, is a fixed nature which is, according to the characterization of Collingwood, less the product of history than its presupposition. [13] That unit which is historically significant is the national subject, and history is therefore one of alternance between true historicity manifested in might, and historical desuetude manifested in subjugation. Might results from cohesiveness and unity, and if this unity were to be lost the body national will lose its spirit or its general will, with the result that "the thrones of its might will fall, and it [the nation] will take its leave of existence just as existence has abandoned it." [14] It is indicative of Afghānī's style that he used the term *quwwa ḥāfiẓa,* which I have rendered as "spirit." The expression, literally "preservative power," is derived from medieval Arabic natural philosophy, in which Afghānī was deeply steeped and concepts from which he often used, where it designates the subliminal quality which keeps together a somatic composite.

The cohesiveness and unity of this body national infused with a vital impulse that yearns for glory is maintained so long as the factors which originally constituted this *Volksgeist* are operative. But once corruption sets in, once the essence is diluted, the auguries of national calamity become manifest. Thus the glorious classical civilization of the Muslim Arabs was corroded from the inside by the snares of esotericist sects, which paved the way for conquest by Crusaders and Mongols. Similarly, the fabric of the Ottoman Empire was weakened by Ottoman Westernizing reformists in the middle of the nineteenth century. As for the French, the glory of their royal past was corrupted by the seductions of Voltaire and Rousseau, which directly led to what he regarded as the calamities of the French Revolution, the Paris Commune and defeat in the Franco-Prussian War. In the same class of universally destructive, disintegrative impulses are socialism, communism, and anarchism, which might cause the annihilation of humanity altogether, being the ultimate forces of corruption and radical antinomianism, the antithesis of order and civilization.[15]

There is no response to weakness and destruction save that of revivalism: the retrieval and restoration of the original qualities that made for strength and historical relevance. No progress without the retrieval of pristine beginnings and the cleansing of the essence from the adulteration of history[16]: such is the fundamental principle of revivalism; the example of Martin Luther was never far from the mind of Afghānī. The Islam that results from the elision of history and the deprivation of time of any significant ontological weight will shortly be taken up; but before this is done it is necessary to take a closer look at the categories that subsist in the trope of authenticity, of absolute individuality and irreducible historical subjectivity.

III

The trope of authenticity described above as less a determinate concept than a node of associations, is premised on a number of important notions and distinctions. Fundamental among these is a conception of history which posits a narcissistic continuing subject, mighty by virtue of its nature but enfeebled by subversion, inadvertence, and what Hegel termed "Oriental ease and repose." This same subject will regain its vital energy and continue the maintenance of its nature—its entelechy —by a recommencement and by the revivication of its beginnings, which still subsist within it just as a nature, in the classical and medieval Arabic and European senses, inheres in a body.

But this subject is inconceivable in isolation from others, which exist alongside it, for the notion is essentially formed in the context of political contestation. These others are, to a very considerable degree, absolute in their otherness, in that they are antitheses of the subject, and, in order for them to be met, their subjectivity has constantly to be objectified, deprived of value except for that which, like forces of corruption, is inessential and contingent, hence transferable. Such was the attitude of Afghānī and all those who adopted the hopes associated with his name toward modern science and technology, of European provenance but not culture-specific and, moreover, necessary for the construction of national might. Throughout, the origin—the positive beginning—is adulterated, but still flows as a subliminal impulse amid degradation and corruption, for the fall from previous heights is inessential, and the essence of the historical subject is in fact suprahistorical and still subsists in the innermost core of the cultural self. The revivalist project is simply one in which this core is again brought to the surface and to the forefront of historical existence, thereby restoring the historical subject to its true nature.

The truth of this nature is an ontological truth, one whose resistance to the vagaries of time is demonstrated by the revivalist belief in its capacity for resuscitation, and whose durability is the measure of its truth. Indeed, this nature, the vital impulse of the body national, is the very reality of the subject in history; corruption is conceivable only as privation. In the light of this, history consists of continuity over a time which knows no substantive causalities, for causality is only manifest in discontinuity.[17] This continuity is in a constantly antithetical relation to all otherness: to other nations, which by virtue of the very nature of bodies naturally seek to subjugate the nation-subject, and to corruptions within, for these are privations of the essence which seek to subvert, and thus to nullify the vital energy which uplifts and allows for glory.

Time is therefore cleft between origins and corruptions, between authenticity and the snares of enemies. Forces of privation, of foreign—that is, inessential—provenance, have no intrinsic extensions: they do not extend to the core of the historical self, for they have no avenues that lead to the fund of subjectivity, either in the past or in the present. They have bearings neither in the past nor in the ontological reality of the present. In contrast, extraneous influences disturb the homogeneity of the subject and confound the bearings of its historical course by repudiating the original inner indistinctness and homogeneity which constitute the stuff of authenticity.

Authenticity, for a contemporary philosopher who has been attempting a left-wing reclamation of Afghānī along the lines of a Muslim liberation theology, designates the self in contradistinction to the other, the essential as against the accidental, the natural as opposed to the artifi-

cial. Only thus can individuality and specificity properly be said to designate any genuine distinctiveness in opposition to "the loss of distinctiveness and dissolution in another specificity [of the West] which claims
universality." Authenticity and its associated notions are, further, said
to extend the cultural ego into history and endow it with "historical continuity and temporal homogeneity and the unity of the national personality."[18]

Authenticity is therefore both past and future linked contingently by
the ontological void of today. The past is the accomplished future and
the future is the past reasserted; history is the past in the future anterior.
History is an even continuum, on the surface of which eddy tiny circuits
which counter the original energies of the continuum and work to suppress them, yet do not quite succeed in more than rippling the surface
and disturbing its evenness. Only thus can teleology be assured: for a
nature to consummate itself, for the future revival to close the circle of
historical appearance and coalesce with the original condition, the end
must be pre-given and inevitable in the sense that it is in accord with
nature.

The body national is thus neither describable nor recognizable if
measured against its contingent existence, or against the sheer temporality and lack of perfection which characterize it today. Time is
devoid of quality, corruption is purely vicarious, and the present is but a
negative interregnum between a perfect origin and its recommencement, which is also its consummation. History therefore takes place in
"two modes of time, one of which has a decided ontological distinction,"[19] the one relevant to the essence and a measure of its duration,
and the other which dissolves into transience and contingency. The former is much like the time of myth as described by Schelling in his *Philosophie der Mythologie,* one which is "indivisible by nature and absolutely
identical, which therefore, whatever duration may be imputed to it, can
only be regarded as a moment, i.e. as time in which the end is like the
beginning and the beginning like the end, a kind of eternity, because it
is in itself not a sequence of time."[20]

The connection of these modes of time is the same as that of different
bodies national: a connection of otherness which, in a social Darwinist
world, is one of subjugation and of antinomy, essentially of negation,
without the possibility of a mutual interiorization such as that inherent
in, for example, the Hegelian dialect of Master and Slave. Indeed, the
polar structuration of the discourse on authenticity is what makes it possible not only to deny essential change in time, thus denying multiplicity over time, but also to deny what we might term spatial multiplicity
of any essential consequence, this being the social, political, and ideological multiplicity at any one particular point in time, except insofar as
such multiplicity is perceived as subversive of a homogeneous essence
which requires evenness. Any unevenness, as has already been indi-

cated, is perceived in terms of antithesis, privation, corruption, atrophy.

It goes without saying that, in the real world, this national subject, an essence which knows neither dysfunction nor transformation but only abeyance, must reassert itself against history. Hence it must bring in train an acute sense of voluntarism. If human history is not to be assimilated to that of brute nature, the only agency capable of restoring nature to its course and directing it to the consummation of its entelechy is the will of the reformer, who stands to his nation as does a physician to a body in distemper.[21] And since this body, the body national, is arbitrarily posited as *sui generis,* it follows that the liberty of the reformer can be best described by following the Hegelian analysis of Jacobinism: it is one possessed by a freedom based on pure self-identity, for which the world is its own will, and whose relation to the reality of the world is unmediated, and therefore one of pure negation.[22]

This will, in a pure, indeterminate element, is pure thought of its own self.[23] It is pure self-reference, a tautological circle, whose impenetrability to reason other than the reason of its own self-reference is very much in keeping with similar outlooks in the German *Lebensphilosophie* of the turn of the century, where life is at once the subject and the object of the mind.[24] The crazed waft of blood in the Rushdie affair is fully accounted for in this context. The authentic self is immediately apprehended,[25] and knowledge of it by its own is a sort of pure and perfect *Verstehen,* an almost innate endowment in the mind of the components that make up this body national, whose self-enclosure is epistemological and not only ontological. Indeed, the epistemological and the ontological correspond perfectly, for knowledge of authenticity is but a moment in the life of this authenticity. For what is such knowledge of a self-identical entity but a form of transcendental narcissism? Indeed, Afghānī specifically designates the *Bildung* of the renascent nation as one whose prime medium is an oratory which exhorts and reminds of the past.[26]

It should be clear from the foregoing that the subject being corrected by oratorical education and which is romantically conceived both beyond history and underlying it, is indeterminate if its conception is left as presented. There are no indications towards its determination except gestures towards historical particularities: events, names, dates. Beyond this, there is reference to a name: Islam. There are analogues to this romantic mode in virtually all cultures. In all these cases, in the absence of historical determination over and above the indication of a Golden Age wherein inhere exemplary glories and utopian exemplars, the discourse of authenticity is socially open, in the sense that its essential emptiness, what Hegel might have termed the boredom of its concepts, renders it very versatile and protean. As this ontological self-identity is epistemologically reflected in solipsism, the result is that the construction of identities here is fundamentally an act of naming.

Naming is not an innocent activity, but lies at the very heart of ideology, one of whose principal mechanisms is the operation of classificatory tokens that determine the memberships of sociopolitical groups. These operations also entail exclusions and inclusions by way of condensations, displacements, and associative interpellation of some complexity.[27] The concrete images put forward as factually paradigmatic—the golden age, the glories of the Arabs, the Middle Ages in some European romanticisms, the idyllic rusticity of Heidegger, of African nativist philosophers, or Westernized Indian sages—serve as iconic controllers of identities and take on general values generated by a truncated and telescoped history; yet these are values which act as carriers of general attributes that no human collectivity can eternally possess and of paradigmatic value that is only imputed to them by the purveyors of the ideological messages.[28] The versatility of the general name—such as Islam—lies therein; that the abstract act of naming engenders as many distinct identities as there are constituted social and political groups which might claim the name as their own. The reality of the historical subject lies not in the head, but in historical reality, and the key to this reality is not the conformity to some self-subsistent essence or some invariant historical Islam which does not exist, but the group which adopts the name by adapting it to its particular form and understanding of the historical paradigm evoked by the name, a paradigm which is metonymically suggested and not specifically indicated by the name itself. The connection between name and historical reality derives its validation and credibility from extrinsic criteria, from the capacity that the group adopting the name has to enforce and consolidate its interpretation and to perpetuate it within institutions both epistemic and social.

IV

This elaborate anti-Enlightenment philosophy of history and of politics which has been read from Afghānī's writings and which was constructed largely with the conceptual apparatus of precritical philosophy is not the only one which could legitimately be attributed to him. There are strands of other orientations as well. In his response to Renan's famous pronouncements of 1883 about the congenital incapacities of the Semitic mind and the inability of the Arab to produce science and philosophy, Afghānī insisted instead that responsibility for the decline of the brilliant civilization of the Arabs was to be borne entirely by Islam. "It is clear," he wrote, "that wherever it becomes established, this religion tried to stifle the sciences and it was marvelously served in its designs by despotism." Islam, he added, is not unique in this respect; all religions are intolerant and inimical to reason, and the progress that the West had manifestly achieved was accomplished despite Christianity.[29]

Freethinking of this kind might be accounted for by many factors, not the least of which was that Afghānī led many lives. An Arabic translation of his reply to Renan was deliberately stalled by his then adept Muḥammad 'Abduh. But in order properly to appreciate the legacy of Afghānī's anti-Enlightenment polemic in its full extent, aspects of which will be taken up presently, it is important to draw attention to one other dimension of his position on Renan. For just as he said that Europe progressed despite Christianity, he also said that the Muslims cannot be denied a similar outcome in the achievement of excellence in science and philosophy despite the heavy burden of Islam.[30] The answer, which he never gave in the text of his reply to Renan, was Reformism.

The Islam he attacked was the traditional Islam of the ecclesiastics. Like Luther, whom he greatly admired, Afghānī can be said to have "overcome the bondage of piety by replacing it by the bondage of conviction . . . [and] shattered faith in authority because he restored the authority of faith."[31] Afghānī, of course, provided some broad strokes, and actual reform—intellectual, social and legal—was to take place at the hands of Muḥammad 'Abduh, who can be said to have stood to Afghānī as St. Simon stood to Condorcet, giving primacy to "social hygiene" over political power as the regulator of society.[32]

Such hygiene is to be had with the reform of religion, which, after all, Afghānī regarded as the backbone of social order.[33] And as Laroui has shown with customary perspicacity, this reformism—which he attributes entirely to Afghānī—is very much in the spirit of the Enlightenment. Of the fundamental motifs of classical Muslim reformism can be cited a utilitarianism in the conception of law, a naturalism in the conception of the world.[34] Indeed, the very core of the reformism is the repudiation of all authority that intervenes between the reformer and the origin to which reform is seen as a return: the Koran and the salutary example of early Islamic history. Islam, according to reformism, knows no authority save that of reason, and what passes for religious authority, such as the Caliphate and the various ecclesiastical offices, are nothing for 'Abduh but secular offices which carry no doctrinal authority.[35] Nothing is authoritative but the pristine condition of Islam.

With historical Islam thus marginalized, 'Abduh could embark on the reinterpretation of the Koran in the light of reason—the historical reason of the time: the fundamental criterion is contained in the notion that Islam is a religion of ease, tolerance, and conformity with the conditions of human life, and is in this sense primeval, and thus the truest, historically the most versatile. Religions are subject to the laws of evolution, for the earliest of the true religions, with implicit reference to Judaism, is in conformity with the earlier stages of human history when right and wrong had to be arbitrarily dictated. A higher stage, implicitly with reference to Christianity, is clear when right and wrong are exhorted with reference to sentiment and to emotional arousal. Finally, with Islam, it is reason that is addressed.[36] Islam is thus transformed into a natural religion, and the reform of society is seen to reside in ridding it of the debris of history and revivifying the general sense of its original texts so they could have a contemporary relevance, in such a manner that Islamic law would become a particular variant of natural law. This reformed Islam is, incidentally, much in keeping with the laudatory ideas some Enlightenment thinkers held about Islam as a natural religion, superior to Christianity on this score, and in keeping with the natural course of social life.[37] After this naturalistic and utilitarian interpretation, little remains, in substantive terms, of Islam as it existed; what remains is a symbolic order.[38]

In the light of this legacy, it is hard to see what remained of Afghānī's irrationalist vitalism, which was the mainstay of his political theorizing and agitation, alongside his reformist notion of restoration. In historical terms, these two facets of his legacy have had separate careers, except to the mind of the Indian philosopher Sir Muhammad Iqbal (1876–1938). Iqbal combined German irrationalism and reformist naturalism and utilitarianism, after the fashion of Syed Ahmad Khan and the very similar efforts of Muḥammad 'Abduh, but he was of course working in a different tradition and circumstance to that experienced in modern Arab history.[39]

In fact, but for the possibilities inherent in the notion of reform as restoration, and therefore the implicit assumption of a subliminal historical continuity, which have been explored above, there is little in Islamic reformism of the romantic politics of Afghānī. Reformist Islam has come to dominate official Islam, but until recently constituted only a subculture in the Arab World, where public life (with the exception of marginal and relatively backward areas like the Arabian Peninsula) has been dominated by nationalism, liberalism, and various forms of socialism, and where the legal and educational systems, traditionally the mainstay of ecclesiastical authority, rapidly became secular.

What vitalist ideologies there were had an altogether different genealogy and had no reference to Afghānī. One would cite here some strands of Arab nationalism, such as the early doctrine of the Ba'th [Resurrection] Party now in power in Syria and Iraq. According to this doctrine, Arabism "does not indicate spatial properties and betrays no passage of time"; it is "the fount of theories, and is not born of thought but is wetnurse of thought." The national self, the historical subject, is itself a criticism of pure intellection and a reaffirmation of life.[40] Similar notions, buttressed with detailed historical researches, can be found in the writings of theorists of the Syrian Social Nationalist Party of the 1940s, '50s, and '60s, and the advocates for infra-historical micronationalisms, such as Maronitism in Lebanon.

Contemporary Islamism, a recent phenomenon which dates in earnest only from the seventies, adapted the vitalist elements in nationalism, the prevalent political and ideological culture in the Arab World, and took advantage of its versatility, which has already been mentioned, to assimilate vitalism to its own purposes. It can be said that Islamism insinuated itself, with a good measure of success, via a process of re-naming of the subject, whose identity is constituted by vitalist associations, into the nationalist ideological sphere and colored itself accordingly. In so doing, it has resurrected the romanticism of Afghānī's and reestablished him as the fount of authenticity and its main proponent and, indeed, its idol.

Islamist political and cultural movements have taken over Afghānī's romanticism with different pitches and emphases. A few have made a thorough reclamation of its abstract Jacobinism, a tendency which we can see in the most acute manifestations in Khomeinist tendencies. Others have seen in it almost a fact of nature, seeing in the indication of raw identities a matter instinctively apprehended by any mind attuned to the workings of nature—in this case, the nature of Muslims; an otherwise excellent history of modern Arabic thought has been written from this perspective.[41] Yet others have adapted this romanticism as a cultural form of an essentially nationalist impulse. To this latter trend belong the hybrid tendencies which seek to translate various aspects of a modern political program into Islamic terminology in order to authenticate and thus authorize them[42] or to develop an authentic "Islamic" method of social science whose metaphysical bearings are not Western, and which, not unnaturally, devolve to a restatement of some modern social science terms in a context where Islam acts as a myth of origin and charter of legislation, with an admixture of a vitalist epistemology.[43] In all these instances, romantic Islamism is the name under which a hypernationalist cultural program is officiated.

More directly relevant to the theme of this essay, however, is the reaction of universalist ideologies to the discourse on authenticity. The discourse of authenticity has rarely come into its own, outside Islamist circles, without being associated with some universalist discourse. Some illustrative examples drawn from the work of contemporary philosophers will suffice to show how this romanticism was received and assimilated, although instances could be multiplied at will. Resistance to the notion of authenticity in the Arab World has been feeble in the recent past due to a number of manifest political circumstances, not the least of which being that the Arab World has not been immune from the worldwide resurgence of atavism, ethnic and religious bigotry, and fundamentalist religiosity.

One primary mechanism according to which linkages between universalism and particularist romanticism are made is the simple act of naming that has already been encountered. The prominent philosopher, Professor Z. N. Mahmoud, a logical positivist by philosophical tendency and a liberal in politics, propounds a program for the construction of an indigenous Arab philosophy starting from "the self." To this end, immediate apprehension is the epistemological key, for it is through introspection, he claims, that we can unveil the principles out of which arise "our" judgments on all matters. Such is his manner of seizing the authentic, which he finds in instances from the Arab past, from which he then derives his liberal principles of liberty and rationality. The combination assures the Arabs not only of the capacity for science, but also human dignity.[44]

Not all attempts have been as crude and awkward as this self-authentication by a very skilled technical philosopher. What Professor Mahmoud did was to bring into prominence—he has a vast readership—a number of staple ideas in Islamist circles since the time of Muḥammad 'Abduh: that revivalism is the axial mode of cultural and political discourse and authenticity the sole means of actual success as of moral probity, that as a result, historical practice is an act of authenticating desires or programs for the present and the future, and that this authentication involves reference to past events still somehow alive at the core of the invariant historical subject, events which are repeatable, in the act of healing the breach between past and future. Thus parliamentary democracy is presented as a simple revalorization of the *shura,* a process of consulting clan chiefs in early Islamic times, and rationality becomes a reclamation of the work of Averroes and of Ibn Khaldun, while freedom becomes a repetition of Mu'tazilite theological theses on free will and socialism is made to stand in direct continuity with peasant rebellions of the tenth and eleventh centuries.

The past therefore becomes the paradigm of a present which must be authentic if it is to be in keeping with the *Volksgeist* and consequently merit serious cultural and political consideration. Past and future are unified by their substratum, the national essence, going beyond which is akin to breaking the laws of organic nature. It is this sense of historical continuity beyond history which has driven some Marxist philosophers to try to assimilate the discourse of authenticity. We can see this clearly in the monumental history of Arab-Islamic philosophy of Hussein Mroueh, assassinated not long ago. In it an attempt was made to separate two modalities of historical time, one of relevance today and the other redundant. The relevant one was, not unnaturally, "materialist tendencies" which might afford a point of linkage between past and future.[45] The past is liberated of its historicity and posited as the fount of desired continuities with a desired future, and the past is again cast in the future anterior, as if the spell of teleology is cast.

The same is discernible in the apologetic tenor of some of the most sophisticated Marxist writings on Arab-Islamic thought. As against the charge made by some writers that time in classical Arabic thought is atomized by occasionalism, one scholar cites the notion of analogy current in Islamic legal theory as well as in theology. Rather than seeing in analogy the primacy of the key term—the precedent—he slants his analysis in the other direction and finds in the practice of analogy a reaffirmation of historicity rather than the denial of history which it in fact is, for it is an affirmation of only one time, a time of superlative ontological weight, the time of the text and precedent.[46] The same author also follows a long tradition in finding in Ibn Khaldun's metaphysical hierarchies a notion of class stratification, and discovers the Marxist theory of accumulation in the theological metaphors with which Ibn Khaldun formulates his discourse on economic activity.[47]

Thus is the anti-Enlightenment polemic interiorized in the bodies of philosophies whose fundamental motifs had been derived from the Enlightenment, and thus is a heritage invented by the elimination of history as past and its retrieval as a form of the present. There is no great secret by which one can explain the invasion by the trope of authenticity and its setting of assumptions that others feel constrained to adopt. But for the understanding of this we must leave the terrain of philosophy for that of society and polity.

Notes

1. See Abdallah Laroui, "The Arabs and Social Anthropology," in *The Crisis of the Arab Intellectual,* trans. by Diarmid Cammell (Berkeley and Los Angeles: University of California Press, 1976), pp. 44–80; and Aziz Al-Azmeh, *Islamic Studies and the European Imagination—Inaugural Lecture* (Exeter, 1986). For a close textual study of otherness in another historical context, see François Hartog, *Le Miroir d'Hérodote: Essai sur la représentation de l'autre* (Paris: Presses Universitaires de France, 1980).

2. The relation of Arabism and Islamism is exceedingly complex, and the reader is referred to the voluminous works of a conference on this matter: *Al-Qawmīya al-'Arabīyya wal-Islām (Arab nationalism and Islam)* (Beirut, 1981). See Aziz Al-Azmeh, "Islamism and Arab Nationalism," *Review of Middle East Studies* 4 (1988): 33–51.

3. *An Islamic Response to Imperialism: Political and Religious Writings of Sayyid Jamal al-Din "al-Afghānī,"* trans. by Nikki Keddie (Berkeley and Los Angeles: University of California Press, 1968). See also Homa Pakdaman, *Djamal-Ed-Din Assad Abadi dit Afghānī* (Paris, 1969). On Syed Ahmad Khan, see Christian W. Troll, *Sayyid Ahmad Khan: A Reinterpretation of Muslim Theology* (New Delhi: Vikas Publishing House, 1978).

4. A. Hourani, *Arabic Thought in the Liberal Age* (London, 1962) is a most serviceable introduction to its topic in English. For a rigorous technical study, see Malcolm H. Kerr, *Islamic Reform: The Political and Legal Theories of Muhammed 'Abduh and Rashid Rida* (Berkeley and Los Angeles: University of California Press, 1966). It must be pointed out that studies on modern Arabic thought in English have achieved none of the seriousness of studies of comparable movements in India, of which one could mention V. C. Joshi, ed., *Rammohun Roy*

and the Process of Modernization in India (New Delhi: National Book Trust, 1975), and Partha Chatterjee, *Nationalist Thought and the Colonial World* (London: Zed Books for the United National University, 1986). Fundamental for the study of modern Arab thought in a European language is Abdallah Laroui, *L'idéologie Arabe Contemporaire* (Paris: François Maspéro, 1967).

5. See Taha Parla, *The Social and Political Thought of Ziya Gökalp* (Leiden: Brill, 1985), and William Cleveland, *The Making of an Arab Nationalist: Ottomanism and Arabism in the Life and Thought of Satic al-Husri* (Princeton: Princeton University Press, 1971).

6. Şherif Mardin, *The Genesis of Young Ottoman Thought: A Study in the Modernization of Turkish Political Ideas* (Princeton: Princeton University Press, 1962).

7. Cf. the approximate sketch of Abdessalam Bin Abdelali, "Heidegger didd Hegel" (Heidegger contra Hegel), *Dirāsāt 'Arabiyya* 19, no. 4 (1983): 93, 96.

8. Jamāl al-Dīn al-Afghānī, *Al-A'māl al-Kāmila* (Complete works), ed. by M. 'Umāra (Cairo, n.d.), pp. 130, 312–313, and *Al-'Urwa al-Wuthqā* (Cairo, 1958), pp. 9–12 and passim.

9. Afghānī, *Al-A'māl al-Kāmila,* p. 147 and idem., *Al-A'māl al-majhūla* (Unknown works), ed. by Alī Shalash (London: 1987), p. 78.

10. Afghānī, *Al-A'māl al-majhūla,* pp. 80–81.

11. For instance, L. Gumplowicz, "Un sociologiste arabe du XIVe siècle" in *Aperçus sociologiques* (New York: Paine-Whitman Publishing, 1963), pp. 201–226 (originally published in 1898); *Geschichte der staatstheorien* (Innsbruck, 1905), par. 59; F. Oppenheimer, *System der Soziologie* 2d ed. (Stuttgart: G. Fisher Publishing, 1964), vol. 2, pp. 173–174. See also Aziz Al-Azmeh, *Ibn Khaldun in Modern Scholarship* (London: Frank Cass, 1981), pp. 157 ff.

12. Afghānī, *Al-A'māl al-Kāmila,* pp. 443–444.

13. R. G. Collingwood, *The Idea of History* (Oxford: Oxford University Press, 1946), p. 91.

14. Afghānī, *Al-A'māl al-Kāmila,* p. 153.

15. Ibid., pp. 157–164.

16. *Al-'Urwa al-Wuthqā,* p. 20.

17. Gaston Bachelard, *Dialectique de la durée* (Paris: Presses Universitaires de France, 1950), p. 52.

18. Ḥasan Ḥanafī, *Dirāsāt falsafiyya* (Philosophical studies) (Cairo, 1988), pp. 52–57.

19. Waḍḍāḥ Sharāra, *Ḥawla ba'd mushkilāt ad-dawla fil-mujtama' wal-thaqāfa al-Arabiyyayan* (Some problems concerning the state in Arab society and culture) (Beirut, 1981), p. 71.

20. Quoted in Ernst Cassirer, *Philosophy of Symbolic Forms* (New Haven: Yale University Press, 1955), vol. 2, p. 106.

21. *Al-'Urwa al-Wuthqā,* p. 20.

22. G. W. F. Hegel, *Phenomenology of the Spirit,* trans. by A. V. Miller (Oxford: Oxford University Press, 1977), pars. 584, 590, 593.

23. G. W. F. Hegel, *Philosophy of Right,* trans. by T. M. Knox (Oxford: Oxford University Press, 1967), par. 4.

24. See the remarks on Dilthey in the excellent work of Stepan Odouev, *Par les sentiers de Zarathoustra: Influence de la pensée de Nietzsche sur la philosophie bourgeoise allemande,* trans. by Catherine Emery (Moscow: Editions du Progrès, 1980), pp. 137–138.

25. Laroui, *L'ideologie arabe contemporaire,* p. 66.

26. Afghānī, *Al-A'māl al-majhūla,* p. 81.

27. Aziz Al-Azmeh, *Al-Turāth bayn al-Sulṭān wat-tārīkh* (Heritage: Power and history) (Casablanca and Beirut, 1986), pp. 91 ff.

28. Cf. the analyses of Hedwig Konrad, *Étude sur la métaphore* (Paris, 1939), p. 88; and Paul Ricoeur, *The Rule of Metaphor,* trans. by R. Czerny et al. (Toronto: University of Toronto Press, 1977), pp. 207–211.

29. Text in Keddie, trans., *An Islamic Response,* pp. 183, 187.

30. Ibid., p. 183.

31. Karl Marx in Karl Marx and Frederick Engels, *Collected Works* (London: Lawrence & Wishart Publishers, 1975), vol. 3, p. 182.

32. Cf. Robert Wolker, "Saint-Simon and the Passage from Political to Social Science" in Anthony Pagden, ed., *The Languages of Political Theory in Early Modern Europe* (Cambridge: Cambridge University Press, 1987), pp. 335–336.

33. Afghānī, *Al-A'māl al-Kāmila,* p. 130 and passim.

34. Abdallah Laroui, *Islam et modernité* (Paris: Editions la Découverte, 1987), pp. 134–147.

35. Muḥammad 'Abduh, *Al-A'māl al-Kāmila* (Complete works), ed. by M. 'Umāra (Beirut, 1972), vol. 3, pp. 287, 289.

36. 'Abduh, *Al-A'māl al-Kāmila,* pp. 448–456.

37. 'Abduh, *Al-A'māl al-Kāmila,* pp. 282–311; and Muḥammad Rashīd Riḍā, *Tārīkh al-ustādh al-Imām Muḥammad 'Abduh* (Biography of Muhammad 'Abduh) (Cairo, 1931), vol. 1, p. 614. In general, see the excellent study of Kerr, *Islamic Reform.*

38. Laroui, *Islam et modernité,* pp. 127–130.

39. Muhammad Iqbal, *The Reconstruction of Religious Thought in Islam* (London: Oxford University Press, 1934), pp. 4–15, 42–55, 126–131, 148–154, 165–169.

40. Michel Aflaq, *Fī Sabīl al-Ba'th* (For the Baath) (Beirut, 1958), pp. 43, 44, 158.

41. Muḥammad Jābir al-Anṣārī, *Taḥawwulāt al-fikr was-siyāsa fil-sharq al-'Arabī, 1930–1970* (Transformations of thought and politics in the Arab East, 1930–1970) (Kuwait, 1980).

42. For instance, Ḥanafī, *Dirāsāt falsafiyya,* and idem., *Al-Turāth wal-tajdīd* (Heritage and renewal) (Beirut, 1981); and cf. Aziz Al-Azmeh, *Al-Turath,* pp. 164–168.

43. For instance, 'Adil Husain, *Naḥwa fikr 'arabī jadīd: an-nāṣiriyya wal-tanmiya wal-dimuqrāṭiyya* (Toward a new Arab thought: Nasserism, development and democracy) (Cairo, 1985).

44. Zakī Najīb Maḥmūd, *Tajdīd al-fikr 'al-arabī* (The renewal of Arabic thought) (Beirut, 1980), pp. 274, 283.

45. Ḥusain Muruwwa, *Al-Naza'āt al-māddīyya fil-falsafa al-'arabiyya al-islā-mīyya* (Materialist trends in Arab-Islamic philosophy) (Beirut, 1978), 3 volumes, ff.

46. Mahmūd Amīn al-'Ālim, "Mafhūm al-zamān fil-fikr al-'arabī al-islāmī" (The conception of time in Arab-Islamic thought), in *Dirāsāt fil-Islām* (Beirut, 1980), pp. 110–111. See Aziz Al-Azmeh, "Islamic Legal Theory and the Appropriation of Reality," in *Islamic Law: Social and Historical Contexts,* ed. by Aziz Al-Azmeh (London: Routledge, 1988), pp. 250–265.

47. Mahmūd Amīn al-'Ālim, "Muqaddimat Ibn Khaldūn—Madkhal ibisti-mulūjī" (Ibn Khaldun's Muqaddima: An epistemological introduction), in *Al-Fikr al-'Arabī* (Beirut, 1978), vol. 6, pp. 37, 41–42, 45–46.

KWAME GYEKYE

TRADITIONAL POLITICAL VALUES AND IDEAS: AN EXAMINATION OF THEIR RELEVANCE TO DEVELOPMENTS IN CONTEMPORARY AFRICAN POLITICAL ORDER

It is a well-known fact that since the euphoric early days of political independence the politics of many an African nation has been blighted in several ways. The political institutions that were bequeathed to the African people by their colonial masters—institutions that were modeled on those of their rulers—did not function properly. This institutional failure may be explained in several ways: (1) the African people simply did not have the ability to operate effectively systems of government that were entirely alien to them; (2) they did not try hard enough to make a success of these alien institutions; (3) not having any emotional, ideological, or intellectual attachments to these institutions, they had no real desire to operate them; (4) they lacked certain moral or dispositional virtues or attitudes (such as patience, tolerance, incorruptibility) which are necessary for the successful operation of these alien institutions; or (5) the institutions may have worked all right but for the disruptions of the political processes by the military. The democratic constitutions that have been fashioned by African peoples themselves, modeled as they invariably have been on European systems, have suffered the same fate. The unavoidable consequence of this constitutional failure for many an African nation has been political instability, uncertainty, and confusion.

In this political uncertainty and confusion, questions are being asked whether viable political structures cannot be forged in the furnace of the Africans' own tradition of political rule. The positive attitude being evinced toward the traditional system stems from the claim or conviction of a number of people that the traditional system of government did have some democratic features which a new political system can profit by. In light of problems of establishing democratic institutions experienced by African nations since regaining their political independence, any talk of African traditions of government having democratic features

487

will undoubtedly evoke cynicism, even scandal. But the facts of anthropology speak for themselves.

In times of wonder and uncertainty, in times when the definition and articulation of values and goals become most urgent, in times when the search for fundamental principles of human activity becomes most pressing and is seen as the way to dispelling confusions and unclarities, the services of the intellectual enterprise called philosophy become indispensable. For philosophy is a conceptual response to the problems posed in any given epoch for a given society. It is therefore appropriate, even imperative, for contemporary African philosophers to grapple at the conceptual level with the problems and issues of their times, not least of which are the problems of government and political stability.

My intention in this essay is to explore traditional African values and ideas of government with a view to pointing up the democratic features of this indigenous system of government, and to examine whether, and in what ways, such features can be said to be harmonious with the ethos of contemporary political culture and hence can be said to be relevant to developments in political life and thought in modern Africa.

Chiefship and Political Authority

An inquiry into the status, nature of authority, and role of the chief and the power relationship holding between the chief and the people will disclose certain political values and ideas espoused in the political setting of traditional Africa. For chieftaincy was certainly the most outstanding feature of the African traditional political structure and the linchpin of the political wheel. In pursuit of this inquiry, I shall first provide facts about political institutions and their manner of operation.[1] I shall then investigate the philosophical underpinnings of the traditional political institutions. It is hoped that this approach, descriptive as well as conceptual, will not only provide insight into the African traditions of politics but also an answer to the question whether or not the indigenous political system exhibited democratic features. For purposes of in-depth study, however, I shall limit my attention to the political thought and practice of the Akan people, the largest ethnic group in Ghana.

Akan Traditional Political Institutions

In this section I am concerned only with the political institutions that bear most directly on the relations between the chief and the people, that is, between the ruler and the ruled—in other words, with the institutions that may be said to be crucial as far as the concrete expression of the democratic idea of the will of the people is concerned.

Every Akan town or village is made up of a number of clans (clan: *abusua*). One of these clans, probably the one whose forefathers founded that town or village, constituted the royal family from which the chiefs or rulers were elected. Each clan comprises many lineages, while each lineage in turn comprises many individuals linked by blood relationships. Each town or village constituted a political unit. A great number of such towns and villages formed a paramountcy, a state *(oman)*, such as the Asante state or Akim Abuakwa state, whose head was the paramount chief, the *omanhene*.

Each town or village had a chief and a council of elders, these elders being the heads of the clans *(mbusuapanyin)*. The chief presided at the meetings of the council. Just as each town or village had a council, so did the state have a council—the state council, described by Danquah as "the great legislative assembly of the nation."[2] The state council, presided over by the *omanhene*, drew its membership from the chiefs of the towns and villages constituting the state.

The chief, who was the political head of an Akan town or village, was selected from the royal lineage by the head of the lineage in consultation with the members of the lineage. The person chosen had to be *acceptable* not only to the councilors—who represented their clans—but also to the Asafo company of young men *(mmerantee)*—the "commoners," in effect, the body of citizens. The paramount chief was chosen in the same way, except that his election had to be acceptable to the chiefs of the constituent towns and villages. Thus, never was a chief imposed upon an Akan community, a fact of which the self-imposed military rulers of Africa today must take note.

Now, having been accepted by the people, the chief on the occasion of his formal installation had to take oath publicly before his councilors and the body of citizens to observe the institutions and laws of the town or state. At the installation ceremony a whole series of injunctions were publicly recited before him. These injunctions defined his political authority. The following are typical examples (taken from Rattray)[3] of such injunctions which were declared to him through the chief's spokesman *(okyeame)*:

> We do not wish that he should curse us
> We do not wish that he should be greedy
> We do not wish that he should be disobedient
>   (or, refuse to take advice).
> We do not wish that he should treat us unfairly *(nkwaseabuo)*
> We do not wish that he should act on his own initiative
>   (literally, out of his own head, that is, acting without
>   reference to the views or wishes of the people)
> We do not wish that it should ever be that he should say
> "I have no time," "I have no time."

It appears that the most important injunction was that the chief should never act without the advice and full concurrence of his councilors, the representatives of the people. Acting without the concurrence and advice of his council was a legitimate cause for his deposition.[4] Thus the chief was bound by law to rule with the consent of the people. Similarly, if a paramount chief abused his power, his subordinate chiefs who were members of his council, could depose him. It may thus be said that the Akan theory of government was a kind of social contract theory. The injunctions submitted by the people to the chief and accepted by him constituted a kind of contract between them. The chief or king was thus to hold power in trust for the people.

The chief's council was the real governing body of the town. The members of this governing council were usually the heads of the various clans. The council was presided over by the chief. The councilors were the representatives of the people, and, as such, had to confer with them on any issue that was to be discussed in the council. That is to say, the councilors, to whom everyone in the town had access, had to seek popular opinion. "The representative character of a councillor," wrote Mensah Sarba almost a century ago, "is well understood and appreciated by the people."[5] The councilor was obliged to act on the advice and with the concurrence of his people, in the same way as the chief was obliged to act after consultations and with the consent of his councilors, whom he had to summon regularly.

The councilors freely discussed all matters affecting the town or state. And in such an atmosphere of free and frank expression of opinions, disagreements would be inevitable. But in the event of such disagreements the council would continue to listen to arguments until unanimity was achieved with the reconciliation of opposed views. The communal ethos of African culture necessarily placed a great value on solidarity, which in turn necessitated the pursuit of unanimity or consensus not only in such important decisions as those taken by the highest political authority of the town or state, but also in decisions taken by lower assemblies such as those presided over by the heads of the clans, that is, the councilors. Thus, it is clear that every command, every move which was adopted by the chief, had been discussed and agreed upon by his councilors (who must have previously sounded popular opinion). For this reason, any publicity made by the chief's spokesman (*okyeame*) regarding a decree, injunction, command, and so forth, was made invariably in the name of the chief and his elders (that is, councilors). Thus, the *okyeame* would announce: "Thus say the chief and his elders . . ." (*Nana na ne mpanyingo se . . .*).[6] Having provided a brief account of Akan traditional political institutions and how they operated, we may now move on to a discussion of the democratic features of these institutions.

Elements of Democracy in Traditional Akan Political Practice

Defining the concept of democracy is not a problem; the famous and perhaps the most widely accepted definition is that it is the government of the people, by the people, and for the people. The centrality of the notion of "the people" is crucial to any definition of democracy. The definition implies, as it must, that the standard by which to judge the democratic nature of a political system is the degree of adequacy allowed for the expression of the will of the people, the extent to which the people are involved in decision-making processes. The problem of democracy, however, is simply the problem of *how to give institutional expression to the will of the people,* how, that is, to make the will of the people explicit in real and concrete terms. In the nations of the Western world, such institutions as the multiparty system, periodic elections, parliaments or congresses, constitutions containing bills of rights, an independent judiciary, and others have been created not only to give expression to the will of the people, but also to guard against the violation of their rights. These are some of the ingredients of the Western democratic political systems.

Now, in what ways, and to what extent, could the Akan political institutions just described be said to have provided a means of expressing the will of the people and popular participation in the political process? Let us explore this question.

The institution of chiefship was definitely the linchpin of the democratic process in an Akan community. For the nature of the political authority of the chief determined the democratic or undemocratic character of the political process. The chief, it was observed, was elected from the royal lineage. Succession to the high office of the chief was, thus, hereditary. And this hereditary element may be said to have imposed a limitation on the choice of rulers, though not necessarily on all other officeholders. Four points may be made that can be said to neutralize the political seriousness and effect of this delimiting factor.

First, unlike some monarchies in the world where the next occupant of the throne—the heir apparent—was obvious to everyone in the nation, the particular person to be chosen and installed as chief in an Akan community was generally not so obvious. The reason is that there were several eligible men in the royal lineage, and each one of them had just about equal claim to the throne. Thus the king-makers or electors, who were elders also of royal lineage, had a number of candidates to choose from. In deciding whom to choose and present to the people, the electors had to exercise the greatest judiciousness and wisdom, for their choice had to be acceptable to the people as a whole. The political history of many an Akan town or state teems with constitutional disputes arising either out of the lack of consensus on the part of the electors themselves regarding the most suitable candidate, or out of the unacceptability of the nominee to the majority of the people. But the point to be noted for the moment is that in choosing the ruler the electors did consider the wishes of the people to whom the nominee was finally to be presented and who had to accept him as their ruler. To the extent that the people had the final say on the suitability of the person chosen to rule them, it could be said that the traditional Akan political structure made it possible for the people to choose their own rulers, even if the initiative was originally taken by some few people.

The second point is that just as the will of the people was of considerable weight in determining the suitability and acceptability of the electors' nominee, so it was most crucial in determining the continuity, effectiveness, and success of a chief's rulership. The "common people" (*mmerantee,* young men) constituted themselves into Asafo companies which were organized for social, military, and political action. "In recent years," wrote Danquah in 1928, "these 'companies' have persistently claimed to possess absolute power to enstool, and chiefly to destool, a chief. This claim seems in a sense to be supported by facts of history and long-established customary practice."[7] Thus even if the people as a whole did not have the power directly to choose their ruler, they had the power directly to remove him or have him removed by the electors. This was another outlet provided in the Akan political system for the expression of the popular will.

The third point is that the limits of the monarchical power were clearly set both by custom and by the series of injunctions publicly recited before the chief and acknowledged publicly by him. These injunctions constitutionally made it impossible, or at least impolitic, for the chief to adhere stubbornly to his views, policies, and actions in the teeth of opposition from his councilors and subjects; they also outlawed arbitrary and autocratic government from the Akan political practice. The injunctions as well as customs so severely curtailed the political authority of the chief that, in the words of R. S. Rattray, an anthropologist in the employ of the colonial administration of the Gold Coast (now Ghana) during the first three decades of this century, "the chief in reality was expected to do little or nothing without having previously consulted his councilors, who in turn conferred with the people in order to sound popular opinion."[8] In connection with the political authority of the chiefs, Brodie Cruickshank, a Scotsman who also served in the British colonial administration in Ghana between 1834 and 1854, made the following observation: "But among none of those chiefs living under the protection of the (British) government, is their authority of such consequence as to withstand the general opinion of their subjects; so that, with all the outward display of regal power, the chief is little more than a puppet moved at the will of the people. . . ."[9] Constitutionally, then, the chief was bound to act only on the advice and with the concurrence of his councilors, and, consequently, of the popular will. As noted before, arbitrary and autocratic actions by the chief would lead to his deposition.

The fourth point that may be made against the view that the hereditary character of succession to chiefship might (potentially) throttle the real expression of popular will is that in any assembly, whether in the council of the chief, or in the palace of the chief, where general assemblies of all the people usually took place, or in the house of a councilor (that is, head of a clan), there was free expression of opinion. No one was hindered from fully participating in the deliberations of the councils or public (general) assemblies and thus from contributing to the decisions of these constitutional bodies. It is thus clear that the Akan traditional political structure allowed for many to participate in making decisions regarding the affairs of the community. "Anyone, even the most ordinary youth," wrote Cruickshank, "will offer his opinion or make a suggestion with an equal chance of its being as favorably entertained as if it proceeded from the most experienced sage."[10]

The observations made by Rattray about the democratic character of the politics of the Ashanti, a subsection of the Akan people, are worth noting:

> Nominally autocratic, the Ashanti constitution was in practice democratic to a degree. I have already on several occasions used this word "democratic," and it is time to explain what the term implies in this part of Africa. We pride ourselves, I believe, on being a democratic people and flatter ourselves that our institutions are of a like nature. An Ashanti who was familiar alike with his own and our (that is, British) Constitution would deny absolutely our right to apply this term either to ourselves or to our Constitution. To him a democracy implies that the affairs of the Tribe (the state) must rest, not in the keeping of the few, but in the hands of the many, that is, must not alone be the concern of what we should term "the chosen rulers of the people," but should continue to be the concern of a far wider circle. To him the state is literally *Res Publica;* it is everyone's business. The work of an Ashanti citizen did not finish when by his vote he had installed a chief in office. . . . The rights and duties of the Ashanti democrats were really only beginning after (if I may use a homely analogy) the business of the ballot-box was over. In England, the Government and House of Commons stand between ourselves and the making of our laws, *but among the Ashanti there was not any such thing as government apart from the people.*[11]

It may be noted that the concept of the divine right of kings which was the basis of the political authority of the Stuart monarchs of seventeenth-century England was never evolved or pursued by the Akan states. On the contrary, the facts do indicate that they had created a political system that not only made real despotism well-nigh impossible, but also gave due recognition to the wishes of the governed.

In all this, the Akan people were *institutionally* expressing, in their own fashion, certain basic ideas of democracy. First and foremost was the idea that the government of a people must be responsive to the wishes of the people. We have noticed that although the chief was not directly elected by all the people, the electors in their choice had to consider the wishes of the people; we have also noted that the chief had to govern in accordance with the popular will. Again, the allowance made for the expression of opinion on public matters enabled the people of an Akan community, or many of them at any rate, to be involved in decision-making at all levels. Public criticisms of government policy and action were inevitable in a system which allowed for the frank expression of opinion. Criticisms of government policy and action were made by people as individuals in accordance with their own light, not as members of "political parties," which did not exist.

The political phenomenon that approximated to "political parties" of the type that obtains in Western countries were the groupings of men and women resulting from disagreements and disputes that emerged—and not infrequently—generally over the nomination or election of a chief, but over other matters as well. But, though such groupings were political in terms of their aims, they could hardly be described as political parties. For their aims were *ad hoc* and ephemeral, and they were concerned not so much with the broad political issues of society as with the issue of the person nominated or chosen to hold the office of the chief. For this reason, such disputes and oppositions never led to ideological rifts, and were submerged before long by the waves of the characteristic demands of solidarity. Because of the nonexistence of political parties, some scholars have supposed that African political culture lacked the concept of opposition. However, the existence both of disagreements, divisions, and groupings along political lines in the deliberations of the traditional councils and assemblies as well as the pursuit of consensus gives the lie to this supposition. Consensus, along with reconciliation, appears in fact to have been a political virtue vigorously pursued in Akan traditional councils and assemblies, and to have become an outstanding feature in the process of reaching decisions. In all kinds of deliberations the aim was to achieve consensus and reconciliation, and this, inevitably, could prolong meetings; but it would allow for argument and exchange of ideas. Consensus logically presupposes dissensus (that is, dissent), the existence of opposed or different views; for it was the opposed views that were, or needed to be, reconciled. If there were not opposition, it would be senseless to talk of reaching a consensus and reconciliation. This is a conceptual truth. Thus, we are forced to conclude that in the traditional Akan politics there was opposition without an organized political party in opposition. Whether or not Akan or African political culture would have in time evolved its own brand of the party system of politics, no one can say for sure. Colonialism slammed the doors against such a possible evolution.

Consensus, as a procedure for arriving at political decisions, was born of the pursuit of the social ideal or goal of solidarity. The concept was thus a feature of the Akan communalist philosophy. It was considered as vital to the Akan conception and practice of democracy; and not without justification. The pursuit of consensus allows for an individual input; it promotes mutual tolerance, patience, and an attitude of compromise, all of which are necessary for the democratic practice in which one voluntarily has to abandon or modify one's own position in the face of more persuasive arguments of the other or others. The pursuit of consensus thus makes for compromise in which the expression of an individual's will becomes effective to a degree, not cavalierly set aside. Consensus must, therefore, be considered a democratic virtue; it is certainly an ideal for any democratic decision-making assembly. I must note at this point that the facts about the democratic political practice of the Akan people are by no means idiosyncratic to them.[12]

The Conceptual Expression of Democracy

In the foregoing section an account was given of the Akan political practice. There is no denying, however, that political institutions take their rise from, and are molded by, a political theory or philosophy. That is to say, underlying political institutions and political practice is a political theory, a philosophy, even though such philosophy may not have been fully articulated or worked out. My intention in this section, therefore, is to attempt to indicate and examine the ideas underpinning Akan political practice and how these ideas were formulated. In the preliterate cultural setting of Africa's historical past, the ideas of politics, as of everything else, were expressed, at the conceptual level, in proverbs and sayings, folk tales, artistic symbols, rituals, and so on. The proverbs, as I have argued in detail in my work, *An Essay on African Philosophical Thought,*[13] are not unlike the fragments of the early ancient Greek philosophers that were a collection of sayings; and, because of their philosophical content or relevance, they were utilized by later thinkers in the reconstruction and resurrection of early Greek philosophy. The same philosophical use, I have claimed, can be made of African proverbs and sayings. In using such sources, one would in fact be involved in an exercise in conceptual ordering, in the logic of ideas.

The well-known Akan proverb, "One head does not go into council" *(ti koro nko agyina),* expresses the political value of consultation or conferring, the idea that deliberation by several heads (that is, minds) on matters of public concern is always better. The proverb (or, fragment) says implicitly that the chief cannot or should not alone deliberate and adopt a policy or an action that affects others, for he is (or, has) one head. Though the fragment may not immediately advocate a democratic practice, it certainly repudiates autocracy or despotism, which is thus defined here as "one head going into council." This fragment is in fact the logical consequence of another one, which is, "Wisdom is not in the head of one person" *(nyansa nii onipa baako ti mu).* If wisdom is not in one person's head, then one head cannot, or should not, go into council, where the exercise of wisdom is required. Since, as the fragment clearly states, every person has some ability to think, and to think about, in this case, matters affecting the whole society, it would be senseless or presumptuous for one person to arrogate to himself or herself the right to think or deliberate for others. The fragment implies, then, that matters concerning the whole society ought to be thought about by all the members of the society, or by as many of them as possible.

But let us explore this fragment a bit further. The fragment means: (1) that other individuals may be equally wise and capable of producing equally good, if not better, ideas; (2) that one should not, or cannot, regard one's own intellectual position as final or unassailable or beyond criticism, but expect it to be evaluated by others; and (3) that, in consequence of (2), one should be prepared to abandon one's position in the face of another person's superior ideas or arguments, or in the event of one's own ideas or arguments being judged unacceptable or implausible by others. The fragment underlines not only the need for, but also the acceptance of, criticism, just as it points up the need to respect the views of others. In the political context, it enjoins rulers to be less dogmatic and more tolerant of the views of others. Logically fleshed out, the fragment also recommends the choice and practice of consensus in political decision-making.

There are fragments specifically about the limited nature of the power of the ruler and the power relations that hold between him and the governed, such as:

1. If a chief reprimands (rebukes, punishes) you for doing something, he does so by the authority of the citizens *(ohen bedi wo kasa a, na efi amanfoo)*.
2. It is when the state kills you that the chief kills you *(oman kum wo a, na ohen kum wo)*.
3. It is when a chief has good councilors that his reign becomes peaceful *(ohen nya ahotrafo pa a, na ne bere so dwo)*.
4. There are no bad rulers, only bad advisors *(ahen bone nni baabi, na asafohene bone na wowo baabi)*.

Fragments (1) and (2) express the idea that the ruler (that is, the chief) acts only on the advice of, or with the concurrence of, or by the authority of the people. Fragment (3) underlines the dependence of the ruler on the advice of his councilors, that is, the representatives of the people, for satisfactory and peaceful government. The implications of fragments (1)–(3) just stated are summed up in fragment (4). The thought expressed in fragment (4) is that theoretically, that is, within the framework of the constitution, there would be no bad rulers, since the ruler would be expected to rely solely on the advice and guidance of his advisors. The presumption is that the advice of the councilors and other lieutenants would be expected to be good, proceeding, as it would, from many heads rather than from one head, that is, the ruler's. But the thought expressed in the fragment is only theoretically plausible, and may in practice be false, insofar as it is possible for the ruler to set aside the views or arguments of his advisors. The thought of the fragment expresses a political ideal, but the realization of the ideal would depend very much on the character, personality, and disposition of the ruler; a stupid, arrogant, and strong-willed ruler may set aside even the good advice of his lieutenants—to his own chagrin, though. But the fact still remains that the thought of the fragment expresses a political ideal the realization of which would give adequate testimony to the effective role of the will of the people in the political process and, *a fortiori,* to the effectiveness of the democratic practice.

An emblem embossed in silver or gold on top of a staff often held by the chief's spokesman at public ceremonies depicts an egg in a hand, and the saying that goes with it is that holding power is like holding an egg in the hand: if you press the egg very hard, you break it; but if you do not press it hard enough, or hold it loosely, it drops and breaks. The symbol expresses an important political thought, which is that a ruler should not oppress his subjects or do anything that could cause them to revolt or rebel, an action that could in turn lead to the possible breakup of his kingdom. On the other hand, if the appropriate and judicious measures, policies, and actions are not adopted as required by particular circumstances, if the firmness and resoluteness a situation demands are not shown by the ruler, his indecision, supineness, and lack of both political will and strength of purpose will wreck his political authority. The symbol is not intended to give the impression that the ruler's position is one of a tangle or paradox; it is intended rather to express an important fact about the judicious or prudent use of political power: neither excessive action nor indolent inaction is a true mark of rulership; political power or authority should be exercised *when* it should, and wisely.

Tradition and Modernity

It may be true to opine that in the development of man and society the cultural factor cannot be ignored or denigrated. The reason is that any meaningful human development takes place in a cultural milieu, and is in fact conditioned or influenced by it. The cultural milieu, even though it cannot be said to be a windowless monad, must nevertheless stay self-identical or internally cohesive in its essentials for a reasonably long period of time for a meaningful and recognizable development to take place. That is to say, the cultural framework of development must continue mostly unscathed for a considerable length of time. This in fact is a necessary condition for the development of human society in all its complexities. In the absence of this condition, development becomes distorted, uneven, and without sure foundations.

Modern Africa is trying feverishly to develop; but it is trying to develop in a cultural setting that historically lacks this necessary condition, that is, a continuity of a cultural framework for its development. The reason is that the colonial interregnum denigrated or set aside the indigenous cultural values and institutions and so failed, or rather refused, to utilize them in building the sociopolitical institutions of the colonial territory. A corpus of cultural values is, to be sure, still in the ascendant, but such values are left in limbo and have, in consequence, hardly been taken into account in the creation of modern political institutions, for instance. Thus the African traditions and values of government, such as have been outlined in this essay, have not had any impact on the modern political setup, even though they are still alive and influential in the politics of the "traditional areas," that is, at the local or provincial levels where the chiefs still exercise some political authority. However, at the level of *national* politics these traditions and values of politics are inconsequential. This means that the modern state apparatus can hardly be said to have evolved from the cultural values of the people, a fact that may well account for at least some of the problems besetting modern African politics.

The search for democracy in postcolonial Africa has been an odyssey, a long and arduous journey the end of which is not yet in sight, but still in the womb of time. Perhaps resorting to the indigenous values and ideas of politics may be a redemptive approach. Some evidence and arguments have been deployed in this essay to show that such ideas and values of politics as popular will, free expression of opinion, consensus and reconciliation, consultation and conferring, and the trusteeship— and hence limited—nature of political power, all of which are ingredients of the democratic idea, were to be found in the African traditions of politics and that they are, thus, by no means alien to the indigenous political cultures of African peoples. But these political values have not been allowed to affect and shape the contours of modern African politics. The consequences have not been palatable: authoritarian politics and illegitimate seizure of political power are the order of the day, features of modern African politics which can hardly be said to derive from African traditions.

To argue that traditional values and ideas be brought to bear on modern political life and thought, however, is not necessarily to apotheosize those values and ideas; it is only to point up their worthwhileness. The Akan fragment, "The ancient (or, the past) has something to say" *(tete wo bi ka),* implies not that the ancient has said everything that needs to be said and can therefore provide us modern people with all the values, ideas, institutions, and so forth, that we may need, but that if we were to examine objectively the "ancient" system of values, we would find *some* values that would be considered relevant to our modern circumstances. But here comes the all-important question: By what criteria are we to accept or reject traditional values, attitudes, ideas, and institutions? How, that is, do we judge that the legacy of the past is or is not worth being given some attention or place within the scheme of things of a present?

There are, I think, at least two important criteria for judging the relevance or otherwise of values, ideas, and institutions of the past to the circumstances of a present. These are: (1) the fundamental nature of a set of pristine values and attitudes, and (2) the functionality of past ideas and institutions in the setting of the present. There surely are values that can be held as so fundamental to human existence that they can, for that reason, be said to transcend particular generations or epochs. Such fundamental and abiding values must be related to, or generated by, considerations of basic, sedimented human desires, wants, hopes, ideals, and sentiments. A present age must ask whether it can abandon such basic human values and continue to exist as a human society. An age or generation that does not pursue the ethic of respect for human life and where wanton killings of human beings are the order of the day cannot survive as a human *society* for any length of time. Thus it is the basic, abiding character of certain values cherished and pursued in the past that makes those values relevant and acceptable to a later age.

I am aware, however, that the view I am urging here is clearly at variance with that of the moral relativist, who would have no truck with a conception of fundamental or abiding or lasting values. Yet I believe that the possibility of a human *society* is grounded on the reality of a fundamental *core* of human values the observance of which makes for the continual existence, stability, and smooth functioning of the society. It cannot be seriously denied surely that, for instance, there are certain things that all members of a society *want* as rational beings. (How to achieve, or whether we shall achieve, all our wants is a different matter.)

The relevance or irrelevance of ideas and institutions of the past to a present would also be determined by their functionality, that is, whether or not they can play any meaningful or efficacious role in the present scheme of things and so conduce to the attainment of the goals and vision of that present. Ideas and institutions that have stood the test of time and have proved their worth can be considered suitable for the purposes of a present moment; otherwise, they must be regarded as obsolescent and consequently jettisoned, to be replaced by new ones. It is the profound appreciation of the efficacy and resilience of values, ideas, and institutions of the past that recommends them to a present age, and underpins the significance of such ebullient utterances as "our *traditions* of democracy," "our *traditions* of humanism," "our *traditions* of hospitality," and so on. All such traditions are of course not a sudden emergence; they are the ideas and values that have been hallowed by time and function. This in fact is involved in the meaning of tradition.

Now, against the background of the views expressed in the immediately preceding paragraphs, I shall briefly examine some of the ideas and institutions of the traditional African political system in terms of their relevance or irrelevance to the modern setting.

It must be borne in mind from the outset that the conditions in which the indigenous democratic institutions operated many decades ago were different from what they are now with the emergence both of large political communities (that is, nations) and of the idea of a central government that controls the political power. The business of government in the modern world is more complex, more ramifying than of yore; we cannot go about such business in the way it was done by our forefathers. The reason is that certain features or aspects of the traditional conceptions of things, but by no means all, may be disharmonious with the modern situation. For instance, the idea of a *hereditary* head of state who is not a mere figurehead but wields (or, wants to wield) effective political power as in the traditional political setting will not be hospitable in a modern political community in which several individuals or groups compete for political power. Also, the concept of a regal lineage from which the chief or head of state was chosen is impossible to entertain and apply within the context of a large modern political community constituted by a medley of ethnic groups. Each of the constituent ethnic groups would want the head of state to come from within it, a desire that would, if not fulfilled, almost invariably engender political wrangles, machinations, and secessions. Ethnicity has been the bane of the party system of politics in postcolonial Africa: party affiliations have generally been on ethnic lines, and ethnicity is known to have played some role in military coups. It is thus undeniable that in the evolution of the democratic system in a large political community some of the traditional political institutions would be a hindrance. Such institutions or practices must therefore be expunged.

On the other hand, there were others to be sure, that today would facilitate democratic political development: the town, village, or state councils that served as instruments of political participation and involvement; ideas of free expression of opinion, popular will, consent, and consensus; and the fact that wealth was not a basis of membership of the traditional councils—so that both the rich and poor found themselves there—all these and others discussed earlier are conducive to the evolution of the democratic practice even in a large modern political setting. It must be noted that both colonial and postcolonial (that is, African) governmental systems created a distance between the government and the governed. This, in turn, engendered attitudes of unconcern and insensitivity to the affairs of the state on the part of the governed. Consequently, the general attitude of the citizen was that it was possible to injure the state without injuring oneself, an attitude that opened the floodgates of bribery, corruption, carelessness about state property or state enterprises, and other unethical or antisocial acts. Traditional ideology, however, positively maintained that any injury done to the community as a whole directly injured the individual. Thus, the traditional system evoked sentiments of personal commitment to the community which the modern state has yet to create in its citizens. These observations undoubtedly suggest the conviction that it is sensible, even imperative, to revivify those of our atavistic political values and attitudes which are evidently relevant to developments in the democratic politics of the modern world.

The upshot of the discussion of this essay, then, is that the ideas and values in the traditional system of government must be thoroughly and critically examined and sorted out in a sophisticated manner. Those ideas that appear to be unclear and woolly but which can nevertheless be considered worthwhile must be explored, refined, and trimmed and given a modern translation. Thus what needs to be done, in pursuit of democracy and political stability, is to find ingenuous ways and means of hammering these autochthonous democratic elements on the anvil of prudence, common sense, imagination, creative spirit, and a sense of history into an acceptable and viable democratic form in the setting of the modern world. When this task has been done, the traditional ideas—some of them at any rate—can be found to be of immense value in the contemporary sociopolitical developments in Africa. Our culture may yet bring us the much-needed political salvation.

Notes

1. In addition to interviews and personal observations the following sources have been consulted in connection with this account:

Joseph B. Danquah, *Akan Laws and Customs* (London: Cass, 1928);

John Mensah Sarba, *Fanti National Constitution* (London: Cass, 1906);

John Mensah Sarba, *Fanti Customary Law* (London, 1897, reissued by Cass, 1968);

Kofi A. Busia, *The Position of the Chief in the Modern Political System of Ashanti* (London: Cass, 1968);

Kofi A. Busia, *Africa in Search of Democracy* (New York: Frederick A. Praeger, 1967), chap. 2;

J. E. Casely Hayford, *Gold Coast Native Institutions* (London: Cass, 1903);

Brodie Cruickshank, *Eighteen Years on the Gold Coast of Africa* (London, 1854);

Robert S. Rattray, *Ashanti Law and Constitution* (Oxford: Clarendon Press, 1929).

2. Danquah, *Akan Laws and Customs,* p. 13.

3. Rattray, *Ashanti Law and Constitution,* p. 82. A couple of the injunctions

have been left out, and some changes have also been made in Rattray's translation from Akan.

4. Rattray, *Ashanti Law and Constitution,* p. 82; Danquah, *Akan Laws and Customs,* p. 116.

5. Sarba, *Fanti National Constitution,* p. 11.

6. Interview with J. A. Annobil, September 3, 1976.

7. Danquah, *Akan Laws and Customs,* p. 119. "Enstool" and "destool" are technical terms for "enthrone" and "dethrone."

8. Rattray, *Ashanti Law and Constitution,* p. 87.

9. Cruickshank, *Eighteen Years on the Gold Coast of Africa,* vol. 1, p. 236.

10. Ibid., p. 251.

11. Rattray, *Ashanti Law and Constitution.*

12. I have neither time nor space to assemble facts about the democratic features of the political systems of other African peoples. Let me just, for the moment, refer to the views of two notable British anthropologists, Meyer Fortes and E. E. Evans-Pritchard, expressed in the Introduction to their book *African Political Systems* (Oxford University Press, 1940): ". . . the societies described are representative of *common types* of African political systems. . . . Most of the forms described are variants of a *pattern* of political organization found among contiguous or neighboring societies . . ." (p. 1). One of their specific observations was, for instance, that "The structure of African state implies that kings and chiefs rule by consent. A ruler's subjects are as fully aware of the duties he owes to them as they are of the duties they owe to him, and are able to exert pressure to make him discharge these duties" (p. 12).

13. Kwame Gyekye, *An Essay on African Philosophical Thought* (New York: Cambridge University Press, 1987), chap. 2.

Cultural Identity

MARIA L. HERRERA

ON THE INTERPRETATION OF TRADITIONAL CULTURES

The old dispute raised by the encounter with and interpretation of alien cultures, which centered on questions of the rationality of traditions or relativism, seems to have shifted toward a new constellation of problems. Among them, we find a profound questioning of the concept of interpretation.

Interpretation has long been recognized as an inescapable dimension of the study of culture: the products of cultural analysis or ethnographic work are after all *texts* about the lives of social groups. However, the emphasis has recently shifted away from a conception of interpretation associated with strong claims of objectivity in which cultures are to be interpreted or 'decoded', under the assumption of what James Clifford called "the ideology of the transparency of representation,"[1] toward an emphasis on 'invention', on the subjective, constructed, character of the texts produced by those who study alien cultures. In addition to a newly acquired awareness by ethnography that cultural studies are forms of 'writing', there seems to be a growing rejection of essentialist conceptions of culture and a recognition of the political dimension of ethnographic work not only as the result of a changed self-image of anthropology, but in consequence of a changed political and cultural climate in traditional societies.

Today the leading image is no longer that of an anthropologist going to faraway places and being confronted by 'radical difference', but rather that of an interpenetration of languages and cultural traditions. Immigration, exile, and travel, have produced interactions of various sorts between people of different ethnic, linguistic, and religious or national origins. Thus the anthropologist working in traditional societies, or with ethnic communities within industrial societies, not only has to move between disciplinary approaches—from a positivistically conceived social-scientific approach to a form of interpretive description closer to literature—but also has to place herself or himself in between cultures. Just as the idea of a detached observer has been gradually

505

replaced by that of an inevitably involved participant, the problems of contending claims of rival cultural traditions may arise not only for different language communities but also for the individual who participates in more than one language community. This not only gives us a changed image of the situation, but raises new problems as well.

For example, not only the objectivity of the (Western) observer has been put into question, but also the problematic notion of 'participation' as it figured in the idea of 'participant observation' of earlier anthropological practice. Beyond the rather romantic (and implausible) idea of treating informants as true co-authors,[2] alien cultures are no longer seen merely as an object domain of study but may be regarded as partners in a dialogical construction or interpretive account of their culture. From these new forms of participation new questions arise, of both a political as well as a conceptual nature, such as: what the extent may be of legitimate intervention in the life of a community, or the need for some form of recompense for the services of informants, and so on. On the other hand, there have emerged the local voices of native scholars, who share with their colleagues from industrial nations a professional training and theoretical commitment, but who perceive the situation from a different angle, so that their concerns may be, for example, with changes in cultural identities of individuals or groups, or with finding criteria to demarcate the identity of ethnic and linguistic communities.[3] There is also, prominently, the question of power: strategies of resistance or integration of traditional societies in relation to dominant groups. However, what concerns us here is looking at the way in which the attempts to take into account the 'point of view of the other' affect the theory and practice of cultural studies—in particular, the way in which this may change our understanding of the task of interpretation.

In this essay, I will attempt to go beyond the old dispute over relativism in order to explore alternative ways to approach the problem of transcultural understanding and interpretation. In the first section (I), I will consider briefly some recent changes in anthropological theory: from objectivist forms of description of traditional societies to an increased awareness of the problems of this notion of cultural interpretation, namely, the fact that neither the alien culture offers itself to the view of the ethnographer as a 'transparent representation', nor that ethnographers themselves are ever completely free from prejudices and assumptions from their culture of origin, which, in turn, prestructure their understanding of alien cultures in non-innocent or potentially distorting ways. Then, in the second section (II), I will attempt a reexamination of some of the central issues in the philosophical debate on anthropology in relation to the problem of the rationality of cultural traditions. In the third section (III), I will turn to literary translation as illustrative of the problems of interpretation and as already suggestive of some possible solutions, such as the ideas of 'partial translatability', of the incomplete and open character of translation, and of the awareness of temporal determinations of language. Then (IV), a model of translation applied to the problem of transcultural understanding will be proposed. Finally (V), the anti-objectivist turn will be completed with the inclusion of the perspective of the point of view of the other, not as a relapse into irrationalism but as a way to look for a rational way to difference.

I

Anthropology is not now and never has been a homogeneous body of theory. The problems mentioned above have been dealt with from different conceptual positions and with varying degrees of political sensitivity by a great variety of scholars. Nevertheless, it is possible to say that there has been a rather general shift from more or less positivistic or objectivist conceptions of the discipline to a kind of interpretive theory of culture.

The limits of objectivism were already spelled out in the work of Pierre Bourdieu[4] among others, in the sixties, and the uncertain theoretical status of ethnography or, more generally, of cultural studies, has recently been articulated by Clifford Geertz:

> Cultural analysis is intrinsically incomplete. And, more than that, the more deeply it goes the less complete it is. It is a strange science whose most telling assertions are its most tremulously based, in which to get somewhere with the matter at hand is to intensify the suspicion, both your own and that of others, that you are not quite getting it right.[5]

From this recognition, however, skeptical conclusions were not derived in all cases. For Pierre Bourdieu, the task was one of correcting an inadequate model. In his critique of structuralist anthropology, or of what he called "structuralist hermeneutics," Bourdieu called our attention to the fact that the position of the anthropologist as an outsider, as somebody who has no part in the real play of the society studied, affects in important ways his interpretation of that society. When social practices are observed from 'outside' they appear to us as a 'representation', as something that has to be 'interpreted'. It is thus, not a coincidence that metaphors from the theater were used in describing those practices: they are presented as 'performances'. For Bourdieu, the anthropologist compensates for his lack of practical mastery in the alien culture by employing the image of a 'map' useful to an outsider "who has to find his way around in a foreign landscape"[6] where there are no familiar reference points. There tends to be an overemphasis on rules, and an artificial way of seeing cultures as totalities, which deprives them of their contingent, temporal, structure. For example, when gift exchanges are explained *via* a model which establishes a 'cycle of reciprocity' that ignores the importance of actual time-intervals between exchanges, and the corresponding effect of these intervals in the process itself, much that is important gets left out—namely, the fact that gifts may not be returned, promises may not be kept, and the gains of real actors can be either minimized or maximized according to the strategy adopted in the exchange.[7] For Bourdieu, to abolish time-intervals means, in fact, to abolish strategies and with that the possibility of understanding the dynamics of social life. What is missing in structuralist models is a way to account for the differential position of the actors and their respective access to resources and, consequently their respective possibilities for the manipulation of strategies. In that way, not only the temporality of practices is ignored but also their political function within a system of domination.

Bourdieu attempted to recover these dimensions in his theory of symbolic domination, in a way that does not reject but rather refines an objectivist approach for anthropology understood as a social science. His later work in the sociology of culture and of education continues to combine a fine hermeneutic sensitivity with a tempered objectivism that maintains the traditional claims of empirical work in the social sciences.

Clifford Geertz, on the other hand, was already going at that time (the seventies) in the direction of a more strongly interpretive approach focusing on the meaning of cultural systems and the role of symbolic forms in human life. His semiotic approach to culture aimed, nevertheless, to avoid the danger of "turning cultural analysis into a kind of sociological aestheticism"[8] by keeping clear and explicit the connections between the symbolic dimensions of social life and its material basis, the frame in which actual conditions of life and questions about legitimacy, violence, revolution, ethnicity, urbanization, and so on are related to the structures of cultural meaning. In doing that, he retained an explanatory function for cultural interpretation that has become problematic in some recent works in anthropology.[9] Before considering that recent anti-objectivist turn, I want to glance back to some of the central issues in the philosophical debate on anthropology.[10]

II

In those earlier debates on the problem of interpretation of traditional societies, discussion centered on questions of the rationality of traditions, or of the problem of relativism. In his well-known essay "Understanding a Primitive Society," Peter Winch asked whether we may learn from these societies, for example, different possibilities of 'making sense' of human life, or whether we may find alternative descriptions of human action.[11] The problem was seen as that of deciding how to establish what will count as 'making sense', and to whom, in Winch's words, "how to make intelligible in our own terms institutions belonging to a primitive culture, whose standards of rationality and intelligibility are apparently quite at odds with our own."[12] Thus, the problem seemed in the first instance to be that of finding ways to make those alien beliefs and practices intelligible to us, and then to decide, or at least to discuss, whether those beliefs and practices could meet some sort of minimal standard of rationality—such as the one suggested by Winch himself in terms of consistency.

This did not really constitute a discussion on other forms of rationality, but was a way rather to attribute to those alien beliefs and practices (incomprehensible from the commonsense perspective of our culture) some kind of internal consistency. If we introduce—as Alasdair MacIntyre did in his "Is Understanding Religion Compatible With Believing?"[13]—a distinction between understanding a belief and sharing it, we might say, in accordance with that criterion of internal consistency, that those beliefs made sense *to them*.

The assumption underlying these attempts to describe and evaluate alien societies is, on the one hand, that of an exotic, static otherness that was there to be observed or described, and on the other, the self-assurance of an unquestioned objectivist position. From such a perspective, the problems of cultural description had to do with finding criteria of intelligibility and rationality. Interpretation means here the rational explanation of actions in accordance with a means/ends scheme internal to the culture in question. Thus, rather than falling under the description of a new form of rationality, their being rational was characterized under the limited sense of being consistent with their beliefs, even if we (or the anthropologist) could not fully comprehend them or accept them as valid.

However, from this strongly ethnocentric perspective it is difficult to see how we could learn from those alien societies as Winch suggested. Even if we attribute to those alien beliefs some form of internal consistency, under what Ernst Gellner called a "principle of charity" or of "contextualist interpretation"[14]—which amounts to attributing to them a form of rationality, namely, instrumental rationality, that is not only typically Western but specifically modern—we could probably make little sense of those beliefs and practices within the context of our modern way of life. In addition, to understand the "principle of charity" in this way may in fact introduce distortions in the description of traditional societies, for it may look for consistency where there may be none.

However, once the apparently irreconcilable distance between cultures or languages as forms of life is rejected, together with the assumptions of this form of objectivism—with the idea of cultures as closed worlds—we may begin to clear the way for alternative characterizations of the relations that may obtain between different cultures.

As long as the encounter with alien cultures was characterized in terms that demanded comparison, or on a model of translation as the matching of words or sentences—such as the one Talal Asad attributed to and criticized in Ernst Gellner[15]—the problem of the incommensurability of the two cultural systems of belief seemed without solution. Neither attributing other forms of rationality to the alien societies, nor deciding what sort of comparison between their practices and ours was called for (for example, comparing magic and ritual not to science but to other Western practices, such as drama or poetry), as suggested by MacIntyre,[16] nor investigating their use of logic, as suggested by Peter Winch, seemed to help in solving the problem.[17]

However, as Richard Bernstein pointed out, there were already indications of ways to go "beyond objectivism and relativism" in the work of some anthropologists, such as that of Clifford Geertz.[18] As mentioned earlier in his work, a hermeneutic approach was developed as a way, if not to solve, then at least to dissolve the problem of relativism.[19]

There are, of course, many dimensions to the problem of interpretation of cultures for which a hermeneutic sensitivity is not sufficient. Nevertheless, getting away from the old relativism dispute as well as from the search for certainties, and accepting the partiality of all accounts of culture as well as the recognition of the fact that these accounts are texts, written from some specific cultural perspective, may help us to avoid some of the old problems.

III

Now, I want to turn briefly to a discussion concerning literary translation, for this may illuminate some important aspects of our problem.

In a 1932 essay, Jorge Luis Borges discussed the problem of translation not only as the central problem for literature, but also as an illustration of aesthetic and philosophical problems.[20] Translation was seen by him both as an inter-linguistic and as an intra-linguistic problem, the temporal distance which separates an interpreter from a text being analogous to differences between languages. However, even though Borges subscribes to the hermeneutic thesis of the need to belong to a tradition in order to be able to understand it, he would also emphasize the productive role of temporal distance in interpretation. According to him, the role of pre-understanding must not be overly stressed, for distance may work as an advantage for the interpreter as well. In fact, exaggerating the former leads to the idea of closed traditions, inaccessible from the structures of prejudices or forms of prereflective knowledge of other traditions. Moreover, this is not the only explanation for the opacity of language and its resistance to translation. Another is that of illusory closeness, that is, believing that one is closer to a given tradition than one actually is. Borges mentions several instances of "productive distancing" from tradition, such as in the case of the reception of literary texts from Spain in Argentina. According to Borges, English and

French authors were better liked and understood by Argentinians than Spanish authors. For Argentinians, says Borges, liking Spanish literature is "an acquired taste."

Temporal distance is certainly a cause of difficulty in interpretation, but we owe to this particular difficulty—that of being unable to distinguish, in an old text written in a foreign language (or even in our own), what belongs to the writer from what belongs to the epoch—the rich testimony of several renditions of the most important texts of Western culture, such as the "Homeric Versions," the title to Borges' essay.[21] To be at some distance from, or not to belong entirely to, a tradition may be an occasion for innovation. This is why, says Borges, the profusion of Irish names in English literature and philosophy cannot be explained in terms of ethnic background exclusively, since among them were some important names of English ancestry, such as Berkeley, Shaw, and Swift. Nevertheless, it was enough for them to feel so different within English culture as to become creative in that culture.[22] Thus, distance is seen not only as a difficulty to overcome but as a condition for innovation.

However, the kind of critical distance that Borges defended presupposed a profound knowledge of the new language and culture. Thus, it is not only distance which works as a condition for criticism and innovation but the ability to see things from the point of view of the new language as well.[23]

There are other interesting conceptual problems that arise in literary translation, such as the need to place actions within what we may characterize as a pragmatic situation in order to be able to understand them adequately. An implicit criticism of the characterization of intentional actions in objectivist accounts, found in literary translations, consists in the practical demonstration of the need to place action in temporal and causal orderings so as to be able to understand the intentions of the agents. As Pierre Bourdieu observed in his critique of mechanical models in anthropology, it is important to determine the strategies of action within concrete situations in order to avoid false generalizations.

In literary translations, on the other hand, there is the need to take into account specific discursive strategies in the making of the new text, the one produced by the translator. This will also become thematized in recent works in anthropology seen as forms of 'writing'.

In *After Babel,* George Steiner describes the steps of the interpretive process of translation, from the initial reconstruction of the linguistic conventions and speech habits of the text in question—through lexical analysis—to what he describes as the reconstruction of the "full intentional quality" of the text under consideration.[24] In order to overcome the temptation of anachronistic readings of texts from remote epochs, the translator is forced to investigate those changes in the meanings of words and in their use, as well as in the associations and special resonances which they might have been able to produce in their original context.

The kind of questions that such an interpreter (the translator) may be inclined to ask are not very different from those that a contemporary linguist working in pragmatics may also want to ask. For example, if we were translating a theater play, and wanted to establish the intentions of a given character, we could ask ourselves, "Did he really mean what he said?" "What was the 'expressive tone' (as Steiner calls it) of his words?" "Are we dealing with conventional expressions (those which belong to the epoch and not to the writer, as Borges said) and, thus, expressions of lesser importance?" or "Are these expressions unusual, and for that reason do they carry greater expressive force?" What concerns us here is, on the one hand, "The complete penetrative grasp of the text," and also, on the other, "the complete discovery and recreative apprehension of its life-forms."[25] But neither "discovery" nor "complete" mean for Steiner a lack of awareness of the necessarily incomplete and tentative character of interpretations. He accepts that since the conditions of origin of a text cannot be fully known (nor can they be fully specified), all interpretations of past texts must remain a conjecture.

In Steiner's model of translation the question of whether it is only from a local conception of validity that we can establish pragmatic criteria for success in translation must remain an open one. Also, this model of translation is not symmetrical; it affords the opportunity of recovering meaning from the privileged position of the interpreter. Steiner describes this process of interpretation in the image of St. Jerome: "meaning brought home captive by the translator."[26] But there is another side to this process, for Steiner recognizes the possibility of the translator being affected in his or her beliefs and values by his or her understanding of the text. Steiner reads the Heideggerian "we are what we understand to be" as entailing that every act of "comprehensive appropriation" brings with it the risk of transformation.[27]

Translation, then, moves in a dialectic of closeness and distance, each new version being seen as a correction to previous versions and as a commentary on the original. It is a problem of technical expertise as much as of cultural and psychological affinities between the translator and the text. The implications of literary translation as a model for interpretation are, in the first place, that it prevents us from either advancing the thesis of the complete transparency of languages or from falling back into its opposite, that of traditions as closed worlds, or of nontranslatability. Rather, from the experience of successful translations, it advances the thesis of partial translatability, as well as that of the historicity or temporal determination of language; as Steiner has said, "No semantic form is timeless."[28]

IV

If the model of interpretation as translation is to be applied to the interpretation of alien cultures, other problems must be taken into account.
To begin with, we must consider the fact that in studying alien cultures
there are no canonical or privileged texts to guide and constrain our
interpretation. There is no common tradition that binds together the
new text to the old one, nor are there shared presuppositions to guide
our interpretation as anticipations of meaning. As compared to the
three components of literary translation—the old text, the translator as
mediator, and the new text produced (by him or her)—we have in the
typical situation of ethnographic studies an interpreter who has to
produce a text from a great variety of sources: voices of actual people,
texts, and cultural institutions and social practices as observed from the
distance provided by a different language and culture.

Thus, the next step in the hermeneutic defense of cultural differences, or of a form of respect for the particularity of cultures, which
strategically avoids the controversy about relativism, will have to be, on
the one hand, a consideration of the need to learn the new language as a
language *in use,* and on the other, a thematization of the new complex of
relations opened up by the *plurality of voices* (rather than a privileged
text) as the material of interpretation. In addition, once idealized,
objectivist conceptions of interpretation are abandoned, we must take
upon ourselves the task of analyzing the actual, empirical conditions of
the act of interpretation.

As I have said before, to reformulate the problem as inter- or transcultural translation in terms of learning the new language as a language
in use is not to solve the problem of incommensurability or incompatibility of the two languages as systems of belief; it is rather a strategy for
approaching the problem in a more productive way. An interesting way
of looking at the problem of conflicts of interpretation is found in Alasdair MacIntyre's *Whose Justice? Which Rationality?*[29] There, the problem
is characterized as that of learning a "second first language." Although
MacIntyre restricts the applicability of his characterization to the problem of the encounter of rival philosophical traditions, it seems to offer
some interesting suggestions for our topic as well.

For MacIntyre the problem is that of assessing rationally the respective merits of contending traditions. He is concerned primarily with the
problem of genesis of philosophical arguments as a dimension that is
constitutive of and not merely external to them. For that reason, his
emphasis is on the historical constitution of philosophical arguments as
narratives. We cannot consider MacIntyre's argument in any detail
here, nor his solution to the problem of the rational assessment of rival
traditions in conflict; we shall, rather, consider his suggestions, includ-

ing the proposed model of translation as learning the new language as a language in use as a first step in the process of understanding alien traditions or cultures, with no conclusive arguments on questions of validity at this point.

MacIntyre proceeds from the assumption that it is possible to learn to see the world from the point of view of other languages and, thus, to achieve understanding without requiring a word-by-word translation. There is no need to assume a complete transparency of languages nor a neutral description that eliminates differences. We may begin by rejecting the assumption that translatability between languages requires a shared framework. In the modified view of translation offered by MacIntyre this is no longer the case because understanding without explicit translation is possible. Something may be untranslatable but nevertheless understood by the speaker of the second language in use. It is precisely from the newly acquired competence in his/her second 'first' language that the speaker can understand and use the new vocabulary, and at the same time realize that the native language does not possess the resources to express such meanings. Literal translation is often not possible; additional explanations are frequently called for, and these very likely include contextual information about the use of expressions as well as explanations about the place of such meanings within a system of beliefs. They might include as well some kind of genetic explanation about their origins, their relation to other practices, and so on.

Learning a foreign language does not assume the symmetry of the two cultures in question nor an exclusively ethnocentric perspective. Although the primary frame of reference remains that of the first language, there might be ways in which the perspective offered by the new language acquires prominence in certain situations. We may see this change as a sort of switch between languages as frames of reference, though we must be cautious at this point. Such switches can only occur in partial settings, with regard to specific meanings, and not as a complete change from one framework to the other. There may be not only incommensurable dimensions (for which a gestalt switch might work as a practical solution, that is, to describe and evaluate things *either* from the point of view of the first language *or* from that of the second, but not simultaneously) but also incompatible beliefs and values.

There may be conflicts that cannot be solved, and if they involve deep commitments on the part of subjects, they may become part of a hidden or forgotten past (as in the case of immigrants) or remembered as belonging to a past, closed stage, for no attempts to reconcile the two are likely to succeed. MacIntyre considers this problem in the context of the historical life of traditions: some may loose coherence and not survive, others may be transformed in the encounter with other traditions, or the debate may be reconstituted at a more complex level. It is, finally, possible that the conflict may have no solution, at least at certain stages of the controversy, with the conceptual means available at those stages in the respective histories of the traditions.

But in addition to the problem of the undecidability of certain conflicts, and to the fact that this does not prevent us from achieving a limited understanding of the alien traditions, what we want now to emphasize is that MacIntyre's proposal is consistent with a pragmatic understanding of language. This is so not only because he stresses the importance of the contextual understanding and learning of a language, but because he regards this learning process as the acquisition of a practical competence whose success is to be judged by pragmatic tests: first, that of being able to innovate in the language; then, being able to extrapolate from the uses of expressions learned in one situation to uses in other types of situations; and, finally, what he regards as the test of successful learning, the acceptance by the native speakers of the language.

However, MacIntyre's emphasis is on the historical constitution and interrelation of traditions, rather than on the problems of interpretation in a synchronic perspective. For this, we want to turn now to pragmatics as the study of language in use. It is important for our understanding of translation as a possible model for intercultural understanding and interpretation that we look into the pragmatic conditions of concrete linguistic exchanges, for they may allow us to propose an alternative to objectivist models.

Pragmatics as the study of language in use establishes additional requirements for the correct use of language. In addition to the normal requirements of clarity, empirical truth, and sincerity, correct usage also requires a specification of the pragmatic conditions of linguistic exchanges, such as who says what to whom and under what circumstances, and the like. It is necessary to use expressions adequately (in addition to being correct) in a given situation. The test is not only in the utterance but on its reception.[30]

Understanding in this view is a matter of degree, and the simile of "deciphering a code" is not a good one, for, as Marcelo Dascal observes, it is not a matter of finding some keys to deciphering a code and thus solving the problem once and for all, but rather of confronting a situation that is vague and ill defined, one that calls for strategies of understanding which may be complementary or have only limited usefulness and validity:

> The rules of understanding, if they are any, are not likely to be algorithmic but are presumably heuristic in nature, and the ability to shift from one set of those rules, i.e., strategy, to another is an outstanding characteristic of a good understanderer.[31]

Part of learning a language in context is the experience of inevitable failure and incomplete grasp of meanings and the full significance of expressions. Learning to follow pragmatic routines begins with limitation, with no full comprehension, as with children, or, in the case of learning a foreign language, there will be a tendency to interpret the new language according to the pragmatic rules of the native language. Normally, the rejections of old rules and the adoption of new ones will not proceed consciously but rather through a process of familiarization with the use of a language in context. What will be required is for one to expose oneself to as many experiences as possible, to live with the new language for an extended period of time. This, of course, does not mean that more restricted forms of learning a foreign language are not possible, as the historical experience of intercultural exchanges has shown us: there is, for example, the partial understanding of a language that comes from involvement in activities related to foreign trade or other transcultural practices. However, without the ability of truly understanding and being able to use a language in context, no interpretation of a foreign culture can be achieved in a way that is even minimally adequate.

The process of learning to speak in childhood has been considered by Dascal as a possible model for the acquisition of pragmatic competence, one that could also be applied to the case of learning a foreign language. However, there are some problems in the latter case, because a subject learning a foreign language is already a linguistic being, unlike a child learning a first language; thus, the relation between understanding and pre-understanding is not the same in the two cases. For instance, in the process of acquiring a first language a child goes through some early stages in which certain distinctions between literal and metaphoric language are not made;[32] once this ability is acquired, though, there is no turning back to previous, undifferentiated forms of speech.

In any case, the taking into account of the pragmatic dimension of language, in the manner indicated by Dascal, has important consequences for a model of intercultural translation: first, we can no longer maintain a conception of translation which assumes that it is possible to achieve increasingly more precise and objective renditions, or 'error free' translation, of foreign discourses into some standardized language,[33] and, second, a contextual understanding of language leads us to consider the empirical dimension of the study of actual linguistic exchanges. We have to see how dialogues and arguments are dependent upon the ways in which they are framed, as well as upon the assumptions and normative commitments of the participants. So, the description of alien cultures is more adequately characterized as a form of 'creative translation' rather than as an implausible neutral description.

V

Finally, the anti-objectivist or hermeneutic turn will not be complete until we find a way to take into account the perspective of the 'other', or of the multiplicity of voices from which interpretive accounts of cultures are constructed. An awareness of the fact that descriptions of alien cultures are not innocent or neutral has to come together with the recognition of the ways in which discursive strategies employed in such descriptions have an impact on the final text produced by the anthropologist.

In the characterization of alien or traditional cultures as 'texts' to be interpreted, the emphasis still rests on the anthropologist as an interpreter with a privileged access to the society observed. Therefore, there is no way to determine the role and weight of native accounts and forms of self-understanding in the elaboration of the final ethnographic text. For example, in the already mentioned work of Clifford Geertz, there is a lack of distinction between his subjectivity and that of the people in the Balinese village he studied, as pointed out by Vincent Crapanzano.[34] Moreover, there is a tendency to describe the Balinese in generic terms as 'they', while the individuality and ethnographic authority is preserved in the 'I' of the first-person narrator. In addition, social practices (such as the Balinese cockfights that give the title to Geertz's famous essay) are characterized as metaphors of social organization, while insufficient attention is paid to the actual description of such practices. So, metaphors remain abstract and there is no evidence to support the attributions of intentions to the Balinese. Thus, Crapanzano argues, "despite his phenomenological-hermeneutical pretensions, there is in fact in 'Deep Play' no understanding of the native from the native's point of view."[35]

However, these problems do not necessarily lead us to the conclusion that all interpretations of alien cultures are "partial"—in the double sense of being incomplete and biased—at least, not entirely. While we accept the fact of the inevitable influence of our ethnocentric interests in any interpretation, as well as the incomplete character of all accounts of culture, we may still find ways to correct or diminish distortions. An attempt to do so is found in the idea of intercultural interpretation and translation as a form of dialogue.

The concept of dialogue has received considerable scholarly attention in recent times, and for that reason we have become more acutely aware of its problems. By this, we mean not only the problematic character of dialogue itself—misunderstandings, failures to communicate—but problems with the theories of dialogue as well. Some of the criticism voiced against these theories is relevant to our topic. Marcelo Dascal, in his introduction to a book on these issues, pointed out the inadequacy of excessively idealized conceptions of dialogue, which cannot account for the actual diversity of dialogues as they take place in real interactions.[36] We have to become aware of the fact that in most interactions between traditions, or, rather, between representatives of traditions—whether actual persons, such as politicians, academics, travelers, and immigrant workers, or 'texts'—what is involved is more than the abstract search for truth. We can think of ritualized political exchanges, or of defensive strategies, or of instances of systematic understanding, or of forms of expressive language, and the like. In fact, we will be compelled to take into account the social, political, and psychological dimensions of actual linguistic exchanges as things that are not merely external but central to the understanding of dialogue. Although the model will still be an idealization, our analysis will gain in richness and precision with a model capable of incorporating greater complexity.

Among the problems with dialogue as a model for intercultural translation is that of the asymmetry of the participants and of the languages themselves—what Talal Asad calls the "inequality of languages." In the first case, this problem has to do with relations between unequal societies, that is, with the political definition of the situation. A postcolonial anthropology, as James Clifford calls it, has to be explicit about the relations of the ethnographers' country of origin with the Third World countries under study, or with the ethnic groups within their own societies, in the form of an "ideology critique" given prior to a definition of the situation. Also, the institutional definition of the practice of ethnography may act as an obstacle to taking seriously any local forms of self-understanding as well as the voices of native scholars. As James Clifford says:

> . . . twentieth-century academic ethnography does not appear as a practice of interpreting distinct, whole ways of life but instead as a series of specific dialogues, impositions and inventions. 'Cultural' difference is no longer a stable, exotic otherness; self-other relations are matters of power and rhetoric rather than of essence.[37]

But in addition to the political dimension of the problem of inequality, there are difficult questions related to the second problem of inequality, the "inequality of languages" in the sense of differences in conceptual resources and linguistic practices. This problem has to do with the suspicion that the very concept of dialogue presupposes a form of argumentation typical of modern, Western societies, and as such, a form that cannot simply be assumed as universal. This dialogue may be a plausible alternative for intercultural translation when the interchange takes place between societies that are not radically different, or which share some crucial aspects of a common tradition, but it becomes highly problematic in the case of relations with non-Western or traditional societies. It may seem that, since we have no recourse to a privileged, neutral, standpoint from which to judge the respective merits of the beliefs and practices of different traditions, the only non-arbitrary way to decide their respective merits will have to be that of giving equal consideration to the arguments and reasons of both parties. This, however, implies that the alien society will have to adopt a practice (rational argumentation) that may be foreign to them, at least in the form we understand it.

Thomas McCarthy has observed in connection with a critique of the "strong program" of the sociology of knowledge, that the conditions of symmetry required by a dialogue situation are not satisfied in this case.[38] For dialogue not only implies that the Western interpreter must attempt to see things from the point of view of the alien society, but that they (the members of traditional societies) will have to do the same with respect to that of the interpreter. In his words:

> To put a very long story in a nutshell: the symmetry of the dialogue situation would require that they try to understand our beliefs and practices— as we must do theirs—including the reasons why we hold the beliefs we do, the justifications we offer for accepting the practices we do, as well as the criticisms we have developed in rejecting other alternatives in our past— some of them rather similar to those obtaining in their society.[39]

Problems arising in this extreme case can be extended to other, less radical cases as well. If we demand that a nonpluralistic society adopt pluralism and accept the idea that all traditions can be put on a par, then in a very important sense, as McCarthy observed, we are demanding that they cease to be what they are. We may ask ourselves to what extent we are willing to change in order to be able to understand their way of seeing the world. But it is not the problem of the radicalization of the notion of participation that concerns us here, but whether by our way of framing the question we have already privileged a type of answer consistent with our beliefs.[40]

Thus, the idea of intercultural learning becomes problematic if we think that radically different societies can be treated "as if" they were on a par. As McCarthy has observed, those things that we might want to learn from traditional societies may be dependent upon a different history and experience, or on *not* having learned some of the things Western societies have learned—such as the contingent character of social and cultural systems, or economic competition, and so on.[41]

On the other hand, these problems are not exclusive of a dialogical model of intercultural exchange; some could also be raised in connection with a conception of the interpretation of alien cultures as a form of translation. For, as Talal Asad points out, it is not the same to attempt to understand a traditional society from the point of view of the Western interpreter and as the production of a text for a specific Western academic audience, as to attempt to provide an interpretation that would make sense to the people under study, or to try to learn from them. In his words:

> The translation is addressed to a very specific audience, which is waiting to read *about* another mode of life and to manipulate the texts it reads according to established rules, not to learn to *live* a new mode of life.[42]

We could imagine that a traditional society would rather understand itself in terms of a narrative constructed around different kinds of problems or issues than those that may interest the anthropologist. However, some middle-ground solution could be attempted, for, as I have pointed out above, our situation is no longer that of isolated, radically different societies, but rather of mixed, changing and interrelated cultures. New forms of nationalism all over the world represent a mode of defense of ethnic groups against assimilation and absorption by the dominant powers. And these, in turn, present the ethnographer and social scientist with new problems, such as the definition of new forms of cultural identity—which occasionally have political implications, as in the case of American Indian land claims[43]—or the processes of resistance and of mutual learning by different ethnic groups under conditions of social disadvantage.

Therefore, we may conclude that dialogue is necessary as an unavoidable form of understanding and of being sensitive to the needs of the people of traditional societies, but it cannot work as a corrective of ethnocentrism if it is understood as an abstract model of intercultural exchange. Rather, its place is in the actual practice of ethnographic research, together with other techniques of the social sciences. For while it is necessary to put an emphasis on the symbolic dimension of cultural life, it is also necessary to draw upon sociology and the social sciences in general, for the problems of subordinated ethnic groups are inevitably related to political and economic conditions that must be taken into account if we are to avoid false idealizations of their situation.

VI

The consequences of all this for the self-understanding of anthropology and the interpretation of cultures are manifold. On the one hand, we can regard the emphasis on invention, and the constructed character of ethnographic texts (redefined by James Clifford as "strong fictions") as completing the anti-objectivist turn in a manner full of internal tensions and contradictions. On the other hand, we can see it as a proposal for a critical hermeneutics that accepts the limits and partial character of interpretation, as well as the need for a corrective to excessive or uncritical ethnocentrism. Critical hermeneutics starts with a recognition of the inescapable moment of interpretation in all descriptions of culture, and of the fact that the final text is *both* something produced from the horizon of the writer—in accordance with his or her presuppositions and the expectations of an audience—*and* a description of another culture. As such, it is an account that selects, classifies, and evaluates— whether implicitly or openly—what is to be described, and that raises claims to objectivity, validity, and correctness in these descriptions. Ethnographic accounts are not neutral, but rather circumscribed and determined by the discursive strategies employed in them, as well as by the descriptions of a given society or group that rest on some kind of controlled observation. This, in turn, constrains the 'creative' dimension of writing, for ethnographic texts are not, after all, 'fictions' *tout court.*

In some recent works in anthropology—that of James Clifford, for example—there is an ambiguity between the idea of "making" texts and the idea of "making [them] up."[44] There is a tension between the idea of "learning" from other societies and of "experiencing" them, on the one hand, and the idea of an "interpretation" or "representation" on the other. Clifford proposes a way out of the paradoxical conception of "participant observation" of traditional anthropological practice in terms of a hermeneutic understanding of a "dialectic of experience and interpretation." But it is not always clear how he wants to dissolve the exclusive authority of the ethnographer as an interpreter, while maintaining that ethnographic texts are inventions constructed by, or experimental products that result from, the writer's strategic choices. This seems to suggest an even stronger form of ethnocentrism than the idea of an interpreter subjected to the constraints of empirical observation. To be sure, empirical observation of alien societies can never be entirely free from the assumptions and cultural biases of social scientists. As Clifford argues, descriptions of social facts are not neutral. However, reducing ethnographic accounts to forms of "invention" (or creative appropriation of the alien culture) by anthropologists amounts not only to renouncing all claims to objectivity, but also to ignoring the alien culture's self-interpretation as a possible corrective to ethnocentrism. One way to dissolve what seems to be an irreconcilable opposition between interpretation and invention may be to understand interpretation not as a representation (under assumptions of correspondence) but as a form of translation that does not suppress the creative moment but restrains it in its willingness to respond to the demands of that which is being translated.

Although Clifford wants to defend the need for dialogical, polyphonic forms of writing ethnography, his excessive emphasis on invention prevents him from incorporating the voices of the other society in any coherent manner. In fact, he seems to reduce the dialogical dimension of ethnographic writing to a technical aspect of the writing of texts.[45] His adoption of the concept of "heteroglossia," which he takes from Mikhail Bakhtin, is thus reduced to the idea that it is possible to understand cultures and languages in partial, incomplete ways. But it cannot account for the ways in which this partial overlapping of languages and cultures (as Dascal has called it) becomes a constitutive part of the final text.

We cannot hope to offer a solution to all these problems in this preliminary exploration of a critical hermeneutics. Nevertheless, even the barest consideration of the conditions of understanding may contribute not only to theories but also to the practices of interaction between different cultures. Thus, I will end with a brief consideration of Marcelo Dascal's concept of "tolerance" as a nonimperialist conception of the relations between cultures.

This principle must be seen in the context of the development of interpretive procedures at the level of the pragmatics of action. It is not a rule or a way to provide criteria to solve conflicts of interpretation, but rather a strategy of understanding that opens up possibilities for learning from other cultures. In an interesting article, Dascal offers a "maximalist" conception of tolerance that not only tolerates the beliefs of others, even if they are mistaken (just as long as they are harmless to the society as a whole), but acknowledges that the 'other' and his or her ideas are capable of being true, or valid, and that they thus deserve actual respect.[46]

The difference between this notion of tolerance and the principle of "charity" or of contextual interpretation as understood by Gellner is that tolerance is not "blind"; that is, it does not come down to granting that seemingly absurd beliefs and practices could make sense *to them*. Instead, tolerance assumes that by learning to see things from the point of view of their language and culture some of those beliefs and practices may come to make sense *to us* as well. In this way, the principle of tolerance works as a corrective for the model of cultural translation, once the idea of learning a foreign language as a language in use is introduced.

The principle of tolerance also springs from the need for the recognition of and by the other. It is anti-dogmatic inasmuch as it incorporates an idea of self-criticism as being capable of correction by others and by oneself as a result of interactions. Learning, in turn, can be seen as an expansion of the expressive capacities of our language so as to accommodate new meanings and new ways of seeing things.

Moreover, we may see this learning process as a way of fashioning redescriptions of ourselves in the new vocabulary (Rorty) or, in other words, as a way of taking into account the transformations of individual and collective identities as a result of intercultural translation. As the process of acquiring a "second first language" affects those who undergo the experience in profound ways, there may be important respects in which it permanently changes their images of reality and basic values. What is accepted from the new language as regards new ways of seeing or describing a situation, new values, and social rules of behavior, is selectively determined by unconscious as well as by conscious motives and reasons. Personal identity, insofar as it can be understood as a narrative,[47] undergoes constant restructuring, so that new forms of self-understanding emerge as a result of this process as well. The latter involves affective and psychological dimensions which prevent us from seeing it as an exclusively cognitive process. On the other hand, intercultural translation induces an awareness of the relative, local character of our prejudices. This can lead to a self-critical attitude, and if it is accompanied by a receptiveness to the reasons of others—our willingness to pass the pragmatic test of recognition by others—we may complete the circle of mutual understanding between cultures.

However, a final objection may be raised at this point, similar to one we have already considered in connection with dialogue as a model for intercultural relations: whether the idea of tolerance itself imposes upon other cultures a principle—or a form of dialogue—that may be foreign to them, or one in which they may not be interested.[48] But the idea of tolerance as a principle guiding cultural translation does not assume a symmetrical relation on the part of the other culture as dialogue does. The principle of tolerance applies to those attempting to understand an alien culture, from the perspective of an inevitably modern, postconventional attitude. As such, it can be seen as a form of liberal pluralism. It is not politically neutral; it assumes, rather, some crucial values of the liberal tradition: not only respect for individual freedom and an egalitarian conception of justice, but also respect for differences and the possibility of dissent.[49] It also excludes dogmatism and intolerance, and the plurality of voices from the other culture enter the final version of the text in the form of questions or concerns guiding the process of interpretation.

However, in order to make the latter possible, we must leave behind totalizing conceptions of an ethnocentric reason, the arrogance of an attitude incapable of understanding that which is not identical to itself, or that rejects anything that does not fit its narrow conception of reason as absolutely alien, as the "other of reason." This is not to adopt an irrationalist perspective, but rather to expand our conception of rationality and our knowledge of the actual conditions of understanding.

The relativization of one's own culture as a result of an encounter with a foreign form of life may result as well in disorientation, or may lead us to become strangers in our own culture of origin. As Georg Simmel observed early in the century, to be placed in a different culture involves both nearness and remoteness, an ambiguity captured by Simmel in the image of the stranger, for whom the experience of new forms of life places his or her own culture under the light of newly acquired freedom and distance.[50]

Notes

1. *Writing Culture: The Poetics and Politics of Ethnography,* ed. by James Clifford and George E. Marcus (Berkeley: University of California Press, 1986), p. 2.

2. Ibid., p. 17.

3. See "Pluralidad Linguistica y Educacion Bilingue," a paper presented at the Simposio Etica y Diversidad Cultural, Instituto de Investigaciones Filosofi-

cas, Mexico (October 1989), by Rodrigo Diaz Cruz. There he questions the extended practice of collapsing linguistic and ethnic categories. He offers examples of Mexican Indian communities where either the same language (Nahuatl) is spoken by several, distinct ethnic groups, or several variants of a family of languages (Zapotec) are spoken by communities that are largely regarded as belonging to the same culture or ethnic group.

4. See Pierre Bourdieu, *Outline of a Theory of Practice,* trans. by Richard Nice (Cambridge: Cambridge University Press, 1977).

5. Clifford Geertz, *The Predicament of Cultures* (New York: Basic Books, 1973), p. 29.

6. Bourdieu, *Outline,* p. 2.

7. Ibid., pp. 5-6.

8. See Geertz, *The Predicament of Cultures,* p. 30.

9. See James Clifford, *The Predicament of Culture: Twentieth-Century Ethnography, Literature, and Art* (Cambridge: Harvard University Press, 1988); also, see over, note 1 above.

10. See: Peter Winch, *The Idea of a Social Science and Its Relation to Philosophy* (London: Routledge & Kegan Paul, 1958); also, *Rationality,* ed. by Brian Wilson (Oxford: Basil-Blackwell, 1979), and *Rationality and Relativism,* ed. by Martin Hollis and Steven Lukes (Cambridge: MIT Press, 1982).

11. Peter Winch, *Rationality,* p. 87.

12. Ibid., p. 94.

13. Alasdair MacIntyre, "Is Understanding Religion Compatible with Believing?" *Rationality,* pp. 62-77.

14. E. Gellner, "Concepts and Society," quoted by Talal Asad, in "The Concept of Cultural Translation in British Social Anthropology," in *Writing Culture,* p. 146.

15. Ibid., p. 147.

16. Quoted by Richard Bernstein in *Beyond Objectivism and Relativism: Science, Hermeneutics and Praxis* (Philadelphia: University of Pennsylvania Press, 1983), p. 102.

17. As Richard Bernstein observed, in ibid., p. 105.

18. Ibid., pp. 105-108.

19. Following Richard Rorty's suggestion of looking for creative re-descriptions of those problems. See *Contingency, Irony, and Solidarity* (Cambridge: Cambridge University Press, 1989).

20. Jorge Luis Borges, "Las Versiones Homericas," *Discusion, Obras Completas* (Buenos Aires: Emece, 1974). According to G. Steiner, there are more than two hundred complete or selected English renditions of the *Iliad* and the *Odyssey,* from 1581 to the present. See *After Babel: Aspects of Language and Translation* (Cambridge: Oxford University Press, 1975), p. 401.

21. Borges, "Las Versiones Homericas," p. 240.

22. Borges, "El Escritor Argentino y la Tradicion," in *Obras Completas.*

23. It should also be interesting to look at empirical studies on bilingualism, as suggested by Marcelo Dascal. I am indebted to him for his critical observations and suggestions on this essay.

24. G. Steiner, *After Babel,* p. 5.

25. Ibid., p. 25.

26. Ibid., p. 298.

27. Ibid., p. 299.

28. Ibid., p. 24.

29. A. MacIntyre, *Whose Justice? Which Rationality?* (Notre Dame: Indiana University Press, 1988).

30. See Marcelo Dascal, "Strategies of Understanding," in *Meaning and Understanding,* ed. by H. Parret and J. Bouveresse (Berlin and New York: Walter de Gruyter, 1981).

31. Ibid., p. 336.

32. As he has pointed out also, see Dacal, "Defending Literal Meaning," in *Cognitive Science* 11 (1987): 280.

33. As it has also been suggested in MacIntyre's works. See *Whose Justice,* chaps. 19–20.

34. V. Crapanzano, "Hermes' Dilemma: The Making of Subversion in Ethnographic Description," in *Writing Culture,* p. 70.

35. Ibid., p. 74.

36. *Dialogue, An Interdisciplinary Approach* (Amsterdam and Philadelphia: John Benjamins, 1985).

37. James Clifford, in *The Predicament of Culture,* p. 14.

38. See Thomas McCarthy, "Scientific Rationality and the 'Strong Program' in the Sociology of Knowledge," in *Construction and Constraint: The Shaping of Scientific Rationality,* ed. by E. McMullin (Notre Dame: Indiana University Press, 1988), pp. 75–95.

39. Ibid., p. 87.

40. As MacIntyre observed in the case of the liberal conception of justice, in *Whose Justice,* chap. 17.

41. McCarthy, "Scientific Rationality."

42. Talal Asad, "The Concept of Cultural Translation."

43. See Clifford, *The Predicament of Culture,* Part Four, no. 12, pp. 277–346.

44. Clifford, in *Writing Culture,* p. 6.

45. See Paul Rabinow, "Representations are Social Facts; Modernity and Post-Modernity in Anthropology," in *Writing Culture,* pp. 244–247.

46. Dascal, "Tolerância e Interpretaçao," in *Crítica, Revista Hispanoamericana de Filosofía,* 21, no. 62 (1989).

47. See Roy Schaffer, "Narration in Psychoanalytic Dialogue," in *On Narrative,* ed. by W. J. I. Mitchell (Chicago: University of Chicago Press, 1981).

48. I want to thank Thomas McCarthy for pointing this out to me. Also, thanks to Carlos Pereda and Carlos Thiebaut for reading earlier versions of this essay.

49. See Javier Muguerza, "La Alternativa del Disenso, en Torno a la Fundamentacion de los Derechos Humanos," Tanner Lectures on Human Values (1988).

50. G. Simmel, "The Stranger," in *The Sociology of G. Simmel,* trans. by Kurt H. Wolff (New York: Free Press, 1964; first published 1908).

ROOP REKHA VERMA

THE CONCEPT OF PROGRESS
AND CULTURAL IDENTITY

Like many other concepts, the concept of progress is loaded with ideological constructions which cloud the concept and create many-faced confusions in the controversies around it. In this essay an attempt will be made to clarify the notion of progress without these ideological superimpositions and then to see what the bearing of cultural identity on progress is. Initially three concepts of progress, available in a common conceptual scheme, will be considered, and it will be noted that they are relative and partial in some one or another way. Later it will be argued that there is also another concept of progress which is not relative in the way in which these three concepts are. Remarks on cultural identity will also include some remarks on modernity. The essay uses some terms of Bergerian analysis of culture, although, it will be found, Bergerian analysis is not fully adhered to. Some of these terms are redefined in this essay and an alternative framework is suggested. The essay does not so much argue for the position taken in it as simply to propose a framework for this position and thus to provide it with a conceptual foundation.

I

At the outset let us note that it may be misleading to talk of *the* concept of progress because in actual use at least three concepts of progress with varying degrees of width of application, are available:

1. Progress as movement or transition in the direction of a certain specified goal;
2. Progress as movement or transition in the direction of a certain specified general value; and
3. Progress as movement or transition in the direction of a certain specified moral value.

Although it may sound trivial, it may be useful to note that defining 'progress' in the ways just mentioned does not commit one to an ontology of goals and values. 'Movement in the direction of a goal and a value' here means precisely movement in the direction of the achievement or realization of that goal or value, and this, in turn, is to be understood as involving greater proximity to, or obtaining higher probability for, the realization of that goal or value. It is obvious that for each of the three definitions just mentioned progress involves comparison between two stages of the agent, which is supposed to have progressed (or regressed), and some other relations like the directedness of a movement or the transition from one stage to another stage. Also obvious are the facts that the relation of comparison involved in progress is transitive and, if the context of progress remains constant, that is, if the agent and the end remain the same, the compared states form a hierarchy, with a conceived and aspired ideal at the top.

Of the three concepts of progress provided by the three definitions given above, the first and the second appear to be nondistinct. However, the distinction between them is that a goal need not be either itself a value or warranted by a value or value system. It need not even be consistent with the value system of the agent. We meaningfully talk of progress in the contexts in which the goals are not implied or warranted by the value system of the agent. Sometimes they are value-neutral, and many times they even conflict with the agent's value system. Yet they can be, and they in fact are, aspired to by individuals and societies, and the task of achieving them is prone to pass through different stages having varying degrees of proximity to the goal. Thus we talk of progress in a scientific experiment or research even when it is value-neutral or positively harmful. The first definition equates progress with any teleologically successful movement or transition, without placing any restriction on the nature of the *telos*. And "teleologically successful movement or transition" means here a movement or transition which shows definite signs of being in the direction of the achievement or realization of a goal.

The three concepts under consideration are, it was said, of varying degrees of width of application. The first one has the widest application range. To every value corresponds a goal, whereas the reverse does not hold true. Therefore in every context in which one can sensibly talk of progress in the second sense, one can talk of progress in the first sense, too, although there are contexts in which one can talk of the latter but not the former. Thus the range of the application of the second concept of progress is narrower than that of the first concept. Likewise, the application range of the third concept of progress is more limited than that of the second. Because, although every moral value is a value, every value is not a moral value. Not being able to appreciate something beautiful is no moral offence. Thus aesthetic values need not be moral values too. Therefore there can be contexts in which one can meaningfully talk of progress in the second sense but not in the third sense, but wherever one can talk of the latter, one can also talk of the former.

Although these three concepts of progress are found in ordinary usage, generally the subject of serious and stable concern is not progress in the first sense but progress in the second and the third senses. Progress in the first sense becomes a subject of serious interest only if it somehow gets linked with the latter two. Further, it is the progress of a society or community, rather than that of an individual, which is of serious and stable concern.

It may seem that one implication of allowing the second concept of progress (in terms of values, moral or nonmoral) is that the question of progress would always be relative to a value or type of value. That is, a statement of the form "The society S_1 has progressed" would always be incomplete and would need the additional mention of the respect in which S_1 is stated to have progressed. Thus, "S_1 has progressed economically" and "S_1 has progressed morally" are complete, whereas "S_1 has progressed" is incomplete in meaning unless used as a shortened version of "S_1 has progressed in some or the other respect." The norms or the value system to assess progress in certain respects would supposedly be provided by the culture of S_1. On these considerations it may be argued that 'progress' has a two-level relativity:

1. Relativity to the respect in which the question of progress is raised. The third concept of progress would not be relative in this manner. Because, by definition, it is confined to only a moral aspect, and thus the question of the specification of the aspect in which progress is made would not arise.
2. Relativity to the culture wherefrom the norms of assessment are derived. Depending upon our theory of moral norms, the third concept of progress, besides the second one, may be relative in this manner.

Let us consider if progress essentially has this dual relativity, and let us start with the first. Suppose a society S_1 at the stage t_1 evolves into a stage t_2 in which it has progressed economically but deteriorated aesthetically, and then it reaches another stage t_3 which shows aesthetic progress but worsening of the economic aspect even in comparison to stage t_1. If we admit only the aforementioned notions of progress, then there is no problem of assessment here. The society S_1 has progressed from t_1 to t_2 in certain respects, where it has regressed from t_2 to t_3 (and also from t_1 to t_3), and has progressed in another different respect from t_2 to t_3 (and also from t_1 to t_3), in which it has regressed from t_1 to t_2. Yet the question of progress of life on the whole does not seem to be satisfactorily answerable by such compartmentalized references to different aspects. It seems that life is not so neatly divisible in its economic, artistic, moral, and other dimensions as the foregoing account of progress might make it appear to be. The question of progress in life is a question of the quality of life, and the question of the quality of life does not seem to be adequately answerable by such truncated and partial references, although nor does it seem to be answerable without taking these dimensions into account. As life is not a quantitative sum of different dimensions but an integrated whole, so its progress, too, is not simply a matter of an aggregate of different 'progresses' nor can it be so quantified as to calculate the balance of progress by deducting the losses in some aspects from the gains in some others. Rather, in this context, it seems to be essentially a synthetic and integrant notion which is truly applicable to the state of a society or an individual on the basis of *harmonious and integrated balance* between different kinds of progresses in the aforementioned second sense. This integrant progress is of a higher and more fundamental order than the other progresses. It is higher because the other progresses are, ultimately, subservient to it. And it is fundamental because the other progresses draw their own value and significance in life from it. Happiness may be defined as an integrated balance between different value orders determining preferences in different dimensions of life. As there are degrees of integrated balance, there are degrees of happiness, too. And progress in a nonrelative sense (that is, nonrelative to an aspect of life) can be defined as a movement or transition in the direction of achieving happiness or as a transition successfully achieving a greater degree of happiness.

If this conception of progress is acceptable, much that is taken as progress would be viewed otherwise. Often the mere increase of quantity or complexity or variety is taken as progress. For example, often we recognize progress in a town if the life-style of its citizens becomes more complex, if it acquires a greater variety of entertainment, or if the number of its industries increases. All this may, in a certain situation, really be conducive to progress. But it need not be, and in some situations it may even be counterprogressive. Whether progress has been made would depend on whether and how far some values are realized by these changes and to what extent they are integrated harmoniously with the other values and needs of life. Let us call mere increases in the quantity or variety of some goods or in the complexity of life 'development' to distinguish it from progress as defined above. A well-known example of counterprogressive development is industrial growth without integrating it with the various value orders of life. Without farsighted planning for the integration of industrial growth with such values of life as health and peace, a very potent force for progress is many times converted into a great obstruction to it.

Now, since progress in all the different senses has been defined above as a movement or transition, it is primarily applicable only in situations in which two different stages of the same agent (individual or society) are to be compared. However, each of these concepts can have a derivative or secondary use also, in which two different agents can be compared and the question of which of them is more progressive can be raised. But this would assume, in cases where the agents belong to different cultures, the nonrelativity of progress with respect to culture, too. This brings us to the second of the two aforementioned relativities. Whether progress is culturally relative or not can be better understood while dealing with the question of cultural identity.

II

Culture has been viewed differently by different thinkers and the alternative concepts of culture are so numerous that it is not possible to examine them presently. Here it is proposed to view culture as a system of the patterns and the modes of expectations, expressions, values, institutionalization, and enjoyment habits of a people in general. Culture is the source of the more-or-less spontaneous actions and reactions of a people and their mode of dealing with objective reality and subjective formations. Three points are noteworthy in this perspective on culture. First, culture is created by a people. Secondly, its main function is to provide a people in general with a mode of dealing with objective reality and subjective formations. "Dealing with" here includes several types of operations: adjustment, manipulation, reaction, response, and so forth. Thirdly, these operations are more or less spontaneous and thus they often get mixed up with the culturally free or natural responses.

That culture is a created phenomenon is admissible in many other perspectives on culture, for example, those offered by Durkheim and Berger. The point regarding spontaneity also is very closely linked with the Bergerian idea of subjective absorption or internalization. The spontaneity of responses flowing from a cultural framework is due to the absorption or internalization of that framework, which itself is a construction or a creation through a complex process. The artifacts of culture range over a variety of concreteness and abstraction. They include dress, food, language, rituals, myths, symbols, codes of relationships, modes of expression, ways of life-sustenance, polity, arts, and values. Ranging over such vast areas of life, culture remains the basic force of, and the focal reference point in, determining one's identity. Culture, and therefore cultural identity, are variable and optional, although, as a matter of fact, in all the cultures their optionality is either not available at all, or only minimally available. Although culture is a human construction and thus a matter of human choice, at the level of the individual this choice is mostly not exerted in freedom and therefore it remains a pseudochoice. Since the primary bearer of freedom is the individual, the optional character of culture, and consequently of cultural identity, remains unfructified or frozen.

This unfructification or freezing of cultural optionality is partly inevitable but to a great extent escapable even though very difficult. For example, in order to recognize and appreciate the options, one needs a language or a framework of categories and therefore has to acquire a language before even seeing what is available for choice. Acquiring a language is thus a condition of the very perception of cultural choices, and therefore this mode of un-opted cultural conditioning is inescapable. This type of inescapable un-opted cultural conditioning or absorption may be called transcendental choice-freeze or choice-closure. There is transcendental choice-freeze when it is demanded by the very conditions of choice-making. Not everything in a culture is subject to transcendental choice-closure. A culture has much that is actually subjected to choice-closure without any transcendental ground. The optionality of such cultural elements is possible although very difficult. Even language, having given the power of categorization and construction of further categories, later emerges out of the choice-freeze, and optionality between different languages opens up.

Explaining how language, a most important artifact of culture, can emerge out of its transcendental choice-closure would involve a whole philosophy of language which cannot be expounded here. To be very brief, it seems that the very conditions of the possibility of language require operations which empower the language user with the capacities and skills to rearrange, reclassify, and reinterpret her or his experiences and construct new categories and conceptual structures. Generalization, comparison, instantiation, abstraction, and so forth are some of such operations. Without these operations language would not be possible, and they are, in their turn, concretized in a specific language. Having mastered these operations by learning a language (in natural course, the language of one's culture), the other languages can be learned and compared with the first language, and new structures can be constructed. Richness of experience and the availability of alternatives would, of course, be required for these tasks.

Like language, a value system also may seem to be subject to transcendental choice-closure. This is because not only *perceiving* choices but also *making* the choices has some conditions. To be able to make a choice there must already be a value system at hand. The value system of a culture handed down to an individual functions as the "natural" value system for the individual and it enables him or her to understand what exerting a choice is like. But in this case again, supported by the natural demands of life, richness of experience, and so forth, the valuation exercise in one's own value system (that is, the value system given by one's culture) makes it possible for the individual to understand alternative value systems, compare them, and either consciously to reaffirm one's own culture's value system or to choose another or else to create a new one. That is, like language, a value system also can emerge out of its transcendental choice-freeze and enter the arena of optionality. Progress is not culturally relative if cultural relativity implies the choicelessness of either the value orders, the integrated balance of which is sought, or the very norm of their integration.

The choice-closures which are not transcendentally required are due to what in Bergerian terminology can be called "objectivation" or Durkheimian "objective facticity," joined with the loss of the recognition that what is "objectivated" or "factified" is still a matter of human creation and human choice and that the objectivation does not annihilate either the alterability or the alterity of the option. In fact, objectivation itself facilitates this loss of recognition, which may be called optionality amnesia. Culture, which is already a very strong and effective force in fixing the identity of the individual, is further strengthened by optionality amnesia and hence becomes almost imperative. This dialectic of creation-objectivation-optionality amnesia is behind most identity formations. In these identity formations, the past or the tradition becomes the most effective and all-enveloping reality, and the ethos of individuals with such identity formations is committed to the past, making tradition the ultimate criterion for the determination of values and thus of progress.

But the temporal locus of a value system is always the present, with an intentionality for the future without making the future a prisoner of the present—the present which would be tradition tomorrow. And the central reference point of a value system is the individual and the society of today. Tradition, by itself, cannot be its own ground or testimony; it cannot authenticate itself. The past, the tradition, is always in the court of life, seeking the lease of approval. The values have to be realized in today's social context and they have to be willed, aimed at, and aspired to by the individuals of today. Without this possibility of forming the ethos of a people and the possibility of the people striving to achieve it, a value system can only be either an item in the thought-museum of cultural artifacts or a fantasy. To guide behavior today, values have to be rooted in today's context. Modernity represents the supremacy of this principle, an attitude of commitment to this dictum. Modernity is not always a rejection of the past. It may be total acceptance of the tradition. But this it can be only if the acceptance of the tradition is conscious, realistic, and critical reaffirmation—a regrounding of the traditional values in the context of the present. The essence of modernity is to recognize new situations and phenomena of life, and to review and modify, if necessary, the institutions and the value system in the light of the new phenomena with the ultimate aim of maintaining the maximum possible harmonious balance between different facets of life. It is perpetual preparedness to make cultural changes with a view to obtaining this balance.

Progress, in a nonrelated sense, was defined earlier as a movement or transition in the direction of achieving happiness, and happiness was

defined as an integrated balance between different value orders determining preferences in different dimensions of life. Progress would,
thus, require determination of value orders for its direction. Whether
progress is genuine or pseudo would depend on whether the value
orders guiding it are consistent with modernity as defined above.
Because if a "value order" is not so consistent, it would not really be a
value order at all in the sense of being a system of norms to guide the
preferential behavior in that temporal context in which the question of
its being value-ordered and consequently the question of progress are
being raised. That is, the time contexts of a value order and progress
supposedly or desirably directed by that value order should be the same.
Otherwise, neither the value order nor progress would be genuine. In
this way modernity and progress go hand in hand.

The point can be understood by using the terminology of Bergerian
dialectic between individual and culture: externalization, objectivation,
and internalization. The dialectic by itself does not explain the possibility of cultural change or a critique of a culture. On the contrary, it
appears to foreclose them by seeming to present only the phenomenon
of the adoption of, or committed adherence to, a culture *given* to the
individual by his social context. What is important to add in this dialectic is that the internalization can be reflective or unreflective. The unreflective or uncritical internalization of a culture is due to nontranscen-
dental choice-closures mentioned earlier, and the identities of
individuals formed by them are inauthentic. An inauthentic identity
militates against the requirements of modernity, and consequently
against those of progress too. The identities formed on the basis of
reflective or critical internalization of a culture, on the other hand, are
authentic, and modernity comes to them as their natural ethos. Internalization, in their case, becomes *validation*. Individuals with such cultural identities are the usherers of progress.

III

The authenticity of identity, of course, implies responsibility, as any
other kind of freedom does. The freedom involved in the authenticity of
identity is wide-ranging and basic. Correspondingly, the responsibilities
which it implies are of a serious and fundamental nature, and consequently they present the individual with challenging situations. Carrying out the responsibilities of freedom requires discernment, assessment, judgment, and confidence, and none of them is so easy a task as
to be performed thoughtlessly or mechanically. However, to call it a
"crisis" or a "metaphysical loss of 'home'," as Berger does, seems an
exaggeration. It seems true that people today suffer from "a deepening
condition of 'homelessness'," and that is a great crisis indeed. But
today's man is really not a fully modern man. Today's person does not

consistently abide by the principle of modernity. He or she lives not only in the midst of, but also along with, a grave conflict between modernity and antimodernity or traditionality. One lives a split personality, with the additional paradox that the two contexts of one's dual personality do not stay apart. Moreover, the developments of what we call "modern times" have not been progressive in many respects and therefore not so in the nonrelative sense of progress. They have been un-integrated, discordant, and imbalanced. Therefore the crisis of present times is not the crisis of modernity as such. It is the crisis of un-integrated and haphazard development.

In fact, modernity and progress, instead of causing the "metaphysical loss of home," would cause the metaphysical restoration of home. What sort of home would a place be if it does not allow its members even the possibility of choice? The comfort of not having to make a choice is a genuine comfort only if not making the choice is itself a choice, and this is possible only if there *are* choices in the first place. The security from hazarding an option is a genuine security only as long as one also retains the freedom of choosing to hazard an option. If the latter is not available, the "security" becomes the security of a prison. A home is essentially that place to which one belongs, and one belongs to a place or situation where one feels that one belongs. In a home an individual is not only a role-player but is also simply an individual. These possibilities of being (and being treated as) simply as an individual and of feeling belongingness are realizable only in situations which allow authentic identities, since the situations generating inauthentic identities are essentially the situations of alienation. It may seem paradoxical, but outwardly it is the individual with authentic identity who appears to be suffering from alienation rather than the one with inauthentic identity. In the case of the latter, one's conformity to the tradition is mistaken for belongingness and the confines of the institution of one's personal relationship for home. But unreflective conformity to tradition is entirely different from belongingness. Belongingness essentially implies a conscious and willing identification that is possible only in the case of individuals who have authentic identity. And authentic identity is not possible without modernity as understood earlier. Thus, progress, modernity, and authentic cultural identity form a network of such conceptual connections that one is not possible without the other.

AGNES HELLER

MOSES, HSÜAN-TSANG, AND HISTORY

In his magnificent essay, *Moses and Monotheism,* Freud engaged in speculations about the wondrous deliverance from perdition of heroes who
were, right after their birth, destined to be protagonists of myths.
Among the numerous, although finite, number of motives which are
normally combined into a few typical patterns in such stories, Freud, in
his quest for the 'truth' about Moses, focuses on three mythological
constants. First, Moses, unlike Oedipus, was not abandoned in order to
die but in order to live. Second, he was "fished out of the water" (not
rescued from a desert or a cliff). Third, he was brought up by another
family, yet he was to find his way back to his 'real' family. As is well
known, Freud inferred from the combination of these mythological patterns that Moses had been an Egyptian who had tried to implant the
then suppressed monotheistic cult of Egypt into the rough and crude
people of Israel. This bold interpretation is not the topic of the current
essay, rather I shall consider the implications of Freud's method. Freud
assumed that there was, there had to be, a complete fit between mythological language and historic truth. If the same motive reappears in two
mythological narratives, it certainly stands for the same historical or
"real" stories or facts. This 'fit' can be deciphered once we familiarize
ourselves with patterns or distortion, reversal, and subterfuge: the work
of our unconscious.

In the last decades of our century, myths have once again become topical for our self-understanding. But the approach to myths, from Levi-
Strauss to Blumenberg, has changed and diversified. Although the
interpretation of bygone ages or the exploration of paradisical or less
than paradisical islands attracts our interest just as it did before, the
main motivation for this inquiry needs to be sought in different quarters. It is not above all the unconscious self of the individual, or the
unexplored Id of the human species that we desire to decipher in a
roundabout way. It is rather our history, our being here-and-now, the
meaning of our own historical existence which is put on the theoretical

agenda with great urgency. One could associate the Freudian approach to myth with the historical consciousness of modernity, and our contemporary approaches with the historical consciousness of post-modernity. The latter will be the topic as well as the standpoint of the following inquiry.

I

One can understand myths as configurations of significations rather than as signs that indicate something else (the historical truth). Actually myths carry truth and/or untruth irrespective of the historical truth to which they may or may not be connected. We are ignorant of whether or not there was a historical figure behind the myth of Achilles. Yet this seemed irrelevant for Alexander the Great much as it did later for Shakespeare. For Alexander the myth was true, and for Shakespeare it was blatantly untrue, but for both, the "message of the myth" was relevant in the highest degree. For in this respect, truth in myth resembles truth in philosophy.

Moses was fished out of the water and subsequently brought up in the court of the Pharaoh. This is why Freud arrives at the conclusion that he was in fact the son of the Pharaoh's daughter. But if myths have their own truth, one cannot establish a direct connection between myth and historical reality. For myth *is* a reality. Stories of heroes of divine origin have been passed down since time immemorial. The man of extraordinary deeds, who spoke with authority, who promised deliverance and kept his promise, deserved a myth, and the myth was indeed bestowed upon him by contemporaries or successors. We have no knowledge of how and when the myth of Moses was bestowed upon 'the man Moses'. But we can be fairly certain that while he spoke with absolute authority about his mission and his encounter with God, he did not believe that he had been put out in a basket on the river Nile as a newborn. Nor did Jesus of Nazareth know anything about the three kings and the star. First comes the mission, then the miracle.

A Chinese novel, *The Journey to the West*,[1] tells us the miraculous story of Hsüan-tsang who traveled from China to the Western Heaven where he was presented to Buddha in the heavenly court. There he received the Scriptures and became a Buddha himself. The Hsüan-tsang of the myth was born to Lady Ying, an unfortunate woman, whose husband was murdered by a knave who immediately usurped the husband's place, threatening to kill the lady's unborn child if she was unwilling to abide by his desires. When the boy is born, Lady Ying fastened him to a plank and put the plank on the river to save the child's life. She also cut his little toe and her little finger, and pinned a letter, written in her own blood, to the boy's garment. The river delivered the boy to a monastery where he was brought up by the monks. As a youth he searched for his mother, found her, and revenged the murder of his father (who had already been resurrected)—and so on *ad libitum*. What a treasure trove for Freudian speculations this story is! Except that this time, we know the real story to the extent real stories can be known. Hsüan-tsang was born into a family of high Chinese officials. He became a Buddhist monk and decided to travel to India (to the West) in order to get hold of certain fundamental Buddhist scriptures. Since the Emperor did not give him permission to leave, he embarked secretly on the journey. After having spent sixteen years in India, he returned home, and—with his nineteen translations and many original writings—marked a new beginning in the story of Chinese Buddhism.

The myth of Hsüan-tsang reminds us of the myth of Moses on several counts. And yet, from the similarities of the myths no similarities between the "real" stories can be inferred. Mythical elements are indeed up for grabs but they cannot be conferred on just anyone. Men and women must deserve their myths. And certain elements fit one particular historical role better than another.

II

Myths are bestowed retrospectively. The owl of Minerva is, after all, a mythological bird and was borrowed as such by Hegel to serve as the metaphor of philosophy. The myth is conferred upon someone or something as the intersubjective authentication of the truth of a message which has already been heard.

We are not familiar with the 'real' story of Moses, while we are with the real story of Hsüan-tsang. But we do not need to be familiar with them in order to decipher some common truth from the respective myths. Both stories are about a 'new beginning' in the life of a religion, a land, and a people, bestowed upon the religious hero by the people in whose land the religion has been newly implanted (or rejuvenated and reformed). The river divides land from land, and whoever is fished out of the water brings new tidings. It is the language of the myth (of the past, the tradition) that makes the strongest statement about these new tidings.

Similarly, it was the language of the past, of a tradition which made the strongest statement about those entirely new tidings carried by the French Revolution. Naturally, I have in mind the language of philosophy. The philosophy of history was merely the intersubjective authentication of the message that a new world had been born in the land of Europe, and that this world was the harbinger of glad tidings for the whole human race.

Just as heroes, prophets, or saints deserve their myths—otherwise the myths would not be bestowed upon them—the modern world, too, deserves its philosophy of history. However, the language of philosophy and the language of mythology are different in kind. Their functional equivalence (as that of spiritual agencies which bestow meaning on agents) does not provide sufficient ground for their equation. If philosophies of history were myths, we could not account for their rapid demise before our eyes. Whatever has happened to the people of Israel, this has not affected the myth of the man Moses. Whatever has happened in our modern world has, however, quickly and deeply affected the truth of our paradigmatic narratives. They turned out to be self-dissolving narratives.

Philosophy was transformed into a depersonified narrative by Aristotle and has remained such ever since. Its major protagonists are not men and women but concepts. Ancient recipients still had difficulties coping completely with the depersonification of the language game. This is why they attributed miraculous stories to philosophers, and endowed them with such paraphernalia of myth as wisdom, cunning, superhuman continence, or subhuman brutishness. Of these myths, only that of Socrates has remained intact. The rest is gone. In the modern philosophy of history, depersonification has been consummated. No wonder, then, that the first onslaught against philosophies of history was related to the attempt at personifying philosophy. I have in mind here Kierkegaard and, above all, Nietzsche. Since this attempt has failed to open up a new avenue in philosophy right to this very moment, and even if it may still do so in the future, I am not going to return to it. This futility, and not the overlooking of important phenomena, brings me to the statement that philosophy, contrary to myth, has been and remains for the time being, stubbornly apersonal, and, in this sense, Aristotelian.

Hans Blumenberg, in his innovative explorations, confronts modern men and women with their own mythologies.[2] Moderns, as much as premoderns, have forged a host of mythological stories and parables. In so doing they have used, sometimes lavishly, traditional mythological materials while reshaping and recasting them. Modern myths, no less than old ones, focus on "great men." Among others, Blumenberg discusses the Napoleon myths, in particular the representative narratives related to the encounter of the two "great men," Napoleon and Goethe, at Erfurt. Although the modern era is extremely attached to heroworship, nonetheless, heroworship does not yield stories which would qualify for foundational narratives and which could bestow intersubjective authentications on the new times. The reasons for this are manifold. Let me mention only one of them. The modern age is future-oriented: the patina of longevity does not attain to the aura of sanctity in the field of acting and doing. Rather, it does so in the field of collecting and remembering. The institutions of modern liberalism and democracy are far from being charismatic. In addition, the short-lived charismatic institutions of the twentieth century, all linked to the worship of totali-

tarian dictators, have taught us a lesson about the dangerous consequences of the institutionalization of charisma under the circumstance
of future-orientation. Simultaneously, they have contributed to the
demise of the great legitimizing philosophical narratives of modernity.

Hegel was a great admirer of Napoleon; once, he termed the emperor
"the world-spirit on horseback." But it would never have occurred to
him to put his philosophy into the emperor's mouth or to make the dic-
tator a protagonist of this philosophy in any sense. No man, not even
the greatest, can be considered the founder of modernity; unlike
Athens, modernity has no Theseus. For disagreement is a constitutive
element of modernity since its "foundation"; universalism and pluralism presuppose one another by definition. To use the language of
Hegel, the universal establishes itself first as an abstraction, and it is
only history as difference, as conflict, as resolve and negation, this painful process of concrete determinations, that will fill the universal form
with contents. The abstract forms, the process, the series of conflicts,
are not founded; they just happen, unfold, grow, and proceed. One of
the reasons that the philosophy of history became so strongly foundationalist is that it denied the philosophical relevance of political foundation.

The universalistic claims of philosophies of history already mark their
difference from myths. Despite disclaimers of their universality, for
example, in the form of singling out particularistic views, images or
interests behind the universalistic facade, a philosophy of history cannot
be unmasked as a new myth—this is how and why the term 'ideology'
has been invented and put to critical or derogative use.

As mentioned, there is a similarity between the truth/untruth of a
myth and that of a philosophy. Neither myth nor philosophy can be
falsified, but we can turn away from both of them. Insofar as we do so,
they become untrue. However, as long as we make painstaking efforts
to show that they are untrue, they are not entirely untrue. They must
still be true for someone else, or otherwise why the effort? They *become*
completely untrue when neither the evaluative term 'true' nor that of
'untrue' is applicable to them anymore. For example, for a long time,
we have not applied the terms truth-untruth to the story of Zeus and
Kronos.

But as the example itself indicates, mythological truth, in an odd and
unexpected fashion, can be shifted into another medium. When a
human group which has had distinct, religious or secular stories of
foundation, is gone for good, the mythical message of its stories also disappears for good. But mythological narratives are, or at least can be,
'representative stories' or parables (where 'representative' means representative also for other groups). As 'typical' stories, they encapsulate
human imagination more generally or universally than does the hero of
a religion or people, on whom the story happened to be bestowed.

These stories remain with us in the form of images, visions and puns, which live their afterlife mostly in the aesthetic medium. 'Afterlife' means (practical) immortality. Stories with an afterlife can always be recalled from the collective memory. This is how they become 'culture'. Can we expect that the same will happen to the representative narratives of philosophy of history?

One expects myths to be alien to facts and modern stories to be inclined to facticity. The picture is, however, more complex. Myths do not recognize the difference between fact, interpretation, and fiction, though believers in myths sometimes do. Since rationalist cultures distinguish between reality and fiction irrespective of the circumstance of how far they divide reality itself into a 'lower' and a 'higher' kind, myths which appear in a fairly rational setting require faith from the believer. For this reason, Christianity needed a credo, while Judaism did not. To have faith means to take everything that happens in the myth for a fact, suspending the practice of telling reality from fiction in the sphere of supreme reality. Philosophies of history as offsprings, advocates, and bards of the modern age are stubborn rationalists in the sense given above. Sympathetic recipients of a philosophy of history are not supposed to believe in it, but to understand it as well as to accept the relevance of its reasoning. But—and this is an important 'but'—the 'authenticating narratives' of the modern (new) age (the ones which lend it authority) do not claim facticity in the same manner as did religious or political myths. Kant, who (together with Rousseau) stood at the beginning of the very short career of great narratives, was the most outspoken here. For him, the distinction between fact and fiction was the hallmark of sound philosophical knowledge. So he termed his own philosophy of history a fiction, but a fiction with the noblest veneer, which makes us understand history, this enigmatic process, which remains inaccessible to perception and so also to mere theoretical understanding. Kant's fiction presents history as a progressive development which unfolds in the direction of the modern age. The Hegelian adventure of the World Spirit was not consciously meant to be a fiction, but neither was it meant to be the reconstruction of facticity. To a lesser extent, this is still true of Marx's story of production, class struggle, alienation and the end of pre-history. All these narratives meticulously follow the pattern of traditional metaphysics, constantly distinguishing between two levels of reality: the lower and the higher. What is real on the lower level is not really, only seemingly, real. What is really real is essential and actual, and it is placed on the upper level. It is the metaphysical (strictly, philosophical) tradition that allows philosophies of history to accept the rationalist tradition (the distinction between reality and fiction) on the one hand, and to tell, in a manner of myths, a fictitious story as a real one on the other. Philosophies of history appeal to our reason and not to our faith. And yet, without a kind of faith, one cannot subscribe to their particular division of reality into a lower and a higher sphere.

The relation between higher reality, fiction, and facticity in philosophies of history cannot be addressed here. The problem is approached by almost every philosophy in a unique way, and space does not allow me to elaborate on them. But all of them agree on four points. And this is so regardless of whether they claim that they have recounted the story of world history 'as it really happened' or whether they rather affirm that only the stories fitted into their account deserve mention and will be recollected in human memory. First, they agree that history is universal; second, that it shows a final tendency to progress; third, that modernity is the consummation of that progressive development; and finally, that everything that has happened, is happening, and is going to happen can be fitted smoothly into the universal framework of progression-toward-modernity, provided that the event in question is not contingent. The same (fourth) idea can be formulated the other way around: every noncontingent event leads toward the consummation of the development of world history.

III

I have already referred to the common experience of our generation: we all saw the great narratives of philosophy of history collapse or slowly disintegrate before our eyes. Valhalla on fire, the twilight of History, awakens mythological reminiscences. The current term 'postmodernity' is rich in such reminiscences. Whenever a myth loses its primeval appeal, the story of a people, a religion, a culture, an institution, draws to its close. Analogical thinking jumps to the conclusion that since philosophies of history have lost their appeal, our own, short-lived, Western politicocultural story has already exhausted all its reserves. Yet this conclusion does not need to be drawn. Insofar as they provided modernity with universal stories of intersubjective self-authentication, philosophies of history were the functional equivalents of myths. And still, as I have pointed out, philosophies of history are unlike myths on several important counts. They can lose their appeal for quite different reasons than myths have done so thus far. Their demise need not be taken, at least not yet, as the clear indication of our having entered another age identifiable with the prefix 'post'. There are alternative explanations.

Myths are experience-resistant, given that fiction and facts merge in them in an indistinguishable unity. Philosophies of history are not. Myths are timeless as long as they live; temporality is their demise. This is not true of philosophies.

By experience-resistance this time I do not mean falsifiability. Philosophical truth is as little open to falsification as mythological truth. Philosophies are not falsified; but, as I have noted, one can simply turn away from them. However, personal experience exerts a qualitatively greater influence on the acceptance or the rejection of philosophies than it does of myths. Commitment to philosophies is always a personal business. Philosophical creeds are not implanted in childhood, and even if they are (as in the case of J. S. Mill), one can shed them and commit oneself to another by mere personal choice. Changing one's version of the world as a result of personal, historical (nonmiraculous) experience presupposes the distinction between fact and fiction, whatever that means. One adopts a rational attitude toward philosophies. The constant flux and change of modern philosophical imagination can be attributed mostly to this particular circumstance. The way the so-called 'great narratives' have been emptied out in our lifetime is very much in line with an already traditional rationalistic philosophical attitude. The life experience of the generation which grew up during or after World War Two is so inimical to the unifying, holistic, and truly self-complacent magnificence of the representative philosophies of history that it could simply not bear with them any longer. It would have been highly irrational to stick to the great narratives after their spirit had left the world (to use Hegel's own metaphor). I need to add parenthetically, as a corroboration of what has just been said, that the less dramatic the generational experience, the less dramatic the philosophical change. The greatest drama took place on the European continent.

What does it mean that the spirit which once enlivened great narratives has left the world? It means roughly what it says. A generation with certain historico-personal experiences can no longer subscribe to stories which do not make sense out of these experiences. This is why they turn away from philosophies of history of the nineteenth-century stock. This is why they can legitimately say that they are untrue.

Yet some caution is warranted here. Though philosophical truth is supposed to be eternal, just like mythological truth, temporality is neither alien nor hostile to philosophy. Depersonification guarantees safe navigation on the ocean of discontinuity. Arguments can be carried from one locus to another like mythological motives, but they are not just conferred upon any deserving man. Rather, the person who made them first can always be taken to task. His views can be discussed as his, and refuted, criticized, altered, or vindicated as such, in any age, by any man or woman of any conviction, even without reference to a whole body of belief. Philosophy of history is gone now, and it seems to have gone for good. But we cannot know, in fact we do not know whether this is the case. Perhaps one day, in a century or just tomorrow, new stories of world history are going to be told; and men and women will turn toward them because they will be true (for them).

'The end of X' language, where X can stand for history, the subject, metaphysics, philosophy, man, the West, and for much more, is the language of philosophy of history. If we seriously intend to leave philosophy of history behind, at least for the time being, it is advisable to leave also 'the end of X' language behind. For the same reason, postmodernity cannot be interpreted as *posthistoire,* as a new period which comes after modernity. At any rate, our life experiences do not bear out this proposition. I recommend, therefore, to understand the term postmodernity as the equivalent for the contemporary historical consciousness of the modern age. Postmodern is not that which follows after the modern age, but what follows after the unfolding of modernity. Once the main categories of modernity have emerged, the historical tempo slows down, and the real work on the possibilities begins. These possibilities are open—thus they can be put to use for better or for worse. This is why statements about future certainties do not appeal to us; nor do reconfirmations of our existence as the very consummation of the whole of human history. Philosophies of history are crutches we no longer need.

IV

When a myth dies, when no one believes in it anymore, the story, the image, which was once a myth, can still remain authentic and true if shifted into another medium. Ormuzd and Ariman, and Leda and the swan are parts of what we term 'culture'. The name of George the dragon killer has been erased from the list of the Catholic saints, but the image of the dragon-killing youth cannot be erased from the world of painting. Philosophy has a status similar to that of art, by which I mean that works of philosophy belong to the realm of 'culture', at least from the time when the Roman age consciously turned back to the Greeks as the source of philosophical wisdom. This is why drawing parallels between the afterlife of myths and that of philosophies seems eminently meaningless. If Aristotle's philosophy survived as philosophy and not as art or religion, the same can be expected from Hegel's. On the other hand, myths and artworks resemble one another more than works of philosophy resemble any of them. One cannot discard a part of a myth and still believe in it. But one can certainly dismiss a few aspects of a philosophy while retaining others. Moreover, this is the normal practice in the preserving of a philosophical heritage. There is very little difference in this respect between the philosophical heritage of the remote past and the legacy of the past of the present.

If postmodernity is indeed but the consummation of modernity, the period where the development of the main categories of modernity have been accomplished and the work within them, with them, and on them begins, then the great narratives of philosophy of history are nothing but exemplary manifestations of the consciousness of the past of the present. The great narratives of philosophy of history have lost their appeal not because they were too modern, but because they were not modern enough. More precisely, everything that was eminently modern in them is going to be preserved as well as constantly recycled.

Moses was put into a basket, Hsüan-tsang was tied to a plank, and both were left to the mercy of the river and to the secret design of God.

Our age experiences itself as being from the past by an ocean. The 'New World' is geographically divided from the Old Continent by the Atlantic Ocean. However, the actual 'New World' is not America, but modernity, and the broadest ocean is not the Atlantic, but the historical-metahistorical divide between the premodern and the modern. Regardless of whether the term 'New World' is meant as a compliment (as in Dvorak's New World Symphony) or as a word of abuse (as in Huxley's Brave New World), we recognize ourselves in it. We understand ourselves as a new beginning, for better or for worse.

The great historical narratives are modern insofar as they make a strong statement for this new beginning. Still, they are not yet prepared to accept the consequences of this new beginning. This is why they are not modern enough. Philosophers of history did not make the simple but meaningful statement: this world is different, it is new. They also felt obliged to prove that the new is the necessary conclusion of everything that happened before in the so-called world history, or that it is the final homecoming of the Absolute Idea. The problem with philosophies of history is not foundationalism, but the way they practiced it. In grounding modernity philosophico-historically, they have robbed modernity of the foundation of its freedom the self-same philosophies were so desirous to establish. Miriam, who put the basket with the little Moses on the river Nile, was replaced by 'World History' writ large and by its laws, although the modern world was supposed to be free and undestined. Yet was it indeed meant to be free and undestined?

The way one starts so one continues. All philosophies of history proceed with the tale until they arrive at the happy ending to which our (modern) age is supposed to be destined. This is a highly unmodern idea. Among others, the novelty of our age consists of the openness of our horizon and the plurality of interpretations of both the present and the past. This openness allows for multiple projects. The multiplicity of projects is promising but at the same time threatening. The point is not that we are ignorant of the end of our story (a feature which we share with every human group and every age), but that we are as yet ignorant as to whether our project will be viable in the long run. We have just began to work in and on modernity. There are formidable problems, both external and internal, to face. Although the project of modernity has spread almost throughout our whole globe, there are high cultures which have put up such a resistance that they can even reverse the trend. It remains to be seen whether the Iran of Khomeini is an exception. And even if the trend is not going to be reversed, we cannot guess whether scriptures will be granted to us in the Seventh Heaven. And we are rightly irritated if someone tells us that he knows all those Scriptures in advance.

Many forms of rationalism are modern and viable, and so are several kinds of universalism. Yet the universalistic use of rationality is highly problematic. Transcendental statements have universal validity. The truth of such a statement is neither old nor new, it is timeless and thus eternal. The idea that the 'new world' and the new world alone has access to the eternal, that we alone can arrive at the self-consciousness of the eternal, will not appeal to many in the postmodern age, for the simple reason that it is just a weaker version of the philosophies of history. Most of the moderns will rather accept confinement in the prisonhouse of historicity, or keep banging at the door of that prisonhouse, than resign to the freedom of uncertainty. Some of them can remain loyal to universalizing rationalism all the same. Difference is our hallmark.

In spite of all their seemingly antiquated aspects, philosophies of history manifest the past of the present. As the manifestations of our own past, they are somehow also the manifestations of our present. To support this statement one needs only to point to the value all moderns share: the value of freedom, both for the philosophers of history and for the rest of us. The only difference is that many postmoderns turn a fairly skeptical eye to the actual status of freedom in the modern age, whereas philosophers of history had, as it were, the happy ending already in sight. The evaluative yardstick has remained unchanged. But, as it often happens, the values on which the narratives are built can be identical, whereas the narratives themselves are not only different, but also exclusive. This can be the case, but in this particular case it is not.

Stories about history can evoke in the reader authentic experiences which have nothing to do with history. If a great narrative could be perceived as the manifestation of one or another authentic modern experiences, it could be called true, albeit not the Truth of History. Let me mention briefly two such experiences of enormous weight: that of human destiny and that of the divine.

Philosophical narratives were said to have been depersonified. Hegel, who adored Napoleon, did not build his story around the vicissitudes of the self-made-man Emperor. Yet one can experience, and also interpret, the whole of the Hegelian system as the disguised biography of a mythical self-made man, and not without certain justification. Modern men and women are contingent. They are also conscious of their contingency. Each is born a bundle of mere possibilities. As I have argued elsewhere,[3] it is only through an existential choice that they can transform their contingency into their destiny, yet once they have succeeded in this, their whole lives will appear to them retrospectively as a progressive chain of self-development through the dialectical unity of freedom and necessity. This is the process that Hegel actually derived or described. And he also added that what he had done could be done only in a retrospective glance.

The narrative is disappointing only if it is about world history. Read as a universalized biography of modern self-made men or women who succeeded in transforming their contingency into destiny, the same story appears in a totally different and new light. There is no Archimedean point from which one can look back at History. But there are certainly Archimedean points from which persons can look back at their own lives, from the height from which they can say with well-deserved satisfaction: I have done it, I have become by choice what I am (and what I have always been). Philosophies of histories are true stories about such men and women. Modern human destiny is not represented in one kind of philosophy, but by different kinds of that genre. Not everyone will recognize her or his autobiography in the great narratives of philosophy of history, but some will. And for them, these stories will be, and remain, true. One does not need to be a Moses or a Hsüan-tsang to embody, or repersonify, world historical narratives.

That men and women project the images of gods following their own imagination is a statement in which both believers and disbelievers can agree. Traditional images of deities survive traditional societies; so do old myths. Nothing indicates that they may wither. And still, modern life experience and world experience do not leave the image and the concept of the divinity unaffected. True enough, modernity seems to be an age without religious genius or fantasy. One might even add to this that Europe in general has never excelled in original religious imagination. But one could also argue that religious imagination is not tantamount to mythological imagination, since philosophies (from Plato onward) have eminently contributed to the conception of religious ideas. Maybe the same will be said about modern philosophies a few centuries from now. There is no knowledge about this. Yet one can convincingly make a case for the innovative impact of modern philosophies on the present. Three philosophers indicate in three different directions: Kierkegaard, Kant, and Hegel. History is central for all three of them. Kirkegaard's Christ is the absolute paradox of History; Kant's God is unknown and unknowable, yet also the postulate of Freedom and of the best world; Hegel's Absolute Idea is the Totality of all that Is in its historical self-development toward itself. The implication is not that modern philosophies of history are but different versions of a theodicea, but that they are also reformulations of the human image about that-which-is-higher-than-human, as it appeared to those who had just entered the modern age.

I have recounted three stories: that of Moses, that of Hsüan-tsang, and that of History writ large. Whatever else they are, they are also stories about crossing the water, stories about crossing the frontier, and stories of rebirth. The first two are also spiritual stories, stories of scripture and revival. They tell us the tale of one particular people, one particular religion, one particular culture. The (modern) spiritual stories of History have so far failed whenever they have aimed at something similar. Modernity encompasses many traditions and cultures; it tells the tale of many peoples, many religions, many cultures. All these tales are different and remain so. Without the spice of common spirituality, there is no shared tale. The condition of a common spirituality has already been named; it is called freedom. The political framework for its appearance has already been set: it is called democracy—yet no spirit has yet filled this framework. As far as modernity is concerned, Moses is still wandering the desert and Hsüan-tsang has not arrived in India. Curious as we are, we do not know when and how and where we are to arrive, or whether we will arrive at all. What we know for sure is that the next installment of the story will be written by us.

Notes

1. *The Journey to the West,* trans. and ed. by Anthony C. Yu (Chicago: University of Chicago Press, 1977).

2. See Hans Blumenberg, *Work on Myth* (Cambridge: MIT Press, 1985).

3. See my *Philosophy of Morals* (Oxford: Basil Blackwell, 1990).

DAYA KRISHNA

SECULARISM: SACRED AND PROFANE

"Secularism," or the secular world view may be considered to be the heart of "modernity," and though the use of such terms as "postmodernism" and "postmodernity" have become increasingly fashionable, there is no such thing as "postsecularism," at least not yet. The secular perspective, or the secular world view, may be said to characterize "postmodernism" as much as it did "modernity" earlier. But it seems that there is a basic misunderstanding about what "secularism" involves among a large and substantive number of contributors to Western intellectual endeavor as it has tried to understand its own history, particularly what has happened during the last four hundred years. And this, to a great extent, may be said to have stood in the way of the understanding of other civilizations and cultures including, perhaps, the West's own premodern heritage, which it finds difficult to own or assimilate through the perspective of "modernity."

The difference between what has come to be called "modernity" and all other past cultures may be said to consist in the denial of all transcendence and the confinement of all that is "real" and "meaningful" to the realm of the "secular" alone, which itself is understood as consisting of only that which is revealed and grasped and felt *by* the senses, *through* the senses, and *for* the senses. The coming of "modernity" has meant a reversal in the attitude to time, to knowledge, to action, and to the world of feelings and emotions in which everyone lives most of the time. This has led to the seeing of all past as something archaic, something full of superstitions, something outmoded and irrelevant to all human concerns in the present. Knowledge itself is seen as provisional, tentative, subject to continuous revision, and justified only by the pragmatic success of the action which it supports. And, action is seen as the satisfaction of desires which themselves are conceived mainly in sensuous, or even sensual terms. Skepticism and cynicism infect all knowledge and value claims, and thought clutches at sensation and the feeling associated with it as the only foundation for knowledge and value that man can possibly have in the world. The denial of essence not merely in the human world but also with respect to objects leads to a situation where all distinctions become contextual and pragmatic in character.

The ultimate thrust of all this logically leads to a questioning of language, *through* which and *in* which all dialogue and discussion take place, as a *meaningful* activity inasmuch as the very notion of 'concepts', 'meanings', or 'images' is sought to be eliminated. Following the lead of the formalist way of looking at mathematics, language itself is seen as consisting of only actual inscriptions or events, that is, "tokens," forgetting that if what the author is writing were to be strictly construed in this way, nobody would know what he is saying, leaving aside the question whether what he or she is saying is correct or incorrect. But, according to some others who are more daring still, there is no author, and no text, and thus no question of who said, or rather "wrote" this, for they make a radical distinction between "speaking" and "writing," or even "what is meant by what is 'written' or 'said'."[1] It does not matter, of course, that their own books carry their own names as authors, and that they do claim royalty and copyright rights and complain if somebody plagiarizes their work; they even "disown" someone else's "understanding" of their work by calling it a "misunderstanding." But if there are no authors and no texts and no meanings, but only "inscriptions" which cannot even be construed as "words" or "sentences," then what are we talking about and why are we wasting each others' time. All "writing" becomes calligraphy, to be characterized only as "pretty to look at" or otherwise, just as we talk about patterns in a textile design or carpet.

The "suicidal intellect" could perhaps go no farther, but such is the logic of the thrust of the way of understanding of the "secular" and its prestige that we accept whatever a Derrida may choose to say or a Scheffler may write.[2] This version of the secular vision wants every entity except those apprehended by the senses to be banished from the realm of the real. The predominant philosophical enterprise of the last hundred years in the Western world may be seen as a sustained attempt to deny ontological status to all nonsensuous entities required for the cognitive enterprise of man. Though seemingly necessary, they must essentially be eliminable in principle. The techniques evolved for achieving this purpose were many, but one thing they all had in common was the translation into terms denoting directly perceivable entities without any residuum whatsoever.

The story or stories of the failure of these attempts are well known to students of the subject, but one thing which is not so well known, or perhaps not so well understood, is that the failure was embedded in the attempt itself as it involved the denial by the mind of its own being, not merely of everything that it produced out of itself, but of its productive activity or energy itself. The mind, thus, became the source of all ontological delusion as it peopled the world with all sorts of entities which had no reason to be called "real."

"Mind" has been treated as a "devil" in the nonempiricist tradition also. But there the attack has been from the side of the self or the soul as it (mind) stood in the way of its turning to God or of its realizing itself, depending upon the system concerned. Here, however, the attack has been from the side of the senses, which do not seem to want any interference in their direct intercourse with the world. Unfortunately for both, mind is the human realm *par excellence,* and without it we would neither have the kind of knowledge we have or the kind of spirituality mankind seems to have had until now. Animals with all their senses do not have the type of knowledge we have, and though we do not know about the angels in heaven, we know that even if such beings were there, they could not have the spirituality evinced by the great spiritual personalities humanity has witnessed in its history. The "human condition," then, is neither that of the beasts about whom we know a little, nor that of angels about whom we "know" nothing.

The acceptance of the "human condition," then, is not only to accept the senses but also to accept the mind with all its diverse capacities and powers, about which we know mainly through the products and creations to which it gives rise. But to accept the mind is not to deny the sense or, at a deeper level, the biological rhythm and cycle of life. The fear of sense-centric thinkers is that once the sure foundation of the senses is gone, there will be no ground left to demarcate between the "real" and the "imaginary." But, as the example of the sensory illusions, particularly those of the structural sort, shows, "to be apprehended by the senses" and "to be real" (in the sense of being veridical) are not the same. The mind may also have illusions of its own, and in case they happen to be structural in nature, they would either never be known as "illusory," or we will have to postulate faculties other than the senses or the mind in man which may expose these illusions. Whether there are faculties other than the senses and the mind may be treated as an open question, as also there is the question whether these faculties are necessarily hierarchical in nature, or unlimited in number. In fact, one of the simple ways to obstruct the proliferation of an infinite number of faculties arranged in a hierarchical order, each correcting the "structural illusions" of the faculty lower than itself in the hierarchy but generating "illusions" of its own about which it can know nothing by the very nature of the case, would be to have a closed circular model where each faculty is treated as coordinate with the other, correcting the other's "illusions" as well as being "corrected" by it, in its own turn. However, in either case, we would have to develop some criteria on the basis of which a faculty would need to be postulated to account for certain functions which presumably could not be explained or accounted for in any other way. The senses, of course, are accepted by everybody, but whether any faculty other than the senses has to be postulated to account for certain aspects of human behavior is the question which has to be raised and answered.

This, of course, is not the place to go into what may be called "The theory of transcendental illusions," but it certainly needs to be stressed that in case there are any such things as "structural illusions," then not only are they "objective" in the sense that they are shared by all persons who have the same structure, but also that life has to be lived—and lived meaningfully—in terms of these "illusions." Also, the realization of them as "illusions" by a "transcendental critique" from a "higher" faculty does not destroy the "appearing" or the occurrence of the "illusion," except in a theoretical sense. Even if one knows, for example, that the sun does not "really" move or that the stick is not "really" bent when seen under water, it continues to appear the "same" as before and this not just to some odd person but to everyone who possesses the same sensory structure of "seeing" as humans do. And, the interpersonal behavior of men has to be geared to the transpersonal "appearing" shared by everybody, except in contexts where the theoretical correction has to be taken into account and the behavior influenced by it in order to achieve the end which would otherwise not be achieved without this correction. In fact, the knowledge of "appearances," even those which are known to be "false," is used by the artist to create a new world of significant forms which seem to convey a meaning which makes life more meaningful, even though it does not happen to be "referential."

To live within the boundaries set by the "structural illusions" generated by every faculty that humans possesses (and we do not know how many we do possess; nor perhaps can we even be sure about the truth of such knowledge in case anyone happens to claim it) and treat the knowledge of this "illusoriness" as it is brought to our awareness by the exercise of a faculty other than itself, as only peripheral to the business of "living," is our fate, and perhaps the necessary condition of any embodied being.

But, beyond this, there is perhaps the even more important fact that one has to act on beliefs which one thinks to be true and thus bring about a situation that would not have existed if one had not had that belief and acted upon it because one thought the belief to be correct or true. Beyond even this is the fact that for the most part action cannot wait and has to be done not only on insufficient information but also on the basis of knowledge that is not only essentially incomplete but also partially false in the sense that its falsity would only be revealed by a later knowledge which we do not have at present. If we add to all these difficulties the fact that most knowledge is probabilistic in character, we will see not only the central dilemma involved in all human action, but also the bewildering fact that through such action something is being continuously brought into existence which is the referent of a descriptive judgment that can be characterized as "true."

Action as the creator of human reality has seldom been the object of philosophical attention either in the past or in the present. It has almost always been seen in the context of ethical discussion, that is, as either being in accordance with a preexistent rule or norm or as realizing an end or value or ideal in terms of which its "rightness" or "goodness" may be judged. But, besides these aspects, which are unquestionably important, especially in the context of the evaluation and judgment of actions, there is what may be called the ontological dimension of action as the creator of reality. This, too, perhaps gives rise to the "structural illusion" of potential omnipotence which all human willing seems subject to in its pure subjective aspect, resulting in the perennial surprise at the nonfulfillment of what one wills or chooses to bring into being. Yet, whatever is brought into being by a person's action, whether it falls short of what was intended or exceeds it or is different from it, demands not merely cognition, recognition, and understanding by others but also further action on one's own part to maintain it as it is or to modify, change, and develop it further. The reality brought into being by action, so to speak, demands further action as the situation brought into being reveals possibilities which could be realized by further action. The realm of action, thus, seems as unending as that of knowledge, though the latter assumes reality to be in some sense finished and completed in order to be known, while the former continuously creates it and, thus, may be said to add to it and change it in a significant sense of the term. It may be thought that the unending character of knowledge derives from the fact that human action is constantly bringing new reality into being, and this seems to be corroborated by the continuous proliferation of all studies relating to any of man's creations, including history. But this will be a misleading impression, as in the knowledge of the natural sciences, where the subject of study seems to be completely indifferent to any human action and the knowledge of it seems as unending as in any nonscientific field. The unendingness of knowledge then, derives not so much from the fact that human beings, by their actions, bring new reality into being as from the fact that the human mind seems to have an inexhaustible capacity for asking new questions and seeking their answers.

Human beings thus have a built-in capacity for innovativeness in the dimensions of both knowledge and action which seem to display an inexhaustibility over time; for, however large the time-span may be taken to be, all that is achieved in the fields of knowledge and action is bound to appear far less than what is needed to be achieved. But this phenomenon is only another name for the transcendent in time, which is anathema to "secularism" as understood until now, a secularism that wishes to banish all inconvenient ontological ghosts that have haunted humanity since its inception. True, the so-called "unendingness" of the human enterprise of knowledge and action belongs to humanity as a whole and not to the individual whose enterprise in these domains is cut short by death, if not by other factors long before death. But humanity itself is not everlasting, and if science is to be believed then it is inevitable that the physical conditions of the planet will make it impossible for any living beings to survive after a certain lapse of time, even if humanity does not commit "collective suicide" much earlier. But, whether the death be that of an individual or a species or of life itself, it raises the same questions, which, as far as I can see, are unanswerable in principle. On the other hand, does the fact of death "nullify" the significance of all that occurs in human life, including those "unending enterprises" which we have mentioned earlier? The evidence of those of us who are "living" seems to give a clear negative answer to this as we continue to celebrate life in the midst of the "death" all round us and pursue all of those things that are necessary for life and for making it meaningful. But if death does not nullify all that occurs, then the "unending enterprises" specific to the human species have to be pursued in any case and the transcendent nature of the human situation has to be accepted.

This "transcendent" dimension here, however, seems totally different from the transcendence that is usually emphasized in the great religions of the world or in the philosophies derived from them. The Hebraic religions usually find this transcendent dimension in the notion of God, which, however differently conceived, is central to Judaism, Christianity, and Islam. The religions of the Indian subcontinent have their quota of gods and goddesses, and even the notion of a supreme God above all others and everything else. But what is distinctive about the latter is the emphasis on a transcendent dimension that lies not so much outside a person as within, and that his or her central task is to realize this and not to establish a relationship either in terms of "dutiful action" or of a "feeling" or "attitude" toward something else. The ontological center, thus, is conceived to be within the person and not somewhere outside. But the secular seekings of humanity have no real place in either of these two traditions; they do not seem to have any firm ontological grounding except in some indirect relationship either to God or to the transcendent self, which seem to be the central concerns of humanity in the two traditions. Ultimately, these seekings have only a secondary status, and even in those rare attempts somehow to link or integrate them into the main body of human thought, they have only a marginal, instrumental role. The heart of the "real" seeker is never in these seekings and, in the final analysis, they have to be, and even *ought* to be, given up. Saints and prophets are not known for their pursuit of knowledge in the empirical realm, and even when they have engaged in an action, it is only action of a particular sort—an action that tries to build the city of God on earth or that turns humans to the true faith that has been revealed to them and which they try to preach to others.

The distrust of the secularist for any postulation of the transcendent perhaps derives from the argument just presented. The secularist's fear of ontological ghosts derives from the traditions where ontology was supposed to be bound with these two positions only. But the transcendent we have been talking about is radically different from these positions and lies at the very heart of the secularist's own activity, enmeshed and involved and rooted in it, all at once, at the same time. Surely, the secularist would not seek to deny the "unending infinity" of human seeking, in the realms of both knowledge and action, even if these realms are conceived only in secular terms, through and through. But once this point is conceded and its significance understood, the presence of the transcendent element can be seen as the distinguishing characteristic of human reality with all the ontological ghosts arising out of it and rooted in it.

The transcendent roots of the secular may be seen not only in the "unending seeking" in the field of knowledge and action where temporality is overcome by making the seeking intrinsically inexhaustible in time, but also in what may be called the atemporal or transtemporal seekings of man. These are evidenced by man's perpetual attempt at creating works which, when contemplated, seem to stand stilled in time, or rather seem to be outside time though tangentially touching it. These are usually known as works of art, but basically they are attempts to create "still islands" in the incessant, perpetual, unending flow of time. Yet, the work of art is an embodied objectification which, when contemplated, stills the mind. The external support, however, is not necessary, and one may directly try to still the mind and its perpetual movement and achieve some sort of transcendence of time, as seems evidenced by the spiritual quest of humanity throughout its history. The seeking of an atemporal transformation of consciousness through contemplation of works created by man primarily for this purpose, or the seeking directly through meditative practices which enable one more directly to be in control of oneself, seem, then, to be the two ways in which man has sought transcendence in his existential consciousness.

But, is this seeking, so immanent in human consciousness, a seeking for the transcendent in the realm of feeling also, or is there some other analogous seeking in the realm of feeling which is distinct from this? Or, to put it in other words, is there a seeking in the realm of feeling, and, if so, what is its nature and how is it different from other seekings that we find in the realm of knowledge and action? The usual answer to this question has been in terms of "happiness," which all persons are supposed to seek all the time. Moreover, almost invariably, the seeking for any other goal, whether in the realm of knowledge or action or consciousness, is seen as an instance of it, the only difference being in the object, purpose, or activity through which one seeks pleasure or happiness. But this, as almost everyone can see from his own experience, is a travesty of the human situation. One does seek pleasure, but not all the time or even most of the time. One also seeks so many other things which have little to do with happiness except in an incidental or accidental way. One may get some "satisfaction" or a "sense of fulfillment" while seeking them, but, firstly, these are not the same as "pleasure" or "happiness," and, secondly, they are seldom, if ever, sought for their own sake. The trick for those who have argued for the thesis that everyone naturally seeks pleasure all the time is to see every other thing as a means to this end, and to ignore or obliterate all distinctions between different states of consciousness and see them only as "pleasant" or "painful." Once these two strategies are adopted, the thesis seems unassailable, since nothing produced as counterevidence will be treated as such. As no counterevidence can even be specified in principle, the position should be seen for what it actually is, an arbitrary definitional statement in the guise of an apparent empirical description.

But, even if it is manifestly untrue to say that humans seek only pleasure and nothing else, would it not be true to say this at least with respect to their life of feelings? In the realm of feelings, what else can one seek but pleasure along with the avoidance of its opposite, that is, pain? This may seem almost self-evident, but self-evidence here derives from the fact that most thinkers have tended to ignore the deep differences between different forms of feeling at the human level. This seems to be facilitated by the fact that almost all states of feeling are either positive or negative, and seem to be paradigmatically illustrated in terms of "pleasure" and "pain." But, while it is generally true that one tries to achieve what is pleasant and avoid what is painful, it is not invariably so. We may genuinely turn away from what is pleasant while attempting to achieve something, even though this may involve some element of pain or discomfort.

In any case, once one sees that the realm of feelings cannot be adequately described merely in terms of "pleasure" or "pain," and that one does not always pursue the one or shun the other, the way is then open to a truer and more adequate articulation of one's seeking in the world of feelings. Perhaps, what one seeks is variety, subtlety, depth, range, significance, meaningfulness, fulfillment, and so forth. These terms, though they may overlap, reveal the diverse dimensions of the world of feeling in which human seeking may operate. This terrain is philosophically unexplored and those who have explored it (literary critics and students of art) have done so only in the context of works of art and not in the independent realm of the seeking of humanity. The relevant transfer of all these insights to man's direct seeking in the realm of feeling is, perhaps, the first thing that needs to be done if any philosophical exploration of this realm is to be undertaken. Yet, even before this attempt, one tentative suggestion may be offered here. And that relates to the observation that perhaps what man seeks in the realm of feelings is, so to speak, a second-order feeling or a feeling about feelings. The first-order feelings are so much at the mercy of objects, situations, and persons that one hardly feels free with respect to them. But one's feeling about these feelings is a different thing altogether. One can, to a great extent, choose what to feel about these feelings—to be perturbed by them, to hanker after them, to be detached from them, to have equanimity about them, and so on. Thus, one may be said to seek in the realm of feelings a state of feeling about feeling which negatively is seen as unaffected by their negativity at the first level and as fulfillment of being by their positivity at the first level. This is, of course, only a tentative suggestion which needs to be explored and developed further. This much, however, seems certain: that something seems to hinder the articulation and the exploration of a man's seeking in this realm even though he continuously lives *with* it and *in* it.

In a sense, people do not know what they seek or why they seek or what is the relation, if any, between their different seekings in the diverse realms of their being and the world or rather the worlds in which they find themselves. Nor does it seem that they can possibly find the "what" or the "why" of it all. The mystery of "unknowability," of "inaccessibility," of "unrealizability" is not somewhere outside us, but within us, at the center of our being, constituting us as we are, as we find ourselves to be. But the so-called "mystery" lies not only in the realm of knowledge but equally, or perhaps even more so, in the realms of feeling, consciousness, and action as well. And, as the ontological creators of a reality which we then try—and find most baffling and difficult—to understand, we share in the deeper mystery of all creation.

To accept humanity, then, is to, accept all of this, and it would be a gross injustice to deny any of it or to accept only a portion and deny the rest or to interpret or understand it in such a way as to drain it of its "seeking character" or to treat it in such a manner as to deny its importance or significance for human life and living. Much of modern thought, especially in the West, has been an attempt to do this for the last few hundred years, if not more. Moreover, all this has been done in the name of "secularism" and "modernity," and as the world of the non-Western intellectual mirrors the Western world, non-Westerners, too, say the same things in their own countries, albeit with a time lag. This is the deeper suicidal impulse, which seeks to deny to persons their essential being as "seekers" and "creators" or to confine them merely to that which is "sensuously pleasant" or reducible to it by one trick or another.

To admit all of this, however, is not to readmit the transcendent in the traditional form as it is found in many religions of the world. First, these religions have never been truly universal, since they have all divided mankind into believers and nonbelievers, into those who are in the fold and those who are outside it. Second, even among believers, religions have created divisions and distinctions based on race, class, caste, or sex. And, thirdly, they have denied the independent importance and reality of the nonreligious seekings of man. There has also been an overplaying of that about which no one can know anything, the situation of man after death. But the denial of all of this does not mean what "secularism" has taken it to mean, that is, the denial of any element of the transcendental or the mysterious in the human situation. Professor Ramchandra Gandhi has argued for the availability of religious ideas in a nonreligious context,[3] and Dr. N. V. Banerjee, more recently, for a deeper, more humanistic understanding of the Buddhist, Socratic, and Christian traditions of viewing the human situation in the world.[4] Ours also is an attempt in the same direction, to articulate the human situation in such a way as to preserve the sacred in the secular and the secular in the sacred, bypassing the traditional religions of the world, which have up until now divided mankind more than unified it.

Notes

1. I have added "said," for presumably these people do go to seminars, conferences and discuss matters by "speaking" to each other, and not just passing "written chits" amongst themselves.

2. Derrida's works are too well known to be specifically mentioned. For Scheffler's contribution, see Israel Scheffler, *Beyond the Letter: A Philosophical Inquiry into Ambiguity, Vagueness and Metaphor in Language* (London: Routledge & Kegan Paul, 1979).

3. Ramchandra Gandhi, *The Availability of Religious Ideas* (London: Macmillan Press, 1976).

4. N.V. Banerjee, *Knowledge, Reason and Human Autonomy* (Bombay, Somaiya Publications, 1986).

Scientific Progress

LARRY LAUDAN

SCIENTIFIC PROGRESS
AND CONTENT LOSS

More than a quarter of a century ago, Kuhn and Feyerabend launched their critique of the notion of scientific progress; that critique has been extraordinarily influential within philosophical circles and well beyond them. It was conducted on several fronts at once, but one of the most effective was the idea that scientific revolutions invariably involve losses as well as gains. It was Kuhn's thesis in particular that, since every choice between paradigms involved rival theories which had different strengths and weaknesses, there was no way in which theory change could be regarded as an unambiguous progression.[1] I shall use the term "Kuhn loss" to refer to this phenomenon—although a fair reading of philosophical texts in the early 1960s makes it clear it had been suggested by numerous workers in the 1950s, including Philip Frank, Stephen Toulmin, and Paul Feyerabend, as well as Thomas Kuhn.

Even if Kuhn loss occurs, why should it exercise epistemologists and philosophers of science so? The answer, in large measure, is that the mainstream traditions in philosophy of science—from Bacon to Whewell to Popper—had made cumulative retention from earlier theories to later ones a central feature of their accounts of scientific progress. It is easy to see why they were tempted to do so. If later theories can show themselves able to do everything that earlier theories can, and more besides, then it becomes wholly uncontroversial to claim that the later theories are better than the earlier ones. The phenomenon of Kuhn loss, if it is real, shows that this straightforward notion of intellectual progress is badly flawed. Indeed, Kuhn persuasively asks whether there can even be a coherent notion of scientific progress if scientific change is noncumulative. It is a question that many of us in philosophy of science have been struggling with for most of the last two decades.

Most of Kuhn's followers have concluded that the traditional notion of progress, which requires full cumulativity between successive paradigms, is indeed the only viable version of progress and that the lack of cumulativity in real science dashes any hope of characterizing large-scale (namely, inter-paradigmatic) change as epistemically progressive.[2] Oddly enough, many of Kuhn's critics (for example, Popper and Lakatos) share his view that noncumulativity is incompatible with cognitive progress; because they do not want to abandon the latter, they find themselves forced to argue that Kuhn loss is a spurious phenomenon, namely, that later scientific theories always have the resources to handle everything that their predecessors did. To this end, they have sought—generally not very convincingly—to retell those episodes in the history of science which appear to involve explanatory losses.[3]

It will be the thesis of this essay that *both* approaches are wrong-headed. The defenders of scientific progress are mistaken in claiming that losses never occur. Indeed, Kuhn loss is so frequent in the history of science as to be a commonplace. More importantly, both the defenders of the classical conception and the Kuhnians are wrong to suppose that warranted ascriptions of progress to instances of theory change require the wholesale retention by later theories of all the achievements of earlier ones. I shall show that *scientific progress does not require cumulativity* of the sort which both the positivists and Kuhn supposed was its *sine qua non*. In sum, a robust version of scientific progress is entirely consistent with a recognition that theory change often involves some losses as well as gains. The remainder of this essay will attempt to show why that is so.

Progress and Well-Testedness

Before we turn to look at the implications of loss, a brief sojourn is necessary into the terrain of theories of scientific progress, for it is progress which is supposed to be threatened by losses of Kuhn's sort. This is obviously not the place to attempt to lay out a general theory of scientific progress; and in any event, that is a task I have discharged in numerous earlier writings.[4] For our purposes here, a few very general remarks about progress will suffice.

To speak of progress, scientific or otherwise, is to speak of a sequence of steps or stages each of which moves us closer to a desired goal state than its predecessor.[5] To find out specifically what *scientific* progress is, we must know something about the goals of science. Although there is much dispute about how precisely those goals are to be understood,[6] this much can be said without too much controversy: whatever else we expect scientific theories to do for us, we expect them to give us reliable knowledge about observable but hitherto unobserved events. One theory is better than another if just in case it can be relied on to give us more accurate anticipations of nature's doings than its rival can. Other things being equal, one theory represents progress over another when it is more reliable or dependable than the other. Now, how can we tell when one theory is, overall, more dependable than a rival? Well, we cannot tell for sure, of course, unless we have examined all their empirical consequences, and that is an inexhaustible class. What we do instead is to suppose that the long-term dependability of a theory can be gauged or estimated by how that theory performs in certain demanding *test* situations. Such tests serve as *indicators* as to the tested theory's future reliability.

On this view of the matter, if one theory passes tests which are more demanding or probative than those passed by a rival, we have (defeasible) grounds for holding that the theory which has passed the more robust tests is more likely to stand up to future scrutiny than the one which has not. Thus, progress and testing are intimately intertwined; progress occurs when we are able to replace a less well-tested theory by a better-tested or better-confirmed rival. And we are justified in calling this "progress" because what the tests indicate is that one theory is more apt to further our goal of achieving dependable theories than its rival. The question we must now address is whether, as Kuhn and many others hold, the existence of loss (that is, violations of cumulativity) threatens scientific progress, so understood.

Kinds of Loss

There are three quite distinct sorts of losses which are often lumped together under the heading of "Kuhn loss."[7] All three involve situations in which one theory or paradigm is replaced by another.

1. The first, and least important, type is *loss of bare empirical consequences*. (I call them "bare" because, unless further delimited, we do not know whether these constitute epistemically salient facts, that is, whether they lent support to an earlier theory.) Such losses occur whenever a successor theory T_s fails to preserve intact all the true empirical consequences of its predecessor, T_p. Losses of this sort are not philosophically insignificant; for one thing, their occurrence undermines Karl Popper's justly famous theory of scientific progress, since that theory required a progressive T_s to possess all the true empirical consequences of its T_p's. But if we can leave Popper to one side, we have to ask whether it is necessarily a bad thing to accept a theory which fails to capture intact *all* the true empirical consequences of its predecessor. The only relevant answer might seem to be that if T_s fails to capture all of T_p's true empirical consequences, then T_p would enjoy some empirical support not enjoyed by T_s.

This answer becomes wholly unconvincing as soon as one realizes that it is an elementary truism about the nature of empirical support that a true empirical consequence of a theory does not necessarily provide evidential support for that theory. Think, for instance, of those many hypotheses specifically constructed ad hoc to account for a particular event or effect. We rightly do not regard those hypotheses as empirically supported or tested by the effects which they entail when those effects were used to generate the hypotheses to begin with.

The significance of this fact should be clear. What it shows is that a theory does not necessarily gain empirical support or confirmation from the truth of each of its true empirical consequences.[8] That is to say, the *supporting (or test) instances* of a theory are, at best a *proper subset* of its true empirical consequences. And from that it follows that a successor theory T_s may fail to capture some of the true empirical consequences of its T_p's. Hence if the Kuhn losses exhibited by T_s occur among the true empirical consequences of a T_p, which were not really supporting instances of that T_p, then it is surely no bar to progress to grant that a T_s may lack some of the true empirical consequences of its T_p.[9] And this means that *if* Kuhn loss occurs among those true empirical consequences of a T_p which are not supporting or test instances for it, then that sort of Kuhn loss is no hindrance to judgments of scientific progress.

2. Having established that the loss of bare empirical consequences does not necessarily pose any obstacle to assessments of progress, let us consider an apparently more challenging case—one that is illustrated by several of Kuhn's and Feyerabend's examples of loss. I shall call them *explanatory losses*. They occur when a certain phenomenon or effect is *explained* by an earlier theory but fails to be explained by its successor. I think that the occasional occurrence of such losses is a well-documented historical phenomenon. Are explanatory losses threatening to scientific progress? Well, they would be *if* the loss of one or more explanatory instances automatically carried with it the loss of empirical support. But I submit that we can run an argument here that is perfectly parallel to the argument I just sketched about empirical consequences. Specifically, we can show that some of the phenomena that a theory explains may fail to be phenomena that lend empirical support to the theory that explains them.

Rather than give a perfectly general argument (which can be given, but it is fairly arcane) let me settle for a single example. Descartes, in constructing his celestial kinematics, was impressed by the fact that planetary motions were co-directional and approximately co-planar. He devised his notorious vortex hypothesis to explain these phenomena *inter alia*. Under these circumstances, we surely want to say that, although Descartes' cosmology arguably provides an explanation for the phenomenon of co-directionality and co-planarity, it fails to derive any empirical support from these phenomena—since it was specifically designed with such phenomena in mind. And that is important because Newton's *Principia* fails to explain either of these regularities. If the existence of explanatory losses were sufficient grounds for denying the progressiveness of a theory transition, then we should have to say that the replacement of Cartesian mechanics by Newtonian mechanics was non-progressive. However, since the "lost" phenomena in question were not legitimately supporting evidence for Cartesian mechanics, the failure of Newton to explain them need not preclude the judgment that Newtonian mechanics represents progress over Descartes.

But that is another way of saying, to put it in general terms, that it is a mistake to suppose that all the explanatory successes of a theory provide weighty empirical support for the theory. This is because there is a difference between the phenomena which a theory explains and the phenomena which provide empirical support for a theory. And since that is true, it does not follow that a T_s that fails to explain some of the phenomena explained by its T_p's is automatically nonprogressive with respect to its T_p's. Indeed, we can imagine circumstances in which a later theory might massively fail to explain many of the things explained by its successor and yet still argue that the later theory represents progress over its predecessor—specifically, when the explanatory losses fall outside the class of supporting instances for T_p and when T_s can claim much new empirical support beyond that enjoyed by T_p.

Yet surely, you might think, high explanatory power is one of the things we aspire to in our theories about nature. Accordingly, loss of explanatory power must be grounds for withholding the claim of progress. There are two points to make in reply.

(a) Explanatory power is a very broad notion, referring to everything that a theory explains. It is thus entirely conceivable that T_s could have greater explanatory power than T_p even if T_p manages to explain some things not explained by T_s. The loss of a few instances need not mean a contraction of the overall explanatory domain.

(b) More importantly, and more radically, I hold that explanatory power is not an unqualified good, to be maximized at all costs. To see why, consider the fact that biblical literalism explains both the creation of the world and the origins of life. Modern science, at least until very recently, failed to explain either. That fact obviously need not preclude our judging that modern science represents an improvement on Old Testament cosmology. What enables us to make such judgments is the fact that *explanatory power per se is a virtue only when exhibited by theories which are otherwise equally well-tested or well-confirmed*. Between two equally well-tested theories, explanatory scope may well be an important desideratum (although I suspect that its importance is more pragmatic than epistemic). But explanatory range ceases to be relevant to a choice between theories which enjoy very different degrees of empirical support. Failure to accept this principle would have the wholly unacceptable consequence that any theory which managed to explain—in however ad hoc a fashion—some one off-beat feature of the world could always claim to be an "acceptable" theory until some rival came along which explained that very fact. In sum, generality of explanation for its own sake is not the *summum bonum* that hand-wringing discussions of loss of explanatory power might lead one to expect.

3. The third form of loss which Kuhn identifies with change of paradigm is what I call *interrogative loss*. Because it looms largest among the forms of loss in Kuhn's discussion, I shall deal with it in rather more detail than the other two. To explain what interrogative loss involves, it might be useful to rehearse some of the general features of Kuhn's model of scientific change. Recall that, for Kuhn, every paradigm consists of several distinct elements. One of the elements making up a paradigm is an inventory of empirical problems or questions that the advocates of that paradigm attach a high premium to solving. For obvious reasons, I call this list of prioritized questions about nature the interrogative agenda of a paradigm. Now, Kuhn makes several startling claims about the interrogative agenda associated with rival paradigms:

(a) that no two paradigm agendas fully overlap, viz., that rival paradigms always have differing views as to the important problems to be solved;[10]

(b) that paradigms will generally do a good job of solving the problems high on their own agenda but fail to solve some of the problems high on the agendas of rival paradigms;[11] and

(c) that, accordingly, the choice between rival paradigms can never be regarded as a progress since accepting one paradigm and rejecting another involves abandoning many of the questions and the solutions associated with the rejected paradigm.[12]

It is this alleged failure of later paradigms to solve all the problems which earlier paradigms indicate to be important which is, for Kuhn, the most serious block to scientific progress.

At first glance, this loss of interrogative or problem-solving scope might seem to be just explanatory loss in another guise. But it is not quite the same because, according to Kuhn, the losses in question here involve lost explanations or solutions for problems which earlier paradigms had regarded as absolutely central. He tells us, for instance, that the advocates of the phlogiston paradigm were very concerned to answer questions like: why are all the metals so similar in appearance? Their theories, moreover, provided answers to such questions. By contrast, the new chemistry of Lavoisier failed to acknowledge the importance of such problems, let alone to solve these problems. As Kuhn puts it:

> Lavoisier's chemical theory inhibited chemists from asking why the metals were so much alike, a question that phlogistic chemistry had both asked and answered. The transition to Lavoisier's paradigm had, like the transition to Newton's, meant a loss not only of a permissible question but of a perceived solution.[13]

I think Kuhn is right in suggesting that rival paradigms or research traditions come with associated interrogative priorities *and* that those priorities often differ from one scheme to another.[14] He may even be right (although I have some doubts on this score) that a paradigm characteristically will do a good job of solving the problems which it identifies as central and will fail at solving problems its rivals regard as central. But, in sharp contrast to Kuhn, I hold that these two facts (if facts they be) are of no epistemic significance and pose no threat to the claim that scientific change has been progressive.

Kuhn's central mistake here lies in his supposition that the ability of a theory or paradigm to solve the particular problems which its advocates regard as especially significant tells us something important about the reliability of that theory or paradigm. Indeed, I shall argue that—from an epistemological point of view—the ability of a paradigm to solve those problems which it specifically set itself to solve is of little moment. This is because the evidential credentials of a paradigm are typically established, not by asking whether the paradigm solves the problems it was designed to solve, but rather by asking quite the opposite question: does this paradigm lead to the solution of problems quite different from those envisaged by its founders?

I have already had occasion to note that there is a broad consensus among philosophers of science that a theory is most robustly tested by an examination of its ability to stand up to empirical tests, which involve the surprising predictions of a theory. Now it is almost in the nature of a case that the surprising predictions of a theory or paradigm will *not* figure on the interrogative agenda of those who developed the paradigm. Generally, the interrogative agenda will identify effects or situations which are already well established and for which one is seeking an explanation. Such phenomena, because already known and well established, will typically not count much towards our confidence in any theory which does solve them, especially not if it was specifically designed to solve them.

Consider, for instance, Kuhn's own example: the ability of phlogiston theory to explain why the metals have similar observable properties (for example, shininess). That fact about the metals was scarcely surprising in the late eighteenth century; indeed, chemists had remarked on it since the Middle Ages. If the phlogiston theory offers an explanation of the known facts of metallic similarity (which it does), that scarcely counts as strong confirmatory evidence for phlogiston theory. Why this matters is that Kuhn's analysis would have us suppose that it is an acute liability for Lavoisier's theory that it offers no explanation for the similarity of metals. But my view is that, if the explanation of the similarity of metals provides no strong support for phlogiston theory (as I have argued it does not), then we should not regard it as a major liability of Lavoisier's that it fails to account for the phenomenon.

What I am supposing here is that it is reasonable to expect progressive successor theories to be able to pass any robust tests which their predecessors passed; failure to meet this condition might well leave the issue of progress in limbo. But we should not hold it against a later theory if it fails to explain some phenomena solved by an earlier theory simply because the advocates of that earlier theory said those phenomena were important. What determines the epistemic importance of a piece of evidence has to do with issues of testing and surprise. The fact that I may want a hypothesis which solves a particular problem, p, is no reason whatever to suppose that—so long as my hypothesis solves p—it is thereby well tested or confirmed. Similarly, the fact that the advocates of one particular paradigm may attach a high premium to solving a particular problem cuts no epistemic ice whatever; quite possibly things are reversed so that we should epistemically discount the ability of a paradigm to grapple with the interrogatory agenda of those who propounded it. Because that is so, the inability of a successor paradigm to address, let alone to solve, all the problems to which its predecessors attached importance—and this is what the most significant cases of Kuhn loss amount to—does nothing to undermine the claim that the latter theory is better than the earlier. Scientific progress would be threatened only if we had no grounds for believing that later theories were no more dependable than earlier ones. But, as I have tried to show here, the presence of the loss of empirical consequences, or of explanatory or interrogative losses is not necessarily any indication that a later theory is less reliable than its predecessors. Lavoisier's theory was better confirmed than Priestley's and thereby represents progress over Priestley's, even though the later theory failed to address some of the problems which Priestley thought to be important.

*   *   *

Progress toward the goal of increasingly reliable theories is thus wholly compatible with all these forms of Kuhn loss. It is for such reasons that I reject the idea that Kuhn loss represents a refutation of the possibility of scientific progress.

Notes

1. As Kuhn summarized his own argument: "There are losses as well as gains in scientific revolutions and scientists tend to be particularly blind to the former" (Thomas Kuhn, *Structure of Scientific Revolutions* (Chicago: University of Chicago Press, 1970), p. 167).

2. The only form of progress which Kuhn and his followers acknowledge as uncontroversial is progress internal to a given paradigm.

3. This is part of the motivation for Imre Lakatos' notorious "rational reconstructions" of the historical record.

4. See especially my *Progress and Its Problems* (Berkeley: University of California Press, 1977); "A Problem-Solving Approach to Scientific Progress," in *Scientific Revolutions,* ed. by I. Hacking (Oxford: Oxford Readings in Philosophy Series, Oxford University Press, 1982), pp. 144–155; and "Progress or Rationality? The Prospects for Normative Naturalism," *American Philosophical Quarterly,* 24:19–33.

5. A weaker notion of progress would require only that the latest step in the sequence be closer to the goal state than the first step in the sequence. I shall stick with the stronger notion both for ease of exposition and because that appears to be the tougher one to defend against Kuhn's criticisms.

6. Witness debates between realists and nonrealists on this issue.

7. The distinction between the three forms of loss that I shall discuss here is my distinction rather than Kuhn's. However, I believe that Kuhn's discussions and examples of loss all fall under one of these heads.

8. As we shall see below, not all the supporting instances of a theory need be among its empirical consequences.

9. Indeed, if the T_p has been falsified, as is often the case when we are talking about scientific revolutions or theory changes, we manifestly do *not* want T_s to exhibit all the empirical consequences of T_p!

10. "To the extent . . . that two scientific schools disagree about what is a problem . . . they will inevitably talk through each other when debating the relative merits of their respective paradigms" (Kuhn, *Structure of Scientific Revolutions,* p. 109). Still later Kuhn writes, ". . . the proponents of competing paradigms will often disagree about the list of problems that any candidate for paradigm must solve" (Ibid., p. 148).

11. ". . . each paradigm will be shown to satisfy more or less the criteria [namely, the problems to be solved] that it dictates for itself and to fall short of a few of those dictated by its opponents" (Ibid., pp. 109–110).

12. ". . . since no paradigm ever solves all the problems it defines and since no two paradigms leave all the same problems unsolved, paradigm debate always involves the question: Which problems is it more significant to have solved?" (Ibid., p. 110).

13. Ibid., p. 148.

14. I have argued this case at some length in my *Progress and Its Problems.*

MARCELLO PERA

A DIALECTICAL VIEW OF SCIENTIFIC
RATIONALITY AND PROGRESS

Progress Thesis versus Variance Thesis: The Whig Solution

As regards scientific change, scientists faithfully subscribe to the view that our theories mark progress over our predecessors'. On the other hand, historians of science have long since espoused the view that epistemic goals and standards of evaluation of theories change. Let us call the former view the *progress thesis* and the latter view the *variance thesis*. As these theses seem to be supported by good reasons, philosophers of science, at least recently, seem to be willing to accept them both. But if we give credit to the scientists' evaluation and take the historians' assertion for granted, we run into philosophical trouble.

The variance thesis seems to be untenable in the face of the progress thesis. For, if standards change, our theories may turn out to be worse, not better, than our predecessors' when evaluated according to our predecessors' standards. On the other hand, in the face of the progress thesis, the variance thesis seems to be unacceptable. For, if our theories may be said to be better than our predecessors', then both our theories and our predecessors' theories must share the same goals and standards. It thus seems that we are faced with a dilemma whose horns are irreconcilable and we must embark either upon finding a new invariant method which satisfies the progress thesis better than the current ones, or upon replacing the idea of scientific progress with something different which is in closer agreement with the variance thesis than the ideas now on the market.

As both programs seem to be unpalatable, various attempts at passing between the horns of the dilemma and reaching a compromise between the progress and the variance theses have been made. The most frequent is perhaps the Whig solution, explicitly advocated by many scholars including Kuhn and Laudan.[1] It consists in maintaining the progress thesis and reinterpreting the variance thesis in the sense that current theories can be said to be better than those of our predecessors only from our vantage point or from the vantage point of the accidental winners. In spite of the fact that this attempt is now disputed by many historians, I have to declare my sympathy with it for several reasons. It does not commit us to what Dudley Shapere has called the "Platonic fallacy,"[2] that is, the view that there must be something immutable —a form, an essence, an idea, or, to put it in non-Platonic terms, the "cunning of Reason"—hidden behind the multifarious ways of doing scientific research. Moreover, the Whig solution does not require us to see things through God's eyes. As a consequence, it has another advantage. It forces us to conclude that progress judgments are our own— human, fallible, disputable as they may be—and not independent from concrete discussions in concrete historical situations.

But, like any other compromise, the Whig solution has some flaws. As it stands, it is faced with considerable objections. First, it is decidedly cynical, for, in its view, whoever happens to score a victory in a scientific controversy has, by this fact alone, the right to declare that he has made progress. Second, it is not realistic. There are many situations in which it is not difficult to find that the accidental winner of a dispute was wrong from the point of view of the subsequent development of science. Third, the Whig solution seems to be either verbal or arbitrary. Since science develops and is open to revision, we cannot know, at any instant, who the true winner is. Only if we assume the position of the last winner can we warrantedly declare that our victory is real progress; but if we project ourselves into that position, our projection is arbitrary and so will be our assessments of progress; if we do not, our evaluation of progress will amount to no more than mere verbal declarations of chance victory with no real grounds. Fourth, the Whig solution seems to be trivial, for any evaluation of progress, being advanced by the winners of a controversy, turns out to be true by definition. The problem whether science progresses would then be solved too much on the cheap. Finally, it seems that we cannot define progress merely in terms of victory, for, as Moore remarked about all attempts at defining "good" in factual terms, given any concrete example of victory, it still makes sense to ask: "Is this victory really progress?"

What seems to be detrimental to the Whig solution are some of the old questions with which Plato enjoyed embarrassing the Sophists. What has scoring a victory in a debate to do with showing that one view is better than another? What has persuasion to do with truth, rhetoric with science, psychology with logic? Cannot people be persuaded to accept even wrong ideas? Or, to reformulate Plato's question for our purpose: should we say that a theory T_2 is progresssive in relation to a theory T_2 because the supporters of T_2 scored a victory over the supporters of T_1, or should we say it the other way round, that is, that the supporters of T_2 scored a victory over the supporters of T_1 because T_2 is better than T_1?

One might object that these questions commit us to just that Platonic fallacy which the Whig solution aims at avoiding. But the questions as such are not involved in this fallacy, only Plato's answer to them is. And rejecting Plato's solution does not amount to rejecting the questions, too. The fact is that such questions are genuine and urgent for the Whig, too. For the Whig cannot realistically maintain that whoever happens to win a debate, however they may have scored their victory, has the right to declare that their own theory constitutes progress over that of their opponents. What the Whig wants to maintain, and must maintain if his or her view is to have an interesting philosophical sense, is that only one who scores an *honest victory* or a *non-Pyrrhic* victory has the right to make a declaration of progress. But, as it stands, the Whig solution to scientific progress has no way of distinguishing between a mere victory and an honest victory.

One might also object that what we are looking for, that is, an explication of the idea of an honest victory, inevitably leads us to deny the variance thesis. For an honest victory is a victory declared by an impartial, neutral arbiter, that is, by a set of firm standards of evaluation, and this contradicts the variance thesis. This objection is more serious. It faces those who want to maintain the variance thesis and the progress thesis as well with an intriguing problem: that of trying to define the idea of an honest victory *without* the impartial arbiter. This essay is devoted to such a problem.

I shall proceed along the following lines: I shall first attempt to show that the demand for an impartial arbiter cannot be satisfied; then I shall try to argue that, if no impartial arbiter can exist, this does not mean that the problems of rationality and progress cannot be solved in an objective way; finally, I shall suggest a dialectical view of scientific rationality and progress and examine a case study to illustrate it. In my view, dialectics replaces both methodology (be it Euclidean, sophisticated, and so forth); it fills in the holes and overcomes the limits of the former without reducing science to the individual and social ingredients of the latter. Thus dialectics intends to face in a new way what Kuhn considers "the greatest challenge" that now confronts both philosophers and historians of science, that is, putting together the "internal approach" and the "external approach."[3]

The Ghost of the Impartial Arbiter

First of all, who is an impartial arbiter? A judge in a court serves our purpose. We say he is impartial when he fulfills two conditions: (a) he is *impersonal*, that is, he interprets the laws without introducing his own wishes, whims, and preferences, but considers only the content of their concepts (the judge is objective); (b) he is *independent*, that is to say, he applies the laws without favoring one of the rival parties of the case he is examining (the judge is neutral). In matters of science, the role of judge is played according to a methodological code. This code is supposed to be impartial in the two senses mentioned above: (a) it is impersonal, for it provides scientists with rules containing objective concepts, which, as Laudan says, are "sufficiently determinate that one can show that many theories clearly fail to satisfy them. We need not supplement the shared content of these objective concepts with any private notions of our own in order to decide whether a theory satisfies them";[4] (b) it is independent, for, as Laudan also maintains, even if different theories or paradigms have their own methodologies and pursue their own values, "there are mechanisms for rationally resolving disagreements about methodological rules and cognitive values."[5] If such a methodological code exists, then an impartial arbiter delivering impartial epistemic verdicts also exists.

But does he? Notice that what is essential here is whether we can disentangle that "mixture of objective and subjective factors, or of shared and individual criteria" which, according to Kuhn, is involved in any interpretation and in any application of methodological standards of evaluation to concrete cases.[6] Laudan maintains that we can. As I have doubts about this crucial point, I shall examine his arguments by focusing on one of them in particular, the "problem-weighting argument."[7]

The typical situation here is as follows. Two scientists holding incompatible theories, T_1 and T_2, accept the rule that one theory is preferable to its rivals if it solves problems that are more important than those solved by the rivals, but disagree about the importance of the problems solved by their own theories; for example, one says that P_1 solved by T_1 is more important than P_2 solved by T_2. The job of the methodologist is to establish which is really the case; more precisely, as Laudan maintains, his job is to distinguish *pragmatic importance* from *epistemic importance* in order to "desubjectify the assignment of evidential significance by indicating the kinds of reasons that can legitimately be given for attaching a particular degree of epistemic importance to a confirming or refuting instance."[8]

Before examining whether the methodologist can attain this desubjectification, let us consider a juridical counterpart of this attempt. Two persons, a father F and a mother M lay the same claim of keeping their child C after divorce. Both accept the law according to which the custody of a child is to be granted to its mother unless she has committed certain deeds D_1, D_2, and so forth but disagree about a particular circumstance, for example F says that M committed D_1, while M denies it. The job of the judge is to make an impartial decision. Suppose he ascertains that M committed D_1—for example, she did not take good care of the child; then the judge can construe the following syllogism:

The custody of a child is to be granted to its father and not to its
mother if the mother committed certain deeds D_1, D_2, and so forth.
M committed D_1.
Hence C is to be granted to F and not to M.

In most cases the construal of such a syllogism is unproblematic. But
this is not necessarily the rule. Suppose the mother admits she committed D_1 but adduces she had a temporary mental crisis, or she lost her job
and had no money, or she had to leave the child for some time because
she had to attend to her old and sick parents. Our judge is now called
upon to find another law which takes the new circumstances adduced by
the mother into consideration. Will he manage to deliver his verdict
without, sooner or later, introducing private elements of his own?

Logicians of law agree that juridical codes do not satisfy any of the
standard properties of formal systems. In particular, they are never precise, because the relevant concepts may be interpreted and applied differently. Usually judges remedy this defect by resorting to jurisprudence, but since jurisprudence is hardly univocal, they have to decide
precisely which precedent serves their present purpose the best. Such a
decision cannot but be dictated by contingent, both collective and personal, factors, such as the culture, training, sensitivity, habits, moral
feelings, philosophical ideas, and so forth of the judges. Moreover,
juridical codes are never complete for they cannot discipline all the
(unpredictable) situations to which they are applicable or cease to be
applicable. Judges remedy this other defect by interpreting the laws as
implicitly containing such clauses as "except in cases beyond control,"
"except in extraordinary circumstances," and so forth, which it is at
their discretion to apply. Although this discretion is not arbitrary, it cannot but depend on the same contingent, collective and personal, factors.
Consider also that, even if juridical codes were precise and complete,
the blind application of a law is usually unjust *(summum jus, summa
iniura);* there is always a tension between justice, which commands generally and indifferently, and equity, which takes differences and specific
circumstances into consideration. And this tension, too, can be settled
only thanks to the personal discretion of the judge. We have therefore to
conclude that, in matters of law, decisions cannot be "desubjectified";
even if judges are independent in the sense specified by condition (b)
above, they cannot be impersonal in the sense of condition (a).

Let us now go back to our scientists. To settle their dispute as to
which theory is preferable, the methodologist consults one of the best
scientific codes on the market (say, Laudan's) and finds the rule that a
theory is preferable to its rivals if it solves problems that are more
important than those solved by its rivals. As the methodologist, like the
judge, aims at an impartial decision, he or she looks for the epistemic
sense of importance. Suppose that, following the code, he or she finds

the explication that a problem is epistemically important for a theory if it is solved by that theory while it is anomalous for its rivals.[9] Then, if he or she ascertains that a problem P_1 is solved by T_1 and anomalous for T_2, he or she can construe the following syllogism:

A theory is preferable to its rivals if it solves problems that are anomalous for its rivals;

T_1 solves P_1 which is anomalous for T_2.

Hence, T_1 is to be preferred to T_2.

Laudan maintains that in many cases syllogisms such as these are not problematic. This can be granted, but the moral Laudan draws from it, namely, that epistemic decisions and preference judgments stemming from such syllogisms are desubjectified, is disputable. To see this point, let us distinguish different kinds of cases.

The first kind of case—let us call them "extraordinary cases"—is that in which the relevant rules of decision are questioned. For example, one scientist advocates inductive method and an opponent defends the hypothetico-deductive method. Here the analogy with the judge does not hold good, because while the judge is always constrained by a code which is the same for everybody (the judge cannot be a legislator), the scientist may question the code's being in force and suggest a different one. Is there a desubjectified procedure for settling the dispute that arises in these cases? As we have seen, Laudan speaks of "mechanisms for rationally resolving disagreements." Consider one of them, reconciling theory and practice. Laudan quotes Lesage, who, attacked by inductivists for his adherence to the hypothetico-deductive method, counterattacked by invoking Newton, the great authority on such a method, with the reply that it is to hypotheses "without any element of [induction or] analogy that we . . . owe the great discovery of the three laws which govern the celestial bodies."[10] And one may remember that Darwin counterattacked a similar objection in the same way: "it has been said that I speak of natural selection as an active power of Deity; but who objects to an author speaking of the attraction of gravity as ruling the movements of the planets?"[11]

But what kind of mechanism of agreement is this? Certainly it is not an impartial, desubjectified arbiter. In the first place, it is not independent of the rival parties, because it is not an authority above them such that both recognize and have to submit to; rather it is a tool of persuasion that *one* party uses in order to convince the other. In the second place, it is not impersonal, because its persuasive efficacy depends on a conflict of personal skills, namely, the skill of one party to catch in the other's set of beliefs a thesis which is inconsistent with the one advocated by that party, and the skill of the other party to reject such an inconsistency or to find a remedy for it. Still this mechanism is an arbiter, but this arbiter lies in the *dispute itself,* and the dispute is not desubjectified.

On the contrary, the dispute is the place where all the different subjective factors openly play their role until they come (when they come) to a unity or agreement. The distinction between pragmatic and epistemic factors can be drawn by saying that epistemic factors are those subjective factors toward which the dispute converges and finally (though still provisionally) stops.

The second kind of case—we may call them "abnormal cases"—is that in which the relevant rules of decision are shared but either their interpretation or their application to the case in question turns out to be controversial. Suppose, for example, the supporter of T_2 admits that the empirical problem P_1 is solved by T_1 but objects it is solved by T_2 as well, though in a different way; or suppose it is admitted that P_1 is really anomalous for T_2 but that a conceptual problem P_2 exists which is anomalous for T_1.[12] A dispute then arises as to the *right* meaning of the term "solution" and as to the *fair* application of the rule that has this correct meaning—for example, as to whether solving a certain empirical problem is more important than solving a certain conceptual one.[13]

These cases are similar to many cases in which judges are involved. Judges, too, have the problem of deciding which is the right interpretation and the fair application of a law. How do they behave? As we have seen, they resort to jurisprudence, and when this is not univocal, they make their decision by using their own personal (though not arbitrary) discretion. Scientists do the same. When a dispute about the interpretation or application of a methodological rule is at stake, they go back to precedents, make analogies, stress similarities, underline differences, or simply decide to constitute a new precedent. All this activity involves a massive dose of personal ingredients, because one party must convince the rival and the community, and this, as we have seen, needs personal skills. Here, too, as above, the mechanism of agreement lies in the dispute; and here, too, the outcome of the dispute is the (temporary) convergence point at which all the personal factors that come out during it reach (if they do at all) unity. Desubjectification follows precisely from this process of unification, it is not the result of the application of a superior, epistemic mechanism.

The third kind of case—we may call them "normal cases"—is that in which neither the interpretation of the rules nor their application is being questioned because the relevant concepts of the rules are quite clear. As an example we may give a rule such as R^*: "Theories are to be rejected if they are inconsistent." Such cases look more favorable to the desubjectification thesis, for here the epistemic decisions and preference judgments seem to follow from the rules (and the factual premises) in a rather mechanical way. But this is misleading. For it does not prove that the concepts contained in such rules are, by their own content alone, so clear and unambiguous that scientists need not supplement them with private notions. Rather it proves that—thanks to that uniform learning and training process to which scientists are subjected during their apprenticeship and to which they are exposed during their ordinary practice—these private notions are so widely accepted, so deeply embedded in scientific culture and made so uniform, that, almost spontaneously, scientists arrive at the same conclusions when they interpret and apply the same rules. To go back to our example, suppose a scientist holding a theory T_1 reaches conclusion p and then conclusion -p. Does it follow automatically that, in the presence of R^*, T_1 is to be rejected? What can be said is that T_1 contains an apparent contradiction. Before any decision concerning T_1 can be taken, R^* is to be interpreted: does it refer to *apparent* or to *real* contradictions? Obviously, this question gives rise to discussion. Then, once R^* is interpreted, for example, in the sense that it refers to real contradictions, it must be applied: is T_1 really contradictory or is it only apparently contradictory? And this question, too, involves a discussion, a reasoning, sometimes a long dispute. It is true that often such disputes are easily solved or do not even arise, but this is no proof that the interpretation and application of the rules cannot be questioned. Not even when they look univocal do concepts speak by themselves. The old saying *"in claris non fit interpretatio"* does not mean that there are concepts that need no interpretative activity, but that in some cases this activity is minimal because it consists of attributing the most obvious, intuitive meaning tacitly accepted by the community of experts.

Granted, not all concepts are ambiguous or equally ambiguous. There are concepts that are univocal. But the univocity of a concept or law or rule is not a function of its verbal content alone but also and mainly of the uniformity of culture of the interpreters. It is thanks to the same juridical culture which they have learned that judges interpret and apply univocally (when they do) the law "All murderers are to be sentenced to death"; likewise, it is thanks to the same scientific culture which has taught them that scientists give the same interpretation and application (when they do) of the rule "All hypotheses falsified by severe tests are to be rejected." In their pretechnical, ordinary use, concepts like "falsification," "severe test," and so forth, are always subjective and rarely univocal; they become objective only when they are submitted to a process of verbalization, conceptualization, and indoctrination which, step by step, leaves out the individual differences and emphasizes what is considered to be essential. In this view, the difference between normal and abnormal cases (and, even more so, extraordinary cases) is a difference in degree. The latter immediately gives rise to a dispute, while in the former case the dispute is either absent, because it is replaced by the received culture, or ancient and forgotten, because it dates back to past times and is now settled. But in either case, desubjectification does not lie in some special, objective quality of the concept (or law or rule) but is the outcome of a process of homogenization of the personal ingredients of its interpreters.

The result of these considerations is that an impartial arbiter in the sense the methodologist aims at does not exist. Or, better, it exists but it is like a ghost, who is dumb unless one attributes intentions to it and transforms it into a real person who manifests opinions. Should we then conclude that our judgments of preference and progress are doomed to be pragmatic, subjective, whimsical, or a matter of taste? What we have just said suggests a negative answer and hints at a different solution. Let us see which one and why.

"Desubjectification" as "Inter-subjectification": The Way to Dialectics

Ghosts are born from fear. Thus if the idea of an impartial method is a ghost, it is to be expected that it, too, has the same origin. If my diagnosis is correct, such an idea is born from a typically philosophical fear which elsewhere I have called the "Cartesian Syndrome."[14]

Those who are affected by this syndrome subscribe, unconsciously or explicitly, to a dilemma: either scientific decisions are governed by impersonal, clear-cut rules, or science is irrational; or, to put it in different terms, either we have algorithms or we are left to judgments of taste. I suspect that Laudan, too, is affected by this syndrome. When he writes that "the *rational assignment* of any particular degree of probative significance to a problem must rest on one's being able to show that there are viable *methodological and epistemological grounds* for assigning that degree of importance rather than another,"[15] he seems to accept the view that the only alternatives to methodology are nonrational, nonobjective decisions. Hence his attempts at distinguishing between pragmatic importance and epistemic importance and his efforts to "desubjectify" the latter notion and expurgate it of the subjective connotations attached to the former. But as these attempts are doomed to failure, at least if our analysis is correct, we must look for a different way out. The only viable one seems to me to recover from the Cartesian syndrome and totally reject its dilemma.

Let us start by stating that "desubjectification" is an ambiguous concept. The term seems to cover at least three meanings. In the first sense, to desubjectify a notion or a decision is to *objectify* it, to make it absolute or independent of the subjects using that notion or making that decision. In the second sense, it means to *socialize* it, to render it dependent on external social factors. In the third sense, it means to *inter-subjectify* it, that is, to make its meaning univocal and its use uniform through a public interchange. Methodologists stick to the first sense. Countermethodologists, especially anarchists and the sociologists of science of the so-called "strong programme," accept the second. The third is still nobody's child, and we must try to see whether it is possible to find a good father for it.

For this purpose, let us go back again to our judge. We have seen that before delivering his verdict he had to take several preliminary decisions concerning the proper choice, the right interpretation and the fair application of the law. To this aim syllogism and deductive logic are not enough, for his problem now is not so much to draw conclusions from premises, as to discover the right premises. How does he find them? For example, how does he establish that the case which he is examining is the same as, or analogous to, or different from, other cases? With the help of certain general principles, he supplies himself with a stock of patterns of reasoning, such as *ex-analogia, a pari, a contrario, a majori ad minus, ab exemplo* arguments, and so forth, which may connect his present case to others. These patterns of reasoning do not belong to formal logic, for they are not formally conclusive; rather, they form the object of *juridical dialectics*. They are *rhetorical* not in the sense that they are verbal embellishments, but in the more important sense that they are forms of reasoning which aim at persuading and reaching, or reinforcing, a consensus on a thesis in conditions in which there are no more compelling arguments.

I maintain that a careful examination of the situations in which scientists take their epistemic decisions shows that the same holds true for them, too. For example, how can they argue that a certain theory is worth working on because it is simple, or promising, or consonant with certain ontological assumptions, or that one problem is more important than another, or that a test is really severe, or that a predicted fact is really novel, and so forth? There deduction and induction do not help them, the former because they cannot infer conclusions from premises when these are disputed, the latter because they cannot rely on empirical evidence. Thus they have no other way than to engage themselves in a dispute with their interlocutors and to resort to rhetorical arguments, that is, arguments that aim at persuading and convincing by offering good reasons for the views they hold.

Rhetorical arguments perform many functions in science. For example, they are resorted to in order to justify a starting point, to suggest a procedure, to recommend a line of inquiry, to criticize or discredit rival hypotheses, to reject objections to a procedure, a hypothesis, an experiment, to emphasize the importance of a prediction or explanation, to offer an explication of a concept, and so on. To take just two examples already mentioned, Lesage argued *ad hominem* against his critics in order to support the method of hypotheses and, through it, his own favorite theory. In the same way and for the same purpose, Darwin made use of an argument by retortion in order to discredit his rivals by mentioning a procedure they could not but consider favorably. It is useless to turn up our noses at these arguments or treat them as fallacious. More realistically, we have to consider that science, including science at its best, also relies on rhetorical arguments, and if science is indebted to them, so much the better for rhetorical arguments, not so much the worse for science.

Therefore, if we are not victims of the imperialism of deductive logic and the arrogance of methodology (which has always been the weapon of inductive logic), we must consider the possibility of adding to them what may be called *scientific dialectics,* or, perhaps more profitably, of making the former special cases of the latter. When this is done, desubjectification in the third sense is achieved. For, since scientific dialectics is the organon of persuasion of interlocutors and the solution of scientific controversies, it desubjectifies epistemic decisions not because it makes them descend from an impartial arbiter (the desubjectified code of methodologists), nor because it makes them depend on this or that external pressure (the social factors of sociologists), but because it makes them the outcome of a debate, of a public interchange of arguments and counterarguments where individualities are transcended, transformed and unified into a uniform, ideal body (the universal audience or scientific community).

But this is a project. To link it to the question of scientific rationality and progress requires that three main steps be taken.

In brief, the first step consists in defining the validity (or strength) of an argument so that it covers the whole variety of arguments, irrespective of their formal structure. Here we must consider that an argument is not a mere string of phrases in a language, but a fragment of a discourse aimed at convincing an interlocutor in a concrete situation of life. As validity or strength is to be distinguished from efficacy, conviction cannot be understood as a function of the style of arguing. On the other hand, as validity or strength is to be referred to a concrete situation of life, conviction must be made dependent not only on the structural, linguistic properties of the argument as such but also on the context in which it is put forward and the challenges it faces, more precisely on the *substantive factors* to which the interlocutors in the debate appeal— such as facts, accepted theories, values, common loci, assumptions, presumptions—and the *procedural factors* which govern the debate—such as the rules for the beginning, prosecution, and termination of the debate.[16] If we now consider that rational conviction (that is, conviction for the ideal body as distinct from psychological persuasion of an individual) can be said to be reached when the interlocutors, whatever efforts they continue to make, turn out to have no more counterarguments, we may propose the following explication:

(Val.)   A scientific argument is valid (strong) if there exists a strategy which, on the basis of a shared set of premises and the accepted substantive factors of scientific dialectics, leads the interlocutors to assent or silence or retreat.

The second step is to define a dialectical norm of rational preference. Here it is natural to link the preferability of a thesis to the kind of arguments supporting it, for in actual practice there seems to be no better way of establishing whether a thesis, for example, a theory, is rationally preferable to its rivals than examining the arguments with which it is defended. Thus we may use *(Val.)* and propose the following explication:

(Pref.)　　A theory T_1 is rationally preferable to a theory T_2 if T_1 is supported by arguments that are stronger than the arguments supporting T_2.

The third step leads us to the question of progress. The natural link here is between progress and preferability. This link may look disputable but, as a matter of fact, it is the same link that both realists and antirealists end up establishing. Realists aim at defining scientific progress in terms of approximation: T_1 is progressive in relation to T_2 if it is closer to the truth or reality. But, as the distance between T_1 (or T_2) and the truth or reality is not a question of observation and measurement like the distance between two points in space, the approximation relation cannot be proven apart from the merits of one theory (the supposed progressive one) as compared with the merits and demerits of the other (the putative regressive one), which, in their turn, cannot be evaluated except by considering the arguments that make the former preferable to the latter. On the other hand, antirealists, for example, the Whigs, define progress in terms of victory: T_1 is progressive in relation to T_2 if the supporters of T_1 scored a victory over the supporters of T_2. But, as we have seen, mere victory is not enough if it is not accompanied by good reasons, and good reasons cannot be but the strong arguments thanks to which the winning theory is considered to be preferable to its rival. We thus propose to make use of *(Pref.)* and propose the following explication:

(Progr.)　　A theory T_1 is progressive in relation to a theory T_2 if T_1 is preferable to T_2.

A synoptical look at our explications of rational preferability and progress may be useful for throwing light on the view suggested here and comparing it with other approaches.

The methodological approach makes rationality and progress dependent on certain properties of theories fixed by a rule; for example, a typical methodological rule of preference says: "T_2 is rationally preferable to, or progressive as compared to, T_1 if T_2 possesses properties x, y, and z," where x, y, and z, are variables to be replaced by constants indicating certain epistemic properties, such as "more testable," "more falsifiable," "tested more severely," "with wider scope," and so forth. On the other hand, the countermethodological approach makes rationality and progress dependent on judgments of taste and propaganda (anarchical mode) or on external factors (sociological mode), or it dismisses the problem completely (hermeneutical mode or mood). On the contrary, the dialectical approach links rationality and progress to the qualities of arguments supporting theories alone. As our *(Pres.)* shows, whatever properties two theories may happen to possess, one theory cannot be said to be preferable to its rival unless the supporters of the former use arguments that are stronger—in the sense specified by *(Val.)* —than those used by the supporters of the latter. The advantages of this view seem considerable.

Compared with methodology, dialectics is more *economical,* for it replaces a whole family of methodological rules by a simple norm of dialectical interchange, and more *liberal,* for it does not link rationality to a single set of desiderata but allows free competition between different values and desiderata.

Compared with Feyerabend's anarchism and his rule that "anything goes" (given that it is to be understood as a rule), dialectics is descriptively more *adequate,* for it makes rationality dependent on arguments and not on tricks or propaganda or the whims of authorities (which is really the case, given that, in actual practice, one theory may happen to be preferred to a rival theory even if it does not explain more facts or does not anticipate novel facts, and so forth, but it is never accepted if it is not supported by the strongest arguments actually advanced in the dispute).

Compared with Rorty's hermeneutics and his rule "respect good epistemic manners,"[17] dialectics is more *precise,* for the norms governing dialectical situations are not mere generic conversational constraints, but constraints stemming from specified substantive and procedural factors. Rorty's hermeneutics neglects the internal factors of scientific dialectics and possesses no tools for distinguishing good epistemic manners from bad. To give an example, Galileo may have tried to convince Bellarmino and his opponents in many ways, but if he succeeded, it is not because he "just lucked out,"[18] but because he was able to offer the strongest arguments at hand. Take away these arguments and hermeneutics will become a passe-partout, a master key.

Finally, compared with sociologism, dialectics is more *realistic,* for it does not dismiss external elements of pressure such as ideological interests, philosophical commitments, or religious dogmas but, by means of the dispute which compels these elements to pass through the filter of the factors of scientific dialectics, brings them inside science. Sociologism, too, bypasses the internal factors of scientific dialectics and links the products of science directly to its cultural environment. But this link turns out to be a short circuit. To give other examples, Victorian England may have influenced the origin, spread, and acceptance of Darwin's theory, and the Weimar republic may also have affected the quantum theory. But such influences were mediated by the filter of scientific dialectics. Take away this filter and the sociology of science will become a tool good for forcing any door. Since dialectics keeps this filter, it also places us in the best position to face Kuhn's "greatest challenge": once social elements are rectified by the factors of scientific dialectics, they are no longer external and separated from the internal.

The dialectical approach enables us to envisage an image of science which is less rigid than the methodological and less elastic than the countermethodological approach, but more realistic than them both. We are no longer forced to choose—to use Popperian metaphors— between a conceptual cathedral erected in World 3 and a psychological byproduct of World 2, nor—to use Feyerabend's metaphor—"to choose either a dragon or a pussy cat."[19] From the point of view of scientific dialectics, there is no need to change science "from a stern and demanding mistress into an attractive and yielding courtesan who tries to anticipate every wish of her lover."[20] The dilemma "either madonna or courtesan" is a typical product of a brothel culture that parallels the dilemma "either algorithm or judgment of taste," which is a typical product of a Cartesian culture. Those who are fond of women will readily admit that there is a middle way between mistresses and madonnas which it is worth going to hell for. Likewise, those who appreciate science will be forced to admit that there is a middle way between science as a cathedral and science as a tavern which makes it worthwhile doing our best for. The dialectical approach promises us that this middle way is attainable. But we still have to try it out.

Dialectics and Progress:
Galileo and Scheiner on Sunspots

As a case study, let us consider the dispute between Galileo and Father Scheiner about sunspots. Galileo maintained that sunspots are clouds located on the body of the sun whereas Scheiner maintained that they are stars not far from the body of the sun. The dispute could not be more radical, because what is at stake is the central assumption of the incorruptibility of the heavens and, with it, Aristotelian cosmology itself. If sunspots are clouds changing shape and dimension and revolving around the sun, how is it possible not to conclude that the heavens are alterable and that other bodies, too, may revolve in the same way? This dispute is therefore a peripheral but essential part of the main controversy between geocentrism and heliocentrism. As Shea writes, for Scheiner, "spots *had to be* stars;"[21] in the same way, we may argue that for Galileo spots had to be clouds or, in any case, alterable bodies.

Faced with our dispute, a methodologist would say there exists an impartial arbiter who can establish which theory is preferable. Thus he would put forward a methodological rule and decide which theory satisfies it best; for example, one of the following rules:

M_1 T_2 progresses in relation to T_1 if T_2 explains all the facts of T_1 and others as well (Popper's rule);

M_2 T_2 progresses in relation to T_1 if T_2 successfully anticipates novel facts (Lakatos' rule);

M_3 T_2 progresses in relation to T_1 if T_2 solves more problems than T_1 (Laudan's rule).

For his part, a countermethodologist discouraged by the failure of the impartial arbiter but still affected by the Cartesian syndrome would say either that Galileo's theory marked progress in relation to Scheiner's because Galileo won the controversy thanks to "propaganda," "psychological tricks," "irrational means," or "means other than arguments,"[22] or that Galileo's theory marked progress over Scheiner's just because he happened to win the controversy and therefore "the question of whether he was 'rational' is out of place."[23]

The dialectical approach follows different lines. It agrees with the countermethodologist's view that such rules as M_1-M_3 are not sufficient by themselves to settle the controversy, but it neither concedes that the only alternative to the dictatorship of rules is propaganda nor dismisses the problem of rationality. Putting the emphasis on the interchange of arguments and counterarguments advanced in the dispute, he would examine the rival theories in the light of the dialectical norms *(Pres.)* and *(Progr.)*. Let us see how this approach works in our case and why.

We have said that when methodological rules are not shared or when they are shared but interpreted and applied differently, scientists have no other way of expressing preference judgments and taking epistemic decisions except to engage themselves in a dispute and try to settle it with an interchange of arguments and counterarguments, including rhetorical ones. This is the case with Galileo and Scheiner.

As Scheiner was an Aristotelian, some of his rules are different from Galileo's. On the other hand, Scheiner was also a scientist in the modern sense and certainly shared some rules with Galileo.[24] If we suppose, as seems to be the case, that both would accept M_3, it becomes immediately obvious that they would give it different meanings. For Galileo "more problems" means "more *empirical* problems"; for Scheiner "more problems" means "more empirical *and conceptual* problems," with special reference to his conceptual problem of not violating the assumption of the incorruptibility of the heavens. M_3, by itself, is ambiguous; nor would a further explication of M_3 explicitly mentioning conceptual problems be better, for what is at stake is precisely whether a certain conceptual problem (Scheiner's) is a real problem. For lack of more precise rules, Scheiner and Galileo had therefore to engage in a dispute and to prove through it the worth of their opposite views. According to our dialectical approach, the outcome of this dispute is what would decide which theory is preferable and progressive. Let us see how things went.

Let A, B, C . . . and r_1, r_2, r_3 . . . stand, respectively, for Scheiner's theses and reasons, as he puts them forward in his *Tres epistulae de maculis solaribus,* written to Mark Welser (1612), and let O_1, O_2, O_3 . . . stand for the observational reports Galileo adduces in his *First Letter on Sunspots* (4 May 1612). Then, to help the reader and make a long story shorter, the dialectical interchange between Scheiner and Galileo can be reconstructed as in Table 1. The Table makes the following three points clear:

Table 1. Dialectical Interchange between Scheiner and Galileo

Scheiner	Galileo
(1) A. Sunspots are real for they depend neither on defects of our eyes nor on the telescope nor on air.	(1) A. Conceded.
(2) B. Sunspots change position.	(2) B. Conceded.
(3) C. Sunspots are not in the air, because: (a) r_1: they rise and set; (b) r_2: they lack parallaxis; (c) r_3: they have their own motion beneath the sun; (d) r_4: the very same phenomena can be seen even through the clouds.	(3) C. Conceded.
(4) D. Spots are not on the surface of the sun, because: (a) r_5: this is unseemly and improbable, for the sun is a most lucid body; (b) r_6: they should return to the same place in fifteen days.	(4) D. Denied, because: (a) r_5 is a *petitio principii;* (b) r_6 presupposes that sunspots are permanent, which contradicts 0_1 (= some of them disappear).
(5) E. Spots are not in the orb of the Moon (or Venus or Mercury), because: (a) r_7: they lack parallaxis; (b) r_8: they have different motions; (c) r_9: they should be seen in the opposite position at night.	(5) E. Denied, because: (a) r_7, r_8, and r_9 presuppose Ptolemy's theory, which has already been rejected by admitting that Venus revolves around the sun; (b) r_8 contradicts r_{10}.
(6) F. Spots are in the orb of the sun but not close to it, because: (a) r_{10}: they move independently; (b) r_{11}: they become smaller close to the edge of the sun;	(6) F. Denied, because: (a) r_{10} contradicts r_8; (b) r_{11} seems to suggest (6), but this is doubtful

Table 1. Continued

Scheiner	Galileo
	because of O_2 (= spots become smaller not in the part turned toward the center of the sun but in the opposite part);
(c) r_{12}: they aggregate close to the edge of the sun, whereas they divide in the middle of the sun;	(c) r_{12} is doubtful because of O_3 (= spots aggregate and divide even in the center of the sun);
(d) r_{13}: they move faster in the middle of the sun than at the edge.	(d) r_{13} suggests F' rather than F because of O_4 (= the difference in velocity of the spots is not imperceptible as it would be if they moved in separate circles from the sun);
	(e) Scheiner contradicts himself for he draws from r_6 the conclusion that spots are far from the body of the sun, whereas r_{11}, r_{12}, and r_{13} imply that they are close to it.
(7) G. Sunspots are stars, because:	(7) G. Denied, because:
(a) r_{14}: they are not clouds or comets: who would ever place them in the sun?	(a) r_{14} is a *petitio principii;*
(b) r_{15}: they are either solid and opaque bodies and then they are stars, or they are denser parts of the sky and then they are stars.	(b) r_{15} is a false dilemma.
	(8) G'. Sunspots are probably clouds because of O_5 (= both of them share six observational properties).

First, to face Scheiner's theses, Galileo uses a complex argumentative strategy. He adduces facts contrary to the ones admitted by his interlocutor (O_2 and O_3), interprets the same facts differently (O_5), and adds new facts (O_5). By playing on these facts and the reasons accepted by his interlocutor, he makes use of different kinds of arguments with the view either to denying the interlocutor's conclusions or to reaching a different conclusion. In particular, Galileo makes use of *modus tollens* (4.b), analogy (8), and *ad hominem* arguments (5.a, 5.b, 6.a, 6.e). Moreover, Galileo charges his interlocutor with committing fallacies (4.a: *petitio principii;* 7.b: false dilemma).

Second, some of Galileo's rhetorical arguments are strong, such as his *ad hominem* arguments, for they show that some of Scheiner's theses are contrary to facts *he himself* concedes during the discussion or to other theses *he* has already granted.

Third, some of Galileo's arguments are rather weak. Consider Scheiner's arguments 4.a and 7.a: "Who would ever place clouds around the sun?" Even though the question may seem ridiculous, it is no more ridiculous than the question "Who would ever place positive electrons around the atomic nucleus?" before the discovery of antiparticles. The fact is that behind Scheiner's question there is the central assumption of the incorruptibility of the heavens. Thus when Galileo says that arguments such as 7.a are "ineffective,"[25] he is both right and wrong. He is *wrong,* if he considers the question from his interlocutor's point of view; he is *right,* if he considers it from his own standpoint. Thus his counterargument 7.a is weak; it is not enough to shift the consensus from Scheiner's theory to Galileo's.

There is a reason for this weakness. An assumption is the protected hard core of a theory or program. What is needed to make it collapse is a complex encircling strategy. One has to behave like a general in a battle; first he will isolate the enemy's lines of defense, for example, by detaching the assumption from the theories it is connected to; then he will weaken these defenses, for example, by showing that the explanatory theories stemming from, or dependent on, the assumption raise considerable empirical problems or are contradictory or are inconsistent with other well-accepted empirical theories; finally, he will concentrate his attack on the assumption itself until it collapses.

Galileo was an excellent strategist and in his *Second Letter on Sunspots* (14 August 1612) and in his *Third Letter* (1 December 1612) he made precisely these moves. For example, in the *Second Letter* he tried to show that the Scheiner thesis F (that sunspots are placed in the orb of the sun but not close to it) raises "manifest objections and contradictions,"[26] while his own thesis F′ (that spots are situated very close to the body of the sun) "saves all the phenomena without any inconvenience and difficulty" *(ibid.).* His main argument for F′ is a *geometrical demonstration* based on new observational facts, while his argument against F is a *deductive proof* based on *modus tollens.* Galileo argues that these facts can be explained by F only if we add to it an auxiliary hypothesis H according to which sunspots are situated "on a little sphere somewhere between us and the sun, so that our eyes were in line with its center and the center of the sun, this sphere being equal in diameter to the sun."[27] But H turns out to be untenable for it faces the "insuperable difficulty that we should unavoidably see the spots moving both ways under the solar disk, which does not happen."[28] In the *Third Letter,* Galileo attacks G and defends G′ with yet another argument. By stressing that spots have nine observational properties different from those of the stars while they share six properties with clouds, he concludes with an analogy to the effect that sunspots are clouds.

At this point, once the explanatory hypotheses have been isolated and doubts have been cast upon them, Galileo attacks the central assumption. In his *Third Letter* he writes that "when trying to defend the inalterability of the heavens, we must not forget the perils to which other positions just as essential to the Peripatetic philosophy may be exposed."[29] And, in a fragment handwritten in the margin of the printed text, more explicitly he writes:

> Peripatetics are like weak defendants of a fortress who, seeing it attacked on one side, rush there all together, without being anxious to defend the other sides to which the enemy, more numerous and seeing them exposed, turn. Thus Peripatetics, in order to find a remedy for the peril of the alterability of the heavens, run to its defense by saying spots are stars; and by so doing leave a hundred entries to the enemy's attacks, for they no longer save the number seven of the planets, nor their revolution around the earth, nor the regularity of their movements, etc.[30]

This is an *ad hominem* argument, for Galileo does not directly prove that the assumption of the inalterability of the heavens is false. He only shows that if his interlocutor sticks to this assumption he ends up by maintaining a set of inconsistent beliefs. Is this a decisive blow? Certainly not, for this assumption does not logically imply this set of beliefs, so that Scheiner can retrieve the latter (or at least some part of it) without feeling forced to abandon the former. The blow he strikes, however, is a hefty one, for the beliefs Scheiner is forced to retrieve lend support and substance to his assumption and are an essential part of his own cosmology; and if this support is missing, the whole building is in danger of collapsing. How is it possible to maintain an assumption when the theses in which it shows itself at its best collapse one after another?

Let us go back to our problem of progress and conclude. It is true that Galileo "converted" many people. But this conversion, if we insist on sticking to this improper term, came about neither because Galileo made use of tricks nor because he "just lucked out," but because he put forward some strong arguments or, in any case, arguments stronger than his interlocutors'. It is also true that, by so doing, Galileo introduced a new "grid" of rationality, but the question as to whether he was right or wrong and did or did not mark progress is *not* out of place. That question can be solved by examining how strong Galileo's arguments were in the dispute and how weak Scheiner's counterarguments proved to be. There it is a *non sequitur* to conclude that, if clear-cut or well-determined methodological rules are lacking, the only alternative is to resort to external factors or to dismiss the problem itself, just as it is a *non sequitur* to conclude that where there are no infallible courts people take justice into their own hands, each in his own way. In science, at least, doing justice means putting forward good arguments.

Concluding Remarks and New Vistas

Aiming at rescuing the Whig solution to the problem of scientific progress, this essay proposes to define such expressions as "T_2 marks progress with respect to T_1," in terms of "The supporters of T_2 scored an honest victory over the supporters of T_1," and tried to define the idea of an "honest victory without an impartial arbiter." The approach we have suggested seems to be promising. Scientific dialectics is not an impartial arbiter because it is not desubjectified in the two senses which correspond to the two horns of what we have called the "Cartesian dilemma," that is, because it does not make epistemic decisions dependent on merely consulting a code, and because it does not make them dependent on external factors transcending the subjects. Scientific dialectics is neither a clear algorithm nor a loaded game; it does not place us under the supervision of God's eye, as methodology still aims at doing, but it does not leave us at the mercy of our personal tastes and whims, as countermethodology suggests we actually are. For scientific dialectics is still an arbiter: it makes epistemic decisions desubjectified in a third, more realistic sense, that is, it makes them public and induces a consensus about them through argumentation.

From the standpoint of scientific dialectics, the standard methodological rules continue to play a role but only if their interpretation and application are subordinated to the outcome of a dialectical interchange; in the same way, personal, social, and pragmatic factors come into epistemic decisions themselves but only if their presence is mediated through the filter of argumentation. Thanks to dialectics we are situated precisely where we are and from where there is no hope of getting away: not in an aseptic World 3 or in an infected World 2, but in a human context of interpersonal relations. We have no other stage than this and no other way of acting our part than trying to convince our audience through argumentation. As we have no bootstrap procedure at our disposal but we are fully entangled in our human context, we can only start from a common basis and go on to play on certain of our interlocutors' convictions in order to modify, or reinforce, or weaken others. What makes our enterprise possible is that we are not starting from scratch. Dialectics starts from a framework, a tradition, a system of beliefs, techniques, practices, ways of arguing. And the firmer the scientific framework, the more effective the scientific dialectics.

If we take this approach several questions arise. I mention only one of them. In order to give a more realistic picture of scientific rationality and cognate notions, scientific dialectics sets itself against methodology and countermethodology (be it anarchical, sociological, or hermeneutical). As we have seen, it defines these notions in terms of the validity or strength of the arguments which are put forward by the interlocutors in a dispute. One might object that if our explication of this validity *(Val.)*

or a similar one works out, then it would amount to a rule of method and therefore dialectics would not differ from methodology. I do not think this objection is tenable. Granted, dialectics is an organon. But, unlike formal logic and methodology, it is not a universal and impersonal logic; it is a local and material logic whose verdicts are delivered on the basis of historically determined substantive factors. As a consequence, dialectics depends on time and considers science as a cultural, historical enterprise; logic and methodology are a-temporal and look at science as a fixed form. Dialectics considers the interlocutors; logic and methodology command impersonally. Just because it aims at convincing an audience, dialectics takes into consideration all kinds of arguments; logic and methodology consider only deductive and inductive arguments. Finally, dialectics is open to revision; methodology, when properly applied, is infallible. Is there a better way of recovering from the Cartesian syndrome without catching the opposite, irrationalistic disease?

Notes

I am very grateful to Aristides Baltas, Adolf Grünbaum, Lorenz Krüger, Larry and Rachel Laudan, Thomas Nickes, and Ilkka Niiniluoto for their criticism, suggestions, and comments on an earlier version of this essay. The fact that I am pleading the role of rhetoric in science does not prevent me from thanking them in a nonrhetorical way. I know that rhetoric is so tricky a game that denying its presence may look like the most subtle way of making its weight felt, but I am confident that these friends, and the readers, too, will appreciate my sincere efforts to cope with their welcome objections.

1. Thomas Kuhn, *The Structure of Scientific Revolutions* (Chicago: University of Chicago Press, 1962), p. 166; and Larry Laudan, *Science and Values* (Berkeley: University of California Press, 1984), pp. 64–66.

2. Dudley Shapere, *Reason and the Search for Knowledge* (Dordrecht: D. Reidel, 1984), pp. 250 ff.

3. Thomas Kuhn, *The Essential Tension* (Chicago: University of Chicago Press, 1977), p. 110.

4. Laudan, *Science and Values,* p. 92.

5. Ibid., p. 96.

6. Kuhn, *The Essential Tension,* p. 325.

7. Laudan, *Science and Values,* pp. 96–102.

8. Ibid., p. 98.

9. Ibid., p. 33

10. G. Lesage, "Premier Mémoire sur la Méthode d'Hypothèse" (1804), quoted in Laudan, *Science and Values,* p. 59.

11. C. Darwin, *The Origin of Species* (London: Everyman's Library, 1972), p. 81. See also the following reply: "who ever objected to chemists speaking of

the elective affinities of the various elements?" (ibid.; both passages were added to the sixth edition of the *Origin of Species*).

12. For the useful distinction between empirical and conceptual problems, both internal and external, see Laudan, *Science and Values*.

13. The history of science provides us with many disputes such as these. For example: in the Copernicus-Ptolemy controversy, is it more important to solve the internal conceptual problem of the "monstrousness" of which the Copernicans accused the Ptolemaics, or the empirical problem of Venus' phases, which the Ptolemaics had the right to consider anomalous for the Copernicans? In the Darwinian dispute, is it more important to solve the internal conceptual problem of the logical inconsistency, which was a flaw of Darwin's later version of the theory of natural selection stemming from his concessions to his critics, or to solve the empirical problem of the colligation of a large class of facts under a single explanation, which was one of the merits Darwin attributed to his own theory? In the controversy opposing Einstein and his Copenhagen rivals, is it more important to solve the external conceptual problem of the completeness of the quantum description of reality which was vital for the former, or the conceptual external problem of the accuracy of predictions and descriptions of phenomena which was essential for the latter?

14. M. Pera, "From Methodology to Dialectics: A Post-Cartesian Approach to Scientific Rationality," in *PSA 1986*, ed. by A. Fine and P. Machamer (East Lansing: Philosophy of Science Association, 1987), vol. 2, pp. 359–374; and "Breaking the Link Between Methodology and Rationality: A Plea for Rhetoric in Scientific Inquiry," in *Theory and Experiment: Recent Insights and New Perspectives On Their Relation*, ed. by D. Batens and J. P. van Bendegem (Dordrecht: D. Reidel, 1988).

15. Laudan, *Science and Values*, p. 99.

16. I have laid down an (incomplete) list of the substantive and procedural factors of scientific dialectics in my "From Methodology to Dialectics."

17. Richard Rorty, *Consequences of Pragmatism* (Brighton: Harvester Press, 1982), p. 195.

18. Ibid., p. 193.

19. Paul Feyerabend, *Against Method* (London: New Left Books, 1975), vol. 2, p. 161.

20. Ibid.

21. W. Shea, *Galileo's Intellectual Revolution* (London: Macmillan Press, 1972), p. 51.

22. Feyerabend, *Against Method*, pp. 81, 153–154.

23. Richard Rorty, *Philosophy and the Mirror of Nature* (Oxford: Basil Blackwell, 1980), p. 331.

24. Galileo says that Scheiner is "a free man and not a servile mind . . . capable of understanding true doctrines" (Galileo Galilei, "Letters on Sunspots," in *Discoveries and Opinions of Galileo*, ed. by S. Drake (Garden City, New York: Doubleday Anchor Books, 1957), p. 96).

25. Galileo, "Letters on Sunspots," p. 99.

26. Galileo Galilei, *Istoria e dimostrazioni intorno alle macchie solari e loro accidenti,* in *Le opere di Galileo Galilei,* ed. by A. Favaro (Florence: Barbèra, 1964–1966), 20 vols., vol. 5, p. 118.

27. Galileo, "Letters on Sunspots," p. 111.

28. Ibid.

29. Ibid., p. 141.

30. Galileo, *Istoria,* p. 232.

ILKKA NIINILUOTO

SCIENTIFIC PROGRESS RECONSIDERED

Philosophy of Science in Progress

Contemporary philosophy of science may seem, both to a casual observer and to an active participant, to be a heterogeneous mess, a wild jungle with various plants sprawling around without any discernible pattern or order. While this impression is not entirely unjustified, it is, however, on the whole misleading.

In spite of diversity and disagreement, philosophy of science is a rapidly advancing field which makes progress in several different branches at the same time.[1] These branches correspond to various "methodological research programmes"[2] which attempt to develop and to refine "theories" about the activities and achievements of science. The contributions of such programs to our understanding of the nature of science can be appreciated only by making retrospective surveys of their development and critical analyses of their current claims.

The years around 1960 are often thought to constitute a decisive turning point in the philosophy of science. During the 1950s, the heirs of the earlier logical positivism—Rudolf Carnap, Hans Reichenbach, Carl G. Hempel, Alfred Tarski, Nelson Goodman, Ernest Nagel, Richard Braithwaite, and their students—had developed an admirably precise and comprehensive account of scientific theories (as partially interpreted sets of sentences), scientific explanations (as deductive-nomological arguments), and scientific inference (as the probabilistic or inductive justification of scientific hypotheses by observational evidence). For this liberal empiricist "Received View,"[3] the main virtues of good science were truth (Tarski), confirmation (Carnap), systematic power (Hempel), and simplicity (Goodman).[4]

Karl Popper's "critical rationalism" emphasized falsification instead of justification, boldness and information content instead of high probability. His attack against Carnap's inductive logic culminated in the publication of *The Logic of Scientific Discovery* (1959), and in his 1960 definition of "verisimilitude" or "truthlikeness." This concept was intended to make it meaningful to assert that one false theory may be "closer to the truth" than another. It also gives us, Popper further argued in his *Conjectures and Refutations* (1963), a good reason to support a realist interpretation of theoretical statements in science: scientific theories are not only tools for making observable predictions, as the instrumentalists claim, but progressive attempts to give more and more truthlike descriptions of reality. Besides Popper, other variants of scientific realism were developed in the 1960s by Wilfrid Sellars, Jack Smart, Mario Bunge, and Hilary Putnam.

Scientific change and the growth of knowledge became hot issues around 1960 through the work of N. R. Hanson on scientific discovery, Thomas Kuhn on normal science and scientific revolutions, Popper and Paul Feyerabend on permanent revolutions, Kuhn and Feyerabend on the incommensurability of rival theories, Stephen Toulmin on the evolution of concepts and theories, and Imre Lakatos on mathematical discovery and scientific research programs. The Popper-Kuhn controversy culminated in the 1965 London Colloquium, which eventually resulted in the book *Criticism and the Growth of Knowledge* (1970), edited by I. Lakatos and A. Musgrave.[5]

While Popper wished to retain a conjectural conception of knowledge with his concepts of corroboration and verisimilitude, Kuhn's *The Structure of Scientific Revolutions* (1962) proposed that the term 'truth' should not enter the analysis of scientific progress. For Kuhn (and for critical realists like Popper), progress does not consist in the accumulation of truths. But unlike Popper, Kuhn recommended that we have "to relinquish the notion . . . that changes of paradigm carry scientists and those who learn from them closer and closer to the truth."[6] For normal science, "solving the problems or puzzles that its paradigms define" must "inevitably be progress."[7] Problem-solving is also the key to progress through revolutions.[8]

In later discussions, Kuhn's views on meaning variance and scientific values turned out to be less radical than some of his followers and opponents had assumed. In particular, he suggested that even in the case of revolutions there is a shared basis of criteria for evaluating rival theories: accuracy, consistency, scope, simplicity, and fruitfulness.[9]

Still, Kuhn's controversy with scientific realism created a highly stimulating problem situation for philosophers. His work was also very influential in another sense: many philosophers of science turned away from the formal and prescriptive accounts of science by the logical empiricists, and directed their attention—in close cooperation with the historians and sociologists of science—to descriptive studies on the actual knowledge production within scientific communities.

New Programs in the Mid-Seventies

Almost ten years ago I edited for the journal *Synthese* (vol. 45, no. 3, 1980) a special issue on "Theories of Scientific Progress." I was confident that the clarification of the concept of progress in science would be an urgent task for philosophers independently of the school that they represent.

Looking back now to the 1980s, I can see that my confidence was not unwarranted. But it also seems fair to say that no important *new* programs are clearly visible in this decade. Instead, the eighties appear to be a period of intensive elaboration of views and ideas which were originated in the mid-seventies, more precisely during the years 1973–1978. The most important of these programs (with examples of their supporters) are summarized in Figure 1.

Both parties of the Popper-Kuhn controversy agreed that the days of *naive realism* are over: science does not typically progress through the accumulation of certified truths, as classical forms of rationalism and empiricism had claimed.[10] *Critical realism* can be viewed as an attempt to find a *via media* between naive realism and *skepticism*. A sophisticated version of such critical realism was developed, already at the end of the nineteenth century, by Charles S. Peirce. His dynamic and fallibilist epistemology admits that we can never be certain that truth has been reached, but still truth about reality is the ultimate limit toward which the opinion of the scientific community is "destined" (with probability one) to "gravitate."

In an important essay in 1973, Larry Laudan showed that critical realism has an interesting prehistory from the seventeenth century, but he also accused Peirce for the "trivialization of the self-corrective thesis."[11] In the same year, David Miller and Pavel Tichý showed that Popper's definition of verisimilitude is not applicable to the comparison of false theories. Some of Popper's followers regarded this damaging result as a reason for giving up the concept of truthlikeness.[12] For example, in *Science and Skepticism* (1984), John Watkins attempts to analyze scientific change in terms of "possible truth" and "information content."[13]

Another reaction was to accept the challenge of developing a logically satisfactory and methodologically relevant concept of truthlikeness. A program for defining verisimilitude, by supplying a concept of "similarity" or "likeness" that was missing in Popper's attempt, was started in 1974 by Pavel Tichý and Risto Hilpinen, soon followed by Ilkka Niiniluoto and Graham Oddie. The results of active research during the decade 1975–1985 are summarized in Oddie's *Likeness to Truth*[14] and Niiniluoto's *Truthlikeness*.[15]

In 1977, I suggested that the concept of progress in science can be defined in a precise way by using my measure for the "degree of

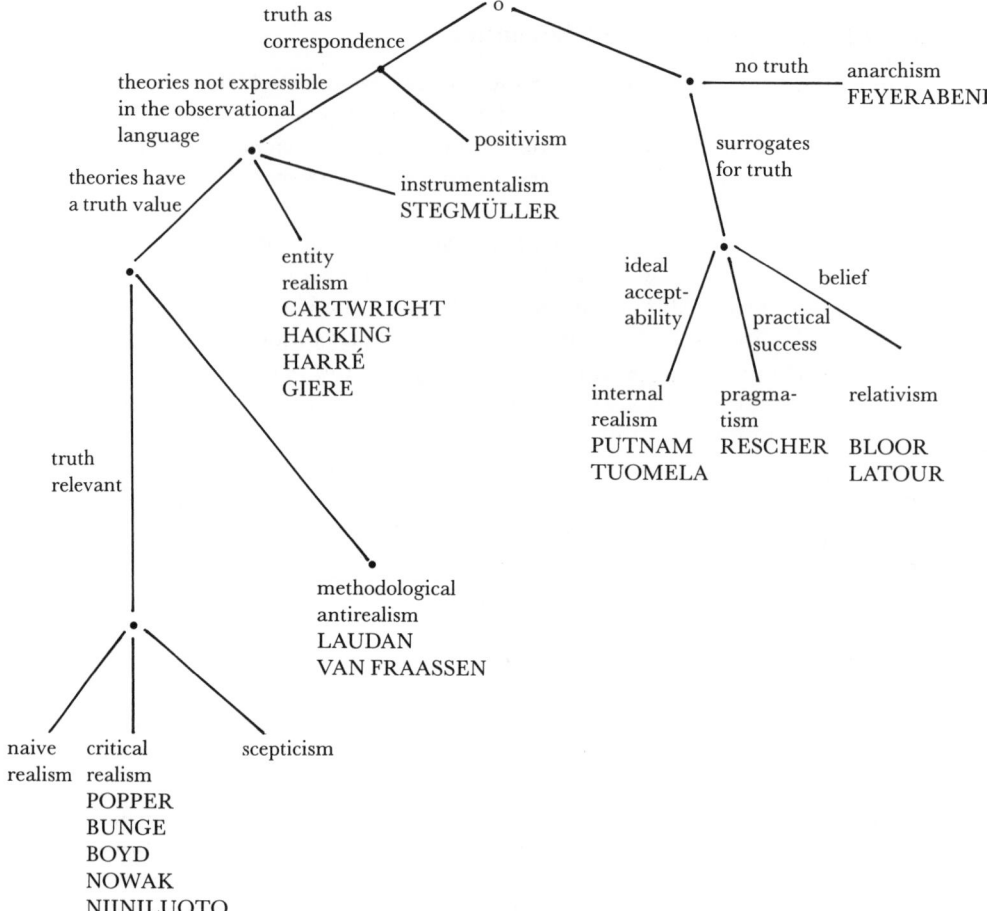

truth as correspondence

theories not expressible in the observational language

theories have a truth value

positivism

instrumentalism
STEGMÜLLER

entity
realism
CARTWRIGHT
HACKING
HARRÉ
GIERE

no truth anarchism
FEYERABEND

surrogates for truth

ideal
accept-
ability

belief

practical
success

internal
realism
PUTNAM
TUOMELA

pragma-
tism
RESCHER

relativism

BLOOR
LATOUR

truth
relevant

methodological
antirealism
LAUDAN
VAN FRAASSEN

naive   critical
realism   realism
          POPPER
          BUNGE
          BOYD
          NOWAK
          NIINILUOTO

scepticism

Figure 1. In an important essay in 1973, Larry Laudan showed that critical realism has an interesting prehistory from the seventeenth century, but also accused Peirce for the "trivialization of the self-corrective thesis" (Laudan, 1973). In the same year, David Miller and Pavel Tichý showed that Popper's definition of verisimilitude is not applicable to the comparison of false theories. Some of Popper's followers regarded this damaging result as a reason for giving up the concept of truthlikeness. For example, in *Science and Scepticism* (1984), John Watkins attempts to analyze scientific change in terms of "possible truth" and "information content."

truthlikeness" of a theory.[16] In my *Is Science Progressive?*[17] this "realist view of progress" is expressed with the definition: science makes progress insofar as it gains highly truthlike information about reality. I also argue that it is possible to make rational assessments or estimates of cognitive progress, if (*pace* Popper) the use of inductive or epistemic probabilities is allowed. Further, the best explanation for the practical success of science is the assumption that scientific theories in fact are sufficiently similar to the truth.

In the 1983 Salzburg Congress I argued that the concept of truthlikeness is applicable also to idealizational theories.[18] Thereby the verisimilitude program was brought together with the Poznan School, which has discussed the "concretization" of idealizational laws in the spirit of critical realism.[19]

The importance of idealizations, especially in the abstract theories of mathematical physics, was the prime motivation for classical *instrumentalism,* as developed by Pierre Duhem and Henri Poincaré in the first decade of the twentieth century. They claimed that, unlike observational statements, no theoretical statements in science have a truth value. During the eighties, this problem stimulated a "half realist" position which accepts the existence of causally interactive theoretical entities (thus, theoretical existential statements have a truth value), but denies a truth value from theoretical laws. Representatives of this *entity realism* include Cartwright,[20] Hacking,[21] and Giere.[22] This program has not yet developed a clear concept of scientific progress, however.

Instrumentalism in a modern form is represented by the "structuralist" approach, exposed by Wolfgang Stegmüller in *The Structure and Dynamics of Theories*[23] and by Wolfgang Balzer, Carlos-Ulises Moulines, and Joseph Sneed in *An Architectonic for Science.*[24] Inspired (and explicitly encouraged) by Kuhn, Stegmüller treats a scientific theory as a set-theoretical construction, which lacks a truth value but can be used to make "empirical claims." This framework leaves room for pragmatic factors and makes possible a semiformal diachronic description of "theory evolution." As theories are not sets of statements, Stegmüller claims that problems of incommensurability can be avoided. Progress can be defined, without the concept of truth, in terms of "theory reduction" on the level of the models of the rival theories.[25]

Partly inspired by Kuhn and Lakatos, Larry Laudan's *Progress and Its Problems*[26] treats scientific change in terms of "research traditions" which aim at "problem-solving" rather than "truth-seeking." Progress is defined by the increase in the "problem-solving effectiveness" of theories. Laudan's view has inspired historical case studies, and there is a promise that the tricky notions of 'problem' and 'answer' could be made precise within Jaakko Hintikka's question-theoretic or "interrogative model" of inquiry.[27]

Laudan is not an instrumentalist, since he admits that theories have a truth value. But he can be said to represent *methodological antirealism,* since for him truth (of a theory) is a utopian and illegitimate aim of science. As Laudan requires that a theory "solve problems" by the derivation of already observed empirical statements or of correct predictions, his concept of problem-solving ability seems to be essentially equivalent to Bas van Fraassen's requirement of "empirical adequacy." Employing the traditional instrumentalist slogan "saving the appearances" (since 1977), van Fraassen demands that "whatever the theory says about the observable should be true." As van Fraassen[28] regards the truth value of the theoretical statements to be irrelevant, his "constructive empiricism" is also a variant of methodological antirealism.[29]

All the programs mentioned above retain the correspondence theory of truth—and find it either suitable (with amendments like "approximate truth" or "verisimilitude"), inapplicable, or irrelevant in the analysis of scientific progress. Another type of reaction to the problem of realism is to replace the semantic concept of truth with some methodological surrogate—such as proved, verified, warrantedly assertable, acceptable, or practically useful. This has been the strategy of mathematical intuitionism (Michael Dummett), verificationism, and pragmatism.

In a series of works, starting with *Methodological Pragmatism* (1977) and *Scientific Progress,*[30] Nicholas Rescher has analyzed science in terms of a methodological notion 'presumably truer'. For Rescher, progress in theory change should be defined on the "pragmatic level" as "the increasing success of application in problem solving and control."[31]

Kuhn's thesis, that observations and meanings, even world and truth, are "theory-laden" or relative to "paradigms" or "world views," has served as an inspiration for thoroughgoing *relativism* about the cognitive pretensions (truth, rationality) of science. In their "strong programme" in the "sociology of knowledge," the Edinburgh School (Barry Barnes, David Bloor) has claimed since 1974 that the scientific study of science should describe and causally explain the beliefs of the scientists—without regard to whether the beliefs are true or the inferences rational.[32] Like an anthropologist studying exotic tribes, a sociologist should investigate through participant observation the activities among the tribes of scientists. This approach is developed in Bruno Latour's and Steven Woogar's *Laboratory Life,*[33] which claims that scientific facts are artificial "social constructions," created in laboratories as consequences of the process of settling controversies.[34]

Finally, Putnam's *internal realism* is an attempt to combine Kantianism and pragmatism without relativism. Rejecting dramatically his earlier "metaphysical realism" in 1977, Putnam now claims that truth is an "epistemic" notion, to be defined as "ideal acceptability."[35] Internal realism rejects all ontological, epistemological, and linguistic versions of the "Myth of the Given"—there is no ready-made world, or privileged languages.[36] Still, this view avoids relativism by identifying truth and reality with the contents of the epistemically ideal "Peircean limit science."

Learning from Progress

A detailed evaluation of the programs of Figure 1 is beyond the scope of this essay.[37] Instead, in this section I try to draw out some consequences that we have learned *from* progress: the debates about scientific change have taught us some important lessons about philosophy of science. This new perspective is then used in the next section to reappraise what we have learned *about* progress in the latest fifteen years.

(a) Formal vs. historical methodology

The message of the Kuhnian revolution was sometimes interpreted as the thesis that philosophy of science should follow a descriptive historical method—and give up the Carnapian quest for the logical and quantitative explication of concepts. While we may agree with Lakatos that "philosophy of science without history of science is empty; history of science without philosophy of science is blind,"[38] a sharp contrast between formal and historical methods in science studies is nevertheless misleading and unnecessary. Logical and quantitative methods are by no means restricted to the "synchronic" study of completed scientific systems, but can be applied as well to the "diachronic" study of scientific change.

At least since Derek de Solla Price's *Little Science, Big Science* (1963), it has been clear that the growth of science (measured by the volume of the literary output of the scientists) can be studied by quantitative methods. *Science indicators,* now investigated in "scientometrics" and widely used as a tool of science policy,[39] are as such not measures of the growth of knowledge, since they simply count publications and citations by ignoring their semantic content. In contrast, the Carnap-Hintikka measures of semantic information or the Tichý-Oddie-Niiniluoto measures of verisimilitude can be used for expressing, in quantitative terms, that a new body of scientific knowledge "tells more" and is "closer to the truth" than an old one. The latter measures also allow us to make precise such Peircean notions of dynamic epistemology as "approach" or "converge towards the truth."

In the same spirit, the advocates of Bayesian "probability kinematics" (Richard Jeffrey, Isaac Levi) have since the mid-sixties employed the quantitative concept of epistemic probability (that is, the degree of belief in the truth of a proposition relative to evidence) in the study of belief-change. Further, it is by now well established and accepted that the study of scientific change can successfully employ concepts borrowed from set theory (Sneed's and Stegmüller's "structuralism") and logical model theory.[40] Besides mathematics and logic, cognitive science and artificial intelligence are currently recommended as sources of "computational" methods that philosophers of science could apply in their work.[41]

(b) Normativism vs. naturalism

Logical empiricism is often portrayed as an attempt to establish by logical analysis and rational reconstruction general prescriptions for sound science, or norms expressing what science ought to be. Thus, philosophy of science is an a priori account of scientific rationality. On the other hand, the pragmatist tradition—exemplified by W. V. O. Quine's "naturalized epistemology" and the historical/sociological approach to the philosophy of science—holds that scientific rationality has to be grounded in the actual practice of scientific research.[42]

Following Lakatos in the "naturalist" demand that methodology should be tested against the actual historical record of the sciences, Laudan required that a methodological theory should capture as rational certain intuitively clear cases of good science. Later he rejected this "intuitionist metamethodology."[43] But even if Laudan explicitly acknowledged the "palpable implausibility" of the claim that "most of what has gone on in science has been rational,"[44] he still insists that theories of scientific change (Kuhn, Feyerabend, Lakatos, Laudan) should be *tested* by the actual history of science. The following quotation suggests that Laudan in fact is willing to include *all* historical cases among the relevant test cases:

> In their original forms, these philosophical models are often couched in normative language. Whenever possible we have recast their claims about how science ought to behave into declarative statements about how science does behave. We have a reasonably clear conscience about such translations since all the authors whose work we have paraphrased are explicitly committed to the claim that *science, because it is rational, will normally behave in ways which those authors normatively endorse.* . . . . It is plain that philosophers of the historical school draw the internal/external distinction so as to include within the range for which their normative views are accountable *virtually all* the widely cited and familiar historical episodes of post-16th century physical science.[45]

The program for "testing theories of scientific change" has already produced impressive and useful case studies.[46] But if the cognitive aims and methods of scientists have changed throughout history, as Laudan convincingly argues in *Science and Values,*[47] and if the scientists have acted on the basis of their methodological principles, it simply cannot be the case that "virtually all" historical cases could exhibit the same shared pattern of methodological rules. Hence, there is no hope whatsoever that any nontrivial normative theory of scientific change could pass "empirical tests."

If a case study reveals, for example, that Galileo or Ampère did not appeal to novel predictions to support their theories, does this "contraindicate" Lakatos' demand that a good theory ought to be successful in making novel predictions? Instead of using Galileo's and Ampère's behavior as "tests" of methodological rules, we may simply conclude that they had not read Whewell's, Popper's, and Lakatos' writings. In this sense, a normative *ought* cannot be derived from, or refuted by, a historical *is*.

Similar problems arise if the naturalist program is applied to contemporary scientists. Ron Giere, in his excellent book *Explaining Science* (1988), gives interesting material to show that high-energy physicists at least sometimes behave as "satisficers." He also suggests that the long debate whether "scientists, as scientists, *should* be Bayesian information processors" is futile:

> We need not pursue this debate any further, for there is now overwhelming empirical evidence that no Bayesian model fits the thoughts or actions of real scientists. For too long philosophers have debated how scientists ought to judge hypotheses in glaring ignorance of how scientists in fact judge hypotheses.[48]

But this view ignores the fact that, already for centuries, theory and practice have been in a mutual interaction in the field of scientific inference. Scientists learn to do science through implicit indoctrination and explicit instruction from their masters, textbooks, and colleagues. So if a case study reveals that a group of real scientists favors "bold hypotheses" and "severe tests," we may judge that they, or their teachers, have read Popper. And if some scientists do not behave like Bayesian optimizers, the reason is probably that the Department of Statistics—and the introductory courses of methodology—in their university is dominated by representatives of the "orthodox" Neyman-Pearson school.

To avoid this kind of vicious circularity in the testing procedure, we should find some strange tribe of scientists who have never been contaminated by any methodological or philosophical ideas. But naturalism is certainly implausible, if it suggests that the best advice for the conduct of science can be learned from those of its practitioners who are most ignorant of methodology!

(c) Methodological norms

Larry Laudan's important article "Progress or Rationality? The Prospects for Normative Naturalism"[49] helps a lot to clarify the debate about naturalism. Laudan suggests that methodological rules can be understood as conditional norms of the form:

(1) If your central cognitive goal is x, then you ought to do y.

Such statements, which express connections between ends and means, are true (or warranted) if y really promotes the goal of x, that is, if

(2) Doing y is more likely than its alternatives to produce x

is true. As (2) is a contingent empirical statement, it follows that the "naturalist metamethodologist" will rely—instead of on pre-analytic intuitions or choices of the scientific elite—on historical data concerning means-ends relationships.

Statements of the form (1) are called *technical norms* by G. H. von Wright (1963). I have earlier suggested that technical norms define the typical form of knowledge that is sought in the *applied sciences.*[50] Laudan's thesis can thus be expressed by saying that methodology is an applied science.

While I agree with this thesis, it seems to me that conditional norms of the form (1) are not typically justified inductively by historical data, but rather by studying theoretical models of knowledge acquisition.[51] Such models study the effectiveness of cognitive strategies relative to epistemic goals and factual assumptions about the world. Examples can be found from disciplines like applied mathematics, mathematical statistics, game theory, decision theory, and operations research.

(3) If you wish to guarantee that a false hypothesis is rejected with high probability, perform a likelihood ratio test.[52]

(4) If your goal is convergence to the true value of parameter p, and if your error of measurement is normally distributed with the mean p, use the average of repeated measurements as your estimate of p.

(5) Given these beliefs and preferences, if your aim is to maximize your expected gain, you ought to choose this act.

An important feature of conditionally normative results of this type is the possibility of proving them a priori by mathematical demonstration. At the same time, their application in some particular situation—that is, deriving from them nonconditional rules or recommendations—requires factual, hypothetical, or empirically warranted knowledge.

Some methodological rules, which express conceptual connections between precisely explicated notions, are purely a priori.[53] For example, a scientific realist may formulate methodological rules of type (1) by means of the following results (Niiniluoto, 1987) which are analytically true (given Hintikka's measure of corroboration and my measure of truthlikeness):

(6) If a generalization has a high degree of corroboration, its degree of estimated verisimilitude is also high.

(7) If a theory is highly truthlike, its deductive consequences are approximately true.

We may thus conclude that Laudan's conception of methodology as consisting of conditional norms legitimates, besides a role for historical data as empirical evidence, also the possibility of formal philosophy of science, so that the approach of logical empiricism is partially rehabilitated.

(d) Constitutive rules and axiology

Laudan's conception of methodology is limited to *strategic rules* that express means-ends relationships. They correspond to principles which tell how one plays chess effectively—how to attack, defend, build strong positions, and eventually defeat the opponent. However, an institutionalized activity also has *constitutive rules* (to use Searle's term), which characterize its legitimate "moves." In the case of chess, such constitutive rules tell how the different chessmen may be moved on the table. Violation of these rules does not lead to *ineffective* playing, but to *not playing* chess at all.

Many debates in the philosophy of science concern the constitutive rules of science. As such rules *define* what science is, they have a "conventional" element, as Popper says. But a demarcation between science and nonscience, or the explication of the concept of science, should also be "close" to the accepted use of the terms "science" and "scientific."[54] The method of justifying constitutive rules cannot be purely logical or empirical, but consists in an attempt to reach a "reflective equilibrium" (to use Rawls' term) between our normative demands for science and its actual practice.[55]

Laudan rejects the demarcation problem: creationism is for him *bad* science rather than *non*science. Therefore, it can be understood that he does not mention constitutive rules for science.[56]

However, Laudan makes the important addition that "methodology gets nowhere without axiology." Unlike Giere, whose version of naturalism admits only instrumental rationality,[57] Laudan acknowledges the "need to supplement methodology with an investigation into the legitimate or permissible ends of inquiry." And in *Science and Values,* he has proposed a "reticulational model" for showing how questions about scientific values can be resolved by appeal to (temporarily) shared theories and methods.

One might object to Laudan's model in that it is not always sufficient: disputes about scientific values may refer or appeal, besides to scientific practices, theories, and methods, also to philosophical principles from fields like logic, epistemology, aesthetics, and ethics.[58] This would not be fair, however, since Laudan may include naturalized versions of such principles among "theories." But still it seems problematic how a network of descriptive statements and conditional norms could ever give a positive justification for pursuing some value in science.

Laudan's reticulational model proposes a negative way of eliminating *utopian* or *unrealizable* goals: "the rational adoption of a goal or an aim requires the prior specification of grounds for belief that the goal state can possibly be achieved."[59] It would be too strong to understand this as requiring that any rational goal can *actually* be reached. For example, epistemological arguments against the infallibility of factual knowledge have lead philosophers to reject the traditional quest for complete certainty as a general value in science.[60] But these arguments gain their strongest support from the observation that in many (though not in all) situations even an *approach* to certainty is excluded, since the relevant hypotheses contain counterfactual or idealizing assumptions and, therefore, are known to be false.

Thus, scientific values should be regarded as respectable if there are reasonable criteria for claiming that we have made *progress* in realizing them. For this reason, it seems to me, Laudan's argument that *truth* is a utopian aim for science is not conclusive. Even if there are no infallible criteria for recognizing whether truth has been realized, it is probable that this goal has been realized in many particular cases. And even in cases where truth is at best the *limit* of inquiry, the measures of verisimilitude help us to assert with empirical warrant that this goal has been *approached*. For example, given the problem described in (4) above, it can be shown that the infinite sequence of point estimates converges *with probability one* to the true value of the unknown parameter.[61]

The axiology of chess is dominated by a single supreme rule: the aim of the game is to win. A secondary rule tells that, if you have lost your chance of winning, you should try to save a tie. When chess becomes an art, the style of playing becomes an end in itself: we try to win with a new, short, and beautiful combination of moves.

In my view, the axiology of science should likewise be governed by a primary rule: try to find the complete true answer to your cognitive problem, that is, try to reach or to approach this goal. As secondary rules, we may then require that our answer be justified, simple, consilient, and so forth. Further, if it is known that the available answers do not include a true one, then our rule is to search for the least false among them.[62]

Learning about Progress

(a) Rationality, quality, progress

By using the concepts introduced in the previous section, we may say that *rationality* is a methodological concept. Therefore, it is also historically relative: in assessing the rationality of the choices made by the scientist in the past, we have to study the aims, standards, methods, alternative theories, and available evidence accepted within the scientific community at that time.[63]

It is now clear why the proliferation of methodological theories is advantageous for the historiography of science. For example, the Carnap-Hintikka inductive logic can be used to assess and explain the behavior of scientists who have happened to endorse inductivism. Similar remarks apply to the philosophies of Popper, Feyerabend, Lakatos, and Laudan.

On the other hand, cognitive *progress*[64] is a goal-relative concept which should be distinguished from neutral descriptive terms ('change', 'development') and from methodological terms ('rationality'). Cognitive progress is an axiological concept: the step from A to B is *progressive* if B is an *improvement* on A, that is, B is *better* than A relative to the ends or *values* of scientific inquiry.

Progress, as a result-oriented or achievement word, should also be distinguished from process-oriented terms like *quality* or *skill* (that is, competence in the performance of some task; how well something is done). There is no necessary connection between quality and progress, even though high quality of research is a good probabilistic indicator of progress.[65]

As Laudan says, progress in science should be evaluated by "our lights" or by "our standards."[66] But here the agreement among present-day philosophers ends: they support different values of science —and, hence, different "theories of scientific progress." In previous sections, I have already observed the fundamental difference between the *realist* philosophers whose axiology includes truth (or some related "veric"[67] epistemic utility, such as truthlikeness) and those who deny the relevance of truth as a value in science.

(b) Systematic power and confirmation

Instead of repeating my arguments for realism,[68] I shall concentrate here on another issue: Laudan demands that aims of science should be detectable or *effectively recognizable* in the sense that "we can ascertain when they have and when they have not been realized."[69] In my view, this demand is too strong. Unless we are naive realists, this condition would exclude the concept of *truth*. But it also would exclude any *truth-dependent* goal. In decision-theoretic terms, this would mean that our definition of progress should not involve any utility which depends on the unknown state of nature.

In his *Progress and Its Problems*, Laudan argued that science is a "problem-solving rather than a truth-seeking process." He proposed that the problem-solving ability of a theory, measured by the number of empirical problems it solves minus the number of anomalies and conceptual problems it creates, would define such an effectively recognizable goal for science.

Here the *empirical problem-solving capacity* is defined relative to "the already observed states of affairs which the theory entails."[70] This syntactical concept is—if we ignore Laudan's insistence on the "importance" of problems—essentially equivalent to Hempel's concept of systematic power, formulated in the classical Hempel-Oppenheim article "Studies in the Logic of Explanation" in 1948.[71] It can be argued that the systematic power of a theory T relative to evidence E co-varies with the degree of *evidential support* for theory T by evidence E.[72] Systematic power of a theory relative to observed facts thus seems to be a fallible indicator of its truth. Moreover, as shown by Juhani Pietarinen, maximizing systematic power as a truth-dependent utility is equivalent to accepting a theory which is confirmed by observational evidence more than its rivals. Again this establishes a straightforward link between the concepts of problem-solving ability and confirmation.

Even a simpler formal argument shows that a theory T which deductively entails statement E is also *confirmed* by E; that is, the probability $P(T/E)$ of T given E must be greater than the prior probability $P(T)$ of T. The only way of denying the confirmational power of E would be to assume in advance that theory T is false so that its probability $P(T/B)$ relative to the background knowledge B is zero, since then $P(T/E\&B) - P(T/B) = 0$.

This argument suggests that a philosopher who thinks that theories have a truth value, but that empirical evidence is incompetent to give any indication of this value, has to assume in advance that all theories are *false*. Hence, methodological antirealism of the type Laudan supports seems to collapse into skepticism about theories.

(c) Progress through verisimilitude

My proposal for defining and estimating verisimilitude is a direct generalization of the Bayesian approach to scientific inference. Suppose that $C_1, \ldots, C_k$ are the strongest potential answers to your cognitive problem, where $C_1, \ldots, C_k$ are mutually exclusive and jointly exhaustive. Then one and only one of them is true. Let this unknown answer be denoted by C_*. What I have shown in detail, in a variety of different cases, is how to define the "closeness" $M(T,C_i)$ of a theory T from a given complete answer C_i $(i = 1, \ldots, k)$, if our cognitive interest is to hit the target C_i and exclude as many distant alternatives as possible. Then the *degree of truthlikeness* $Tr(T,C_*)$ of theory T is its M-distance from the true answer C_*. But since this value is unknown, when C_* is unknown, the best choice of T is that which maximizes *expected truthlikeness*, defined by

(8) $ver(T/e) = \sum_{i=1}^{k} P(C_i/e)M(T,C_i),$

where $P(C_i/e)$ is the epistemic probability that C_i is true given evidence e, and $M(T,C_i)$ is the gain due to T in case C_i happens to be the true alternative.[73]

The distinction between unknown truthlikeness $Tr(T,C_*)$ and estimated truthlikeness $ver(T/e)$ allows us to define absolute and evidence-relative concepts of progress:

(9) Step from T to T′ is (absolutely) *progressive* if $Tr(T,C_*) <$ $Tr(T′,C_*)$.

(10) Step from T to T′ *seems progressive* on evidence e if $ver(T/e) <$ $ver(T′/e)$.

Here (10) is a decidable concept, applicable retrospectively to historical cases by taking e to be the old evidence or our present theory.[74]

Function ver also suggests that there is a fallible "upward path" from empirical success to high truthlikeness.[75] There are cases where $ver(T/e)$ is high or approaches to its maximum value, when e is our currently accepted evidence. If evidence e is regarded as reliable, and if the probability measure P in (8) is a rational one, then it is rational to assert (fallibly) that T in fact is close to the truth (or closer to the truth than the available rivals).[76]

Function M allows us to show that the deductive consequences of an absolutely highly truthlike theory must be approximately true (*confer* (7) above). It thus helps to express precisely in what sense the assumption of truthlikeness serves as an abductive reason for thinking that successful scientific theories are truthlike in relevant respects—and grounds for defending critical scientific realism.[77]

Realism, as an attempt to "estimate the character of reality," is therefore not only a "realism of intent" but also of "achievement";[78] science is not merely a truth-*seeking* activity, but has also found methods for making progress in truth-*finding*.

(d) Incommensurability

By providing a tool for making the notorious concepts of critical realism precise and respectable, the theory of truthlikeness shows that the days of *metaphorical realism* are over.[79] But I do not try to pretend that the doctrine of verisimilitude would solve all problems of scientific progress. It still needs to be developed in many directions, and it should be applied to case studies from the real life of science.

One particular problem deserves attention here: the Kuhn-Feyerabend thesis of incommensurability. In its extreme form, this thesis is not very interesting, since it would make every theory an isolated unit which could not be a rival to any other theory. As there could be no reasons for rejecting a theory, strong incommensurability would make science cumulative in an extreme sense.[80]

But a weaker form of incommensurability—meaning variance—is still a relevant problem for all major programs in the philosophy of science. Attempts to get rid of this problem have not been successful.[81] If we wish to speak of competing theories, rival research traditions, and scientific progress, in cases where the relevant conceptual frameworks are to some extent different, methods for finding links between them (or between their statements, applications, problems, and so forth) are needed.

In the case of truthlikeness, this means that meaningfully to compare two theories we have to be able to regard them as rival answers to the same cognitive problem. This in turn can be accomplished by translating one theory to the other, or by translating both of them to a richer third language.[82] Fortunately, work on these important problems of translation and reduction is in progress, too.[83]

Concluding Remark

A recent article by Wang Shun Yi, published in *Journal of Dialectics of Nature* in Beijing, discusses my debate on scientific progress with Larry Laudan.[84] The author acknowledges that the concept of truthlikeness can be applied to the comparison of rival theories developed within one culture—such as Western science. But, he claims, the relation of incommensurability obtains between theories from different cultures, for example, between Western and Chinese science.

A thesis of this kind could be based on the assumption that the vocabularies of Western and Eastern languages are radically different and, hence, nontranslatable from one to the other. But perhaps a more plausible case could be made for the claim that the axiologies of the activities called "science" in East and West are fundamentally different. In particular, there is a remarkable difference in the links between scientific values and social progress: science has been an indispensable element in promoting the Western project of modernity. The truth-seeking and problem-solving accounts of scientific progress are different expressions of this Western heritage.

Through this connection to the main theme of this volume, the debates on the concept of scientific progress within modern analytical philosophy may provide a contribution to the comparative study of Eastern and Western ways of thinking.

Notes

1. I am speaking here about the so-called general philosophy of science (i.e., the study of scientific theories, scientific inference, scientific knowledge and its

growth, etc.) rather than the foundations of various disciplines (i.e., philosophy of physics, philosophy of biology, etc.).

2. Cf. Lakatos' paper in *Method and Appraisal in the Physical Sciences: The Critical Background to Modern Science, 1800–1905,* ed. by C. Howson (Cambridge: Cambridge University Press, 1976). We shall see below in Learning From Progress that "methodological research programmes" are concerned not only with methodology (i.e., the best means of achieving the aims of science) but also with axiology (i.e., the aims and values of scientific inquiry).

3. For a good survey of the Received View, see *The Structure of Scientific Theories,* ed. by F. Suppe (Urbana: University of Illinois Press, 1977).

4. For early attempts to explicate these concepts, see *Probability, Confirmation, and Simplicity,* ed. by M. H. Foster and M. L. Martin (New York: Odyssey Press, 1966). More sophisticated treatments are developed in *Information and Inference,* ed. by J. Hintikka and P. Suppes (Dordrecht: Reidel, 1970).

5. Recent reassessments of this volume are given in *Imre Lakatos and Theories of Scientific Change,* ed. by K. Gavroglu, Y. Goudaroulis, and P. Nicolacopoulos (Dordrecht: Kluwer Academic Publishers, 1989).

6. T. S. Kuhn, *The Structure of Scientific Revolutions* 2d ed. enl. (Chicago: University of Chicago Press, 1970), p. 170.

7. Ibid., p. 166.

8. Ibid., p. 169.

9. See Kuhn, *Scientific Revolutions,* p. 206; Suppe, *Scientific Theories;* and T. S. Kuhn, *The Essential Tension* (Chicago: University of Chicago Press, 1977), p. 322.

10. But see M. Pera, "In Praise of Cumulative Progress," in *Change and Progress in Modern Science,* ed. by J. Pitt (Dordrecht, Boston: Reidel, 1985), pp. 267–282.

11. L. Laudan, "The Trivialization of the Self-Corrective Thesis," in *Foundations of Scientific Method: The Nineteenth Century,* ed. by R. Giere and R. Westfall (Bloomington: Indiana University Press, 1973), pp. 275–306.

12. For discussions about this strategic question, see *Progress and Rationality in Science,* ed. by G. Radnitzky and G. Andersson (Dordrecht, Boston: Reidel, 1978); *The Structure and Development of Science,* ed. by G. Radnitzky and G. Andersson (Dordrecht: Reidel, 1979); I. Niiniluoto, "The Significance of Verisimilitude," in *PSA 1984,* ed. by P. D. Asquith and P. Kitcher (East Lansing: Philosophy of Science Association, 1985), vol. 2; I. Niiniluoto, *Truthlikeness* (Dordrecht: Reidel, 1987), chap. 12. Cf. also L. Laudan, "The Confutation of Convergent Realism," *Philosophy of Science* 48 (1981): 19–49, and *Science and Values: The Aims of Science and Their Role in Scientific Debate* (Berkeley: University of California Press, 1984).

13. J. Watkins, *Science and Scepticism* (Princeton: Princeton University Press, 1984).

14. G. Oddie, *Likeness to Truth* (Dordrecht: Reidel, 1986).

15. See also I. Niiniluoto, "The Significance of Verisimilitude" and the col-

lection *What-Is-Closer-To-Truth?* ed. by Theo Kuipers, Poznan Studies in the Philosophy of Science (Amsterdam: Rodopi, 1987).

16. See the conference proceedings in I. Niiniluoto and R. Tuomela, eds., *The Logic and Epistemology of Scientific Change,* Acta Philosophica Fennica 30 (Amsterdam, 1979).

17. I. Niiniluoto, *Is Science Progressive?* (Dordrecht: Reidel, 1984).

18. I. Niiniluoto, "Theories, Approximations, Idealizations," in *Logic, Methodology and Philosophy of Science,* vol. 7, ed. by R. Barcan Marcus, G. J. W. Dorn, and P. Weingartner (Amsterdam: North-Holland, 1986).

19. The journal *Poznan Studies,* ed. by Leszek Nowak, started to appear in 1975. See also W. Krajewski, *Correspondence Principle and the Growth of Knowledge* (Dordrecht: Reidel, 1977), and L. Nowak, *The Structure of Idealization: Towards a Systematic Interpretation of the Marxian Idea of Science* (Dordrecht: Reidel, 1980).

20. N. Cartwright, *How the Laws of Physics Lie* (Oxford: Oxford University Press, 1983).

21. I. Hacking, *Representing and Intervening* (Cambridge: Cambridge University Press, 1983).

22. R. Giere, *Explaining Science; A Cognitive Approach* (Chicago: University of Chicago Press, 1988).

23. W. Stegmüller, *The Structure and Dynamics of Theories* (New York, Heidelberg, Berlin: Springer-Verlag, 1976).

24. W. Balzer, C. U. Moulines, and J. D. Sneed, *An Architectonic for Science* (Dordrecht: Reidel, 1987).

25. For a critical discussion, see I. Niiniluoto, *Is Science Progressive?,* chap. 6, and David Pearce, *Roads to Commensurability* (Dordrecht: Reidel, 1987).

26. L. Laudan, *Progress and Its Problems: Toward a Theory of Scientific Growth* (London: Routledge & Kegan Paul, 1977).

27. See the special issues vol. 47, no. 1 (1981) and vol. 74, nos. 1–2 (1988) of *Synthese.*

28. B. van Fraassen, *The Scientific Image* (Oxford: Oxford University Press, 1980).

29. For a critical discussion of van Fraassen, see I. Niiniluoto, "Theories, Approximations, Idealizations."

30. N. Rescher, *Scientific Progress: A Philosophical Essay on the Economics of Research in Natural Science* (Oxford: Blackwell, 1978).

31. See also Rescher, *The Limits of Science* (Berkeley: University of California Press, 1984), and *Scientific Realism: A Critical Reappraisal* (Dordrecht: Reidel, 1988).

32. See D. Bloor, *Knowledge and Social Imagery* (London: Routledge and Kegan Paul, 1976) and the Laudan-Bloor controversy in J. R. Brown, ed., *Scientific Rationality: The Sociological Turn* (Dordrecht: Reidel, 1984). Bloor could also be understood as not denying objective truth but rather as asserting its methodological irrelevance. This would bring him to the same box in Figure 1 as his sharpest critic Laudan. Surprisingly, Bloor describes his own sociological work in a traditional empiricist, Baconian, and causalist way—demanding true

and objective descriptions and explanations of belief change in science. For effective arguments against the consistency of radical forms of relativism, see H. Siegel, *Relativism Refuted* (Dordrecht: Reidel, 1987).

33. B. Latour and S. Woolgar, *Laboratory Life: The Social Construction of Scientific Facts,* 2d ed. (Princeton: Princeton University Press, 1986).

34. Also evolutionary epistemology, if it refuses to use the concept truth in the biologist study of belief change, may be a version of relativism (e.g., Toulmin). Cf. I. Niiniluoto, *Is Science Progressive?* chap. 4; W. Callebaut and R. Pinxten, eds., *Evolutionary Epistemology* (Dordrecht: Reidel, 1987); and P. Thagard, *Computational Philosophy of Science* (Cambridge, Massachusetts: MIT Press, 1988).

35. H. Putnam, *Reason, Truth, and History* (Cambridge: Cambridge University Press, 1981).

36. R. Tuomela, *Science, Action, and Reality* (Dordrecht: Reidel, 1985).

37. Some attempts toward this direction are given in I. Niiniluoto, *Is Science Progressive?;* I. Niiniluoto, "Progress, Realism, and Verisimilitude," in *Logik, Wissenschaftstheorie und Erkenntnistheorie,* ed. by P. Weingartner and G. Schurz, Akten des 11, Internationalen Wittgenstein-Symposiums, 1986, (Wien: Verlag Holder—Pichler—Tempsky, 1987), pp. 151-161.

38. *Method and Appraisal in the Physical Sciences,* ed. by C. Howson (1976), p. 1.

39. See *Toward a Metric of Science: The Advent of Science Indicators,* ed. by Y. Elkana et al. (New York: Wiley & Sons, 1978); and N. Rescher, *Scientific Progress* (1978).

40. D. Pearce and V. Rantala, "A Logical Study of the Correspondence Relation," *Journal of Philosophical Logic* 13 (1984): 47-84; D. Pearce, "Critical Realism in Progress: Reflections on Ilkka Niiniluoto's Philosophy of Science," *Erkenntnis* 27 (1987): 147-171.

41. See R. Giere, *Explaining Science* (1988); and P. Thagard, *Computational Philosophy* (1988).

42. For a careful commentary of this distinction, as exemplified by Carnap's method of explication and by Kuhn, see C. G. Hempel, "Valuation and Objectivity in Science," in *Physics, Philosophy and Psychoanalysis,* ed. by R. S. Cohen and L. Laudan (Dordrecht: D. Reidel, 1983).

43. L. Laudan, "Some Problems Facing Intuitionist Meta-Methodologies," *Synthese* 67 (1986): 115-129.

44. Laudan, "Some Problems," p. 117.

45. L. Laudan et al., "Scientific Change: Philosophical Models and Historical Research," *Synthese* 69 (1986): 148-149 (my emphasis).

46. *Scrutinizing Science: Empirical Studies of Scientific Change,* ed. by A. Donovan, L. Laudan, and R. Laudan (Dordrecht: Kluwer, 1988).

47. Laudan, *Science and Values* (1984).

48. Giere, *Explaining Science,* p. 149.

49. Larry Laudan, "Progress or Rationality? The Prospects for Normative Naturalism," *American Philosophical Quarterly* 24 (1987): 19-31.

50. I. Niiniluoto, *Is Science Progressive?* (1984).

51. Laudan acknowledges that methodology is a "mixed empirical/conceptual discipline." See Larry Laudan, "Relativism, Naturalism and Reticulation," *Synthese* 71 (1987): 221–234.

52. Laudan's claim that "every good textbook on experimental design goes much further towards explaining why science works than all the writings of scientific realists put together" uses a misleading contrast, since methodological rules about experimental design (e.g., (3)) normally employ realist goals (e.g., eliminating falsity, finding truth). See Larry Laudan, "Explaining the Success of Science: Beyond Epistemic Realism and Relativism," in *Science and Reality,* ed. by J. T. Cushing, C. F. Delaney, and G. M. Gutting (Notre Dame, Indiana: University of Notre Dame Press, 1984), pp. 83–105.

53. See Laudan, "Progress or Rationality?" in which Laudan admits in a footnote that one can imagine ends/means connections which are analytic, but repeats with emphasis in the conclusion the claim that his naturalistic theory of methodology does *not* promise any a priori or incorrigible demonstrations.

54. Thomas Kuhn, "Rationality and Theory Choice," *The Journal of Philosophy* 80 (1983): 563–570.

55. Thagard, *Computational Philosophy of Science.*

56. For my view on the continuing importance of the demarcation problem, see I. Niiniluoto, *Is Science Progressive?* chap. 1.

57. Giere begs the question about axiology, since he simply assumes that the general goal of science is "finding out what the world is like." Many antirealists, instrumentalists, pragmatists, and relativists of Figure 1 would not agree with this goal description. See R. Giere, "Scientific Rationality as Instrumental Rationality," *Studies in History and Philosophy of Science* 20 (1989): 377–384.

58. I. Niiniluoto, "Progress, Realism, and Verisimilitude."

59. Laudan, *Science and Values,* p. 51.

60. Note that fallibilism is not based upon empirical studies of the psychological certainty or uncertainty that the scientists feel, but rather upon the logical strength and inconclusiveness of the possible arguments for scientific statements.

61. I. Niiniluoto, *Truthlikeness;* and I. Niiniluoto, "Corroboration, Verisimilitude, and the Success of Science," in *Imre Lakatos and Theories of Scientific Change,* ed. by K. Gavroglu, Y. Goudaroulis, and P. Nicolacopoulos (Dordrecht: Kluwer Academic Publishers, 1989).

62. For further discussions on axiology, see Kuhn, *The Essential Tension,* chap. 13; C. Dilworth, *Scientific Progress: A Study Concerning the Nature of the Relation Between Successive Scientific Theories* (Dordrecht: Reidel, 1981); Hemp, "Valuation and Objectivity in Science"; M. Sintonen, *The Pragmatics of Scientific Explanation* (Helsinki: Acta Philosophica Fennica, 1984), vol. 37; Thagard, *Computation Philosophy of Science;* I. Niiniluoto, *Is Science Progressive?* and Niiniluoto, *Truthlikeness.*

63. G. Doppelt, "Relativism and Recent Pragmatic Conceptions of Scientific Rationality," in *Scientific Explanation and Understanding,* ed. by N. Rescher

(Lanham: University Press of America, 1983), pp. 107–142; Laudan, "Progress or Rationality?"

64. Progress with respect to knowledge is here distinguished from educational, methodical, economical, technological, and social progress. The latter are related to science, but are not discussed in this essay.

65. Science indicators, if they indirectly rely on the judgment of scientific experts (publications, decisions, awards, favorable citations), may to *some* extent reflect the quality of research. But as such they are not measures of scientific progress.

66. Laudan, "Progress or Rationality?"

67. This term is used by Sintonen in *The Pragmatics of Scientific Explanation.*

68. I. Niiniluoto, *Is Science Progressive?* and *Truthlikeness.*

69. Laudan, "Progress or Rationality?" p. 31.

70. Cf. the discussion in I. Niiniluoto, *Is Science Progressive?* p. 165.

71. C. G. Hempel, *Aspects of Scientific Explanation* (New York: Free Press, 1965), pp. 278–288.

72. See I. Niiniluoto and R. Tuomela, *Theoretical Concepts and Hypothetico-Inductive Inference* (Dordrecht: Reidel, 1973).

73. Instead of (8), we could also define a function of *probable verisimilitude* that expresses the probability that T is close to the truth. See I. Niiniluoto, *Truthlikeness* and "Corroboration, Verisimilitude, and the Success of Science."

74. In R. Wachbroit, "Progress: Metaphysical and Otherwise," *Philosophy of Science* 53 (1986): 354–371, Wachbroit argues interestingly that the step from Aristarchus to Ptolemy not only *seemed,* but in fact *was,* progressive, so that considerations regarding "which hypothesis is closer to the truth appear thus to be beside the point." My reply is that truthlikeness does not depend on truth value only: Ptolemy's powerful and informative geocentric system was indeed more truthlike than the isolated heliocentric hypothesis of Aristarchus. See I. Niiniluoto, "Is There Progress in Science?" in *Pragmatik, Handbuch pragmatischen Denken,* vol. 5, ed. by H. Stachowiak (Hamburg: Felix Meiner Verlag, forthcoming).

75. See Laudan's criticism of abduction in *Science and Values.* If a tentative fallible inference to the best explanation is denied in science, then Laudan owes us an explanation why we constantly rely on it in everyday life. See also A. Musgrave, "The Ultimate Argument for Scientific Realism," in *Relativism and Realism in Science,* ed. by R. Nola (Dordrecht: Kluwer, 1988), pp. 229–252.

76. Truth is here a "local" matter—the target is represented by the strongest true answer to our cognitive problem. It need not express the "whole truth about reality" (whatever that might mean). The target may also be defined counterfactually as the strongest statement that *would* be true if certain idealizing assumptions were true. Cf. I. Niiniluoto, *Truthlikeness.*

77. Cf. R. Boyd, "The Current Status of Scientific Realism," in *Scientific Realism,* ed. by J. Leplin (Berkeley: University of California Press, 1984), pp. 41–82; I. Niiniluoto, *Is Science Progressive?* and Musgrave, "The Ultimate Argument." Arthur Fine, who has untimely announced the death of realism (and all

its alternatives in Figure 1) (see Leplin, *Scientific Realism,* p. 83), argues that every realist explanation for the instrumental success of science can be replaced by a "better instrumentalist one" (see A. Fine, "Unnatural Attitudes: Realist and Instrumentalist Attachments to Science," *Mind* 95 (1986): 149–179). The trick, he claims, is "to replace the realist conception of truth by the pragmatic conception." Fine fails to note that the proposed "instrumentalist explanation" is then a mere tautology without any explanatory power—the realist's argument. "Theory T is instrumentally successfully, since T is truthlike" is transformed to the trivial "Theory T is instrumentally successful, since T is instrumentally successful."

78. Cf. Rescher, *Scientific Realism.* Rescher points out correctly that the efficacy of a theory in prediction and explanation is not a proof of its actual truth. He argues further that truth (or approximate truth) is not even the *best* explanation for empirical success. A better explanation for the successes of theory T (e.g., Ptolemaic astronomy) is provided by a more adequate theory T' (e.g., Newtonian astronomy) which explains how T was able to generate successful applications. I find Rescher's argument as such quite reasonable, but he fails to tell why the deeper explanation by T' would indicate that T (or some part of T) is *not* approximately true. In order to show why T was able to generate successful applications, T' has to refer to some connections—partial or approximate correspondence—between T and reality.

79. I. Niiniluoto, "Progress, Realism, and Verisimilitude."

80. I. Niiniluoto, *Is Science Progressive?*

81. See Pearce's account of Stegmüller and Laudan in D. Pearce, *Roads to Commensurability.*

82. See Pearce, "Critical Realism" and I. Niiniluoto, *Truthlikeness,* chap. 12.

83. Cf. W. Balzer, C. U. Moulines, and J. D. Sneed, *An Architectonic for Science;* Pearce, *Roads to Commensurability.*

84. S. Y. Wang, "Niiniluoto's Theory of Progress of Science" (in Chinese), *Journal of Dialectics of Nature* 10 (1988): 7–14.

LORENZ KRÜGER

DOES PROGRESS IN SCIENCE
LEAD TO TRUTH?

Does progress in science lead to truth? If this is to be a real, as opposed to a merely rhetorical, question, we have to admit the possibility that progress in science might *not* lead to truth. Is that conceivable? The term "progress" seems to imply the notion of a certain goal that can gradually be approached. In this essay I hope to show that this implication is only apparent: there may be progress without a goal. Nevertheless, truth may still be the distinctive achievement of science. If, in spite of that, truth should be denied its function as the final goal, or the point of convergence, of scientific endeavors, what alternative account of truth could be offered? To address this further question is the main purpose of this essay.

Before we turn to it, it is useful to remind ourselves of what else could be the goal of science if not truth. We are all familiar witn some alternatives that have been advanced in the last decades. These alternatives share a common feature: they emphasize the *practical* side of science, in particular its problem-solving capacity. "The unit of scientific achievement is the solved problem," says Thomas Kuhn;[1] and Larry Laudan has written a classic book on scientific progress whose main text (after a Prologue) starts with the sentence: "Science is essentially a problem-solving activity."[2] True, problems may not only be practical problems, they need not necessarily belong to a context of production, control, or prediction; they may be theoretical puzzles of understanding. But the stress on their character of being *problems* is meant to indicate that solving them is something like clearing, perhaps even tracing, a path, so that it be viable for further thought or action. Problem solving is removing anomalies or obstacles, and as such has nothing to do with truth. Indeed, in what sense can we say that discovering the truth about a thing solves a problem? Granting that there is such a thing at all as recognizing or knowing the truth, it would seem to be neutral as to whether or not it solves a problem. The problem-solving qualification of a truth, if any, will depend on the place or function the recognition of the truth has within the specific context of action which makes the problem problematic, that is, renders it a matter of concern.

This conception of science appears very natural, once we acknowledge the intimate relationship between science and technology that is so typical of our era. To think that the highest form, indeed the only genuine form, of science or *scientia* is contemplation seems very old-fashioned and irrevocably outdated; the literal meaning of "theory" has long been forgotten. We have come to adopt a thoroughly *dynamic* view of science: science is *research*—an activity that is, moreover, deeply intertwined with technological development and production, possibly also social engineering. It is perhaps the only type of action that, though highly competitive, leaves no room for fundamental antagonisms concerning its standards of method and success, even across cultural boundaries.

If this dynamic conception and the optimistic hope of its global unifying function are granted, the notion of truth will at best appear superfluous for the characterization of the enterprise and at worst a harmful source of confusion about the real nature of science, at any rate a relic of European metaphysics without transcultural value. Scientific theories have always been superseded by new theories; we all expect that our best present theories will inevitably meet with the same fate. Hence, what counts, according to the dynamic view, is not their truth but their use. And useful they are. They help enormously to direct expectations, take precautions, protect health and life, and produce means of living, including material and cultural luxuries. The efficiency of science in all these respects is increasing rapidly, and in this very real sense there is progress in science. Of course, science-induced changes also involve losses in life quality and serious dangers, and this is rightly a matter of great concern. Practical progress is problematical and ambivalent; but this is nothing but another sign of its undeniable existence.

In another sense, however, the pragmatic picture of science as a problem-solving activity denies that there is progress in science: science does not advance our knowledge of what the world itself is really like. Kuhn originally announced this idea in the following way: on the one hand, he trusts that "both the list of problems solved by science and the precision of individual problem-solutions will grow and grow"; yet on the other, he wants to "relinquish the notion that changes of paradigm carry scientists and those who learn from them closer and closer to the truth."[3] This position, he claimed, implements a Darwinian evolutionary view: science develops unidirectionally to higher forms of knowledge and achievement, but it has no goal; it does not approximate or approach anything. Hence, the notion of truth loses its possible place and function. Laudan, exploiting the fallibility of all our claims to knowledge, has put this idea more provocatively thus: "To retain the view that science aims at presumptively true theories, in the face of the admission that we would not know how to recognize a true theory if we had it, is to render science an irrational enterprise; for . . . it is irrational to adopt a goal (scil. true scientific theories) which (a) we do not know how to achieve, (b) we could not recognize if we had achieved, and (c) was such that we could not even tell whether we were gradually moving closer to achieving it."[4]

Laudan's view is, indeed, convincing—at least as long as its explicit assumption that we would not know how to recognize a true theory if we had it stands up to scrutiny. It is here where my doubts begin. I shall devote this essay to expose them, at least in outline, and submit them for discussion. My leading question is: do we *know* what truth is? More specifically: can we hope to say what truth is, or what the term "truth" means, *independently* of what we believe to be our candidates for the status of being true? Laudan, in defending his title on being a scientific realist, has talked about truth as if there were one and only one acceptable notion of it; presumably he had Tarski's semantic notion of truth in mind.[5] In this respect he agrees with his opponents, who contest his realism. Now, it has always puzzled me that both parties readily, often tacitly, accept the assumption that there is one and only one clear and fixed notion of truth. How does one reconcile this view with the dynamic view of science? *If one's central concerns are scientific change and something so deeply historical as progress, should one not be prepared to find that also our notion of truth is something historical?*

It is a common and usually unquestioned presupposition of the debate about progress in science that either science approaches the Truth (with a capital T)[6] or that progress has nothing to do with truth but rather with acceptability, problem-solving efficiency, or something else of practical significance. It is true, there are proposals that soften this alternative to some extent. But they do not really get away from it. On the one hand, Niiniluoto has dropped the assumption that there is a single ideal theory expressing *the* truth about the world and replaced it by the truth about a specific problem area, so far as it is expressible in a certain language L.[7] On the other hand, truth has been relativized to paradigms or theories.[8] But Niiniluoto continues to take for granted that we can find scientific languages whose maximally specific sentences are fully descriptive and simply true or false; indeed he adopts the postulate that "for each scientific problem or problem area, there exists an ideal or practically ideal language."[9] This means that, though he is willing to restrict the extension of knowledge, he continues to insist on its unimpaired and unique representativity within limited domains. In other words, he sacrifices some of the scope but nothing of the conceptual character of the classical concept of truth. Conversely, his opponents, by granting truth-with-respect-to-a-theory, do not concede very much to the adherents of correspondence and realism. Their relativization of truth will inevitably appear as no more than the adaptation of the *word* "truth" to a new use, but not as the rediscovery of the real thing in a new theoretical dress. Indeed, they continue to claim that significant progress occurs in theory change, while not accepting the persistence of truth across such changes. In short: the familiar concessions by both parties in the dispute tend to disguise the basic opposition between them. As a matter of fact, the controversy does continue, if in a modified form. One may, therefore, suspect that it will prove irresolvable. This suspicion offers a motive for probing into the hidden presuppositions of the dispute.

In this essay, therefore, I want to examine what I take to be an essential presupposition of the controversy: the mistaken belief that scientific realism implies a static notion of truth. From it the following dilemma is derived: either scientific theories are qualified by their progressive dynamics, so that their distinctive feature cannot be truth; or truth is still taken to be the distinctive feature of scientific success, so that truth cannot actually be available but degenerates to the content of a hope for an indefinite future. Both views offer an utterly unrealistic picture of truth. *We need an improved conception of truth in order to reconcile the historical reality of science with a realistic interpretation of its results.* In attempting such a reconciliation I want to join forces with Laudan; but I think that he, in his defense of realism,[10] severely underestimated how much is at stake. It is, indeed, no less than an alternative account of truth—a way out of the controversy that is mentioned but not pursued by both Laudan[11] and, before him, Kuhn.[12]

The revised account of truth, in order to be adequate, should fit a conception of science that involves the following features.

1. Science is realistic. By this I mean that scientific representations, on the average, are not a matter of social arrangement but of contact with nature, where nature is defined as that part of our environment which is invariant with respect to intentional human actions, a part that includes, of course, physical and mental features of human beings. To the extent that this contact is mediated by symbolic (verbal, mathematical, diagrammatical, and so forth) representations, those latter can qualify as true or false. Since scientific representations can be used for many different purposes, the intended qualification needs to be distinguished from qualifications such as "useful for purpose X."

2. Science is reflective. It does not just produce symbolic representations or beliefs about its subject matter, it also develops views of what it means to have such representations or beliefs and to be justified in having them. In other words: the contents of science are inseparable from our ways of understanding what makes them scientific and *vice versa.* Truth is always intended truth, it is truth under some interpretation or other.

3. Science is dynamic. Scientific accounts of the world are invariably replaced by new accounts that are different, often at variance with ear-

lier accounts, though typically resembling them to some extent in some respects. According to the reflective nature of science just stated, this continuous change will not leave the notion of truth unaffected. We ought to expect correlations between those scientific findings that are distinguished as true and the views about what it means for them to be true.

4. Science is individual. By this I mean that science is not the partial and imperfect realization of an a priori, well-defined corpus of potential knowledge that is, as it were, determined by the nature of things, so that it could, in principle, be reproduced anywhere at any time in the same form. Rather, we should take the term "science" to refer to a singular chain of events: as it happens of Greek origin, of Mediterranean and European development and, by now, of global impact and recognition. Granted the unity of this cultural phenomenon, and granted the first point about the realistic nature of science, we should be prepared to accept the unifying distinctive feature of it: truth. If we do, the notion of truth cannot only be no more unchangeable than the notion of science itself, as just pointed out under (3), but it will not even be a simple generic concept. Rather, the term "true" will be of the nature of the name of a biological species that, while being applicable to indefinitely many instances, nevertheless also refers to something unique, namely, the species as an historical individual.

I should perhaps add an important reservation in order to avoid serious misunderstandings. Nothing of what I have just said is intended to patronize the term "true"; still less is it meant to claim some kind of higher wisdom or value for the historical phenomenon we call "science." In English the word "true" may be used to praise things that have no recognizable relationship to science or its foundation in ordinary everyday experience. I presume that the same is true for many languages in various ways. I take this to be an interesting problem rather than an objection. It is an important task to investigate these uses of "true" in order to assess either distinct and unrelated meanings of "true" or possibly discover connections with science that have so far been hidden. More importantly, to promote science to the paradigm locus of truth does not imply that scientific contact with nature is better than other possible or actual attitudes of humans toward nature: for example, better than some venerable form of ancient wisdom, be it of Eastern or Western origin. Recent experiences with science have suggested serious misgivings about it to many of us, even though most of us may not want to devalue science for that reason, let alone make the futile attempt to get rid of it altogether.

Returning to my fourfold characterization of science and its implications for truth, I am facing the task of describing a concept of truth that combines the following properties.

(a) It is realistic; that is, it interprets truth in terms of contact between human representations and represented contents that are beyond the control of the representing individual.

(b) It applies to indefinitely many instances (representations, especially propositions) separately, yet also to the set of such instances through time collectively.

(c) It changes with time and in correlation with its changing paradigmatic instances.

Most likely, it strikes one as obscure and overly speculative to think that these properties could possibly be united in a single concept. Indeed, we may be steering into highly uncertain philosophical waters here. Yet, the mystery is not darker than that of the nature of science, once science is conceived as a unified historical phenomenon. Science is not just historical; it is about something beyond human history as well. But if we had asked scientists of diverse periods, including our own, what they had thought science to be, we would have received different answers; and yet we may reasonably believe that all these answers are contributions to a growing, hence changing and incomplete, understanding of one and the same thing: science. Of course, once we have come to see science as a historical and developing individual, we can no longer detach our own answer from those given earlier in our history. Rather, we shall wish to relate it explicitly to those earlier views in one way or another.

In the rest of this essay I shall try to indicate how one might substantiate two of my claims: (1) that the concept of truth changes in correlation with views on what instances are paradigmatic applications of it, and (2) that scientific change—scientific progress, if you like—contributes to an understanding of how the different notions of truth relate to each other. Of course, I can at best give you a very rough and to some extent perfunctory, outline of this program. Its execution will need an enormous amount of work. Perhaps I should hold back the programmatic ideas until I can give them more support. On the other hand, critical objections at this point may save me much misplaced labor.

In order to illustrate the temporal character of truth I propose tentatively to distinguish four different views of truth. For easy reference I shall label them as follows: (1) the eternity view of truth, (2) the present-centered view of truth, (3) the future-centered view of truth, and finally (4) the past-centered view of truth. Not accidentally the eternity view is placed on top of the list. It is not only older than the other views, but presumably is still preferred over the others by most people. Therefore I will talk about it first.

The eternity view claims that every truth that exists at all can, in principle, be referred to at all times invariantly. If the changing symbolic means of reference should not completely harmonize with each other, they ought to be criticized and, if possible, improved. Science offers itself as an efficient means to this end. Our everyday language is not particularly well suited for talking about the more sophisticated details of, say, heat or rheumatism; hence it is complemented or partly replaced by the technical language of the physicist or the physician. More generally, indexical reference with the help of particles like "here," "yesterday," "you," and so forth, are replaced by indications of places, dates, persons, and so forth. This method of constructing a comprehensive system of symbolic expressions is familiar. Its aim is to dissociate truth from time, to make truth timeless and in this sense eternal.

This solution to the problem of truth agrees with certain intuitions we all share. What we can say truly today is something we may truly repeat tomorrow. And if, or as far as, we have divinatory or prognostic capacities, we would have been able, or were able, already yesterday to anticipate the same truth as that which we are expressing today. This view of truth appears still more indubitable when applied to contents that are themselves invariant in time, as we may assume for basic natural laws, or even timeless, as in the case of mathematical theorems. Conversely, such timeless or invariant states of affairs are the historical root of the eternity view of truth.

Indeed, the long tradition of this view as well as its enduring attraction today are certainly related to the dominance of mathematics and the mathematical sciences of nature in the European history of knowledge. The replacement of cosmological stories by the idea of a lawlike order marks the transition from a mythical to a scientific understanding of the world. In the Pythagorean-Platonic tradition, it has even led to the extreme philosophical claim that nothing can be truly known except insofar as it participates in the timeless order of things. For brevity's sake I can no more than mention the Christian transformation of this idea. We all know that it crystallizes in a suggestive metaphor of truth: the representation of something is true to the extent that it coincides with the view the omniscient God has of this thing. It is well known that this view directed the founders of modern science. In 1599 Johannes Kepler wrote (in a letter to Herwart of Hohenburg): "God created man in his image, so that we may have his thoughts. What is really in the mind of man except numbers and quantities? These alone we understand correctly and . . . with the same kind of knowledge that God has of them."[13] What Galileo says on the same topic in his *Dialogo* some thirty years later reads almost like a quotation from Kepler.[14]

But mathematics and the mathematical form of reality is not everything; science needs experience, and that surely consists of a temporal chain of events. How could the experiential side of science, natural history as it was also called, be reconciled with the eternity view of truth? Does it not consist of very human, noneternal truths? In the long run the problem could not be suppressed or solved. But a temporary solution has proved surprisingly stable. Briefly and roughly, it was based on two moves: (a) to interpret "experience" as "experiment," and (b) to accord universal laws the central position in the overall representation of nature. Experiments are defined as something that can be repeated at any place and time, and fundamental laws are taken to be temporally and locally invariant. Under these assumptions it appears possible, indeed necessary, to separate truth from all circumstances under which it is actually found or preserved.

Only in a supplementary second step, the truth of contingent statements—for example, about unrepeatable historical events—is then assimilated to that of permanent or arbitrarily repeatable states of affairs. From God's point of view, they can be captured in timeless representations once and for all. Of course, it is then conceded that we humans usually cannot reach these representations; but this is also the case for natural laws. Although Kepler and Galileo would have protested, it is even true in the case of mathematics. We have become wary to postulate the existence of mathematical objects that conform to one and only one true form of speaking about them. If, however, we are, along this line of thought, led to dissociate our actual ways of getting access to the truth from God's truth *everywhere,* the eternity notion of truth becomes empty.

I do believe that the atemporal notion of truth of the Frege-to-Tarski tradition, if taken seriously, commits us to a certain brand of metaphysics that has widely lost its credit. The dubious feature consists in the total separation of questions of being from questions concerning the possible human recognition of being. Indeed, in the eternity view one defines the truth of a statement or an opinion without considering in any way the possibilities of access to such a truth. In other words: this view of truth belongs to an ontology that is completely free of epistemological ingredients. But that is something which we have been inclined to reject since Descartes or, at the latest, since Kant. All signs we have appear to indicate that we ought to take into account our human possibilities of reaching the truth when we try to define a concept of truth.

Now, this last maxim is at the heart of the *present-centered view of truth,* to which I now turn. According to it we can call "true" only something that can be shown to be true, that is, verifiable from the position of the person who claims the truth. This view, as is well known, has found a particularly radical articulation in the logical empiricism of our century. To its adherents a concept of truth that ignores the procedure of verification was banished as metaphysical, because immune to criticism and inapplicable in our real, cognitive life. In other words: the transition from the eternity view to the present-centered view of truth is the transition from an ontological to an epistemological extreme.

An adequate discussion of the present-centered view is beyond the scope of this essay. I want to restrict myself to two remarks concerning the fate of this position. The first remark concerns the development of this view. The entire history of the conception of truth in modern philosophy is structured by the fact that the eternity view and the present-centered view of truth overlap. Only the emphasis gradually shifts from the former to the latter, until the extreme present-centered view of our century is reached. I understand overlap in terms of the following phenomenon: on the one hand, truth was thought to be anchored in the knowing subject since Descartes; this agrees fully with the present-centered view. On the other hand, the paradigm of truth continues to be mathematical knowledge. This part of the conception of truth is inherited from the eternity view; it is indeed consciously borrowed from this view in order to avoid the pitfalls of sense perception.

The second remark aims at a systematic criticism of the present-centered view of truth. an especially far-reaching objection against it is the following: all procedures of examination and confirmation of a truth that can be applied here and now depend on previous (real or alleged) knowledge. Therefore, their reliability is to be measured by the amount of truth contained in those previous convictions. Charles Sanders Peirce once expressed this condition in the following way: "each chief step in science has been a lesson in logic." He illustrates this claim with the work of Lavoisier, of whom he says that "his way was to carry his mind into his laboratory, and literally to make of his alembics and cucurbits instruments of thought."[15] Under this interpretation logic comprises not only the art of inference but all procedures that help to confirm a truth claim in science. This realistic conception of the conditions of access to present-centered truth obviously transcends the limits of the present and puts truth in a historical context. In accordance with this idea, Logical Empiricism, which most uncompromisingly propagated the epistemological extreme of the present-centered conception of truth, has almost inevitably led to the contemporary historical philosophy of science. Kuhn's *Structure* has shaken the philosophy of science not least because it made clear that the present-centered view of truth is untenable.

Now, Kuhn disavowed the historical or cultural relativism that is so often attributed to him. I believe that his disclaimer will continue to meet with resistance as long as *the concept of truth* has not been adapted to the new historical perspective. Put in more abstract terms, as long as the qualification of representations as scientific remains based on the present-centered view of truth, all the wealth of historical wisdom does not suffice to achieve the transformation of the empiricist conception of science into a new coherent view. To me at least it has remained a paradox that the working textbook-trained scientist on the one hand and the historian of science on the other should *necessarily* have different pictures of science.[16] Either the historicity of science is superficial, as the eternity view of truth would have it, or historical relativism is unavoidable. In short: to tie truth to a shifting specious present does not make enough room for the real historical dimension of truth.

This, at last, forces us to consider the relationship of truth and the temporal course of history. Therefore I shall now go on to the most prominent view that takes up this consideration: the *future-centered view of truth*. The enlightened belief in the moral progress of mankind has prepared the ground for this view. Revolutionary discoveries of the nineteenth century added to its moment: Darwin's theory of natural selection and the irreversibility of the entire material process in the universe that is the consequence of a generalized conception of the second law of thermodynamics. Toward the end of the last century these developments induced a few philosophers to claim that the classical world picture of modern science, with its immutable world order governed by immutable laws, was outdated, and to adopt a new evolutionary world picture. Minds as different as Charles Peirce and Friedrich Engels are part of this same movement.

Emerging from the shadow of their great predecessor Hegel, each in his own way applied the idea of evolution not only to the world but also to the concept of truth: Truth is neither eternal nor something that could be made available just here and now. Rather truth develops in the course of time in a process of research that continues indefinitely. Peirce expresses this conception of truth in the following sentence: "The opinion which is fated to be ultimately agreed to by all who investigate, is what we mean by the truth. and the object represented in this opinion is the real."[17] Engels, in a similar way, speaks of the "infinity of the knowable subject matter," so that its investigation "can, according to the nature of the case, only be carried out . . . in an asymptotic process."[18] These two names and citations may be taken as representative of the entire group of future-centered theoreticians of truth.

The future-centered theory of truth is plausible. Truth is not a matter of the present moment, except in the most trivial cases, and even then only under the presupposition of a far-reaching context. In almost all practical questions of life, truth is at best the final product of a chain of questions, investigations, doubts, errors, and renewed attempts at reaching it. Even opinions that count as settled are preliminary and subject to revision—at least so far as their deeper significance and wider context is concerned, a context within which they may always change considerably in meaning and function.

Perhaps the most recent and most important expression of the future-centered view of truth is found in the writings of Karl Popper and the theory of verisimilitude that he initiated. Popper compared truth with "a mountain peak which is permanently, or almost permanently, wrapped in clouds." He who seeks the truth is like a climber; the summit is only present to him as an anticipated goal of his endeavor. Even if he has reached a point from which the ground descends in all directions, he cannot exclude that he has only reached a subsidiary peak. Usually the only sure thing for him is that he is not yet on the top.[19] Popper's attempt at proving that research is a process converging toward truth is in accordance with this picture: all criteria that he can offer in order to measure the closeness of a claim to the truth, its verisimilitude, concern the local comparison of neighboring stages of the research process. Since the truth itself is (still) unavailable, there can be no question of knowing the distance between it and any of our actual claims. I am not aware that refined versions of Popper's ideas on verisimilitude have managed to overcome this predicament, however nicely they model the idea of approaching an optimal state of knowledge within a given linguistic or theoretical framework.[20]

But if this is so, why should the summit exist at all, Truth with a capital T?[21] At least the hiker should have seen it once, if only from a distance. But we can no more look into the future than our hiker through the clouds. Nor do we have a chance of proving the existence of the limit of a convergent series of truth claims from a kind of conceptual convergence of our scientific theories. Against this conception Quine has rightly objected that it involves "a faulty use of numerical analogies."[22] This remark was directed against Peirce, but it fits his successors just as well. The future-centered view of truth in all its diverse modifications is invariantly based on the purely speculative assumption that there is this convergence of our cognitive endeavors: the Truth that awaits us in the indefinite future. It is not hard to see that here we have a contamination of a time-related view of truth with the eternity view of truth. The product of a convergent research process placed at the end of time is just as far from our earth as the thoughts of God. The future-centered view of truth does not directly appeal to an eternal order of things, but still it relies on an eschatological order.

The same point may be made by saying that the future-centered view is teleological. Seen from the perspective of biology, it is then a mistake to call it evolutionary or evolutionist, as for example, Popper does.[23] A Darwinian evolutionary view of science will have to abandon the idea of convergence,[24] hence of truth-as-convergence. For this reason I finally turn to what I tentatively call the *past-centered view of truth*. According to it, truth consists in a present reference of propositions, opinions, or the like to an object, but a reference that is only possible on the basis of an appropriate prehistory. Put in simple terms: truth is only possible as the result of a learning process. The distinction from the future-centered view may be expressed thus: if we did not already possess truth now, we could not possess any truth at all. The distinction from the present-centered view of truth may be expressed by saying: if we should attempt to ascertain a truth solely from the resources of the present, we would fail to secure any truth at all.

The past-centered view admits of very simple illustrations. The most ordinary examples for it are everyday claims which each of us utters all the time: for example, about an open door. It is an inconspicuous but trivial fact that these claims are based on a learning process which each of us has gone through when she or he acquired the command of perception and speech. The present perception or act of listening is only a preliminary last part of this process. The same statement is valid a fortiori for more complex states of affairs: for instance, of assertions that one may make about the character of a person. The development of the sciences needs a further *collective* learning process beyond the cognitive efforts of the individual. The last case makes clear that the past-centered view of truth is also a *historical* view of truth. It is the view of truth that agrees with our earlier observation according to which science is a unique historical phenomenon.

To bar misunderstanding I should perhaps add that the past-centered view does not commit us to a naturalistic fallacy. For the learning process that is included in the definition of truth need not simply be a causal process; not every explanation of how people come to adopt a certain opinion is the justification of a truth claim. Someone may believe a notorious liar, and we all may be deceived by illusions that are rooted in our nature or our common history of prejudices. The road of learning or experience necessarily leads through disillusions. Nevertheless, it is the only one that can, under favorable circumstances, legitimize our claims to truth.

One of the advantages that I tend to attribute to the past-centered view is that it is fully compatible with the currently prevalent evolutionary view of the world, especially the world of organisms, including the species *Homo sapiens*. The choice of the term "compatible" is deliberate; I do not see that the present stage of evolutionary theory justifies a stronger expression. The classical field of epistemological studies continues to be history, paradigmatically the history of science. Although this history remains an independent subject of research in its own right, it can no longer be viewed in teleological, let alone eschatological, terms. At least, this seems to me a fair expectation, if every tenable notion of truth is to be correlated with its paradigm applications, among which evolutionary theory occupies a prominent place.

At this point one may perhaps wish to object that my claim of correlation is at variance with my own illustrations: for example, those concerning the discovery of evolution and the future-centered view of truth. I did not mean, however, to imply a simple one-to-one relationship. History is much too complex for that; it contains the "simultaneity of the non-simultaneous" (I borrow the term from Reinhart Koselleck),[25] that is, the co-presence and interaction of developments that originate from, and are typical for, different periods. I consider the convergence view of truth as an instructive example of the hybridization of the eternity view of truth with the idea of evolution. Among other things, it illustrates my second heuristic idea: only the progress of science as a whole is likely to provide an adequate notion of truth; and conversely, only the specific relation to truth (as opposed to use) is likely to make us understand the internal coherence and progressiveness of science as a distinguished cultural achievement that may be contrasted to other such achievements.

Notes

1. Thomas S. Kuhn, *The Structure of Scientific Revolutions* (Chicago: University of Chicago Press, 1970), p. 169.

2. Larry Laudan, *Progress and Its Problems* (Berkeley: University of California Press, 1977), p. 11.

3. Kuhn, *The Structure of Scientific Revolutions,* p. 170; cf. p. 206.

4. Larry Laudan, "The Philosophy of Progress," in *PSA 1978,* ed. by P. D. Asquith and I. Hacking (East Lansing: Philosophy of Science Association, 1981), vol. 2, pp. 530–547.

5. Ibid., pp. 533–534.

6. Karl R. Popper, "Truth, Rationality and the Growth of Scientific Knowledge," in *Conjectures and Refutations* (London: Routledge & Kegan Paul, 1963), pp. 215–250.

7. Ilkka Niiniluoto, *Is Science Progressive?* (Dordrecht: Reidel, 1984).

8. Thomas S. Kuhn, "Reflections on my Critics," in *Criticism and the Growth of Knowledge,* ed. by Lakatos and A. Musgrave (London: Cambridge University Press, 1970); and W. V. O. Quine, *Word and Object* (Cambridge: Massachusetts Institute of Technology Press, 1960).

9. Niiniluoto, *Is Science Progressive?* p. 90.

10. Laudan, *PSA 1978,* pp. 533 ff.

11. Ibid., p. 535.

12. Kuhn, *The Structure of Scientific Revolutions,* p. 206.

13. Johannes Kepler, *Works,* vol. 13, p. 209.

14. Ibid., vol. 7, pp. 128–129.

15. Charles Sanders Peirce, "The Fixation of Belief," in *Collected Papers* (1877) 5.363.

16. Kuhn, *The Structure of Scientific Revolutions,* chap. 11.

17. Charles Sanders Peirce, "How to Make Our Ideas Clear," *Collected Works* (1878) 5.407.

18. Friedrich Engels, "Uber Nägelis Unfähigkeit, das Unendliche zu erkennen," *MEW,* vol. 21, pp. 501–502.

19. Popper, *Conjectures and Refutations,* p. 226.

20. Niiniluoto, *Is Science Progressive?* chaps. 5 and 7; and Ilkka Niiniluoto, *Truthlikeness* (Dordrecht: Reidel, 1987), chaps. 5–7.

21. Popper, *Conjectures and Refutations,* p. 232.

22. Quine, *Word and Object,* sect. 6, p. 23.

23. Karl R. Popper, *Objective Knowledge* (Oxford: Oxford University Press, 1972), p. 261.

24. Kuhn, "Reflections on My Critics," pp. 170–171.

25. Reinhart Koselleck, "Geschichte, Historie," in *Geschichtliche Grundbegriffe,* ed. by O. Brunner, W. Conze, R. Koselleck (Stuttgart: Klett, 1975), vol. 2, pp. 593–717; specifically, p. 674.

CONTRIBUTORS

Aziz Al-Azmeh is Sharjah Professor of Islamic Studies at the University of Exeter. He received the Doctor of Philosophy degree in Oriental Studies from the University of Oxford in 1978. Dr. Al-Azmeh has written extensively on cultural authenticity in articles in Arabic and European languages. Among his books are two on Ibn Khaldūn, the subject of his doctoral dissertation.

Roger T. Ames holds a Ph.D. from the School of Oriental and African Studies, University of London. He is Professor in the Department of Philosophy at the University of Hawaii and editor of the international journal *Philosophy East and West*. Dr. Ames' recent publications include *The Art of Rulership: A Study in Ancient Chinese Political Thought*, *Thinking Through Confucius* (with David L. Hall), and *Nature in Asian Traditions of Thought: Essays in Environmental Philosophy* (edited with J. Baird Callicott). He is also a translator of Chinese classics.

Karl-Otto Apel received a Ph.D. at the University of Bonn and has held full professorships at the Universities of Kiel and Saarbrücken, and currently holds the chair for social philosophy at the Johann Wolfgang Goethe Universität, Frankfurt am Main. Dr. Apel has been Visiting Professor at universities in Canada, Italy, France, and the U.S.A. He is a leading scholar of the Frankfurt School, one of his most recent publications being *Understanding and Explanation: A Transcendental Pragmatic Perspective*.

Richard J. Bernstein is Vera List Professor of Philosophy at the New School for Social Research and was recently Visiting Professor at Frankfurt University. He received a Ph.D. at Yale University in 1958. Dr. Bernstein served as editor-in-chief of *Praxis International* from 1980–1984 and has written extensively on political philosophy, metaphysics, and American philosophy, as well as on topics in hermeneutics and continental philosophy. He is a past President of the American Philosophical Association (Eastern Division).

Margaret Chatterjee received a B.A. and M.A. at Oxford University and a Ph.D. at the University of Delhi. She was Head of the Department of Philosophy at Delhi before assuming the post of Director of the Indian Institute of Advanced Study, Simla. Dr. Chatterjee has published seven books and fifty-six articles on Indian and comparative philosophy. She has also published poetry and has written, lectured, and broadcast on Gandhian thought.

Antonio S. Cua is Professor of Philosophy at the Catholic University of America. He received a Ph.D. at the University of California, Berkeley, in 1958. Dr. Cua is co-editor of the *Journal of Chinese Philosophy* and consultant to four other periodicals. He has published four books and over fifty articles on Chinese and comparative philosophy. He has served as President of the International Society for Chinese Philosophy and as President of the Society for Asian and Comparative Philosophy.

Arthur C. Danto was educated at Wayne State University, Columbia University, and the University of Paris. He received a Ph.D. at Columbia in 1952. Dr. Danto has taught at Columbia since 1951 and is presently Johnsonian Professor of Philosophy and Co-director of the Center for the Study of Human Rights. He has published eleven books and served as editor or consulting editor for four journals. Dr. Danto is past President of the American Philosophical Association (Eastern Division). He is art critic for *The Nation* and received the George S. Polk Award for Criticism in 1986.

Eliot Deutsch is Professor of Philosophy at the University of Hawaii and former editor (1967–1987) of the international journal *Philosophy East and West*. He received his doctorate from Columbia University and has been a visiting professor at the University of Chicago and Harvard University. His publications include *Studies in Comparative Aesthetics, Advaita Vedānta: A Philosophical Reconstruction,* and *On Truth: An Ontological Theory.*

Ferenc Feher received a Ph.D. from the Hungarian Academy of Sciences in 1972 under the supervision of Georg Lukács. He is Senior Lecturer, Committee on Liberal Studies, Graduate Faculty, at the New School for Social Research in New York. Dr. Feher has written thirteen books, edited six, and published over a hundred articles in a number of European languages.

Lenn E. Goodman is Professor of Philosophy at the University of Hawaii. He received a D.Phil. from Oxford University and a B.A. from Harvard University in Philosophy and Near-Eastern Languages and Literature. Dr. Goodman has edited the Brown Judaica Studies-Medieval Approaches to Judaism Series and served as Vice President of the Institute for Islamic-Judaic Studies. He has published eight books including several translations from the Arabic, and over fifty articles and reviews.

A. C. Graham has taught for thirty-four years at the School of Oriental and African Studies, University of London. He received a Ph.D. in 1953, and has subsequently been Lecturer, Reader, and Professor of Classical Chinese. Dr. Graham became a Fellow of the British Academy in 1981. He has held visiting professorships worldwide, including a current post at the University of Hawaii. He has published nine books and over sixty articles in leading journals.

Kwame Gyekye is Professor of Philosophy at the University of Ghana, Legon. He was educated at the University of Ghana and Harvard University, receiving a Ph.D. from the latter in 1969. Dr. Gyekye has published two books on Graeco-Arabic philosophy, two books on African philosophical thought, and thirty articles.

David L. Hall is Professor of Philosophy at the University of Texas at El-Paso. He received a Ph.D. at Yale University in 1967. His publications in Western philosophy include *Civilization of Experience* and *Eros and Irony.* He has also published widely in Chinese and comparative philosophy, including *The Uncertain Phoenix* and *Thinking Through Confucius* (with Roger T. Ames), which is forthcoming in a Chinese translation.

Agnes Heller is Hannah Arendt Professor of Philosophy at the New School for Social Research, New York. She has studied and worked under Georg Lukács at the Lorand Eotvos University of Budapest and the Hungarian Academy of Sciences, and was dismissed from her academic position together with Lukács for political reasons in 1958. Dr. Heller joined the New School in 1984. Her present research includes a philosophical monograph on Lukács and *A Treaty of History* (second part).

Maria L. Herrera received a B.A. at the Universidad Nacional Autonoma de Mexico in 1975. She received an M.A. in applied anthropology in 1978 and a Ph.D. in philosophy and social sciences in 1985 at Boston University. Dr. Herrera is currently Assistant Professor at the National University of Mexico, teaching courses in aesthetics, philosophy and literature, and political philosophy.

Jiang Tianji was educated at the National Southwest Associated University, and the Graduate School of the University of Colorado at Boulder. He has held professorships at Beijing and Guangxi Normal Universities and is currently Professor at Wuhan University. Dr. Jiang has served as both President and Honorary President of the Chinese Society for Studies in the History of Western Logic. He is co-editor of two works forthcoming in English, *Chinese Essays in the Philosophy of Science* (Reidel) and *Popper in China: Proceedings of the Popper Conference. Wuhan. 1987* (Routledge & Kegan Paul).

Thomas P. Kasulis has a Ph.D. in philosophy from Yale University. He has taught comparative philosophy at the University of Hawaii, Harvard University, and the University of Chicago. Dr. Kasulis is presently Professor in the Department of Philosophy and Religion at Northland College, Wisconsin. He has published widely in Japanese philosophy, including *Zen Action, Zen Person,* and is at present working on a history of Japanese philosophy. He is currently President of the Society for Asian and Comparative Philosophy.

Daya Krishna is former Professor of Philosophy and Ex-Pro-Vice-Chancellor at the University of Rajasthan, Jaipur, India. He has been a member of twelve learned societies and an active participant in seventeen international conferences, including the Fifth East-West Philosophers' Conference in 1969. Dr. Krishna has published nine books and over eighty articles in philosophy, the humanities, and the social sciences.

Lorenz Krüger was educated at the Universities of Heidelberg and Göttingen in physics and philosophy, respectively. He was Professor of Philosophy at Bielefeld and the Free University, Berlin, before assuming his present post at the University of Göttingen. Dr. Krüger is concurrently a Fellow of the Berlin Institute for Advanced Study. He has been a Research Fellow in the United States, Israel, and Germany. He has published or co-published eight books and over fifty articles in philosophy and the philosophy of science.

Joel J. Kupperman received an A.B., S.B., and A.M. at the University of Chicago, and a Ph.D. at Cambridge University in 1959. He is Professor of Philosophy at the University of Connecticut. Dr. Kupperman's publications include two books on ethics and two textbooks, one on logic and the other on fundamental problems in philosophy. He has published articles in several major subdisciplines of philosophy, including Asian and comparative philosophy.

Larry Laudan was educated at the University of Kansas and Princeton University in physics and philosophy, respectively, receiving a Ph.D. from the latter in 1965. He has taught at the University of London, the University of Pittsburgh, and Virginia Polytechnic Institute and State University. Dr. Laudan is currently Chairman of the Philosophy Department at the University of Hawaii. He has published extensively on topics in the philosophy of science and is at the forefront of current discussions in scientific method, progress, and the history of science.

Li Zhilin was educated at the Shanghai University Literature Institute and the East China Normal University, receiving his doctorate from the latter in 1988. He worked under Feng Qi. Dr. Li is currently Professor of Philosophy at the East China Normal University. He has published five books and over forty articles on topics in Chinese and comparative philosophy.

Alasdair MacIntyre was educated at Queen Mary College (University of London), Manchester University, and Oxford University. He was W. Alton Jones Distinguished Professor of Philosophy at Vanderbilt University and concurrently Henry R. Luce, Jr. Visiting Scholar at the Whitney Humanities Center, Yale University. He is currently Professor of Philosophy at the University of Notre Dame. Dr. MacIntyre is past President of the American Philosophical Society (Eastern Division). He has published eighteen books and over one hundred twenty articles.

Bimal K. Matilal was educated at Calcutta University, the Sanskrit Association of West Bengal, and Harvard University. He received a Ph.D. at Harvard in 1965. Dr. Matilal is concurrently Spalding Professor of Eastern Religions and Ethics at the University of Oxford, Fellow at All Souls College, Oxford, and the founder-editor of *Journal of Indian Philosophy*. He has published thirteen books and over eighty articles and reviews on Indian logic, language, and religion.

Ilkka Niiniluoto was educated at the University of Helsinki in mathematics and philosophy, receiving a doctorate in philosophy in 1974. He was a Visiting Scholar at Stanford University in 1972. Dr. Niiniluoto is concurrently Professor of Theoretical Philosophy and Chairman of the Department of Philosophy at the University of Helsinki. He is the author of *Theoretical Concepts and Hypothetico-Inductive Inference* (with R. Tuomela), *Is Truth Progressive?* and *Truthlikeness*.

Lucius Outlaw attended Dartmouth College, Fisk University, and Boston College, receiving a doctorate from the latter in 1972. He is Associate Professor of Philosophy at Haverford College. Dr. Outlaw has published widely in African philosophy, African-American philosophy, social and political philosophy, and phenomenology.

G. C. Pande was educated at Punjab University and the University of Allahabad, receiving a D.Phil. from the latter in 1947. He has taught at four Indian universities and has been since 1985 a National Fellow at the Indian Council of Historical Research, New Delhi. Dr. Pande has published sixteen books and over forty articles on Buddhism, Indian culture and history, philosophy of history and values, and poetry.

Graham Parkes is Associate Professor at the University of Hawaii. He received his doctorate from the University of California, Berkeley, and his B.A. from Queen's College, Oxford. He has been active in film work, including the making of an audiovisual presentation celebrating the centenary of Nietzsche's *Zarathustra*. Dr. Parkes is the editor of, and contributor to, an anthology entitled *Heidegger and Asian Thought*.

Marcello Pera is Professor of Philosophy at the University of Catania, Italy. He received a Ph.D. in philosophy at the University of Pisa in 1972. Dr. Pera has been a Visiting Fellow at the University of Pittsburgh Center for Philosophy of Science, and has helped organize three international conferences. He has published three books and eight papers in English on problems in the philosophy of science.

Karl H. Potter was educated at the University of California at Berkeley and Harvard University, receiving a Ph.D. from the latter in 1955. He has taught at Carleton College and the University of Minnesota. Dr. Potter is presently Professor of Philosophy and Chairman of the Department at the University of Washington. He has published six books, including three volumes of the *Encyclopedia of Indian Philosophies*.

Hilary Putnam is Walter Beverly Pearson Professor of Modern Mathematics and Mathematical Logic in the Department of Philosophy at Harvard University. He holds a Ph.D. from U.C.L.A. as well as two honorary degrees. Dr. Putnam has written extensively on the philosophies of mathematics, natural science, language, and mind. In recent years his interests have centered on the relations between scientific and nonscientific knowledge. His most recent books are *The Many Faces of Realism* (Open Court, 1987) and *Representation and Reality* (MIT Press, 1988).

Richard Rorty was educated at the University of Chicago and Yale University, receiving a Ph.D. from the latter in 1956. He has taught at Wellesley College, Princeton University, and the University of Virginia. Dr. Rorty is currently University Professor of Humanities at the University of Virginia. His books include *The Linguistic Turn, Philosophy and the Mirror of Nature, Consequences of Pragmatism, Philosophy in History,* and *Contingency, Irony and Solidarity.*

Megumi Sakabe was educated at the University of Tokyo, completing the doctor's course in the humanities in 1965. He is currently Professor in the Faculty of Letters at the University of Tokyo. Dr. Sakabe has published five books and over eighty articles on Japanese and Western philosophy.

Svetozar Stojanović received a Ph.D. at the University of Belgrade, Yugoslavia, in 1962. He is Professor, Center for Philosophy and Social Theory at the University of Belgrade. Dr. Stojanović was Visiting Professor at Washington University, St. Louis, in 1988, and at Freie Universität, West Berlin, in 1989. He is editor-in-chief of the journal *Praxis International* (Oxford) and Chairman of the International Humanist and Ethical Union (Hague). He has published five books and over eighty articles in Serbo-Croatian, English, German, French, Swedish, and Spanish.

Frederick J. Streng was educated at Texas Lutheran College, Southern Methodist University, and the University of Chicago, receiving his Ph.D. from the latter in 1963. He is currently Professor of History of Religions, Southern Methodist University. Dr. Streng has edited four books, including the sixteen-volume *Religious Life of Man* series. He is the author of *Emptiness—Study in Religious Meaning* and *Understanding Religious Life*.

Roop Rekha Verma received her doctorate from Oxford University and is currently Professor of Philosophy at Lucknow University, India, and concurrently Director of the Indian Council of Philosophical Research, Lucknow. She has taught abroad at Oxford University and at Krakow University, Poland, and has participated in many national and international seminars. Dr. Verma has published thirty-five articles in Indian and international journals of philosophy.

Richard Wollheim was educated at Westminster School, London, and Balliol College, Oxford, in history, philosophy, politics, and economics. He has been a Fellow of the British Academy, an Honorary Associate of the British Psychoanalytical Society, and a Fellow of the American Academy of Arts and Sciences. Dr. Wollheim has taught at University College, London, and Columbia University. He is presently Mills Professor of Intellectual and Moral Philosophy at the University of California, Berkeley. His latest publications include *The Thread of Life* (Harvard, 1984) and *Painting as an Art* (Princeton, 1987).

Index

Adorno, 10, 13, 21, 96
Advaita Vedānta, 389, 430
Al-Afghānī (1839–1897), 471–473
Africa: and democratic institutions, 487; modern, 497–499; traditional political structure of, 488
African culture, community ethos of, 490
Ames, Roger T., 107, 121, 197
Analects, The, 228, 232, 236
Aquinas, Thomas, 106, 214
Arendt, Hannah, 103n.44
Aristotle, 106, 208, 315, 401, 413, 415, 538, 543; and al-Ghazālī, 422; his distinction between *phronēsis* and *epistēmē,* 268; on imitation, 333; on metaphor, 63; and Plato, 412
Argument, validity of, 580
Aufhebung, in Hegel and Marx, 72
Austin, J. L., 214
Averroes, 401, 482
Avicenna, 401
Ayer, A. J., 213

Bacon, Francis, 52
Barnes, Barry, 163, 170, 598
Berger, Peter, 533
Berlin, Isaiah, 143, 301, 308, 310
Bernstein, Richard J., xiv, 510
Berque, Augustin, 343–350
Bourdieu, Pierre, 507, 511
Bloor, David, 163, 170, 598
Blumenberg, Hans, 538
Buddhism, 155, 249; Madhyamaka, 125; Mahāyāna, 430; scripture, its view of, 444; Shingon, 217; and substantialist language, 462; Tendai, 217; Zen, 306

Carnap, Rudolph, 157
Chang Tsai (Zhang Zai) (1020–1077), 194, 249
Chih (zhi), conventional translation as "to know," 227; as experiential, 234; and *jen (ren),* 239; as moral prompting, 240–241; as performative, 239–240; as social, 236–238; three parts of, 246
China: and modernization, 50–51, 251; as postmodern, 59
Chinese philosophy: and epistemology, 248; and formal logic, 245; method of reasoning in, 246
Chuang Tzu (Zhuang Zi), 60, 61, 246
Chuang-tzu (Zhuang-zi), The, 61, 197
Chu Hsi (Zhu Xi), 119, 249, 251, 279, 282
Chün-tzu (jun-zi) ("paradigmatic individual"), 283
Community, 267
Comparative study: central goal of, 402–403; and the meaning of human expressions, 368
Conceptual scheme, 124, 193; and chains of opposition, 196; as a metalogical pattern of names, 200; and syntactic structure, 208
Confucianism, 59; central characteristic of its moral theory and practice, 116; its doctrine of the rectification of names, 65; and Neo-Confucianism, 110; reasonable challenges to, 284; respect for authority in, 280; three types of, 281
Confucius, 106, 280, 288; and the language of deference, 62–66; language and music for, 66
Correlative thinking, 209, 232–234

637